Adolescent Development

Charles E. Merrill Publishing Company
A Bell & Howell Company
Columbus   Toronto   London   Sydney

Adolescent Development

An Ecological Perspective

James Garbarino

The Pennsylvania State University

with
Robert H. Abramowitz
C. Elliot Asp
Aaron T. Ebata
Nancy L. Galambos
Wendy C. Gamble
Anne C. Garbarino
Cheryl R. Kaus
Andrew F. Kelly
Cynthia J. Schellenbach
John E. Schulenberg
Janet M. Sebes
Joan I. Vondra

Published by Charles E. Merrill Publishing Company
A Bell & Howell Company
Columbus, Ohio 43216

This book was set in Palatino
Production Coordinator: Christina Anagnost
Copyeditor: Tracey Dils
Text Designer: Cynthia Brunk
Cover Designer: Cathy Watterson
Cover Artist: Charles Reid

Credits:
Selections on pages 5, 6, 7, 8, 9, 10, and 11 from *At the Shores*. Copyright © 1980 by
Thomas Rogers. Reprinted by permission of SIMON & SCHUSTER, Inc.
Table 5.2, page 216, from R. Liebert, R. Poulos, and G. Marmor, *Developmental
Psychology*. Copyright © 1977 by Prentice-Hall.
Table 7.1, page 312, adapted from E. Maccoby and C. Jacklin, *The Psychology of Sex
Differences*. Copyright © 1974 by Stanford University Press.
Pages 446–447 from Selman's Stages of Interpersonal Conceptions. Reprinted from
PSYCHOLOGY TODAY MAGAZINE. Copyright © 1979 by the American
Psychological Association.

Library of Congress Card Catalog Number: 84–62704
International Standard Book Number: 0-675-20301-5
Printed in the United States of America
1 2 3 4 5 6 7 8 9 10—90 89 88 87 86 85

*To John Lennon, who has brought adolescents
of three decades through the exhilarating
and difficult process of growing up.*

To the Instructor

What do I want to teach these students?
What's the best way to teach it?
How do I make it stick?

These are the questions in my mind as I approach my course in adolescence. They have guided the writing of this text, both the context and the style.

I was guided also by my efforts as a scholar to understand how the social environment creates risks and opportunities for adolescents. These efforts have been influenced by my involvement in human services for adolescents as a secondary school teacher, as a youth counselor, and as a consultant to a wide variety of social service agencies. In all this, my collaborators and I have tried to work through an "ecological framework," which I understand to mean an approach that emphasizes the processes of human development. These stages occur when the individual interacts biologically and psychologically, with the social and physical environment (called the *micro-, meso-, exo-* and *macrosystems*). We have carried this systems perspective through each chapter, beginning with an introduction to the chapter topic's relevance to each level of the ecological system and concluding with an ecological wrap-up that briefly reminds the student of key issues at each system level.

In writing the book I brought together a group of talented Penn State graduate students as my collaborators, each of whom has special expertise in studying adolescence. All have worked with me in my seminar on adolescence and each took special responsibility for one or more of the book's chapters. These collaborators include Andy Kelly, John Schulenberg, Aaron Ebata, Elliott Asp, Nancy Galambos, Joan Vondra, Wendy Gamble, Janet Sebes, Cheryl Kaus, Cynthia Schellenbach, Robert Abramowitz, and Anne Garbarino.

Let me say a few things about each chapter.

Chapter 1 begins an inductive approach to adolescence, the cornerstone for the entire text. It presents a kaleidoscope of adolescent images and follows these with principles for answering the question, "What is adolescence?" Chapter 2 presents an ecological model and the concepts of sociocultural risk and opportunity. It also introduces *social competence* as a way to understand adolescence. Chapters 3 and 4 present the key phenomena of physical and cognitive maturation and development. Chapter 3 details the processes and structures of puberty as well as the psychological and social factors. Chapter 4 presents adolescent reasoning (intellectual and social) and thus integrates scientific and moral reasoning. In these chapters we continue our inductive approach by introducing issues of theory—what a theory is and how different theories approach the same topics. This background sets the stage for Chapter 5's full-blown analysis of theories of adolescence.

Chapters 6, 7, 8, and 9 discuss family relations, identity, sexuality and intimacy, and academic and vocational development. In each case, we use our ecological perspective to show how a systems framework links together research findings and practical issues, on the one hand, and individual and social change, on the other. Issues of *how* one studies adolescence run through these discussions.

Chapter 10 presents the adolescent in the community of peers—how friendships and peer groups form and work and how adult institutions respond. Chapters 11 and 12 are linked. Chapter 11 presents the psychological and social adjustment problems faced by adolescents, while Chapter 12 analyzes the theory and practice of intervention with adolescents. Throughout the text we have included first-person accounts of adolescence contributed by my students and by me. In Chapter 12 we include first-person accounts of human service professionals dealing with school problems, suicide, anorexia nervosa, drug abuse, and delinquency.

Chapter 13 focuses on social changes affecting the transition to adulthood, and the epilogue concludes with thoughts on the meaning of adolescence.

Note that rather than having a separate chapter to deal with cultural and ethnic issues, we have incorporated these issues throughout the text. The index can also help you trace ecological discussions that are presented in each chapter of this book.

I have called upon my undergraduate students to read and comment upon the text at various stages, and I have used some of their reflections on their own adolescent years to help personalize the analysis. I hope you find it useful in your own teaching as I have in mine.

On the next few pages, I have written a brief preface for your students. Since they are going to be listening to me for the next weeks and months as they read the text, I thought it only fair that I lay my cards on the table for them at the outset and let them know some of my assumptions and goals. I'll leave it to you to let them know where you disagree or choose a different emphasis.

Acknowledgments

We first would like to thank those who typed the manuscript and helped put its pieces together: Alice Saxion, Joy Barger, and Kathie Hooven. Also, we would like to thank Ed Rydelek at the Number Four Trading Post, who helped arrange for the manuscript to make its appointed rounds. Second, we thank our editors at Charles Merrill; Jane Sudbrink and Tracey Dils. Third, we thank the outside reviewers who commented upon and helped us improve successive versions of the manuscript: Craig Barclay, University of Michigan; Robert Enright, University of Wisconsin; Ellis Evans, University of Washington; Douglas Sawin, University of Texas at Austin; Lawrence Shelton, University of Vermont; Elizabeth Susman, National Institute of Mental Health; Kenneth Tokuno, University of Hawaii at Manoa; John Williamson, North Texas State University; and Steve Jorgenson, Texas Tech University.

To the Student

When I begin teaching a class in adolescent development, I begin by telling the students where I stand on several important educational issues. I want to do the same for you here, since you will be reading this text.

I think adolescent development is a special course for most college students. Unlike courses on child development or aging, a course on adolescent development deals with issues and experiences immediately accessible. Most college students (but certainly not all) are not parents, so they do not have intimate experience with young children. Sometimes it's not easy to clearly recall the events of childhood. Similarly, many college students are not living that closely with the elderly to have an intimate understanding of that experience. Lastly, many of the issues of early adulthood are too close for college students to analyze objectively. But adolescence is just the right (and intriguing) topic for study by most college students. It is recent enough to be remembered clearly, without the distortions of childhood, yet far enough away to permit at least some objectivity. I count on my students being objective. One way of showing the type of recall I encourage is my inclusion in this text of brief statements on "my most vivid memory of adolescence" written by some of my students *before* they took the course. I hope you will compare your own memories with those of my students. Perhaps your instructor will ask you to write down your most vivid memories to supplement what I've included in the text.

When I teach about adolescent development, I have in mind four goals for the student: to become a better professional providing human services to adolescents; to become a better parent of an adolescent; to become a better citizen dealing with public issues affecting adolescents; and to become a better researcher studying adolescent development. While I think all four goals are important, I want you to understand that this text emphasizes the first three— professional, parental, and citizen roles. Most of the students in my classes will be active in one, two, or all three of the first three roles; few will become research scientists. I think the text reflects this orientation in that each chapter has its eye on understanding the life stage of adolescence so that you can understand individual adolescents.

Finally, I want you to know that I believe *what* you understand adolescence to be depends partly upon *who* you are (including what your own adolescence was like). For this reason I've tried to personalize the book as much as possible, including the most vivid memories of adolescence from me and the other people who produced this text. We, too, were once adolescents. We have had first kisses, great embarrassments, great successes, peer pressures, conflicts with brothers and sisters, and parents who were usually loving but sometimes just didn't understand, just as you have had.

I hope you'll enjoy the book. In any case, I'd welcome your comments or suggestions. Feel free to write to *me* in care of the publisher (c/o Chris Cole, Charles E. Merrill, 1300 Alum Creek Drive, Columbus, Ohio 43216).

Contents

1 What Is Adolescence? 2

Adolescents in Fact and Fiction 4

What Is Adolescence? 11

Youth and History 12

The Demography of Youth 16

Health and Mortality 21

Domestic Violence 22

Family Relations 24

Images of Adolescence 26

Adolescence as a Political Issue 29

What's Normal for Adolescents? Professional Stereotypes and Empirical Realities 30

Adolescents on Adolescence 37

2   *Human Ecology and Competence*
in Adolescence   40

Human Beings as Social Animals   42

The Interaction between Person and Environment   42

Nature and Nurture   44

*The Great Depression as a Source of Developmental Risk and
Opportunity   46*

A Systems Approach to Adolescent Development   49

Microsystems   51

Mesosystems   56

Exosystems   59

Macrosystems   60

An Ecological Map   72

The Meaning of Competence   75

A Synthesizing Approach to Competence   80

The Development of Social Competence   81

Conclusion   86

3   *The Biology of Adolescence   88*

What Is Puberty?   90

The Onset of Puberty   93

Physical Growth at Puberty   106

Sexual Development   112

The Psychology of Puberty   122

Adolescent Health   131

Conclusion   137

Ecological Wrap-Up   138

4   *Adolescent Thinking   140*

Cognitive Development: An Overview   142

Adolescent Egocentrism   154

Alternative Views of Adolescent Thinking   157
Creativity and Intellectual Exceptionality   158
Reasoning about Moral Issues   166
Ecological Differences and Moral Reasoning   175
Alternative Approaches to Moral Development   176
Reasoning about Political Issues   183
Conclusions   188
Ecological Wrap-Up   188

5   Theories of Adolescence   190

An Introduction to Models and Theories   192
Relating Theory to Research   200
Criteria for Evaluating Theories   200
Prescientific Theories   203
Nature Theories   207
Psychoanalytic Models   211
Nurture Theories   218
Social Learning   224
Cognitive Theories   228
Toward a Synthesis: A Biologically Sound Cognitive Learning Theory   230
Ecological Wrap-Up   232

6   Families and Their Adolescents   234

Naturalistic Observations: Watching What Families Really Do   236
Laboratory Analogues: Assessing What Families Would Do   237
Interviews or Surveys: Listening to What Families Say They Do   237
Choosing a Method   238

An Introduction to the Meaning of the Family in Human Development   239

The Role of the Parent   241

Definitions of Family   243

Family Size and Composition   245

Birth Order   247

Contemporary American Families   248

Parent/Child Relations   258

Schaefer's "Circumplex"   259

Baumrind's Four Styles of Parenting   260

Elder's Typology of Family Styles   264

Adolescent Maltreatment   265

The Challenge of Adolescence: Maintaining the Family System in the Face of Adolescent Autonomy   267

Influence of Other Kinship Relations   278

Conclusion   280

Ecological Wrap-Up   281

7   Knowing Who You Are   284

Definitions of Self, Self-Concept, and Identity   286

The Special Role of Self-Concept in Adolescence   287

Erikson's View of Identity Development   292

Dominant Stage Models of Identity   293

Individual Characteristics Related to Identity Development   297

Summary of the Possibilities and Impediments to the Development of Positive Self-Concept   301

Social Characteristics Related to Identity and Self-Concept   306

Establishing Sexual Identity   308

Collective Orientations to Identity   314

Macrosystem Issues in Identity   322

Identity and Enhancement of Self-Concept   323

Ecological Wrap-Up   325

8 Sexuality and Intimacy in Adolescence   326

Theoretical Perspectives   329

Cultural Perspectives   331

The Nature of Intimacy   334

Sexual Attitudes and Behaviors   342

Sexual Encounters   347

Variations in Sexual Orientation   361

How Does It Feel? What Does It Mean?   363

Sexual Knowledge: What and from Where?   364

Issues in Adolescent Sexuality and Intimacy   369

Conclusion   373

Ecological Wrap-Up   375

9 Adolescents in Schools and at Work   378

Schools and Education   380

Current Issues in the Schools   383

School Success   387

Dropping Out or Leaving Early?   391

Characteristics of the School Context   396

The Family and the Academic Environment   402

Careers and Work   404

The Process of Choosing a Career: Theoretical Perspectives   405

Vocational Choice   407

Employment Opportunities   418

Adolescents at Work   419

Reciprocity between Schools and Careers   423

Ecological Wrap-Up   427

10 Beyond the Family: Peer Group and Community   428

Adolescents in the Community of Peers   431

Fitting In: The Adolescent Peer Group   433

Friendship as Relationship 439
Who Becomes Friends? 440
The Nature of Adolescent Friendships 445
Identity and Intimacy through Interaction 451
Peer Relations and Social Adjustment 453
The Life-Long Significance of Friendship 455
Adolescents and the Community 458
The Community as an Influence on Adolescent Development 459
Adolescents in the Community 466
Ecological Wrap-Up 467

11 *Adjustment in Adolescence* 468

Delinquency 473
Theories of Delinquency 479
The Adolescent Runaway 481
Juvenile Prostitution 490
Physical, Psychological, and Sexual Abuse 497
Substance Abuse 503
Suicide 507
Classification of Psychopathology 509
Depression 513
Schizophrenia 516
Eating Disorders 517
Ecological Wrap-Up 520

12 *Human Services for Adolescents* 522

General Issues in Human Services 524
Special Issues in Services for Adolescents 527
Models of Human Services for Adolescents 534
Rehabilitative Approaches 541
Residential Treatment 548
Substance Abuse 551
Juvenile Delinquency 557
Abuse and Neglect 558

Adolescent Pregnancy   559
Eating Disorders   560
Juvenile Prostitution   562
Adolescent Suicide   562
Ecological Wrap-Up   565

13 The Transition to Adulthood: Youth and History   568

Adolescence and History: A Community Case Study   570
The Meaning of Youth as a Period in the Life Course   571
What Is Adulthood?   573
Cohort and Generation   576
The Role of Work in the Transition to Adulthood   581
The Role of College in the Transition to Adulthood   583
The Role of Marriage and Parenthood in the Transition to Adulthood   586
Social History and the Transition to Adulthood   596
Intergenerational Conflict   599
Youth and the Future   600
Ecological Wrap-Up   602

Epilogue   603
Glossary   607
References   615
Author Index   653
Subject Index   663

Adolescent
Development

Preview

- Adolescence is the period in life between childhood and adulthood.

- In modern societies adolescence begins before age 13 and ends after age 19.

- In the last century, more and more young people in North America have come to experience longer and longer adolescence.

- The schooling available to and required of adolescents is a critical influence on their development.

- The ratio of youth to adults in a society influences the experience of adolescence.

- One of the big issues for adolescents is coming to terms with sexuality and intimacy.

- The major health problems of adolescents involve decisions made about lifestyle— smoking, drinking, drugs, driving habits.

- Adolescence requires families to change and adapt.

- Popular and professional stereotypes abound concerning what is normal and abnormal for adolescent behavior.

1

What Is Adolescence?

*T*he Chinese philosopher Lao-tzu who lived in the sixth century B.C. tells us that "A journey of a thousand miles must begin with a single step." How are we to begin our journey into the study of adolescence? We do so one step at a time. Each step builds upon what we have learned in the step before. This will become apparent as we proceed. Our discussions will follow a particular pattern. In each case, we will first look at specific information about adolescents, *then* wrestle with what it might mean, and then introduce some general concepts to help organize what we have learned so that we can then use those ideas as a foundation for looking at and wrestling with more information, on the way to introducing additional general ideas.

The process of moving from specific information to general principles, ideas, or concepts is often called an *inductive* approach to learning. It contrasts to the *deductive* approach, which begins with principles, ideas, and concepts, *then* introduces specifics to illustrate them. Both have their strengths and weaknesses. The inductive approach often seems confusing *initially.* The deductive approach often seems clearer *initially.* At the start, students using the inductive approach may be hungry for some general ideas to make sense of the specific pieces of information confronting them. But if students can deal with that hunger, they are likely to find that when they do come face-to-face with general ideas, they can appreciate and evaluate them better. For example, students in training to become high school teachers often find that if they have some first-hand experience in the classroom, in the halls, and in the lunchroom with adolescents *before* they take their courses in educational psychology or principles and practice of teaching, these courses mean much more to them and they get more out of them than when they take the courses first and then confront the realities of the school.

This chapter is designed to introduce our inductive approach to studying adolescence. Our approach is a series of discussions of specific aspects of adolescence: issues, controversies, topics, debates, and information. We have built the inductive process into each discussion, and as a whole these discussions themselves feed into Chapter 2, which presents some general ideas and principles with which to organize and make sense of the material as a whole. In Chapters 3 and 4, we return to specific information—the biological and mental changes that occur in adolescence. These chapters pave the way for the ideas and principles in Chapter 5, which deals with how the major theories of adolescence make sense of this interplay of biological and mental changes. To return to this chapter, we will begin with literature as the best exposure to the specifics of adolescence and then introduce some general ideas and principles concerning the definition of adolescence.

Adolescents in Fact and Fiction

We often find the richest analyses of human behavior in fiction. Adolescence is no exception. Novels and short stories provide some of the best insights into the adolescent experience as it exists in different times and places. However, we must acknowledge that one of the difficulties in studying adolescence is that so much of what people say and write is neither based on rigorous empirical research nor conforms to what that research has to tell us (this is true of professionals as well as the general public). Compared to *child* development, the study of *adolescent* development has been more infrequent and often less sophisticated. This is changing somewhat. In the 1970s few universities offered courses in adolescence (L'Abata, 1971); 26% offered graduate courses and only 48% offered undergraduate courses. Many were very impressionistic and were not oriented to research. Today, most universities have filled this gap. One evidence of this is the proliferation of scholarly journals devoted to adolescence; there were five as of 1983, including *Adolescence*, the *Journal of Youth and Adolescence*, *Journal of Early Adolescence*, *Journal of Adolescence*, and *Youth and Society*. Although good literature can *communicate* effectively, we must look to research to sort out the empirical realities of adolescence.

The box on page 5 lists some twenty novels containing major adolescent characters that document historical, cultural, ethnic, racial, and economic, and geographic differences in the experience of adolescence. Read them all and you will have a rich store of human detail with which to illustrate the science of adolescence.

To demonstrate the richness of fiction as a source of insight into the adolescent experience, we can examine passages from a superb novel of adolescence, *At the Shores* by Thomas Rogers (New York: Simon and Schuster, 1980). Each passage tells us something we need to know, discover, or remem-

Novels with Adolescent Characters

Pride and Prejudice	Jane Austen
A Family Gathering	T. Alan Broughton
Rubyfruit Jungle	Rita Mae Brown
One of Ours	Willa Cather
The Red Badge of Courage	Stephen Crane
Great Expectations	Charles Dickens
Ordinary People	Judith Guest
Too Far to Walk	John Hersey
A Separate Peace	John Knowles
Sons and Lovers	D. H. Lawrence
How Green Was My Valley	Richard Llewellyn
The Member of the Wedding	Carson McCullers
Song of Solomon	Toni Morrison
Lolita	Vladimir Nabakov
The Chosen	Chaim Potok
The Trees	Conrad Richter
The Catcher in the Rye	J. D. Salinger
Memoirs of an Ex-Prom Queen	Alix Kates Shulman
The Adventures of Huckleberry Finn	Mark Twain
A Boy's Own Story	Edmund White

ber about adolescence. The fact that the novel describes an affluent teenage male (Jerry Engles) growing up in the 1940s demonstrates that there are aspects about adolescence that are universal while other aspects are bound up in who, where, and when you are. It has something to say about each aspect of adolescent development, so much so that it provides an outline of the topics covered in this text.

From the novel.   Gloria herself had changed. She was now intensely social. She moved through the corridors of Blaine Hall surrounded by a bevy of best friends, all of whom looked at Jerry significantly whenever they saw him. Gloria had told them something, though Jerry could never be sure exactly what. "What does she say about me?" he asked Gloria's friends, who would only laugh and roll their eyes. When he asked Gloria herself, she grew lofty and remote. "What do you mean?" she said, as if there had never been anything between them worth talking about. "You know," he said, referring to that first kiss in the cloakroom and to the other kiss he had earned by his fighting. "I don't know anything," she said, as if they were perfect strangers, but the next time she passed him in company with her friends Jerry felt all eyes were upon him, and then from behind his back he heard half-smothered giggles. He was wild with curiosity. He knew he was supposed to have Done Something. Furthermore there seemed to be notes he was supposed to have written Gloria. He sometimes saw her and her friends looking at pieces of paper they hid when they saw him coming. If these were really love letters, then Gloria must have written them to herself, but she would not admit that either. She teased and mystified him unmercifully, and because of her behavior he was acquiring a new reputation at school. This new reputation was that of a Lady Killer. He was supposed to be a dangerous boy where girls were concerned.

Commentary. *Sexuality and prestige are where the action is, was, and probably always will be. Early adolescence is a time of intense orientation to peers. When peers and sexuality are put together the result is powerful feelings. Chapter 8 deals with sexuality and Chapter 10 with peers.*

From the novel. She was a bewildering girl. Sometimes he thought she actually disliked him. Other times she seemed glad to receive the attention he now openly paid her. At a Colony Club party in the spring they roller skated together at the White City all one afternoon, and afterward he felt that at last things were on a simple and natural footing. She would be his girlfriend and he would be her boyfriend and henceforth things would go swimmingly, but before the year ended she had become mysterious once more, and then in seventh grade she changed again, this time physically. She was now taller than he was by an inch or so, and she had developed one of the most noticeable busts in class. When they ate fudge sundaes together at Stineway's she would lean across him to get another napkin, thus pressing her soft breast against his chest, reminding them both that she was getting to be a big girl. She dressed up, too, and when they went to the movies together she began appearing in heels that lifted her a good three or four inches above his level. He seemed to be losing ground with her, sinking almost, a sensation that deepened during the sudden clinches she sometimes initiated as they sat together at the back of the Piccadilly Theater or when he walked her home after a party at Carolyn Webster's house.

Commentary. *Physical maturation is the indisputable central fact of adolescence, and the fact that females usually race ahead as adolescence begins is a challenge with which both boys and girls must wrestle. We deal with physical maturation in Chapter 3, with its influence on self-concept in Chapter 7, and with its significance for sexuality in Chapter 8.*

From the novel.   He wondered sometimes if the indulgence that people, especially women, showed him was due to the fact that he was getting to be good-looking. He was thirteen now, and he could see he looked nicer than most of the other boys. He had no spots. He was neither thin nor fat. He was beginning to grow.

Commentary.   *Early maturing boys, particularly boys who are spared the ravages of acne, are at a distinct advantage in the social environment of adolescence. Adults as well as peers grant them a position of leadership, as we shall see in Chapters 3, 7, and 10.*

From the novel.   Dating, real dating with an almost sure goodnight kiss at the end, began in ninth grade, and he plunged into it with enthusiasm. He dated widely, spending most of each week considering which girl he would ask to the movies or to a party that weekend. There were more parties than ever now that the war was over and everything was getting back to normal, which was how he liked things. The war had been sort of interesting while it was going on, but he realized it had imposed a strain on him. It made him feel he ought to be doing something he wasn't doing, which was not a sensation he liked. Now he felt he was doing exactly what he ought to do—leading a normal life.

Commentary.   *Dating provides a context in which adolescents can learn and test important social skills. A big issue is whether or not dating leads to the development of intimacy and friendship. We consider the role of dating in sexuality in Chapter 8, its role in peer relations in Chapter 10, and the role that intellectual development plays in social relations in Chapter 4. In Chapter 13 we look at how the historical events of one's adolescence (such as World War II for Jerry) mark a generation in ways that can carry over a lifetime. Chapter 2 explores such effects on youth who were children of the Great Depression in the 1930s.*

From the novel.   In seventh and eighth grades they talked about the facts of life. Murphy, whose father was a doctor, brought books to school, and not just medical textbooks. One day he turned up with Mantegazza's *Human Sexual Customs*, from which he read them choice passages about exotic initiation rituals in Africa and Asia. In ninth grade they were more grown-up, of course, though still there was a lot of joking and talking about sex. They speculated one day about the possible effects of administering Spanish Fly to Miss Collins, a conversation that both disturbed and fascinated Jerry, who listened avidly but contributed little. Often he was relieved when such conversations were stopped by Phil, or more usually by John Williams, who said from time to time, "You guys are *sick.*" Often the talk was sick, though fascinating, and the point was that Ernie Hill had more to say along these lines than anyone except Bill Murphy himself. The thought of Ernie alone with Shirley was distinctly worrisome, although at the same time Jerry felt that Ernie was a great guy. Next to Phil Forson, Ernie was probably his best friend.

Commentary. *Sex stands for power, intimacy, love, prestige, and self-esteem. It's a complicated challenge to sort it all out that occupies much of the adolescent's time as we shall see in Chapter 8.*

From the novel. They were laying face to face on her unmade bed. In addition to the usual chaos of clothes in her room there were Christmas wrappings all over the place. Jerry began to feel the comfortable, unbuttoned sense of intimacy he often felt in his sister's presence. He went on voluntarily. "She (Carolyn) hasn't got big breasts," he said, "but she's very sensitive." Anne nodded. Their faces were close together. He was feeling now as close and as intimate as he had felt in the old days when he snuck into her room to play Orphans. "I don't love Carolyn, though," he said, "I don't love anyone now." "Why not?" Anne asked. "I don't know," he said reflectively.

Commentary. *Adolescence is a time when siblings often serve important functions for each other—as sounding boards, as confidants, as someone to call upon for help. Family relations in adolescence is the topic of Chapter 6.*

From the novel. His whole future depended on his education. His family had no money. Their Chicago apartment, their summer cottage, his tuition at U-High and Anne's at Swarthmore all came out of what Mr. Engels earned at Standard Oil. If Jerry wanted his own children to enjoy private schools and summer homes and long car trips to New England and to the West Coast and to the Florida Everglades he would have to earn a good salary, which meant studying hard not just in high school but in college, and not just in college but in graduate school. Mr. Engels had a Ph.D. in Chemistry from Johns Hopkins. Did Jerry think he was going to get into a college like Swarthmore or a graduate school like Hopkins without studying? And if he didn't get into such schools what would he do, what would become of him? To belong to the educated upper-middle class you had to be educated, and to get an education you had to study. It was axiomatic.

Commentary. *For all that we think of adolescence as a time when the present is the only thing that matters, much of the adolescent's concern focuses on how activities today will affect prospects for the future. Schooling has come to figure centrally in those calculations for more and more adolescents. Chapter 9 discusses the links between educational and vocational development.*

From the novel. Mr. Engels avoided details at this stage of his argument. He was a clearheaded, lucid, scientifically trained man quite capable of helping Jerry with his algebra and his Latin and his English grammar and his biology, but he allowed a certain cloudiness to envelop the whole question of what was wrong with adolescent sex. Nevertheless there was no loss of meaning in what he had to say. He used words like "dangerous" and "unhealthy" which in Jerry's mind translated easily into the grand old story aired in a thousand locker-room conversations and passed on faithfully from generation to generation of school-boys. Jerry knew his father was talking about premature ejaculation and early impotence induced by self-abuse, and of clap and syphilis picked up from bad women that led to paresis and madness. Or alternately, you could knock up a nice girl, which led to scandal, outraged fathers and brokenhearted mothers, shotgun weddings, marital unhappiness, and divorce. Or, if you did not face the music and stand by the girl you'd gotten in trouble, there was another se-quence of miserable events which involved the girl's killing herself with an amateur abortion while you ended up in a gutter somewhere, dead drunk from trying to forget it all. It was perfectly clear, and Mr. Engels' warnings about sex led to a conclusion as axiomatic as his warnings about grades. To provide his family with the same kind of good life he himself had enjoyed, Jerry would have to be well educated. To have the kind of married love his parents en-joyed, Jerry would have to control himself sexually for the next eight to ten years. "You do understand?" his father would ask him, and Jerry would nod, impressed by the reasonableness of it all.

Only. . .

Commentary. *Sex is often a difficult issue for parents to deal with as they ac-commodate to adolescence. The issues of pregnancy and morality endure, al-though in recent years we have seen much greater acknowledgement, if not ac-ceptance, of adolescent sexuality and its many consequences (e.g., teenage pregnancy without marriage). We consider sex education in Chapter 8, as well as a variety of sex-related issues in Chapters 10, 11, 12, and 13 (including teen-age pregnancy and parenthood).*

From the novel. Girls listened to each other more than boys did. Nancy was telling Rosalind and Shirley about some friend of hers who had dieted until she was sick. It was a long story and to Jerry not a very interesting one. He could not imagine telling Alec Walker anything like that. He could hardly imagine telling Alec about anyone Alec didn't know, nor could he imagine Alec listen-ing. Yet both Rosalind and Shirley listened. Girls were just more polite or maybe less self-absorbed than boys. They seemed to be interested in hearing about people they didn't know. Shirley began to talk about her cousin Jessica who was studying ballet. Nancy listened to that. So did Rosalind. Next it would be Rosalind's turn, Jerry thought.

Commentary. *Boys and girls often have different orientations to the social environment—particularly if they are encouraged to adopt and act out tradi-*

tionally masculine and feminine roles. Some of this is changing, but some differences are likely to remain. We explore sex roles in Chapters 7 and 8.

From the novel.   Jerry began kissing Rosalind's throat. He put his lips to the base of her throat and murmured, "I love you," as if he were talking directly to her soul without having to go through her ears and her brain. Nearby Malcolm's heavy footfalls added a new sound to the night. A droning mosquito added something more. Then somehow they were no longer sitting up. Enormous things seemed to be happening. Rosalind grew still beneath him. Then he felt her arms around him, and at that point he didn't see how he could not go ahead.

He woke up the next morning feeling very serious. His first thought was, *I may have gotten her pregnant.* His second thought was, *then we'll have to get married.* His third thought was, *only they won't let us marry.* Then he got up and went to the bathroom where he showered for a long time. Finally he put on clean clothes and went out to the porch to face the new day.

Lying back against the dune he began to think more seriously about Rosalind. Why had she let it happen, he wondered. She had not been driven by passion. Neither, for that matter, had he. Why had he done it? It was a crazy thing to do, without precautions, with mosquitoes biting his back, and no blanket for Rosalind to lie on. His knees were chafed. It had really not been much fun for either of them, particularly Rosalind. He'd enjoyed it with Elaine more than he had with Rosalind, yet there was just no comparison between the two experiences. Elaine meant very little; Rosalind meant everything.

Commentary.   *Sex is a challenge for adolescents whether they are active or inactive. And it's rare that sex is not serious business. We return to sex in our discussions often. Sexuality, its origins and social significance, is one of the issues with which all theories of adolescent development must come to terms. Chapter 5 is where we review the major theories of adolescence to see how they understand the interplay of psychological and social forces in shaping development. Most adolescents still do not use contraception when they become sexually active.*

From the novel.   . . . the whole world came back to him. His mother. His father. Anne. A feeling of absolute despair came over him. He couldn't even drown himself! They wouldn't let him. And it wasn't just them. It was Phil and Shirley. It was Rosalind herself. It was his whole family. Polly. Joanne. Rufus. His grandmother. His uncles and aunts. They just wouldn't let him do this. He couldn't swim out and drown as he wanted to drown. He had to go back.

He was treading water, rising and falling with these waves which were ready to bear him back to the shore if only he wanted to ride them. From the top of each wave he could see a host of waves crowding in toward him. He could feel the wind blowing in his face. Waves and wind and family all seemed to urge him away from his death. He felt completely helpless. Not being able to die was worse than dying. In fact dying would be a relief, only the shoreward tug of his family was too strong, as strong as the waves themselves. He felt almost angry about it. He had to go on living, even when he didn't want to live. He looked longingly toward the wave-shaped horizon. If only he could get out there, but he couldn't.

Commentary.   Death wish. Adolescents sometimes seem to flirt with death as much as they flaunt their vitality. They wallow in fantasies of despair and joy and may even seriously attempt suicide. If they are not connected to life by the positive bonds of family and friends, they may even succeed in destroying themselves. Social connection is vital. It plays a role in the formation of identity (Chapter 7) and in the dynamics of most social and psychological problems affecting adolescents (Chapters 11 and 12) from suicide to depression.

From the novel.   Friendliness would be his chief emotion. It already was. He felt friendly toward everyone. Being brokenhearted much of the time had widened his sympathy, and he now paid much more attention than before to classmates like Betty Lomax who had never been popular or well liked. She had beautiful hair, but she was a little overweight, and her skin was a bit sallow, and she was not particularly witty or bright. Yet he felt she was a sweet and lovable person, and he smiled at her in the hall and talked to her when he had the chance.

Commentary.   Resolution. Crisis. Resolution. A successful adolescent resolves each crisis and goes forward strengthened and more mature to face the next challenge and in so doing advances forward in the transition to adulthood. Most theories of adolescence assign a central role to this crisis/resolution motif, as we will see in Chapters 5 and 7.

What Is Adolescence?

What is adolescence? Thomas Rogers has given us some answers in *At the Shores*, but we will spend the rest of our time in this book providing a more complex and detailed answer. Put most simply, adolescence is the period of life between childhood and adulthood. That period may be short (so short, in fact, that it seems to disappear entirely), or it may be long (so long that it may seem endless to everyone involved). It may be marked clearly by elaborate ceremonies called *rites of passage* or be ambiguous and ill-defined, with some aspects of adulthood beginning earlier than others and no ceremonies or symbols that say clearly who is an adult and who is not. Adolescence results from the interplay of individual characteristics and the social systems in which the individual participates directly (family, school, church, peer group, etc.) or that have an indirect effect upon the individual's behavior and development (e.g., the parent's workplace, the school board, the state legislature). This is what we mean by an *ecological* perspective on adolescence, and we will spend our time in Chapter 2 examining it.

Although we will make mention of the experience of adolescence throughout history and in societies around the world, we are most concerned with understanding adolescence in North America in the 20th century. With modern North America as our target, we can be a bit more specific in defining adolescence. Adolescence is the period of life that begins *around the time* when the processes of physical and sexual maturation (*puberty*) move into high gear and ends when young people have assumed responsibility for the major roles of adulthood (economic, sexual, and political). For most people, adolescence begins before the start of the teenage years (ages 11–12) and ends after the teenage years pass (in the early 20s). In general, more and more young people have come to experience a longer and more fully felt adolescence in North American society in the last three centuries. And in recent decades the traditional period encompassed by the seven years from 13 to 19 has grown to the current adolescent period that spans a decade. The main reason for this seems to be an historical increase in the time spent in school and a decrease in the time spent in work during the teenage years.

Youth and History

In order to understand where we are, we need to know where we've been. Such an understanding is essential here. For help we can turn to Joseph Kett (1977), the leading historian of adolescence. Kett points out that the emergence of adolescence as a distinct life stage did not occur in isolation. It was part and parcel of the decline of child labor and the rise of secondary education as a socially-mandated practice. Furthermore, each of these historical developments took place as part of a larger phenomenon, the industrialization of North America. Kett tells us that many of the current problems and conflicts adolescents face, such as juvenile delinquency, sexual awakening, and the "generation gap," are not new. They appear over and over again in our history. Education and occupation have, along with other social forces, transformed the North American continent from a rural, agricultural wilderness with a small native Indian population to a modern urbanized and industrialized society. In the course of this transformation, schools have become the dominant social context for young people, while work has become a part-time experience. As a result, adolescence has come to occupy a larger and larger role in the lives of more and more young people. The history of the relation between education and work *is* the history of adolescence in many ways.

The majority of the schools in 18th century America were primary schools that served children and focused on the "three R's" and, of course, religion. Such schools were open to both boys and girls. However, the grammar schools (the counterpart to today's high schools) were reserved for only a small minority of boys who had interests in the professions (Greenleaf, 1978). Attending school was not mandatory. The individual, and usually the family, made the choice. However, the Puritans were unique in making education more than an individual or family decision. As Bailyn (1960) indicates, unruly and uneducated youth had no place in the Puritan society of the 17th and 18th centuries, and community leaders feared that the family's ability to impart piousness, literacy, and industriousness was diminishing, so the government stepped in and made schooling mandatory, a development that began to spread in the 19th century. Then as now, adults asked, "What's the matter with kids today?"

As society became more complex, the traditional method of the family making decisions about the education of their children was no longer sufficient. Schools developed as a necessary institutional response to changing conditions and to new needs for socialization (Greenleaf, 1978). The 18th century Rationalist Movement bolstered the image of the school as a constructive social force. Curriculum became a burning issue towards the end of this period. As Oscar Handlin (1976) reports:

> Well before 1776, American education felt the pressure of competing, even contradictory, impulses that continued to create cross-currents in its development for two centuries. An endlessly unravelling argument thus echoed through the decades between those who insisted that the primary function of the schools was to transmit an inherited body of culture and those who wished to focus attention on training useful skills. (p. 126)

Of course, this sounds quite relevant to today's educational system. These common concerns link today with yesterday: What is the proper role of home and school? How much education is enough? When should young people be free to leave school? Vocational or classical curricula? Secular or religious themes? In the past, the notion of publically financed schools was not widespread and these educational issues applied only to those who could afford to pay for schooling out of their own pockets.

After the 1860s, population on the continent quadrupled. Immigration, which slowed to a trickle after the Revolutionary War, increased sharply during this period (Tyack, 1978) as North America became a refuge for the poor and persecuted of the world. North American society was quickly becoming urbanized, industrialized, and specialized.

This was a period of tremendous expansion for the elementary and high schools, and thus the experience of adolescence increased in scope. Several of the events and processes that occurred were instrumental in shaping today's educational system. For one thing, school became compulsory. Starting with Massachusetts in 1852 and ending with Mississippi in 1918, each of the United

States passed compulsory attendance laws (Pounds & Bryner, 1973). While high schools began to appear in the 1820s, it was not until the 1870s that the high school replaced the academy as the major secondary educational agency. In 1874, the Kalamazoo decision by the United States Supreme Court legalized the use of public funds for high schools (Pounds & Bryner, 1973), but opposition to public funding for an even broader educational system continued.

During this period, the educational system began to develop many of its modern characteristics. Schools became systematic and organized. The grouping of students into separate grades (the *ladder system*) became dominant, and objective examinations and standard courses of study developed (Pounds & Bryner, 1977). School organization became bureaucratic and centralized. The teaching profession also underwent changes. Prior to this time, teachers had to meet few if any formal qualifications. In addition, with education being a marginal institution, teachers had little authority, and discipline was a major problem (as it is today in many schools where cultural and social conditions again conspire against education for teenagers). Conditions improved, however. With a graded school system, teachers became more specialized. Qualifications became more stringent and schools for training teachers emerged. As education became legitimate, and students were separated according to age, discipline became an easier task. More and more, teaching was becoming a professional— and a female—occupation (Perkinson, 1977).

The schools seemed to offer a way of socializing the masses in a uniform manner. With the great influx of immigrants, the schools served to assimilate those of diverse backgrounds into North American culture. As North American life became more recognizably different from European life, immigrants were viewed as a threat with mass education as the solution (Perkinson, 1977). In practice, however, this solution was not perfect. Immigrants were not always willing to give up their past, and thus immigrant young people faced conflicts between the worlds of home and school. To resolve this dilemma, immigrant parents often kept their children out of school, just as affluent American-born elites often resorted to private schools to avoid contact with foreigners (Tyack, 1978). All in all, however, and especially as the middle class grew, the public educational system came to be a major force in creating a uniform society in which more young people were experiencing adolescence.

Schools also took on the function of rectifying social ills and providing a refuge for socially problematic youth. Horace Mann, a leader in the common school crusade, maintained that social problems, be they drunkenness, slavery, inequality of rights for women, poverty, blindness, or insanity, could only be solved by uniform education. Schools were the starting point of reform (Tyack, 1978). In addition, the great influx of immigrants and the movement towards urban living created a large population of youth for which delinquency was a major problem (Kett, 1977). Furthermore, labor leaders saw education as a way to improve adult wages (Perkinson, 1977), since if children of employable age were in school, they did not compete with adults in the job market. All in all, the expansion of schooling for young people served many social goals. A major outcome of this expansion was the extension of the scope and duration of adolescence.

Although compulsory education was legally mandated and child labor outlawed, neither was enforced. As a deputy constable appointed to enforce child labor and training laws in Massachusetts wrote in 1870:

> Nobody looks after it—neither town authorities, nor school committees, nor local police—and the large cities and many towns of the state are full of unschooled children . . .and nobody thinks of obeying the school laws. In fact, most persons are ignorant that there is any such law (from Kaestle & Vinovkis, 1980, p. 76).

In the 20th century, education has become a nearly universal experience for youth. Participation by youth aged 14–17 in school rose from 32% in 1920 to nearly 90% in 1960 and has remained at about that level ever since (U.S. Bureau of the Census, 1978). During the same period, the percentage of those graduating from high school increased from less than 20% to over 65% (Carnegie Commission on Higher Education, 1973). Two of the major forces that served to increase enrollment and graduation were the Great Depression and improved industrial technology (Havighurst & Neugarten, 1977). During the Great Depression, the majority of adolescents were unable to get jobs, and thus were encouraged to stay in school. The school took on a "cold storage" function: keeping adolescents fresh but out of circulation. With the improvement of industrial technology, fewer unskilled and semiskilled jobs were available, and this made it difficult for adolescents to get jobs after the Depression. In addition, as jobs requiring high school and college degrees increased, the incentive to stay in school and graduate also increased. Certification, which began during the previous period, was now in full swing.

The curriculum of the high school underwent further changes. Educators and theorists became concerned that the existing system would perpetuate class differences. The main focus thus was no longer to prepare adolescents for college or jobs, but to teach adolescents to "get along with others" and to "fit in." In the beginning of this period, "social efficiency" was stressed; in the 1940s and 1950s, "life adjustment" (Tyack, 1978). However, the function of the school to select youth for future high status education and work persisted, as successful adolescents were given the society's stamp of approval and sent on to college and to jobs with higher status and monetary rewards.

Colleges and businesses began complaining that the schools were neither properly selecting nor training students for their future (Perkinson, 1977). Studies emerged during the 1950s showing that America had too few skilled technicians and professional workers and too many unskilled laborers. In 1957, the Soviet Union launched the first earth satellite, Sputnik 1. North Americans (particularly those in the United States) viewed this event as an indictment of their educational deficiency. Within a year, the U.S. Congress passed the National Defense Education Act to provide funds for improving the quality of instruction in science, math, and foreign languages. In addition, it provided funds to improve guidance and counseling services as well as vocational education programs. This served to reinforce the role of schools in the adolescent experience.

Social justice has been the overarching theme of the post-World War II period, and this has had an important impact on the experience of adolescence. Social movements developed that were aimed at changing the educational and occupational prospects of minority groups. In 1954, the U.S. Supreme Court ordered that all states proceed with the racial desegregation of all public schools. This was followed by the Civil Rights Act of 1964, which prohibited discrimination of any kind in any agency that received public funds, and the Elementary and Secondary Education Act of 1965, which provided schools with funds to use for desegregation purposes (Havighurst & Neugarten, 1977). The process of desegregating the public schools was far from easy. It became apparent that since many communities and neighborhoods were racially segregated, integration could only take place through the mass transportation or *busing* of students. Dissatisfaction with busing was and still is widespread, and it continues to involve adolescents in political protest, violence, and challenging interpersonal situations in the halls, classrooms, and buses of their schools. We shall examine the effects of desegregation when we return to the topic of schooling in Chapter 9. If this historical review tells us anything it is that the basic educational issues facing North America today grew out of the nature of our society as it has developed over the last two hundred years.

The Demography of Youth

One way of examining the meaning of adolescence is to consider how many youth there are in relation to the rest of the population. Studying the size and composition of the adolescent population (their *demography*) can tell us much of importance. Figure 1–1 summarizes demographic trends for the youth population (age 14–24) for the hundred years from 1890–1990.

Note several things in this figure. First, in 1890 the ratio of youth to adults was higher than it has ever been (.57). This means that more of the population was young in 1890 than ever before. Why? For one thing, life expectancy was shorter in 1890, so people remained in the adult population for a shorter period of time. For another thing, immigration was high then, and immigrants tended to be young and to have large numbers of children. But does all this mean that adolescents dominated society? Although young people were in great numbers, relatively few of them were living as adolescents, as we use the term today. Very few were in school, for example.

A Case Study: School Size and Adolescent Development

One interesting historical trend that illustrates the role of schools in shaping the adolescent experience is the dramatic increase in the size of secondary schools since World War II, from an average of 500 per school in 1950 to 1500 per school in 1980 (Garbarino & Asp, 1981). As we shall see later, this increase in school size was prompted in part by a massive increase in the size of the youth population, but it goes beyond that in both its origins and consequences and tells us something about society and its values. As such, it is a good introduction to our ecological perspective on adolescence.

Why are schools getting bigger? Schools could be small but seldom are for two reasons that are rooted in our culture and its values (what we call its *ideology*). First, as Conant (1959) and Jackson (1966) point out, the emphasis of educational experts on the formal academic aspects of the school's curriculum has led to a concern for and interest in the strength of large schools. In this line of reasoning, bigger is better because it increases the school's ability to provide diverse intellectual resources for students (e.g., an advanced math class for seniors). A disregard for the social issues involved in school size may have stemmed from the assumption that the only real issue facing schools is academic sophistication. This may have been true in the 1950s, when the major drive to eliminate small schools gathered momentum. An analysis by Heath (1970) reports that many states in the 1950s mandated the consolidation of small schools (with enrollments of 400–600) into large schools with enrollments in the thousands in order to achieve more sophisticated and high-powered academic curricula. This is interesting in light of recent demands for a return to the basics.

The second major ideological reason for increased school size stems from the notion that bigger is always better. As Schumacher (1973) and Sale (1980) report, modern societies are characterized by the impulse toward bigness in all social institutions—business, government, religion, and education. "Enrollments" in all institutions have either been *allowed* to grow in a generally haphazard and unplanned manner, with little or no consideration given to the impact of such growth on social dynamics, or they have been *forced* to grow as a sign of institutional health. Hence, it appears that largeness in schools is a reflection of largeness in the broader social spectra—government, industry, and so on. For schools, the assumption is that bigger means more power, diversity, and opportunity for educational specialization and differentiation. What is more, many administrators have concluded that bigger schools provide more benefits per dollar spent (are more cost-effective) and are a more efficient use of tax money.

Research increasingly disputes these claims and warns us against big schools on psychological grounds (Garbarino & Asp, 1981). In their classic study, Barker and Gump (1964) investigated 13 Kansas high schools varying in size from 35 to 2,287 students. They focused on the *behavioral settings* present in each school. By behavioral settings, Barker and Gump mean the different formal and informal activities that make up the school. These include "math class," "chorus practice," "lunchroom," "study hall," "home economics class," "gym class," "the football game," "detention after school for misbehavior," "waiting for the bus," "smoking in the bathroom," "chess club," and all the other regular situations existing in the school. Barker and Gump refer to them as "organized assemblies of behavior, episodes, physical objects, space, and duration" (p. 19). In other words, they are the psychological and social *units* of which schools are composed. Certain types of behavioral settings, however, such as academic classes, athletic contests, and libraries were common to all schools. Beyond such settings, the number and variety of settings available to students increased directly with school size. For example, in the smallest school, there were 60 behavioral settings, and in the largest school, there were 189 behavioral settings. Thus, in the larger schools students had more curricular and extracurricular options.

Increased options, however, do not mean increased participation. In fact, the reverse seems to be true. That is, larger schools may have increased options, but they have lower participation rates. Gump and Friesen (1964) studied 11th graders in five of the above mentioned schools. One school was large (over 2,000 students) and four were small (83–151 students). They found that the average participation rate per student was higher in the small schools than in the large school. Thus, even though the large school offered more behavioral settings (189 compared to 48 for the small schools), the students in the small schools were active in more settings. Furthermore, not only did students in small schools participate in more settings, they also participated in a wider variety of settings. Students in the large schools were more "specialized." The larger the school, the higher the level of talent and expertise necessary for participation. In the smaller school the average student

had a much better chance of both having a chance to participate and to participate successfully. As Gump (1977) stated:

> Satisfactions in the small schools are more related to improvements of one's capacity, to challenge and action, to close cooperation among peers, and to 'being important.' Large school satisfactions tended to be more passive; that is, they were derived from somebody else's actions. (p. 383)

This leads us to worry that adolescents in big schools are being taught to be passive, and it shows us that social systems do much to shape the adolescent experience.

Social systems usually affect different individuals differently, however. It appears that school size affects academically unsuccessful students ("marginal students") more than academically successful students. Willems (1967) studied this in the five above-mentioned schools, and in an additional large school (2,015 students) and five other small schools (81–183 students). He calculated a student-to-activity availability ratio (S/A) in each school. Low S/A referred to more activities than students ("undermanning"), and high S/A referred to more students than activities ("overmanning"). Undermanning occurs more often in smaller schools, and overmanning occurs more often in the large schools. Willems compared marginal students—i.e., low scores on intelligence tests (an IQ of less than 99), two or more D grades in previous semester, and parents who had dropped out of high school—with regular students (i.e., IQ above 105, at least C grades, and a father employed in white collar occupation) in both large and small schools. In the small schools, there was no difference in reported sense of obligation to nonclass activities between marginal and normal students. In the large schools, however, the regular students had significantly higher sense-of-obligation scores than the marginal students. Furthermore, when marginal students in large schools did participate, they received little positive feedback. Other research takes this a step further and finds higher dropout rates for large schools (Garbarino & Asp, 1981). All in all, it seems the anonymity of the large school lessens personal accountability.

In broad terms, school size can have an impact on the character development of the student (Garbarino, 1973, 1980). Specifically, large schools tend to exert a negative influence on the character development of most students by depriving them of important experiences in participatory roles. Such experiences are essential for effective socialization to adulthood and for orderly social relations. We can suggest that school crime, alienation, and dropping out is related to school size. Large schools are less likely to offer a personalized climate; there is a weaker *connection* between the human adolescent and the often impersonal inflexible system.

Remember, however, we are speaking in broad terms. For some students and for some purposes, large schools can be beneficial in many ways. The superior athlete may benefit more from the publicity and greater competition afforded by larger schools. Furthermore, as Grabe (1981) indicates, failure to compete successfully may be more detrimental to those in small schools, where success is more common, than in large schools, where failure is

more common. His 1981 study reports that while participation rates are higher in small schools, the *pressure* to participate successfully can *increase* alienation when students lack the ability, motivation, or interest to respond positively to the situational pressure. Nothing comes without costs. That is one of our messages in this text. But, when we are speaking of the average adolescent, bigger schools usually denote a more overall negative experience. And big schools represent the culmination of a trend begun in the 19th century for schooling to assume an increasingly dominant role in defining adolescence.

The length of the school year as well as the number of students completing twelve years of school have also increased, another example of the increased role of the school in adolescent life. In 1870 the average student had a 132-day school year but was out of school some 41% of the time. By 1920 the average year was 162 days, and the average student was out 25% of the time. By 1968, the school year was 179 days, and the average student out only 9% of the time (Coleman, 1974). Whereas in 1937 only 42% of those who were enrolled in the fifth grade actually completed high school and only 15% entered college, by the late 1970s these figures were 85% and 49%, respectively (Garbarino & Asp, 1981). In Chapter 9 we explore the dynamics of schooling for adolescents.

The second point to note in Figure 1–1 is that the ratio of youth to adults declined from 1890–1960 (and the actual *number* of youth even declined between 1940–1950). The major reason is longer life spans for adults and a sharp decline in the birth rate during the Depression years of the 1930s (when the youth of the 1950s were born). Also, of course, immigration slowed down in the 1920s and a significant number of young people died in World Wars I and II. One consequence of this was a relatively small number of youth in the

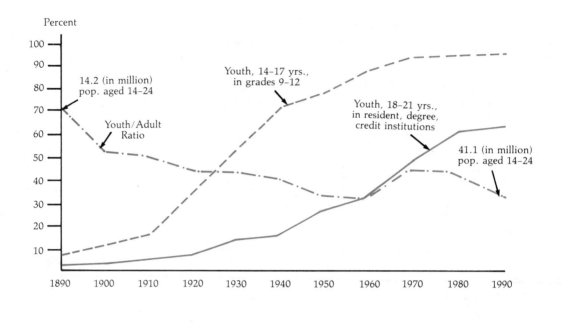

Percent

Enrollment statistics by decade
Digest of Education Statistics, 1975 Edition, DHEW Education Division National Center for Education Statistics, U.S. Government Printing Office 1976. Table 30, p. 37, Table 80, p. 80. Historical Statistics of the United States, Bureau of the Census 1975, p. 383. Projections of Education Statistics to 1984–85, National Center for Education Statistics 1976. Table 3, p. 18, Table 5, p. 21, Table B-2, p. 154, and Table B-3, p. 155.

Aging ratio
Ratio of population 14–24 to population aged 25–64 from Table 2, Chapter 3 of PSAC report 1973. Chapter 3 prepared by Norman Ryder.

FIGURE 1.1

Secular trends in population aging and enrollment rates for secondary and higher education, United States, 1890–1990. (Reprinted with permission from J. Adelson, (ed.) Handbook of Adolescent Psychology, N.Y. John Wiley & Sons, Inc.,© 1980.)

1950s and correspondingly good job prospects in the post World War II period because of less competition for entry-level jobs.

Third, note the enormous increase in the number and ratio of youth from 1960 to 1970 (increases of unprecedented magnitude). This is the "baby boom" generation, who were born in the wake of World War II and dominated the Youth Culture of the 1960s.

What is the significance of the baby boom generation and the fact that in the 1980s the number and ratio of youth are declining again? It means that commercial opportunities decline in one market (e.g., youth-oriented products such as record albums) and increase in others (e.g., physical fitness facilities for young adults). It may also mean a shift in political priorities and media attention away from adolescent concerns. Of course, the most dramatic changes occur in institutional efforts to serve youth, most notably in schools. As the baby boom reached school age, communities mobilized to enlarge first elementary schools and then, in the 1950s, to expand high schools, and finally, in the 1960s and 1970s, to develop colleges and universities. In the 1980s, communities are expanding facilities for adult education, while closing elementary and secondary schools.

Although the baby boom slowed down in North America in the 1970s, it has been continuing nonstop all over the world since World War II (Brown, 1981). Declining death rates (due to improved basic health care and preventive medicine) and high birth rates have meant mushrooming population growth in Africa, Asia, and South and Central America. As more and more nations have become industrialized and urbanized, their massive young populations have come to include more and more young people who actually experience adolescence as we are describing it here. In Brazil, for example, 60% of the population is 15 years old or younger. In Chapter 13 we will return to demographic issues as we look at the history of and future for youth.

Demography helps us see where and when to look for changes in the social meaning of adolescence. It tells us where the markets are, where the institutional needs are, and where the issues will be for professional services.

Health and Mortality

By all rights, it seems adolescence should be a time of peak physical condition, when the biological organism comes into its full powers. Advertisements portray adolescents as robust, glowing, and alive with vigor. And adolescents *are* healthy in most respects, as we shall see in Chapter 3. They are spared many of the degenerative diseases that afflict old age and are well past most of the communicable childhood diseases. And yet, some health problems are particularly serious in adolescence. Venereal diseases are a major problem, for example, with herpes being a growing crisis. What is more, social and mental crises are often tied to threats to physical well-being. As the following report indicates, social violence, often related to drug abuse, ends the lives of many adolescents each year.

WASHINGTON, Jan. 8, 1983 (AP). Death rates in the United States are declining for everybody except people from 15 to 24 years old, a Federal report says.

Accidents, murders, and suicides were responsible for three out of four deaths among that group, up sharply from 1950 when they accounted for about half the deaths in the grouping.

Automobile accidents are the leading cause of death among young whites, accounting for 40 percent of the deaths in 1979, but homicides account for the largest portion of deaths among young blacks, 39 percent.

The figures were included by the Department of Health and Human Services in a report titled "Health, United States, 1982." The figures used were for 1979, the latest full year available. . .

The report said that in 1979, the death rate for young men was three times higher than that for young women and the mortality rate among blacks was 20% higher than among whites.

The data also showed that death rates from such external causes as accidents, homicide, and suicide, which have at times been as much as 85% higher for black youths than for white youths, are beginning to converge.

In 1979, the rate for young black women was four percent higher than that for young white women and the rate for young black men was 12 percent higher than that for young white men. The convergence can be explained by a decrease in deaths from homicides and from non-motor vehicle accidents among young blacks, along with more deaths from motor vehicle accidents among young whites, the report said.

There were 34.4 deaths of young people per 100,000 population from motor vehicle accidents in 1950, and 46.8 such deaths per 100,000 in 1979. (*New York Times*, January 9, 1983, p. 21)

While health-care professionals have come to see that "life-style" is an important influence on adult health, they have long realized that it is *the* major influence on adolescent health. Adolescent health depends mainly upon social rather than strictly medical care, since the issues revolve around encouraging safe habits (e.g., with respect to alcohol, sex, and tobacco) and discouraging high-risk activities (such as high-speed driving, the use of dangerous drugs, unprotected sexual activity, and criminal behavior). All these contribute to the social violence adolescents experience at their own hands, directly or indirectly. And beyond the violence involved in accidents and high-risk life-styles, is the violence that involves adolescents in their families.

Domestic Violence

Violence is deeply embedded in our way of life, and adolescents are part of that culture of violence—on both the giving and the receiving end. Table 1–1 presents the results of a national survey of violence in two-parent families (Straus, Gelles, and Steinmetz, 1980). "Severe violence" includes kicking, biting, hitting with a fist or an object, beating up, threatening, or using a gun or a knife.

Note how common violence is between siblings: 76% report some form of violence (including 48% in the severe category). Note also that 18% of the

TABLE 1.1
Violence in the family.

	Violence Index	Severe Index
Spouse-to-Spouse	16%	6%
Parent-to-Child	64%	14%
Child-to-Parent	18%	9%
Sibling-to-Sibling	76%	48%

SOURCE: Based on Straus, Gelles and Steinmetz, 1980, p. 266.

kids are reported to behave violently towards their parents. This contrasts with 64% of the parents who behave violently towards their children. Violence is taught and learned first in the family, as we will see in Chapter 6 when we discuss parent-adolescent relations.

A recent study by Martin and Kourany (1980) showed that violence is a significant problem when teenagers babysit for younger children outside their families. Figure 1–2 reports the results.

With over one million teenagers employed regularly in babysitting in the United States, the fact that 7.7% of the adolescent babysitters reported hitting their charges means tens of thousands of adolescents are doling out this form of violence to children outside their own families. Extreme cases like the following are documented and may be all too common.

> Robert J., an 11-year-old white male was recently charged with beating three young children for whom he was babysitting. All three girls, ages 2, 4, and 6, were treated and released from a local hospital following the attack, labelled as aggravated assault. He had been hired by the mother to care for the children for one evening. The mother had minimal contact with the sitter prior to engaging his services, and despite this fact, she was stunned by his impulsive angry episode. The Department of Human Services investigated the case. (Martin and Kourany, 1980)

Adolescent violence can take many forms and arise for many reasons. One of the most dramatic and disturbing forms is when adolescents kill their parents—*parricide*. Youth kill their parents for various reasons, but many incidents tell the story of adolescents who retaliate against brutal parents—*reactive parricide* (Post, 1982). Such cases reveal the desperation of brutalized teenagers and how poorly our society prevents violence in the family, often not even recognizing it or intervening before it takes its horrible toll in human destruction. This terrible theme was brought to continental attention in 1982–1983 when two teenagers in Wyoming conspired to kill their brutally abusive father.

Richard, Deborah (his sister), and Mrs. Jahnke were terrorized by Mr. Jahnke for years. This abusive treatment included psychological, physical, and

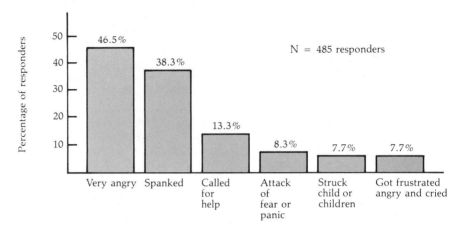

FIGURE 1.2

Negative experiences while babysitting. (Reprinted with permission from Child Abuse and Neglect, 4, *J. E. Martin and R. F. C. Kovrany, Child abuse by adolescent babysitters,* © 1980, Pergamon Press, Ltd.)

sexual brutality. At age 16, Richard struck back. He killed his father with a shotgun blast.

> I told my sister that night, "Don't worry, Deborah, I'm going to protect you. He's never going to hurt you again." She was going crazy—she was being hurt so much. She needed to be free. I had to free my mother and myself. . .free them from the pain and misery my father had caused us, and would always cause us. (James, 1983)

Post (1982) tells us that this case is a classic example of reactive parricide. As such, of course, it represents the negative extremes of family life for adolescents. It also reveals some of the major normal issues in the family dynamics surrounding adolescents: a changing balance of power, more autonomous decision making, sexuality, and a coming to fruition of patterns established in childhood. Even in normal and successful families, adolescence can be a challenge.

Family Relations

What does adolescence mean for the family as a whole? For one thing, it means adjusting patterns of authority and interaction to incorporate a new person, as we shall see in greater detail in Chapter 6. Developmental psychologist John Hill (1980) has looked at the research on this matter, and he concludes that:

> Studies where family interaction is directly observed suggest that there may be a period of temporary disequilibrium in early adolescence while the family adjusts

to having a "new person" in the household—"new" in stature, "new" in approaching reproductive capability, "new" in cognitive competence—but this disequilibrium in no way approaches the shoot-out that many parents are led to expect from media reports. Instead, in most families, there appears to be a period of adaptation to the primary changes, a period when both parents and their newly adolescent children work out—often not consciously—what these changes mean for their relationships. (1980, p. 33)

At its heart, the task of being parent to an adolescent (and adolescent to a parent) is substantially different from the parent-child relationship in several ways (Garbarino & Gilliam, 1980).

- *The adolescent's power is much greater than the child's.* This includes physical power, of course, including the capability for physical retaliation if assaulted by a parent. It goes beyond this, however, to include the power to stimulate and influence family conflict, to leave the family situation, to harm self and others, to embarrass the parents, to compare parents with other adults, and to help oneself and others. All this suggests that the role of adolescents themselves in producing destructive parent-child relations may be a quite significant factor.
- *The adolescent has a broader field of other significant individuals with whom the parents must come to terms.* Autonomous relationships with other adults and with peers increase, including sexual relationships that many parents may perceive as threatening.
- *The adolescent's intellectual abilities are likely to be more advanced than are the child's.* Adolescents tend to reason much more like adults, and this injects a new element of complexity into the parent's task. It may also increase the importance of how intellectually sophisticated parents and youth are, for harmonious family relationships may depend upon the ability of each to figure out the other.

These factors and others come together to change the standards that guide appropriate behavior in family relationships when a child reaches adolescence. Some forms of behavior by parents toward their offspring that were appropriate (if not particularly wise) in childhood may become abusive in adolescence. For example, the psychological connotations of spanking a three- or four-year-old are usually different from those of spanking a 15-year-old, and most families have ceased to use physical punishment by that age. Likewise, types of affectionate touching and other intimate physical contact that are quite appropriate, even desirable, between a father and his infant daughter are inappropriate between the same father and his teenage daughter because of their sexual connotations. Also, efforts to exert a high level of control over the details of a four-year-old's daily existence may be acceptable, while the same intrusiveness with a teenager would be entirely inappropriate.

In some ways, parents can "get away with more" in their interactions with young children than in their treatment of adolescents. Adolescents have a broader base of experience with which to compare parental actions. If treated badly, teenagers are more likely than young children to perceive the deviance of their treatment and to report it to someone outside the family (Garbarino & Gilliam, 1980). Many adolescents have developed the mental capacity to enable them to better understand flaws in parental reasoning and character and have the physical capacity to do something about it. On the economic side, U. S. Department of Agriculture figures indicate that the yearly cost of maintaining a teenager is about 140% that of a young child. This increased cost is stressful for many families and may be a source of family conflict, particularly in blue-collar families where wages peak early in life so that the increased financial demands of adolescence are not matched by increasing income as they usually are in white-collar families.

Put it all together and it is little wonder that surveys such as that done by Pasley and Gecas (1983) report that a majority of parents say that the adolescent years are the most difficult ones for childrearing. They found that the ages 14–18 were ranked most difficult, followed by the 10–13-year-old period.

And yet, while many parents view adolescence as a difficult time, many adults (including parents some of the time) look nostalgically at adolescents because they see the bittersweetness of their own departed youth: first love, first job, first poetry, first everything. It's worth noting here that we must always be cautious of conclusions based upon what people remember; adults are liable to misrepresent adolescence—both their own and their children's. Data drawn from memory (*retrospective data*) are subject to a variety of distortions ranging from simple forgetting to subtle and often unintentional efforts to make the past make sense in terms of the present and to justify actions taken in the past in light of knowledge only possessed in the present.

Examining cultural images of adolescence is important to understanding the social meaning of adolescence, although as we have said, it is not the whole story. It is an important part of our ecological perspective, as we shall see in Chapter 2, because it helps show us the cultural blueprints upon which society is built.

Images of Adolescence

Many adults recall adolescence as a bittersweet time. The 19th century British poet Wordsworth captured this feeling with exquisite poignancy in his "Ode. Intimations of Immortality" (1807):

> Though nothing can bring back the hour
> of splendor in the grass, of glory in the flowers,
> We will grieve not, rather find
> Strength in what remains behind. . .

Consider the following anonymous poetic tribute to youth that captures one way our culture attributes social meaning to adolescence.

On Youth

Youth is not entirely a time of life, it is a state of mind. It is not wholly a matter of ripe cheeks, red lips, or supple knees. It is a temper of will, a quality of the imagination, a vigor of the emotions.

Nobody grows old by merely living a number of years. People grow old only by deserting their ideals. You are as young as your faith, as old as your doubt; as young as your self-confidence, as old as your fears; as young as your hope, as old as your despair.

In the central place of every heart, there is a recording chamber; so long as it receives messages of beauty, hope, cheer and courage, you are young.

When the wires are all down and your heart is covered with the snows of pessimism and the ice of cynicism, then and then only have you grown old.

We do need to go beyond nostalgic images of adolescents (which usually apply to teenagers in ones or twos) and recognize the sinister images of adolescents. Stereotypes of adolescents abound in the media and in the attitudes of most adults, even professionals in the field. And many of these stereotypes are negative.

Youth can serve a symbolic function for adults. Other writers see different images when they recall adolescence and even when they observe real teenagers at work on the challenge of experiencing adolescence. Writing in *Esquire* magazine, Bob Greene gave us a vivid picture in an article called simply "Fifteen." His article reminds us that while we may speak generally of adolescence, there are important sub-periods, with middle adolescence (14–16 years old) being a time when the feeling of being "between" may be at its height, particularly for boys.

FIFTEEN. WHAT a weird age to be male. Most of us have forgotten about it, or have idealized it. But when you are fifteen. . .well, things tend to be less than perfect.

You can't drive. You are only a freshman in high school. The girls your age look older than you and go out with upperclassmen who have cars. You probably don't shave. You have nothing to do on the weekends.

So how do you spend your time? In 1982, most likely at a mall. Woodfield is an enclosed shopping center sprawling over 2.25 million square feet in northern Illinois. There are 230 stores at Woodfield, and on a given Saturday those stores are cruised in and out of by thousands of teenagers killing time. (Greene, 1982, p. 17)

Some of the most prominent observers of adolescence in the 1950s and 1960s saw these negative stereotypes as both the cause and effect of adolescent alienation from the adult world. Classics such as Paul Goodman's *Growing Up Absurd* (1956) and Edgar Friedenberg's *The Vanishing Adolescent* (1959) and *The Dignity of Youth and Other Atavisms* (1965) explored this pessimistic theme. Goodman's title is self-explanatory. Friedenberg emphasized the way adults regard adolescents with fear and often contempt. High schools are the principal arena in which adult society plays out this theme:

> They are problem-oriented and the feelings and needs for growth of their captives and unenfranchised clientele are the least of their problems; for the status of the "teenager" in the community is so low that even if he rebels, the school is not blamed for the conditions against which he is rebelling. What high school personnel become specialists in, ultimately, is the *control* of large groups of students. . . (Friedenberg, 1965, pp. 92–93)

Twenty years later, as controlling school crime and meeting basic scholastic requirements have become dominant issues, Friedenberg's analysis remains timely.

Consider this view of adolescents discovered in a 1972 book by Leonard Wolf entitled *A Dream of Dracula: In Search of the Living Dead:*

> Adolescents recognize him at once. (His bad breath, his red, red lips.) If he kissed you once, will he kiss you again? They lie in the torpor of their pupa stage, waiting for something better to happen to them, dreaming about transformations. Pimpled, gawky, swollen with blood and other juices they do not quite understand, they know about being loathed, and loathing. Like Dracula, they avoid mirrors. Like him, they know about drinking blood. Haven't they been told what sacrifices have been made in their behalf? Who ruined their mother's figure? Whose education has cost their father his most brilliant hopes? In revenge, when I ask a classroom of college freshmen who, in their experience, most nearly resembles a vampire, they unhesitatingly set down their answers: "My father"; "My mother."
>
>   Blood surges in and soils the young. Hearing the world "suck," they look about warily, in the grip of strange confusions: they know what all those films are about—ego, power, parasitism, loneliness, immortality, youth, youth, youth and thirty-eight kinds of sex. The living-dead. Finally it comes down to this: When Dracula's lips approach the delicate throat of the beautiful girl on the screen, *they* know. . . . (p. 17)

One common conception of adolescence particularly prevalent in the 1950s and early 1960s was that of the happy-go-lucky, impressionable, sometimes emotional and moody individual who could become caught up in sentiment or some worldly concern, but only in a transient, uncommitted fashion. It was not that adolescents did not take themselves seriously, but the adult world considered them to be in the age of "pre-responsibility." Adelson (1964) has labelled this adolescent stereotype the "fool."

Perhaps as a natural extension of the innocence in the "fool" stereotype, adolescents came to be viewed as the "victims" of adult society. In this view, adolescents were helpless and vulnerable and were often exploited by unscrupulous adults who would take advantage of their innocence. As if to counterbalance this conception, there was the image of the adolescent as a *victimizer* of society. This image pictured the adolescent as a leather-jacketed, rebellious hoodlum bent on destroying society and all the adult world held precious (Adelson, 1964). This "anti-hero" conception was perpetuated in the films and books of the era, most notably in James Dean's portrayal of the "Rebel Without a Cause." Adolescents in this view are a feared group; the term adolescent is synonymous with delinquent (Anthony-Caplan & Lebovici, p. 55). In the 1960s, the teenager came to be viewed as a lazy "peacenik" who would rather lie back in a state of drug-induced euphoria than wash, defend his country, or get a job. Drugs, sex, peace, and love were seen as the values of these adolescents, and contributing to society was their last concern. The 1980s have seen a proliferation of images. Some portray the adolescent as sophisticated but lacking a clear role in society. David Elkind captured this in his 1984 book *All Grown Up with Nowhere to Go.*

Adolescence brings special challenges to those who are part of racial or distinct ethnic minorities, in which even the positive stereotypes can have a negative impact. A young American of Japanese descent pictures it this way in a poem entitled "Turning Hakujin" (which means "turning white" and is a parody of a popular song entitled "I think I'm turning Japanese").

TURNING HAKUJIN

"I" was an Asian   It was a bummer
'Til I discovered the American way
No more odori   No more sashimi
Not while I'm living in the US of A
I think I'm getting whiter every single day
(J. K. Yamamoto, 1982 in *Echoes from Gold Mountain*)

Progress has been made in integrating some aspects of adolescent culture, however. Black pop singer Michael Jackson became a dominant and nearly universal star in the 1980s, cutting across racial lines. What impact has that had? It is hard to tell, as we shall see in Chapter 7 when we deal with self-concept.

Adolescence as a Political Issue

Adolescence are often at the center of political controversy. Many of these controversies center on efforts to control adolescent behavior, particularly adolescent sexual behavior, and may include laws to enact community-wide curfews, to regulate drinking and driving, to require schooling, or to prohibit adolescents from working in "inappropriate" settings. On one side is usually a liberal coalition that argues for "liberating" youth from adult authority in the belief that this will encourage the development of responsibility and character. On the other side stand conservatives who believe that adolescents need to be protected from their immaturity if they (and the society) are to avoid serious harm—be it physical or moral. The debate was hotly contested in Ancient Greece, in Medieval Europe, in Colonial America, in the Roaring Twenties, and in the turbulent 1960s. Each side claims victories and defeats, successes and disappointments. Both sides contain well-intentioned and wise individuals. Which is right? As always, it depends. It depends upon the particular mix of historical forces that define the issues for a particular generation of adolescents.

In recent years, one of the big political controversies concerning adolescents has arisen around efforts to discourage sexual activity and limit access to contraception. One issue that drew public attention in the early 1980s was the proposal that publically-supported facilities be required to inform parents when adolescents requested contraception. This "squeal rule," as it has been called, polarized the traditional sides in the long-standing debate over the rights of parents vs. the rights of adolescents. One legislator, Senator Jeremiah Denton (R-Ala.), went so far as to introduce federal legislation designed to promote sexual abstinence. Responding to Denton's proposal, conservative Republican Senator Barry Goldwater asked: "How the hell are you going to regulate that? They've been trying ever since the apple. It's just like abortions. You can make them unconstitutional but they're still going to go out and have one."

What's Normal for Adolescents? Professional Stereotypes and Empirical Realities

It's very easy to get caught up in describing the many problems of adolescents since they often evoke concern, sympathy, alarm, and interest. A smooth, uneventful adolescence is not going to generate a lot of interest. But focusing on the problem adolescent is misleading. Such an approach often hides the fact that most young people manage the challenges of adolescence, most of the time. In addressing the personal and social adjustment issues of adolescence, the one question that naturally comes to mind is "What is a normal adolescent?"

Normality in human behavior is a difficult concept to define for any age, but in adolescence, determining what constitutes normal behavior is a special problem because of our stereotypes about adolescence. The very definition of a stereotype tells us that the actual contrary behavior of adolescents has little immediate effect on the way adults view adolescents because adults selectively perceive information that is consistent with the stereotype. Stereotypes often serve a useful function for those who hold them. They justify the way things are and make complex situations seem simpler, and perhaps more easy to deal with.

While we should not be surprised by the existence of these stereotypes among the general public, it is surprising to realize that many of those who work with and study adolescents also hold distorted views, and that this has colored the kind of treatment adolescents have received by practitioners and theorists alike.

Professional Stereotypes

An old and enduring view of adolescence has been that this period is necessarily *stormy and stressful* (often referred to by the German words *Sturm und Drang*). In this view, adolescents experience conflict and turmoil as a normal part of their development. They will exhibit unstable, troubled, disturbed behavior that may be barely distinguishable from (or may actually be, depending on one's viewpoint) full blown mental illness—*psychopathology.* Many theorists have subscribed to this view, each with a special description and explanation of the process. Most who do and do so most strongly have worked professionally with or studied disturbed adolescents engaged in deviant behavior. What is more, when they have looked at normal adolescents firsthand, they have usually looked at males, and white males at that. This has tended to produce an adolescent psychology in which the key principles and concepts may invalidly overemphasize the special problems and characteristics of the troubled, the male, and the white. We must keep this in mind as we proceed.

The founder of the storm and stress stereotype was the psychologist G. Stanley Hall (1844–1924), who was the first to publish a textbook on adolescence (1904). Hall was very much influenced by Darwin and the 19th century biologist Ernst Haeckel. Darwin hypothesized that human beings have evolved from "lower" forms of life, with apes, monkeys, and other mammals being our closest relatives. Haeckel studied the development of human embryos and compared this process to the development of the embryos of other species. With the primitive equipment available in his day, Haeckel mistakenly observed that the human embryo changed in such a fashion as to first resemble a fully developed fish embryo, then a frog embryo, later a rat embryo, a monkey embryo, and at last an ape embryo. In Haeckel's view, this was a manifestation of the evolutionary development of man as hypothesized by Darwin. Thus, it was said that *ontogeny* (the biological development of an organism) *recapitulates* (mirrors or repeats) *phylogeny* (the historical evolution of a species).

Hall grasped this notion and applied it to the postnatal development of the human. Thus, as he saw it, the stages of childhood reflected the stages in human evolution. As Gallatin (1975) has described Hall's theory:

> During early infancy the child was recapitulating a "monkey-like" stage in the history of the human species. The years between eight and twelve allegedly represented a reenactment of a more advanced but still rather primitive form of man-

kind, perhaps a tribe that had managed to support itself through hunting and fishing. Similarly, adolescence was supposed to be a recapitulation of a stage midway between savagery and civilization—when still-primitive man had begun to develop the rudiments of a culture. (p. 30)

In Hall's view, the adolescent is struggling to balance the more primitive impulses of the savage with the more humane ones of the civilized person. This attempt to reconcile these two divergent sources of influence results in the turmoil or storm and stress that Hall defined as an inevitable part of the adolescence.

This early formulation of human development did not gain wide acceptance, partly because it relied on the tenuous extension of Darwin's evolutionary theory. One of the problems with the theory was addressed immediately by the psychologist Thorndike (1904). He pointed out that one could not account for the behavior of a two-year-old child by stating that he was recapitulating a monkey-like stage of human evolution, because the two-year-old is already more advanced in ability than monkeys, apes, or any of the creatures the developing human is supposed to be "recapitulating." For an in-depth review of the specific critiques aimed at the theory, the interested reader should seek out Hodos and Campbell (1969), Gallatin (1975), and Thorndike (1904).

Although Hall's specific theory of human development as reflecting the Darwinian evolutionary process did not gain wide acceptance, Hall was responsible for starting the field off on the "nature" orientation, the view that human behavior was more under the influence of genetic rather than environmental determinants (a topic we will return to in Chapter 2). The general idea that adolescence is characterized by "storm and stress" also exerted an enduring influence on psychological theories of adolescent development, as we shall see more fully in Chapter 5 when we consider what theories are and how they work.

The psychoanalytic view of adolescence is one that has had a profound impact on the way in which mental health professionals have dealt with adolescents. While the theory is very different from Hall's formulation in content, it shares Hall's view of adolescence as being necessarily stormy and chaotic and rooted in biological influences. Anna Freud (1958) wrote of the difficulty of distinguishing normality from psychopathology in adolescence:

> . . .adolescence constitutes by definition an interruption of peaceful growth which resembles in appearance a variety of other emotional upsets and structural upheavals. The adolescent manifestations come close to symptom formation of the neurotic, psychotic, or dissocial order and merge almost imperceptibly into borderline states, initial, frustrated or fully fledged forms of almost all the mental illnesses. Consequently, the differential diagnosis between the adolescent upsets and true pathology becomes a difficult task. (p. 267)

This quote illustrates Anna Freud's view of adolescence as a developmental disturbance. While a complete discussion of the psychoanalytic perspective is the province of Chapter 5, a brief and much simplified presentation is in order here. Sigmund Freud (Anna's father) saw the infant as dominated by unrestricted sexual drive *(Id)*. This drive was expressed during a series of stages of psychosexual development, each of which involved a different part of the body for expression. Eventually the child developed a strong sexual attachment to the parent of the opposite sex, leading to a desire to get rid of the same-sexed parent, the child's rival for the object of his/her sexual desire. Freud labelled this combination of desires and emotions the *Oedipus Complex* for males and the *Electra Complex* for females. As children mature, they become aware that this desire is inappropriate, and the ensuing guilt causes a repression of these desires. Thus, at about the age of five, children enter the *latency period* during which the desires are held out of consciousness, and some degree of balance is obtained.

Anna Freud (1936, 1958, 1966) emphasized that the impulses of the latency period are reawakened at the onset of puberty, and teenagers experience psychic conflict as they try to balance their Oedipal impulses with what society dictates as correct behavior. Children may utilize a series of defenses (called *repression, rationalization,* and *projection* in Freudian terminology) in order to keep these Oedipal desires from awareness, thereby escaping the uncomfortable and threatening turmoil that results from the conflict. So, in the psychoanalytic view, while there appears to be a balance during the latency period, it is only a preliminary and precarious balance. As the individual comes closer and closer to adulthood, this balance becomes more and more inappropriate. It cannot handle the powerful sexual drives. Thus, the adolescent has to overthrow his or her old system and build a new one. This process results in the rebellion, the ups and downs, and the dramatic changes that Anna Freud saw as being typical of adolescence.

This period of upheaval is a healthy, normal expression of development, but during this period adolescents will reject their parents (in response to the unacceptable desire to possess the opposite sex parent) and enter into a series of intense but brief romantic involvements with their peers, as they learn to accept and adapt to their rediscovered sexuality. This behavior will be perceived as *rebellion*. (Note here that this provides a theoretical explanation for the stereotyped view of adolescents as being necessarily *rebellious*). It is interesting to note what Anna Freud (1958) wrote concerning what is occurring when such *structural upheavals* and *rebellious* activities do *not* occur.

> . . .we all know individual children who as late as the ages of 14, 15, or 16 show no such outer evidence of inner unrest. They remain, as they have been in dealing with the latency period, "good" children, wrapped up in their family relationships, considerate sons of their mothers, submissive to their fathers, in accord with the atmosphere, ideas, and ideals of the childhood background. Convenient

as this may be, it signifies a delay of normal development and is, as such, a sign to be taken seriously. . . .These are children who have built up excessive defenses against their drive activities and are now crippled by the results, which act as barriers against the normal maturational processes of phase development. They are, perhaps more than any others, in need of therapeutic help to remove the inner restrictions and clear the path for normal development, however "upsetting" the latter may prove to be. (p. 265)

Thus, it is clear that in the psychoanalytic perspective, the exhibition of storm and stress in the form of conflict with parents is not only a *natural* experience, but is also a *necessary* occurrence for normal adolescent development to occur. The "upholding of a steady equilibrium during the adolescent process is in itself abnormal" (A. Freud, 1958, p. 275). For a further elaboration of the psychoanalytic view of the process of adolescence, the interested reader should turn to Bernfeld (1938), Geleerd (1957), Eissler (1958), Harley (1961), Fountain (1961), Ackerman (1962), Blos (1962, 1979).

But is this psychoanalytic view correct? Answering in the negative were two of the leading anthropologists of the 20th century, Ruth Benedict and Margaret Mead. Mead's fieldwork in the South Pacific (*Coming of Age in Samoa*, originally published in 1928) led her to propose that adolescence *can* be a smooth time devoid of storm and stress, if society allows it to be. In particular, she concluded that an easy-going sexuality eliminated most of the problems we tend to think of as dominant in adolescence. Ruth Benedict took this argument further by arguing that the key is the continuity of experiences and expectations from childhood into adulthood. We will take a closer look at these anthropological theorists in Chapter 5 when we review the role of theory in understanding adolescence. It is worth noting here, however, that Mead's observations about Samoa have been challenged by an Australian anthropologist Derek Freeman, who has spent many years in the area. According to Freeman (1983), the young Mead was misled by the young people she met in the 1920s. Contrary to Mead's view, Freeman concludes that Samoan youth were racked with repressed sexuality, guilt, and violence—perfect candidates to support the storm and stress explanation rather than invalidate it. The controversy rages still, and no one set of data will resolve it one way or the other. But the issue has many practical implications for the task of understanding adolescents.

The basic practical question that emerges from a storm and stress conceptualization of adolescence is whether adolescents who are experiencing problems should be cause for concern. Indeed, if one accepts the psychodynamic perspective on this issue, the *lack* of problems is a cause for concern, and in a sense, the absence of problems becomes a problem. This is a rather confusing state of affairs. The implication is (and many have asserted this) that most problems in adolescence are just a phase, will pass, and therefore should *not* be treated by professionals. The question remains: Will problems pass, or should they be treated before they get worse? What *are* adolescents really like gener-

ally? Do they usually experience problems, or is this just a professional stereotype based on faulty theory?

Research Data on the Nature of Adolescence

The first research *(empirical)* evidence that teenagers in modern westernized societies do not necessarily experience major problems of adjustment was presented by two sociologists, Westley and Elkin (1956). Their small sample of
middle-class adolescents in Montreal, Canada, reported little turmoil. Instead,
they presented a picture of relative calm and stability. These findings were criticized as being biased because of the small, privileged sample used in the study.
In time, however, other studies with larger, more representative samples
emerged that validated these findings.

Douvan and Adelson (1966) conducted a study in which they extensively
interviewed over 3,000 adolescents. The sample was constructed in such a way
as to be representative of the entire United States population of boys and girls
facing adolescence, although it was restricted to teenagers in school and somewhat underrepresented low income and racial minority youth. In this broad,
more representative sample, there also was little evidence of major turmoil and
conflict. In fact, their data presented a picture of the "typical" adolescent as a
somewhat conservative and conforming individual:

> The adolescent at the extremes responds to the instinctual and psychosocial up-
> heaval of puberty by disorder, by failures of egosynthesis, and by a tendency to
> abandon earlier values and object attachments. In the normative response to ado-
> lescence, however, we more commonly find an avoidance of inner and outer con-
> flict, premature identity consolidation, ego and ideological constriction, and a
> general unwillingness to take psychic risks. The great advantage of the survey
> technique is that it allows us to study these adolescents who make up the middle
> majority, who evoke neither grief nor wonder, and who all too often escape our
> notice. (p. 351)

It is important to make note of this last point. Many observers have noted that psychologists and psychiatrists see a rather selected sample of adolescents, those who are brought to professional attention usually because they are
experiencing some form of psychological distress. Because of this, psychologists and psychiatrists may have a rather limited, skewed perception of what
most adolescents are like. To avoid this pitfall, it is important when construct-
ing an image of the typical adolescent to look at nonclinical, nonpatient samples of teenagers. Only by following this procedure may we reasonably expect
to get a realistic view of life as an adolescent, although even that is difficult to
accomplish.

Douvan and Adelson's study has been criticized for the fact that their in-
terviewers were not mental health professionals (and thus presumably were
more likely to miss signs of distress), but subsequent studies that *have* em-

ployed mental health professionals interviewing nonpatient populations have confirmed the finding that the majority of adolescents do *not* show overt signs of disorder. (Of course, the psychoanalytically-oriented could respond that this shows that most adolescents suffer from the "problem" of no problems noted by Anna Freud.)

One of the most extensive studies of this topic was the Normal Adolescent Project carried out by Daniel Offer and his colleagues (Offer, 1969; Offer & Offer, 1973, 1974, 1975), an eight-year project using a sample of 73 typical middle-class, *male* teenagers in the Midwest United States. The boys were assessed at various times from their freshman to senior years of high school. The assessment procedure consisted of parent interviews, psychological tests, and psychiatric interviews. In addition, 61 of the original 73 subjects were assessed in the same manner during their four years of college.

Offer and his colleagues identified three major patterns of growth for these adolescents, which may or may not apply equally well to females. *Continuous growth* refers to a gradual, smooth transition from adolescence to young adulthood, free from the turbulence and turmoil predicted by the storm and stress theorists. *Surgent growth* refers to a less gradual developmental pattern, where growth occurs in "spurts," between which development appears arrested. Most of the teenagers in this study developed in one of these two modes, experiencing little or no stress and discomfort on their way to normal, adaptive adjustment to adulthood. A third pattern of growth was termed *tumultuous growth* and corresponds to the kind of inner turmoil and crisis pattern the storm and stress proponents predict for all adolescents. Twenty-one percent of the sample evidenced this kind of developmental process, a large enough minority to show that there are enough troubled adolescents (at least among males) to sustain the professional stereotype of storm and stress.

In another study, Rutter, Graham, Chadwick, and Yule (1976) studied a large representative sample of all of the 14–15-year-olds on the Isle of Wight (in Great Britain). They found only a very slight increase in psychopathology from middle childhood to adolescence and a very low incidence of rejection or relationship difficulties between adolescents and parents. Interestingly, however, they found that about 22% of their sample reported that they *often* felt miserable or depressed and were having trouble sleeping. This is almost the exact percentage that reported this pattern in the studies by Offer (1973, 1974, 1975), and helps reassure us that the Offer study has something to say about females as well as males. (About 44% reported feeling miserable and depressed *at times*—but then, who doesn't?) We should note that in Michael Rutter's study (1976) the incidence of psychopathology (as assessed by a formal psychiatric interview) was 16.3% among their sample, so that there is a difference between reporting depression and being considered clinically depressed.

Therefore, we have evidence from two fairly large-scale studies that about 20% of nonpatient adolescents will report experiencing serious turmoil as they grow up. This is far short of the majority predicted by storm and stress theorists.

In their study of middle-class families of adolescent boys, Bandura and Walters (1959) also found little evidence of storm and stress. When teenagers did exhibit aggressive behavior, such as fighting physically with their parents, it was found that they had the same problems as younger children, but when they became bigger and stronger, they could overpower their parents. Bandura and Walters concluded: "Our findings suggest. . .that the behavioral characteristics exhibited by children during the so-called adolescent stage are lawfully related to, and consistent with, pre-adolescent behavior" (Bandura, 1964, p. 196).

The general conclusion that profound conflict and turmoil across all life's domains is not the typical pattern of development for adolescents receives support from other studies of nonpatient populations (Grinker, Grinker & Timberlake, 1962; Hamburg, Coelho & Adams, 1974; Oldham, 1978; Weiner, 1982). It seems fairly well established then that when one looks at the data, the typical (or *modal*) adolescent is *not* one who is experiencing far-reaching psychic disturbance as a matter of predetermined developmental course. Keep in mind also, that no period in the human life course is totally free from stress and conflict. Thus, the storm and stress hypothesis does seem to be a professional stereotype after all. This is worth keeping in mind throughout all our discussions of adolescence.

Adolescents on Adolescence

Although we have been attempting to make general statements about adolescents and the experience of adolescence, we should recognize the diversity that exists among adolescents and the variety of adolescent experiences. Some adolescents cope with families disrupted by divorce while others live in the midst of stability. Some sample new life-styles including experimenting with drugs and sex, while others live according to traditional values and patterns of behavior. Some live in fast-paced cities and suburbs, while others live in more slow-paced rural areas. Some live in extreme poverty, while others live in affluent splendor.

Research often focuses upon similarities in adolescent development. However, the following stories reveal the particularities of adolescent experience.

June: In general, what my parents expected of me is what they got. I knew which situations to avoid since I had an older brother.
Mara: The conflicts began when I started dating an older boy. I was just recovering from a bout of anorexia nervosa, and I had a bad self-image. I rejected the love I received at home and searched for the reassurance of a boyfriend.

Mike seemed to be the answer to my problems. He introduced me to drugs, alcohol, and sex. But, finally, I realized what a louse he was and what a fool I'd been. When I realized how I had tortured my parents, I felt ashamed and embarrassed.

Armond: If I missed my curfew, my parents grounded me for a week. My friends and I never took drugs, or drank alcohol. Therefore, I felt there was no reason why I couldn't go when and where I wanted to go. Thinking back on it, I suppose my folks just wanted me to spend more time with them. What bothered me most about these discussions was that my parents always compared me with my older sister. I realize that my problem with my parents was nothing compared with what some kids go through.

Eloise: My biggest conflict with my parents was over love. I had decided that the best thing that could ever happen to me was to date the school's football star. Jim was worshipped for his athletic excellence and he developed a severe case of the "head swells." His egotism shaped my parents' opinion of him. A typical date consisted of an invitation to watch his muscles ripple, and I spent so much time waiting for Jim to show up for dates that I sacrificed other social activities. After too many of these selfish incidents, mom told me to break up with him. "But he's my whole life," I shouted. Then she backed down saying, "It's your life." She was right about that. But she was right about Jim too.

Devon: The worst conflict occurred after my brother and I had been home alone. We had a big fight, and when my parents got home, the house was a mess. They blamed me, and I ran away to Denver. My parents found me, and we actually talked it out. They admitted they had treated me harshly, but they did it to keep me out of trouble.

Anne: I suppose my only conflict with my parents was over curfew. In general, my parents were very supportive. I only hope that I will be able to handle my own kids in a similar way.

Frank: I don't really remember who threw the first punch. All I remember was the fight. I was bigger than he was, but he wasn't alone. Suddenly she was hitting my back. I flipped her off of me and onto him and, they fell to the bottom of the stairs. I shook until the rage passed, and I realized what I had done. As my mother and father got up from the bottom of the stairs, I knew I won the fight, but I felt sick and exhausted. Later my father beat me with a belt. Looking back on it I realize that he wanted to prove he still had authority over me. At the time all I knew was that he was spanking me. I'd been spanked so many times that I could tolerate the pain without a sound or a tear. I never heard the lecture he gave me. I apologized to him, but to this day, I'm not sure why.

Marsha: My parents were divorced, and I lived with my mom. My mother and I became close, but I had a strained relationship with my father, who I saw a few times each month. When my mother announced that she was going to get remarried, I was terrified of losing her. However, I grew to love my stepfather.

Mindy: My parents thought I was the greatest, but I was so busy striving to please them that I forgot about myself. My mother was always telling her friends that I was her best friend, but I resented her for lying to everyone, just so we would appear to be a perfect family. This went on until I just couldn't take it anymore. I had started dating a boy. My parents thought it was nice, but they didn't notice all the sexual, emotional, and psychological changes I was going through. When I tried to talk to my mother about my problems, she said I was too happy to have any real problems. Although I yelled that we weren't really "best friends," she still couldn't face it and will not to this day admit it.

Carlos: My mother had taught me to dislike my father and told me I was lucky I wasn't like him. After my mother died my father decided to move back into the house. But before he would move in he wanted to redecorate the house because the old stuff reminded him of my mother. When the work was being done he insisted that I stay at the house. Soon I had a regular party going. When my father found out, I expected the worst from him. But on this occasion he just smiled, and evicted my friends in such a nice way that I saw him in a new light.

Geneva: Pregnancy was the most dramatic crisis I experienced as a teenager. I moved into a home for unwed mothers and gave my baby up for adoption. My parents could detach themselves from the situation whereas I was very much attached, and a barrier built up between us. They were nice to me, but I could feel that they were just waiting for this unpleasantness to be over. They failed to recognize that I had to face reality to get through the experience. I could have used their help.

Paul: I had a typical adolescence in many ways. But when my best friend died in a car crash, I was devastated. I became cautious, and I really started thinking about what was important in life. It scared me that death could just happen and that life can be grim. But most of all it made me face reality.

Our task in this book is to do our best to face reality about adolescence. But, as we have seen already, and will continue to see, it's not so simple. In this chapter we have raised in one way or another the many issues that command our attention in the chapters that follow: competence, conflict, identity, sexual exploration, intimacy, mental and physical health, and preparation for the future. In Chapter 2 we present an ecological framework for understanding social competence in adolescence.

Lao-tzu told us that the only way to begin a journey of 1,000 miles is with the first step. In this first chapter we've tried to get off on the right foot to take that first step.

Preview

■ Biology and the social environment combine to shape the experience of adolescence.

■ An ecological perspective on adolescence helps us understand the interplay of biological and social influences.

■ The Great Depression of the 1930s provides a case study that demonstrates that who you are and where you experience adolescence matters a great deal.

■ The ecological perspective organizes experience into systems: individual organism (the person as a psychological and biological being), microsystems (e.g., the situations and relationships of day-to-day life—family, school, and peer group), mesosystems (the relationships between microsystems, e.g., school and home), exosystems (the systems in which the individual does not participate but which affect that individual, e.g., government), macrosystems (the values and institutions that guide society, e.g., capitalism or communism).

■ Social competence is the set of abilities and characteristics necessary to succeed in the real world and feel good about yourself.

Adolescence is a time of life when the interplay of physical, social, and psychological influences is particularly important. The diversity of people, all the various combinations of gender, age, family, position, temperament, personality, intelligence, culture, economic resources, and social climate, makes the discussion of this interplay a unique challenge. As we saw in Chapter 1, the very essence of adolescence lies in the way a culture defines and shapes the years between childhood and adulthood. The physical characteristics of the child are eventually replaced with the physical characteristics of the adult. The start of these physical changes is usually the start of adolescence. However, the end of adolescence is much more a social matter. This has led developmental psychologist Jerome Kagan (1975) to observe that: "Adolescence begins in biology and ends in culture." In this chapter we propose a way to think about the interaction of the biological, the psychological, the social, and the cultural.

2

Human Ecology and Competence in Adolescence

Human Beings as Social Animals

Adults and adolescents often appear self-reliant, but it is easy to see that human infants are entirely dependent upon others for their very survival. This dependence on others does not end in early childhood, however. Rather, it is transformed and develops into a set of social relationships that define the human condition in its many aspects: linguistic, intellectual, economic, political, religious, and sexual. The Greek philosopher Aristotle correctly called us *social animals*, and this is nowhere more true than in adolescence when biological and social changes abound. To understand adolescence, we need to be keen observers of adolescents as social animals.

Like the biologist who must study an animal by learning about its habitat, sources of food, predators, and social practices, the student of human development must address how people live and grow in the social environment. The study of the interrelationships of organisms and their environment is called *ecology*. Ecologists study how the individual and its habitat shape the development of each other. We must, then, recognize the habitat of the developing adolescent as including family, friends, neighborhood, church, school, the physical environment, as well as less immediate forces that constitute the social geography and climate (e.g., laws, institutions, and values). The interplay of these social forces and physical settings with the individual defines the range of issues in the forefront of an *ecological perspective*. The most important characteristic of this ecological perspective is that it both reinforces our inclination to look inside the individual and encourages us to look beyond the individual to the environment for questions and explanations about the individual's behavior and development. It emphasizes development in context. It constantly reminds us that human development results from the interplay of biology *and* society, from the characteristics individuals bring with them into the world and the way the world treats them, from nature *and* nurture.

The Interaction between Person and Environment

Those who study adolescence from an ecological perspective view individuals and their environments as partners in development: each changes over time and each adapts in response to changes in the other. Different people react differently to the same environment (just as different environments react differently to the same person). One adolescent loves school while another hates it. An adolescent may be a big success in the classroom but a flop at parties. These things change over time as well.

The relationship between parent and adolescent, for example, changes and becomes more complex as each participant learns from and responds to the other. During infancy the child has limited channels for communicating with its parent and the parent has only limited ways to communicate with the infant.

As the child grows up, he or she learns to talk and reason while the parent learns which techniques for influencing the child work well and which do not. Parent and child develop a history and a consistency to their relationships.

Neither can be viewed as a constant causing the other to develop; rather, *the relationship itself* is a cause of change in both parents and adolescents. One of the reasons brothers and sisters often have different relationships with the same parents is that the experience of rearing one child changes the parents in ways that may show up in the way they raise a second child. Thus, for example, the second adolescent in a family may find that his or her parents have preconceptions about adolescence based upon their experience with adolescence the first time around and may have decided they need to be more strict or lenient. If the first and second children are of different sexes or temperaments, or if the community context is different, what worked well for the parents the first time may backfire the second. One reason for this obsolescence is the character of the second child. Another involves changes in the society in which that second child experiences adolescence. Even a matter of a few years can be important in presenting a different cultural climate or political context (Nesselroade & Baltes, 1974) as in the case of a war beginning or ending, a change in governments, relaxed or tightened rules on drinking, changes in the availability of drugs, or alterations in standards concerning sexual behavior. This is one major contribution of an ecological approach to our understanding of adolescence: it focuses our attention upon the role of these more distant cultural environments in individual development.

The ecology of human development is oriented towards culture and society because it is really the study of how a whole society functions to raise the children and youth who will eventually take their place within that society as its parents, workers, and citizens (Garbarino, 1978). Adolescents are the bridge between past and future. Society is always renewing itself, remaking itself, and transforming itself through them. "Individual" development is only part of the story, and we must understand it in conjunction with the main plots in the human story—history and culture. This means we must always keep in mind the big picture of society as we seek to understand the snapshots of individual lives.

Although societies differ in what they value, in their norms for behavior, and in their characteristic forms of social relations, some basic human needs are found everywhere. All humans have physical needs (food, shelter, etc.) and psychological needs (e.g., affection and continuity) (Mead, 1970). Amidst these universals, social class, gender, region, ethnicity, and genetic endowment all shape development. Rich and poor, male and female, city and farm, black, white, Asian, and Hispanic, quick and slow—all these variations can make a difference. They present opportunities and risks for development. For example, a female living in a big city is likely to be much more savvy and "street wise" about men than a similar female living a sheltered middle-class life in a small town. Individuals face different opportunities and risks for development because of their mental and physical make-up *and* because of the type of environment they inhabit. The combination of individual characteristics and characteristics of the habitat is the central concept of human ecology. This combination is called the *ecological niche.*

By *opportunities for development* we mean relationships in which adolescents find material, emotional, and social encouragement compatible with their needs and capacities that exist at a specific point in their developing lives. The best fit between adolescent and environment must be worked out through individual experience within some very broad guidelines of basic human needs and specifically adolescent issues, and then renegotiated again as development proceeds and situations change. We consider some of the guidelines for this process of adjustment later in this chapter.

Risks to development can come both from direct threats and from the absence of normal, expectable opportunities. Besides such obvious biological risks as malnutrition or injury, there are sociocultural risks that threaten development. Sociocultural risk is the process of impoverishing the adolescent's world of essential experiences and relationships; sociocultural opportunity is the opposite. For example, an orphan may suffer from his or her lack of family ties, while another adolescent may have many and diverse role models as part of a large close-knit family. Similarly, an adolescent graduating from high school during the low point of an economic depression is likely to have fewer job opportunities than one graduating during a booming economy. Understanding these sociocultural risks and opportunities is one of our goals in this book and it runs as a theme through each chapter.

Nature and Nurture

Understanding the interaction between nature and nurture in development is so difficult that most researchers do not even try to handle both parts of the equation at once. Rather, they tend to hold one side constant while letting the other side vary. Scientists try to identify situations in which they can limit the sources of variation and thereby isolate effects. One way to do this is to study identical twins. Such twins have the same genetic make-up because they result from one fertilized egg (the same *nature*). Thus, differences between them that show up as the twins develop are due to differences in the way they are treated (*nurture*). This can then be compared to the results for nonidentical twins, siblings, cousins, and unrelated individuals to try to isolate the impact of nature and nurture. This is a difficult task (Bronfenbrenner, 1975).

Studying genetically identical twins (*nature constant*) reared apart (*nurture varied*) can shed light on the role of nature and nurture in intelligence. In contrast, we might examine how unrelated teenagers (nature varied) respond to the same stimulus (nurture constant), such as the ingestion of alcohol. Or, an investigator might systematically vary one while letting the other vary randomly, as in presenting adolescents of different ages in a school with three different teaching styles and observing the overall effect of each. A researcher is rarely able to look directly at the interplay of nature and nurture in development. It's often too hard to carry out the necessary research, *particularly* in adolescence when physical change is so important yet so variable from individual to individual.

Because of this complexity, we rarely know what the real limits, potentials, and costs are of alternative social arrangements. What kind of schools do adolescents need? How do we deal with drug abuse? Why do some teenagers become sexually active while others do not? How do we prevent vandalism? How serious are divorce and remarriage as influences on adolescents? Where adolescent risk and opportunity are concerned, our lack of a scientific basis is extremely unfortunate because the inevitable issues of making policies and delivering services require a scientific analysis of the costs and benefits of alternative approaches to the individual and to the society. In computing these costs and benefits, we have much to learn from how history shapes individual and cultural development. Understanding what has come before in human societies can illuminate the questions we seek to answer today and in the future.

When we do compute these costs and benefits, moreover, we rely upon a definition of development that is itself socially grounded. Our definition of development grows out of Bronfenbrenner's view of development as "the person's evolving conception of the environment, and his relation to it, as well as the person's ongoing capacity to discover, sustain, or alter its properties" (Bronfenbrenner, 1979). We can see in this definition a respect for the human mind and heart. It tells us to look at how a person's life evolves, how the person gains intellectual and emotional awareness, and how the person becomes a more influential actor in the social environment. It focuses on the story of an adolescent's development.

In a sense, then, our interest in development is really an interest in biography. We must discover how the lives of individual adolescents and the lives of their societies intermingle. Events taking place at the level of nations—the big picture—often reverberate right down into the day-to-day life of the individual family—the little picture. We see this when the actions of an oil-producing cartel affect whether or not a teenager can find work or whether parents can help a youth finance a car or horseback riding lessons. Conversely, millions of individual decisions can add up to major social changes, such as when millions of adolescents decide to become sexually active without birth control and the result is an upsurge in teenage pregnancy. This interplay of biography and history is at the heart of our interest in adolescent development. While easy enough to convey in generalities, this ecological conception of development is very difficult to apply in practice.

One important thing about this ecological perspective is that it reveals connections that might otherwise go unnoticed and helps us look beyond the immediate and the obvious to see where the most significant influences lie.

Trying to understand many important developmental phenomena is like a shell game. You think you are sure where the pea is, only to find it is really somewhere else. Let's consider a specific example.

The Great Depression as a Source of Developmental Risk and Opportunity

What was the effect of the Great Depression of the 1930s on adolescents and their families? This question is actually like the one that asks, "What is more important, nature or nurture?" The answer is, "it depends." Few events—even events like economic depressions that may seem obviously and totally negative—have a guaranteed, universal, and inevitable significance. Most derive their importance from the context in which they occur and the people they affect (e.g., adolescents or their parents). In the case of the Great Depression, we have more than just speculation to go on and will consider Glen Elder's (1974) classic study designed to illuminate the processes involved.

Economic deprivation is generally recognized as the principal source of sociocultural risk to young children, although its impact on adolescents is less clear. Within the space of two years (1976–1978), two major analyses of family life conducted by blue-ribbon panels of experts separately concluded that poverty is the principal threat to family life. The National Academy of Sciences (1976) and the Carnegie Foundation (Keniston, 1977b) both cited inadequate economic resources as the central villain in undermining the adequacy of families as contexts for child development. Inadequate income is not the only source of troubles for families, of course. Wealthy people have family troubles as well. But anyone who looks at the data on the connection between poverty and family life must agree that a life lived in poverty is tougher than one lived in wealth, or as actress Sophie Tucker put it, "I've been rich and I've been poor and rich is better."

What are the consequences of economic deprivation for adolescent development? Sociologist Glen Elder (1974) conducted his study to answer this question with reference to the impact of the Great Depression of the 1930s on the youth of that era. Two long-term (longitudinal) studies of child development had been launched by an earlier generation of investigators in the period of 1929–1932 in Northern California, one in Oakland, the other in Berkeley. The first dealt with children born 1920–1921, the second with children born 1928–1929. Both studies included middle-class and working-class families. A wide range of information was obtained about the adolescents and their parents. The data were collected for more than forty years using questionnaires, interviews, clinical assessments, and direct observation of the families. When Elder came to the project in 1962, he saw a unique opportunity to explore the impact of the Great Depression on the life course of the young people in these two studies.

The data permitted Elder to look at how the Depression affected adolescents as a function of the following:

1   *Age*   The Berkeley children were just entering school at the worst of the Depression, while the Oakland children were teenagers by that time. That factor, of course, is critical for our interests.
2   *Social class*   Both middle-class and blue-collar families were included.
3   *Level of economic deprivation*   Some families were relatively unaffected, while others lost more than 35% of their income.
4   *Sex*   Both males and females were included.
5   *Pre-Depression quality of family-life*   Both strong and weak marriages had been identified.
6   *Self-concept*   Individual feelings about self differed to start with.

Elder found a very complex pattern of results. These findings are worth noting here because they demonstrate just how complicated this matter of sociocultural risk and opportunity really is, and just why we need the ecological framework to make sense of the data. They also suggest some ways in which adolescents and children differ in how vulnerable they are to some kinds of sociocultural risk and in their ability to benefit from some forms of sociocultural opportunity.

In the Depression era, the husband was usually the predominant breadwinner. In families where the husband lost his job or much of his income and the marital relationship was weak, the mother often led the way in blaming the father for "his" economic failure. When this happened, girls seemed to be encouraged by the dominant performance of their mothers and boys were disillusioned by their father's failure. The result was that such girls reported fewer personality and emotional problems than their male counterparts. All these factors were intensified if the sons and daughters were young children rather than adolescents when the economic deprivation occurred, because they were then more dependent upon their parents and were exposed to the new situation for a longer period of time in the home. On the other hand, a strong marital bond led to strengthened families under the pressures of economic loss as parents banded together in response to the crisis. The effects were greatest for middle-class families: the positive effects on teenagers from homes with strong marital bonds and the negative effects on young children from homes with a weak marital relationship. One explanation for this is that blue-collar families were more accustomed to dealing with unemployment and income loss.

We should note that all these findings come from families with a pre-Depression record of relative stability: parents were married and had an adequate work history. These were not the chronically unemployed, nor were they single-parent households. For the families in Elder's study, the experience of economic deprivation was an *event*, not a permanent condition. That is a significant part of the story and cautions against making simple generalizations about other groups, such as the single-parent, chronic welfare case.

As if all this complexity were not enough, we must remember that the Great Depression preceded the economic boom of World War II and the 1950s. Some teenagers were ready to benefit from that opportunity when it presented itself. Youth who reached early adulthood in the late 1930s got behind in their life timetable and many never caught up. What is more, one response to events of the Depression itself was the creation and expansion of our whole social welfare system: unemployment insurance, Social Security, and the like. Ironically, many now consider this very system to be part of today's problems because, for example, it may be seen to encourage pregnant teenagers to keep their babies and set up separate households supported by welfare funds such as the Aid to Dependent Children program.

Another historical change is cultural in nature. Depression-era families were more likely to see their economic deprivation as being their own fault, as opposed to today when we have a greater appreciation for the influence of impersonal economic forces arbitrarily imposing financial hardship. This theme emerges from interviews with people who were adults during the Depression (Terkel, 1963). All these things add to the already large number of variables that we must take into account.

To be an adolescent during a time of economic or social disaster adds an element to potential risk (and perhaps opportunity) that is not present in less troubled times. However, whether or not the impact of those troubled times will produce damage depends upon how the family and community experience those forces and how they are transmitted to the adolescent. Elder's study makes this clear. Families who were not directly hit with income loss did not show the effects that deprived families did; some occupations were more affected than were others; some communities suffered more than others.

What is more, we must keep in mind that the individual is not a passive participant. While Elder's account stresses the *average* effects of economic change and development, there was, of course, substantial individual variation. Some suffered blows to their feeling of self-worth, self-confidence, and overall mental health that lasted the rest of their lives. Others felt pride in their ability to overcome adversity. Some individuals were more affected than others; some capitalized upon opportunities while others did not. It is precisely this joint emphasis upon characteristics of each individual in concert with social factors that makes the ecological approach a valid model of the real world. Rarely are risk and opportunity totally separate and absolute, nor are they static. The individual's vulnerability changes. Adolescents seem less totally dependent upon their families than are young children, but they may be *more* vulnerable to direct influence by forces *outside* the family, such as economic pressure. Risk can be overcome or disarmed, opportunities created or enhanced. This comes through in Elder's study. However, the more impoverished a person's world is to start with, the more likely he or she is to fail when hurt by social, economic, or psychological stress (as in the case of families with a pre-Depression record of weak marital bonds or conflicted marriages). The experiences of childhood play an important role in determining the resources teenagers bring to bear on situations faced in adolescence. To make sense of the complex interrelationships of the adolescent and the environment we need a framework that incorporates the variations in individuals, families, communities, and societies that Elder's analysis uncovered. We can find such a framework in a systems approach to the ecology of adolescent development.

A Systems Approach to Adolescent Development

What does it mean to adopt a *systems approach* to adolescent development? While people use the term systems approach in various ways, there do seem to be several common themes when the approach is applied to studying people. A systems approach is based upon the idea that all living entities share some common characteristics. The simplest biological entities (cells and bacteria, for example) exhibit many of the same processes and functions as larger and more complex biological entities (such as people).

Systems analysts even approach nonliving entities such as computers with the same basic orientation. What is this orientation? The systems approach uses a set of basic concepts to account for the workings of all living beings. We do not intend to present all such concepts or to explore them fully, but we do want to mention them here. All systems run on *energy*. They may draw energy from the environment outside their *boundaries* (as when a person eats food) or generate it from resources they contain within their boundaries (as when a person burns fat stored in the body).

Just mentioning boundaries tells us that a system has some identity and existence apart from everything else. A *closed system* has very impermeable boundaries; an *open system* allows energy, material, and information to flow freely across its boundaries. Of course, systems are ordinarily neither totally open nor totally closed. Systems are always in a state of disequilibrium seeking equilibrium; they alter themselves and the environment in an effort to seek a *steady state* or a balance. Indeed, much of the action that goes on in the world results from systems reacting to changed conditions within and outside their boundaries. Living systems can develop regular patterns of response when they repetitively face the same kind of situations. These patterns are *automated* or routine. When faced with new situations, however, the living system may construct a new response. They are *adaptive*. As each individual system goes about its automated and adaptive way, it influences other systems that are part of the same environment and open to changes in that environment. To a greater or lesser degree systems are linked; action by one influences another.

The adolescent is a system, made up of the many organ systems within the boundaries of the body. Each of these organ systems is composed of other *subsystems*. But the adolescent is also part of some larger systems as well. The adolescent's family is itself a system. The school is a system in which the adolescent is a part. The physical environment plays an important role in the various systems that comprise and include the adolescent. Ultimately, the entire Earth is a system, and the fate of an individual adolescent is linked to the fate of the Earth (Schell, 1982). For more about systems analysis as it applies to human development, see Anderson and Carter (1974), Berrien (1968), and Urban (1978).

Our goal here is to make use of a systems approach to adolescence in ways that will clarify the complexity we face in the interplay of biological, psychological, social, and cultural forces at work in transforming a child into an adult. A systems approach helps us discover the connections between what might at first seem to be unrelated events. It also can help us see that what often seems like an obvious solution may actually only make the problem worse. Systems analyst Jay Forrester (1969) concludes that because systems are linked and therefore influence each other through *feedback*, many of the real solutions to social problems are not readily apparent and may even be exactly the opposite of what seems sensible on the face of things (they are *counter-intuitive*). This will become apparent as we proceed.

The framework proposed by developmental psychologist Urie Bronfenbrenner (1979) provides a useful systems approach to the ecology of human development. It offers some tools to sort out the phenomena, highlight the issues, and formulate the questions we need to ask and answer about adolescence. Like most frameworks, it relies on some special terms that we need to define. We will use them in our discussion of how adolescents develop in interaction with the immediate social environment of family, friends, school, church, and neighborhood, and how aspects of the larger social context affect what goes on in the situations in which adolescents find themselves (Garbarino, 1982).

Remember that the individual adolescent is a system in a world of systems. All the concepts we introduced earlier apply to individual adolescents. What is more, the defining characteristic of adolescence itself is the changing nature of the individual adolescent as a system. As the adolescent strives toward a new dynamic equilibrium, the level of energy changes, boundaries change, and the sources and nature of feedback change. As the automated patterns of childhood become obsolete, the adolescent must act in the adaptive mode to seek new strategies and tactics for living successfully.

The adolescent plays an active role in an ever-widening world. Newborns shape the feeding behavior of their mothers but are confined largely to cribs or laps and have limited means of communicating their needs and wants. Ten-year-olds, on the other hand, influence many adults and other children located in many different settings and have many ways of communicating. The adolescent's world is still larger and more diverse, as is his or her ability to influence that world. Individuals and environments negotiate their relationships over time through a process of reciprocity—neither is constant and *each* depends on the other. One cannot reliably predict the future of one without knowing something about the other. We see this when we ask "Does economic deprivation harm development?" We answer, "It depends on how old one is when it hits, what sex one is, what the future brings in the way of vocational opportunity, what the quality of family life was in the past, and what one's economic expectations and assumptions are. In short, it depends."

We see the individual's experience as part of a set of subsystems working within larger systems within even larger systems, "as a set of nested structures, each inside the next, like a set of Russian dolls" (Bronfenbrenner, 1979, p. 22). In asking and answering questions about development, we can and should always be ready to look at the next level of systems "beyond" and "within" (Garbarino, 1982). If we see parents and teenagers in conflict over lost income (the family system), we need to look beyond to the general economic system. We also should look to the culture that defines a person's personal worth in monetary terms and that blames the victims of economic dislocation for their own losses (social systems). And we must also look within the individuals (as psychological systems) that are affected by the changing roles and status of the parents to know why and how they adjust in ways that generate family conflict. In addition, we must also look "across" to see how the several systems involved (family, school, workplace, and economy) adjust to new conditions. These social forces are the keys to ecological analyses. They exist as linked social systems. We can express these concerns in a systematic way that permits us to organize empirical information, theoretical issues, and public concerns (Bronfenbrenner, 1979; Garbarino, 1982). This systems approach examines the environment at four levels beyond the individual organism—from the micro to the macro.

Microsystems

The *microsystem* is the immediate setting in which the adolescent develops and in so doing experiences and creates reality. It includes people, objects, and events that occur directly to and with the individual adolescent as a system. Look around you and see where the adolescents are. They are at home, in peer groups, at work, and in schools. Each of these places implies the existence of a set of enduring roles and relationships: parents and children, leaders and followers, supervisors and employees, teachers and students. The shared experiences that occur in each setting provide a record of the microsystem and offer some clues to its future, because microsystems evolve and develop much as adolescents themselves do from forces within and without.

At first, for most *children*, the microsystem is quite small. It is the home and involves interaction with only one or perhaps two people at a time (*dyadic or triadic interaction)* in relatively simple activities such as feeding, bathing, and cuddling. As the child develops and becomes an adolescent, complexity normally increases: the adolescent does more, with more people, in more places, and dyadic and triadic relationships expand to include more participants. Church, school, peer group, and work may be added to the list of relevant microsystems. Indeed, the expanding capacity to do more is the very essence of development.

Play figures prominently in this process from the early months of life, and eventually is joined by productive labor (work). Working, loving, and playing (what Sigmund Freud called the essence of normal human existence) are the principal classes of activities that characterize the microsystem and are the core issues in adolescence and the transition to adulthood. However, how much one does of those activities and how complex they are differ from person to person and from environment to environment. For example, one expects to find more love at home than in school, more play than work in the peer group. Prayer and other religious activity also play a greater or lesser role, depending upon the spiritual orientation of the microsystem.

One of the most important aspects of the microsystem as a force in development is the existence of relationships that go beyond simple dyads (two people). To be able to observe and learn from being exposed to other dyads (such as mother and father) by being part of a triad enhances development. Being able to observe differences in dyadic experience because a third party is present enhances development. One way we learn to love is by observing parents who love each other. The psychological developments of adolescence produce special resources for the teenager who profits from exposure to model dyads. So long as increased numbers in a microsystem mean more enduring reciprocal relationships, larger and more complex microsystems mean enhanced development, particularly if this complexity is matched to the individual's age (Bronfenbrenner, 1979). Adolescents can handle more than children. We measure the social riches of an individual by enduring, reciprocal, multifaceted relationships that emphasize playing, working, and loving. And these relationships change, because microsystems, like individuals, change. The setting "school," for example, is very different in June than it was in September for the same youth, who, of course, are themselves not the same as they were at the beginning of the school year.

It is also important to remember that our definition speaks of the microsystem as a pattern *experienced* by the developing person. Adolescents influence their microsystems and the microsystems influence them in turn. (Indeed, one of the challenges parents face is creating a smooth and mutual sharing of power in the microsystem of the family.) By their participation, youth have a say in the character of the microsystem, while at the same time the microsystem provides youth with ongoing values, standards, regularities, and experiences that come to be understood as "normal." We carry around in our heads ideas about the way things are, pictures of reality. These "cognitive maps" are the reality we live by and act upon. Shakespeare said it well in *Hamlet* (II, ii, 259): "There is nothing good or bad, but thinking makes it so." Perhaps this idea was still more clearly expressed by sociologist W. I. Thomas, who said, "If men define situations as real, they are real in their consequences" (Thomas & Thomas, 1928, p. 572). Adolescents (more than children, but less than adults) construct their microsystems as much as they are shaped by them.

The adolescent's microsystem becomes a source of developmental risk when it is socially impoverished. Development suffers whenever the microsystem is stunted, be it because of too few participants, too little reciprocal interaction, psychologically destructive patterns of interaction, or some combination of the three.

A microsystem should be a gateway to the world, not a locked room, because our definition of development emphasizes the expanding ability of the individual to deal with more microsystems and more complex relationships within those microsystems (Bronfenbrenner, 1979). The "product" of a healthy microsystem is an adolescent whose capacity for understanding and successfully dealing with ever-wider spheres of reality increases. Such a person learns to have self-respect and self-confidence, to be socially and intellectually competent. Let us take a brief look at two examples of developmental risk, socially impoverished microsystems, microsystems that are too one-sided and too negative, and how they work against competence and self-esteem. The contrast—microsystems that excel in being well-balanced and communicating positive feelings—exemplifies social opportunity.

The Role of Imbalanced versus Balanced Microsystems in Developing Competence

One of the essential features of a healthy microsystem is *reciprocity*—the give and take interaction that both respects and challenges, that stimulates and responds appropriately. When this essential reciprocity declines significantly, it jeopardizes development. How does this happen?

It happens when the balance of power within the family microsystem breaks down. In childhood this usually means that one or both parents seize complete control of the parent-child relationship and seek to dominate the family. In so doing, they may thwart development. But in adolescence, it is often the adolescent who seizes control over family relations. It *is* appropriate for the adolescent to play an active role in shaping parental behavior, just as it is natural for the parent to influence the adolescent's (Bell, 1968). This is a healthy family microsystem; both sides share control. When parents *refuse* to be influenced *or* adolescents take over, they upset the essential principle of reciprocity.

For the older child and the adolescent, the issue of reciprocity is found in the childrearing "style" adopted by the parent(s). Of course the style parents "choose" or "adopt" may be influenced by many factors: their own family experiences, their marital status, and their experiences outside the home in the world of work. Diana Baumrind's studies (1978) of childrearing styles and their consequences for development provide an insightful look at how important the principle of reciprocity is to the family microsystem. She found that where reciprocity was maintained in day-to-day interaction, what she called an *authoritative* orientation, the child enjoys the greatest number of opportunities to develop successfully. Where parents systematically violated the principle of reciprocity, development suffered. An authoritarian style violated the principle of reciprocity by loading excessive power in the hands of the parent and placing the youth in a passive role. A *permissive* style inappropriately gave *carte blanche* to the adolescent and his or her unformed drives and, thus, placed the *parent* in a passive role. Neither does justice to the youth's developmental needs because both undermine the social richness of the family microsystem.

Consider an incident in which a 13-year-old shows up at 6 o'clock when dinner was scheduled for 5 o'clock. The authoritarian parent might respond with, "You're late. Go to your room. There will be no supper for you!" When the adolescent responds with, "But I. . . ," the parent interrupts with, "No but's. Go to your room." In contrast, the permissive parent might respond with, "Welcome home, dear, I'll cook your supper now." The authoritarian parent has not permitted the youth to offer a response and has short-circuited the potentially useful process of bargaining and negotiating. The permissive parent, on the other hand, has not set the adolescent's behavior against a standard, and in that way has done him or her a disservice. For different reasons, the permissive style joins the authoritarian style in shutting off the developmentally enhancing process of negotiation.

In contrast, the authoritative style emphasizes negotiation. The parent greets the youth with: "It's 6 o'clock, and dinner was scheduled for 5 o'clock. You're an hour late. What's the story here?" When the teenager responds with, "But I was with my friends and lost track of time, then I had to help the other kids clean up the recreation center. . . ," the parent responds with, "I can see how you could lose track of time, but having dinner together is pretty important, and besides it makes more work when you're late. I suggest you find a way to keep track of time better, or you'll have to come straight home from school. Let's work on that. For tonight, your dinner is in the oven. I'll expect you to clean up your own dishes when you're done." When the family microsystem is working this way, the balance of power between parent and youth, and standards and impulses is appropriate and developmentally enhancing. It offers developmental opportunity. When it is too one-sided, it places the adolescent at risk.

Negative versus Positive

Adolescent experiences in the microsystem color their whole view of the world. The family is the headquarters for human development. Adolescents incorporate these experiences into their emerging concepts of themselves, the world, and their place in that world. Probably the single most important microsystem issue is emotional climate *(affective tone)*. A *negative tone* can find expression in the full range of microsystem behaviors, including what is said (or not said), what is done (or not done). A positive climate produces a kind of "social momentum," while a negative climate produces "social deadweight." Positive climate contributes to success in the world because it gives the child a reservoir of self-confidence or *ego strength* that is an important foundation for competence (McClelland, 1973). Negative climate makes youth vulnerable to being easily discouraged by everyday problems and turns them away from full and satisfying participation in the world.

Coopersmith (1967) demonstrated that the microsystem plays an extremely important role in determining whether young people experience their world and themselves in positive or negative terms. Nurturing, involved, and actively contributing parents give adolescents a positive view of themselves *(high self-esteem)*, while passive, neglecting, and uninvolved parents give adolescents a negative view of themselves *(low self-esteem)*. We tend to construct an image of ourselves based on the feedback from significant others. This view of personality is in the classic tradition of George Herbert Mead (1934) and others who argue that by defining the role a person plays, we go far towards defining the person. It figures prominently in our discussion of identity in Chapter 7. To rob adolescents of positive self-regard, either by deliberately deprecating their accomplishments or by conveying a sense of worthlessness by neglect, is to place them at developmental risk and constitutes psychological maltreatment (Garbarino, 1978a, 1980b; Garbarino & Garbarino, 1980).

To develop a positive sense of self, adolescents need warm, responsive, and active "partners." The microsystem can fail in many ways, but the most serious threat comes from neglecting parents who starve the youth of emotional sustenance. These parents are likely to exhibit what Norman Polansky (1976) calls the *apathy-futility syndrome*. The elements of this pattern are a kind of emotional deadness, an unwillingness to initiate or respond to actions, a pervasive sense of ineffectiveness, and a general unresponsiveness to the initiatives of other family members. The developmental threat posed by adults who suffer from the apathy-futility syndrome is that they are unable or unwilling to provide the intense, responsive interaction necessary for the adequate development of competence and self-esteem. Rather, these caregivers project a world view of passivity, depression, and rejection. None of the active encouragement needed to develop a personal reservoir of self-esteem and positive regard exists. A childhood colored by the apathy-futility syndrome is likely to produce an adolescence plagued by hostility and social failure.

Like all concepts, the apathy-futility syndrome needs to be understood in terms of actual behaviors. Burgess and Conger (1978) provided such behavioral documentation. They observed families interacting in their homes, both in unstructured interaction and in pursuit of several tasks provided by the investigators. The principal conclusion of these studies was that parents who abuse and neglect their offspring characteristically ignore positive behavior, have a low overall level of interaction, and emphasize negative behavior. This is certainly a "social engine" well-suited to the task of producing psychologically damaged human begins and, as is the case with most childhood problems, it is in adolescence that the scope and magnitude of the damage become apparent.

Emotional starvation is bad for development. It is part and parcel of a broader risk: rejection. Youth who are rejected are in trouble. This is the conclusion of anthropologist Ronald Rohner's wide-ranging studies of the problem. Rohner (1975) examined rejection—its antecedents and consequences—in cultures all over the world. He found that across cultures, rejection is a kind of emotional malignancy, a psychological cancer that eats away at the individual's capacity for self-esteem, social competence, and hope. Rohner concluded:

> . . .that parental rejection in children, as well as adults who were rejected as children, leads to: hostility, aggression, passive aggression, or problems with the management of hostility and aggression; dependency; probably emotional unresponsiveness and negative self-evaluation (negative self-esteem and negative self-adequacy); and probably, emotional instability as well as a negative world view. (Rohner, 1975, p. 168).

In support of the ecological perspective, Rohner also found that rejection increased when a child's caregivers were isolated from the nurturing and feedback of interested others—friends and relatives, kith and kin. This is, of course, an issue that implicates the systems outside the family, and it is one we will consider shortly. At this point, suffice it to say that we cannot understand either type of microsystem risk and opportunity (balance and affective climate) without looking at its antecedents and consequences in the other systems involved—the individual and the community. Just as parents guide and protect their children, the community is parent to all its families (or should be).

Mesosystems

Mesosystems are relationships *between* microsystems in which the adolescent experiences reality. The links themselves form a system. We measure the richness of mesosystems by the number and quality of connections. One example is the case of the adolescent's peer group and home. We ask, do friends visit the adolescent at home? Do the adolescent's parents know his or her friends? A second example is the link between church and home. Do parents attend? Does the minister visit the home? Do the adolescent's friends attend? A third case involves school and home. Is there only a single link between home and school—the adolescent's participation in both? If this is only a single link, the mesosystem is weak and this may place the adolescent at risk, particularly if there is little cultural agreement between home and school.

The central principle here is that the stronger and more diverse the links between settings, the more powerful the resulting mesosystem will be as an influence on development. At one extreme we have the case where the youth is the only connection, for example when parents have no contact with a youth's peers. At the other, we have the case where there is total overlap between two or more settings, for example life in a religious commune. We define mesosystem risk first by the absence of connections and second by conflicts of values between one microsystem and another.

A rich range of mesosystems is both a product and a cause of development. The social competence of well-connected individuals increases, and that in and of itself increases the adolescent's ability to form further connections. A poor set of mesosystems both derives from and produces impaired development, particularly when home and school are involved. What determines the quality of a youth's mesosystems? The initiatives of the adolescent and the adults who care for him or her play a significant role, of course. Their role is particularly important when the adolescent enters a new microsystem.

A mesosystem arises at the point where a developing person first enters a new setting. This is what Bronfenbrenner calls an "ecological transition" (1979, p. 210). The two critical issues here are how this is done and who is involved. If, for example, the ecological transition (e.g., starting school) is defined as a very positive event by the adolescent's parents, if the adolescent's peers are supportive, if the adolescent is well prepared for the new setting, if the adolescent is accompanied by the parents, and if the new setting receives the adolescent with enthusiasm, the adolescent is on his or her way to a strong and developmentally enhancing mesosystem. In such a positive case the whole (the mesosystem) will be greater than the sum of its parts (the microsystems). Chapter 8 explores the ecological transition of becoming sexually active in this light.

Negative versus Positive Connections

The stronger, more positive, and more diverse the links between settings, the more powerful and beneficial the resulting mesosystem will be as an influence on development. A rich range of mesosystems is a developmental opportunity; a poor set of mesosystems produces impaired development. When the microsystems work in concert—a strong mesosystem—youth benefit. When they work in isolation or in opposition, youth are at risk.

The School-Home Relationship as an Example of Mesosystem Risk and Opportunity

All this is easiest to see when we look at the school-home mesosystem. For some adolescents, this mesosystem is strongly positive. There are many connections, and there is mutual support between the two settings. Parents ask about school work, attend the school's parent functions, and perhaps even volunteer their time for school activities. The home trains the adolescent to be comfortable and competent in dealing with the school's basic activities. It conveys a positive regard for written materials and the use of language and concepts in formal, problem-solving, and systematic question and answer sessions, organized around the solution of problems involving objects, quantities, and relationships. Adolescents raised with this pattern are more likely to work to the fullest of their potential at school (Garbarino & Asp, 1981). This pattern might be called the *academic culture* (Garbarino & Asp, 1981), and it includes what J. W. Getzels (1974) calls *language codes* and *value codes.*

> The language code gives the child the categories for structuring and communicating this experience. The value code tells him what in his experiences is important. For one child the codes learned in the family and those required by the school may be continuous (the same); for another they may be discontinuous (different).

That is, one student will find that the approach learned at home is well-suited to school; the two settings use the same *codes* and are therefore continuous. Another student will find school different from home—unrelated and even irrelevant, perhaps in active opposition, but certainly discontinuous.

Some children come to school well equipped to be students, while others are aliens to the microsystem of the school and find its requirements alien to their own experience. By the time they reach adolescence, many individuals find these differences have become overwhelming. In a world such as our own where academic success is important, to be an alien to the academic culture is to be at developmental risk. This theme is developed in Chapter 9. Failure in school sets the individual up for a whole series of socially and personally risky experiences, e.g., conflicts over rules, economic penalties, threats to self-esteem, and further alienation from the mainstream of cultural and social experiences that the society has to offer. Trouble with school is a major contributor to juvenile delinquency (Gold, 1963).

Beyond this issue, there is the question of how well school and home work together to provide a healthy balance of objective and subjective responses to the adolescent. Getzels (1974) has written persuasively that one measure of a healthy social environment is the balance between *universalism* and *particularism.* Universalism is based on treating everyone by the same standards (*what* you are); particularism looks at each person individually (*who* you are).

While home and family tend to emphasize particularistic concerns, schools tend to emphasize universalistic ones. However, for an adolescent to experience a healthy balance of particularistic and universalistic concerns, school and home must complement each other. Neither should be so extreme as to place the role of the other in jeopardy. Also, some adolescents may need the school to provide a compensatory dose, either of particularistic or universalistic orientation, if the home is unable or unwilling to do so. This is clearly a mesosystem issue. Too much particularistic treatment undermines the ability to deal with the abstract and the bureaucratic world. Too much universalistic treatment impairs the ability to deal with genuine intimacy. The implicit danger of the family is typically that it will go overboard on the particularistic end; the danger of the school is that it will overemphasize the universalistic. While there is no hard and fast rule to judge these matters, it does seem clear, as we said in Chapter 1, that large secondary schools, because of their inherent tendency to overemphasize universalistic orientations, pose the danger of psychologically starving students, particularly students who are borderline academic cases (Garbarino, 1980). Like the small family, where there is a high ratio of adults to children, the small school provides more opportunities for the reciprocal interaction that enhances development (Barker & Gump, 1964).

The school-home mesosystem is one of the most important in the adolescent's life. When it is strong and positive, it provides the adolescent with an opportunity to develop intellectually and socially, to become a more complete human being. When it is weak and negative, it burdens the adolescent with conflicts of values, style, and interest. So burdened, adolescents are held back from their fullest development. As schools have become more isolated from neighborhoods and other community institutions, the demands for academic success have increased and the stresses on families have magnified. The potential for developmental risk related to the school-home mesosystem seems to have increased (Garbarino & Asp, 1981). However, studies of intervention programs aimed at strengthening this mesosystem have documented that this goal can be accomplished (Bronfenbrenner, 1975).

Exosystems

Exosystems are situations having a bearing on the development of adolescents but in which they do not play a direct role. The exosystems affecting adolescents are those settings that have power over their lives, yet in which they do not participate. These exosystems include the workplace of the parents (for most youth, since they are not participants there) and those centers of power (such as school boards, church elders, and planning commissions) that make decisions affecting day-to-day life for adolescents.

In exosystem terms, risk and opportunity come about in two ways. The first is when the parents or other significant adults in an adolescent's life are treated in a way that impoverishes (risk) or enhances (opportunity) their behavior in the microsystems of home, school, church, or peer group. For example, Melvin Kohn (1977) has found that when parents work in settings that demand conformity rather than self-direction, they reflect this orientation in their childrearing style. Other examples include elements of the parent's working experience that impoverish or enhance family life, such as low pay, long or inflexible hours, traveling, or stress, on the one hand, and an adequate income, flexible scheduling, an understanding boss, or pleasant surroundings on the other.

The second way risk and opportunity flow from the exosystem is when decisions made in those settings affect an adolescent's day-to-day life. For example, when the school board suspends extracurricular programs in the youth's school or the planning commission closes the youth center, they jeopardize adolescent development. When they expand extracurricular programs for youth, they increase developmental opportunities since extracurricular activities are the lifeblood of social life for many adolescents who otherwise would have little to motivate academic activity. Thus, exosystem risk occurs when youth lack effective advocates in decision-making bodies. Psychologist George Albee (1980) has gone so far as to identify powerlessness as *the* primary factor leading to impaired development and mental illness *(psychopathology)*. It certainly plays a large role in determining the fate of *groups* of adolescents and may even be very important when considering individual cases, such as whether or not a teenager's parents have the pull to get him a second chance when he gets into trouble at school or with the police. Risk and opportunity at the exosystem level are largely a political matter because *who gets what* is the basic political issue.

One of the ground-breaking accomplishments of the ecological approach is that it highlights situations where development is significantly shaped by the actions of people with whom the individual has no direct contact. This relates social *policy* to adolescent development. Consider this example: because of fluctuations in the economy, a corporation board decides to shift operations from one plant to another, and hundreds of youth are affected, because their families are forced to move to a new location, because they cannot get part-time work now or full-time work later, or because their parents lose their jobs. This is a classic illustration of an exosystem effect, and it is one that touches the lives of many adolescents each year.

When adolescents have friends in high places, the opportunities for development increase and risks decrease. It is worth noting, however, that the ecological perspective forces us to see risk beyond the narrow confines of individual personality and family dynamics. In the ecological approach, both are "causes" in the child's development and "reflections" of broader sociocultural causes. Perhaps you are familiar with Mark Twain's saying: "if the only tool you have is a hammer you tend to treat every problem as if it were a nail." If we only think about youth at risk in terms of personality and interpersonal dynamics, we will never see the many other avenues of influence that might be open to us as helpers or that might be topics of study for us as scientists. This message guides our discussions of intervention (Chapter 12).

Macrosystems

Meso- and exosystems are set within the broad ideological and institutional patterns of a particular culture or subculture. These are the *macrosystems*. Thus, macrosystems are the blueprints for the ecology of human development that reflect a people's shared assumptions about how things should be done, as well as the institutions that represent those assumptions. To identify a macrosystem is to do more than simply name a group—Israeli, Arab, Swiss, American, Latino, Black, Anglo, Indian—and is more like labeling a cultural system such as Judeo-Christian, Communist, or Democratic. We must compare these groups systematically on some common scales of measurement, such as *collective versus individual orientation* or *schooled versus unschooled.* Religion provides an important example of the macrosystem in operation because it defines the relation between human beings and the rest of the universe. Sociologists such as Max Weber have proposed that religion in the form of the Protestant work ethic is responsible for how economic institutions work in European and American societies. Religion is a good illustration of the macrosystem concept because it involves both a definition of the world and a set of institutions reflecting that definition, both a theology and a set of roles, rules, buildings, and programs.

Macrosystem refers to the general organization of the world as it is *and as it might be.* The existence of historical change demonstrates that the *might be* is quite real and occurs through evolution (many individual decisions guided by a common reality) and through revolution (dramatic change introduced by a small cadre of decision makers). The suburbanization of America in the post-World War II era happened because of an intricate set of individual decisions, technological developments, and corporate and governmental initiatives. All together, they reshaped the experience of a great many adolescents in families and schools (Wynne, 1977). The Iranian revolution of 1978–79 overturned a *modernizing* society and indicated a changed institutional and ideological landscape. We can assume that these changes have reverberated through Iran's schools and homes to shape the experience of adolescence. First-hand reports from Iran tell of pervasive effects that include extreme pressures to conform in schools.

What are risk and opportunity when it comes to macrosystems? Risk is an ideology or cultural alignment that threatens to impoverish microsystems, mesosystems, and exosystem relations for adolescents; opportunity promises to enrich adolescent development by enhancing other ecological systems. Risk is institutionalized support for high levels of geographic mobility that disrupt neighborhood and school connections, versus policies that promote stability. It is a pattern of nonsupport for parents, tolerating or even condoning intense conflicts between the role of worker and parent instead of promoting parent-oriented policies and practices in the workplace. It is a pattern of racist or sexist values that demeans minority groups and thus threatens the development of self-esteem versus a pluralistic ideology that welcomes diversity and increases self-worth. In general, macrosystem risk is any social pattern or societal event that impoverishes the ability and willingness of adults to care for adolescents and adolescents to learn from adults. Opportunity is a social pattern or event that encourages and supports adults in caring for adolescents or adolescents in learning to be competent and responsible. It is an essential aspect of the human ecology because macrosystem forces shape day-to-day life, and thus the experience of adolescence.

Although we experience reality and construct it in the immediate settings in which interpersonal relationships take place (microsystems), and can extend our view to see the relevance of connections between settings (mesosystems) and the indirect influence of settings in which we do not ourselves participate (exosystems), many of the most important influences on our lives come from social, economic, and political changes that occur at the level of nations and whole societies. For example, World War I and World War II exerted profound effects on the day-to-day lives of nearly all Americans, including adolescents. Patterns of migration brought blacks out of the South and into the North in response to World War I and the resulting need for factory workers in the North's industrial cities. In both World War I and II, women entered the work force, taking traditionally male jobs, primarily to fulfill the needs of the war. Thousands of children and youth experienced the temporary or permanent loss of a father. The economic face of the nation changed dramatically. Many men and women saw so many new worlds that they were motivated to reconstruct their own. These macro-events produced myriad technological changes that have diffused into day-to-day life, perhaps most of all in Europe, Asia, and Africa where the fighting took place and the post-war reconstruction was most dramatic. And as Roger Rosenblatt (1983) has shown in his eloquent book *Children of War*, war continues to be a potent force shaping the character of adolescents everywhere it rears its ugly head.

We think of macrosystems as cultural blueprints that underlie the organization of institutions, the assumptions people make about social relations, and the workings of the political and economic system. Two aspects of this definition are particularly important for our purposes.

The first is that this treatment of culture goes beyond simple description. That is, in specifying culture as the blueprint for society, we leave open the possibility that those blueprints may be in error. The ecological perspective offers us the possibility of criticizing culture and society on the grounds that they impede human development and generate social risk. While this may seem self-evident, it does represent something of a departure from the way many social scientists think of culture. Using the term *cultural relativism*, many social scientists argue that all cultures are equivalent, that one cannot and should not criticize other cultures since all cultures arise as a specific adaptation to circumstances (cf., Tulkin, 1972). Translating culture into the concept of macrosystem, on the other hand, raises the possibility that such consistencies may not be in the best interests of adolescents and their development. This, as we shall see, is an important point.

The second and related aspect of our definition is found in the statement that macrosystem refers to consistencies "that *could* exist" (Bronfenbrenner, 1979, p. 26). As we said before, the ecological approach is intimately bound up with social policy (the decisions and principles guiding the behavior of public and private institutions). It necessitates a serious consideration of social engineering as a way of dealing with individual developmental problems; it broadens the base for intervention. Naturally, this is of special relevance in the discussion of sociocultural risk and opportunity, where the focus of attention is on problems in just those "consistencies in the form of lower-order systems" that do exist and have a particularly positive or negative developmental effect on individuals. Thus, an ecological approach has a moral imperative attached to it; it both describes and prescribes. It tells us that to reduce risk and increase opportunity at the most immediate level of the microsystem, we *should* consider changing things in the big picture. This means that the topic of sociocultural risk brings together the *helping* and *describing* traditions in human development. The meaning and implications of this moral and scientific approach to culture will emerge as we look at five examples of the macrosystem issues implicated in understanding competence.

The Effects of Pluralistic versus Totalitarian Societies in Fostering Individual Competence

At the very start, we can look at the sociopolitical organization of the society. The development of children, particularly their moral development, depends in part on the *political* structure of their experiences (cf., Almond & Verba, 1965). While we will consider moral development in more detail in Chapter 4, here we need to note that children and youth need a world that combines stability and diversity, consensus on basic principles combined with alternative and competing expressions of those principles. Very young children need to form powerful attachments that provide the basic prosocial motivation to develop morality. Once they have developed that basic prosocial motivation (to obey, to attend to rules, and to develop the rudiments of conscience), they need more (Garbarino & Bronfenbrenner, 1976). Adolescents need to be faced with moral choices, but in a reasonably secure, nurturing, and supportive setting.

Two extremes, and therefore two dangers, are possible. On one hand, there may be such a diversity of irreconcilable alternatives that adolescents cannot choose and at the same time avoid the hostility and alienation of those they choose against. On an interpersonal level, Bateson (1972) has called such situations *double binds* ("damned if you do and damned if you don't") and linked them to mental illness in the form of schizophrenia. Youth should be protected from these conflicts since they are unfair and developmentally threatening (e.g., when a parent makes sexual advances to a child).

One can imagine a society that irreconcilably pitted school and government against family, for example. In such a situation, the adolescent would be faced with an intense double bind. To remain loyal to the family would mean to estrange one's self from peers, from teachers, and in fact to place oneself in political jeopardy. To side with school and government would mean to make the intolerable choice of turning one's back on kin. Many totalitarian societies force this choice upon children as a matter of course; Nazi Germany did so (Shirer, 1960). Democratic societies do not do so as a matter of policy, although such dilemmas may occur when there are irreconcilable differences between family and state. This is the situation facing some fundamentalist Christian sects that have been frustrated in their efforts to set up religious schools by state regulations concerning accreditation.

In contrast to the society in which there is irreconcilable conflict between family and state, there stands the society in which all social agents are unified in single-minded devotion. Here the developmental problem is not one of double binds but rather is the lack of diversity, which will impede moral development. For example, when church and state are under the same rulers *(theocracy)*, such as in Iran under the Ayatollah Khomeini, there is unchecked absolutism, and moral sensibility languishes. Where there is no diversity, the youth can too easily satisfy society's demands. This stands in contrast to the democratic society in which a measure of social diversity necessarily exists, where there are competing allegiances that youth must sort out and in so doing learn to develop high order thinking and judgment (Garbarino, 1968). Adolescents learn to live by principle in the society that promotes diversity within consensus.

We believe that the greatest danger to moral development lies in the totalitarian society that commands total allegiance to the state. This authority is manifested in the authority of adults such as teachers and youth group leaders. One study of these data (Garbarino & Bronfenbrenner, 1976) looked at the moral judgments of youth (12 years old) in countries with varying degrees of social and political diversity. At issue was the degree to which the moral judgments of youth reflected a balance of adult and peer influences in totalitarian versus democratic societies. The study used the term *pluralistic* to refer to the middle ground between irreconcilably intense conflict on the one hand and the extreme absence of conflict on the other. In a pluralistic society, there are competing allegiances that operate within a common framework: a consensus on basic principles, agreement to the rules of the game, and appreciation for the need to spare individuals impossible choices as much as possible. The results of the study indicated that among both communist and noncommunist societies, the less pluralism a society manifested, the less balanced were the moral judgments of the youth (Garbarino & Bronfenbrenner, 1976). The issue is one of totalitarian versus pluralistic societies, not necessarily one of political East versus political West.

What does this have to do with sociocultural risk? It tells us that when looking at macrosystem matters we should attend to whether or not the political culture of a society forces youth and parents into intolerable dilemmas. It tells us that there are developmental grounds for supporting the pluralistic society. In fact, White (1959) illuminated these developmental grounds in creative detail. He speculated that there is an inherent drive to master the environment and a natural ability to recognize when forms have changed (an *incongruity mechanism*). In White's view, the human being thrives on a balance of the familiar and the different, of the known and the novel, on *optimal discrepancy*. Environments that provide the individual with this kind of optimal discrepancy serve to stimulate and enhance development. They provide the kind of social and intellectual richness human beings need. Thus, classic, philosophical traditions of democracy stand on firm ground. A democratic society—a pluralistic society—is in fact a healthy environment for humans to grow in. It offers them the greatest exercise of many processes, such as evaluating, deciding, and comparing, that are innately and particularly human. Therefore, a nondemocratic social system—a macrosystem dominated by totalitarian influence—presents a sociocultural risk for adolescents while a pluralistic society presents an opportunity for development.

The Economic System: Costs and Benefits for the Development of Competence

The economic system is one of the most powerful aspects of the macrosystem. It connects work, goods and services, and the social, biological, and physical environments that more than anything else define the kind of life we lead. The type of economic system—for example, laissez-faire capitalism or state-run socialism—and a person's place in the economy—rich or poor, working or unemployed, superior or subordinate—have an enormous effect on one's relation to one's family, community, country, and oneself.

The American economy finds its identity in the free-market assumptions first advanced by the classical economist Adam Smith, as tempered by 20th-century innovations of government intervention and welfare policies. Laws and regulations, taxes, and government programs attempt to fine tune the economy so it works better and ensures the survival and minimum well-being of all Americans. How well is the economic system working to support our nation's youth?

At the heart of this question stands one of the great political, economic, and social debates of our time. As we said earlier, human needs are constant and basic; societies with much fewer technological advances than ours have had long and happy histories. We can all easily cite the benefits of our economy: material wealth, social and geographic mobility, rising health and educational standards, to name but a few. At the same time, we must ask about the costs of our system to people and to the environment. One way to consider this is in terms of the underlying assumptions that determine how things are done in the economy.

For example, our economy is based on the principle of permanent growth as a necessary condition for progress. This belief seems rooted in the "Protestant work ethic" we mentioned earlier as part of Max Weber's analysis of the role of religion in Western societies. Growth constantly requires new markets, resources, changing demands, and an emphasis on consumption. As a cultural blueprint, this idea seems obvious, even indisputable. Yet many observers question the wisdom of continual growth as a blueprint (Brown, 1981; Daly, 1980). Starting from the idea that Earth is a finite environment, we can see the most sensible economy as a steady-state system, a sustainable society with basically fixed levels of population and economic output. Indeed, this is the kind of world system analyst Jay Forrester (whom we mentioned earlier) envisions.

As technology advances, productivity and time, rather than increased production, would be gained. The economy would strive toward stable levels of consumption and economic activity and *maximum* durability and quality of goods, leaving people the means and freedom to concentrate on meeting their psychological and spiritual needs. One can imagine a combination of advanced technology and cottage industry, as people devote themselves to satisfying labor and minimizing unpleasant work. Our ecological situation, of course, would be much improved by a system based on stability and the sustenance of all life, rather than constant growth and the exploitation that it requires. How does this affect adolescence? Some question the wisdom of electronic games and gasoline-powered recreational vehicles in preparing youth for an ecologically sane society (Garbarino, 1979).

Another aspect of the economic macrosystem is the use of the profit motive as a basis for economic decisions. Rather than directly considering basic human needs of consumption, satisfying labor, and human relatedness, our economy is based on the pursuit of profit and the accumulation of wealth. Unemployment, poverty, worker alienation, pollution, and stress, as well as the whole "malaise of affluence" (Lasch, 1979) are unfortunate by-products of our economic status quo. While the riches we have accumulated may be unparalleled, so are the problems and dangers from which we suffer. Adolescents face our economic situation with the hope and expectation of finding a job and a career that will allow them to develop economic independence. But many have trouble doing so. Unemployment among youth is higher than among any other age group, and most youth who do find work do not find it very satisfying or uplifting (Steinberg et al., 1982).

Finally, the current blueprint incorporates the economic notion of *efficiency* as the only basis for making decisions. In a time of scarce energy and jobs, common sense would argue that an approach to production that focuses on creating permanent jobs (i.e., is *labor intensive*) would provide work for more people by using less nonhuman energy. Yet the trend throughout the economy (in North America and the rest of the world) is toward *increasing* the mechanization and automation that puts people out of work and requires massive amounts of nonhuman energy. The agricultural sector, for example, has "released" 25 million people from the farms of the United States since 1940 by utilizing more and more sophisticated machinery. Yet, agriculture has never been in a more precarious state than it is now, as farmers are forced to farm larger acreage and go deeper and deeper into debt to afford land and machines, while the topsoil that must sustain us forever is being depleted at an alarming rate because of the necessity of "mining the soil" to reap short-term yields

(Brown, 1981). Moreover, food production is in the hands of fewer and fewer people, and a high level of unemployment, particularly for youth, is a permanent problem, especially for those at the bottom of the society who need work most.

The fact that these basic economic assumptions are not questioned frequently testifies to the extent to which they are ingrained and have become a part of the macrosystem. Market payoffs, rather than human concerns, dictate what is to be the structure of our social relations. The point here is not the injustice or inefficiency *per se.* It is the fact that so much of what happens in the economic realm affects adolescents (e.g., their personal identity) and their families (e.g., in conflict over the costs of raising a teenager). It is precisely the way we *think* of our involvement (or fail to think about it) in the economy as workers, consumers, investors, and taxpayers that keeps the problems from getting solved. Because they may be more ready to challenge accepted assumptions than adults, adolescents may be amenable to rethinking these assumptions if encouraged to do so.

Individualistic Competition versus Interdependent Cooperation

One of the clearest ways to identify the operation of a macrosystem is to consider what people take for granted. Particularly when comparing macrosystems, one finds that what is taken for granted in one society is hotly disputed in another. American culture views independence and autonomy as a part of "human nature" and as a positive goal towards which individuals should strive. It assumes that individual competition and independence are universally the norm. This belief is so firmly fixed in our macrosystem that many of us would find it hard to consider an alternative. We see dependency as basically unhealthy *(pathologic)* or at least immature (Rotenberg, 1977). Our culture denigrates interdependency and sees it as a form of weakness. Just to present the issue this way is to raise the question: Is independence a self-evident good, or is it only good as defined within a particular culture, a culture subject to criticism on the grounds of its effect on development?

We need to look at the social benefits and social risks of our culture. Our individualistic culture gives us a sense of personal responsibility, a rationale for achievement, and a justification for success. It provides a justification for our social system, differentiated as it is by economic and social levels. Our narrowly individualistic culture provides the freedom, individuality that collective societies cannot.

On the other hand, it clearly implies (and often makes painfully obvious) that if success is a matter of individual virtue, failure is a matter of individual deficiency. The other side of individualism is alienation, a sense of estrangement, of isolation, and of being perilously alone (Slater, 1970). Many social philosophers have argued that it is in the interdependencies and interconnections of one's social life that one finds enduring sources of what is meaningful.

This position receives increasing scientific support as survey data and other investigations show that people who are well-connected on an interpersonal level are the happiest and most satisfied with their day-to-day existence (Campbell, Converse, & Rodgers, 1976; Whittaker, Garbarino & Associates, 1984).

The fact that social connectedness and enduring social relationships are what keeps us going in life suggests that our individualistic culture, and the competition and denigration of interdependency it implies, place us at sociocultural risk. Our culture tends to say "every man for himself" while our nature as human beings says "no man is an island." We face a real, enduring, and intense conflict here. Adolescents with their fuller participation in this culture feel a pull to be both an "individual" and "one of the crowd." This issue is an important dynamic in the process of forming an identity (as we will see in Chapter 7).

This conflict has been identified repeatedly in social and historical analyses of our society. Sociologist David Riesman called it "the lonely crowd"; Philip Slater discussed it in his book, *The Pursuit of Loneliness;* James Webb, an historian, saw it throughout our history as "the parabola of individualism." It means that we value individual autonomy and privacy so much that we are always threatened with social isolation. And, because adolescents are at a very culturally sensitive point in their lives (some call them "cultural weather vanes" because they point where the winds of change are blowing), they are prone to feeling isolated and alienated more than children or adults who are more clear about their social positions and actually have clearer social rules.

We seem to say that everyone should be on their own, free, without recognizing that the price for such independence is the risk of alienation, a pervasive sense of dissatisfaction, and a heightened vulnerability to depression. Adolescence is a critical period in life for developing interdependence as well as independence, a capacity for tenderness as well as intellectual objectivity, and respect for diverse forms of human competence as well as pride in their own achievements. Most males are so oriented to autonomy they risk losing touch with intimacy. Many females are made to feel guilty about their sense of social connectedness (Gilligan, 1982). Altogether, our excessive and unrealistic valuing of independence sets us up for unhappiness, including clinical depression (Weissman & Paykel, 1973).

Just as in moral development where pluralism is the key, the matter of competition, individual responsibility, and interdependence requires a balanced solution. Without a notion of individual responsibility and accountability, it is unlikely that people can develop sufficient belief that individuals themselves rather than external forces determine the course of life (a belief in self-responsibility that we call *internal locus of control*). The very cornerstone of our society is individual self-motivation and competition, with cooperation seen mainly as a means toward the goal of the individual's greater gain. On the other hand, without an appreciation for interdependence, for how much we need each other, and for the intrinsic worth of social connectedness, we are constantly in

jeopardy of alienation and depression. Both of these are potentially serious social problems affecting adolescents, among whom they may provoke suicide.
Excessive dependency can make the individual unequipped to face the demands
of our society, while extreme independence can make one unable to share life's
joys and hardships with others (Gilligan, 1982).

That this is a macrosystem effect is demonstrated by the fact that it permeates all our institutional life. In schools we see it in the fact that individual
competition—primarily for grades—is a corrosive force undermining the self-
esteem and development of the majority of students who inevitably must be
losers (Dreeben, 1968). On a broader scale, we see it in our virtual inability to
restrain commercial exploitation of adolescents, all of which goes forward under the banner of individualism. Advertisers have an *individual* right to play to
youth, while parents have an *individual* responsibility to counteract this advertising blitz that emphasizes materialistic gratification. We see it in one of its
most virulent forms in our society's apparent inability to do anything about the
sexual exploitation of adolescents in prostitution and pornography (a topic we
consider in Chapter 11). This leads us to consider the cultural roots of another
social risk to adolescents, violence in the family.

Violence as a Norm in the Macrosystem

As we hope has become clear in this discussion of macrosystem issues, to speak
of the macrosystem is to consider the meaning of human nature. This is evident as well if we look at normal violence. Just as our culture sees individual
competition as a fact of human nature, it tends to define violence as an inevitable and normal part of domestic relations (Gil, 1973; Straus, Gelles, & Steinmetz, 1980). The use and approval of violence in domestic relations is common
in our society. The most recent and comprehensive study (Straus, Gelles, &
Steinmetz, 1980) documents that among normal American (two parent) families, domestic violence in some form is almost universal (involving at least
some hitting in 90% of the families surveyed), and serious assault occurs in
some 15% of our families.

The very fact that we define only the most damaging and extreme forms
of physical punishment as *abuse* and permit the rest to be classified as only
normal discipline is testimony to the status of violence in our culture. This,
too, is a macrosystem issue, because violence figures prominently in the blueprint of our domestic and institutional life. It is, in fact, a normal part of our
experience. According to survey evidence, many if not most educators, clergy,
and police generally approve of the use of physical force and corporal punishment in disciplining children and youth (Parke & Collmer, 1975). Few parents
can conceive of—let alone implement—alternatives to the use of physical force
in social control and discipline with their children. The incredulous or hostile
response given to calls for domestic *nonviolence* is testimony to this.

When Sweden's legislature reaffirmed and strengthened its opposition to
the use of physical punishment by parents, the American press treated the ac-

tion as a ludicrous bit of nonsense. The parallel is illuminating. When psychologist John Valusek issued a booklet under the title *People Are Not For Hitting*, he found that most readers assumed that he did not include children in that message. He had to add *And Children Are People, Too* before the message was clear to many readers (at which point they rejected it). Is it any wonder that when adolescents are frustrated or angry they resort to violence, as we showed in Chapter 1?

There are grounds for believing that the use of physical force is not inevitable, that it is a reflection of social stress, and that alternatives can and do exist. The same investigators who found such widespread support for and use of domestic violence found that the level of such violence rises in direct proportion to a host of predisposing stress factors such as economic inadequacy, marital conflict, social isolation, and personal inadequacy. Rather than being an inevitable expression of human nature, the use of violence is a culturally conditioned expression of distress. Desmond Morris made the following observation about domestic violence based on his look at nonhuman species: "The viciousness with which children. . .are subjected to persecution is a measure of the weight of dominant pressures imposed on their persecutors" (1970).

Cultural support for violence against fellow humans represents sociocultural risk because it presents and legitimizes a dangerous outlet for stress. Some other cultures, mainly technologically primitive, tribal cultures, do not legitimize this outlet, and they have less domestic violence (Korbin, 1977). Some social stress is inevitable, and when we provide an outlet that can easily escalate into physically and emotionally damaging behavior, we place adolescents in general at risk and the adolescents of distressed families in special jeopardy. Where we condone the slapping of one teenager, we inevitably increase the likelihood that another will be punched. Where we accept physical abuse against wives on the grounds that it is a husband's right, we make it almost inevitable that youth will be battered. The insidious thing about macrosystem effects is that they send ripples throughout the human experience. In supporting and accepting violence as part of the macrosystem, we set in motion a chain of events that inevitably places substantial numbers of young people at risk in their microsystems. On the other hand, insofar as we are able to start a countermomentum of nonviolence, we may serve to protect adolescents who find themselves in stressful circumstances. Domestic violence is one of the most poignant and pressing areas of sociocultural risk with which our society must deal.

Sexism and Racism as Cultural Issues

One of the important principles guiding our efforts to enhance human development states that we should attempt to encourage the best possible match between individual characteristics and social settings. As we noted before, the ecological definition of development involves the idea that the more differentiated one's conception of reality and the greater one's skill in mastering reality, the greater the fulfillment of individual potential. This definition of development argues that ideologies or institutions that unnecessarily or unfairly limit the opportunities of individuals are a threat to development. Such factors unnecessarily and unduly restrict the experience, and hence the development of those affected. Two such factors are sexism and racism because they oppose the goal of individual development. They narrow the range of *social* contexts to which *individual* characteristics must be matched, and therefore increase the risk of injustice. Thus, even if the average male is stronger and faster than the average female, it is unfair to superior females to limit the participation of females in athletics.

As an ideology, sexism asserts that there are rigid, inherent, and inevitable differences between males and females that are and should be the basis for the differentiation of activities (Maccoby & Jacklin, 1974). In its best form, it is a *separate but equal* approach to development. In fact, according to research from a variety of sources, it contributes a "separate but unequal" macrosystem effect. It forces females into unduly and unnecessarily narrow choices of activity (the male role is also limited, of course, but offers some potent rewards as compensation—e.g., power over females). Thus, sexism exerts a depressing effect on many aspects of female competence. For example, research on occupational development has shown that young males cite a very wide range of potential occupations, ranging from the close-to-home (policeman, doctor, and mailman) to the far-flung (spaceman, baseball star, and president). Young females, on the other hand, as early as four years of age will restrict most of their choices to teacher, nurse, and mother. Clearly, this does an injustice to the diversity of interests and abilities that exist among females. Therefore, there are developmental grounds for seeing sexism as a source of sociocultural risk.

Sexism also forces males and females into roles and personality styles that may be difficult for them to maintain; it violates the principle of fit or match. It means that males who are temperamentally inclined to nurturing roles may assume such roles only with decreased self-esteem and a sense of failure. It means that females who are temperamentally inclined to adopt aggressive, athletic roles must cope with the role incongruity this implies. All of this flies in the face of the principle of matching individual characteristics to situations and is therefore developmentally threatening. Whatever *group* differences there may be (and there *are* grounds for believing that such average differences between the sexes do exist—Hutt, 1972), they do not justify values and institutions that run roughshod over quite significant *individual* differences (Rosenberg & Sutton-Smith, 1972).

In the same manner, racism is a macrosystem threat to development. By postulating racial differences in intelligence, moral character, and general competence, racism undermines the development of those it defines as inferior and even impoverishes the development of those judged superior (Tulkin, 1972). It places the inferior individuals at risk by creating a negative reality with which they must contend at serious psychological cost. It has a demonstratively depressive effect on competence and contributes to a wide range of personality disturbances. Because it is a macrosystem effect, it permeates the institutional life of the society, and thus forces its victims into extraordinary measures to cope. Adolescents, trying as they are to cope with their *individual* development (e.g., rapid physical change), are especially vulnerable, as the racial differences in juvenile problems we will discuss in Chapter 11 show.

Attributing characteristics to individuals within a group presents a threat to the development of those individuals, particularly if they are cast in a negative light. There is almost always overlap between groups, whether the differences are due to actual genetic differences (such as the height of Chinese versus Bantu people) or discriminatory testing (such as when Jews, immigrating into the United States in the early 1900s, were judged to be intellectually inferior on the basis of intelligence tests administered to them in English, which they did not all speak).

Human development proceeds *through individuals*, although aggregate differences can and do exist. *Isms* (Sex*ism*, rac*ism*, etc.) that limit and define the range of possibilities for groups have an inevitably adverse effect on the individual by disrupting the natural process by which individual and environment are matched to facilitate development. Science and ethics merge in rejecting sexism and racism. These ideologies are not consistent with the process of fullest human development at any age. Adolescents, as fledgling adults, are open to damage from these macrosystem effects.

An Ecological Map

In sum, then, the ecological perspective on human development offers a kind of map for steering a course of study and intervention, for assessing and dealing with risk and opportunity. Remember that here it is a map drawn from the perspective of the adolescent. A parent's or teacher's map would be different e.g., work might be an exosystem for the adolescent but a microsystem for the parent. With that in mind, examine the picture presented in Figure 2.1 and Table 2.1. It gives some visual approximation of our ecological framework.

Systems at each level have distinctive characteristics that are relevant to an adolescent's development, and therefore different criteria are appropriate for assessing the impact of each level. Furthermore, these effects may be either positive or negative, either opportunities or risks. And, while the family microsystem is usually the most important system, the overall impact of the environment emerges from the dynamic balance among all levels of influence. These forces, which extend beyond the family, grow in number, importance, and complexity during childhood and assume a critical role in adolescence. Indeed, in adolescence the individual begins to construct new bridges from the family

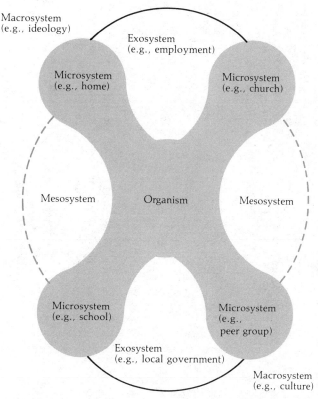

FIGURE 2.1
The ecology of human development.

to the other systems in the human ecology, for example, to the peer group. Whether or not adolescents succeed in this task depends upon how well their personal resources stack up against the social challenges they face.

But what are these personal resources? What does it take to meet these social challenges? Take a moment to think about it. Can you define competence? One common response is to list a series of characteristics: "intelligence," "courage," "empathy," "strength," "self-control," "mathematical ability," and "verbal ability" all come to mind. But are all of these equally important for everyone? Do boys need different characteristics than girls? Does a poor kid growing up in a tough neighborhood need the same skills as a rich kid in a safe suburb? Does a Canadian need different personal resources than a Russian? All these issues come into play when we try to specify what we mean by *personal resources.* They are tough issues, but we have to face them as we try to define social competence.

TABLE 2.1
A summary of the ecology of sociocultural risk and opportunity.

Ecological Level	Definition	Examples	Issues Affecting Adolescents
Microsystem	Situations in which the adolescent has face to face encounters with influential others	Family, school, peer, group, church	Is the adolescent regarded positively? Is the adolescent accepted? Is the adolescent reinforced for competent behavior? Is the adolescent exposed to enough diversity in roles and relationships? Is the adolescent given an active role in reciprocal relationships?
Mesosystem	Relationships between microsystems; the connections between situations	Home-school, home-church, school-neighborhood, peer group-home	Do settings respect each other? Do settings present basic consistency in values?
Exosystem	Settings in which the adolescent does not participate but in which significant decisions are made affecting the adolescent or adults who interact directly with the adolescent	Parent's place of employment, school board, local government, parents' peer group	Are decisions made with the interests of adolescents in mind? How well do supports for families balance stresses for parents?
Macrosystem	"Blueprints" for defining and organizing the institutional life of the society	Ideology, social policy, shared assumptions about human nature, the *social contract*	Are some groups valued at the expense of others (e.g., sexism, racism)? Is there an individualistic or a collectivistic orientation? Is violence a norm?

The Meaning of Competence

What is human development all about? We each might have our own particular answer to that question. Some might say the point of human development is "to fulfill your potential." Others might say, "to help the world progress." Others might say, "to help humanity." Others, "to serve the state." Still others might say, "to serve God" or "to become more spiritually perfect." Our task here is to aim our sights a bit lower than proposing some overall purpose to life, although we do believe that most adolescents need to have a strongly felt purpose. Our intention is to offer some tools for understanding the events and processes of adolescence in terms of our ecological model.

What is it that is threatened by social risks? What does social opportunity promise to enhance? The answer is *competence*, the ability to succeed in the world. Competence is the currency of development. We need to understand more about competence before we can go further in identifying developmental risks and opportunities in adolescence. We can start with the basic dictionary definition of competence as "means sufficient for the necessities of a good life." It is a good definition to start with but it is not enough for our purposes. We need a more detailed one that gives more attention to the implications of competence for understanding adolescent development.

We can start by noting that the *means* talked about in the definition exist in actual settings in real social and physical environments. As we shall see, one of the thorniest problems in defining competence is working out how much of it is specific to certain situations *(situation specific)* and how much is general (or even universal). For example, do the same people and qualities succeed in the freshman year of college as do (or would) in the first year of military service? Do the two settings require the same characteristics? Is competence the same in both settings? Is competence the same for teenage girls as it is for boys? Do the roles the two groups play or are expected to play by adults and institutions differ sufficiently to require different "means sufficient for the necessities of a good life?" We'll try to keep these questions in mind.

Perhaps the most basic issue in understanding the meaning of competence is "*who* defines competence?" Consider the issue of competence in the high school. Who defines the meaning of academic competence or school success? Is it the taxpayers who support public education (or the parents and trustees of a private school)? Is it the educators who have responsibility for the curriculum and classroom instruction? Is it legislators who make laws about education? Is it mental health professionals who have a concept of psychological well-being and who may deal with youth who are disturbed by their experiences at school? Is it the adolescent students themselves who must cope with schools and schooling on a day-to-day basis and live with its results in their adult lives?

It is a tough question in general (what is competence?) and in this particular case (what is academic competence?). We will deal with the former here, and the latter in Chapter 9. Two of the general issues flowing from the general question are these:

■ Can a definition of competence remain "value free" or neutral? Can we be objective about something so socially fundamental and personally important as competence?

■ Is a definition based on personal opinions and observations or systematic research? Is it based on what we know or what we wish to believe?

We can keep these questions in mind as we review some of the major efforts to define and explore the meaning for competence.

We start with Greenspan's (1979) concept of *social intelligence*. He defines it as the

> ability to understand and to deal effectively with social and interpersonal objects and events. Included are such variables as role taking, empathic judgment, person perception, moral judgment, referential communication, and interpersonal tactics. (p. 483)

Figure 2.2 presents the components of social intelligence as Greenspan has arranged them.

This is a useful framework. Of course we need to figure out what *exactly* goes in each of the boxes. That takes some doing if we take seriously the questions we raised earlier about culture, social class, and sex. But we can keep Greenspan's scheme in mind as we look at four major approaches to social competence: *Level of Functioning, Bag of Virtues, Interpersonal Success,* and *Maturity-Oriented.*

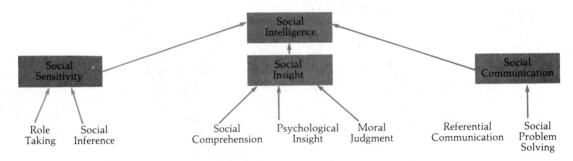

FIGURE 2.2

A proposed model of social intelligence. (Greenspan, S. "Social intelligence in the retarded." In N. Ellis (Ed.) Handbook of mental deficiency, (2e), Hillsdale, N. J.: Lawrence Erlbaum Associates, 1979.)

Level of Functioning emphasizes the idea that we can compare people, that we can assess each individual's competence relative to other individuals. This comparative approach tends to be quantitative—"How well is an adolescent doing at school?" The Bag of Virtues approach focuses on whether or not an individual possesses important characteristics. It is inclined to ask questions such as "Is this adolescent creative?" The Interpersonal Success approach emphasizes that the successful attainment of goals must occur through social interaction, through people. Thus it might ask, "Can this adolescent communicate with peers and adults?" Finally, the Maturity-Oriented approach compares the individual with that same individual's potential. Competence is thus being all *you* can be, and this approach might ask "How far along is this adolescent in becoming all that he or she can become?"

Level of functioning. These approaches emphasize the situation-specific aspects of competence and argue against generalized definitions. For example, McClelland (1973) argues that intelligence (IQ) testing (assessing general intellectual ability) tells us little about how well people are doing and will do in the specific situations they face in their lives. Each situation has its own agenda. Success in the classroom makes different demands than success in the video arcade for example. Having said that, however, McClelland does indicate some behaviors and characteristics that *often* seem important if one is going to function well in life's situations. These are patience, the setting of moderate goals (neither unrealistically low nor high), effective communication skills, and a general resilience in the face of frustration or adversity *(ego strength)*. The overriding point in McClelland's view is adequate functioning in real life situations rather than general "intelligence" or "intellectual development" (more on this in Chapter 4).

Bag of virtues. These approaches (so-called by Kohlberg and Mayer, 1972) attempt to specify the set of traits that characterize a healthy, functioning person. Foote and Cottrell (1955), for example, say that competence is synonymous with being able to marshal one's resources to achieve one's desired outcomes or goals. This defines competence as simply having what it takes (the means) to get what one wants (the ends). And, it says there is a set of traits that promotes this.

- health: optimal use of physical resources
- intelligence: ability to organize and mobilize resources
- empathy: ability to predict the feelings of others
- autonomy: a stable, positive sense of self
- judgment: ability to estimate and evaluate alternatives
- creativity: the capacity for innovation and the ability to evoke new roles in the self and other

Any list such as this makes some sense, even if it is based on common sense (such as Foote and Cottrell's) rather than research. But where do we stop in listing traits? Anderson and Messick (1974) go so far as to list 29 characteristics representing social competence. What would your list include?

Interpersonal success.   Some have emphasized the social aspects of competence and focused on competence within interpersonal relationships (e.g., O'Malley, 1977; Weinstein, 1969). Indeed, in many studies, social competence is often taken as synonymous with (or at least crucial for) peer acceptance and social adjustment. After reviewing studies of social competence in children, O'Malley, (1977) defines it as:

> productive and mutually satisfying interactions between a child and peers or adults. Productive interactions attain personal goals of the child, whether immediately or in the long run, which are adaptive in classroom settings. Interactions will be satisfying to the child when goals are attained, and to others if actions in pursuit of the goals are received in either a benign or positive manner. (p. 29)

According to Weinstein (1969), the stability and functioning of any social system depends on individuals being able to "effectively pursue their personal goals" and be "successful in achieving personal purposes." Although a social system may define expectations for the performance of roles, everyday living requires negotiating with others who may have opposing motives or purposes in order to establish a pattern in which most people's basic needs get met. To participate in society, people must be able to control the responses of others. Therefore, the acquisition of skills needed to engage in these negotiations is central to the socialization process. Incidentally, Wynne's (1977) book about the effects of suburbanization on youth that we mentioned earlier postulates that suburban life is deficient in teaching this competence in negotiating.

Defining interpersonal competence as "the skills and abilities allowing an individual to shape the response he gets from others," Weinstein has outlined three major components of this ability. The first characteristic on Weinstein's list is *empathy* or what others have called *role-taking*. It is the ability to accurately "take the role of the other" and to be able to accurately predict consequences that one's actions will have on the perceptions of the other. The second component is the availability of "a large and varied repertoire of lines of action" or *interpersonal tactics*. This implies that an individual needs to have a wide range of alternative behaviors from which to choose, such as being assertive in one setting and accommodating in another. Finally, an individual must have the *interpersonal resources* to be capable of employing effective tactics in situations where they are appropriate. These resources are personal orientations or traits that may predispose an individual towards displaying or inhibiting particular kinds of behaviors, such as patience and courage. The particular strategy an individual uses in an interpersonal situation would depend on these intrapersonal resources and would characterize an *interpersonal style.*

Greenberger and Sorensen (1974) have proposed that "the capacity to interact effectively with others" is an essential component of "psychosocial maturity." In order to be *interpersonally adequate,* an individual must develop:

1 *Communication skills:* the ability to convey and receive messages (of which empathy plays an important part);
2 *Enlightened trust:* learning whom to trust and under what conditions, including recognition of individual and situational factors in making judgments of trustworthiness; and
3 *Knowledge of roles:* an awareness of social conventions and the understanding of role requirements relevant to interpersonal functioning.

The importance of good interpersonal relationships for personal satisfaction and social stability seems obvious. Several theorists (including Hartup, 1978; Sullivan, 1953; Youniss, 1980) have argued that good peer relations, particularly during adolescence, are essential for healthy psychological development (we will discuss this further in Chapter 10). Research supports this view. Several studies show that poor peer relations not only relate to poor mental health, but are also related to problems such as delinquent behavior (Roff, Sells, & Golden, 1972), poor school achievement (Westman, Rice, & Berman, 1967), and various forms of mental illness and personality and behavior disorders (Cowen et al., 1973; Kohlberg et al., 1972; Roff, 1972; Roff & Sells, 1968; Roff, Sells, & Golden, 1972; Watt, 1978).

Maturity.   Some have tried to link competence to socialization and development by invoking the concept of maturity. Maturity here means a full flowering of all that a person can be, biologically, psychologically, and socially. Heath (1977) is in this tradition when he views maturity as a "determinant of generalized competence" involving a set of universal traits. These traits include: "ability to anticipate consequences; calm, clear thinking; fulfilling potential; ordered; predictable; purposeful; realistic; reflective; strong willed; and unshakable" (p. 204). Greenberger and Sorenson (1974) define the link between competence and maturity as the integration of a subjective sense of worth, behavior that facilitates interpersonal contacts, and being in tune with the society at large. Buhler (1969) offers the same message.

While a person may need particular skills, abilities, or characteristics to function successfully in different environments, some theorists feel that an important part of competence is *believing* that one is competent, *wanting* to affect the environment, and *feeling* good about doing so successfully. Having an internal sense of competence or "drive for mastery" means an individual *wants* to be competent and is intrinsically motivated to engage the environment (Harter, 1978; White, 1959).

A Synthesizing Approach to Competence

We have tried to bring together these themes in a working definition of competence that we can use throughout our discussions. We see competence as a set of skills, attitudes, motives, and abilities needed to master the principal settings that individuals can reasonably expect to encounter in the social environment of which they are a part, while at the same time maximizing their sense of well being and enhancing future development. Having said all that what does it all mean?

We think it means several things. First, it establishes competence as the goal of socialization and development. We are (or at least should be) moving adolescents towards fully competent adulthood. They need to *be* good at something to *feel* good about themselves and to be good citizens (and workers, and eventually, perhaps, good parents). This gives us goals, and thus standards, with which to evaluate the performance of institutions and individuals that assume responsibility for the well-being and nurturance of youth. It gives us an ecologically valid definition of competence, appropriate to our perspective.

Second, our definition emphasizes positive capacities rather than simply describing the absence of negative characteristics, deviance, or pathology. Some individuals function competently despite these handicaps. Third, our definition recognizes that different social environments—as defined by social class, ethnicity, or culture—encourage and reward different things and thus establish different kinds of competence. This is evident in the work of those who study the diversity of socialization among groups that differ on the basis of culture and ethnicity (Laosa, 1979; Ogbu, 1981), social class (Coles, 1980; Kohn, 1977; McCandless, 1970), or gender (Parsons, 1960; Chodorow, 1978; Gilligan, 1982). But it also asks us to consider how different social environments for adolescents relate to each other. Are they separate but equal? Is one dominant over another? The answers have significant implications for assessing competence in adolescence.

Settings characterized by economic deprivation, cultural aggression, racism, or psychopathology pose one of the challenging issues facing us—the issue of what is *normal* development and competence. Can we use the same criteria in defining and evaluating competence in these settings? Some say yes. They argue that all adolescents need to learn certain basic skills and how to get along in the mainstream culture. Others argue that we must understand people in terms of their specific experiences. Ogbu (1981), for example, says that the "ghetto theory of success" reflects the demands and resources of certain socioeconomic conditions. A competent youth in such a situation is one who can function within that setting, regardless of its deviance with respect to the rest of the society. We will return to this issue again in considering juvenile delinquency.

A second, related issue is *bicultural competence.* Many people who are part of a minority culture function successfully in both their subgroup and in the majority culture. Of course, this is sometimes a strain. The tension between the two identities is often great, for example when one is part of an ethnic or immigrant minority disparaged by the majority culture or when the subgroup's values are very different from the mainstream.

A third issue challenging the meaning of competence is found in the development of children and youth who overcome earlier difficulties as they grow up and seem to function successfully despite adverse conditions—e.g., having psychologically disturbed or abusive parents (Garmezy & Neuchterlein, 1972; Garmezy, 1977). These resilient or *stress-resistant* youth call into question our assumptions about how the environment nurtures development. Although some have attributed their success to superior constitutions or a *self-righting tendency*, they often are found to have some less than obvious social resources to draw upon for psychological support (Goldberg, 1977; Sameroff & Chandler, 1975). For example, longitudinal research by Werner and Smith (1981) found that both personal and social factors were important in whether children categorized as "at high risk for behavior disorders" actually showed those problems at eighteen years of age. In general,

> the invulnerable child developed a strong early attachment and autonomy during the preschool years, mastered competencies in childhood, and had a sense of some control over life events during adolescence. The home environment had at least one stable caregiver (a parent, sibling, or grandparent) who was supportive but not over protective and fostered the child's growing autonomy. (Ulrey, 1981, p. 37)

These three special cases (deviant settings, bicultural experience, and stress resistance) demonstrate the importance of two general principles:

- ▓ Human beings strive to meet some universal needs, but do so in ways that are culturally diverse and society specific
- ▓ Human beings are notable for their resilience and adaptability

Competence is based on the striving to meet personal and cultural goals, goals that have a basis in the very nature of the human organism. In a nurturing environment the competent youth thrives; in a hostile environment the competent youth adapts in order to survive. Thriving and surviving translate into environmental terms as the human ecology of developmental opportunity and risk and the development of social competence is the crucial outcome.

The Development of Social Competence

The development of social competence in childhood is the product of physical and environmental factors and a factor in the future development of competence in adolescence as well. We have stated that competence is the goal of socialization and development. Whether and how the individual acquires specific competencies and whether individuals are seen as competent members of society is an ecological issue; it depends on an interplay of personal and environmental factors.

From conception onward, biological and genetic factors play a critically important role in development. Genetic characteristics can put a child "at risk" for impaired development by preventing a child from developing required competencies. Mental and physical handicaps, congenital health disorders, physical attributes and appearance, and temperament all fall into this category.

Although these factors may have direct influence on the acquisition of social competence, they commonly exert their influence through the social environment, particularly by affecting how other people treat the individual. Thus, for example, mentally or physically handicapped adolescents could be at risk for impaired social development if they are not able to elicit the kinds of responses from peers and adults that would establish the kind of secure nurturing attachment they need (Ulrey, 1981).

Some researchers consider individual differences in style of behavior (temperament) as an adaptive response that has genetic origins and historical implications for the development of adaptive cultural modes of childrearing (Freedman, 1974; Super, 1981). Several authors (e.g., Thomas & Chess, 1980) suggest that individual differences in temperament are associated with differences in functioning. It is not so much that individuals with one particular temperament are more competent than individuals with other temperaments. Rather, outcomes in development and the influence of temperament lie in the "fit" between the individual and the demands of significant environments such as family and school (Lerner et al., 1982). This highlights the ecological principle of assessing individual social competence in terms of the ecological niche, rather than in general terms. For example, an aggressive, striving female finds a better fit in a society in which there are entrepreneural roles for women than in a society that insists upon keeping women at home as childbearers and homemakers only. Some researchers have concluded that certain methods of childrearing are more often related to desirable outcomes in adolescence, in general. Others call this into question by arguing that under special circumstances the usually wrong approach may be right, and vice versa. We find one example of this in the case of Chaim Potok's novel The Chosen in which a loving father subjects his genius son to a decade-long "withdrawal of affection" in order to teach the boy humility and an appreciation for human suffering.

In viewing empirical studies of the effects of different styles of childrearing, (which we will explore further in Chapter 6) Rollins and Thomas (1979) conclude that:

> Socially competent behavior of children, that is, behavior that is valued in society as desirable and has instrumental utility, is positively correlated with parental support, power of same sex parent, inductive control attempts, and the impor-

tance of such socially competent behavior to parents; it is negatively correlated with coercive attempts of parents. (p. 348)

Most investigators have concluded that social class plays an important role in this respect: According to a review by Gecas (1979), higher socioeconomic status has been related to:

1   the use of reasoning instead of physical punishment to control behavior;
2   the use of discipline on the basis of the child's intentions and motives rather than on overt acts;
3   egalitarian as opposed to autocratic relationships with children;
4   high degree of parental affection;
5   greater emphasis on independence and achievement.

Not surprisingly, researchers have linked use of these methods to socially desired outcomes in children. Rollins and Thomas, however, suggest that recognizing specific styles of interaction or techniques and methods used in child-rearing may be a necessary part of the equation but is not enough by itself to predict outcomes in children and adolescents:

Social competence in children is facilitated by parental support and control attempts of an indirect type *if at the same time the parent values such competence in the child.* These parental behaviors without valuing the social competence, or valuing social competence without these parental behaviors, would probably *not* result in social competence in the child. (1979, p. 342, emphasis added)

So, these techniques permit the parent to influence development, but they must have a plan, a set of values, some content to teach when they assert control and influence. Melvin Kohn's classic work, *Class and Conformity* (1977), forms the basis for investigating parental values as an important link between family situational variables and childrearing practices. In 1969, Kohn asked a national sample of fathers (with children aged 3 to 15) to rate the desirability of 13 characteristics of children. These valued characteristics were shown to fall into two general categories (or *dimensions*), one being labelled *self-direction versus conformity*, and the other labelled *maturity*. In subsequent analyses, Kohn found consistent social class differences in parental values, with working-class parents valuing behaviors reflecting conformity to external standards, while middle-class parents valued behaviors relating to self-direction and adherence to internal standards of behavior.

Experience at work can influence behavior as a parent, and thus qualifies as an exosystem effect. We mentioned earlier Kohn's work showing that the type of work people do can influence what they value as parents: jobs that require initiative lead to emphasizing independence; jobs that demand conformity are associated with demands for obedience at home. Kohn's work is generally consistent with Miller and Swanson's (1958) studies in the 1950s of how the wives of middle class husbands in bureaucratic jobs sought to encourage different things in their children than did the wives of men engaged in entrepreneural enterprise (conformity in the former case and assertive independence in the latter). More recently, research on mothers who work outside the home has shown that their daughters are trained to be more career-oriented and their sons more involved in household tasks (Bronfenbrenner & Crouter, 1982).

According to Kohn, the primary influence on values is by the degree to which the parent is able to exercise self-direction (as compared to having to conform) at work. Thus, parental values link the socioeconomic system in society to family dynamics. This ecological perspective shows us how differences in conditions of life give rise to parental values and perspectives that are adaptive and transmitted to children "both directly as conscious attempts to inculcate values in their offspring, and indirectly through different styles of interaction" (Gecas, 1979, p. 379).

Although the effect of social class has been shown to be consistent and fairly sizable in studies using national samples, there is evidence that among some groups and in some places, other factors such as locale, ethnicity, and religion may equal (or perhaps surpass) socioeconomic indicators in accounting for differences in parental values.

In an attempt to partially replicate Kohn's work with a more recent national sample of mothers and fathers, Wright and Wright (1976) report that although indicators of social class do explain a significant proportion of variation (10–14%) in childrearing values, the addition of ethnicity and geographic locale add almost as much. Winetsky (1978), in examining parental preferences for educational activities, found that middle-class parents had a higher degree of preference for self-directed activities than working-class parents. Among the working-class parents, however, Anglos had significantly higher preferences for self-directed activities than non-Anglos.

The results of Winetsky's (1978) work suggest that there may be significant effects of combining SES and ethnicity. In noting the numerous ethnic differences in both achievement and abilities in a longitudinal study of children in Hawaii, Werner and her colleagues concluded that "It seems quite apparent that from our study that SES differences alone do not explain the differences in capacity and achievement among children from different ethnic subcultures" (1968, p. 56). Along with evidence that show high correlations between social competence and academic achievement, these results point to the usefulness of examining cultural factors (ethnicity and associated values) along with socioeconomic indicators in investigating the conditions that promote the development of social competence in children. Recall our earlier mention of the Protestant work ethic, for example.

Adolescence is an important time for both the development and demonstration of competence. During this period individuals are testing their abilities to function successfully in the world and trying to feel good about that ability. Often deficits that were only potential in childhood become real in adolescence when demands for mainstream characteristics and skills increased markedly in school and the world of work, as we shall see in Chapter 9. With some skills and confidence as a foundation, the adolescent will be ready to develop further skills that may be important during their adult years.

Adolescence is a time when individuals begin to influence the course of their own development to an unprecedented degree (Lerner & Busch-Rossnagel, 1981). Adolescents have increased opportunity to select particular environments and situations, and in many cases are able to arrange the quality of their experiences. What they have arranged can influence the course of their growth. This is both the promise and the danger of adolescence. Their appearance and behavior stimulates those around them to treat them in certain ways, ways that may be different from when they were children as their image changes with their bodies. An "ugly duckling" may blossom into a swan while an attractive child may become an unattractive teenager. In addition to selecting roles, adolescents are assigned to roles and duties and are expected to act in adult-like ways in making decisions and taking responsibility for their actions. Thus, adolescents must now confront directly a set of stresses *and* resources from which they may have been shielded previously. Beyond just being influenced by these forces, adolescents can make something out of these risks and opportunities (recall Elder's study of adolescents in the Great Depression). This highlights the cost of social incompetence: missed opportunities for enhanced present and future development.

Our discussion of competence brings us to several questions we need to keep in mind while considering other aspects of adolescent development:

1   *Does competence carry over across situations?* Does being successful in an academic situation carry over into dating or work situations? Are there some skills, attributes, and attitudes important for competent functioning in each of these settings?

2   *Does competence carry over across relationships?* Does being competent with adults carry over to being competent with peers?

3   *Does competence carry over across time?* Does the competent child become the competent adolescent, then the competent adult? Can the relatively unsuccessful child become competent in adolescence? What about the successful adolescent who fails in adulthood?

4   *Does competence carry over across history?* Was competence in the 1960s the same as in the 1980s?

We will hold these questions in mind as we proceed with our study of adolescence.

Conclusion

With this ecological perspective on social competence, risk, and opportunity as our guide we are now ready to look at adolescence directly. We begin with the individual as a biological system in transition. Adolescence is first and foremost the biological stimulus of physical maturation to the psychological and social environment. After we investigate the nature of this biological stimulus in Chapter 3 we will examine the parallels in the maturation of intellectual functioning in Chapter 4. With these discussions of developing body and mind behind us we will be ready to look at theories of adolescence in Chapter 5.

Preview

- Biological maturation is a vital part of adolescence.

- Puberty is the complex set of changes that transform the child's body into the mature body.

- The timing of puberty depends upon the body's own biological clocks and the influence of diet, health, and social conditions.

- The body's biological clock is run by a series of glands and organs that produce hormones affecting growth and maturation.

- Sexual maturation involves both the reproductive organs and other organs that differentiate males and females (e.g., hair, voice, etc.).

- The emotional and behavioral reactions of the individual, peers, parents, and other adults affect the way each adolescent experiences puberty, particularly when maturation comes relatively late or early.

- The major health issues affecting adolescents, such as smoking, drinking, drug use, accidents, and violence, concern lifestyle and personal safety.

We begin our discussion of adolescent development with the person as a physical being. The human organism is the system at the center of our ecological map as we drew it in Chapter 2. We followed that map outward from the organism into the micro-, meso-, exo-, and macrosystems that define the *human* meaning of changes in the physical organism in adolescence. This leads us to consider the psychological, social, and cultural dimensions of adolescent physical maturation and well-being.

Most of us can remember (or keep trying to forget) awkward moments in adolescence (particularly early adolescence) when our bodies seemed to be strangers to us, tried to play tricks on us, refused to do what we wanted, or just appeared (to us, at least) to be different from everyone else's. The reality of these experiences is echoed in popular stereotypes and survey research that portray adolescents as preoccupied or even obsessed with their bodies. Physical change does provide the organizing events of adolescence. It poses the issues with which different theoretical perspectives must wrestle, as we will see in Chapter 5 when we review major theories of adolescence. It provides the major stimuli for all the psychological and social adjustments we group together under the heading, *the adolescent experience*.

In this chapter we examine four principles. First, physical maturation *(puberty)* is a long-term process, occurring over many years, rather than a single event. Second, there is more to puberty than meets the eye. We often think of puberty only as a series of events leading to sexual maturity, but along with the development of the reproductive system and the sex characteristics, a number of other equally important biochemical changes are

3

The Biology of Adolescence

taking place. Third, the significance of puberty for the individual adolescent arises from the interaction of biological changes, psychological developments, and social roles that operate within a broad cultural context. We find the meaning of puberty in the ecology of adolescence. Physical maturation lends itself to an ecological perspective because it reaches from the individual as a biological system to the society as a macrosystem in its significance and because all the levels of systems reach down to influence it. Fourth, issues of adolescent health are highly social in nature, as much as, if not more, than they are "medical" in the narrow sense.

What Is Puberty?

The word *puberty* comes from the Latin *pubescere*, which means "to be covered with hair" (Brooks-Gunn & Petersen, 1983). A typical dictionary definition describes puberty as being "the period or age at which a person is first capable of sexual reproduction" (Random House Dictionary, College Edition, 1975).

To gain a better understanding of puberty as a process, we need to understand how the events of puberty fit into the general processes of growth and maturation. As the culmination of reproductive development, it is part of a process that had its origins long before birth. Sexual maturation really begins at conception, with sexual differentiation completed in the womb—*in utero* (Petersen & Taylor, 1980; LeBaron, 1972). Along the same lines, puberty is just one component of the broader pattern of human growth. Even in its own right, puberty lasts much longer than we may think. Its initial phases begin as early as eight years of age, and the process continues until the mid- to late-teens (Petersen & Taylor, 1980).

But there is more to puberty than just sexual development. It involves a whole series of physical changes, many of which are not directly related to reproduction. While each of these involves significant *physical* change, it is, as we shall see, the translation of these physical events into a psychological and social context that defines adolescence. To highlight this we must consider the psychosocial implications for each physical event. The overarching point is that there is quite a lot of normal variation in the timing of pubertal events. This means that on almost any measure of puberty some individuals will be early in comparison with their peers, while others will be late. As we shall see again and again, the perception of oneself as early or late *can* have very important psychological implications.

We can group the processes that occur during the course of puberty on the basis of their outcomes. Marshall and Tanner (1974) present a five part scheme that is helpful in understanding the full extent of pubertal development. Based upon their analysis, we see the major events in puberty as being:

1   The acceleration, then deceleration of skeletal growth. We note that early vs. late maturation is an important influence on personality development that extends its influence into adulthood.

2   An alteration in body composition resulting from skeletal and muscular growth and a change in the distribution and amount of body fat. We note that the shape of an adolescent's body does much to influence the shape of his or her social life and that body size and shape problems are a major issue for adolescents.

3   The development of the circulatory and respiratory systems, which results in increased strength and endurance. We note that the ability to participate in sports is a prized commodity for adolescents and a major reason that early maturing boys have a social advantage.

4   The development of the gonads, the reproductive organs, and secondary sex characteristics. We note that as adolescents begin to look like adults they and the people around them begin to shift their expectations and invoke a new set of expectations that includes but goes beyond sexuality.

5   Changes in the nervous and endocrine systems that coordinate and bring about the other changes. We note that the adolescent's brain changes in ways that may make it possible to reason in more mature ways, with many psychological and social implications.

The most vivid memory of my adolescence is the fact that all of my friends were beginning to look like young women. I still looked like a little girl. My best friend, Bonnie, was fifteen going on twenty-five. We used to go to parties together and guys would ask her if I was her "little sister." All of my friends were getting boyfriends. I was still lagging behind. Who wanted to out with a little girl? I used to wear baggy clothes so no one could see my lack of a figure. Not even makeup helped. I thought I would never grow up.

I remember having a large circle of friends, but feeling anxiety over not looking as mature as my girlfriends. My first boyfriend (should I hold his hand?). These are the memories of my adolescence.

I moved to a new state when I was in eighth grade. It was hard trying to fit in with these new people who had known each other for years. It took almost the entire year. But eventually I was accepted.

Entering high school was a new experience. Everyone was getting high in the bathrooms. Drugs were a new thing to try.

I think the most difficult thing for me was that all my friends were beginning to look like young women. I still looked like a little girl.

It is clear then that puberty is a complex and interrelated set of phenomena that is much more than simply physical and involves much more than the development of the capacity to reproduce. However, the use of the term often seems to reflect a conception of puberty as a singular event, rather than a process. This issue of "event" versus "process" is an important one in defining puberty, and deserves some attention.

The Nandi of East India inflict pain and test the male's ability to suffer in silence. In Central Africa, a girl is separated from her family for fattening up to marriageable proportions. Some societies define puberty through official events such as these (Sommer, 1978; Rogers, 1981). Within these cultures—mostly technologically primitive ones—the onset of puberty is marked by celebration and ritual, a *rite of passage*. Such rituals are more common and more intense for males.

However, even though youth in modern Western societies experience prolonged and relatively ambiguous adolescence, we are not without puberty rituals. Granted, we do not have a rite of passage marking the transition from childhood. In fact, we have a confusing mass of minor ceremonies and ritual events that makes it difficult to define the official time of maturity. Because we seem to view puberty as erupting suddenly and lasting only a short time, we may underestimate its influence on other aspects of development and often fail to see how the biology of adolescence is interwound with its psychological and social counterparts.

Besides the physical, there is also a social dimension to puberty. There are two ways of looking at this. First, the living conditions (nutrition, health care, and so on) in a particular area influence the timing, duration, and outcomes of puberty (Katchadourian, 1977). (We will examine this phenomenon in detail later.) This reveals the ecology of puberty, as micro-, exo-, and macrosystems of the youth's environment influence the physical experience of puberty. Second, the events of puberty are given meaning by the society in which they occur. Culture influences what youth experiencing puberty think and feel about their own development. It is those around adolescents—peers, parents, and the society at large—who tell young people what these events mean. The message adolescents hear is influenced or *mediated* by their own level of psychological development. Thus, while puberty may be a process of physical change, it is the interaction of the biological, the psychological, and the social that really defines puberty as a human phenomenon and gives it ecological significance. As an aside, we should note what Thornburg (1974) has called *social puberty*, defined as the direct involvement in some way with members of the opposite sex before physical-sexual maturation. We will have more to say about this in Chapter 8, when we consider sexuality.

Up to now it may seem as though we are treating puberty as a constant, and that it is only variations in the social context in which it occurs that account for differences among individuals in pubertal experiences. This is not the whole story. The rate of physical development follows many normal patterns, and there are even variations in the sequence of events in some cases. Of course, not every adolescent's physical growth can be called normal, but the range of normality is very wide. A glance in a typical eighth grade classroom will confirm this. It would not be unusual for a visitor to see some youngsters who look like adults, while others would not be out of place in an elementary school. Yet, all of these adolescents could probably be labelled *normal*, at least in terms of physical development. Therefore, it is important to remember that when we speak of general trends in pubertal development (as we will throughout this chapter), the timing, sequence, pace, duration, and, ultimately, meaning of puberty vary greatly among individuals (Dewhurst, 1969; Marshall & Tanner, 1970). Diversity, not uniformity, is the rule in adolescent physical development, a message that must be communicated to adolescents (and preadolescents) to save them anxiety and anguish when they are a bit late or early in developing.

We can now return to our original question: What is puberty? We answer in terms of its biological outcomes, but with a disclaimer. Puberty results in the attainment by the child of "the physique and physiological capabilities of an adult, including reproductive capacity" and includes the full flowering of adult sex differences in appearance and physiology *(dimorphism)* (Katchadourian, 1977, p. 23). Further, this long-term process is universal, but not uniform. It is mediated by individual variations in timing, rate, and duration, and derives its human meaning from the psychological and social context in which it occurs.

The Onset of Puberty

The two most important questions regarding the onset of puberty are: When does it occur? Why does it occur? Researchers have developed a pretty good picture of the events of puberty, although questions do remain. In general, we can say that puberty begins when a complex network of systems within the body begins to send and receive information to each other. These messages build up into major biochemical changes that alter growth rates, affect the size and composition of some tissues, and cause the maturation of sex organs. We know this happens, but some controversy and uncertainty remains about exactly why the feedback buildup starts (Petersen & Taylor, 1980).

When Does Puberty Occur?

We do have a little more information about *when* puberty occurs than *why.* Therefore, we will deal with that issue first. As we do, we need to keep in mind that the changes in hormones associated with puberty begin in middle childhood, but we are usually not aware of the onset of puberty until several years later when the more obvious signs appear.

The onset of puberty is related to a number of genetic and environmental factors that interact with each other to influence the timing of physical maturation. Therefore, the time at which the process of puberty begins to unfold seems to be a highly individual matter. However, there *appear to be* some general trends in physical development (of which puberty is a part) over the past 100 years that may signal a reduction in individual diversity in the onset of puberty (although not all scientists agree that these trends are actually occurring). Changes in height and weight and the decrease in age of the onset of menstruation *(menarche)* over successive generations during the past 100 years are summarized by the term *secular trend*.

The evidence supporting the existence of a secular trend comes from several sources. Data from several countries show that preschool age children have been getting taller and heavier, on the average, by about 1.0 cm and .5 kg per decade since 1900 (Falkner, 1972). Comparison of the same individuals at puberty reveals an increase of 2.5 cm and 2.5 kg per decade over past generations. The significance of this phenomenon is mainly in terms of earlier maturation, rather than a large increase in overall eventual adult height across generations (adults appear to have gained about 1.0 cm per decade). Not only does pubertal growth begin sooner now, it stops earlier as well (Badwin & McLaughlin, 1964; Maresh, 1972).

The most well known evidence for a secular trend in the onset of puberty comes from the work of the English physician, J. M. Tanner. Tanner's (1973) data show that the age at menarche has declined for West European and American females over the past 140 years. For example, the average age at menarche for Norwegian females has declined about four years from 1840 to 1980, with the general rate of decline being about four months per decade. A similar decline is apparent for American women. On average, adolescent American females in 1900 experienced their first menstrual cycle at about 14, while their counterparts of 1980 did so at about 12.

These data seem conclusive, but we need to be careful for several reasons. One is the tendency to make more out of the trends than really exists. For instance, if we use Tanner's data and project it into the past, we could conclude that women in the middle ages experienced menarche in their thirties. There is no evidence to support this conclusion. Also, some recent data show a lack of change in the age of menarche in Western societies for the past 30 years or so (Zacharias, Rand, & Wurtman, 1976). A report issued by the National Center for Health Statistics (1976) states that any previous steady increase in size of American children has come to a halt in the past decade. In fact, some scientists propose that if the changes reported by Tanner were plotted over several centuries, we would see that the secular trend is actually part of an oscillating pattern in which the age of the onset of puberty swings back and forth (Falkner, 1972). Another problem in taking Tanner at face value is that his sample may not be a representative one. If the different years used in Tanner's data tapped different groups of children and youth the results could easily give a misleading picture. There have also been questions raised about the accuracy of the early data.

In any event, even if there has been a secular trend in the age of pubertal onset, it appears to have stopped (Petersen, 1979). This is true for males as well as females, although there are no comparable data for boys because there is no event in males as obvious as menarche to use in comparing the age of pubertal onset across generations. It seems doubtful that puberty will come any sooner in modern industrial societies (Petersen, 1979), which may be a fortunate thing for us because, as we shall see in Chapter 8, we wonder whether society, families, and schools could adjust to an even earlier onset of puberty, given the trouble they have now dealing with pubescent seventh graders!

Why is puberty not likely to begin any earlier? The answer to that question has to do with the factors affecting growth, in particular the levels of nutrition and health care within a society. Although there has been some speculation that the secular trend results from genetic changes in the population due to intermarriage among groups—*the genetic hybrid hypothesis*—most observers attribute the change to social factors producing changes in physical conditions. The historically observed decreased age at menarche seems to result mainly from the improved nutrition and the decrease in illness and disease that has occurred in modern societies over the past 100 years. But the decline seems to stop when nutrition and health care reach an optimal level (Petersen, 1979). In other words, growth is no longer retarded by poor health and nutrition.

This does not mean that we will eventually see puberty beginning at the same time for everyone, and we will always have to cope with a wide variety in early adolescent growth. There are a number of genetic and social factors that influence physical development besides nutrition and health care and that will act to keep our "diversity as opposed to uniformity" rule in force.

Factors Affecting Growth

We can conveniently divide the factors affecting growth into two groups, genetic and environmental. However, we must remember that these factors are interrelated. A set of specific genetically controlled features may have evolved in response to a particular set of environmental conditions, and certainly environmental factors can modify a genetically programmed set of events. As we said in Chapter 2, nature and nurture are inextricably intertwined. Given "normal" circumstances though, it is heredity that largely determines our physical development, and therefore, the timing of puberty as well.

Genetic influences on growth operate at both an individual and species level. Our particular pattern of growth and the role of puberty in the overall process seems to be a unique feature of primates, especially monkeys, apes, and humans (Tanner, 1962). In other animals who experience a pubertal cycle, the interval between birth and puberty is relatively short, and growth does not slow down between these points and accelerate again at puberty as it does in humans and their close evolutionary relatives. Some theorists of human evolution speculate that this delay in sexual and physical maturation allows a greater degree of intellectual and social development (including play) while the child is not in sexual competition with potentially aggressive adults (Tanner, 1970). We call this kind of speculation *sociobiology* when it includes efforts to explain social structure and values on the basis of evolution (van den Berghe, 1979). Whatever its evolutionary origins and rationale, the pubertal pattern in humans probably evolved early in our species history and, except for minor changes such as the time of onset, has remained basically unchanged.

Familial and sex effects are examples of genetic influences on growth that operate at a more individual level. The influence of heredity on physical growth is probably most obvious in family relationships. We tend to look like our parents, and there is a strong positive correlation between the height of parents and their offspring, particularly between mothers and daughters, and fathers and sons. There is also a relationship between mother's and daughter's age at menarche (Tanner, 1962). Tanner reports that the average age difference at menarche between unrelated, randomly selected girls is 13 months; for nonidentical twins, the average difference is 10 months. Identical twins raised in the same household (under modern conditions) show an average age difference at menarche of only 2.8 months.

Sex is also a genetic influence on growth. Its most noticeable effect is the fact that girls begin puberty about two years earlier than boys (Higham, 1980), but sex also influences the sequence of pubertal events. For example, girls experience the adolescent growth spurt about two years before boys (with many social consequences, including orienting younger girls to older boys), but both sexes reach sexual maturity at around the same time, and there is very little difference in the age at which the secondary sex characteristics (such as pubic hair) first appear (Finkelstein, 1980). The commonly held notion that the development of secondary sexual characteristics occurs earlier in females is probably due to the fact that their appearance is more evident in girls even when fully clothed (e.g., breast development). Corresponding events in boys (e.g., growth of the genitalia) are not apparent when males are dressed. The noticeable markers of sexual development in males (e.g., growth spurt, facial hair, and voice change) are later events in the cycle of male puberty and, therefore, males appear to reach sexual maturity at a later age than females (Finkelstein, 1980).

It also seems that body build or shape (which is primarily genetically determined) has an effect on the timing of puberty. Some studies report that individuals who are short and stocky mature earlier than those who have a taller and leaner linear build. However, obesity and excessive thinness are both associated with delayed puberty and with cessation of menstruation (Frisch, 1978). Whether this is due to the fact that shortness leads to early maturation, or that early maturation results in a shortening of the growing period is not clear (Daly, 1966). (We will deal with the effect of sexual maturation on physical growth in more detail later.)

A genetic influence on development sometimes thought to affect the timing of puberty is race. However, while there are marked racial differences in some physical characteristics (e.g., skin color), it seems that pubertal pattern is not one of these. Evidence regarding differences in age at menarche from around the world shows that race does not seem to be a significant factor in determining the age of the onset on puberty (Hiernaux, 1968). For example, blacks include both the earliest and latest maturers (Cuban blacks and the Bundi from New Guinea), while whites vary within a more moderate range. It seems that factors other than race (e.g., health care and nutrition) are responsible for the international differences in age at menarche reported by researchers around the world. An Israeli study showed that age at menarche for Jewish women differed widely depending on whether the women were born in Europe or the United States as opposed to Asia or North Africa (Halbrecht, Sklorowski, & Tsafriv, 1971). The father's birthplace was also a factor.

If race is not important in explaining these inter- and intranational differences in the onset of puberty, what is responsible? What we are observing in these variations is the operation of environmental factors. Like genetic factors, environmental factors can influence development on both a species and an individual level. Specific constellations of environmental factors can bring about the evolution of a set of genetic characteristics. Here we will deal with only the immediate effects of environmental conditions on individuals and not consider species effects.

The most pervasive environmental influence on the timing of puberty is health in general and nutrition in particular (Petersen & Taylor, 1980; Warren, 1983). Growth depends on the intake of various nutrients, and thus malnutrition stunts or interferes with the growth process. The severity of the effects of malnutrition depends on both the amount of nutritional deficiency in conjunction with the individual's caloric needs and how chronic the problem is. Caloric need is related somewhat (but not exclusively) to age because age is associated with growth rate, size, and metabolic rate. Thus, the greatest need for food is at puberty, a fact well known to parents who buy groceries for teenagers! The effects of acute malnutrition can be quickly corrected when proper nutrition is instituted, but prolonged and severe nutritional deficiency usually results in permanent problems (Frisch, 1983).

The effects of nutrition on puberty are reflected in the differences in age at menarche across and within countries and cultures. It seems that the more adequate nutrition is (other things being equal), the earlier puberty will occur, within limits set by genetics (Petersen, 1979; Tanner, 1970; Frisch, 1978). As we mentioned earlier, there appears to be a limit to the effects of nutrition on the timing of puberty. Once nutrition is optimized, the age of onset seems to stabilize (Petersen, 1979). However, the effects of nutrition do not occur in a social vacuum. When nutrition improves, usually other aspects such as health do as well. Thus, it is difficult to isolate the exact effects of nutrition from other influences. A good illustration of this is found in the relationship between socioeconomic status (SES) and physical development.

SES is determined by a set of variables (income, education, occupational prestige) and many of these have an indirect effect on growth. Differences in cultural attitudes and economic resources between SES groups also imply differences in nutrition, health care, and childrearing practices. Several researchers have found a relationship between SES and height, with the children of upper class parents being taller than those from working class homes (Tanner, 1970). This probably results from the higher standard of living of upper class children, and in particular, better nutrition and greater availability of high quality health care, both of which are associated with better living conditions.

In a similar vein, there appears to be a correlation between higher SES and lower age at menarche, at least in some countries (Tanner, 1973). Again, this is probably related to general living conditions and especially nutrition. Some studies report no such correlation, but this could be due to the relative nature of SES classifications—the lower class in one country may be fairly well nourished compared to the same class in another country (Douglas & Simpson, 1964). Therefore, one would expect to find a relationship between SES and the onset of puberty in developing nations, but not in more industrial societies. Such macrosystem influences illustrate an important aspect of the ecology of human development.

Several other influences on growth may also be interacting in this SES effect. For example, both illness and emotional state have an effect on growth (Warren, 1983). Both of these are likely to be operating in a negative manner when children are raised in impoverished microsystems, i.e., in institutions that cannot meet basic psychological needs. This tells us that delayed puberty may be an aspect of sociocultural risk.

Some environmental factors that influence puberty are a direct reflection of the physical environment. For instance, children grow faster in the spring and autumn than in other times of the year. Height increases more during spring, while weight accumulates faster in the fall (Sinclair, 1973). Menarche also varies by seasons. There seems to be a decrease in the incidence of menarche in the spring. In countries with great seasonal variation, the onset of menarche peaks at certain times of the year (Zacharias, Rand, & Wurtman, 1976; Kantero & Windholm, 1971). Altitude is another factor that seems to affect the onset of puberty by influencing the general growth rate. Females who live at lower elevations begin to menstruate earlier than those from the same SES who live at higher elevations (Petersen, 1979). Thus, the physical as well as the social ecology plays a role in puberty.

One physical influence commonly thought to be a major factor in the timing of puberty turns out to have little impact—climate. Many people assume that youngsters living in hot, humid areas experience puberty earlier than those living in colder climates. This was sometimes referred to as *ripening*. Research has refuted this proposition. Thus, for example, Nigerians average 14.1 years of age at menarche, while English average 13.1.

What Initiates Puberty?

Our ecological perspective helps organize the influences in our discussion of puberty: Systems at all levels from micro- to macro- contribute to the onset of puberty. We now turn to the timing mechanism itself for further illumination of the ecology of adolescence.

Several explanations attempt to account for the onset of puberty. One seems particularly intriguing. This theory put forth by researchers, Frisch and Revelle (1970), is often called the *critical weight hypothesis.* Frisch and Revelle speculate that the onset of puberty occurs when a youngster reaches a certain critical weight, and the underlying process that triggers puberty is the attainment of a specific metabolic rate (Petersen, 1979). Their theory is based on evidence that reveals that menarche occurs at a relatively constant weight in girls, and that the adolescent growth spurt seems to begin at a constant weight in both sexes. Recent data suggests that fat must make up 17% of an individual's body weight if menstruation is to begin and continue (Petersen, 1979). This idea is supported by the case of teenagers who starve themselves (anorectics) and by female athletes in some sports (gymnastics, running, and swimming) who experience a cessation of menstrual activity *(amenorrhea)* when their body's fat content drops below normal levels.

In summary, Frisch and Revelle feel that the attainment of a critical body weight causes a change in metabolic rate that in turn lowers the sensitivity of specific areas in the brain to levels of certain chemicals in the blood. This causes the body to produce more of these chemicals, and it is their increased concentration in the blood that sets the pubertal process in motion. (We will discuss the hormonal control of puberty in some detail later.) While this explanation is plausible and has some empirical support, many scientists remain skeptical. They believe that Frisch and Revelle's hypothesis fails to rule out competing explanations (Petersen, 1979). Many feel that critical weight is more *associated* with the onset of puberty than a *cause* of it (Petersen & Taylor, 1980). This kind of objection is an important part of the scientific process, one that we will consider further in Chapter 5 when we discuss theories and theory building.

Part of the problem in studying the onset of puberty lies in the nature of puberty itself. The actual beginning of puberty is not marked by great physical changes, but rather by minute increases in hormonal levels in the bloodstream. It is much easier to determine that a youngster is experiencing puberty than it is to discern its exact beginning and end (Petersen, 1979). We do know that a network of chemicals (called *hormones*) produced by the endocrine glands initiate and mediate the pubertal process.

Hormonal control of puberty.   Before we can examine the role of hormones in puberty, it is necessary to have some basic information about hormones and their place in bodily functioning. Hormones are specialized chemicals that act as messengers for a group of glands known as the endocrine system. The endocrine system is made up of eleven glands or gland areas located throughout the body. These glands form a linked set of systems in dynamic equilibrium or *homeostasis*. That is, the action of one serves as feedback to another. They interact with each other in a way that strives for overall system balance. If one malfunctions seriously it can overwhelm the ability of the others to compensate and cause real problems for the entire biological system.

Endocrine glands are really groups of hormone-producing cells that may be closely packed together to form glands or distributed throughout an organ whose primary function is not endocrinal. These are gland *areas* rather than true glands. For example, the cells that produce the hormone insulin are found in small, widely dispersed groups in the pancreas, an organ whose main role in the body is to produce digestive enzymes that are sent to the small intestine. (Insulin enables the cells to metabolize sugar to produce energy for various bodily functions.) The cells that produce the sex hormones, on the other hand, are grouped together in glands we label the *gonads* (although the adrenal gland produces sex hormones in relatively smaller quantities).

The endocrine glands are unique within the body because they have no ducts. That is, they use the blood stream as a communication channel, while other glands possess ducts (well-defined passageways from the gland to a single spot in the body). For example, the saliva glands deliver saliva to the mouth through tubelike ducts (LeBaron, 1972). The hormones produced by the endocrine glands (the only cells in the body that produce hormones) are channeled throughout the body by the circulatory system. Thus, hormones are much more widely distributed in the body than the secretions of nonendocrine glands (LeBaron, 1972).

This far-ranging distribution is in keeping with the function of the endocrine system. Indeed, hormones affect almost every facet of our lives as biological organisms. They control growth and reproduction, maintain balances of minerals and water, synthesize many compounds needed by the body, and control the storage and use of nutrients (LeBaron, 1972). Some hormones act only on a single organ or a specific set of cells within that organ, or even another endocrine gland (and are thus *targeted*), while others act on all cells in the body (and are *untargeted*). Hormones that have other endocrine glands as their targets are called *tropic hormones*. For example, gonadotropic hormones are hormones from the pituitary gland (part of the endocrine system) that act on the gonads (another part of the endocrine system).

Hormones are part of a group of chemicals called organic compounds, because they are organized around groups or chains of carbon atoms. Chemically, there are three types of hormone molecules within this organic category: *proteins*, *steroids*, and *amines*. Typically, all the hormones produced by an endocrine gland are of the same type. The hormones that are important in pubertyare either proteins or steroids.

At this time we are not exactly sure how hormones work in individual cells (on the *cellular* level), but we are aware of several factors that mediate their effects (LeBaron, 1972). The first is how accessible the cells are to the influence of the hormones, the receptivity of the target cells. The target cells must be open to and thus able to utilize the hormone. Second, the circulating level of the hormone is important. Until the amount of the hormone working its way through the body reaches a high enough level to activate target cells, it is a neutral factor in the body, not causing any direct effects. A good example is the case of the sex hormones that bring about the changes at puberty. These hormones are in the blood throughout childhood, but in such low concentrations that the target cells are unaffected. It is only when circulating levels reach a certain point (a *threshold*) that the events of puberty begin. The action of a hormone depends on the interaction of the sensitivity of the target cells and the concentration of the hormone in the blood stream. As we shall see, changes in this receptivity and concentration are important in the process of puberty.

The amount of a certain hormone produced by an endocrine gland and its effects ultimately are controlled by a mechanism known as a *negative feedback loop*. Besides responding to a hormone and carrying out some needed activity, target cells also produce a "message" that goes back to the secreting gland to let it know if the hormone is having the proper effect. Sometimes this "message" is a particular substance produced by the target cells and sometimes it is the concentration of the hormone itself that is the messenger. This lets the producing gland know if there is enough of the hormone available or if more needs to be produced. Endocrine feedback systems can be simple loops or involve several glands as well as the nervous system. The events of puberty are controlled by a complex feedback system that involves the *hypothalamus* (part of the nervous system) and the interaction of several different endocrine glands. In order to understand how this system works we need to break it apart and examine the role of each component before looking at the system as a whole. Table 3.1 outlines how and where the key glands and hormones function.

Hormones are powerful and subtle chemical forces in the body, and the physical effects of the sex hormones have been well documented. More controversial is the view that testosterone and estrogen also influence behavior. The evidence is mixed on this issue, but does suggest some effects (Daniel, 1983; Petersen & Taylor, 1980; Tobin-Richards, Boxer, & Petersen, 1983). Testosterone certainly has some effect on both sexual responsiveness and aggression in males, and it may be more difficult to produce a comparable level of nonviolence in males than in females. Males castrated before puberty are almost always impotent, and many of those who have their testes removed after puberty have difficulties functioning sexually. Castration also seems to leave young males less aggressive, and research with monkeys reveals some evidence for a link between testosterone levels and aggressive behavior (Rose, Holaday, &

TABLE 3.1
Glands and hormones involved in puberty.

	Location	Function
GLANDS:		
Hypothalmus	Underside of brain	Controls action of pituitary gland
Pituitary Glands: posterior	Underside of brain, below hy- pothalmus	Posterior regulates blood pressure, water retention, contraction of uterus in childbirth, and release of milk from mammary glands.
anterior		Anterior pituitary secretes hormones that regulate puberty: GH, TSH, ACTH, FSH, and LH
Gonads	Genitals	Produce sex cells and sex hormones
HORMONES:		
GH-Growth Hormone	Acts throughout body	Stimulates growth and regulates metabolism
TSH-Thyroid Stimulating Hormone	Thyroid	Thyroid hormones affect metabolism rate, growth rate, bone and teeth growth
FSH-Follicle Stimulating Hor- mone + LH-Luteinizing Hormone	Gonads Gonads	Both control production of sex hormones in both sexes and stimu- lates production of sex cells (sperm for males, ova for females); *however*, after puberty FSH and LH are at constant levels for males but vary cyclically in females.
ACTH-Adrenalcortotropic Hormone	Adrenal Gland	Controls production of sex hormones in *both sexes*: estrogen, pro- gesterone, and testosterone (sex steroids)
Estrogen	Female reproductive organs and other organs such as breasts and pubic hair	Controls sexual maturing—reproductive systems and secondary sex characteristics (eg. figure, voice, pubic hair)
Progesterone	Female reproductive organs	Controls ovulation and maturation of mammary glands
Testosterone	Male reproductive organs and other organs such as skele- ton, facial hair, vocal cords	Produces sexual maturation, secondary sex characteristics, and growth spurt

Bernstein, 1971). However, there is no evidence that treatment with testosterone will heighten the sexual drive of normal males. Rather, it appears that a certain level of testosterone is a necessary, but not sufficient, condition for adequate sexual functioning. There also seems to be some evidence to support a relationship between sexual responsiveness and testosterone in women, but this has not been conclusively demonstrated (Katchadourian, 1977).

Female sex hormones (estrogen and progesterone) seem to influence the behavior of women, to some extent, as well. The effect of hormonal variation on female animals has been well documented. Many mammals copulate only when the female is at a peak of hormonal activity (in *estrus*). Often referred to as "being in heat," this is closely tied to ovulation. When the ovaries are removed from mammals other than humans, sexual activity no longer occurs. No such link between sexual behavior and ovulation has been demonstrated in humans, but there is evidence that women do go through mood changes in association with the menstrual cycle, in particular the level of estrogen. In some studies women have rated themselves as more active and pleasant during the first part of the cycle and less so during the remainder (of course, there could be psychosocial reasons for this). Also, right before menses itself, when there is a drastic reduction in hormone level, there appears to be a greater likelihood that women will experience anxiety, irritability, and depression (Moos, 1969). In extreme form, this condition has a clinical label, *Premenstrual Syndrome* (PMS), which has been experimentally treated with synthetic estrogen.

We need to be cautious in attributing behavioral and emotional variation directly and exclusively to hormonal fluctuation, however. Biological variables do have direct influence on all forms of human behavior—emotional and cognitive. There may indeed be some link between sex hormone level and behavior in both males and females, but there is no evidence to support powerful stereotypes of women descending into the depths of mental illness during their menstrual periods or of males running amok because of testosterone-flooded brain cells. These stereotypes are apparent in all segments of our society. Several "rock music" tabloids have attributed the popularity of "heavy-metal" rock bands with adolescent males to the aggressive tendencies of the youngsters brought on by the high levels of testosterone "flooding their brain cells" at puberty (Rolling Stone, 1980).

Up to this point we have examined the parts of the endocrine system and their respective hormones that are important in puberty. Now let's see how the hormonal control mechanisms of puberty work. Recall that the levels of the various hormones that regulate the events of puberty are controlled by a series of interrelated feedback systems. These biological feedback systems operate much like a thermostat furnace system in a house. When the house is too cold, a sensing device in the thermostat causes the furnace to come on and produce more heat; when the temperature reaches the level set on the thermostat, the sensing device shuts off the furnace. The hormone levels in our blood are similar to the heat in a house. When this process reduces the concentration of hormones in the blood below a certain point, the appropriate endocrine gland or glands are stimulated to produce more.

This type of system is called a *negative* or *inhibitory* system, because as the level of a certain hormone rises, its production is inhibited. There are *positive biological feedback systems* as well. In a positive feedback system, an increased level of a hormone would cause more of it to be produced. Such systems cannot operate for long or the body would be flooded with that hormone.

The feedback mechanism that regulates puberty is a negative or inhibitory system involving three levels. Figure 3.1 illustrates this system in males. Here we can see that the hypothalamus is in charge. It produces neurohormones that cause the pituitary to release FSH and LH (ICSH). These, in turn, stimulate the production of testosterone by the testes, and testosterone acts on various organs and cells in the body to bring about physical development. There is a feedback system operating between the gonads and the hypothalamus that uses the testosterone level in the blood as a messenger. When the concentration of testosterone reaches a certain point, the hypothalamus reduces the level of neurohormone output, which in turn inhibits or slows down the release of gonadotropins by the pituitary. Lower levels of LH and FSH inhibit the production of testosterone by the gonads and thus reduce the concentration of testosterone. When the testosterone level declines far enough, the inhibitory effect on the hypothalamus terminates and it increases output of FSH and LH releasing factors, causing the cycle to begin again (Katchadourian, 1977).

Figure 3.1 shows that there is also a short feedback system in operation here involving the levels of LH and FSH and the hypothalamus. High levels of these gonadotropins also inhibit the production of hypothalamic-releasing factors. There is speculation that the hypothalamus regulates itself with the ultrashort feedback system. The physiological role of the short and ultrashort systems is not understood either. The female hormonal control system operates in much the same way as the male, except that it is cyclic in nature resulting in the phenomenon of menstruation. We will deal with the menstrual cycle in some detail later.

We now have some notion about how puberty is regulated, but why does it start in the first place? We are not exactly sure, but it seems to involve the decreasing sensitivity of the hypothalamus to the blood concentrations of the sex steroids. This is sometimes called the *hypothalamic thermostat* or *gonadostat.*

The hypothalamus-pituitary-gonad feedback system is intact before birth, so we know that puberty results from the readjusting of an intact system rather than the creation of a new one. It appears that the setting of the hypothalamic gonadostat decreases during childhood, resulting in greater and greater amounts of gonadotropins being produced and thus increasing gonad activity. This process continues until finally levels of sex steroids rise above the sensitivity threshold of their target tissues and the changes that characterize puberty result (Root, 1973). This readjustment process continues throughout adoles-

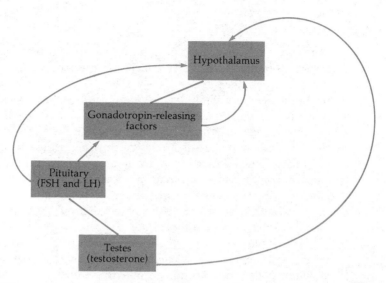

FIGURE 3.1

Gonadotropin-releasing factors cause the anterior lobe of the pituitary to discharge FSH and LH into the blood, stimulating the testes and promoting testosterone production. Concentration of releasing factors, gonadotropins, and testosterone regulates output of hypothalamic gonadotropin-releasing factors by feedback mechanisms. (From O. Vilar, E. Hafez, and T. Evans, Human Reproduction, Conception and Contraception, *Harper and Row, 1973.)*

cence until an adult equilibrium point is reached and hormonal output remains relatively constant. This process is a slow one. It begins in childhood with the initial increases in gonadotropins and sex steroids occurring only during sleep and returning to prepuberty levels when the child is awake (Finkelstein, 1980; Petersen & Taylor, 1980). Eventually the higher concentrations of gonadotropins and sex steroids are present during the day as well. We should remember this when in Chapter 5 we discuss Freud's theory of preadolescent sexuality (the *latency period*).

Although we are fairly sure about the "decreasing gonadostat sensitivity theory," we do not know *why* this occurs. As we pointed out earlier, some support a critical weight hypothesis and hypothesize that the attainment of a critical weight causes the resetting of the gonadostat. However, many remain unconvinced, and the mechanism of pubertal onset is still considered something of a mystery (Brooks-Gunn & Petersen, 1983; Grumbach et al., 1982; Petersen & Taylor, 1980).

Now that we have some idea of why puberty occurs and how it is regulated, let's take a look at the actual physical changes that take place. A convenient way to do this is to organize these changes into two groups: physical growth and sexual development. We will deal with the physical part of puberty first and the sexual second.

Physical Growth at Puberty

When we consider growth at puberty we need to remember that it is part of a life-long process. Growth at puberty is spectacular, but people actually grow more at other times in their lives. The period of most rapid growth is before birth; the newborn infant weighs about three billion times as much as the fertilized ovum (Sinclair, 1973). A high rate of growth continues in infancy when the birth weight is tripled by the end of the first year and quadrupled by age two. In childhood there is a relative slowing of the growth rate until the onset of puberty when growth then accelerates rapidly. During adult life growth becomes a compensatory mechanism, replacing losses from the normal wear and tear of living, along with those due to illness. Ultimately, replacement cannot keep up with decline and with an unbalanced physiological budget the organism becomes unable to function.

We have been using the term *growth rate* as a general descriptor of increases in body size and weight. Actually, while all parts of the body do grow simultaneously, they do not grow at the same rate. A look at Figure 3.2 will make this clear. The horizontal axis here is age and the vertical axis represents size as a percentage of total growth. The four curves describe the growth patterns for various parts of the body. The general curve refers to increases in height and weight including growth of the muscles, the skeletal system, respiratory and digestive organs, the kidneys, the spleen, and overall blood volume. You can see that this curve increases only gradually after infancy until about age 12, indicating the onset of the adolescent growth spurt. The reproductive curve refers to the growth of the sex organs and the external genitalia and reflects the dramatic effect of the increasing sex hormone levels that signal the onset of puberty. The differences in general and reproductive growth are due to the fact that the tissues of the reproductive system are not as sensitive to the influence of growth hormone as are the components of the general pattern. The reproductive system does not "grow" until sex steroid levels exceed a sensitivity threshold, which happens during puberty.

The neural curve refers to the growth of the brain, the skull, the spinal cord, and other aspects of the body's neurological system. These mature sooner than any other part of the body (Daniel, 1983). The head, in particular, is more developmentally advanced than any other part of the body and the top parts (eyes and brain) grow faster than the lower portion. Although brain weight shows some interesting spurtlike increases during adolescence, the neural system has reached almost full adult size by puberty.

The final curve in Figure 3.2 represents the growth pattern for the lymph system, keys to fighting disease and infection. These glands reach a developmental peak during late childhood, and afterwards, while the rest of the body continues to grow, actually shrink to arrive at final adult size (Katchadourian, 1977).

The most characteristic physical (in contrast to sexual) change at puberty is the sudden increase in height, usually called the *adolescent growth spurt*. In

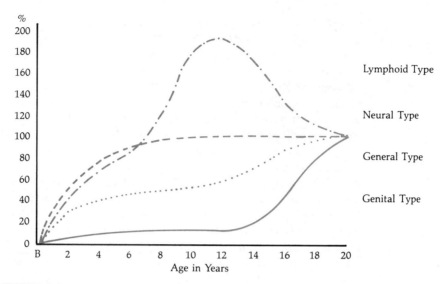

FIGURE 3.2

Growth curves for the four main types of growth in humans. (Redrawn with permission from R. E. Scammon, in The Measurement of Man, ed. J. A. Harris, C. M. Jackson, D. G. Patterson, and R. E. Scammon, University of Minnesota Press, 1930.)

girls it begins at about 10½, and reaches a peak at about 12. Boys usually do not begin their spurt until about 12½, with the peak coming at about 14 (Tanner, 1973). However, these are *average* figures; individuals differ a great deal. As we have seen, many factors influence growth, and the normal range is quite wide. This is a vital message to convey to adolescents and adults who are responsible for adolescents. Both groups are concerned about the normality of specific individuals and need to know that most differences among young people are normal.

The adolescent growth spurt is a dramatic event because of the great increase in the *rate* of growth, not the overall increase in stature (Tanner, 1973). Data on the average height *gained* from year to year and the *velocity of growth* for boys and girls based on North American and West European averages show there is a sudden increase in the *rate* of growth in adolescence, but little overall height increase relative to final adult stature. This too is normal, and both adolescents and caregiving adults need to know this lest they fear the adolescent is going to grow until he or she becomes a giant!

There are average sex differences in both velocity and final outcome of the growth spurt (Tanner, 1970). Peak velocity is a little higher in males than in females, with boys growing 7–12 cm during the year they reach peak velocity, while girls grow about 6–11 cm during their peak year (Tanner, 1970). Also, the average height for adult males is about 15 cm taller than the average female (Tanner, Whitehouse & Takaishi, 1966).

This adult height difference is linked to the action of the sex hormones. Before puberty, boys and girls are about the same height, but the earlier physical growth of girls causes them to end up shorter than boys. This happens because the bones (particularly the long bones of the extremities) grow almost exclusively at the ends, in places called the *epiphyseal growing plates*. These plates are made up of a ring of cartilage at each end of the bone, which, unlike bone, is not solidified, and therefore, can grow. Growth continues until the epiphyses unite with the shaft of the bone (Damon, 1977). High concentrations of the sex hormones, especially estrogen, bring about a deposit of more calcium in the growing plates and also cause the cells to slow down and finally stop their division (LeBaron, 1972). Since females enter puberty before males, they have less time to grow before the increasing level of sex steroids stops bone growth. There is, however, some additional bone growth beyond adolescence in both sexes because some bones grow at the ends of the bones (by *apposition*), rather than between the epiphyses and the shaft. The head and the face also continue to grow into late adulthood. During the growth spurt the relative size of the head (in proportion to the rest of the body) decreases. This occurs because the head matures early and the rest of the body catches up at puberty.

The increase in height at the growth spurt is due to an increase in leg and trunk length (Daniel, 1983). The legs grow first, and then the trunk follows about a year later. But the final increase in height is due more to the growth of the trunk than the legs. The rate of growth is quicker for parts of the body at the extremities where there are many bones, each of which can grow at its ends (e.g., hands and feet). This difference in rates is called a *maturity gradient*, and it may be a temporary problem for some adolescents who find themselves with disproportionately large hands and feet. They need reassurance that the rest of their bodies will eventually catch up.

Weight also increases substantially at puberty. In fact, the pubertal increment in final *weight* is greater than *height*. Boys have accumulated only about 55 percent of their adult weight and girls 59 percent by age 11 (Heald & Hung, 1970). This weight gain is a composite of increases in the size of the skeleton (the bones become thicker as well as longer), the muscles and internal organs, and in the amount of fat. It is obvious that a substantial change in velocity occurs at puberty. However, weight depends more on environmental factors such as diet and exercise than height, and thus is a more variable indicator of growth. As we shall see later, weight problems are a significant health issue in adolescence and exemplify the psychosocial theme of adolescent health issues.

Along with increasing size, adolescents also become stronger. This results from an increase in both the number of muscle cells and their size, although a gain in strength lags behind these increases in muscles by several months (Root, 1973). Although prepubescent girls and boys are equal in strength, a substantial difference in muscular strength appears at puberty. In males, there is a greater gain in muscle cell number, and muscle cell size continues to increase

My most vivid memory of my adolescent years occurred on a field trip I took to Acapulco, Mexico. A close friend of mine had asked me to teach him how to swim. He was about six foot tall and 180 pounds. I was a mere five foot-four.

The first chance we got, we headed for the pool. I began by showing him how to get his head wet. My friend had always been the nervous type. He was rather uncoordinated and clumsy. This should have been my first warning. I was a fairly good swimmer, but certainly not competent enough to teach someone else. That should have been my second warning—but I was an overconfident teenager.

After demonstrating how to hold my breath and going under water, I asked my friend to do the same. As he came back up, his long hair was covering his eyes and he began screaming that he couldn't see. I tried to calm him, but the next thing I knew he had wrapped his arms and legs about me and was dragging me toward the deep end of the pool.

I struggled to free myself from his grasp, but my attempts were in vain. Everytime I got one hand free, he would grab on somewhere else. Once I got to the surface for air and tried to scream, but the Spanish word for "Help!" had suddenly escaped my vocabulary.

I was quickly running out of air and knew I was dying. As I tried to wrestle free, I found the strangest thoughts going through my head—how would they return my body? My grandfather was dying of cancer, would my family have two funerals? Then I uttered a short prayer. "Lord, let your will be done. If I'm to die, I'm ready." Suddenly I was free and on the surface. I turned to see my friend being towed toward the edge. We were saved—Praise God!

into adulthood. Boys experience about a fourteen-fold increase in the number of muscle cells between five and 16, with cell size continuing to grow until the mid-thirties. In girls, the number of muscle cells increases about ten times with maximum cell size occurring by 10½ (Root, 1973). Boys also appear to have greater speed and coordination of body movements for activities like throwing balls, but girls seem to have more finger dexterity (Maccoby & Jacklin, 1974).

The characteristic sex differences in body proportion arise at puberty as well. Males develop broad shoulders and relatively narrow hips, along with long legs in comparison to the trunk. Females develop narrower shoulders, wider hips, and shorter legs in relation to the trunk than males (Daniel, 1983).

Despite the maturation experienced by adolescents, there are many misconceptions concerning their strength and coordination. For example, it is commonly thought that adolescents "outgrow" their strength or are easily tired. Also, many believe that adolescents are typically awkward and clumsy. While not technically correct (adolescents do not become less strong), these beliefs do reflect the fact that size does increase faster than strength in many cases, which leads to a lower ratio of strength to size. Height and muscular size do precede increases in strength, so that an adolescent may be less strong than an adult of similar stature and muscular development for a year or so, but there is no real decrease in strength. Similarly, coordination may lag behind height and strength increases, but there is no deterioration in this area. As Tanner (1962) states: "a clumsy boy in late adolescence is likely to have been a clumsy child before adolescence and . . . is likely to end up a clumsy man."

While most other body components increase rapidly at puberty, body fat actually decreases. With the onset of puberty there is a progressive loss in body fat. Females typically do not lose as much fat as males, however, and tend to have more fat as adults in the areas of the pelvis, breasts, upper back, and upper arms. Fat distribution accounts for the fact that highly muscular female athletes do not appear as developed as their male counterparts. Females also have more fat in layers beneath the skin (subcutaneous fat), which hides their muscles and results in less visible surface veins (which are easily seen in the male).

Besides the changes in fat content and distribution, there are other changes in body proportion and appearance that occur during the growth spurt. The appearance of the head itself changes. The facial bones grow faster than the cranium and the face appears to emerge from the skull. Also, the jaw and the nose become more prominent. The recession of the hairline in both sexes enhances this shift in facial appearance (although this occurs more in males). At the same time the lips become fuller.

These external changes are dramatic, but the growth spurt at puberty also brings about internal changes of equal importance. The development of the cardiovascular and respiratory systems are prime examples. The heart goes through the growth spurt like other muscles in the body, not only increasing in size, but nearly doubling in weight. Systolic blood pressure increases at puberty (particularly in boys) and so do the number of red blood cells, blood hemoglobin (the oxygen carrier in the blood), and the total blood volume (Katchadourian, 1977). However, these "blood increases" are more pronounced in men. Adult women have about a million fewer red blood cells per millimeter of blood than men.

At the same time, the lungs increase in size and respiratory capacity, but again more markedly in boys. Also, the exchange of oxygen in lungs becomes more efficient. These changes in the circulatory and respiratory system result in an increased tolerance for exercise by producing a greater capacity for physical exertion and faster recovery from its effects. The gains are greater in males.

We have pointed out several aspects of physical growth and maturation in which sex differences appear at puberty. It is easy to overstate these differences and exaggerate their importance. For one thing, these differences are usually expressed as averages, and there is a great deal of overlap between the sexes. *Some* females are faster, bigger, and stronger than *many* males, for example. Second, greater physical ability and endurance depend to a large extent on exercise, practice, and training, which are generally encouraged for males in our culture and discouraged in females (although this is changing). In fact, some women may have a greater capacity for dealing with long periods of physical exercise in long distance running and swimming than men, particularly in early adolescence when females take the lead in the onset of puberty. Many feel this will become apparent as participation in physical activities and athletics becomes more and more acceptable for females. Third, even given the known male superiority in terms of some physical capabilities, we need to keep the significance of such differences in mind. In the modern world, where brain is usually more important than brawn, existing sex differences are probably less important than ever before in human history. Remember this when we consider sex differences in self-concept and identity in Chapter 7.

> . . . If men and women were free to choose their own modes of work and play, they would sort themselves out according to a variety of determinants of which physical characteristics would be one in relation (to many others). (Katchadourian, 1977, p. 50)

Another internal change that deserves mention here concerns the growth of the brain at adolescence. The brain actually grows very little after childhood, and the number of cells remains constant from birth. However, there is some evidence for spurtlike increases in brain weight followed by periods of no change. This pattern has been referred to as *brain growth periodization* (Epstein, 1977). These spurts appear to be the result of increasing complexity of the neural networks within the brain. Some believe that these spurts are related to the stages of cognitive development outlined by Piaget that we will discuss in Chapter 4 and have gone so far as to propose changes in the curriculum offerings for early adolescence based on this hypothesized relationship (Epstein & Toefler, 1977). However, at this time there is no conclusive evidence linking cognitive ability and brain growth periodization (Petersen, 1983).

One final class of internal changes at puberty deserves attention. These are changes in bodily functioning that affect an adolescent's nutritional needs. Two examples are body temperature and basic metabolism rate (BMR). Normal body temperature declines from birth, reaching adult levels in girls by about age 12, but continuing to drop in boys for a while longer (Katchadourian, 1977). BMR declines from birth to old age, but this trend slows temporarily during puberty, an indication of the increased physiological activity at that time. Therefore, the need for food is at its height during puberty. The peak caloric requirements in girls usually coincides with menarche, while for boys it occurs at the time of the peak growth spurt. (Caloric requirements decline continuously after adolescence into old age, the reason why it makes sense to establish wise eating habits in adolescence.) The changing physiological processes are reflected in two potential adolescent health problems, obesity and malnutrition. We will deal with these in a later section.

Up to this point, we have considered only those physical changes at puberty that are not directly part of sexual maturation. We now turn our attention to the most spectacular events of puberty, those which culminate in the development of the capacity to reproduce.

Sexual Development

Sexual development is marked by the emergence of two groups of features, the primary and secondary sex characteristics. Primary sex characteristics are structures that are directly related to reproduction (for example, the sex organs). Secondary sex characteristics are features that contribute to the differences in appearance between the sexes, but are not directly related to reproductive capacity (e.g., facial hair in males and breast development in females). It is these secondary sex characteristics, of course, that are of greatest psychological and social significance to adolescents on a day-to-day basis.

We will deal with sexual development by examining the emergence of the primary and secondary sex characteristics and then putting them together with the physical changes we have already described to get an overall idea of the sequence and timing of the events of puberty.

Primary Sex Characteristics

Males.   The most distinguishing primary sex characteristics in males are the external genitalia: the penis and the scrotum (the saclike structure that holds the testes). During childhood these change very little, but both begin to grow markedly after the onset of puberty. Tanner (1962) has divided genital growth at puberty into five stages, as shown in Figure 3.3. Stage 1 shows the prepubertal state where the external genitalia look much the same as in early childhood. In stage 2 the skin of the scrotum becomes larger (average age 11.7). This continues in stage 3, when the penis also becomes larger while the scrotum becomes even more coarse (average age 12.8). Penis growth continues through stage 4, and the scrotum turns darker and becomes more pigmented (average age 13.6). In stage 5 the genitalia attain adult appearance (average age 15.0). These stages are often used to categorize adolescent pubertal development, although pubic hair is often used as an additional indicator.

The penis serves both an excretory and reproductive function and has been the object of much cultural preoccupation in both modern societies (e.g., Freud's concept of penis envy as a basic dynamic in the relations between females and males) and technologically primitive societies (e.g., phallic idols). It has been worshipped as a symbol of power and fertility, and even today is the object of many folk beliefs, all of which attach an intense set of emotions to all aspects of it. Because of these beliefs, the size and shape of the penis can be-

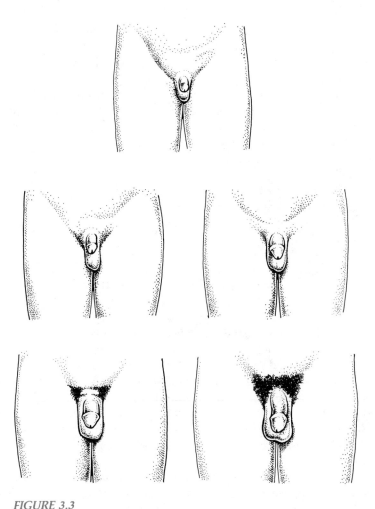

FIGURE 3.3

Stages of male genital development: 1. prepubertal in which the size of the testes and penis is similar to that in early childhood; 2. testes become larger and scrotal skin reddens and coarsens; 3. continuation of stage 2, with lengthening of penis; 4. penis enlarges in general size, and scrotal skin becomes pigmented; 5. adult genitalia. (From J. M. Tanner, Growth at Adolescence, *2d ed., Oxford: Blackwell, 1962.)*

come a source of concern for adolescents (and adult males as well), and it is important that they receive accurate information about this area of the body. The size and shape of the normal penis are *not* related to physique, race, or virility (Katchadourian, 1977). While penises (like any other organ) may differ in size, these differences tend to diminish when the penis is in an erect state (Masters & Johnson, 1970). Also, the penis neither atrophies with lack of use or enlarges because of frequent activity.

As the scrotum and penis grow, the contents of the scrotum (the *testes*) do so as well. (Recall that the testes are the site of sex cell and sex hormone production in males.) Unlike the ovaries, infantile testes do not contain all the sex cells they will ever produce. The testes produce new sperm continuously after puberty until old age. Testicular growth during puberty is quite dramatic and is a marker for the onset of puberty in males. It occurs quite early in the pubertal sequence and continues throughout adolescence. Testes may be of different sizes, and even when the same size, one often hangs lower, giving the impression of being larger.

Concurrent with the development of the external genitalia and the testes is the maturation of the *delivery system.* This system consists of a series of tubes that convey sperm from the testes to penis. These are the epididymis, vas deferens, ejaculatory duct, and urethra. Note that the urethra carries urine from the bladder as well as sperm from the testes. This dual function is often confusing to children, and even for adolescents it may add to the emotional and cultural complexity of coming to terms psychologically with the penis and with sexuality in general. Surrounding the urethra are a number of spongelike tissues that are filled with blood vessels and nerve endings. When the penis is flaccid these tissues contain little blood. An erection occurs because the vessels fill with blood and expand, to give a very mundane description to a very psychologically intense physiological event. The ability to have an erection is present from birth and thus is not a pubertal development.

Besides the maturation of the delivery system, some accessory glands also enlarge at puberty, most importantly the prostate gland. Its secretions account for much of the volume of the fluid and the characteristic odor of ejaculate when orgasm occurs in a sexually mature male. It is the maturation of the prostate that makes ejaculation possible because it provides a medium for the delivery of sperm.

It is important to keep in mind that orgasm and ejaculation are not the same thing. Ejaculation is the discharge of semen (consisting of sperm and fluid from the accessory glands) during orgasm. The capacity for orgasm is present (in both males and females) from birth, but it is not until puberty that it is accompanied by ejaculation in males. A boy's first ejaculation is often a dramatic event. Like menarche in girls, first ejaculation has important psychological dimensions. As we will see later, both events can be very stressful and disturbing if they occur in a climate of fear, ignorance, and guilt concerning sexual development.

Females.   The external genitalia in females are not quite as noticeable as in males, but they do undergo significant changes at puberty. The female genitalia are the mons pubis (a soft protuberance over the pubic bone), the major and minor labia, the clitoris, and the vaginal opening. All these structures become larger and more sensitive to stimulation during puberty, especially the clitoris.

This organ, like the penis, contains spongelike tissue that becomes engorged with blood in an excited state, causing it to become erect. However, this event has not received the same psychological and cultural treatment as the male erection, perhaps because it is less visible. Indeed, the relative internality and subtlety of female sexual functioning has permitted male-biased observers to systematically denigrate and misinterpret female sexuality. Because of their internalized position, the female genitals are not as useful as an index of pubertal development as are the external genitalia in males. Therefore, they are not often used to determine the extent of sexual maturation.

As in males, the female delivery system changes at puberty. This system is made up of the ova ducts, the uterus, and the vagina. The ova ducts transport the ovum to the uterus. If fertilization occurs, it takes place in the ova duct. It is in the wall of the uterus that the fertilized ovum implants itself and matures. The vagina or birth canal is both the entry point for sperm (enclosing the penis during intercourse) and the exit for the fetus, another functional overlap that emotionally and symbolically complicates the psychological and cultural dynamics of sexuality. During puberty, the uterus, ova ducts, and vagina increase in weight and size. The uterine wall becomes more muscular, and the inner lining goes through a number of changes in preparation for its role in nurturing the fetus. The lining of the vagina also gets thicker. In fact, this thickening of the vaginal lining is an indication of impending puberty and is one of the first events in the pubertal process (Marshall & Tanner, 1974). The interior of the vagina also changes chemically, becoming acidic, rather than alkaline as was the case in childhood. This shift in chemical balance creates a suitable environment for sperm, and thus increases the chances that fertilization will occur.

The female gonads (the ovaries) become larger and heavier at puberty, but the increase is not as dramatic as with other female organs. As we mentioned earlier, the ovaries at birth contain all the ova they will ever produce, although these remain in an immature state until menarche. Rather than a large increase in size or weight, the dramatic pubertal changes in the ovaries are chemical, involving the maturation of the immature ova (called *oocytes*). Although there may be some prepubertal cyclic patterns in the girl's body, it is at puberty that the cyclic phenomena of ovulation ordinarily begin, a process that is controlled by the interaction of the hypothalamus, the pituitary, and the ovaries. The sequence of events leading up to ovulation and that process itself are the menstrual cycle.

The easiest way to understand the complex processes of the menstrual cycle may be to follow the development of the ovum itself. Recall that the hypothalamus causes the pituitary to secrete the gonadotropins FSH and LH. In Figure 3.4 we see that at the beginning of the cycle the level of FSH is somewhat higher than that of LH. Under the influence of FSH, the oocyte begins to enlarge and becomes surrounded by a single layer of follicle cells. As the oocyte continues to mature, a second layer of different follicle cells forms outside the first and becomes several layers thick. The follicle continues to increase in size and a hollow cavity, filled with fluid, forms in the middle, as the cycle proceeds.

When estrogen concentration reaches a threshold, it causes the pituitary to shift its output to LH, rather than FSH production. By this time the follicle has matured into a structure called a Graafian follicle, which is near the surface of the ovary. The sharp increase in LH causes the Graafian follicle to rupture and the ovum to be released *(ovulation)*. The ovum then moves down the ova-duct toward the uterus, arriving at the point of implantation in about seven days. It spends about three to four days moving through the ova-duct and the rest of the time floating around the uterine cavity.

Besides triggering the release of the ovum, LH also transforms the ruptured follicle into the corpus luteum. The corpus luteum secretes progesterone (it is the original inner layer of follicle cells that produces progesterone). Progesterone stimulates the final preparation of the uterus for the ovum. If the ovum has been fertilized, implantation in the uterine wall occurs on the seventh day after ovulation. Implantation causes a signal to be sent to the ovary that stimulates it to keep the corpus luteum secreting progesterone. Continued high levels of progesterone maintain the uterine lining so that the implanted ovum grows to maturity (the process of pregnancy).

If the ovum is not fertilized, implantation does not occur, and no message is sent to the ovary. In that case, the corpus luteum shrivels after the seventh day of the cycle and no longer secretes progesterone or estrogen. As the concentration of these hormones drops, the uterine wall can no longer be maintained, and its thickened lining begins to break down. The bleeding and discharge that results are called menstruation. Once again we have offered a scientific description of what we must recognize as a miracle once we stand back and look at it with wonder and amazement that our bodies go about this business of living month after month. Looked at this way, it is easy to see why "primitive" cultures attach mystical significance to the process.

A drop in progesterone levels causes the pituitary to slow its production of LH and to increase FSH secretion. This stimulates the development of a new follicle and the cycle starts all over again, with ovulation occurring about 14 days after menstruation. Both FSH and LH are present throughout the cycle, but the nondominant hormone is always at a much lower concentration. Also, when estrogen dominates before ovulation, and progesterone after, during the progesterone phase, a fairly high concentration of estrogen is present, much higher than the level of progesterone during the estrogen phase of the cycle (Le-Baron, 1972).

The primary sex characteristics provide a backdrop for the social side of sexual development because the possibility of pregnancy and the management of that possibility is one of the central, core issues in the ecology of adolescence, as we shall see when we discuss sexuality in Chapter 8.

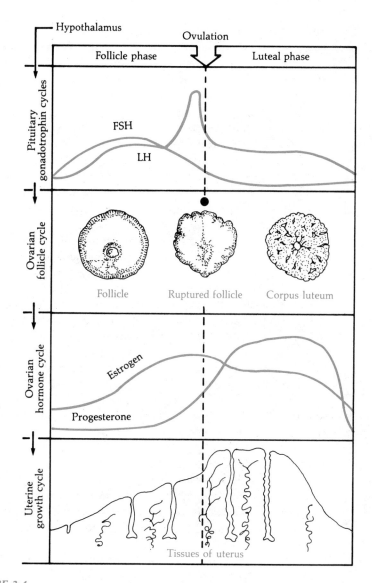

FIGURE 3.4

The relative concentrations of the pituitary tropichormones and the ovarian hormones as they relate to stages in the development of the ovum and corpus luteum and to the growth cycle of the uterine wall. (Drawn with permission from Le Baron, R., Hormones: A Delicate Balance, Indianapolis, IN: Pegasus Books, 1972.)

Secondary Sex Characteristics

Male.   Two of the most distinctive male sex characteristics are body shape and facial hair. From our previous discussion, we know that the male sex hormone testosterone acts on the body to produce a masculine body type, consisting of relatively broad shoulders, narrow hips, and a long trunk. Deviations from this norm are a source of concern and sometimes discrimination for adolescent males. The emergence of facial hair, also prompted by high levels of testosterone, occurs late in puberty, at about 16 or 17, although some fine hair first appears on the upper lip at around 14 (Daniel, 1983). From the upper lip, facial hair spreads to the upper cheeks and the area under the lower lip, and finally to the sides and lower edge of the chin. All this presents an opportunity for an important rite of passage—beginning to shave.

At this same time many boys start to experience problems with acne, due, in large part, to the growth and increase in activity of the oil glands (sebaceous glands) on the face. Using acne treatment products is another kind of rite of passage marking the onset of adolescence and, like shaving, offers an opportunity for parents and youth to engage in problem solving and intergenerational solidarity. The sebaceous glands are closely associated with the hair follicles and oil from the sebaceous glands may trap dirt and plug a follicle. This can result in a blackhead or pimple (when the follicle becomes infected because of the bacteria trapped by the clog). This increase in sebaceous gland activity also occurs in girls, but at an earlier age. Armpit (axillary) and body hair appear concurrently with facial hair, with body hair continuing to spread after puberty. Chest hair has symbolic significance for many, indicating virility in some circles (a function that has led more than one youth to shave his chest in an effort to stimulate thicker, coarser hair).

Preceding the appearance of facial, axillary, and body hair by about two years is the emergence of pubic hair, a major event in puberty. Pubic hair first appears at the base of the penis as long strands of slightly curly hair. It then spreads over the scrotum, becoming darker and more coarse. In males, pubic hair continues to spread until the mid-twenties and often beyond, particularly along the center line of the abdomen. Pubic hair is another feature of physical maturation with cultural/symbolic significance, and thus psychological intensity. It and the other changes can transform the locker room into a testing ground, a humiliating source of worry, or an arena of pride.

Another distinctive male pubertal event is the lowering of the voice. This does happen in girls, but to a much lesser extent. The lowering or deepening of the voice occurs because of the enlargement of the larynx. This comes late in the pubertal process and may be either a gradual process or happen quite quickly. It is not unusual for boys to experience more than several awkward moments when their voices are changing, as when their new bass suddenly and uncontrollably becomes a soprano.

Males normally experience some breast development because of normal hormonal action, although not nearly as much as females. Breast development in males usually occurs as the emergence of a hard node under the area surrounding the nipple (the *areola*). However, many boys experience a degree of breast enlargement as well. Katchadourian (1977) reports that one study of adolescent boys revealed that 40 percent of all boys showed some breast development. This enlargement usually disappears within a year or two, although the areolar increase is permanent (Nydick et al., 1961; Roche, French, & DaVila, 1971). The psychological disruption produced by significant breast development in males can be a serious matter, one that demands informed parental concern, sympathetic treatment, and perhaps even medical or mental health intervention. Severe enlargement of the breasts is called *gynecomastia* and can result in breast size (usually only on one side) reaching the normal mature size for females. The hormonal imbalance that produces gynecomastia (insufficient male hormones or excess female hormones) usually requires hormone therapy coupled with counseling to resolve the psychological distress, but may include removal of tumors that have caused the imbalance in the first place.

Females.   As with males, body shape is distinctive in females. Estrogen acts on body tissues to give females narrower shoulders, wider hips, and shorter legs compared to trunk length than males. The most obvious female sex characteristic is the development of the breasts. As is the case with the penis, breast development has much symbolic cultural significance and thus many psychological and social ramifications.

Breast development is an early pubertal event that begins, on the average, at about age 11 and is usually completed by 15. However, onset varies between 8 and 13 and completion from 13 to 18. Breast development follows a predictable sequence and is often used as a pubertal index. Tanner (1962) describes five stages, which are shown in Figure 3.5. Stage 1 is the prepubescent stage. At stage 2 a small protuberance under the nipple (called a *breast bud*) is present. Stage 3 involves general enlargement. By stage 4 mammary glands and adipose tissue deposits have developed that will eventually give the breasts their adult shape (stage 5). During adulthood the breasts continue to change, becoming larger during pregnancy and smaller and less firm after menopause. One breast often develops faster than the other during puberty, and this may be a cause of concern in the adolescent. Many adult women have one breast larger than the other, a situation that may present special challenges to females, (Faust, 1983).

As in males, the emergence of pubic hair is a major pubertal event for females and is often used as a pubertal index. Like the other signs of puberty, the relatively premature or late appearance of pubic hair can be psychologically unsettling. Here, as elsewhere, it makes sense to communicate the wide normal range of onset and to help early and late maturers cope with their peers and themselves in this matter. Pubic hair usually appears between 11 and 12 and the adult pattern is established by 14. Pubic hair precedes axillary (armpit) hair by a year or so. Pubic hair first appears as a sparse growth of downy hair at

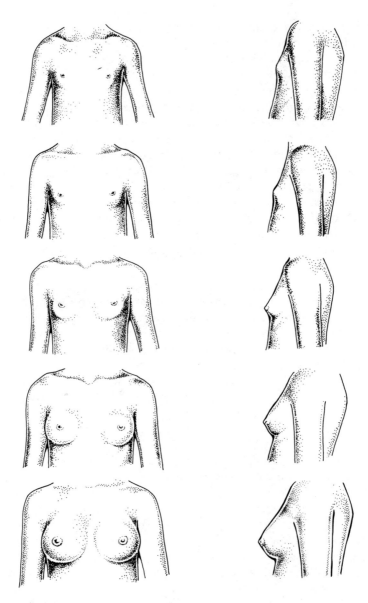

FIGURE 3.5
Stages of breast development in adolescent girls: 1. prepubertal flat appearance like that of a child; 2. small, raised breast bud; 3. general enlargement and raising of breast and areola; 4. areola and papilla (nipple) form contour separate from that of breast; 5. adult breast-areola is in same contour as breast. (Used with permission from J. M. Tanner, Growth at Adolescence, 2d ed., Oxford: Blackwell, 1962) p. 36.

the sides of the labia. This is followed by curling, coarsening, increased pigmentation, and an increase in the amount of hair. The adult pattern has a relatively distinct upper border as compared to males, because females are less likely to have pubic hair on the abdomen.

Having discussed the primary and secondary characteristics that emerge at puberty, we need to review their timing and sequence. Table 3.2 shows the sequence of pubertal events in each sex and the approximate ages at which they occur. As we have mentioned earlier, many of the events that are common to both sexes occur one to two years earlier in females. The length of puberty is evident here; even some of the physical changes in the process occur fairly early

TABLE 3.2

Average approximate age and sequence of appearance of sexual characteristics in both sexes.

Age (Years)	Boys	Girls
9–10		Growth of bony pelvis Budding of nipples
10–11	First growth of testes and penis	Budding of breasts Pubic hair
11–12	Prostatic activity	Changes in vaginal epithelium and the smear Growth of external and internal genitalia
12–13	Pubic hair	Pigmentation of nipples Mammae filling in
13–14	Rapid growth of testes and penis Subareolar node of nipples	Axillary hair Menarche (average: 13½ years; range: 9–17 years) Menstruation may be anovulatory for first few years
14–15	Axillary hair on upper lip Voice change	Earliest normal pregnancies
15–16	Mature spermatozoa (average: 15 years; range: 11¼–17 years)	Acne Deepening of voice
16–17	Facial and body hair Acne	Arrest of skeletal growth
21	Arrest of skeletal growth	

SOURCE: L. Wilkins, ed. *The Diagnosis and Treatment of Endocrine Disorders in Childhood and Adolescence,* 1957. Courtesy of Charles C. Thomas Publisher, Springfield Illinois.

NOTE: The age of menarche given here is later than that given in the text because it is based on older data.

in middle childhood, particularly for girls. It is also clear that sexual maturity in both sexes is attained relatively late in puberty, with many other events preceding it.

Tables such as Table 3.2 are helpful in understanding the sequence, timing, and duration of puberty, but we need to remember that these are based on averages derived from fairly specific adolescent populations. Not only do these averages vary from population to population (due to the influence of genetic and environmental factors), but the range of normality contained within these general guidelines is very wide indeed. For instance, even though the growth of the testes in males begins at about 11½ and is completed by about 15, it is normal for testicular growth to begin as early as 9½ or as late as 13½, and to end any time between 13½ and 17 (Tanner, 1973). It does seem that the general sequence of events is more predictable than their timing, but even that is not immutable. When changes occur close together in time, they may even appear to occur in reverse order.

Describing the nature, sequence, and timing of puberty tells only part of the story, however. Such lists, while informative, give us no information about how the process *feels* to the adolescents and the people who care for and about them. As we stated at the beginning of this chapter, the meaning of puberty is defined by the social, psychological, and cultural context in which it occurs. For many adolescents, the normal events of puberty are not experienced as normal at all, and may be a source of wonder, surprise, embarrassment, or even fear and loathing. The timing and sequence of events are most important to adolescents, for they are most concerned about whether or not they are in step or out of sync with the development of most of their peers.

The Psychology of Puberty

Both individual pubertal outcomes and the entire process itself have psychological consequences for adolescents. Having examined the physiology of puberty we now turn to how the developing individual's psychology and relationships with others in microsystems influence the experience and consequences of maturation. We start with two propositions grounded in research and folk wisdom: how you look influences how people treat you (Adams, 1981) and what's going on inside your body affects how you feel and act (Petersen & Taylor, 1980). These two principles set up the complex interaction of psychology and biology in adolescence (Brooks-Gunn & Petersen, 1983).

Our macrosystem establishes and maintains norms for beauty, attractiveness, and appropriate appearance for each sex. Individual adolescents (and even some groups who differ from majority norms) may feel that they are out of line with what the culture deems "normal." Early-maturing females and late-maturing males, in particular, seem to have the most negative feelings about their bodies (Petersen & Taylor, 1980).

Well, I can't say this is my most vivid memory of adolescence, but it is certainly one which indicated to me the pivotal nature of the age.

It was late one evening, when some friends and I had maneuvered ourselves into the unenviable position of having to walk through Central Park at a rather late hour. We got about halfway through, and then started horsing around and generally got lost in having fun. We finally realized that we had better get moving. We collected as a group, and began walking East once again. Immediately we noticed a gang of guys headed our way. "What the hell am I doing in Central Park late at night?" I wondered. We all held our breath, and kept walking. Finally we met up with the gang. They collected to our right, and we attempted to keep walking. They cut us off, so we had no option but to wheel around and face them down. As we did, they seemed to lose interest, and soon walked on. Well I was astounded—I was sure we were going to get into a fight. We all laughed out of relief, and continued our way East.

Later on that night, I told my brother about the incident, and related my surprise that they didn't give us more trouble—I mean I thought they were going to whomp us for sure. My brother said, "well you know, you guys aren't so small anymore—I mean you've all grown about two inches in the past two days!" It was then that I realized that we all really had grown a lot. At that moment my body-image changed to conform more to how my body really was. No longer was I such a little kid.

A typical concern is height. Because of cultural stereotypes, boys fear being too short, while girls are often afraid of being too tall. Certainly, stature may be a real problem for individuals at the extreme ends of the continuum. Even at these extremes, however, some people make good use of their special characteristic (e.g., jockeys and basketball players). Most adolescents are well within the normal range (and will certainly end up in the normal range), but do feel concern. Stature among children is as varied as it is among adults (Tanner, 1962). Puberty may temporarily exaggerate these height differences because of differential growth patterns and variation in timing, as in the case of a tall child who is an early maturer or a short child who is late. Early puberty also brings differences in height among youngsters who were of similar stature in childhood, simply because one grows faster than the other. Toward the end of adolescence, however, the slower maturers usually catch up. It is important for children to understand the pubertal contribution to adult stature and to have realistic expectations about their own eventual height. We cannot overstate the need for knowledge about puberty and physical development among adolescents and the adults who care for them. An information-rich microsystem can provide the nurture needed as adolescents cope with the vagaries of their nature.

Besides height, our culture has norms regarding other physical features affected by the pubertal process (Faust, 1983). These include weight, breast size and shape, facial features, and body shape (Petersen & Taylor, 1980; Lerner, 1969). Culture is not uniform, however. Expectations differ somewhat among social class and ethnic groups, but the dominant macrosystem does set norms through the mass media and the arts that many adolescents may feel they cannot (and will never be able to) meet. As adults, we need to be aware of the strength of these norms and provide adolescents with information about the dynamics of pubertal process and the wide range of *normal* individual differences in the rate and timing of pubertal development.

Two major developmental markers in puberty are likely to be a source of difficulty for some adolescents. These are first ejaculations and menarche. These two signals of approaching sexual maturity are often misunderstood by adolescents *and* adults. Some people create unnecessary and potentially harmful guilt among males by conveying the message that the occurrence of nocturnal emissions or wet dreams is linked to sexual indecency and perversion. Along the same lines, the increasing sensitivity of the genitals to erotic stimulation can lead to emotional conflict regarding masturbation, which is reported by 80% of males and 40% of females by age 14 and by more than 90% of the males and 60% of the females by age 18. The figures for females are lower but are approaching the levels reported by males (Dispold & Young, 1979). Many adolescent males experience embarrassment and humiliation when an unwanted and seemingly uncontrollable erection occurs while the youth is in a public place such as a classroom. Literature is full of descriptions of the struggles of pubescent boys to gain some measure of control over their uncooperative minds and bodies as they and their world become "hopelessly" erotic. First person accounts tell this story also.

Similarly, menarche can be an emotional challenge for girls (Brooks-Gunn & Ruble, 1983). Lack of information and support may lead to embarrassment or even terror for some pubescent females as the boxed stories on p. 125 illustrate. Certainly, stereotypes of menstruation as the "curse," or as a time when a woman should not exercise and should expect to be in an "awful mood" do not promote the development of a healthy attitude toward this process in females, or in males for that matter. Konopka (1966) linked inadequate preparation for or response to menarche by parents to social maladjustment in adolescent females.

In the case of both menarche and ejaculation, adolescents need to know what is happening to them and what they can expect to happen. They need to know that menstruation, ejaculation, and related events are part of the process of growing up, can be viewed with pride, and need not be the object of shame or embarrassment. (Removing the guilt from masturbation for both sexes is likewise important, as we will see in Chapter 8.) Nocturnal emissions and men-

First Hand Accounts of Nocturnal Emission and Menarche

I remember the first time it happened. Or maybe I should say I don't remember the first time it happened. What I do remember is waking up in the morning with this gooey wet spot on my bed . . . and then I remembered! It was some dream alright. All my dream girls at once and me right there in the middle of it all. Wow. But I paid the price for it the next morning. Yuck. I think my mother guessed something was up. After all I never volunteered to make my own bed before.

When I woke up that morning I didn't know what had happened. I guess I was pretty naive (I guess maybe I still am). I had no idea what the hell this mess was on my sheet. At first I thought I'd wet the bed. That was it. I remembered guys joking about "wet dreams" and maybe this was what they were talking about. I couldn't talk to anyone about it. But when it happened again I figured out what was going on, because that time I remembered having a very sexy dream the night before. It felt good during the dream but I felt pretty guilty the next morning.

I'll never forget the way my Mom and Dad handled things the first time I had a wet dream. I was pretty confused about it when I woke up in the morning. I remembered the dream and I guess I had woken up after I came. My Mom didn't say anything to me about the sheets. But that afternoon my Dad sat me down to fill me in on how things worked. I knew about babies and intercourse and all that, but this wet dream stuff was

news to me. Anyway, he made me feel it was normal and O.K. That evening my Mom gave me an extra hug. She never said anything, but that hug told me everything was alright. Thanks, I needed that.

My first period came when I was 12. I was scared when it started. It hurt too, and I thought there was something wrong. I went to my mother and told her. She seemed pretty sad. Not shocked. Just sad. She told me what to do and bought me some sanitary napkins. Later that day I heard her crying in her room. I knew it was about me.

My first time I got my period . . . boy was I ready. I had been waiting for this day when I would finally become a woman. When it finally happened I was so proud I couldn't wait to tell Mom. She had told me all about it and how it meant I was growing up. She smiled and hugged me. That night my Dad took the three of us out to dinner to celebrate. He even proposed a toast to "the new woman." I felt so lucky. Other girls have such a hard time with it. I felt so lucky. I still do.

I was 11 when I first had a period. It was no big deal. We had had films at school and my mother had asked if I knew about that stuff. Sure, no problem. I still can't understand what all the fuss is about. It's just your body doing its thing. It's like the first time I had sex. Same thing. You do it. Sometimes it's great; sometimes it's just O.K. It's your body. What else can you do?

arche are involuntary occurrences. It is the responsibility of the significant adults in the lives of adolescents to help them understand and deal with these important events, and part of the responsibility of professionals who are involved in sex education for parents.

Along with concerns about specific pubertal events and outcomes, the timing of puberty in relation to peers can have psychological consequences for the adolescent. Evidence for this comes from longitudinal studies of growth in which individuals were followed from birth to maturity. Investigators of the effects of pubertal timing compare those who matured relatively early with those who matured relatively late, looking for developmental outcomes that are correlated with timing. We will consider some of the effects here, but will return to the psychobiology of puberty in Chapter 7 as an influence on self-concept and identity.

The Effect of the Timing of Puberty on Psychological Development

While the timing of puberty does seem to have an effect on psychological development, there are conflicting views as to what and how significant those effects are (Petersen & Taylor, 1980). Also, these psychological outcomes seem to differ according to what sex one is, when one was born, and what social class one is. For females, early maturation appears to have both benefits and costs. One study done some forty years ago reported that female early-maturers were conspicuous because of their size, frequent bad complexion, and by the fact that they were menstruating (Stolz & Stolz, 1951). On the other hand, some investigations have found early maturation to be related to increased social prestige in grades seven, eight, and nine, while being "average" was important to social standing in sixth grade (Faust, 1960). Some studies show that early-maturing girls rarely achieved a high degree of social status, popularity, or leadership, and that they were perceived by others as being listless or indifferent and lacking poise in social situations (Petersen & Taylor, 1980). Late-maturing girls seemed to be generally better off than early maturers. They were usually described as more confident, outgoing, and assured. However, differences between early- and late-maturing females appear to be temporary. They tend to wash out in early adulthood and may even be replaced with reversed benefits. Peskin (1973) reports that as 30-year-old adults, early-maturing females cope better and are more self-possessed and self-directed in the cognitive and social domains.

For males, the findings are also mixed. Some researchers report that early-maturing boys are better off than their late-maturing counterparts. They are seen as more relaxed, as more popular with peers, and as more attractive to adults. At 17, early maturers showed less dependency, greater self-confidence, and more adultlike behavior than late maturers. These differences seemed to carry over into adulthood. Jones (1965) found that at age 30 early maturers outscored late maturers on measures of socialization (greater conformity), dominance, and making good impressions, while late maturers scored higher on an index of psychological difficulties. However, follow-ups show that by the late 30s many of these differences disappeared and the late maturers showed themselves to be more flexible, insightful, and creatively playful (Jones, 1965). It seems one cost of early maturing is a more conventional, rigid, humorless, conforming, and moralistic adulthood (Jones, 1965).

Some data suggest that early-maturing boys may have some difficulties during adolescence, especially when popularity, peer relationships, and the like are not the primary criteria for comparison (Petersen & Taylor, 1980). For example, one research found that early maturers:

> were more somber, temporarily more anxious, more submissive, less exploratory, less intellectually curious, and less active after the onset of puberty . . . the late-maturers displayed no consistent changes on these dimensions. (Petersen & Taylor, 1980, p. 143)

Our ecological perspective tell us it is important to remember that the effects on both males and females are influenced by other factors. It depends upon what setting you are in, what everyone else is doing, and how people interpret and respond to your experiences. For example, early maturation predicted leadership among working-class boys, but not for middle-class adolescents. Early maturation was found to be positively related to self-confidence in middle-class girls, but to *lack of* confidence for working-class girls (Clausen, 1975). In addition, Blyth and his colleagues (1978) report that the effects of the timing of puberty also appear to differ on the basis of what kind of school one attends (being more positive for seventh graders in two- or three-year junior high schools than for seventh graders in three- or four-year middle schools, for example).

As should be clear from our brief review, much important research remains to be done in this area to clarify which effects occur when and for whom. Not only are the data sparse, but most of the existing studies are seriously limited because they may be outdated. The danger is that the limits of the evidence will create or reinforce stereotypes that interfere with the kind of sensitive, individualized attention adolescents need in coping with the timing and nature of bodily changes.

For our purposes, though, the most important thing to keep in mind is that effects do indeed occur. As concerned adults, we have an obligation to acknowledge the psychological effects of puberty and help adolescents deal with them. Here, as in so many other areas, knowledge can be power. Puberty is a challenge, with all that implies for individual adolescents and the people who care for them. One aspect of that challenge lies in cases where adolescents experience health problems related to puberty.

Disorders Related to Puberty

The most common health problems related to puberty are those related to nutrition, particularly obesity and malnutrition. Malnutrition is not as great a problem in North America as it is in other areas of the world, but wherever it occurs, it can hinder normal physical growth and even cognitive development as well.

Obesity, on the other hand, is a major problem for North American adolescents (and also adults). A Canadian survey shows that while 5% of young adolescents are obese, 15% of middle adolescents are greatly overweight (Santrock, 1981). As we have already seen, as adolescents grow older, metabolism rate slows and caloric needs decline. However, food intake often does not match this decline in caloric needs, resulting in a gain in weight. This is the main reason why there are more overweight older adolescents than younger ones.

However, obesity also depends on factors such as basic metabolic rate (BMR) and amount of physical activity as compared to food intake. BMR is genetically determined (although it can be altered). Adolescents with a high BMR can eat almost anything and not put on weight, but if those who have a low BMR are to avoid gaining weight they have to be much more careful about what and how much they eat. However, amount of physical activity may be even more important in obesity than BMR, in part because it may affect BMR and even the target weight the body seeks to maintain.

Studies show that fat teenagers may actually eat *less* than their thinner counterparts, but they also exercise less. For example, a study of girls at a summer camp showed that, although obese adolescents did engage in a number of sports, they were inactive 60 to 70% of the time they were playing a game, as compared to 10 to 20% for nonobese girls (Rice, 1981). We need to stress here, though, that obesity is also related to self-concept, amount of stress in one's life, and may have genetic bases other than BMR (Frisch, 1983). Also, our culture's current obsession with being thin is more than likely a factor in both obesity and its reverse—self-induced starvation *(anorexia nervosa).* Anorexia nervosa is most prevalent among adolescent girls (more about it and other pathologies in Chapters 11 and 12).

While we have stressed that the range of normality in adolescent growth is wide, there are some who fall outside these limits. For example, if a person's height is more than 20% greater or less than the norm for her age and sex, she would be labeled short or tall. If she deviated more than 40% from the norm, the individual's growth would be abnormal, and she would be labeled as either a giant or a dwarf (Katchadourian, 1977). Under present adult norms, males under 4 feet 8 inches in height are considered dwarfs and those over 6 feet 7 inches are termed giants. For women, those shorter than 4 feet 5 inches and taller than 6 feet 1 inch are labeled dwarfs or giants, respectively (Lerner & Spanier, 1980).

Excess or overgrowth is usually genetic in origin, although it is sometimes due to pituitary action, usually resulting from the presence of a tumor in the gland. Short stature can result from a number of causes, but pituitary disorder is the most common reason. This often takes the form of underproduction of GH by the anterior pituitary. Other adolescent health problems stemming from puberty include growth disturbances and menstrual dysfunction. Growth disturbances can involve both excessive and insufficient growth, precocious and delayed puberty, and menstrual disorders (Cutler et al., 1983; Daniel, 1983; Frisch, 1983; Waner, 1983). All present intense psychosocial challenges to adolescent self-concept and self-esteem.

Delayed puberty occurs when an individual goes through the pubertal process at a much later age than usual. (If a person never, or only partially, becomes sexually mature, the condition is referred to as *sexual infantilism.*) Delayed puberty can result from malfunction of the hypothalamus, pituitary, or the gonads (as well as other sources), but the end result is a delay in, or insufficient production of, the sex hormones.

Precocious puberty is the condition in which the onset of puberty occurs much earlier than normal (Cutler et al., 1983). The age limits for this are somewhat arbitrary, but are usually set at eight for girls and nine for boys. If there is development at these ages comparable to normal growth at 12 for females and 13 for males, then precocious puberty is said to be occurring. This condition is twice as common in females as it is in males, but it is usually a far less serious condition in females unless it is extreme. Some efforts have been made to develop a physiological treatment for extremely precocious females utilizing synthetic hormones. While promising, these treatments have not been demonstrated to succeed completely (Cutler et al., 1983). Psychological counseling and managing the social environment remain critical to resolving the problem. Girls who have this problem are much less likely than their male counterparts to have another serious disease of some sort. Precocious puberty occurs for a number of reasons. In girls the most common cause is an ovarian tumor, while in boys brain tumors (or other intracranial lesions) are the most frequent cause.

Menstrual disorders comprise a third set of adolescent health problems that arise at puberty. The most common menstrual problems are a failure to menstruate, excessive menstrual bleedings, premenstrual tension, and painful menstrual periods (Klein & Litt, 1983). Menstruation is the result of a complex series of interrelated events that take several years to reach an adult pattern. An adolescent's first cycles may be quite irregular; she *may* not be fertile until she reaches her early twenties. Amenorrhea can occur for a number of medical reasons but is often due to emotional disturbances. For example, some adolescents who have had sexual intercourse may be afraid that they will become pregnant. They may become extremely anxious while waiting for their period to occur, and this may upset their cycles, causing menses not to occur. Amenorrhea, while it may be only a natural fluctuation in the course of development, should be carefully monitored, as it may require medical or psychological treatment. One effect of a girl's involvement in a rigorous program of athletics (particularly swimming and long distance running) may be a cessation of menses. This fact bears noting given the increasing involvement of adolescent girls in sports, with one effect being the "normalization" of this sort of amenorrhea.

Excessive menstrual bleeding also has several causes (Warren, 1983). Normally, the menstrual flow is only about two ounces, brought about by a drop of estrogen, and particularly, progesterone levels. But uterine bleeding, especially in adolescence, can be caused by either a sudden withdrawal of or continuous administration of estrogen or progesterone. This is referred to as estrogen/progesterone withdrawal and breakthrough bleeding respectively, and it accounts for the infertility (ovulation does not occur) of the early menstrual cycles in many adolescents (although it would be foolish to use this in place of contraceptive protection).

The main cause of excessive bleeding in adolescence is estrogen breakthrough bleeding. Tumors of the uterus are sometimes the cause, but these are rare in adolescence. Occasional excessive menstrual flow is not a problem, but on a continuous basis it can result in anemia. Hormonal therapy has been found to be an effective treatment that brings the problem under control until the normal process of maturation occurs (Katchadourian, 1977).

Premenstrual tension (in its extreme forms called *premenstrual syndrome or PMS*) is really a series of difficulties, not just a single problem. These occur for a few days just prior to menstruation and may involve pain in the lower back; a feeling of heaviness, with or without weight gain due to fluid retention; headache; and fatigue. These symptoms may be accompanied by emotional upset as well, although the extent of this has been exaggerated and used as justification for discriminatory policies and practices. For example, women suffering from premenstrual tension are often irritable and easily upset, moody, or even depressed. About 60% of all females experience some form of premenstrual tension. However, most are able to deal with these difficulties and the problem does not inhibit normal functioning for most women. Public attention focused on an alleged extreme form of premenstrual syndrome in the early 1980s when lawyers for a woman charged with murder pleaded "temporary insanity" on the basis of extreme premenstrual tension syndrome.

Sometimes premenstrual tension merges with the symptoms of painful menstruation *(dysmenorrhea)*. However, dysmenorrhea may also occur in the absence of premenstrual syndrome. Dysmenorrhea usually involves cramps or pain in the pelvic area, and occasionally backache, headache, and nausea as well. There are a number of possible physical causes (hypersensitivity of the uterine lining, flexing of the uterus backward or forward, congestion from constant standing, allergies, and so on), but psychological variables also seem to be important (Bowman & Spanier, 1978; Klein & Litt, 1983). This is evident in the finding that religions that tend to instill guilt about sex are associated with higher rates of menstrual problems.

Menstrual disorders begin at an early age but are typically associated with fertile cycles so they usually do not first occur at menarche. If a woman has not experienced some problem by 20, then she probably will not until she approaches menopause (Katchadourian, 1977). Also, for many women, menstrual disorders disappear after childbirth. In both cases, physiological, psychological or both sorts of factors may be involved.

A final, related problem which is relatively prevalent in adolescent females is vaginal infections. These are caused by microorganisms. Symptoms are itching and inflamation of the genitals, and they may involve large, malodorous discharges. These infections are easily treated medically but often reoccur. These vaginal infections should not be confused with gonorrhea, which also produces a discharge (see Chapter 8) or a normal premenarche discharge which is a normal event (although it does not occur in all girls). This whitish discharge is not pathological and does not irritate tissue or have a bad odor. It disappears at menarche.

Adolescent Health

In some ways, the major health issues in adolescence are similar to those in adulthood. A number of the diseases affecting the adult population are also seen in adolescence, including hypertension, arthritis, and cancer, to name but a few (Kovar, 1979). For example, health statisticians estimate that about 5% of all adolescents have significant cardiovascular problems, and about 8% of adolescent males and 4% of the females have high blood pressure (Kovar, 1978). However, the most common medical disorder of adolescence is acne, which affects about 70% of all adolescents (Kovar, 1978; Katchadourian, 1977). Tooth decay and vision problems are also common in this age group, with about 55% showing some sign of tooth decay and 34% wearing corrective lenses. Some diseases that frequently occur in the adolescent years are infectious mononucleosis, epilepsy, diabetes, allergies (especially hay fever), and asthma. Some of these are chronic disorders that first emerge in adolescence and continue into adulthood (e.g., diabetes and allergic conditions), while others are short-term diseases that are most prevalent in adolescence or young adulthood (e.g., infectious mononucleosis).

Among the most challenging chronic health problems facing adolescents are physical handicaps. Because issues of body image are so salient in adolescence it should come as no surprise that physical conditions that impair participation in normal activities (e.g., heart conditions resulting from rheumatic fever or seizures associated with epilepsy) or produce marked deviation from standards of physical attractiveness (e.g., scoliosis—curvature of the spine—and hunchback) are serious threats to self-esteem and popularity.

When I think back about my adolescence, I immediately recall the heartbreak of acne. Until my early teens, I had a very clear complexion; but once age fourteen rolled around, my problems with acne started. At first my acne was minor and the problems associated with it equally minute. However, as my acne increased, so did my troubles.

This was a time when appearance was extremely important to me and my self-concept was greatly deflated with each new pimple. I slowly adopted the attitude that there was something wrong with me more than just my complexion. My posture even suffered as I slouched, showing my inner feelings about myself. I never shared these feelings with anyone which probably added to my stress.

To further complicate matters, my acne would worsen during stressful periods. Anticipation of upcoming social events such as dates or dances caused me to break out even more and as I worried about this, my problem only increased.

I finally decided to see a doctor when I went to college. This helped somewhat but my acne still exists. Having acne all these years has taught me to cope with it better. It still bothers me to look in the mirror, though. My doctor says that as I age, my acne will decrease and finally vanish, but the scars it left behind will always remind me of the pain.

In September of my seventh grade year, I found out that I had scoliosis and would have to wear a backbrace. The following February, I finally picked it up. It was a Friday and there was a band swim party that night. I can still remember how I felt that night as I tried to get in and out of my Milwaukee brace without help. It was embarrassing and humiliating. But, as I look back on the memory now, I was the only one who felt awkward. The loss of that kind of independence was a blow to my pride.

My adolescent years were filled with many events that I'll always remember. As I look back now, a few special memories seem to stick out in my mind. One in particular was that I was one of the first girls in my class to get braces. I was so self-conscious about them and never liked to smile. I was always known to be talkative, but the braces seemed to quiet me down. It seems silly that braces could change part of a personality. It took me awhile to realize that in the long run I would have beautiful straight teeth. During the next few years, many other children got braces and were going through what I did. Looking back now, I realize that my reaction to braces was similar to most others. Now, it doesn't even phase me to see someone with braces, no matter what the age.

The most vivid memory of my adolescent days was biking with my friends. The reason this stands out so clear in my mind is because while I was riding my bike one day with two of my friends, I was hit by a car. Needless to say, I was pretty messed up and I spent two months in a hospital and three months in a body cast. What a way to spend the summer! Although I missed two and a half months of school, I was allowed to enter my sophomore year without making up any of the classes. The most important thing I learned from the accident was that it pays to have friends, they can pull you through the worst of times. Friends you never even knew you had stop by just to say hello and get well soon. And those who were the true blue friends sat by the bed every day to get you anything you needed. Yes, if there is one thing I learned during my adolescence, it is how your friends are always with you through good times and bad times.

Physical handicaps present an acute challenge in the area of emerging sexuality. Rogers (1981), for example, reports that a majority of females and males admit they would not marry a physically deformed person. Depression and suicidal thoughts are an important issue for the seriously handicapped adolescent. The adults around them must recognize this and strive to be sensitive and yet not overprotective. Be it sexuality or career education, supportive, informed adults, and peers can play a constructive role in the life of the physically handicapped adolescent.

In general, however the overall rate of disease among adolescents is low. The leading cause of death in this age group is accidents (see Table 3.3), with a majority of these being auto accidents (Califano, 1978). Auto accidents are an even greater problem than these figures show; for every adolescent killed in a car accident in 1976, 43 were injured and many of these were permanently disabled.

Violence—either against themselves or by others—is also a leading cause of death among adolescents. Adolescent suicide, in particular, has been on the increase. For example, there was a 40% increase in the number of deaths due to suicide among 15 to 19 year olds from 1970 to 1975 (Califano, 1978). (For every actual suicide experts estimate there are approximately 100 unsuccessful attempts.) Besides an increase in the number of suicides, the proportion of adolescent deaths from suicide has also increased. Certainly, these figures indicate our need to deal with depression and other mental disorders that are problems for adolescents (for more on this, see Chapters 11 and 12).

The other major health concerns of adolescence are life-style related social problems and difficulties that arise at or as a result of puberty. Here we are referring to such things as smoking, drug abuse, pregnancy, sexually transmitted diseases, obesity, malnutrition, and pubertal growth disorders. We will examine the issues in adolescent health in three categories: life-threatening ill-

TABLE 3.3
Death rates for the five leading causes of death for children and adolescents.

Cause of Death	Rates per 100,000	
	Ages 5 to 14 Years	Ages 15 to 24 Years
Accidents	18.1	60.3
Motor vehicle accidents	8.7	39.2
All other accidents	9.4	21.1
Drowning	3.2	2.9
Fire	1.5	1.3
Falls or poisoning	0.4	4.2
Malignant neoplasms (cancer)	4.8	6.8
Congenital anomalies	2.0	N.D.
Homicide	1.0	13.7
Suicide	N.D.	11.8
Total	35.7	118.9

SOURCE: Adapted from U.S. Bureau of the Census, Current Population Reports, 1978a. From Lerner & Spanier, 1978.
NOTE: "N.D." means no data specified.

nesses, disorders related to the pubertal process, and life-style related difficulties. Let's take a brief look at each of these.

Life-Threatening Illness

We have already mentioned many of these, so we will discuss only the two most problematic and common: diabetes and cancer. Diabetes, which is a disease involving disruptions of the body's metabolic mechanisms, is a chronic illness. It can arise in both childhood and adult life, with current estimates of its prevalence in young people as 40 cases per 100,000 youngsters 15 years old or younger (Katchadourian, 1977). Forty percent of juvenile diabetics display their symptoms between 10 and 15. The disease is most likely to occur first at ages 6 and 12 (Weil & Kohrman, 1968).

Treatment of diabetes has improved remarkably in the twentieth century. The life expectancy of a juvenile diabetic was only one year after the onset of the disease in 1914, but today with the use of sophisticated diet programs and insulin injections, the child diabetic can expect to lead a reasonably normal life. However, there is no cure. The illness is only controlled by a fairly strict treatment routine, which may sometimes become tedious and even overwhelming to the adolescent.

Cancer is fast becoming one of the major causes of death in adolescence. In fact, it is even more frequent in young children than in adolescents and is the leading cause of death for people between the age of 1 and 15 (Fernbach &

Starling, 1975), although some forms of cancer (leukemia and bone cancer) peak during puberty. The cause for this is unknown, but some speculate that it may be related to the accelerated bone growth occurring at that time (Katchadourian, 1977). Dealing with cancer (and the possibility of death) poses some very difficult psychological problems for the adolescent (as well as for adults), including threats to self-concept, self-esteem, body image, and autonomy. No treatment regime makes sense without careful attention to the difficult psychosocial issues involved.

Life-Style Related Health Concerns

Some of the most alarming—to adults at least—are problems related to lifestyle such as smoking, the use of alcohol, and drug use by adolescents. Smoking is a problem that is particularly acute in adolescence. Teenage smoking has been on the rise through the 70s, particularly among females. For example, from 1968 to 1974, the number of adolescent smokers increased 50% while the number of teenage girls who smoked doubled (Califano, 1978). In 1978, researchers estimated that 4,000 teenagers per day became regular smokers, with six million American adolescents aged 13–19 in the United States being regular smokers. About one-third of all high school students are regular smokers. These trends continue despite adolescent awareness of the hazards of smoking: one study showed that 99% of children 7 to 14 thought smoking caused cancer (Rice, 1981).

Drug use among adolescents is also a major problem. During the early seventies, drug use among teenagers increased dramatically. Although this trend has stopped (and in some instances reversed), drug use is still high in this age group. For example, by 1976 about 40% of 16- and 17-year-olds had tried marijuana and 21% were regular users. The near-daily use of marijuana among high school seniors rose from 6 to 11% from 1975 to 1978, but the upward trend halted in 1979 (*Today's Education*, 1981). In 1978, health statisticians estimated that 4% of Americans 12 to 17 years of age had had some experience with cocaine (Califano, 1978). Among high school seniors, the rate of cocaine use doubled from 6% in 1975 to 12% in 1979, although only one in six had ever tried the drug (*Today's Education*, 1981). Use of amphetamines and inhalants increased among high school seniors in the mid- to late 70s, and it is estimated that about 9% of 12- to 17-year-olds have used inhalants. Heroin use is on the decline, with 1% of high school seniors doing so and a similar percent of 12- to 17-year-olds report having experimented with it.

By far, the most widely used drug among adolescents is alcohol. One study of tenth, eleventh, and twelfth graders in New York State reported that 85% had used alcohol, compared to 27% who had used marijuana and 8.6% who had experimented with LSD (Yancy, Nader, & Burnham, 1972). Drinking by adolescents has increased steadily since World War II. The age at which adolescents take their first drink declined from 13.4 to 12.6 years of age from the mid-60s to the late 70s (Califano, 1978). However, by most standards the problem is not drinking *per se*, but rather excess drinking that leads to impaired functioning and physiological damage.

Figure 3.6 presents the percentage of adolescents who report some type of heavy drinking (becoming drunk). This figure increases through the secondary school years. Almost 10% of high school seniors, for example, say they get drunk once a week or more. Among all adolescents, boys drink more than girls, although females are "catching up" here as they are with smoking. Since the late 60s, the number of teenage girls who drink has tripled, and the use of alcohol among female adolescents has begun to approach that of males. This trend in females in socially problematic behavior has been observed across the board, e.g., in juvenile delinquency (see Chapter 11).

The most vivid memory of my adolescence, or ironically my least vivid memory was of my first drinking experience. This occurred at about age 16, at a Friday night party a friend told me about. "Everyone is going to be there," so I felt obliged to go as well. Well, everyone was indeed there, and alcohol was pouring like water, and I drank as fast as they poured. After what seemed like 500,000 glasses of grain punch, I decided I had had enough and left to go home. I was sure it had to be at least 3:00 A.M. . . .in fact it was before 11:00. My parents were just going to bed when I walked in, being extremely careful, walking as straight as an arrow, and being as cool as they come. I knew if I could just get out two words ("GOOD NIGHT"), I would be home free. I managed this beautifully, and now very proud of myself turned and walked into a wall. The rest of the evening was spent in the bathroom, and is now, as it was then, only a blur. But the lesson lingers on, and despite all my best attempts since, I've never again been able to match the feelings (or lack of them) that I had that night.

Learning about boys and booze in the space of one day. I was about 13 or 14, it was a Friday. Fridays were big days because there were football games on Friday nights. One of my classmates who I had a crush on asked me to the game that night. I was to meet him at 6:30. He didn't show up until 8:00, he says "hello" and lays a huge wet kiss on me. What a shock having never been kissed before. I pushed him away, ran off, and found my older sister and her friends. They were all drinking. I was curious about it, so I started drinking, too. I drank too much, spent the whole night and the next day sick. So much for finding out about things in a good way.

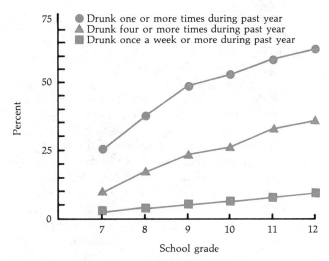

FIGURE 3.6
Percentage of teenage drinkers who report getting drunk or very high, by frequency and school grade, U.S.A., 1974. (From U.S. Department of Health, Education and Welfare, Public Health Service, Alcohol and Health, *Second Report to the U.S. Congress, 1974 [Rockville, MD.: National Institute on Alcohol Abuse and Alcoholism, 1975], p. 21.)*

Conclusion

Many problems in adolescent health, particularly life-style related social difficulties, are often dismissed or explained away through the use of the stereotype of the risk-taking adolescent. Recall the discussion in Chapter 1 of "storm and stress" as a rationale for adolescent psychopathology. The popular press, the general public, and even professionals often believe that adolescents are more prone to take chances than adults, with the result being drug use or accidents of various types. However, there is no evidence that adolescents are more prone to risk-taking in general than are adults (Petersen, 1982). In fact, "adolescents are less likely than adults to smoke, to drink, to use drugs, and to be sexually active" (Petersen, 1982, pp. 14–15). It is the amount of *experience* with these behaviors that differentiates adolescents and adults. Because of their limited experience, adolescents are more likely to make poor judgments and behave unwisely in risky situations. Adolescents probably have more traffic accidents largely because they have less driving experience than adults and are also not as familiar with the effects of drugs or alcohol (Petersen, 1982). These factors are more important than thrill-seeking.

> If experience is the key factor, then the appropriate focus of interventions for adolescents is to give them the information, skills, and practice necessary to behave more wisely, in a manner consistent with their values and needs. (Petersen, 1982, p. 16)

Some adolescent health problems derive in large part from society's unresponsiveness to the health care needs of adolescents (Jenkins, 1978; Califano, 1978). Their needs are

> . . . poorly represented, in health policy debates and their problems are inadequately addressed in health education. In delivery of health services, their care is frequently age inappropriate and unresponsive . . . (Jenkins, 1978, pp. 29–30)

It seems that many members of the health care profession, like many parents, lack information about how to deal with adolescent health problems e.g., pediatricians who treat adolescents as they do young children (Califano, 1978). Also, many adolescents have no access to health care. They may not know where to go or feel they cannot afford to get help. Some may fear that if they go to a doctor or clinic, their parents will find out about some sensitive medical or emotional problem that the adolescent does not want them to know about. There are encouraging signs, however. The number of teaching hospitals offering special training in adolescent medicine for physicians is growing, and the American Academy of Pediatrics is encouraging its practitioners to see adolescents in pediatric practice until age 21.

Our society needs to come to grips with these issues. As we pointed out, there are a number of health problems that are specific to adolescence or at least are prevalent in this age group. Also, it is in adolescence that a number of crucial habits and attitudes are formed, which, "in the future, can make or break a person's health" (Califano, 1978, p. 13). Society's perceptions and responses to the adolescent as a physical organism are quite variable. To some extent, society's response to the physical adolescent grows out of our theories of adolescence, how we understand the meaning of adolescence as the interplay between biological and social forces. This leads us to Chapter 4 in which we examine the processes of cognition as they apply to understanding adolescence. Cognitive development is the partner to physical maturation as a foundation for the distinctive characteristics of adolescence that we observe in home, peer group, school, work, dating, and community activities.

Ecological Wrap-Up

Organism.   The human organism is a system made up of many subsystems. It is genetically programmed to go through the events of puberty in a predictable sequence. Each subsystem links up with others in an orchestrated symphony of physical changes. The impact of these changes is far-reaching. It touches the adolescent's self-image, relations with peers and parents, and health. While there may not be any direct effect on intellectual functioning, puberty does challenge all aspects of the adolescent's psychological make-up and functioning.

Microsystem.   The psychosocial *consequences* of physical development are shaped by the adolescent's microsystems, particularly family, peer group, and school. The way parents, peers, and educators react to menarche, breast enlargement, differences in height and voice, pubic hair, and asynchronous development will do much to shape the adolescent's response to these developments. Microsystems can also play a role in directly influencing the course of physical development, e.g., in the case of nutrition's link to pubertal onset.

Mesosystem.   The consistency of response to the events of puberty influences their psychosocial consequences. Adolescents are likely to discount supportive parental advice concerning the timing of their own physical development if their peers do not corroborate this information. Adolescents who are at either end of the normal variation on some physical characteristic need to experience a positive consensus from their microsystems; the microsystems should reinforce each other in reassuring the concerned adolescent.

Exosystem.   Institutions play a role in the well-being of the adolescent as a biological system. Programs aimed at improving nutrition, reducing smoking, teaching safe driving, controlling venereal disease, and otherwise promoting adolescent health can do much. A key feature of the exosystem picture is whether institutions support sex education designed to help adolescents cope with puberty, particularly its normal variability in timing. As research on school structure indicates, policy decisions about grouping adolescents (e.g., in middle vs. junior high school) can affect the likelihood that early maturation will have significant psychosocial consequences.

Macrosystem.   Historical changes have had a significant effect on the timing of puberty. This secular trend seems to have reached its limits, however, in communities in which adequate nutrition and health care are standard. But cultural differences remain in how societies respond to puberty, how they celebrate the rites of passage, and how they mark adulthood. What is more, cultural images of attractiveness play a critical role in the psychosocial consequences of physical development. As fashion changes with respect to preferred body types, some adolescents are automatically "in" while others are "out." The cultural trends can also increase the risk of health problems, such as when a mania for thinness worsens the problem of anorexia nervosa.

Preview

■ Intelligence is the ability to acquire knowledge and make use of it in understanding the world. Individuals differ in this ability, as well as in their characteristic style of thinking about things.

■ The human mind is organized around the processes of *organization* (putting together mental structures to form complex patterns) and *adaptation* (the general tendency to interact with the environment and to change and to be changed).

■ Adolescents learn to see themselves and their place in the social world more realistically as they mature cognitively and experience a wider circle of micro- and mesosystems.

■ Changes in moral judgment relate to changes in cognitive ability. The adolescent gains new tools for evaluating the value and consequences of alternative paths of behavior.

■ Females and males tend to reason differently about the social environment. Both approaches contain advantages and disadvantages for getting along in the world.

■ Adolescents translate intellectual and moral development into political reasoning. Their new-found cognitive abilities and ambiguous social role often make them attractive to political movements seeking alternatives to established power.

*I*n this chapter we are interested in the abilities of adolescents to reason and think about the world around them, to ask questions about social and scientific issues, and to explain human behavior including their own. We are interested in changes in the way individuals acquire and use knowledge, what developmental psychologists call *cognitive development* (Elkind, 1968). And we are also interested in introducing some of the major theories of human development. Having seen these theories in action here in this chapter we will be ready to examine them in their own right in Chapter 5. This is our inductive approach at work again. It may be unsettling to be dealing with theories before we have fully discussed what exactly they are, but the uncertainty here will be rewarded by a better grasp of the issues later.

Intellectual ability, the ability to acquire and use knowledge, is an important aspect of competence. The cognitive skills that the individual brings to adolescence have arisen and developed during infancy and childhood, and a normal adolescent is capable of moving on to advanced levels of thinking more like those of adults. In fact, according to most theorists and researchers, adolescence is the time during which individuals first attain the cognitive skills that are characteristic of adult thinking. Of course, some acquire these advanced skills earlier than others (and some never do), and further development and refinement of skills and abilities occur during the years following adolescence. What is more, across the life course these cognitive skills provide the basis for reasoning not just about scientific matters, but about social matters as well. They apply not just to how physical things work but to how psychological, social, and moral things work.

4

Adolescent Thinking

From our ecological perspective, we see that the development of advanced reasoning is related to other processes occurring within the adolescent as an individual (e.g., physical maturation and brain growth) as well as in social systems of the adolescent's world (e.g., family, school, and community). Cognitive development and its application to physical and social phenomena occur within the child's home and family environment, the school and community, and the macrosystem that sets standards and values for the adolescent. In order for adolescents to deal with the social and scientific world, they must have the ability to reason clearly and effectively. Surely the skills called for in effective problem-solving, be it in the social or academic spheres, are an asset for the adolescent. Thus, thinking ability or reasoning is one aspect of competence that underlies effective social relationships and success in school.

This chapter consists of four major sections. In the first, we review ideas and concepts that represent current thinking about the development of reasoning. We give special attention to concepts of intelligence and theories of cognitive development. We devote the second part of the chapter to understanding how the adolescent's overall social competence is linked to the processes of cognitive reasoning. In the third section, we look at current approaches to the study of moral development, surely the most studied application of reasoning to social phenomena. In the final section of the chapter, we discuss the political attitudes and reasoning of adolescents.

Cognitive Development: An Overview

Intelligence

In discussing the development of reasoning skills we first turn to the issue of intelligence and the role it plays in reasoning ability. Most people agree that cognitive development and intelligence are intimately related. Both have something to say about the character of a person's knowledge. One emphasizes how much one knows relative to similar others and is thus a *quantitative* approach (because it focuses upon the *quantity* of knowledge), emphasizing the development of the intellect as an *information processor*. It seeks to explain how and why some individuals are more effective and efficient in processing and storing sensory information and in discerning patterns in that information. The other emphasizes the types and styles of knowing that people exhibit and is thus referred to as a *qualitative* approach (because it addresses the *quality* or character of knowing). The qualitative approach emphasizes the development of mind. It seeks to explain how ideas and the ability to generate and use ideas arise. As we shall see, however, most research on adolescent intellectual functioning reflects one or both of two traditions.

Of course, human development incorporates both themes: ideas without calculation are chaotic; calculation without substance is sterile. However, each has its corresponding methodology for assessing its development and its characteristic research issues. Each has its patron saints: the Swiss Jean Piaget for the development of mind and the British Sir Francis Galton and French Alfred Binet for the information processor model. Remember these two orientations as we proceed to consider adolescent intellectual development.

The history of attempts to define and measure intelligence spans thousands of years, but current conceptions of intelligence and intelligence testing have their roots in the assessment movement that began in the 19th century. This movement toward developing tests to measure an individual's intellect (the *psychometric approach*) gained impetus when, in the late 1800s, Sir Francis Galton used tests to determine how effective different individuals were in discriminating among sights, sounds, and other sensory input, as a measure of intelligence. In both world wars, the military used intelligence tests to place its personnel, and throughout the 1900s, many American and European scientists developed measures of intelligence (Anastasi, 1976).

Intelligence has been defined in many different ways. Some definitions see intelligence as one generalized ability while others present it as groups of abilities that together comprise intelligence. Intelligence remains, however, something that *cannot be observed* directly but is *inferred* from psychological tests. In theory it is an ability or set of abilities. In practice it is a set of behaviors on tests. These tests, such as the Stanford-Binet and the Wechsler Intelligence Scales, use the IQ score (intelligence quotient) as an indicator of intelligence. This score is determined by the individual's performance on the test, adjusted for the chronological age of that individual, with a score of 100 indicating a normal match of performance to age (a score greater than 100 indicates greater intelligence and a score of less than 100 suggests lesser intelligence).

The Multidimensionality of Intelligence

Today most researchers think of intelligence as being *multidimensional, that is,* composed of many different related factors and abilities. Earlier theorists, however, viewed intelligence as a single generalized ability. Pioneering researcher Louis Terman (1916), for example, claimed that intelligence was comprised of an inherited general factor g that indicated the individual's ability to verbalize and think abstractly. A few years later, Charles Spearman (1927) expanded on Terman's theory and hypothesized that in addition to the g factor there is a second factor, the s factor, that accounts for specific aptitudes of the individual, such as mathematical or spatial abilities.

More recently, Guilford (1967) proposed a *structure-of-intellect* model to conceptualize intelligence. He postulated at least 120 distinct factors or abilities making intelligence a very complex phenomenon indeed. Guilford extended previous conceptions of intelligence by including in his work measures of the ability of the individual to arrive at many different solutions or alternatives to a problem *(divergent thinking)*. Most intelligence tests had attempted to measure only the ability to solve a problem that has one specific answer *(conver-*

gent thinking). As we shall see, contemporary studies of creativity tend to use measures of divergent thinking and find that it is to some extent distinct from convergent thinking.

We cannot say exactly how many abilities or cognitive skills make up intelligence, partly because that number varies from one definition of intelligence to another and partly because of the tremendous investment of time and energy involved in devising tests that could measure those abilities.

Although research on the development of intelligence and its constituent abilities does not provide us with conclusions about how intellectual abilities change, the multidimensional conception of intelligence is popular. Available intelligence tests usually include a number of items that tap such skills as memory, verbal comprehension, recognition of objects, reading, and arithmetic. The Stanford-Binet Intelligence Scale (Terman & Merrill, 1960) yields one overall IQ score that is derived from performance on a number and variety of different tests. The Wechsler Adult Intelligence Scale (WAIS) (Wechsler, 1955), the Wechsler Intelligence Scale for Children-Revised (WISC-R) (Wechsler, 1974), and the Wechsler Preschool and Primary Scale of Intelligence (WPPSI) (Wechsler, 1967) all yield an overall *(Full Scale)* IQ based on all items in the test, a Verbal IQ based on a subset of verbal and mathematical test items, and Performance IQ based on several items requiring manipulation of various objects. Several subtests make up each of the Wechsler Scales, and subtest scores can be obtained in addition to the three major IQ scores. Along with these tests of multiple aptitudes, other tests such as The Primary Mental Abilities Test (Thurstone & Thurstone, 1962) testify to the widespread belief that intelligence comprises several different abilities.

Researchers are also interested in how the structure of intelligence changes, how it develops from infancy to old age. One study that addressed the development of intellectual abilities in adolescence (Fitzgerald, Nesselroade, & Baltes, 1973) tested the hypothesis that intelligence becomes less generalized and more composed of ever-more diverse specific abilities (i.e., more *differentiated*) as one grows up (Burt, 1954, 1966; Garrett, 1946). This *age-differentiation* hypothesis suggests that during early childhood there is the development of a general type of intelligence consisting of several related abilities (the *integration period*). According to the age-differentiation hypothesis, during adolescence there is a gradual emergence of several distinct groups of abilities in a process known as *differentiation*. In late adulthood, however, the developmental trend is towards a less differentiated pattern of cognitive abilities or, to use an awkward word, *de-differentiation.* This approach seems consistent with a general picture of human development emphasizing people's similarities at birth and old age, in contrast to their diversity in between.

In order to examine how the organizational pattern of intellectual abilities changes during adolescence, Fitzgerald and his colleagues (1973) selected a random sample of students from the ages of 12 to 18. The students were divided into three groups according to grade (grades 7 and 8, grades 9 and 10, and grades 11 and 12). The Primary Mental Abilities Test (Thurstone & Thurstone, 1962), which was derived from the multifactor perspective of intelligence, was administered and then the scores were analyzed by statistical techniques to determine if, with increasing age, the number of abilities was more differentiated, as the age-differentiation hypothesis suggests. The results of this study showed that there was *no* differentiation with time, and that the number of abilities or factors (verbal, number, reasoning, and spatial factors) remained constant. Thus, the authors concluded that differentiation of these four abilities occurred prior to adolescence, and that the adolescent-oriented age-differentiation hypothesis was unsupported. This points our attention toward the childhood origins of intellectual competence and the pioneering work of Jean Piaget.

Piaget's Theory of Cognitive Development

No discussion of intelligence is complete without reference to the Swiss psychologist Jean Piaget (1896–1980), who formulated a theory of cognitive development that continues to stimulate research and debate today. In his writings (1950, 1952, 1960) Piaget presented his model of the development of intellectual functioning from early infancy through adolescence. Piaget saw cognitive growth proceeding through four stages in which the content and nature of thinking in each *stage* is different from the other stages. Chapter 5 presents a discussion of this as an example of a more general approach to development that is implied in such stage theories, namely that development proceeds through a series of distinct changes in the way the individual functions rather than as simply through the gradual accumulation of new skills and abilities.

Piaget defined intelligence as a *biologically*-based adaptation, in which the developing individual attempts to establish a balance or state of equilibrium between the environment and itself as an organism. The individual accomplishes all this through patterns in the brain that arise, develop, mature, change, and are replaced. These patterns are the *structures* of thought.

Thus, Piaget's theory emphasizes the individual as a system, as an active organism, an organism that interacts with its ecological surroundings in order to adjust to those surroundings and to make those surroundings more to its own liking. As the child plays, explores, and becomes familiar with the environment, growth in cognitive functioning occurs and the capacity to adapt increases. This, of course, casts adolescence as a crucial time in intellectual development, because it is a period of intertwined profound biological and social changes. And, as we shall see, it is a period critical to the development of fully mature thinking.

Organization and Adaptation

Piaget believed that children inherit two cognitive functions or tendencies as part of their basic human equipment and that these functions enable them to cope with the environment. These two functions are *organization* and *adaptation*. Organization is the tendency to "integrate structures, which may be physical or psychological, into higher-order systems or structures" (Ginsburg & Opper, 1969, p. 18). "Structures" refers to those mental patterns that exist in the brain, be it the neurological patterns required to bring hand to mouth or the complex of associations required to describe justice. For example, the developing child coordinates physical structures such as hand, arm, and leg movements with each other and with other physical abilities such as vision and hearing in order to be physically competent. Children also organize their psychological structures (their concepts of number and time, for example) so that they can better reach a state of equilibrium or "fit" with the environment. Adolescents and adults can use complicated abstract ideas in this same way, e.g., by combining the ideas of justice and equality into a political ideology that can guide behavior aimed at social change.

Adaptation refers to the individual's general tendency to interact with or adapt to the environment. Adaptation occurs through two continually functioning, complementary processes called *assimilation* and *accommodation.*

Assimilation is the process in which a person interprets an environmental event using mental structures that already exist (what the individual already knows or can do). This process is based upon the individual recognizing a situation and fitting it in somehow with structures that already exist. The individual can grasp the situation (be it an object, an idea, an experience, or a *stimulus*) as something familiar, something that makes sense. For example, the newborn's usual response to the bottle or breast is to begin sucking motions. The baby recognizes them and they fit in. When other stimuli are placed near the infant's mouth, however, the same response occurs. The infant's existing structures for organizing the world do not change when an external stimulus, such as a finger, comes into contact with the infant. The object is perceived as having the same functions or properties of the breast. The same process operates throughout life. A teenager who treats every adult the way she treats her parents is engaged in assimilation ("all adults are the same as my parents").

Accommodation, on the other hand, involves modifying the existing psychological structures in order to adapt to an event. It is what the organism does when it meets up with something that is not X or cannot be treated as if it is X. When the infant begins to discriminate between finger and breast, so that the sucking response does not occur when the finger is placed near the mouth, accommodation has taken place. The finger does not elicit the old response, but may, in fact elicit a new one, such as grasping. In adolescence the individual learns that one standard concept of parent/adult will not suffice.

In the process of accommodation, the organism has changed, and as a result can become even more active in the assimilation mode. It now has use of two different structures and will go on to add others *as needed.* This process fits well with the definition of development we proposed in Chapter 2, and it reflects our overall systems orientation. Recall that in Chapter 2 we presented the basic idea of systems analysis as that of each functioning entity sharing

My most vivid memory of adolescence is the hardship I had in fitting in with the cliques; in general being popular (à la Square Pegs on NBC) during high school. Since I lived in a rural area I found that the students from town, who were a majority in the school system, felt I wasn't good enough for them. I ended up always being left out of activities, being picked last in gym class for games, etc., and I was always trying to prove my abilities to my fellow students. Usually this only succeeded in my becoming a butt for their jokes and pranks. Fortunately, during my high school years I met people in the same situation as me, and in a sense we formed our own little group of "outcasts."

some fundamental processes for seeking dynamic equilibrium. Piaget's analysis is clearly within this approach.

Organization and adaptation occur throughout life. Their interplay is responsible for intellectual development. Thus, these processes serve to move the individual through the stages of cognitive development.

Piaget's Stages

Piaget's four stages of cognitive development are: (1) the *sensorimotor period* (from birth to approximately 2 years); (2) the *preoperational period* (from approximately 2 to 7 years); (3) the *concrete operational period* (from approximately 7 to 11 years); and (4) the *formal operational period* (from about 11 to adulthood). Before we discuss formal operational thought and cognitive development in adolescence, it is necessary to provide a basis for understanding changes in cognitive development in adolescence by briefly reviewing Piaget's first three stages.

Sensorimotor period (birth–2 years).   During the first two years of life the infant develops from an individual who interacts with the world by way of innate responses to external stimuli to an individual who has many structures available, enough to provide the beginnings of symbolic thought and the ability to remember an object although that object is not in sight. This ability is termed *object permanence*. In fact, one of the major attainments of the sensorimotor period is the "conquest of the object" (Elkind, 1967). Of course *objects* here includes people as well: mother, father, brother, and sister receive the attention of object permanence as well. Their comings and goings can be assimilated as can the comings and goings of nonhuman objects.

Many of the changes in cognitive development that occur within the sensorimotor stage are the result of changing *schemes*. Piaget used the term *scheme* to designate organized patterns of behavior, both physical and intellectual. For example, the infant's sucking response is a scheme, as is the grasping reflex.

As the child develops, schemes change from hereditary, innate responses to complex learned responses, and in so doing become more and more like concepts and ideas instead of just wired-in computer programs. The youngster who has not attained the concept of object permanence has a different scheme for understanding objects in the environment than the child who does have object permanence. The latter child, through interaction with the surroundings, has modified the old scheme of "out of sight, out of mind" and replaced it with another scheme about relationships between individuals and objects, "what goes away is somewhere else." It is also in the sensorimotor stage that children begin to imitate behaviors that have been witnessed a day or two before (an accomplishment called *deferred imitation*) and to have rudimentary problem-solving abilities. These advances are made through the organization and adaptation processes of the child and open up a widening social field beyond the dyad in the family microsystem.

Preoperational period (2–7 years).   Broken down into two stages, the first stage of the preoperational period, *preconceptual thought* (2–4 years), represents the child's increasing ability to form mental images of objects and events that are absent. The major acquisition of this stage is the conquest of symbols (Elkind, 1967). During this time the child's language abilities are rapidly improving and in part consist of attaching names to objects in the environment and describing the properties of those objects. Thus, the child's attainment of symbolic thought allows symbols or words to represent various stimuli that the child sees as important. Also developing during this stage is imaginative or pretend play. Because the child can substitute a symbol for an actual object, the child can pretend that absent objects can be seen and touched, and that children can pretend to be adults, animals, fire-fighters, and a variety of other figures.

During the second stage of the preoperational period, *intuitive thought* (4–7 years), children begin to perform certain mental operations such as classification of objects according to one attribute, although they are generally unable to *articulate* what that attribute is. One characteristic of the child's thought in this stage is the tendency to focus on only one dimension of an object *(centration).* If a child is given one set of poker chips containing blue chips and yellow chips and one set of blue marbles and yellow marbles, the preoperational child will tend to separate the objects according to either color (blue and yellow) or type of object (marbles and chips) but not both. Also, the child at this stage is limited in the ability to take another person's perspective, i.e., is *egocentric*. Thus, preschool children may not understand effects of their behavior on another person. For example, young children often say such things as, "Why are you so fat?" or "I don't like you" without realizing how such comments might hurt the listener's feelings. Egocentrism is a big issue throughout development and takes on a special character in adolescence.

Concrete operational period (7–11 years).   During this period the child becomes less egocentric, is able to focus on more than one attribute of an object, and develops the ability to recognize that, although the shape of a substance has changed, the quantity remains the same *(conservation)*. In short, the child masters classes, relations, and quantities (Elkind, 1967). One of Piaget's classic tests of conservation of mass is to show two equal balls of clay to a child and ask if the quantity of clay in each is equal. The young child can determine that the quantity is the same. However, if one ball of clay is rolled into a thin, long piece the child who has not yet attained conservation of mass will say that the long, thin piece of clay contains a greater quantity of clay than the ball. The preoperational child moves into the concrete operational period when conservation is attained.

There are several characteristics of the child's thinking in the concrete operational stage that allow the development of conservation abilities. One characteristic is that the child can focus on more than one attribute or dimension of an object, i.e., the child has *decentered.* In our example of the blue and yellow poker chips and marbles, we noted that in the preoperational stage the child will tend to focus on either color or type of object, but not both. The child in the concrete operational period, on the other hand, is more likely to focus on color *and* type of object and therefore can classify objects by both color and type (e.g., blue marbles, blue chips, yellow marbles, yellow chips).

Reversibility is another characteristic of concrete operational thought. Piaget defined reversibility as "the permanent possibility of returning to the starting point of an operation in question" (Inhelder & Piaget, 1958, p. 272). Thus, the child who is able to determine that the long piece of clay, in our previous example, has the same amount of clay as it did when it was in the round shape, has attained the quality of reversibility. He can retrace the steps made in transforming the ball of clay into another longer shape, although the ability to do so is still tied to seeing the objects involved. Only later will the child be able to do these kinds of problems using symbols.

Also attained during the concrete operational period is the ability to see that objects can be part of a larger category of objects *(class inclusion).* Thus, strawberries, apples, and peaches are understood as all being fruits. The child in the preoperational stage is less likely to identify distinct fruits as part of a larger category. In addition to class inclusion, the child in the concrete operational period is able to order or rank objects on a scale of large to small, short to tall, and so on. This ability is called *seriation.*

Egocentrism in the concrete operational period is still present but to a lesser extent than in the preoperational stage of cognitive development. For example, children in the preoperational stage are unwilling to change rules of a game regardless of other children's reasons and opinions for doing so. In the concrete operational period, however, children do not see rules as absolute and are willing to change them in response to the different perspectives of other individuals (Piaget, 1932).

Formal operational period (11–adult).   In summarizing Piaget's conception of the formal operational period, Elkind (1967) refers to the formal operational period as "the conquest of thought." Piaget himself described it as, "a transformation of thought that permits the handling of hypotheses and reasoning with regard to propositions removed from concrete and present observations" (Piaget & Inhelder, 1969, p. 131). Whereas children in the concrete operational stage are able to hypothesize about concrete objects and experiences in the present, the adolescent moves further and is able to think about multiple possibilities including those hypothetically existing in the future (Inhelder & Piaget, 1958). The adolescent with formal operational thought can imagine the unlikely and impossible. For example, ask most adolescents to work through an argument based on the assumption that the sky is purple and they will be able to do so. Children, in the concrete operational stage, however, are more likely to respond that "the sky is blue and cannot be purple" and be unable to proceed. The crucial difference, however, is that adolescents in the formal operational period can think *logically* about contrary-to-fact situations. They can deal logically with the *form* of an argument independent of its content, while concrete operational children get caught up in the specific validity of the content and thus cannot address pure form. The issue then is not imagination or creativity but the ability to abstract, to engage in "pure" formal thought.

___

Among the several vivid memories of my adolescence is the time when the mysteries of sex were revealed. As I entered my early adolescent years, I had a few vague notions about what sex was. I knew that certain words would result in disapproval, and while I managed to see a few explicit pictures in various magazines, I knew little about what it all meant. My parents were of some help, but their uncomfortableness about the topic, coupled with my inability to grasp the whole idea, left me with a sense that sex was something mysterious that only a few people "did." I pretended, along with my friends, that I knew more than I did. I remember laughing at jokes even when I had little idea about the meaning. The puzzle just wouldn't fit together, and I was becoming more and more curious.

One day, when I was about 12 years old, my family and I were out in the country visiting some friends that lived on a farm. There was no one my age to play with so I was walking around the farm alone. Suddenly, I caught sight of two huge horses, making strange noises, with one on top of the other "piggyback" style. Obviously, they were copulating, but at the time I had no idea what they were doing. At first, I thought something was wrong. Either they were fighting, or the one on top was hurt and the one on the bottom was trying to carry him to help. I was going to run for help, but then it occurred to me that sex was somehow involved. I stood and watched, somewhat scared, but mostly in awe. If this had to do with sex, I was more confused than ever, for this position had nothing to do with the scrambled picture in my mind. I really had to figure this out.

A few days later, I was hanging around the neighborhood. I ran into one of my friend's older brothers who was friendly towards me (probably because he liked my older sister). I started telling him about my experience with the horses. He became excited and exclaimed "they were doing 'it'!" I tried to maintain my facade of knowing all about "it" and made what seemed to be reasonable comments. But he told me that I had it all wrong, and went ahead and explained the details in terms that I understood.

All the notions that I'd been carrying around were finally all fitting together. I was amazed. After he finished talking, he told me to not tell anyone that he told me, which was fine with me for that meant that my previous ignorance wouldn't be revealed.

As I walked home, so many realizations struck me at once. Everybody did "it," or would do it at sometime or another—my parents, my teachers, my neighbors, even people I saw in the supermarket! The most striking thing was that this had been going on all along, probably right in front of me, and I didn't know it.

I caught a glimpse that things were much more than they appeared to be. I began wondering what else I was missing, and possibilities and hidden meanings multiplied in my mind. It was not a good feeling, for the world now seemed infinitely more difficult to figure out. But it wasn't an unpleasant feeling either, for now I was on to one of the great mysteries. Best of all, I realized that some day, probably later than I wanted to, I would also do "it."

The adolescent ability to think about possibilities is extended into the scientific realm. For example, given a number of jars containing colorless solutions and asked to combine them to produce a colored liquid, the adolescent who has attained formal operational thought can systematically mix various liquids and eliminate others in order to find the appropriate combination. He or she will act as a scientist, figuring out which combinations will provide the critical tests, which are unequivocal. This stands in contrast to the less mature mind, which will probably end up proceeding haphazardly, randomly, and easily getting misled by coincidences and deceptive ambiguities. The steps taken in order to solve the scientific problem involve, first, analyzing the problem at hand, and, second, developing hypotheses about what could occur if certain actions are taken. As Ginsburg and Opper (1969) state, "these hypotheses are numerous and complex because the adolescent takes into account all possible combinations of eventualities in an exhaustive way" (p. 206).

After considering possible solutions, the adolescent experiments with the hypotheses so that, one by one, they can be either eliminated or supported. Faw (1980) cites as an example a word problem in which the respondent is given the letters A, E, M, S, and T and told to generate as many words as possible. The formal operational adolescent systematically tries out 120 possible combinations of letters, probably discarding groups of combinations that violate word construction rules.

The adolescent reaches a conclusion after testing hypotheses. The problem has been solved. "The adolescent's thought is now so flexible and powerful that it has reached a high degree of equilibrium" (Ginsburg & Opper, 1969, p. 206). Piaget designed several scientific problems (such as mixing liquids to isolate chemical effects) in order to determine whether children and adolescents have attained formal operations (Inhelder & Piaget, 1958). The kind of thinking characteristic of formal operational thought is termed *abstract thinking*. Piaget saw abstract thinking as the major attainment of the formal operational stage. It allows the individual to be able to think about thinking and to think about the thoughts of other people. This results not only in an increasing ability to solve scientific problems but also in improved ability to understand the perspective of others. Thus, abstract thinking applies to social problem-solving, too. Brazee and Brazee (1980) offer the following criteria for deciding whether adolescents are concrete, transitional, or formal thinkers.

Concrete

1 Do they need to have things explained exactly?
2 Are they able to go from one task to another without explicit instructions?
3 Are they able to see the relationship between ideas?
4 Do they make only literal interpretations of content and material?

Formal

1 Do they have the ability to perceive relationships between two ideas?
2 Can they perform complex tasks without teacher direction?
3 Can they go beyond the surface level of information to offer interpretation and application?

Transitional

1 Does their performance depend upon the nature of the task? That is, do they respond concretely to some tasks but formally to others?

As we shall see throughout our discussion, moving from concrete to formal operations has implications for all aspects of the adolescent experience from self-concept to ethical values to vocational development.

How Universal Is Formal Operational Thought?

Piaget's work seems to imply that the attainment of formal operational thought during adolescence is nearly universal. Recent work on the attainment of formal operations, however, brought forth the suggestion that such advanced thought may not be as widespread as originally believed. What is more, it seems to be more likely among more intelligent youth who live in intellectually stimulating environments (Peel, 1971; Dulit, 1972). We should note, however, that Piaget did say that "a particular social environment remains indispensible for the realizations of those possibilities. It follows that their realization can be accelerated or retarded as a function of cultural and educational conditions" (Piaget & Inhelder, 1969, p. 337). Even with this disclaimer, however, it seems fair to conclude that Piaget overestimated the rate at which youth develop formal operational thought. To some extent this may have resulted from the restricted samples of young people he studied and the very limited measurement techniques he employed, techniques that increase the likelihood of falsely concluding that higher order thinking is present. Epstein (1979) reports that by age 15 no more than 32% of the adolescents he studied were capable of any formal operational thinking, and only 13% were mature formal thinkers. By age 18 these figures were only 34% and 19%.

A number of studies conducted by Elkind and others (see Elkind, 1975, for a brief review) agree in showing that many young adolescents, college students, and older adults are *not* at the formal operational level of thinking, and that the highest level of such thinking is quite rare at any age. In addition, abstract thinking, as Piaget conceptualized it, may be used by adolescents in certain situations more than others and thus may not always be evident (Martorano, 1974). That is, even when individuals possess the ability to engage in formal operational thought, they do not always display that ability. We refer to this as the difference between competence and performance, and it is quite important. We must always be careful about concluding that someone *cannot* do something when we only know for sure that we have not *observed* them doing it. Performance proves competence, but lack of performance does not necessarily mean incompetence.

Could There Be a Fifth Stage?

If formal operational thought is not as characteristic of adolescents and adults as initially hypothesized, then even fewer may reach what has been postulated as a fifth stage of cognitive development. Piaget conceptualized formal operations as an end state in cognitive development. Once having achieved formal operational thought, he believed, there is no more advanced stage of reasoning that the individual can reach. The work of Gruber (1973), however, led to the suggestion that there may be a more advanced stage of cognitive development, beyond that of formal operations. This suggestion led to Arlin's (1975) study of a possible fifth stage.

Arlin (1975) proposed that the stage of formal operations is really a problem-solving stage that is the basis for a fifth stage, the *problem-finding* stage.
Arlin's work with young adults supported the notion that some individuals first
attain formal operational thought, and then move on to a fifth stage. According to Arlin, the *discovery* of scientific problems and the *identification* of new
questions are characteristic of problem-finding. Of course, Arlin's conclusions
are tentative and research needs to be conducted before we accept or reject this
tantalizing idea of a more advanced stage. When we think about the most active intellectually competent individuals we have known, however, it makes a
lot of sense. Arlin's view has been criticized as being merely "an improvement
in content rather than in cognitive development" (Fakouri, 1976, p. 472). It is
premature to be sure whether Arlin's proposed fifth stage is really a higher type
of thinking (a qualitative change) or simply the fourth stage applied to additional issues (a quantitative change), as Fakouri believes.

Adolescent Egocentrism

During the formal operational period the young adolescent becomes more able
to consider other perspectives. Hence, there is a decrease in the type of egocentrism witnessed in the previous cognitive stage, although it hardly disappears.
There is, however, another kind of egocentrism characteristic of the formal
operational stage. In part it seems to derive from the way formal operations
tend to permit and even encourage a kind of self-reinforcing form of speculation. One gets involved in going further and further into a topic, driven by the
ability to generate the next hypothetical "What if." What if leads to further
"what ifs," and a spiralling deeper and deeper into the topic often occurs. This
happens when the topic is oneself.

The young adolescent begins to better recognize that other people have
their own unique thoughts, perspectives, and experiences, but believes that the
focus of the others' thoughts and attention is on the adolescent him- or herself
(*adolescent-style egocentrism*). The adolescent's self-consciousness and attention to personal appearance are typical of the adolescent's emotionally egocentric qualities. When added to the cognitive sort of egocentrism, this makes for
a very egocentric period in the life course.

*During adolescence I have some very vivid memories of confusion,
anticipation, and suspense. I was so unsure about my future and what was
going to happen to me as well as to my family. Would I be married? Would I
finish college? Would I be ugly or fat or well liked? And most importantly,
would I fit in? Would people like me?*

The most discouraging, depressed time of my short life—I could always be found eating, watching TV or studying. We had moved from a 15-room country farmhouse to a four-room townhouse in downtown New Orleans, and I had to learn to adjust to new surroundings and new people with different ethnic backgrounds.

Adolescence was a time of struggle—to keep my skin clear—my clothes right—my grades good—my family happy, etc.

I must have eaten three times what I do now and it certainly was obvious. Exercise was a bike ride to the local 7–11 for a candy bar.

I don't have many good memories of adolescence. The few I do are greatly overshadowed by all the bad!

We were just 15, my friend and me. And we were on our way to the big city, for the first time ever. There we were sitting in the seats of an Amtrak train, watching the scenery of New York State roll by. Suddenly we were thirsty. Other people were walking to the front of the train. It looked as though there might be a water fountain up there. "Should we walk up there?" I asked. "I don't know. I'm scared." "Well, I'm pretty thirsty but there are an awful lot of people who stare on this train." My friend said, "I'll go if you go." I said, "You go first." She replied, "I can't. How about if I follow you?" "Should we try it?" I asked. "I don't know. Maybe we can walk fast." She went first. Then I followed. Soon we were back in our seats flushed with excitement but comfortable at last. And extremely happy because we had survived that entire train load of people who had nothing to do but stare at two adolescents.

The alarm went off at 6:45 a.m. sharp. It hardly needed to wake me on that cool, crisp September morning. It was my first day at East Allegheny High.

To this point in my life, school had consisted of sixteen familiar faces. There were 365 students in my new class—over 1,000 (gulp) in the entire school. I could not begin to imagine how one could remember this many names and faces. The task was staggering, but the possibilities and potentialities were exciting.

As I stepped off the bus I was awestruck with the massive cement buildings with their funny green windows. I suppose it was beautiful, after all it was newly built and had cost thousands, maybe millions to build.

Suddenly, my handmade dress seemed all wrong. The style was out-dated, it was too long, the colors weren't right and I was sure that everyone else was noticing and disapproving. As I bobbed among the endless streams of other adolescents who peopled the vast corridors, I realized that perhaps the opposite was also true. Nobody knew or cared what I looked like. I was one more "Freshie."

The reality of this situation was that both of these perceptions were partially true. As time went on I came to know many of the faces and names, to love a few, but the others remain bobbing, vague faces going down the corridors.

Being a cheerleader from the ages of 13 to 17 was probably one of the greatest time periods of my life. My entire high school career was built around my experiences as a cheerleader and my experiences with my fellow "rah, rahs," During my senior year after football seasons and a long bout of "senioritis," I was kicked off the squad. The incidents leading up to my removal are tedious and boring. It is the specific day I was kicked off that I remember so vividly. My initial reaction after hearing the news was extreme anger. But in the weeks and months to follow, I experienced some of the most depressing times of my adolescent years. One teacher told me the day I found out about my removal, "If that's your worst tragedy in life, you'll be very lucky." He was right, but it still hurts.

David Elkind (1967) hypothesized the existence of two beliefs common to adolescents that are derived from egocentrism, the *imaginary audience* and the *personal fable*. The imaginary audience encompasses the young teenager's belief that all eyes are focused on his or her behaviors, physical appearance, and other personal attributes. Elkind uses the term imaginary audience because it portrays the adolescent as an actor who is constantly being observed (or so the adolescent believes). An example of this belief is the young teenager who would rather go thirsty than have the whole classroom observe him leaving the desk and walking out of the door. On the other hand, some adolescents might revel in the glory of leaving the classroom while everyone is watching. The point is that both assume all eyes are on them, whether they like it or not.

The personal fable is a story that adolescents believe to be true of themselves by virtue of their immortality, uniqueness, or other special qualities. In essence, the adolescent believes he or she is an exception to the rule. We will see in a later chapter that many teenage girls apparently tell themselves in a personal fable that "I can't get pregnant" and thus, are victims of their own cognitive functioning when they engage in sexual intercourse without benefit of contraception. Elkind believes that adolescent egocentrism decreases by the age of 16 when many have made the transition to formal operational thought. This is one reason why we should be sensitive to differences between early and late adolescence. However, it seems clear that many people retain personal fables well after age 16, particularly when such fables pertain to sexuality and power.

Alternative Views of Adolescent Thinking

While Piaget's theory has attracted many followers, it has also attracted some criticism. In his review of work on Piagetian notions and theory (as outlined by Piaget and his colleague Inhelder), Keating (1980) claims that:

> I am led to conclude by the evidence . . . first, that we know very little about how adolescents' thinking differs from children's thinking beyond the obvious (but important) performance descriptions; and second, that Inhelder and Piaget's (1958) general theoretical model is not an accurate account of the change. (p. 238)

As alternatives, Keating (1980) considers *psychometric* and *information-processing* research that emphasizes the elements of intelligence and the computer model as potentially more promising approaches to understanding cognitive development in adolescence than the emphasis on the development of mind. In the psychometric approach, performance on intellectual and abilities tests is examined for shifts at various age levels. The study by Fitzgerald and his colleagues (1973) that tested the age-differentiation hypothesis, as previously mentioned, is an example of psychometric research in this area. Recall that this research didn't document clear and dramatic qualitative shifts. Recall also that Epstein (1979) found that only a minority of even older adolescents were consistently demonstrating formal operational thought. Brazee and Brazee (1980) reported similar though less negative results. In seventh grade they classified 31% of the students as formal operational thinkers (about double what Epstein reported).

Information-processing approaches view the mind as a computer and take into account the mind's encoding, storage, and retrieval of information abilities. One such approach is to focus on individual differences in cognitive processing. For example, Keating and Bobbitt (1978) found age differences in such cognitive processes as efficiency in long-term memory retrieval and memory search rate. Research seems to suggest that rapid maturation of the information-processing system occurs in pre- and early adolescence (Keating, 1980). These alternatives to Piaget may be best thought of as challenges to the idea that cognitive development occurs in qualitative changes, that "a child thinks differently from an adolescent." The alternatives say that children do *less* of the same things that adults do (perhaps so much less in some ways that it looks as if they are not doing them at all). In any case, adolescence seems to be a critical point, when individuals either start thinking in new ways, or they get substantially better at and more motivated to perform complex intellectual operations. As we will see in Chapter 5, building and testing theories hinge upon just this kind of issue.

Creativity and Intellectual Exceptionality

Both the psychometric and stage approaches recognize the existence of differences among individuals in matters of intellectual competence (although the former accentuates such differences while the latter downplays them). The existence of mental retardation is undeniable, for example. Indeed, adolescence is usually a critical point in the life course of the seriously retarded because it is a period when expectations for self-sufficiency and competence increase dramatically. It often becomes a "make it or break it" time as retarded adolescents and the adults who care for them must make important arrangements for autonomous or sheltered lifestyles based on the level of competence already achieved and likely to be achieved.

But retardation is not the only form of intellectual exceptionality. Some individuals exhibit extraordinary intellectual proficiency, and these individuals are often labelled *gifted*. When IQ tests are used as the criterion, a score of 130 (putting an individual in the top 2% of the population) is often used to identify the intellectually gifted (Hogan, 1981), although other indications of intellectual talent are often used in schools (e.g., some special scholarly accomplishment such as a science project or mathematics demonstration).

We should note here that such singling out of the intellectually gifted is no simple matter. Many voices have been raised in support of a broader conception of gifted to encompass any exceptional mental talent including artistic and musical abilities as well as excellence in science, humanities, and the social sciences. The issue is taken a step further by including creativity in the assessment of exceptionality. As we noted earlier in considering factorial models of intelligence, most sophisticated approaches recognize multiple components of intellectual ability. Where does creativity fit in?

Rogers (1981) defines creativity as "the capacity to recombine with unusual sensitivity and spontaneity, the products of experience into new forms" (p. 148). Tests for creativity usually differ from intelligence tests in that intelligence tests determine whether the youth can generate the prespecified correct or most appropriate or likely answer *(convergent thinking)*, while tests of creativity seek multiple, new, unusual answers or solutions *(divergent thinking)*. The former might ask the youth to define a word or solve an equation; the latter might request the youth to propose possible uses for a turnip. However, for all their interest, tests of creativity fall short of predicting later creative *achievement*, which, like all forms of competence, depends upon nurturing, support, and opportunity at all levels of the human ecology and does so in ways that are complicated and often difficult to recognize.

It is important to recognize that the intellectually exceptional adolescent is likely to be socially competent as well (Hogan, 1981). Highly creative adolescents are likely to be strong and independent, if somewhat unconventional, personalities (Getzels & Csikszenthmihalyi, 1976). Those who combine high intelligence and high creativity constitute a true elite (Hogan, 1981). As such they are a natural resource for society to nurture and encourage.

Cognitive Style

One way to interpret differences in creativity is to say that they reflect differences in cognitive style, the manner in which individuals approach an intellectual task. Some people characteristically engage in divergent thinking. If they do it well, we say they are creative. Some people characteristically approach questions in a methodical, systematic manner; others are impulsive and intuitive. When the former are effective we call them "thorough and thoughtful." When the latter succeed we call them "brilliant." Each is a cognitive style. Most individuals display a characteristic cognitive style (Ewing, 1977). Ausburn and Ausburn (1978) have identified eleven dimensions of cognitive style, including those we have mentioned already as well as *tolerance for unrealistic experience* ("willingness to accept perceptions which contradict what is known to be true") and *field independence/field dependence* ("ability to perceive figures as distinct from their backgrounds"). Different *combinations* of these dimensions represent different cognitive styles, and they may make adolescents well suited for different types of tasks. For example, an individual who is high on tolerance of unrealistic experiences and field independence may be perfect for writing science fiction, while a person low on these characteristics may be well-suited to anticipating how most of his or her peers will respond to an advertising message.

Differences in style may reflect differences in temperament as well as the effects of training—some of us are born quick and others patient. Some researchers report cultural differences (e.g., Cole & Scribner, 1974): technologically primitive people living in a nonliterate culture do not use verbal concepts in solving problems as people living in modernized, literate societies characteristically do.

Many situations permit different styles to succeed equally well. However, some problems may be more suited to reflective styles (e.g., when errors are costly), while others favor impulsive approaches (e.g., when errors are cheap and quick results count). We will return to the issue of cognitive style when we discuss the formation of self-concept in Chapter 7, where we will find that these differences can affect how an adolescent goes about the task of answering the question, "Who am I?" Considering this and other issues will lead us to the topic of moral reasoning, the most widely studied aspect of social reasoning.

One of the most important contemporary issues in social reasoning is to be found in how children and adolescents deal with divorce. As we will see in Chapter 6 when we discuss family relations, divorce has become very common throughout North American society, with some one in three marriages eventually ending in divorce. All told, about half the children born in the 1980s are expected to spend some of their first 18 years in a single parent household, for one reason or another. Many people, professionals and the general public alike, are concerned about this. For example, psychologist David Elkind (1981) fears that divorce hurries children into growing up too fast. As he sees it, divorce makes too many demands on children to mature, assume responsibility, and cope with parental needs (including sexuality). Social critics Vance Packard (1983) and Marie Winn (1983) express similar concerns in their books *Our Endangered Children* and *Children Without Childhood.*

But how do children and adolescents differ in their ability to meet the challenge of parental divorce? Researchers tell us children have trouble comprehending divorce. Their explanations of divorce and family conflict tend to reflect the same kind of unsophisticated reasoning they use in dealing with physical problems. Adolescents tend to be more able to grasp parental divorce as an idea. Both groups, however, are likely to have trouble dealing emotionally with family break up. The box on page 161 presents some young children's views of divorce and family conflict. How might an adolescent present these issues and experiences? The box on page 161 presents two mature adolescent views of parental divorce.

These views on divorce demonstrate that the children are wrestling with powerful emotions and traumatic experiences as best they can. Their reasoning is simplistic, however. Contrast them with the adolescent analyses. Reasoning in general and the social applications of reasoning constitute a very important part of social competence, and we can call these "social cognition."

Impression Formation

One area in which social applications of reasoning are vital to social competence is in the ability to form accurate impressions of other people encountered by the adolescent. We can separate impression formation into five categories of related processes—*differentiation, decentration, abstraction, inference,* and *organization* (Hill & Palmquist, 1978). In the case of the first, *differentiation*, research on children in late childhood and adolescence has found that with an increase in formal operational thought there is also an increase in the ability to differentiate among people on the basis of categories beyond sex and race. The number of attributes used to describe people increases most before puberty and during the transition to formal operational thought (Bigner, 1974; Peevers & Secord, 1973; Rosenbach, Crockett, & Wapner, 1973; Yarrow & Campbell, 1963). There is a similar increase in the ability to use increasingly complex and differentiated self-descriptions (Livesley & Bromly, 1973; Montemayor & Eisen, 1977; Mullener & Laird, 1971).

The second category, decentration, represents the ability of the early adolescent to understand that others can and do have different viewpoints. Several researchers have shown that decentration begins in middle childhood and continues in adolescence (Livesley & Bromley, 1973; Peevers & Secord, 1973; Wolman, 1967). Hill and Palmquist (1978) have noted that abstraction, the third process, is another impression formation skill that increases as the child moves into adolescence. Used in the social-cognitive sense, abstraction refers to the increasing ability to describe people in terms of motives, attitudes, and personality traits rather than in terms of appearance and other concrete characteristics. Several researchers have found such shifts in the pre- and early adolescent period

Children's Views of Divorce

My mother and father got divorced because our house wasn't big enough for both of them. They broke some dishes too. Also the checkbook was always empty.

Age 7

Divorce is sad. My Mom is sad about hers. I know because she looks sad when it's her birthday (and she's not even old). I am sad sometimes too, but I talk to my dog about it. He listens real good.

Age 8

My father left home. He said he needed space. Now we live in a smaller apartment and so does he.

Age 6

My mother and father still love each other. And they love me too. They say we will all be better off someday. I think I was just too bad for them.

Age 7

When I grow up I'm never going to get divorced. I think I'll just live with my sister.

Age 8

Adolescents' Views of Divorce

My parents had been having problems for a long time before they actually split up. They didn't fight with each other in front of us kids. But we knew something was wrong from the way they were so *extra* polite sometimes *or* they'd be totally silent to each other. I've tried to talk with them about it, but I still don't quite understand it. I think the big problem was that my dad wanted someone more exciting than my mom (he's living with a younger woman now), and she wanted someone who appreciated her more. But I'm not sure. I just wish they could have worked things out. Nobody is any happier now that they're divorced.

Age 16

My father and mother were fighting all the time. I couldn't wait to get out of the house to go to school, and I'd stay out as late as I could after school to avoid the whole mess. On weekends I'd visit friends. My father had a drinking problem and he and my mother would battle all the time about money. I was glad when they got divorced. Even though it makes everything more complicated (like money) at least it's quiet at home now.

Age 15

(Livesley & Bromley, 1973; Montemayor & Eisen, 1977; Peevers & Secord, 1973).

Inferences regarding the attribution of motives to real or fictitious people is the fourth process (Baldwin & Baldwin, 1970; Collins, Berndt, & Hess, 1974; Shultz, & Butkowsky, 1977). It refers to the ability to conduct a hypothetical assessment of why people do things without having direct evidence of their motives. It requires that the observer identify clues and make inferences. Clear-

My most vivid memory of adolescence perhaps is when I got stranded in the Greyhound Station in Baltimore, Maryland. Being from an all-white community and attending a Catholic high school, at the age of 17 I still really had not seen that all people were not like me. Between the bag ladies, the man who was clucking like a chicken and spitting up blood on the floor in front of me, and the pimp (who was wearing a bright orange, velvet suit) who tried to recruit me to "work" for him, I was very shocked to see reality is not very pretty or sugar coated.

ly it depends upon having experiences and concepts to draw upon that become more available with the transition to adolescence. The more an individual has seen and done, the more that individual has to go on in making inferences about why others do or say what they do and say.

Organization of both negative and positive impressions into a larger picture of the whole person (Livesley & Bromley, 1973) is the fifth process of impression formation. It involves the ability to form a coherent and consistent concept of another person based upon the available data. As we will see in Chapter 7, this applies to oneself as one seeks to formulate a self-concept and eventually a personal identity.

Clearly the research on impression formation documents a link between cognitive development and the socially-relevant ability to make judgments about people on the basis of abstract qualities. This desirable increase in social cognition aids in adaptation and seems to be related to the onset of formal operations.

Role-Taking Abilities

In Chapter 2 we noted that role-taking, perspective-taking, and overall interpersonal relations comprise one aspect of social competence. Selman and colleagues (1974, 1971, 1976a, 1976b, 1977) believe that pre- and early adolescents develop increasing ability to think about the thoughts of other people and to eventually consider the society's point of view as a whole. Selman has postulated a model of development of social perspective-taking that considers this ability as a hierarchy of stages through which the individual passes enroute to a fully mature ability to consider the needs of the greater good, of the society's perspective.

Even if we accept the premise that social cognition does increase in adolescence, this does not necessarily mean that the individual with great perspective-taking skills has correspondingly great interpersonal skills. As Selman (1976b) found, preadolescent boys who were maladapted and had interpersonal difficulties as a whole had lower social cognitive reasoning abilities than normal preadolescents. However, some of the maladjusted boys performed *well* on the social cognitive measures and still did not exhibit interpersonal skills. Social reasoning skill thus seems to be a necessary component of social competence, but is not the only skill that is needed (i.e., it is not sufficient to ensure competent social behavior).

Research and theory on cognitive and social reasoning skills has spurred an interest in developing intervention programs designed to teach interpersonal problem-solving abilities, part of which involve perspective-taking and recognizing others' emotions. Most of the pioneering work in this area has been done with children in their early or middle school years (see e.g., Gesten, Flores de Apodaca, Rains, Weissberg, & Cowen, 1979; Weissberg, Gesten, Rapkin, Cowen, Davidson, Flores de Apodaca, & McKim, 1981; Spivack & Shure, 1974). Spivack, Platt, and Shure (1976), however, report that adolescents who are maladjusted are much more likely to be deficient in such social-cognitive skills as perspective-taking. In fact, Spivack and his colleagues (1976) concluded that:

> Perspective taking was found to be quite significantly related to adjustment among teenagers. Findings using similar though simpler tasks among latency-period children are less impressive. . . suggesting that even simple role-taking ability may make little direct contribution to the level of social adjustment in this age group, though it may perhaps contribute indirectly by enriching the quality of interpersonal cognitive problem-solving thinking. Being able to appreciate and integrate multiple perspectives may very well take on significance with age, to the point where in adolescence it functions in more intimate relationships to social adjustment. (p. 100)

Thus, we can see that perspective-taking skills have much relevance for actual interpersonal skills and eventual social competence in adolescence.

Reasoning about Issues of Social Interaction

In an attempt to bring what is known about cognitive development to bear on the understanding of everyday social behaviors of the adolescent, Elkind (1980) referred to Goffman's (1969) work concerning strategic interactions and Piaget's theory of cognitive development. Elkind's interesting and thoughtful account is not based on research but is taken from his own personal view of how an adolescent operates. In a sense, he presents his nonempirical understanding of various psychological principles such as formal operational thought and how they relate to human behavior.

"According to Goffman, strategic interactions are interpersonal encounters that have as their aim the acquisition, concealment, or revelation of information" (Elkind, 1980, p. 432). Thus, the card player who succeeds in bluffing other participants has engaged in a successful strategic interaction (Goffman, 1969). Elkind postulates that strategic interactions require a complex thinking process, i.e., formal operational thought. Because the adolescent can think about thinking, possibilities, and the thoughts of other people, interactions between the adolescent and others take on new forms. Of course, Elkind hypothesizes that the personal fable and the imaginary audience are central to strategic interactions in the sense that they perpetuate the enhancement of self-esteem on which the interactions are based. To illustrate the concept of strategic interactions, Elkind looked at a number of different behaviors such as phone calls, friendships, "cutting," dating, and forbidden acts.

Adolescents engage in strategic interactions with their telephone behavior. In order to enhance self-esteem and perceived popularity, the adolescent may talk on the phone for a long time, so that other callers will hear the busy signal and become awed at the popularity of the adolescent. Another telephone behavior of the adolescent is to remind the friend on the other end that another call is expected, so they should only speak for a brief period of time. The need for self-esteem also results in associations with friends who are attractive, wealthy, or who in some other ways have special qualities. Through the association the adolescent feels important. Through the strategic interaction of "having valuable friends," the adolescent communicates that feeling.

Elkind used the term "cutting" to describe strategic interactions in which the adolescent refuses to recognize another "friend" in a public place. This act of cutting or humiliating the friend impresses the adolescent's audience because it demonstrates power. Likewise, there is a decrease in the adolescent's self-esteem if cut. Young adults gain self-esteem through their occupations. For example, some occupations have higher prestige than others and cutting behavior can be extended to subordinates. This raises the social status of the individual doing the cutting. As the individual matures, friendships are not used so much for exploitative purposes as for satisfying relationships based on mutual interests and support. This is the true test of social competence.

Dating is another source of many strategic interactions in which the adolescent attempts to diminish the chances of being rejected by, for example, asking sly questions such as "Are you busy Saturday night?," which is less risky than saying "Would you like to go out with me Saturday night?" Such strategies are used throughout the dating process in order to attempt sexual encounters and to effectively call a close to the date, and we will refer to them again in Chapter 8 when we discuss adolescent sexuality and intimacy.

Elkind (1980) also refers to strategic interactions for forbidden acts. These acts include such illegal or forbidden behaviors as drinking, smoking, and skipping school. The adolescent thinks of many clever ways in which to engage in illicit acts and to reduce the chances of being caught. In successfully completing these behaviors, adolescents impress themselves as well as the audience for which they are performing.

Most of these strategic interactions are clearly evident during early adolescence. Elkind postulates that such strategies develop and change through three processes during later adolescence and adulthood. The first process refers

The most vivid memory of my adolescent years took place one summer when I had little to do and decided to get involved with this Bible study group at a nearby Methodist Church. At first I was a little reluctant because I thought that Bible studies weren't "cool" but since I was bored, I decided to go anyway.

When I arrived at the church, I remember stopping just outside the door and wondering what my friends would think when my mother told them that I was going to a Bible study. I suppose it was my concern about my self-image but since I had grown up with a knowledge of Jesus Christ and what he stood for, I soon discovered myself inside the church. When the kids were divided into small groups, I discovered that they looked pretty ordinary and not at all what I had imagined them to look like because after all, I thought normal young people just don't read the Bible during the summer if at all during the other seasons. However, I soon discovered that my thinking was all wrong and these kids who were in their early teens not only read the Bible but were so very deeply interested in living a Christian life. Now that seemed even more strange because my friends back home were only interested in girls and whether or not they could sneak a Playboy or Penthouse from their older brother's room and these guys talked intently about Jesus and how he had changed their lives. I remember this boy who was slightly older than the rest of us and who seemed to be the leader of our group. He had been in a halfway house because he had been caught smoking pot and sniffing airplane glue in the lavatory at the end of the day, and I had not seen him in a long time. Something drastic had changed with him and after one of the Bible studies, I discovered that he had tried to kill himself but when his attempt had failed, he had been placed in a mental institution for treatment. It had been at that mental institution that a pastor had talked to him about the Lord and how the Lord gave abundant life to those who followed him.

After I heard him talk like he had to me, I went home and really had a fun time mocking what he had said to my friends while deep down what Matt had said to me had touched me deeply. I played hooky from the Bible study for the next two days and I had planned to drop out of it because it was wearing away at my nerves. However, this boy came and told me that Jesus loved me and that my pride was standing in the way of a wonderful life. It was then that I discovered that the life I had led was all a clever deception and that what I thought was cool was really not.

to the mechanical way in which older individuals engage in strategic interactions *(automatization)*. Through repeated practice, strategic interactions become automatic and no longer occupy such a prominent place in the individual's thinking. Many of the forbidden acts become legal as the community grants adult status *(legalization)*. Other acts such as prostitution, drug use, or gambling are still illegal and require further development of strategic interaction skills. The developing elaborateness of strategic interactions in later adolescence and adulthood is called *transformation*.

Reasoning about Moral Issues

As we can see from the social applications mentioned so far, cognitive development and reasoning are linked to the development of social competence (Ford, 1982). One aspect of social competence that has received extensive attention is thinking about moral issues. One of the major theorists in the field of moral development is Lawrence Kohlberg, who expanded Piaget's cognitively-oriented conception of moral development into a six-stage theory with broader social foundations.

The theories of Piaget and Kohlberg focus on the way individuals negotiate their way through life by moving in and out of equilibrium. These systems orientations are called *cognitive-disequilibrium* theories for that reason. In an earlier part of this chapter we noted that Piaget's theory of cognitive development assumes that individuals seek a state of equilibrium with their environment: children, adolescents, and adults strive to adapt to other people and things around them. When the individual feels tension because assimilation cannot handle new input, the result is disequilibrium and accommodation takes place. The individual attempts to reduce disequilibrium by a combination of changing the environment and changing the self, and in the process can advance into a higher level of cognitive development. The new more elaborate and differentiated schemes represent developmental progress.

In addition to being cognitive-disequilibrium theories, Kohlberg's and Piaget's conceptions assume that the development of moral standards and values occurs in an unvarying sequence of stages that have distinct characteristics. Each stage builds upon the previous stage through reintegration and reorganization of moral perspectives (Hoffman, 1980).

Similarly, the individual can feel tension when in contact with other people who have slightly higher levels of moral reasoning. The need to fit with one's environment causes the individual to accept and attain a higher level of moral judgment. Thus, exposure to more advanced stages leads to advanced moral reasoning processes, although systematic "backsliding" in response to lower-order thinking is unlikely, except in isolated circumstances such as a threat to life and limb (Hoffman, 1980). An adolescent who has figured out how to do the "which liquid makes the colors" problem described earlier is unlikely to revert back to random, superstitious trail-and-error thinking. The same is true of moral reasoning.

Piaget's Theory

Through observation, study, and questioning of children playing the game of marbles with all of its many rules, Piaget (1932) developed a theory of moral development that was broken into two stages. The first stage is called the stage of *moral realism* (or *heteronomous morality*). During the period of moral realism, which is predominant from early childhood until late childhood or early adolescence, the child views actions as either right or wrong according to the standards set by law. Therefore, if an action is illegal, then no matter what the intentions or circumstances, the action is wrong. An action that is not punishable by law, on the other hand, cannot be wrong. Piaget and Inhelder (1969) view the stage of moral realism as objective because as far as the child is concerned issues of right and wrong are resolved without consideration of intent or feeling. Rather, the belief that morally wrong actions will always be punished by an external force prevails *(imminent justice)*. The world is thus composed of "Good Guys" and "Bad Guys." Young children watching the news frequently want to know, "Which ones are the Bad Guys?" when they see stories about military action and are puzzled by civil wars in which it's hard to tell the Good Guys from the Bad Guys. Adults and adolescents are *more likely* to appreciate the ambiguities, complexities, and subtleties involved.

As children develop cognitively, become less intellectually egocentric, and have a greater range of experiences, they begin to develop a greater appreciation of how complex feelings, motives, right, and wrong really are. This growth sets the stage for Piaget's second period of moral development, *autonomous reality*. Now the child views actions as distinct from the law and its consequences (punishable or not) and is able to judge actions in their own right, with respect to the intentions involved and the consequences for other people. Subjectivity (but as empathy rather than egocentrism) rather than objectivity dominates the child's moral reasoning in this second stage.

Kohlberg's Theory

Kohlberg (1958) based his theory of moral development on Piaget's ideas, and studied the reasoning of children and adolescents (initially only males) to determine with more specificity how moral reasoning changes when confronted with moral dilemmas whether they be tough ethical issues, difficult choices, or philosophically ambiguous situations. He presented his subjects with several moral dilemmas and assessed the reasons these individuals gave for their choice of the "right" way to deal with the dilemma. The particular solution was not important; the reasoning involved in arriving at the solution was Kohlberg's interest. The following paragraph describes the most commonly cited of those dilemmas that Kohlberg used.

A woman was near death from cancer. One drug might save her, a form of radium that a druggist in the same town had recently discovered. The druggist was charging $2,000, ten times what the drug cost him to make. The sick woman's husband, Heinz, went to everyone he knew to borrow the money, but he could only get together about half of what it cost. He told the druggist that his wife was dying and asked him to sell it cheaper or let him pay later. But the druggist said 'no.' The husband got desperate and broke into the man's store to steal the drug for his wife. Should the husband have done that? Why?

Kohlberg's six stages of moral reasoning were derived from his examination of the subjects' responses to several hypothetical moral dilemmas such as these. There are three general levels of moral reasoning in Kohlberg's approach, preconventional, conventional, and postconventional, and two stages within each level.

What I witnessed between two of my best friends, Molly and Betsy, taught me much about relationships. Molly was going steady with Bill and had been for two years. (They were actually listed in the yearbook together as "Mr. and Mrs. _____ High School").

Molly began to suspect Bill of seeing someone else, secretly, for several months. I had just received my driver's license and can remember driving Molly around to try and catch Bill with the other girl. You can imagine our shock when we discovered that the other girl was Betsy.

It was awful to witness the withering of their friendship after that. Molly did not tell Betsy that she knew right away but instead, pretended to continue confiding in her about this "other girl" to see how Betsy would handle it. The hurtful game-playing on Molly's end was cold and calculated, like a cat playing with a mouse before doing away with it. I walked to school with Betsy every day but I was sworn to secrecy. She looked so unhappy much of the time.

When Molly accumulated enough lies and evidence, the whole school heard about it. It's strange because although Betsy was objectively "in the wrong," I felt most sorry for her. She told me how Bill had pushed for the relationship and of how powerless she felt in her feelings for him. However, the guilt was unbearable and she broke it off soon after it had started. It was terrible to hear her describe how the guilt didn't stop but just got worse, especially with Molly's questions. Betsy was afraid and ashamed to disclose her lack of loyalty to Molly.

It was very sad. Betsy was always popular, social, and active. But no one saw much of her after the news got out. The whole situation caused me to struggle for the first time with the moral issue of fairness in treating others. Does disloyal behavior mean that someone is a bad person? Should the principle of loyalty in friendship be a yardstick to measure someone's worth?

Preconventional Moral Reasoning

The first two stages of Kohlberg's theory fall under the preconventional category of moral reasoning. Basically, the child's moral standards are based on the child's wish to avoid punishment and to gain rewards, to conform to the *rules* of society. Thus, the individual avoids the action that is punishable and tries to perform acts that bring rewards.

Stage 1: punishment-obedience orientation.   During this stage of moral reasoning, which is very similar to Piaget's stage of moral realism, behaviors that are punishable by an external authority are wrong. Actions that are obedient to the demands and laws of external authority are judged to be right.

Stage 2: instrumental hedonism and concrete reciprocity.   In this stage of moral reasoning, actions that satisfy one's needs and that therefore are personally rewarding are considered to be right. Furthermore, reciprocity is present only in the sense that one who receives a reward or favor for a particular action will repay that reward or favor at a later date.

Conventional Moral Reasoning

The two stages under this level of reasoning reflect the individual's desire to conform to the *roles* that society dictates. Actions are judged to be wrong when they transgress the established boundaries.

Stage 3: good boy/good girl orientation.   In this stage, one conforms to rules in order to avoid the dislike or disapproval of significant others. Thus, actions are wrong when they result in censure by parents, peers, teachers, and so on. Actions are right if they are approved by these significant others.

Stage 4: authority maintaining orientation.   Actions are right if they maintain the social order as prescribed by superior authorities. One gains respect by "doing one's duty" and being a good, law-abiding citizen. The aim is to avoid the guilt and shame that results from criticism by legitimate authorities.

Postconventional Moral Reasoning

Under this level, the individual is able to see that laws are relative and flexible. Rules of society are not always based on inherent rightness or wrongness, but are established subjectively. Thus, some rules may, in fact, conflict with the needs and rights of certain members of the society and the individual recognizes this conflict. The individual seeks to conform to what reason says are the *rights* involved in a given situation.

Stage 5: social-contract orientation.   In this stage, actions that are right are held up as those actions that have been examined and evaluated by the whole society as the right actions. General standards of behavior are set up, but the individual in this stage of moral reasoning understands that these standards may change if change is needed. That is, the standards are not necessarily right in and of themselves. Personal opinions and values about standards are acceptable.

Stage 6: universal principle orientation.   This highest stage of moral reasoning reflects the individual's belief in universal principles with respect to the value of, equality of, and respect for human rights. The individual in this stage does not conform to *rules* or *roles* for any reason other than that the rules and roles represent abstract and ethical principles that should be followed in order to respect the *rights* of human beings. The person forms moral standards on universal principles of virtue and justice that transcend rules developed by the peer group, the community, and even the nation.

The levels and stages of Kohlberg's theory of moral development and their correspondence to illustrative behaviors and values for human life are shown in Table 4.1. It is easy to see that with the higher stages there is an increase in the abstract nature of moral reasoning and standards. This abstraction coincides with the development of formal operational thought in the adolescent and is thus subject to the limitations imposed by cognitive development. For example, the adolescent who does not attain formal, abstract thought cannot attain postconventional moral reasoning. As we saw earlier, only a minority of adolescents appear to attain formal operations. Consequently, postconventional reasoning is by no means the dominant form of moral reasoning among adolescents. The two are linked together.

Several studies have found that individuals who have attained principled moral reasoning have also attained the higher thought processes typical of formal operational thought. For example, Tomlinson-Keasey and Keasey (1974) found that young school-age subjects just crossing over into formal operational thought, as well as college students who frequently use formal thought, had high levels of moral reasoning. Other studies have shown similar relationships between formal operational ability and postconventional reasoning (Faust & Arbuthnot, 1978; Langford & George, 1975).

Critique of Kohlberg's Theory

There has been much research conducted to assess the validity of Kohlberg's theory. Some of that research has found that Kohlberg's sequence of stages is not necessarily universal or invariant (Garbarino & Bronfenbrenner, 1976; Hoffman, 1980). Cross-cultural studies show that stages 5 and 6 may occur mainly in a modern democratically-oriented country such as the United States where the emphasis is on principles such as "liberty and justice for all" and "constitutionality." Several studies conducted in societies that have little political freedom or modern style social complexity have found very few subjects

TABLE 4.1
Kohlberg's moral development stages.

Stages	Illustrative Behavior
Preconventional	
1. Punishment–obedience orientation	Conforms to rules in order to avoid punishment.
2. Instrumental hedonism and concrete reciprocity	Conforms to rules in order to obtain rewards or to have favors returned.
Conventional	
3. Good boy–good girl orientation	Conforms to avoid disapproval or dislike by others.
4. Authority maintaining orientation	Conforms in order to avoid censure by legitimate authorities and resultant guilt.
Postconventional	
5. Social-contract orientation	Conforms to maintain the respect of the impartial spectator judging in terms of community welfare.
6. Universal principle orientation	Conforms to avoid self-condemnation.

SOURCE: From "Moral and Religious Education" by L. Kohlberg. In T. Sizer, ed. *Religion and Public Education* (Boston: Houghton Mifflin, 1967), p. 171. Copyright 1967 by Houghton Mifflin. Reprinted by permission.

beyond stage 4 (Edwards, 1975; Gorsuch & Barnes, 1973; Kohlberg & Kramer, 1969; White, 1975). It has been suggested that in industrialized nations, individuals pass through the first stages of Kohlberg's theory more rapidly than people in less industrialized countries (Edwards, 1975). Clearly the dynamics of moral reasoning are related to macro-, exo-, and microsystem variation.

While many studies have found that level of moral reasoning does advance with age (Davison, Robbins, & Swanson, 1978; Surber, 1977), they suggest that the progression does not proceed necessarily in stages (Hoffman, 1980; Lerner & Spanier, 1980). That is, characteristics of reasoning that are supposed to be peculiar to a particular stage have been shown to be present in other stages as well (Surber, 1977). It has also been observed that reasoning typical of a higher stage may be evident at one time and in some situations, but not be a characteristic response. Individuals may even revert to a "lower" form of reasoning (Kuhn, 1976). Thus, reversibility of reasoning *can* occur, a process that is contrary to Kohlberg's notions and more characteristic of the information-processing approach we noted earlier (and more in accord with common sense). Turiel (1974) offered an integrating analysis of "conflict and transition in adolescent moral development" that helps resolve this issue. As Turiel sees it, the transition from one stage to another involves a phase of conflict or disequilibrium during which existing ways of reasoning are reevaluated en route to a higher level.

Many of the studies investigating Kohlberg's theory have been criticized on methodological grounds. For example, a subject's response to a moral dilemma can be affected by the social desirability of the response or the subject's need and desire to appear morally right to outside observers (Tracy & Cross, 1973), thereby calling into question whether or not the subject actually uses that level of reasoning or is just telling the investigator what the subject thinks is a desirable approach. In addition, scoring for level of moral development is difficult (Kohlberg, 1975) and may be subject to cultural bias (Simpson, 1974). What is more, the dilemmas themselves are remote from typical adolescent experiences and controversial in ways that may impair the adolescent's ability to bring to bear their best judgment skills. They may be sidetracked by the strangeness of the content. All told, these objections suggest that some respondents may show only that they *can* reason at a higher level than they typically do, while other respondents may test out at a lower level than they characteristically employ in real moral decision-making.

Rest and his associates have attempted to overcome some of the methodological problems by devising a standardized, objectively scored test, the Defining Issues Test that also measures Kohlberg's stages (Rest, Cooper, Coder, Masanz, & Anderson, 1974; Rest, 1975, 1976). This scale is interesting because it is a recognition rather than a production test in that subjects choose from a variety of responses to moral dilemmas presented by the examiner. They do not have to produce spontaneously their own responses. For example, they might be given a choice among several responses to Heinz's dilemma as we posed it earlier. One might be to condemn Heinz for breaking the law. A second might be to justify Heinz because the druggist was acting immorally and thereby forfeited his rights. The point is that the respondent need only be able to discriminate among the options, not produce them. This method detects the *ability* to reason on a more advanced level than does Kohlberg's method (i.e., more people score in the more advanced categories), just as multiple choice tests produce more correct answers than do short answer tests of the same material since recognizing is easier than producing. Rest's (1975) longitudinal study supports Kohlberg's ideas of a developmental trend toward more advanced moral reasoning throughout late adolescence, however, and illustrates the usefulness of this new scoring procedure.

Kohlberg's Reformulation

In Chapter 5 the discussion will focus on the value of theories as a means for approaching and understanding the nature and course of development. Theories advance knowledge and, in the process, may themselves change. Perspectives are often revised because of new evidence that is contrary to the assumptions of a theory or because the scientist rethinks and reconceptualizes old ideas. Kohlberg's own theory has recently undergone a reformulation, a change which shows us how theories develop and progress.

Kohlberg (1976, 1978) reformulated his basic six stages into five stages that describe the development of moral reasoning and that show how the development of moral judgment parallels the development of the ability to put oneself in someone else's position *(social perspective-taking)*. In so doing, he looked at the work of Selman (1976a, 1976b, 1977) who presented a hierarchy of stages to describe the development of social perspective-taking. Kohlberg and Selman see this social-cognitive ability as related to the person's level of moral judgment. Thus, cognitive reasoning and social role-taking both influence the extent to which the individual moves on to higher-level moral reasoning processes.

Table 4.2 presents Kohlberg's new five stages and the kind of social perspective-taking that is characteristic of each stage. Perspective-taking relates to the process of impression formation we discussed earlier in this chapter. It is important because it determines how people see and understand others, how they interpret others' motivations and emotions, and how they see the roles of individuals in society (Kohlberg, 1976, 1978). Thus, the ability to take the perspectives of the other directly impinges upon one's view of moral rules, expectations, and conventions. It adds emotional information to the more "objective" character of moral judgment as reasoning. Having said that we ought to consider the important distinction between moral judgment and moral behavior.

Moral Judgment and Behavior

Before we address other issues in the area of moral development, it is important to clarify the distinction between moral judgment and moral action. It is easy to assume that the ability to engage in moral judgment and the willingness to perform moral behaviors are related and that one's reasoning about a moral issue *leads to* action that reflects that level of reasoning. Observation of others and our own experience tell us, however, that we do not always behave in ways that we think are right. Moral behavior is subject to the influence of our peers, our needs and motivations, and the influence of situational context. Consider, for example, Milgrim's (1961) study of the willingness of normal individuals to resist the orders of an authority figure (a doctor in a lab coat) to administer electrical shocks to a helpless victim who was failing a test of word association learning. Despite the fact that most participants judged their own

TABLE 4.2
Levels and stages in the revised version of Kohlberg's theory of moral-reasoning development.

Level 1: Preconventional

Stage 1. *Heteronomous morality.* "Egocentric point of view." The person doesn't consider the interests of others or recognize that they differ from the actor's; the person doesn't relate two points of view. Actions are considered physically rather than in terms of psychological interests of others. There is a confusion of authority's perspective with one's own.

Stage 2. *Individualism, instrumental purpose and exchange.* "Concrete individualistic perspective." The person is aware that everybody has interests to pursue and that these can conflict; right is relative (in the concrete individualistic sense).

Level 2: Conventional

Stage 3. *Mutual interpersonal expectations, relationships, and interpersonal conformity.* "Perspective of the individual in relationship with other individuals." The person is aware of shared feelings, agreements, and expectations—which take primacy over individual interests—and relates points of view through the concrete "golden rule," putting oneself "in the other guy's shoes." The person does not yet consider generalized system perspective.

Stage 4. *Social system and conscience.* "Differentiates societal point of view from interpersonal agreement or motives." At this stage, the person takes the point of view of the system that defines roles and rules and considers individual relations in terms of play in the system.

Level 3: Postconventional, or Principled

Stage 5. *Social contract or utility and individual rights.* "Prior-to-society perspective." The rational individual is aware of values and rights prior to social attachments and contracts. Such a person integrates perspectives by formal mechanisms of agreement, contract, objective impartiality, and due process; considers moral and legal points of view; and recognizes that they sometimes conflict and finds it difficult to integrate them.

SOURCE: From *Human Development: A Life-Span Perspective* by R. M. Lerner and D. F. Hultsch: (New York: McGraw-Hill, 1983), p. 261. Copyright 1983 by McGraw-Hill. Reprinted by permission.

behavior to be wrong they went ahead and followed orders. This lead the experiment to be called a test of the *Eichmann Effect*, after the World War II Nazi death camp commander who justified his behavior on the grounds that he was "just following orders." For a vivid depiction of a massive breakdown of morality, read Shirer's (1960) classic account of *The Rise and Fall of the Third Reich.*

There is some link between level of reasoning and quality of behavior, however. For example, researchers report that juvenile delinquents are more likely to have lower levels of moral reasoning than nondelinquents. Also, some research finds that individuals at the higher stages of moral reasoning are more altruistic and honest. There is little support, however, for the hypothesis that postconventional reasoners are more likely to resist pressure to conform (Blasi,

1980) or that there is a fixed powerful relation between moral reasoning and ethical behavior.

Ecological Differences and Moral Reasoning

We have already mentioned that there are cross-cultural differences in how far and how fast people move along the Kohlberg scheme of moral development stages. This suggests that ecological differences, particularly macrosystem differences, influence moral development. But what is the nature of those ecological differences that affect moral reasoning?

We know that *within* the North American culture there are differences in the stage that individuals of different backgrounds attain. There is evidence to suggest that attending college increases the likelihood of moving into the post-conventional level. For example Rest (1975) observed that in a group of high school graduates, those who knew they were going away to college did not differ significantly with respect to the stage of moral development from those who were pursuing other alternatives. Two years later, however, when the same subjects were retested, those subjects who had attended college were much more likely to be principled moral reasoners than those who did not attend college. Turiel (1974) also indicated that college students had more advanced levels of moral reasoning than noncollege youths. College populations are self-selected, however (they chose to be at college), and this may influence the results of such research.

Nonetheless, it appears that college is one microsystem conducive to higher moral reasoning processes. Lerner and Spanier (1980) suggested that the college environment exposes individuals to a wide variety of people, situations, attitudes, and values that in turn result in greater and more diverse perspective-taking skills on the part of the student. Such perspective-taking skills reflect a higher level of cognitive development and hence, the potential for higher levels of moral reasoning.

The microsystems of college and their impact on students through exposure to multiple experiences and individuals can be likened to a society that, in general, is characterized by multiple roles, ideas, and people. Such a macrosystem reinforces diversity and independent thought and hence principles moral reasoning. Indeed, Garbarino and Bronfenbrenner (1976) examined the possible effects of living in cultures that differ in their expectations, sanctions, and rewards for individuals with respect to deference for diversity. The *pluralistic* culture is the "setting in which social agents and entities represent somewhat different expectations, sanctions, and rewards for members of the society" (p. 75). A variety of roles and people with differing values is characteristic of the pluralistic culture. On the other hand, a *monolithic* setting refers to the setting in which one overriding set of goals or principles is in existence. Members of a monolithic culture agree that there is only one right way to live. The *ano-*

mic setting is a rather disorganized setting that has no integration of principles or goals. This culture is characterized by general chaos.

Garbarino and Bronfenbrenner concluded that it is the pluralistic society that facilitates higher levels of moral reasoning, first through the child's attachment to the parents, which results in motivation to internalize values, and second, through the child's interaction with diverse social agents that represent life according to different values, ideas, and perspectives. This social interaction directs and allows the child to be autonomous in judging different views and finally accepting a set of standards or ethics. Children in a monolithic setting, however, have no choice. They are forced to accept the single set of rules that exists. They cannot exercise autonomy, and therefore face more limited opportunities to develop higher levels of moral reasoning. The anomic society fails to encourage advanced levels of moral reasoning because the attachment that is necessary for internalization of others' values and standards may not form in the disrupted and disorganized society.

The family (microsystem), the relations between family, school, and neighborhood (mesosystem), and the larger work, civic, and political organizations (exosystems) can also be characterized as pluralistic or not (Garbarino & Bronfenbrenner, 1976). Thus, for example, the family that is democratic and that allows autonomy and negotiation while setting certain limits is more pluralistic than the authoritarian family in which rules that are set by the parents are inflexible and continually enforced. Some research has shown that children and adolescents in the former family setting are more responsible, autonomous, and competent, characteristics that seem to be associated with moral maturity (Baumrind, 1967, 1968, 1971), as we shall see in Chapter 6.

Alternative Approaches to Moral Development

Gilligan's View of Moral Reasoning

One of Kohlberg's students, Carol Gilligan, has developed an alternative approach to Kohlberg's stage theory. Gilligan was dissatisfied with Kohlberg's scheme because it seemed to represent the moral development of males better than it did the moral development of females (which is not surprising, since it was developed using male subjects). Kohlberg's stage theory fails to recognize that males and females may respond in a different manner when faced with moral dilemmas (Gilligan, 1982).

Kohlberg's scoring procedure often places females at a lower level of moral reasoning than males. Gilligan became dissatisfied with Kohlberg's approach while doing a study of *real* rather than *hypothetical* dilemmas. As she studied the moral reasoning of pregnant young women contemplating abortion, Gilligan saw a characteristic feminine focus on caring and interdependency in contrast to the masculine "voice of reason." Gilligan's (1982) conception of the two modes of moral reasoning does not assume a hierarchy of stages, however. Rather, she pays significant attention to both styles of reasoning as legitimate responses to moral issues. Kohlberg's stage theory obscures these differences in the development and style of reasoning.

Generally, according to Gilligan, females are more likely to approach a moral dilemma by considering not how the law conflicts with certain rights and needs (the logical male orientation) but how the resolution of the dilemma will affect relationships between or among individuals involved in the dilemma, or alternatively, how the dilemma could be averted through communication, help, and caring between the individuals. Kohlberg's theory does not have any system of measuring this important avenue of moral reasoning. Gilligan would rather see moral judgment assessed by examining the "two views that are complementary rather than sequential or opposed" (p. 208). Does a person hear and speak both voices? Instead of assuming a hierarchical sequence of stages, Gilligan would observe human moral development as a process of understanding relationships between people. Gilligan's approach derives in part from the recognition that males and females are socialized differently. Women are brought up to have a sense of caring and to consider the consequences of moral decisions for their social relationships. They fear separation and seek connection. Males, on the other hand, are raised to reason in an objective manner distinct from the "messy" details of emotion and particular relationships. They fear dependency. These modes of moral reasoning are probably quite distinct by the time individuals approach adolescence. Because Gilligan's approach is rather new, more empirical work must be done before we understand to what extent the sexes exhibit different modes of reasoning. One issue is the degree to which observed differences reflect gender differences rather than just the response of submissive individuals (in this case females) to dominant individuals (males). Anthropologists like Sarah Hrdy (1984) believe this is the real phenomenon being observed, not sex differences *per se*.

The most vivid memory of my adolescence started when I joined the Girl Scout troop in my area. Unfortunately, these memories are not the most happy memories. The beginning of my adolescence was an unhappy time for me.

Girl Scouts was a great opportunity for most girls. A chance to grow and be independent of Mom and Dad was what every girl should want except, of course, for me.

During my earlier childhood I became very attached to my parents and any time spent away from them was devastating to me. However, the very first time was a girl scout camping trip to the mountains for a weekend. Naturally, I was homesick. But the worst of it is the camp leaders had no sympathy for my feelings and treated me very unfairly.

When I returned home I was a very unhappy girl. My parents had many problems with me for quite a time. I would not eat or sleep. And I never left my mother's side. I was a mommy's girl for at least a year later, and it had a strong effect on my life both at school and at home.

I have outgrown those feelings and become an independent person now. But I will always have my memories of how a girl scout camping trip affected my adolescence.

One evening as I sat in my room reading, my brother came in and announced that he wanted me to shoot him.

"What?"

"Shoot me," he said as he sat on the other end of my bed.

The look on his face made me choke back the urge to say "bang-bang." He was totally serious.

"If they put me on one of those machines, I want you to shoot me and put me out of my misery," he blurted out.

"What machines? What are you talking about?"

He then told me about a movie he had seen about two brothers, one of which was being kept alive on respiratory machines. He explained that the one brother had asked his younger brother to shoot him in the head if he was put on a respirator. He didn't want to live that way. Tears started to roll from his eyes as he told me that he'd thought it out and that he thought he might die that way because of his Cystic Fibrosis. (A disease that plugs the lungs with a thick mucous. Average life-span: 16 years.)

My first reaction was anger. "What are you talking about?" I screamed. "What the hell kind of person do you think I am? I couldn't kill you! I won't do it!"

"You'd do it for a sick animal."

"I'm not so sure, and you're no animal, you're my brother. I want you to have every chance to live! I won't kill you, it's murder. They'd put me away!"

"I'll put it in my will," he said. "They won't prosecute. . ."

"Like hell!" I interrupted. "Just get out, leave me alone!"

"When the time comes, please, do it if you can," he pleaded as he left the room.

About twenty minutes later, I checked in his room, he lay on his bed, as I had, quietly sobbing. I said, "I don't think I could. I'm afraid."

"So am I."

We sat there crying and holding each other closely until we couldn't cry anymore. I kept thinking, "You couldn't, you won't."

The man in the movie did.

My most vivid memory of adolescence was the relationship I had with my boyfriend throughout the four years of high school. We went to school together since first grade and were always assigned seats next to each other because of the alphabetical proximity of our last names. I remember hoping in grade school that we would date when we became old enough to do so. We began pairing off in group activities after eighth grade and stayed together until college. Our relationship was both romantic and companionate. I spent a great deal of time with his family and was included in everything they did.

Ours was a very intimate friendship but I don't remember feeling enveloped or stifled. Independence issues were strong for both of us and we seemed to pursue our different interests and goals and maintain separate friendships without any threat to our relationship. Looking back, our relationship, in fact, provided a strong foundation of mutual respect, love, and security that probably contributed greatly to our development as separate individuals.

We never discussed marriage but our break-up was heartrending nonetheless. It was time to part for college. Although the break-up was a mutual decision, soon after I began seeing someone else. So the end was a bit stormy. We corresponded for a short while and then he met someone else. He married her and has begun a family.

That was ten years ago and although I don't think about him too frequently, I believe that I still feel the effects of that relationship today. I'm very glad for having experienced, in adolescence, a warm and loving intimacy.

Suffice it to say here that Gilligan's view has ramifications for many aspects of adolescent development. For example, in Chapter 7 we will consider how her view helps us see that males and females may seek personal identity in different ways. Males believe they need to become a well-defined individual *before* they can "risk" intimacy, while females seek self-definition *through* intimate relationships. As we shall see, each "strategy" has its costs and benefits, as the box on pages 180, 181 shows.

The Psychodynamic Approach

The psychodynamic approach to moral development draws heavily on Sigmund Freud's theory of development, a major topic in Chapter 5. In Freud's view, the adolescent's moral development comes from a need to channel strong sexual and aggressive impulses into safe expressions. By adolescence, a healthy individual has developed a conscience (a *superego*). In adolescence they examine and affirm the values taught to them by parents and lodged in the superego (Solnit, 1972), and they reformulate those values to deal with issues that had not been resolved at an earlier stage (Blos, 1976). Others, such as Erikson

Decisions, Decisions

The following excerpt from an article by journalist/essayist Ellen Goodman illustrates the distinction between the two kinds of reasoning described by Gilligan (1982).

They are going out to dinner.

He turns to her and asks, "Where do you want to eat?" From his point of view it is a simple matter for which there is a direct answer.

She hears him, holds his question in the air and looks it over. From her point of view it is the opening line of an exploration, the beginning of a process.

Slowly, she runs through her Rolodex of local options. One place was too crowded last time, another too expensive, a third she liked, but he thought too "veggie." Three or four possibilities finally present themselves before her mind for screening purposes. She responds to his question with her questions: "What about Chinese food? Are you in the mood for pizza? How did you like the fish place last time?"

"Tonight, I'll go anyplace you like." He repeats, "Where do you want to go?" There is an edge of impatience now lining his voice.

The woman senses something familiar about this dialogue. They have been here before. She begins to see a choreography to the way they make plans. She remembers now all the other performances, prompted by all the other questions: What time should we leave? Which movie do you want to see? Which color do you like?

As a rule, he thinks that she has trouble making up her mind. As a rule, she thinks that he is impatient. But this evening, she finally realizes how different their goals are, how differently their minds are working. He is always looking for a decision. She is always searching for a consensus.

What do you want for dinner? He is asking, literally, for the name of a restaurant. She, on the other hand, wants to find out what he feels like eating, what she feels like eating, what their first choices are, what their second choices are, whether there is a choice that will satisfy him, her, them.

His question is simple; hers is complex to the point of absurdity.

She thinks of the women in her family. To make a date with her mother, sister or aunt requires at least two, possibly three, phone

(1970), have contributed to the psychodynamic approach to moral development by postulating a need to form an identity during adolescence. Part of that identity is the acquisition of ideologies and moral values. Moral development thus helps consolidate identity formation (our topic in Chapter 7).

Criticism of the psychodynamic approach has focused on two issues: it does not specify the motive for moral behavior and standards and it lacks empirical support (Hoffman, 1980). Those inclined to favor the psychoanalytic (the best developed psychodynamic approach) approach respond that Freud calls. As a group, they can barely compose a menu for a family dinner without the services of a polling agency. They are famous for conference calls, often driving each other crazy in the need for agreement.

It happens even with her women friends. They are not, individually, uncertain. One makes editorial decisions about national policy with confidence; another makes plans for natural conservation with aplomb; a third makes a career of challenging conventional wisdom. But put before them the question— Your place or mine?—and they begin to waffle. "What do you want to do?" "I don't know, what do *you* want to do?"

The woman is, of course, exaggerating, but not by that much. There seems to be a problem, somewhat endemic to her sex, about this kind of decision making.

The way she figures it, women are, as a whole, more likely to consider relationships in making decisions. They think in context. A choice as simple as picking a restaurant is recast as a concern about pleasing everyone.

Like members of some Japanese quality circle, they prefer to spend the time reaching agreements rather than writing directives. At

worst, their pursuit of consensus ends in paralysis, or stifled differences.

Their men, on the other hand, often regard this process as interminable and chaotic. At worst, their pursuit of decisions ends in bossiness or submission.

Of course, there are other movements in this dance of indecision. An arabesque of martyrdom, a plie of self-sacrifice. Sometimes, under the guise of pleasing others, the women she knows waltz away from conflict and responsibility. If the movie is lousy, if it rains at the seaside, if the pizza is cold, it isn't their fault.

Her own motivations are, probably, one part thoughtful, one part self-protective, one part chicken.

The woman considers all of this. She has, as usual, gone too far. They are only talking about dinner, after all. One dinner. No one will arrest her for selfishness if she chooses the restaurant. In fact, the consensus is in: it's her turn to make the decision. (1982, The Boston Globe Newspaper Company/Washington Post Writers Group. Reprinted with permission.)

did say that avoiding guilt was the primary motive for engaging in moral behavior and that the special method of psychoanalysis does validate the model. In Chapter 5 we will return to these issues as we consider how one goes about proving and disproving theories.

Hoffman's Empathic Arousal Approach

Empathy is the ability to feel and appreciate the feelings of others, the ability to put yourself in the other person's shoes. Empathy may be crucial to morality because it both motivates the individual to behave in humane ways (because it stimulates an impulse to do unto others as you would have them do unto you) and because it improves the accuracy of one's judgments about the motives of others and the consequences of our own actions. It should come as no surprise, for example, that adults who abuse their children are likely to be deficient in empathy (Bolton, 1983). Hoffman (1980) bases his approach to moral development on the belief that there is a biological predisposition for people to be empathic and understanding (albeit in varying degrees from person to person). As Hoffman sees it, empathy has three components. The affective component reflects the *feeling* of empathy. The cognitive component reflects the developing child's increasing ability to *take other perspectives* and *recognize distress*. The motivational component involves *wanting* to do good for others, putting aside self concerns. This is altruism, a motive that is generated by empathic arousal. This approach to understanding moral development of the adolescent ties together the increasing cognitive ability of the adolescent and the predisposition to be empathic into a system of morality in which feelings and thoughts work hand in hand. It may be the unification of heart and mind that Gilligan seeks.

Socialization

Research on socialization takes into account the importance of parents and peers in the internalization of values and moral standards. We should note, however, that much of this research relies upon demonstrating *associations* between parental behavior and child behavior that are ambiguous as to cause and effect. That is, we often don't know if the parental behavior causes the child's behavior or if the child's behavior stimulated the parent's behavior, or if something else (such as a genetic predisposition) produced both. We will deal with family relations in Chapter 6 and peers in Chapter 10, but here we do need to examine how parents and peers shape moral development.

From the socialization perspective, the child internalizes values and standards in response to three types of discipline: *power assertion* (in which parents punish wrong or immoral behavior), *love withdrawal* (in which disapproval of behavior is expressed verbally and nonverbally, by showing less affection), and *induction* (in which parents explain reasons for engaging or not engaging in a particular behavior and the consequences of doing so). The use of induction results in guilt and a moral orientation that is independent of external sanctions. Power assertion is associated with fear of external authorities, while withdrawal of love is not consistently related to any particular moral orientation (Hoffman, 1977). Power assertion combined with induction is a particularly potent socialization strategy because it tends to produce both compliance and moral reasoning.

During adolescence, the influence of peers grows in importance. It seems that association with peers, especially with a large gang, may facilitate the breaking of moral standards. There is more of a diffusion of responsibility among a gang of peers, and at this time (particularly in early adolescence) the

A memory which comes to my mind during adolescence is when me and three of my girlfriends decided to have a Chinese fire drill. The problem was none of us knew what one was and we decided to do it during a film in science class. There were 12 that were supposed to do it, but only us four did it and we ended up only running around one lab table. As a result, we were sent to the office and each received one day of inhouse suspension. This consisted of sitting in a room all day, about the size of a bathroom, by ourself and doing work which was sent to us from our various teachers. We had all been terrified of what our parents were going to do to us, but each laughed when they heard of the reason and punishment.

home is not as strong a motivator of guilt as it was in preadolescence and childhood (Devereaux, 1970). However, not all peer groups are deviant, and some peer groups may even lead to *higher* moral reasoning levels as long as some of the group members already reason at higher stages and they articulate their views (Kohlberg, 1973). Thus, parents remain important role models and peers become more influential, and the characteristics of both have a lot to do with how the adolescent as a moral agent deals with the world.

Reasoning about Political Issues

We now turn to the topic of political reasoning, which we consider as partly a special topic within the more general matter of reasoning about reality and partly as a subissue within the broader topic of moral judgment, because it involves a combination of techniques and principles. Thinking about political issues depends upon the adolescent's cognitive functioning and moral reasoning as well as his or her position in society (and the very nature of that society). Consider the following case study of 1960s political activism.

In attempting to decipher what influenced the political activism of the 1960s, Kenneth Keniston (1969) turned to the relationships among moral development, behavior, and political protest. He attributed college protests to many cultural and historical changes that were occurring at the time. For example, the wider availability of higher education lengthened the period of time in which youths were exposed to different perspectives, values, and standards. As we noted earlier, college-educated youths tend towards higher levels of moral reasoning. Thus, the educational and social atmosphere facilitated a wide-ranging critique of society, of the macrosystem as well as its exosystems. The end result was a higher percentage of students attaining postconventional reasoning and participating in political protests aimed at effecting change (Chapter 13 will discuss this in greater detail).

Keniston (1969) reported data from a few studies that attempted to discern the relationship between participating in student protests and levels of moral reasoning according to Kohlberg's stages. College students were separated into two groups based on their political activities on campus (protestors and nonprotestors). One finding was that the protesters were significantly more likely to be postconventional reasoners than the nonprotestors. The majority of nonprotesters were conventional reasoners, a finding that shows moral reasoning plays an influential part in political reasoning and behavior. Political developments like this demand that we develop a clear picture of how adolescents come to reason about political phenomena.

Models of Political Socialization

Gallatin (1980) identified four perspectives from which researchers have viewed the development of political reasoning. Each model has a different focus for understanding political socialization and different methods for studying that process. One emphasizes the specific events that teach political values through example and by rewarding statements and actions supporting three values. The second is based upon the idea that differences in personality correspond to differences in political values. For example, individuals with an authoritarian personality are drawn to authoritarian politics. The third approach emphasizes the way conflicts and harmonies between generations within a family shape the younger generation's inclination to accept or reject the values of the older generation. The last approach focuses on the way changes in the quality of thinking (from concrete to formal operational) influence the individual's approach to political values and decision-making. In Chapter 5 we will see how these approaches to political socialization correspond to the major broad theories used to interpret and explain all of human development. Major theories offer an interpretation of specific phenomena that shows those specific phenomena to be part of a larger general picture.

Political values are taught, modelled and reinforced: the behavioral/social learning model. Proponents of this particular model see political views and attitudes (indeed all views, attitudes, and behavior) as being acquired through experience and learning in response to parents, peers, and schools. Some researchers suggest that most of the critical political socialization of the individual takes place *prior* to adolescence (Easton & Hess, 1961; Hess & Torney, 1967) whereas other researchers who are proponents of this model believe that late adolescence is an important period in which political opinions and attitudes form (Jennings & Niemi, 1968a, 1968b). But all these researchers argue that youth *learn* their politics rather than creating or discovering them.

The research of the behavioral group points to the adolescent's apparent lack of knowledge about politics. Langton and Jennings (1968), for example, disappointedly reported that most teenagers could not answer even the simplest questions about politics and government in the United States (e.g., what is the term a U.S. Senator serves?). Political *awareness* and *opinion* do appear to be present in young children between the ages of three and six (Schwartz, 1975), but the beliefs and attitudes of how the political system works appear to be copied from adults, often in a simplified or unrealistic form (Hess & Torney, 1967). Of course, adults too exhibit both meager knowledge and simplistic thinking when it comes to politics (as in sexual matters, as we will see in Chapter 8). In several informal surveys conducted in the 1970s randomly selected adults were asked to read and endorse the Bill of Rights. Many thought it was subversive and refused to sign, and very few recognized it for what it was. By the way, what is the term of a U.S. Senator or Canadian member of Parliament?

Political values meet an emotional need: the psychodynamic model.   Proponents of the psychodynamic model focus on the relationship between patterns of personality and political ideologies. Thus, as they see it, certain personalities are attracted to particular sets of political attitudes, beliefs, and values (Gallatin, 1980). The individual's emotional needs make some political value systems feel better than others. For example, Knutson (1972) claims that the individual who is self-actualized or who favors personal fulfillment and competence by developing one's capacities is more likely to respect democratic attitudes. The assumptions of democracy are similar to the self-actualized person's own philosophy: trust in others, willingness to change when necessary, openness, and creativity (Knutson, 1972). The major population of interest to researchers in this area has been adults, but the study of adolescent personalities and political orientation gained attention in the wake of 1960s political activism (Keniston, 1969; Renshon, 1974; Sigel, 1975).

Political values are a reaction to one's parents and the society they represent: the generational model.   Researchers who follow the generational model are interested in determining how political orientations are passed along from one generation to the next and how political reasoning differs from one generation to the next. Proponents of this model have traditionally regarded adolescence as the critical period for the acquisition of political beliefs because it is in adolescence that people either reject or accept their parent's way of living (Gallatin, 1980). Much of the concern with the so-called *generation gap* was fired by the influence of the generational school. We will return to the generation gap presently.

Political values evolve in response to cognitive development: the cognitive-developmental model.   Cognitive-developmental researchers have used Piaget's notions as the basis for understanding political socialization. They argue that political ideas follow the same path as all other ideas. They arise through assimilation and accommodation and become more sophisticated as the individual matures cognitively (Gallatin, 1980). Representative research from this area in-

cludes studies that compare trends in political reasoning and moral development and report that the two are very closely connected (Kohlberg & Gilligan,
1971; Kohlberg & Kramer, 1969). Keniston's (1969) effort to summarize the relationship between political activism and moral development is one example of
the cognitive-developmental school of thought because it traces moral and political motivations and development.

As we will see throughout our discussions of adolescence, the major theories all offer interpretations and each offers a particular focal point for research. In the present case, the behavioral/social learning model seems to have
little interest in the *content* of political values. Rather it focuses on the process
of transmitting those values. The psychoanalytic theory, in contrast, is very interested in content, but mainly because content is a clue to underlying personality. So the real interest is in political values as an expression of the state of
one's psyche, in the psychological *significance* of content. The generational
model seems most interested in *changes* in the content of political values. It focuses on why some youth accept the previous generation's political values
while other youth reject those values because they reject the people associated
with those values. Finally, the cognitive-developmental model rests upon the
principle that it is *how* people understand political values and the *implications*
of those values that is most important. All four theories have an interpretation
of the topic, but each has its own way of defining the key issues. We will return to this matter in Chapter 5. Here we turn to the generation gap as an illustration of how different theories define issues differently.

The Generation Gap and the Development of Ideology

Student activism in the 1960s led some researchers to hypothesize that there is
a large gap between the attitudes, ideas, and values of parents and their children. Some researchers have reported little correspondence between parent and
child political attitudes (Bengston, 1970; Bengston, Furlong, & Laufer, 1974;
Thomas, 1974), a finding that supports the possible existence of a generation
gap. Other researchers, however, have demonstrated the opposite. Some have
found that attitudes and beliefs about politics are surprisingly similar for parents and their children (Douvan & Adelson, 1966; Offer, 1969). In her review
of the research, Gallatin (1980) concluded that the generation gap has been
overstated and that the empirical evidence, overall, does not document its existence.

Lerner and his colleagues shed some light on the relationship between
parent and child attitudes and the generation gap (Lerner, 1975; Lerner &
Knapp, 1975; Lerner, Karson, Meisels, & Knapp, 1975). These researchers designed a questionnaire, The Contemporary Topics Questionnaire (CTQ), which
includes 36 statements on issues such as drugs, war, dress codes, sexual activities, and other contemporary topics. One such item to which the subject responds is: "Political power of the United States military establishment is reaching

a dangerous level." Subjects respond on a scale of 1 (strongly agree) to 7 (strongly disagree).

Lerner (Lerner & Knapp, 1975; Lerner et al., 1975) selected groups of adolescents and their parents to participate in the studies. Adolescents completed the questionnaire in order to give their own attitudes, and, in addition, completed the questionnaires as they *thought* their parents would. Parents also gave their own attitudes and perceptions of how their children would respond. Thus, there were measures of *actual* attitudes of the parents and children, as well as *perceptions* of attitudes of each group by the other group. The researchers found that the actual attitudes of parents and children were similar; they were generally on the same side of the issue. What differences did exist were usually in intensity of feeling about the issue. For example, parents might strongly agree with an issue while their children agreed only slightly. From the perspective of actual attitudes, then, there was not much of an indication of a generation gap.

Where the gap did exist was in perceived attitudes. Students overestimated the degree to which parents' actual attitudes differed from their own. Parents were perceived to be on the opposite side of an issue more often than they, in fact, were. Furthermore, parents *underestimated* the degree to which their children had different opinions. The attitudes of the children were perceived by the parents to be more similar to their attitudes than they, in fact, were. Thus, there was much more of a generation gap with respect to youth-perceived rather than actual attitudes (or parent-perceived). Lerner (1975) explained these differences by hypothesizing that adolescent egocentrism (Elkind, 1967) leads to the belief that youth's ideas are unique. Others have emphasized the idea that any generation gap that does exist tends to be selective rather than general, that is it exists on some issues (particularly issues of style) and not others (particularly basic orientations toward life). We will return to this in Chapters 6 and 10 when we discuss adolescents in relation to parents and peers.

In attempting to chart the course of political ideologies in adolescence, Adelson (1975) chose to examine how adolescents "conceive of and judge the fundamental workings of society, politics, and government" (p. 64). Summarizing findings from a number of different studies, Adelson concluded that the adolescent is not as idealistic or optimistic as is frequently believed. Indeed, adolescents may become cynical or pessimistic about the world once they come to understand its workings (and we will see in Chapter 9 that this is often what happens when adolescents work part-time in low-level jobs). The child and the preadolescent have more romantic and unrealistic imaginings than the adolescent, and the increasing realism in adolescence is associated with the increasing presence of advanced cognitive abilities.

Adelson linked the development of ideology in adolescence to five achievements that are usually attained by late adolescence: abstract thinking, a better sense of the past and future, a better sense of change, recognition that political decisions have both costs and benefits, and an advanced understanding of principles. Formal operational thought is thus related to political reasoning. Whereas the adolescent has a higher degree of political realism than the younger individual, Adelson noted that most adolescents are not deeply involved in political questioning nor do they as a group demonstrate sincere concern for knowing and understanding political processes. In addition, Adelson reported that North American adolescents' thinking with respect to politics emphasizes morality and political reasoning. That is, politics is seen as being inextricably related to moral issues, actions, and decisions. Other cultures are notably less inclined to portray politics as a subdomain of morality and define politics simply as the exercise of power on behalf of group interests.

Conclusion

Looking at cognitive and moral reasoning in adolescence from our ecological perspective, we see three important things. First, adolescents face a special opportunity to increase their individual resources by increasing their cognitive powers. Second, the support from the various systems of the human ecology plays an important role in shaping the nature and extent of cognitive development. Third, the use made of cognitive as opposed to affective abilities in social reasoning varies in important ways as a function of who one is in the larger scheme of things. This will become even more apparent in Chapters 7 and 8 as we discuss how adolescents develop a coherent sense of self and social identity and how they come to terms with sexuality. First, however, we turn our attention to theories of adolescence to help resolve the disequilibrium brought on by the heavy demands for assimilation and accommodation in this chapter's inductive introduction to theory. Chapter 5 offers a deductive analysis of what theories of human development are, how they work, and how they can help us understand adolescence.

Ecological Wrap-Up

Organism.   The development of reasoning is a vital aspect in the humanizing of the individual. But we must understand it in the context of other individual developments, most notably the development of an empathic, caring orientation. Recognizing this is Gilligan's contribution, as she shows us that humans speak with two voices.

Microsystem.   Family, school, and peers can influence the pace, course, and outcomes of cognitive development. The quality of the individual's environment can accelerate or retard the processes through which the adolescent attains formal operational thought. Microsystems are also important in providing some of the content for cognitive processing and in developing links between reasoning and behavior. They play a role in the development of intelligence as well.

Mesosystem.   For adolescents to make the greatest use of their emerging cognitive abilities, it helps to have a pluralistic social environment in which microsystems differ but do so in the context of a basic consensus concerning the "rules of the game." This implies harmonious but not dictatorial mesosystems, diversity within basic consensus.

Exosystem.   Community institutions play a role in the development of adolescent reasoning through the policies they adopt that either encourage or discourage discussion, debate, and critical thinking in adolescent microsystems such as schools. What is more, these community institutions set policy concerning the allocation of resources that can be critical for the intellectually exceptional and the unusually creative, either nurturing or squandering special talent on the one hand, and either providing remedial assistance to the intellectually retarded or allowing them to languish on the other. Adolescence is a crucial time in shaping the life course of exceptional individuals of all types.

Macrosystem.   Individual cognitive development takes place against the background of individual versus collectivist themes, and modern versus traditional ideology. These blueprints shape the direction and content of thought. They provide much of the content for reasoning about moral issues and stake out the rewards for intellectual development and creativity. Cross-cultural differences exist in the development of formal operational thought. The political system also provides an ideology that each adolescent must cope with: perhaps to simply assimilate it if it is consistent with other values; perhaps to accommodate to it if it differs from moral values but demands compliance; perhaps to seek to change it if morality demands and the realities of power permit it.

Preview

■ A theory has two parts: a *model* that provides an *idea* of how things work and a series of coordinating definitions that link the model to observations of the real world.

■ A paradigm is a broad framework for viewing the world, in which some theories seem to make more sense than others.

■ We evaluate the worth of theories by how efficiently they account for what we observe and want to understand.

■ Theories of adolescence are as old as philosophy itself, and certainly date back to the ancient Greeks.

■ Religious philosophies of adolescence were challenged and supplanted by the biologically-oriented Darwin and Hall in the nineteenth and twentieth centuries.

■ All the major psychological theories of the twentieth century—Freudian, behavioral, cognitive, anthropological—have something to say about adolescence.

■ Efforts continue to produce a theory that incorporates the diverse biological, physiological, cultural, and social influences that give meaning to adolescence.

5

Theories of Adolescence

*N*ow that we have examined physical maturation (Chapter 3) and cognitive development (Chapter 4), it should be clear that there are many ways to interpret the meaning of adolescence. How we understand adolescence depends upon what we take for granted, what we choose to study and what to ignore, what the current issues are in our time and place, and how we *feel* about adolescence (and adolescents). With an ecological perspective as our guide and two chapters worth of substance in mind, we now consider theories of adolescence. Theories are how people arrange all the questions, answers, and facts into a coherent, meaningful pattern. They are based on a set of fundamental principles and assumptions for the purpose of making predictions and interpreting events expressed as cause/effect statements.

In dealing with theories *after* covering the foundations of adolescent development in physical maturation and cognitive functioning, we have continued the inductive approach that we introduced in Chapter 1. We have offered examples of theories in action, and now will speak more generally about theories and more systematically about theories of adolescence. Had we adopted a deductive approach, we would have *started* with generalities about theories and then moved to specific examples. In this chapter, our goal is to present our ideas of what a theory is and how it works. We then use these ideas in presenting brief summaries of some major theories of adolescence. So armed, we will be ready to push on to the major issues and topics of adolescent development that remain before us: family relations, self-concept, sexuality, academic and vocational development, peers, psychological and social problems and intervention. The issues about theories and the theories themselves will run through all of these topics.

The ecological perspective we presented in Chapter 2 serves as a map on which to plot theories of adolescence. From the ecological perspective, each level (micro to macro) has its own allied scientific disciplines. Biologists look mainly at the organism, although they often look to many levels within the organism right down to the individual cell and its component parts. Psychologists examine the individual as he or she relates to the microsystem, although often they examine processes and mental structures within the individual. Sociologists emphasize the meso- and exosystems, although often they explore the inner workings of these systems as microsystems themselves. Anthropologists are most concerned with the macrosystem, although they do have something to say about all system levels. As we shall see, however, some theorists aspire to use their basic principles and assumptions to integrate all the levels, to present a comprehensive view of adolescent development.

An Introduction to Models and Theories

To understand how the concept of adolescence evolved, we first must consider how theories of development themselves arose historically. Inquiry into the phenomenon of adolescence could only emerge when adolescence itself was recognized as a unique, distinct stage in human development. For this reason, interpretations of adolescence have depended upon the prevailing views of development in general. Theories of development and conceptions of adolescence are therefore linked both intellectually and historically.

Defining a Theory of Development

We can think of a theory as having two fundamental parts: a *model* and a series of *coordinating definitions*. Some models are not the foundation for a theory, however. They stand alone as descriptions of a particular set of phenomena without aspiring to broader general explanation of reality. A model is a hypothetical representation of a particular phenomenon that for one reason or another cannot be observed directly. Through the use of a model, we can organize and make sense of complex events or circumstances. For example, Freud's model of personality (described later) defines three essential hypothetical constructs that he labels the id, ego, and superego, none of which we can observe directly. Furthermore, Freud's model describes the interactions and influences between each of these constructs so that it presents a coherent, functional portrait of the personality. A model is a kind of invisible picture. A good model simplifies and summarizes what appears to be an overwhelmingly complex system of individual characteristics. A good model does this for us, with the attendant risk of oversimplifying, of course. A good theory gives us a set of ideas about *why* the model works as it does.

The coordinating or operational definitions link the model to observable events and thus allow both the application of the model to real life situations (through explanations) and tests of the theory on the basis of empirical data (through predictions). One example of a coordinating definition might present intelligence (perhaps related in a model to creativity) as the score on a standardized IQ test. In another theory that relates habit, drive, and inhibition to the probability of performance, *drive strength* may be defined in a laboratory context as hours of food deprivation.

The goal of any theorist is to specify carefully many such definitions, spelling out relationships between the model and observable events in the most detailed but concise terms possible. Most precisely, a coordinating definition becomes a mathematical function relating two or more variables. Importantly, the more precise the definitions, the easier it is to test the adequacy of the model. Critics of Freud's psychoanalytic theory, for example, say the theory is of little value because of the inherent difficulties of testing the hypothesized influence of each of the three forces within the personality. Although Freud's theory tells us that personality is multiply determined, the relative contributions of each of these forces is not specified. Thus, a personality characteristic such as *dependency* could evolve along numerous pathways. This kind of observation limits the explanatory power, and therefore the usefulness of the underlying model. And it calls into question the theory's own validity.

Theories versus Paradigms

Growing out of scholarly traditions called "the philosophy of science" and "the sociology of knowledge," in recent decades, scientists in all areas have come to see that *what* they think (their theories) is influenced by *who* and *where* they are in time and space (Pepper, 1950; Marx, 1910). Being Caucasian or being Asian in a society dominated by racial status predicts that some theories may appear more attractive and even more self-evident than others, in the same manner that being wealthy in a society dominated by social class can have this effect. Thus, for example, Festinger's (1954) cognitive dissonance research showing that people tend to believe whatever will bring consistency between their perceptions and their behavior would predict that theories attributing racial differences in intelligence to genetic factors will be more persuasive and more easily adopted by those ethnic subgroups commanding superior social positions than by those in subordinate positions. There is a psychology and a sociology of knowledge at work in theory-building.

The psychological value of a theory is greater when a theory is adopted from a mentor early in the education process and used later as the foundation for a career. It is more difficult to accept new data that challenge a theory in life later than earlier. Thomas Kuhn (1976), a philosopher of science, called all these social and psychological considerations combined with the ideas they revolve around a *paradigm*.

We may conceive of a paradigm as a broad framework for viewing particular phenomena and for conducting research. It represents a perspective or world view that is common to many scientists (usually in a particular period and location) and that shapes the way they observe, interpret, and measure events. The growing shift towards a systems approach or ecological perspective that we identified in Chapter 2 represents a paradigm change. Why is it happening? One reason seems to be that many scholars have come to feel dissatisfied with theories that do not reflect the interconnectedness that we see all around us in the world.

Because it is a *perspective* and may, in fact, exert subtle as well as major influences on many different theories, a paradigm is considered more general and ultimately more inclusive than any single theory. It influences which groups of theories will seem plausible and worth pursuing and which will seem ridiculous. Thus, for example, theories that rely upon spiritual forces (e.g., devils cause mental illness) are dismissed as ludicrous by those who are part of the scientific paradigm. In the sense that it influences how, why, and for what content area a theory is constructed, we may consider a paradigm a part of the ecological context for theory development. An example of a particular paradigm and its impact on theory development will help to illustrate this point.

In the period following World War I, psychologists "knew" that IQ was fixed at birth. Thus, when Howard Skeels presented results of an experiment showing that social intervention had raised the IQ of a group of institutionalized infants from subnormal to normal levels, his findings were dismissed by the psychological establishment as absurd. Years later, when the paradigm concerning intellectual development had shifted to permit the idea of changing IQ through social intervention, Skeels was finally recognized as an insightful psychologist (Bronfenbrenner, 1979).

It is inevitable that human beings formulate and adopt explanations consistent with the subjective viewpoints dominating a particular time and place. However, it is essential that we be sensitive to the existence and influence of these paradigms. If we combine this with efforts to avoid them or at least state them clearly, we will be more accurate in explaining and understanding ourselves and the world we live in. Although progress in generating information may proceed within a context dominated by an unyielding paradigm, truth may be neglected or even stifled.

Conceptual Issues in Developmental Theories

By surveying developmental theories through history we can identify several recurrent conceptual issues that theorists characteristically address. Their stands on these issues reflect their own paradigms. We can think of each position described below as a particular paradigm that has had an important impact on the theories that subscribe to it.

Issue #1: Nature versus nurture.   From the very earliest theories of development dating back to the philosophers of ancient Greece, developmentalists have been caught up in an intense, and, as some see it, often unproductive debate over which is the major influence on development, biological inheritance or environmental shaping. There have been those who claim that genetic inheritance predetermines a narrow range of potential developmental outcomes. Others, however, argue that humans are fundamentally malleable and that individual development is primarily a consequence of specific environmental circumstances.

An illustration of this controversy is provided by opposing reactions to the *sturm und drang* view of adolescence mentioned in Chapter 1. Some theorists hypothesize that adolescence is universally experienced by the individual as a period of storm and stress, a time when day-to-day living is fraught with internal and external conflict, disequilibrium, and uncertainty. It is important to note that developmental positions emphasizing terms such as "global," "universal," and "inevitable" almost invariably imply a biological or at least genetic basis for developmental processes. How else could we find such similarity across the diversity of human experiences? Thus, these theorists believe that inherent, biologically-based factors invest this period with conflict and turmoil.

In contrast to this view, other theorists hypothesize that the experience of adolescence is an environmentally determined circumstance. In their view, biological processes have very little to do with the experience of this period. Instead, the relative conflict or pleasure experienced by adolescents depends upon cultural values, cultural expectations, and the discrepancy between child and adult roles in a given society.

Cross-cultural studies that examine the consistency or discrepancy between findings for individuals of different social and cultural milieus are important in resolving this issue. Noticeable differences in development in various settings highlight the role of environment. When quite different settings produce similar outcomes, on the other hand, such results indicate an important role for heredity. An ecological perspective tries to integrate nature and nurture by emphasizing the interaction of the two forces, as we saw in Chapter 2.

Interaction here means that each factor affects the other, and we cannot predict the outcome with knowledge of only one. Nature interacts with nurture. Biological differences shape how particular environmental influences will affect an individual. For example, some individuals are better equipped to benefit from intellectually stimulating experiences. Likewise, environmental conditions may determine which genetic factors will have an effect. In one technologically unsophisticated hunting society nearsightedness may be a devastating disability, while in a technologically sophisticated society, it may be no more than an occasional inconvenience.

Issue #2: Critical periods versus compensation.   Proponents of the critical period view say there are certain developmental milestones that can be achieved *only* during specific chronological periods and that, if not accomplished at that time, *cannot* be achieved spontaneously at another point later in development. Alternatively, development may be viewed as a flexible, or *labile*, process of change. Theorists maintaining this position see compensatory processes as providing individuals with *repeated* opportunities to develop competencies or characteristics that were not acquired during earlier phases of development or to acquire alternate, compensatory abilities that help to offset the absence of previously available qualities. In the case of sexual identity, for example, it appears that individuals become committed to their gender in the first few years of life. Efforts to change gender identity fail later on.

A critical period linked to adolescence involves what Sigmund Freud saw as conflict between sexual impulses, on the one hand, and inhibitions arising from the conscience on the other. In Freud's view, the individual must resolve this conflict and strike a suitable balance during adolescence or face an adulthood filled with anxiety and disrupted psychological functioning. Development unhampered by subsequent neuroses or unchecked gratification of sexual and other impulses depends upon prior resolution of this conflict. It is the *only* way to achieve it, in his view.

In contrast, other theorists conceive of development as a series of situation-specific social learning experiences that build up, but do not necessarily change the character of the individual. From this perspective, characteristics of the individual (attitudes, expectations, understanding, skills, and so forth) do not depend upon the outcome of any single situation, event, or stage of development. Instead, specific deficits may be remedied by new learning. Similarly, skills that are absent in one setting (in the home, for example) may be fully functioning in another setting (in the peer group). Development is thus a patchwork quilt; each piece has its own origins and each piece can be modified or replaced.

Clarification of this issue requires researchers to intervene at some later point in development to remedy a particular deficiency or resolve a developmental impasse. The success of such efforts suggests the extent to which compensatory functions may operate. Most persuasive would be documenting the relative frequency of spontaneous resolutions occurring well after a conclusion of the hypothetical critical period. These are cases in which individuals went ahead and developed a characteristic later in life that they were supposed to have developed in an earlier critical period.

Issue #3: Continuity versus discontinuity.   Some theorists see development occurring in a gradual, incremental fashion towards greater complexity, organization, and integration. Such a conception sees adolescence as a relatively smooth series of biological, psychological, and social increments in development. It recognizes that these may or may not occur in synchrony with one another. In fact, from this perspective (with its emphasis on continuity of development across the entire lifespan), isolating a particular chronological sequence and labeling it adolescence is an arbitrary act that may be lacking in purpose or meaning. The alternative view sees discrete stages that are achieved and subsequently surpassed. Development, in this case, is an irregular and sporadic progression from one phase to the next (Brim & Kagan, 1965).

Intelligence: Fixed or Malleable?

The work of Howard Skeels represents one example of the kind of evidence necessary to test the notion of critical periods of development. Skeels' work had its origin, as is often the case, with a fascinating but accidental discovery resulting from simple observation and an inquiring mind. Briefly, Skeels observed a dramatic change in the behavior of two one-year-old female orphans who had been removed from their orphanage and placed in a home for the retarded. Despite previous clear indications that both were retarded, repeated testing after the transferral revealed the two girls to be functioning in the normal range, both behaviorally and intellectually.

In attempting to explain this surprising finding, Skeels noted specific environmental differences that may have had a major role in effecting the individual change. In particular, whereas the orphanage personnel could provide only the most basic and routinized care for their many charges, certain retarded patients were only too happy to "adopt" the only little girls on the ward and offer them individual attention and elaborated care.

To test the possible therapeutic effects of this transferral, Skeels arranged for ten other orphans (with an average age of 19 months) to be assigned to similar wards in the institution for the retarded. Of this group of 12 children, the mean intelligence score before transferral was 64—clearly within the retarded range of functioning. A comparison group of 12 chil-

dren remaining in the orphanage was later identified and their average IQ at 17 months documented. Although less than normal, the mean of 87 was still considerably higher than that of the experimental group. What were the results at follow-up?

> After an average of 19 months in the institution for the retarded, the mean IQ of the experimental group children was 92. By the age of six [at which time 11 had been adopted], their IQs averaged 96. Parallel testing of the contrast children showed IQs of 61 and 66. (Achenbach, 1982, p. 240)

These differences, noted when the children were about three years old, on the average, were maintained and even accentuated when other information (e.g., educational, occupational, income, and marital status) from a follow-up during adulthood were included in the analysis (Skeels, 1966). It is data such as these that provide arguments against the idea that particular aspects of development crystallize at particular ages, remaining resistant to later efforts at amelioration or improvement. Obviously, the sample chosen, the age of the subjects, the nature and breadth of the intervention, and especially the domain of development studied will all have bearing on the findings. Nevertheless, it is obvious that serious challenge may be offered even to very basic assumptions about development.

Some cognitive developmentalists base their approach upon a belief in a distinct sequence of stages that progress in orderly fashion. According to Piaget's theory, for example, adolescence marks the transition from concrete operations (engaging in logical operations on information that is concrete in content) to formal operations (engaging in abstract reasoning). This transition is abrupt and represents a discontinuity in the course of development. Identifying adolescence as a qualitatively distinct stage therefore has significance to the cognitive developmentalist; the developmentalist may then begin to infer specific characteristics about the reasoning processes of a given individual during the adolescent stage in contrast to him or herself in earlier or later stages.

When examining this issue empirically, it is often necessary to study individual differences rather than group functions. Although patterns of development may, in fact, occur in stages, these patterns may not be evident if group averages alone are examined. For this reason, individual developmental "curves" are plotted in order to determine whether children and youth attain related developmental competencies and milestones in a gradual, stepwise fashion or in a more rapid, all-or-none manner (see Figure 5.1).

Issue #4: Stability versus instability.   One final issue concerns the stability of individual differences in development. Is one's relative position constant? Or do some individuals speed up or slow down in their development compared to others? Another way to ask this question is to consider whether development is consistent and always travels in the same direction (*monotonic*) or whether (temporary) regressions are possible. Can individuals ranked relatively high in developmental maturity regress at some point so that they lose their high position compared to others? In summary, one may ask whether the rate of *individual differences* are stable and also whether *change* is stable.

Some psychoanalytic theorists propose that the second Oedipal complex during adolescence represents a temporary regression to an earlier developmental stage when sexual impulses and inhibitory forces were in conflict. Therefore it is possible for individuals who reach puberty ahead of others of their age to experience psychological regression that places them at a level of functioning that is now immature relative to their slower developing peers. Furthermore, the duration of the regression may be longer (or shorter) than that of others.

FIGURE 5.1

Often it is not meaningful to plot group averages when one is studying developing. The solid lines in this drawing represent individual growth curves (and demonstrate rapid change in physical status over time). Note how misleading the gradual and incremental plot of average growth is (the broken line).

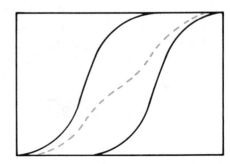

In contrast, psychosocial theorists postulate that adolescence represents a single dynamic sequence in a series of developmental tasks that must be confronted and resolved. At this particular life stage, individuals must struggle to attain a unique identity or they risk inconsistency and ultimately confusion among the many psychosocial roles made available by the family, the community, and the culture. Achieving such an identity is a relatively stable developmental advance. Once acquired, it is not lost, although elaboration and refinement are inevitable. On the other hand, conflict or irresolution during any one stage may interfere with the successful achievement of subsequent stages and one may lose ground in comparison with peers. The individual who struggles unsuccessfully to discover a meaningful personal identity may, for instance, become "morbidly preoccupied with what others think of him" (Muuss, 1975, p. 66) and, as a consequence, find great difficulty in establishing an intimate interpersonal relationship, the next developmental task (see Figure 5.2). He or she thus falls further and further behind his or her peer group with respect to psy-

FIGURE 5.2
The individual who struggles unsuccessfully to discover a meaningful personal identity may become "morbidly preoccupied with what others think of him" (Muuss, 1975, p. 66). (Courtesy of Erick Vondra.)

chosocial development. Change, according to this theory, is stable; individual differences are not.

Relating Theory to Research

Developing and refining theory is a mixture of hard work and exciting break-throughs of information and interpretation that captures the very essence of what is meant by the phrase *creative science*. Just as facts provide the foundation for ideas, so do ideas direct our efforts at fact-finding. The development of a theory depends equally upon creative and insightful conjectures and detailed, methodologically precise research. We introduced the concepts of deductive and inductive thinking before, in Chapter 1. As we said before, we switch back and forth from one to the other throughout this text, first building up ideas for examining specific events, then using general principles to pinpoint and illuminate specific incidents. Developmental theorists themselves follow this back and forth process (which is often called a *dialectical* process). Sigmund Freud is a good example.

Freud was using an inductive approach when he relied on clinical case studies (primarily of women during the Victorian era in Vienna, Austria) to suggest ideas about human development from which he developed his psychoanalytic theory. From his observations and interpretations of the psychological make-up of *these* individuals, Freud developed a theory of personality that he believed applied to *all* individuals. However, as Freud developed his set of concepts and models into comprehensive theory, he was ready to use that theory deductively to interpret and explain new cases and new phenomena that he encountered. We are trying to do this as well in our discussions.

Criteria for Evaluating Theories

Let us now turn our attention to the important task of evaluating theories. We must begin with an appreciation of the principle that theories can be neither proven nor disproven, but only assessed according to their scientific utility. As the great social psychologist Kurt Lewin put it: "There is nothing so practical as a good theory." For a theory to be valuable in the scientific community it must be able to assimilate existing data in a scheme that conveys both order and meaning (we use this wording to recall Piaget's model of how children form and evaluate their theories of the world). Discrepancies between what we know or understand and what a theory predicts do not disprove the *theory as a whole* any more than consistencies between data and theory prove it. Instead, the theory must accommodate to new data if that is possible. When the theory can no longer accommodate to the existing facts, it eventually must be discounted.

As a new theory emerges, it competes with the old and eventually displaces it if the old theory cannot withstand the challenge. Therefore, an essential factor in evaluating theories is *time*—time to test specific predictions, time to accumulate relevant data, time to compare theory with data, time for a new theory to prove its superiority in assimilating and accommodating to new data. There are, however, several specific evaluative guidelines that serve as general criteria in evaluating or comparing theories. These are parsimony, generality, explanatory value, testability, and heuristic value.

Parsimony.   A parsimonious theory accounts for a relatively large number of observations using a minimum of theoretical constructs. The criterion of parsimony tells us that the fewer elements a theory needs to explain the phenomenon (assuming it does so accurately), the better the theory is. This makes intuitive sense, since the goal of a theory is to organize and *simplify* what might otherwise appear as a large, diverse, and unrelated set of observations. Often a sign that a theory is not holding up well is that it needs a modification each time research produces a new finding.

Generality.   How far a theory has application to a broad range of phenomena defines its generality. The more it explains, the greater its generality. There is typically, however, a trade-off between the parsimony and the generality of a theory. It is so often true that the fewer the elements in a theory (parsimony), the fewer coordinating definitions connecting these elements to external events and, as a consequence, the more limited its application (generality). Theories seek to strike a balance between being specific (but not narrow) and being general (but not unwieldly).

Explanatory value.   This aspect of a theory refers to its capacity for explaining and predicting events. If all the data relating to the phenomenon under study are accounted for within the theory, that's a good sign. When relationships or events not currently assessed may be accurately predicted from the theory, that's even better, and the theory has high explanatory value. Explanatory value is distinguished from generality by its emphasis on accounting for the many circumstances and occurrences related within a *single* topic, rather than a distinct *series* of topics, all of which are addressed by the one theory.

Testability.   This is, perhaps, the most fundamental criterion for evaluating a theory. A testable theory stipulates coordinating definitions with clearly defined and concretely described (*operationalized*) terms. It allows us to state detailed hypotheses and then to test them in an unambiguous manner. These then serve as a measure of the accuracy of particular elements or relationships within the theory. It is impossible to determine the adequacy of the theory for explaining any phenomena at all if its coordinating definitions are so broad and vague that they preclude hypothesis-testing. When this is the case, even diametrically opposed results might be equally "explained" according to the theoretical model, because there is almost no limit to how one could empirically interpret its elements (through nonspecific coordinating definitions). This is an oft-cited problem with Freudian psychoanalytic theory.

An example of the dilemma posed by poorly specified coordinating definitions might clarify this point. In a model concerned with brain functioning, a particular reading disorder might be hypothetically linked with minimal brain damage to the left neural hemisphere. However, the organic dysfunction (the mechanical problem) termed *minimal brain damage* is not considered large enough to be detected by abnormal EEG patterns or by any *particular* pattern of behavior other than a reading disability (i.e., it lacks a carefully conceived operational definition). Therefore, a child who exhibits a reading disability and who also exhibits other clear but minor manifestations of dysfunction in the left hemisphere—including an abnormal EEG pattern—is labelled minimally brain damaged. Unfortunately, this is also the case of the child whose *only* symptom is the same difficulty in learning to read. How do we know that each reading problem represents the same disability or, in fact, any disability at all? We "know," because both are hypothesized to be the result of minimal damage to the left hemisphere. How do we know such damage exists? Because both exhibit a reading "disability." A circular definition of this type has little meaning and utility to both the researcher and practitioner alike. Unless we have clearer evidence that these two children share the same disability, our efforts to find common factors to understand the disability will be fruitless, and our efforts to help the children themselves misguided. Thus, it is clear that both theory evaluation and theory refinement depend upon carefully defined coordinating definitions and testable hypotheses that allow unambiguous feedback about the accuracy of theory elements.

Heuristic value.   The extent to which a given theory both unifies and organizes scattered or unrelated observations *and* generates a great deal of research and debate is an indication of its heuristic value. A dictionary definition states that something is of heuristic value that helps to discover or learn or guides or furthers investigation. A heuristic theory effectively organizes data so that scientists are better able to perceive and comprehend patterns implicit in that data. The more novel and insightful—and therefore revealing—a perspective offered by the theory, the more consideration, discussion, and debate it generates. This, in turn, stimulates more research, and eventually culminates in more knowledge (which may then be used to modify, refine, or even discard the theory). Thus, the greater heuristic value attached to a theory, the more effective its interpretation of the data and the greater its power for stimulating further knowledge and, ultimately, further understanding.

Let's keep these criteria in mind as we review some theories of human development with applications to adolescence.

Prescientific Theories

Prior to the invention and widespread use of scientific methods, the scholarly community relied upon the views and propositions of philosophers and theologians for an understanding of human development. Adolescence as a distinct developmental stage was almost absent in the theories developed in this early era in the history of developmental theory. More often, these theorists were concerned with the human life as a whole, and debate over the theoretical *nature* of humanity and the developmental process took center stage. Because these early theories do, nevertheless, play an important role in subsequent views of both development in general and in adolescence in particular, we will outline them here. When reviewing these prescientific theories, it is especially meaningful to trace the origins of later developmental stands and to recognize specific elements incorporated into more recent theories. Much of the current debate over nature and nurture, for example, is found in the old theories.

Greek Philosophy

The two primary figures of ancient Greece who contributed theories of human development were Plato and Aristotle. Their theories focus on the meaning and dynamics of mental development.

Plato (427–347 B.C.).   The philosophical treatises of Plato represent some of the earliest recorded inquiries into human development. The foundation for many of Plato's theories was a belief that every individual is the product of two distinct and independent entities: the body and the soul. As Plato saw it, the two might interact somewhat, and each contributed uniquely to the make-up of the individual. Of the two, however, the soul was clearly the more significant. Since the physical body was characterized by certain weaknesses (e.g., physical needs and susceptibilities), its tendency was to restrict the opportunity and ability of the soul to "perceive . . . and reach higher realities" (Muuss, 1975, p. 12). Understandably, it is on the soul that Plato focused his attention. This emphasis on the abstract (pure reason) over the concrete (body) seems to parallel the masculine/feminine distinctions drawn by Gilligan in Chapter 4's discussion of moral development and identifies Plato's conception as a very masculine one.

Plato's model of the soul described three layers arranged in order of increasing quality and value. The basest of layers and the lowest in the physical anatomy were the *desires and appetites*. These characteristics appear to be the very early precursors to the construct that Freud later termed the id. A more elevated property was the *spirit*, a collection of such praiseworthy qualities as courage, forbearance, endurance, and convictions, in addition to aggression and ferocity (Muuss, 1975). These two layers, common to all animals, were contained within the physical body. In contrast, the third layer, *reason*, was an immortal quality that represented what was divine in the universe. This was the layer that distinguished humans from animals and that, consequently, was the last to develop. Prior to the development of reason, Plato argued, perception was the dominant mode of cognitive functioning, a sequence echoed much later in Piaget's theory of cognitive development.

Aristotle (384–222 B.C.).   Although he rejected Plato's position on mind/body dualism, Aristotle elaborated on his predecessor's characterization of mental development (i.e., the development of the human soul). Aristotle also divided soul and body, inextricably united into three layers. According to Aristotle's model, these layers corresponded both in nature and in development to the natural biological order from the simpler plants to the more complex animals (the *phylogenetic order*) he perceived in the world around him. In his more clearly delineated stage theory, Aristotle conceived *Infancy* (0–7 years) as a period when plantlike functions (nourishment and reproduction) were dominant. During *Boyhood* (7–14 years—note the male bias that we will encounter again), dominant functions were more animallike in nature, consisting of sensory, perceptual, and locomotory functions. Aristotle believed that it was not until *Young Manhood* (14–21 years) that humanlike functions took precedence. This third layer was directly analogous to Plato's Reason and Piaget's formal operations.

Aristotle's conception of development provided a basis for the evolutionary stages of development that G. Stanley Hall proposed in his Recapitulation Theory over 2,000 years later (we mentioned this in Chapter 1 and will describe it again later). It is also interesting to note the possible origins of the present-day concept of adulthood beginning at the age of 21 years. One final note worth mentioning is the masculine orientation adopted both in Aristotle's and in Plato's models. To what extent does the 13-year-old female exhibit the characteristics of "boyhood" or the 15-year-old female those of "young manhood?" Developmental theory has had a masculine bias from the very start.

We should point out that both Plato and Aristotle emphasized the relatively greater importance of nature over nurture. The best the environment can do is provide fertile ground for the natural development of human characteristics. The worst it can do is retard that natural course of development. Looking to another one of our general issues concerning theory, Aristotle sees development as discontinuous and stagelike, while Plato outlines a developmental process that is more gradual and continuous in nature. However, they agree that a mental component (which they term the soul) is the primary element of the developmental process, although it is initially almost indistinguishable from lower life forms.

Christian Theories

The Greek view of human development was joined by Christian theories. Much earlier Christian thought reflected classical Greek ideas about the natural order of things. However, the Reformation injected new theoretical orientations (i.e., new paradigms) into efforts to understand human development. Perhaps the one that was most influential and innovative is represented by John Calvin.

Calvin (1509–1564).   A French theologian whose highly influential convictions were later reflected in the religious beliefs and practices of the Puritans, Calvin espoused a view of humanity and of development that represented a sharp break from the earlier and long-heralded Aristotelian philosophy. In conjunction with new developments in Christian theology that made their appearance in the Middle Ages, Calvin preached a philosophical doctrine that reversed the concept of man as a developing organism. While not dismissing physiological changes, Calvin and his followers minimized developmental processes by adopting the notion of *preformation.* They argued that the human mind and soul were entirely preformed before birth. Medieval diagrams of human sperm portray a miniature man, the *homunculus,* curled up within the head of the sperm (see Figure 5.3). Development was merely a process of physical maturation in which the preformed individual gradually achieved adult size.

In addition to this extreme view of development, Calvin was a proponent of the belief in innate original sin. The combination of these two views, preformation and innate sin, formed the basis for a model of human nature in which sinfulness and impurity of character were the natural state of the child. Hope for positive development resided in early intervention. This model supported stern and harsh childrearing practices aimed at converting unprincipled, corrupt, and resisting minds into socially and religiously responsible consciences. This attitude was so popular that nearly 100 years passed before the Greek developmental concepts were once again applied to mental functioning and physiological growth. Despite scientific repudiation, the Calvinist model remains explicitly strong among some groups in today's society; it is implicit in much of what is said and done about controlling adolescent behavior by those who define the task as combatting sin and impurity.

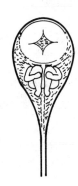

FIGURE 5.3
The homunculus, a miniature man curled up within the head of human sperm demonstrates the medieval conception of preformation. (Louis Breger, FROM IN-STINCT TO IDENTITY: The Development of Personality, © 1974, p. 4. Reprinted by permission of Prentice-Hall, Inc., Englewood Cliffs, N.J.)

Epigenesis/Empiricism

Locke (1632–1704). John Locke offered a developmental view that recalled the positive tone of the Greeks. It was during Locke's era, moreover, that the term *epigenesis* was coined to refer to the gradual unfolding process, the progression towards increasing complexity and organization that was more characteristic of Plato's than of Aristotle's model of development. Locke, however, described the human infant as a *tabula rasa*, a blank page upon which the events and conditions of the environment would write their developmental saga. In this respect, Locke differed both from Calvin and his doctrine of innate sin *and* from the Greek philosophers who believed in inborn natures that were more neutral in orientation. For instance, children were characterized by Aristotle as exhibiting "anger and wishing and desire" and the adolescent as being "changeable and fickle in their desires, which are violent while they last, but quickly over," and also, "owing to their love and honour they cannot bear being slighted, and are indignant if they imagine themselves being unfairly treated" (Muuss, 1975, pp. 17–18). Locke's model, in contrast, assigned an important role to the influence of environmental experiences in shaping the human character and qualifying the nature of its development. Locke claimed the adolescent is the sum total of previous experiences and is not predestined for bad behavior any more than good behavior unless the experiences of childhood point that way.

Rousseau (1712–1778). Just as Aristotle's model simultaneously represented an elaboration of and a divergence from his predecessor's views, so Rousseau's model both supplemented and challenged Locke's view. For the first time, development was viewed as an interaction between the forces of nature and nurture. The young child, inherently good from its earliest days, was soon subjected to the detrimental, corrupting impact of a poor education and a restrictive society. If preventive measures were not employed from the start, the child would swiftly degenerate into the misguided, ill-natured, and unnatural adult bred *en masse* by society. Note how this viewpoint significantly contradicts Calvin's doctrines. Rousseau's remedy was lenient, nondirective childrearing practices combined with efforts to keep children totally untutored and ignorant of formal learning until they had attained the age of 12 years, when reason emerged and education would find a receptive and unadulterated mind. Thus, Locke's environmental role was expanded in Rousseau's model but set within the context of a strong belief in an intrinsically good human nature.

Rousseau, like Aristotle before him, also adopted a stage model of development in preference to the incremental approach his predecessor hypothesized. In assuming such a position, Rousseau was once again confining the epigenetic process to discrete periods of development. Furthermore, the stages he postulated reflected in some measure the natural phylogenetic (species evolutionary) order, progressing from animallike infancy (0–5 years), when pleasure and pain are the predominant experiences, through a "savage stage" (5–12 years) (analogous to a primitive human evolutionary period), when the five senses dictated experience, to the advanced stages of development when uniquely human qualities were attributed to the maturing person.

Preadolescence (12–15 years) saw the emergence of reason, but also of self-consciousness, while self-esteem, the development of the conscience, and the social orientation necessary for productive membership in society evolved during adolescence (15–20 years). The adult years of life, again delineated by the marker age of approximately 21 years, were distinguished by the exercise of the newly operative will, the quest for self-determination (Muuss, 1975). Thus, the child's mind was once more characterized as qualitatively different from that of the adult. In Aristotle's model, sensory experiences progressed from childhood when mental images but not mental cognitions were accessible to the older youth's ability to reason. This presaged Rousseau's conception, just as Rousseau's set the stage for Piaget's cognitive theory (Gallatin, 1975).

It is significant to note that Rousseau, during the 18th century, encouraged a movement toward the use of empirical, observational methods for collecting the information on which to base theoretical projections. This, in itself, was an important contribution to developmental theorizing. However, it was not until the following century that scientific methods were applied to developmental theory, and this ushered in a new era of knowledge and understanding about human development. Table 5.1 summarizes the key themes in the theories presented by Plato, Aristotle, Calvin, Locke, and Rousseau.

Nature Theories

The publication of Darwin's text, *On the Origin of Species*, in 1859 heralded a swing of the pendulum back towards a developmental paradigm that emphasized the role of biological and genetic factors in predisposing the path and outcome of development. As we shall see, this set the stage for later efforts to draw out the best of the earlier prescientific theories and incorporate them into new more scientific approaches.

Darwin (1809–1882). The theory that Darwin proposed in his 1859 text described a cycle of biological change and adaptation of species (*phylogenetic change*) culminating in the formation of all modern species, including human beings (Homo Sapiens). This cycle involved random biological variations that would be passed on to later generations if they increased the survival rate. All beings are constantly threatened with extinction. Inheriting characteristics that enhance survival increases the likelihood that those same characteristics would continue to be expressed by surviving species (they would live to reproduce). In contrast, alternative, nonadaptive characteristics would die out with the ill-equipped individuals or species. "Survival of the fittest" became the catchphrase for interpreting Darwin's theory. Interestingly, Darwin could not discover his theoretical missing link, the *process* by which characteristics were

TABLE 5.1

Contrasting views of prescientific theorists.

		Course of Development	
Theorist	**Nature at Birth**	**Qualitative**	**Quantitative**
Plato	Neutral disposition (both innate virtues and faults)	Gradual change from "appetites" and "spirit" to reason	Development restricted to third "layer" of soul primarily
Aristotle	Neutral disposition (both innate virtues and faults)	Discrete changes from plantlike to animallike to human functioning	Three stages: "Infancy," "Boyhood," and "Young Manhood"
Calvin	Innate sin	Gradual physical growth without development (preformation)	No development
Locke	"Blank slate"	Gradual change that is dependent upon environmental forces	No discrete stages
Rousseau	Inherent virtue	Discrete changes from animallike to savage to "civilized" human functioning	Five stages: Infancy, childhood, preadolescence, adolescence, and adulthood

transmitted from generation to generation. Gregor Mendel accomplished that with his genetic theory of inheritance.

The implications of Darwin's theory and its impact on Western thinking have been enormous. It is, in fact, a prime example of a theory possessing great heuristic value. The notion that the human species had developed over a course of gradual, incremental evolutionary change (phylogenetic change) simultaneously affirmed the direction developmental theorists had been taking in the past and stimulated refinement of their models. Accordingly, the phylogenetic stages that Aristotle and Rousseau proposed for individual (ontogenetic) development (i.e., plantlike, animallike, and finally humanlike functioning) were expanded and explicated in the Recapitulation Theory that G. Stanley Hall proposed soon after.

Hall (1844–1924).   The approach that Hall took in his theory of development is an extension of concepts that had been evolving over a long period of history. However, the approach that he took in providing *evidence* for his theory was a turning point in the science of knowledge and how it is acquired (*developmental epistemology*) that cannot be overstated. For the first time, information related to development was surveyed in a systematic manner, and the study of developmental processes was undertaken according to the scientific method. Science and philosophy were united in the examination of human development.

Hall derived his theory from his interpretations and applications of Darwin's evolutionary theory, but indirectly from the conceptions of development that were a legacy of the early Greek philosophers, Aristotle in particular. His Recapitulation Theory had its immediate foundation in a series of experiments that Ernst Haeckel had conducted on embryonic development. Haekel compared the developing embryos of a number of mammalian (including human), reptilian, and amphibian species and discovered similarities during the earliest stages considerable enough to cause them to appear identical. This was a mistaken conclusion, however, and one that he erroneously interpreted according to Darwin's theory. Specifically, Haekel reported his findings as a confirmation of Darwin's theory, since individual embryonic development (the earliest stages of ontogeny) appeared to retrace phylogenetic evolutionary stages in a manner consistent with Darwin's ideas. The human embryo, in other words, seemed to pass through an evolutionary sequence of stages in which it took the form first of fish and amphibian embryos, followed by avian (birds), and finally mammalian embryos, before assuming distinctly human features. Haeckel's studies played a major role in popularizing Darwin's theory and suggested to Hall the validity of the recapitulation principle, which states that ontogeny (individual organismic development) recapitulates (repeats the steps of) phylogeny (the evolution of species). See Figure 5.4.

Hall applied this principle, in much the same way that Aristotle and Rousseau had, to stages of human social and cognitive development. Hall's ver-

Fish   Turtle   Chick   Hog   Rabbit   Human

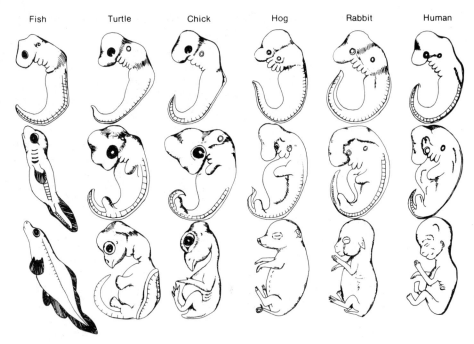

FIGURE 5.4
Ontogeny recapitulates phylogeny. It is easy from these diagrams of embryonic devel-
opment to see why Haeckel should conclude that ontogeny (individual—in this case,
human—development) retraces phylogenetic (species) evolutionary stages. The human
species, in Haeckel's thinking, evolved from "lower" life forms like the chicken and liz-
ard. (Reprinted by permission from HEREDITY, EVOLUTION, AND HUMANKIND by
A. M. Winchester. Copyright © 1976 by West Publishing Company. All rights re-
served.)

sion, however, identified four individual (*ontogenetic*) stages, differentiated on
the basis of hypothesized discontinuities in development. Hall believed these
stages reproduced in a condensed form the phylogenetic history of the human
species. The animal stage (0–4 years) was characterized by the primacy of four-
footed locomotion and by a reliance on sensory information. The years of middle childhood (4–8 years) represented the hunting and fishing "caveman" stage
of human phylogeny, when pleasure in outdoor motor activities (sports,
games, fighting) was paramount. A more advanced, but still primitive, epoch
was manifested during preadolescence (8–12 years), when the "humdrum life of
savagery" took precedence (for an illuminating look at this read William Golding's novel *Lord of the Flies*). Routinized activities and rote learning were particularly favored at this time. But it was during adolescence that the final transition from primitive to civilized humanity was reenacted. Indeed, this was the
period that Hall considered the most significant of all human development, and
it was to this period that he devoted the greatest portion of his attention.

From the age of 12 to 25 years, youth experienced a turbulent transition from the excesses due to "barbaric and bestial proclivities" to the civilized complexities of a "higher kingdom of man" (Hall, 1904). Extremes in temperament, attitudes, and behavior resulted from advances in cognitive, moral, and socioemotional functioning, combined with the awakening and temporary dominance of sexual impulses. Hall coined the phrase *sturm und drang* (storm and stress) to summarize the conflicts, uncertainties, and inconsistencies inherent in this kind of "second birth," when "the old unity and harmony with nature is broken up," but the "new sphere" or "higher kingdom" is not yet achieved (Hall, 1904). It was also described as:

> the most critical stage of life, because failure to mount it almost always means retrogression, degeneracy, or fall. One may be in all respects better or worse, but can never be the same . . . the consciousness of childhood is molted, and a new, larger, better consciousness must be developed, or increased exposure and vulnerability will bring deterioration. (p. 72)

Adolescence represented a critically important stage in development for another reason as well. Hall theorized that this was the period when nurture took over from nature as the dominant influence on development. Whereas evolutionary and genetic forces dictated the nature and sequence of earlier childhood stages, Hall believed it was the social, educational, and religious environment that determined the resolution of adolescent transitions. For the first time in the history of developmental theory, adolescence received prominence and recognition within a scientific framework for its unique and significant contribution to development, for standing at the watershed between nature and nurture.

Psychoanalytic Models

Sigmund Freud (1856–1939).   At about the time Hall was applying knowledge about evolutionary processes to development, Sigmund Freud was applying observational data on the psychology of clinical patients to the formation of personality. His background in physics led him to propose what has been described as a *hydraulic model* of personality (so-called because pressure on one part is transmitted to another, as happens in a car when pressure on the brake pedal is transmitted hydraulically to the brakes).

Freud conceived of a fundamental psychic energy that drove the human personality and dictated the attitudes, perceptions, and actions of the individual. This psychological energy, termed the *libido*, operated according to a *pleasure principle*. That is, it constantly demanded expression in the form of immediate gratification. The characterization of the libido as a force operating in accordance with the principles of physics determined the hydraulic quality of its activity. A concentration of such energy required expression—if not in one form, then in some other—in much the same way that a hydraulic steam engine operates. Its expression might be manifested in overt behavior or in the activity of the subconscious through fantasy or through psychological defense mechanisms (techniques for guarding the individual from harm because of the expression of powerful feelings). Sometimes, however, these feelings slip by the guards and surface, often through revealing misstatements that we all know as *Freudian slips*. See Figure 5.5.

Across the course of development, the libido becomes concentrated in particular portions of the anatomy (*erogenous zones*). Since this psychological movement occurred in a set and systematic way for all individuals, Freud offered labels for each of these five stages.

Initial concentration of the libido in the mouth of the infant and very young child defined the first, *oral stage* of personality development (0–2 years). Pleasure during this period is derived from stimulation of this area by eating, sucking, biting, and other movements of the mouth. During the *anal stage* (1½–3 years), pleasure is obtained by exercising control over elimination, either retaining or releasing body wastes. Libido is concentrated in the anal region during this phase, presumably in reaction to parental efforts in the context of toilet training.

During these two initial stages, only the first of three eventual personality structures is operating in full force. This is the id, which embraces and is embodied in the libido and acts solely to achieve gratification of psychosexual impulses. Not until the onset of the third period, the *phallic stage* (3–5½ years) does a personality structure develop in which the child's thoughts and actions are controlled through a regard for reality. This is the ego, which operates according to what is called the *reality principle* because it seeks to accomplish the id's goal through socially acceptable and appropriate means.

Libido becomes localized in the genitals during the phallic stage, and pleasure results from physical stimulation of this area. At this time, as Freud saw it, children develop a sexual desire for opposite sex parents. In boys, this is called the *Oedipal complex* (after the Greek myth about Oedipus who killed his father unknowingly and married his mother). In girls it is called the *Electra*

FIGURE 5.5
This cartoon illustrates one of the most commonly referred to Freudian concepts, the Freudian slip. (From SALLY FORTH by Greg Howard. © 1983 Field Enterprises, Inc. Courtesy of Field Newspaper Syndicate.)

complex (after another Greek myth with a similar plot). Conflicts between their incestuous desire and fear of parental retribution—either castration by the father (in boys) or possibly maternal disapproval (in girls)—are resolved in the formation of the superego, the final personality structure. There are two essential components of the superego, having distinct but related functions. The creation of the *ego-ideal,* the first component, symbolizes adoption of the same sex (rival) parent figure and his or her characteristics as the ideal role to strive for, prompting identification with this parent. The second component is the newly acquired conscience, dictating a set of morals and principles that may be unrealistic, though acquired by way of societal standards. We all know that some of the simple rules of morality learned at home may not be realistic.

We should point out that, as Freud sees it, difficulties in resolving any one of these stages (through, for example, excessive parental restrictiveness or indulgence), result in *fixation* at that particular developmental stage, and the origins (*etiology*) of later personality problems (*neuroses*). Thus, *anal compulsive* adults who require both the physical and socioemotional conditions of their lives to be arranged in strict, unvarying terms, presumably have had inordinate conflict during the anal stage (perhaps due to heavy demands on the part of parents for early toilet training).

Freud thought the final two stages, covering the period from middle childhood through adolescence, were substantially *less* significant in forming the adult personality than what came before. Instead, the critical period of life with regard to personality development is those first five crucial years (and three initial developmental stages). Nevertheless, events and influences occurring during the later phases were in fact hypothesized to make some contribution to adult functioning.

During the *latency stage* (5½–12 years), libidinal energy becomes diffused throughout the body and to some degree submerged (*latent*) in the system. For this reason, the period is one of relative easygoing stability, when libidinal energy is diverted into play and the acquisition of basic skills (e.g., reading, writing, and arithmetic). By the onset of the next phase, the *genital stage,* however, the libido emerges once again and, for the second time, focuses in the genital area. In this case, libidinal energy assumes a more mature expression, since the goal of reproduction now supplements the earlier simple pleasure-seeking orientation. On the condition that fixation has not occurred during some earlier stage, stable heterosexual relationships can form and the individual can enter a healthy, adjusted adulthood.

It is clear that Freud's theory provides a role for both genetic predisposition (an inherent pattern of libidinal movement, a genetically based and unalterable level of psychic energy, a universal stage progression, etc.) and for environmental influences (primarily childrearing practices, but also, for instance, experiences of childhood trauma). On the other hand, it gives much more emphasis to the role of the environment in shaping how successfully individuals master their personal biological agenda. In Freud's view, successful resolution of each psychosexual stage, and therefore, one's adult psychological status in terms of both personality and adjustment, is the outcome of these environmental forces. As a consequence, Lerner and Spanier (1980) refer to the psychoanalytic model and definitions as a "weak interactional" theory; both nature and nurture factors are incorporated, but their interaction is limited. In addition, Freud emphasized early childhood and downplayed the role of adolescence as a significant period of development. This became the task of Freud's daughter, Anna, who elaborated the psychoanalytic theory.

Anna Freud (1895–1982).   The extensions that Anna Freud made to her father's theory referred primarily to the late childhood and early adulthood years. In particular, she expanded upon the concept of a second awakening of libidinal urges during the pubertal period (i.e., genital stage) and its impact on the developing personality. In responding to biological and physiological (hormonal) changes at this time, she hypothesized that id impulses were, in fact, made more powerful than they had been during previous stages (e.g., anal or phallic). Consequently, the precarious equilibrium that had been established among id, ego, and superego during latency was entirely disrupted and psychological conflict was rampant. This adds significance to the period of adolescence as an influence on personality and resonates with Hall's view of storm and stress.

With the recurrence of these sexual impulses, Anna Freud postulated the experience of a second Oedipal complex. Incestuous desires for the opposite sex parent once again induced conflict and turmoil within the individual. This time, however, the existence of a conscience internalized the struggle. No longer was the fear of parental action paramount. Instead, the dread of violating personal morals instituted by the superego and the accompanying loss of self-esteem took primacy. Parents were rejected in favor of peers, youthful romances, and infatuations, not because of the parents' authority, their attitudes, or their ethos, but because of the mutual emotional attachment between parent and youth that prompted Oedipal conflict in the first place.

Anna Freud viewed the ability to resolve the rekindled conflict between id and superego as a function of the strength and flexibility of the ego. Mature responses on the part of the ego in restraining and coping with libidinal impulses were partially determined by the previous adaptations and outcomes of earlier stages. The individual's efforts to manage the tensions it feels as id and superego struggle for supremacy are called *defense mechanisms*. Employing a defense mechanism was a more competent response in her view than relying on other persons (e.g., turning to peers for emotional support). In addition, two new defense mechansims were added to the repertoire of the unconscious around the period of the genital stage: *intellectualization* and *asceticism*. The former entailed elaborate, abstract rationalizations for avoiding, denying, or in some manner justifying one's attitudes, actions, or emotions: "By casting his own internal struggle in the form of an abstract argument, the adolescent could

manage to gain some distance from it. Rather than having, say, to face his re-
newed feelings of hostility for his father, the youngster could content himself
with denouncing the 'tyranny of all authority'" (Gallatin, 1975, p. 71).

In reverting to the second defense mechanism of asceticism, the adolescent was exercising a policy of strict self-denial as a response to the new bar-
rage of impulses:

> Young people who pass through the kind of ascetic phase which I have in mind
> seem to fear the quantity rather than the quality of their instincts. They mistrust
> enjoyment in general and so their safest policy appears to be simply to counter
> more urgent desires with more stringent prohibitions. Every time, the instinct
> says, 'I will,' the ego retorts, 'Thou shall not,' much after the manner of strict par-
> ents in early training of their children. (A. Freud, 1936, p. 154)

Although both mechanisms were presumed available prior to puberty, their use
was particularly characteristic of adolescents in the genital stage.

In summarizing her additions to psychoanalytic theory, Anna Freud described two general threats to subsequent adjustment arising from genital stage
disharmony and disequilibrium. On one hand, adolescents might yield to the
influence of the libido and thereafter entertain meager, if any, efforts as adults
to put a rein on their impulses or inclinations. Alternatively, adolescents might
invest too heavily in defense mechanisms and imprison themselves in a lifelong
pattern of repression and self-denial. Regardless of this issue, Anna Freud was
thus affirming adolescence (for different reasons) as the critical period of storm
and stress that Hall had previously discerned. The same orientation was again
reflected in the writings of Erik Erikson, another theorist in the psychoanalytic
tradition, who postulated an identity *crisis* that was activated during the adolescent years.

Erik Erikson (1902–   ).   Erikson's work represents a divergence from the
psychosexual framework adhered to by both of the Freuds. While still maintaining the psychoanalytic perspective (the belief in the existence of instinctive,
psychic energy motivating human behavior and the role of the unconscious),
Erikson shifted the emphasis from psycho*sexual* to psycho*social* development.
His theory evolved in response to cross-cultural studies. These studies suggested that the specifics of the Freudian conception of development were not universally applicable. As Erikson saw it these studies did suggest the commonality of certain *general* developmental needs and experiences that were very
social in nature. Erikson thus pictured development within an expanded context—society and culture. He moved beyond the family to devise a series of developmental tasks that would represent individual development across all cultures.

As Erikson saw it, every individual, regardless of culture, requires a certain degree of encouragement, self-mastery, and social recognition for development of what he termed the *ego-identity*. By focusing on the *ego* rather than

the *id,* he was establishing his topic as psychological development from a *social* (externally-oriented) versus *sexual* (internally-oriented) perspective. Erikson thus retained Freud's concepts, but reorganized their structure, giving ego primary importance and a force of its own. In this, Erikson was joined by White (1959). Furthermore, Erikson emphasized the positive and normal themes rather than the negative and problematic, future adjustment rather than adult pathology.

Erikson also linked his theory of development to the epigenetic (gradually unfolding) principle described earlier. He interpreted this to mean that "anything that grows has a ground plan, and that out of this ground plan the parts arise, each part having its time of special ascendancy, until all parts have arisen to form a functional whole" (from Muuss, 1975, p. 55). He then outlined a series of developmental endeavors that formed the ground plan for psychosocial development. The psychosocial tasks roughly conformed to the chronology of Freudian psychosexual stages, but the individual was building upon the foundation of the previous stage, not simply moving on to the next challenge. The two sequences, Freudian and Eriksonian, are summarized and compared in Table 5.2. Each of Erikson's tasks has its "time of special ascendancy" and depends upon the outcome of the preceding tasks.

During the first stage (0–1½ years), infants depend upon capable parental handling, consistent interaction, and sensitive fulfillment of their needs in order to develop a sense of *trust* in the world around them, in the microsystem. Basic feelings of security evolve from experiences of the environment as a well-ordered, responsive, and reliable system of nourishment and care. Having established essential trust, infants become active in seeking out new experiences and relationships. Without basic trust, the growing child becomes less open to new experiences and less willing to explore and master new situations.

As childhood progresses, new psychosocial challenges confront the developing individual, and successfully achieving autonomy versus shame or doubt (1½–3 years), initiative versus guilt (3–5½ years), and industry versus inferiority (5½–12 years) propels the youngster to the threshold of adolescence. The

TABLE 5.2
Psychosexual and psychosocial stages of development.

Chronological Stages	Freudian Stages	Eriksonian Stages
Infancy	Oral	Basic Trust vs. mistrust
1½–3 years	Anal	Autonomy vs. shame, doubt
3–5½ years	Phallic	Initiative vs. guilt
5½–12 years	Latency	Industry vs. inferiority
Adolescence	Genital	Identity vs. role confusion
Young adulthood		Intimacy vs. isolation
Adulthood		Generativity vs. stagnation
Maturity/old age		Ego identity vs. despair

goal of this stage is to establish a personal identity, to formulate a concept of self that spans past, present, and future existence. Individuals must search for and seek out consistencies in their own personality, attitudes, and behaviors that endure across time, across place, and across social context. Learning how others perceive them suddenly assumes great importance as a pathway to self-definition. Erikson states that adolescents "are sometimes morbidly, often curiously, preoccupied with what they appear to be in the eyes of others as compared with what they feel they are" (Erikson, 1959, p. 89).

By affiliating with a peer group, young people of this age (beginning about age 12) are typically less challenged by the task of independently achieving their identity, since many of the details of appearance, behavior, interests, and ideals are dictated by group codes or standards. Heterosexual relationships in adolescence similarly contribute to self-awareness and self-concept by affording intimate feedback about personal attributes. A true commitment to such a relationship, however, requires fusion of two separate and already established identities. This fusion is deferred until the next psychosocial stage in young adulthood—at least for males in this very masculine conception of identity as the production of autonomous individuals.

Failure to relinquish the peer group and achieve an independent identity results in role confusion: the submersion of a single, integrated identity beneath the bewildering array of personal, family, social, and career roles offered by society. Role confusion prompts self-doubt, obsession with the opinions of others, or withdrawal from social interaction and disregard for social functioning. In the extreme, role confusion is implicated in the evolution of delinquency and psychopathology, as well as in the absence of consideration for others or even an awareness of social reality. Such a state of identity disorder could even provoke suicide attempts, since the adolescent often "would rather be nobody or somebody bad, or indeed dead . . . than be not quite somebody" (from Muuss, 1975, p. 67).

If on the other hand, youth successfully achieve identities for themselves, they are better prepared to encounter successive stages fostering either intimacy or isolation (young adulthood), generativity or stagnation (adulthood), and ego integrity or despair (maturity/old age). Adolescence, in Erikson's theory, assumes a more prominent position than that which was proposed in the original Freudian model. In a manner similar to the way Anna Freud expanded the role of adolescence in Sigmund Freud's theory, James Marcia elaborated on the adolescent identity quest first proposed in the Eriksonian model. We will deal with Marcia more fully in Chapter 7 when we examine the development of personal and social identity in adolescence. Here it is sufficient to say that Marcia's research convinced him that adolescents use different strategies for coping with this issue of identity and that these strategies vary along two dimensions: crisis and commitment. Being in the active process of examining and choosing between alternative roles constitutes crisis, and being personally invested in and committed to that choice constitutes commitment. Marcia devised a four-stage model and typology of the adolescent identity crisis that we will present in Chapter 7.

It is clear that Erikson and Marcia, as Freud and Hall before them, assign the primary causal role in setting the agenda for development to nature. As they see it, inherent factors in human functioning predetermine a sequence of universal stages and the issues and challenges that characterize each adolescent. Simultaneously, however, they postulate environment to be an important influence, the source of developmental fine-tuning. Thus, the final course of development was considered the outcome of a weak interaction between biogenetic and environmental forces, as it was for our next group of theorists, the cultural anthropologists.

Nurture Theories

Cultural Anthropological

As we have seen, the theories discussed so far all assume a greater role for nature over nurture in the developmental process. The views shared by cultural anthropologists Margaret Mead and Ruth Benedict offer an alternative. Both deal explicitly with the period of adolescence, and both are centered on the belief that nurture takes clear precedence over nature in specifying the adolescent experience. A discussion of their observations and conclusions serves to illustrate this alternative developmental position.

Mead (1901–1981).   Although certain of the theories predating or concurrent with Mead's findings (especially Erikson's) took anthropological data into account, most proposed a developmental sequence or pattern based on limited observations from a single cultural tradition (contemporary Western society). They assumed the patterns that these theories built up were universal and that the theories were generalizable to all societies and cultures. By presenting data collected from several "primitive" societies Mead seriously challenged the universality of these theories. The observations she offered from her anthropological studies provided evidence that was in direct contradiction to all theorists who claimed adolescence to be a period of inevitable conflict and strife.

Mead documented several non-Western cultures (the Samoan and New Guinean societies) in which there was not only an absence of storm and stress, but where adolescence was considered a smooth and pleasurable period, even a high point of life. In Samoa, diminishing childhood domination by siblings and the lack of adult marital responsibilities and sexual restrictions distinguished adolescence as a relatively carefree and enjoyable period when external authority diminished, casual sexual liasions were acceptable, and personal responsibilities minimized. It was a time for some experimentation and self-indulgence, a phase of development in which the individual was subject to few demands and allowed to lead a life free of conflict.

Mead's observations also challenged the concept of critical periods early in life. Her data instead attested to the wide variability in the timing, methods, and expectations of childrearing practices across cultures, with comparable success rates for producing "adjusted" adults. These data called into question theories such as Freud's, which predict serious and irreversible adult consequences of very strict or very lenient childhood training or discipline.

As an alternative to the claim that developmental theories are universal, Mead introduced the concept of *cultural-relativism*. This is the idea that our views of development are determined by the macrosystem in which we live. As Mead saw it, this meant that the psychological experience of developmental stages, for instance, is a product of a sociocultural system that fosters discontinuities across the lifespan. In a more uniform, consistent macrosystem, the idea of stages makes less sense.

Although it might, at first, appear that Mead entirely dismissed the influence of biological factors, she did acknowledge the role of heredity and individual life history. She noted that marked differences "in physique and apparent temperament" within single societies and the contribution that the "unevenness of physical puberty" can make for adolescent adjustment problems

Were Samoan Youth Pulling Margaret Mead's Leg?

How does the public respond when the work of an eminent researcher and theorist is challenged, if not refuted? In the following box taken from a national newspaper, several reactions to Freeman's challenge of Mead's position on cultural continuity are apparent. First, the conservatism of human theory and belief systems is quite evident. Reputation and renown, as well as elapsed time, are clearly factors working against the invalidation of an accepted theory or model. On the other hand, the heuristic value of a theory such as Mead's can be greater than the vulnerable components that comprise the model and its coordinating definitions—or the data on which they are based. Through the gradual accumulation of *multiple* positions and *multiple* investigations, developmental theory has evolved beyond dependency on any single piece of research or even any single conceptualization, no matter how monumental in its time. Indeed, scientific progress can only take place in the *absence* of such dependency. A major edifice may remain intact despite some weak foundation stones-

. . . but only so long as the remainder of its foundation is broad and deep enough to counteract those weaknesses. Theory development must *not* measure its strength in terms of any *single* weakest link.

Coming of Age with Dr. Mead

A number of important questions rise out of the latest controversy over the work of anthropologist Margaret Mead. The controversy has been set off by a forthcoming book in which an Australian anthropologist sharply challenges the findings in Dr. Mead's celebrated 1928 study, "Coming of Age in Samoa." The questions echo from South Seas villages, to adolescence in America, to the world problems which Dr. Mead eventually saw as requiring a change in human thinking.

The new book, "Margaret Mead and Samoa: The Making and Unmaking of an Anthropological Myth," is by Derek Freeman. According to its publisher, the Harvard University Press, he studied Samoa decades after the young Margaret Mead's field work there in the 1920s. But he chose a village location likely to have been little changed. Where she found tranquillity, sexual freedom, and lack of jealousy, he found tensions, strict sexual prohibitions, and proneness to jealousy.

Why should the general public care about what is at this stage mainly fuel for academic debate? Because of the widespread influence of the Mead book and because of those far-ranging questions mentioned above.

One of these is the possibility that even the most accepted or entrenched human idea is subject to rejection or modification on the basis of later information. Dr. Mead's findings began being challenged during her lifetime. She spoke of her Samoa book as true to the state of knowledge in the '20s.

Is there still something true in what she said about American adolescence even if her Samoan evidence was wrong? *She argued that adolescence did not have to be the time of tur-* *moil and anxiety familiar in American stereotypes.* She attributed the problems to the impact of the society, not to innate biological reasons. Many American families have helped their teen-agers cope with society and proved that adolescence need not inevitably be turbulent.

Another question is the general underlying one of nature and nurture—heredity and environment—as influences on societies and individuals. The new book is said to enter in on the currently vocal heredity side in this perennial debate. But the intellectual trend is toward some kind of synthesis in which heredity plays a part but individuality emerges through acceptance or rejection of various cultural and environmental influences.

Part of the contribution of Dr. Mead's kind of cultural anthropology has been to see that people are not bound by geography, for example, since neighboring tribes can develop differing ways.

One of her latter-year assertions was that no one is limited to thinking of people as "fragmented by our previously deficient methods of thinking about them as primarily physical or biochemical creatures." The notebook explorer of Samoan villages embraced the new age of communications and information. Because of it, she wrote, "we have an opportunity to correct our mistakes, take another breath" with a wider understanding of the needs of the whole world than human beings have ever had.

There were valuable insights here. They will be remembered whatever the scholarly judgment on Dr. Mead's early researches. (© 1983 The New York Times, Inc. Reprinted by permission.)

(from Muuss, 1975, p. 108). Despite this limited concession to the developmental biases created by nature, however, Mead remained committed to the predominance of nurture in producing character and personality. She wrote that: "At whatever point the society decides to stress a particular adjustment, it will be at this point that adjustment becomes acute to the individual" (Mead, 1952, p. 537).

Interestingly, as we noted in Chapter 1, Mead's data have been challenged by an Australian anthropologist who claims that Mead systematically misperceived Samoan culture and particularly Samoan adolescence (Freeman, 1983). This raises questions about Mead's conclusions, certainly, but it also reveals how vulnerable the anthropological approach is. An outsider attempts to form a picture based on the testimony of native witnesses and may be misled for fun, for self-protection, or for gain.

Benedict (1887–1948).   Ruth Benedict expanded Mead's ideas about how the concept of cultural relativism should help us understand development. It was she who first examined the role of cultural continuity across the lifespan, particularly as it related to the transition from childhood to adulthood. Her theory emphasizes cultural conditioning as the main force at work to shape human development. The variable of interest, consequently, is not the objective events but the subjective *experience*. More specifically, she believed that when childhood training is consistent with later adult roles, the individual will experience a relatively smooth and orderly process of transition to adulthood. To the extent that childhood training must be "unlearned" for appropriate functioning in adulthood, adolescence will be experienced as a period fraught with inconsistencies, ambiguities, and conflicts.

Benedict went on to propose that contemporary Western culture is characterized by just such sociocultural inconsistencies. Therefore, it was not surprising that theorists basing their data on Western samples should construct sturm und drang theories about adolescent development. Their limitations in generality were swiftly exposed, however, when any cross-cultural comparisons were attempted.

Drawing on Mead's data collected from the Samoan culture (and thus making her conclusions vulnerable to the distortions made possible by vulnerable data) and contrasting them with Western principles and practices, Benedict was able to differentiate three general paths along which continuity and discontinuity could operate. These are the responsibility inherent in being a child versus an adult; the relative dominance of children versus adults; and the consistency in sex roles. Brief comparisons between Samoan and North American cultures on each indicator will illustrate this point.

Although both American and Samoan adults were expected to fulfill certain labor commitments within their societies, the degree to which children and adolescents were seen as possessing a similar responsibility was hardly comparable. Samoan youngsters were required from an early age (6–7 years) to contribute to household functioning; young girls participated in childcare, cooking, and weaving, while young boys fished, planted, and gathered food. In contrast, North American children spent and still spend much of their homelife at play and are, in fact, forbidden by law to participate in labor outside the home. Moreover, their play bears little resemblance to future labor, unlike the leisure activities frequently engaged in by Samoan children. A Samoan girl, in addition, had wielded authority over younger siblings from the outset, and in fact, assumed most of the responsibility for their discipline.

Parents had never appeared as major authority figures and a Samoan youth who found himself in disagreement with his parents merely moved in with nearby relatives. Thus, dominance appeared not to be a uniquely adult characteristic. This is far from the case in North American society, where socially-sanctioned parental authority may go unchallenged until the adolescent begins to seek autonomy from home and parents.

The discrepancy in American sex roles from youth to adulthood is likewise apparent (and we will discuss them in Chapter 8). There are many who consider thirteen- and fourteen-year-olds too young for formal dating, let alone for sexual relations. Sex is a topic strictly taboo for younger children, and premarital virginity remains an ideal in many circles. But, as Mead saw it, a Samoan adolescent was free to experiment with sex. With the strict exception of incest, sexual activities were accepted as commonplace. "Parental indulgence toward masturbation is common. The postpubescent girl expends 'all of her interest . . . on clandestine sex adventures'" (Muuss, 1975, p. 101). These attitudes are entirely consistent with relatively relaxed sexual customs in adulthood.

Given these descriptions of role in a more continuous culture, it is hardly surprising to discover the noticeable contrasts that marked the adolescent experience. In the West, adolescence is characterized as a period of internal turmoil, psychological stress, and behavioral extremes. In Samoa, it is perceived as an enjoyable and unburdened stage of life, anticipated and recalled with pleasure. The anthropological point is made, as is the unique contribution that Mead and Benedict offered to adolescent theory and to more general paradigms of development.

Anthropological research often challenges the universality of interpretations based upon specific cultural experiences. For example, Malinowski (1955) challenged Freud's interpretation of the son's resentment of his father (the Oedipal complex). Based upon his observations in cultures where uncles rather than fathers are authority figures, Malinowski concluded that it was power rather than sex that was involved.

Along the same lines, Japanese psychoanalyst Heisaku Kosawa proposed an alternative to the Oedipal complex based upon Japanese culture. He called it the Ajase complex. Like the Oedipus complex, it refers to an ancient myth. Ajase was a young prince who felt betrayed by his mother because of her sex-

In *Centuries of Childhood* (1962), Philippe Aries describes the discontinuity in the early 1600s, at least among royalty and the well-to-do, in attitudes toward appropriate sexual behavior for children of very early versus middle or late childhood:

> One of the unwritten laws of contemporary morality, the strictest and best respected of all, requires adults to avoid any reference, above all any humorous reference, to sexual matters in the presence of children. This notion was entirely foreign to the society of old. The modern reader of the diary in which Henri IV's physician, Heroard, recorded the details of the young Louis XIII's life is astonished by the liberties which people took with children, by the coarseness of the jokes they made, and by the indecency of gestures made in public which shocked nobody and which were regarded as perfectly natural.
>
> During his first three years nobody showed any reluctance or saw any harm in jokingly touching the child's sexual parts. 'The Marquise [de Verneuil] often put her hand under his coat; he got his nanny to lay him on her bed where she played with him, putting her hand under his coat . . . These jokes were not limited to the servants, or to brainless youths, or to women of easy virtue such as the King's mistress. The Queen, his mother, made the same sort of joke: 'The Queen, touching his genitals, said: "Son, I am holding your spout . . ." '
>
> When he was between five and six, people stopped talking about his sexual parts, while he started talking more about other people's. Mille Mercier, one of his chambermaids who had stayed up late the night before, was still in bed one morning, next to his bed (his servants, who were sometimes married, slept in his bedroom and do not appear to have allowed his presence to embarrass them). "He played with her, toyed with her toes and the upper part of her legs, and told his nanny to go and get some birch twigs so that he could beat her, which he did . . . His nanny asked him: 'What have you seen of Mercier's?' He replied calmly: 'I have seen her arse.' 'What else have you seen?' He replied calmly and without laughing that he had seen her private."
>
> . . . After 1608 this kind of joke disappeared; he had become a little man—attaining the fateful age of seven—and at this age he had to be taught decency in language and behaviour. When he was asked how children were born, he would reply, like Moliere's Agnes, 'through the ear.' Mme de Montglat scolded him when he 'showed his genitals to the little Ventelet girl' . . . .The boy of ten was forced to behave with a modesty which nobody had thought of expecting of the boy of five. (From *Centuries of Childhood* [pp. 100–102] by Philippe Aries and translated by Robert Baldick. Reprinted by permission of Jonathan Cape Ltd.)

Adherents to the one theory of cultural relativity would have to question the relative ease or difficulty of the transition *to* adolescence among individuals of this social group.

ual relations with his father. Ajase kills his father, but could not carry through on his plan to kill his mother as well. Then Ajase broke out in sores so disgusting that everyone else avoided him. His mother put aside her feelings about Ajase's act and cared for him in his time of need. This reconciled mother and son; each forgave the other. As Kosawa saw it, this myth better expresses the Japanese dynamic of indulgence, dependence, love, and hate than does the Western-oriented Oedipal myth.

Social Learning

Another school of thought on development evolved from the behaviorist or learning tradition. As is true of cultural anthropology, this tradition emphasizes the role of nurture over nature in shaping development. Whereas anthropological theory focused on *continuity* of experience, learning theory focused on *content and contingencies* of experience. Anthropology emphasizes the ways in which society is a woven cloth, while behaviorism endeavors to describe how each thread is spun. The major concerns to behaviorists are the particular lessons acquired, the variables that influence that acquisition, and the contexts in which those lessons are later acted upon. Adolescent behavior is thus a function not only of culture and society, but of the particular situations and contexts in which individuals found themselves—of the specific interactions occurring in microsystems. Principles of learning dictated that "behavior" includes actions, attitudes, interpretations, and even emotions. The rising and falling of all these "behaviors" depends upon what is reinforced; anything is possible.

Although each school of behaviorist thought has its own individual history, an overview of the work of their most influential advocate, B. F. (Burrhus Frederick) Skinner, should furnish the background information necessary for later applications to developmental theory.

Skinner (1904–   ).   We have discussed the limitations on generalizability that result from culturally bound data bases. Many observers believe we should keep this in mind when we note that Skinner developed his theory of learning from extensive laboratory studies of rats and pigeons. Nevertheless, the conclusions he drew from that work and the model that he set forth have been shown to make sense in subsequent studies involving human subjects. Skinner's fundamental belief is that the probability of any particular behavior (whether it be thought, deed, or emotion) is increased by rewarding its occurrence. Thus, if adolescents gain the esteem of their peers (assumed here to be a rewarding event) by participation in sexual relationships, the likelihood that they will be sexually active in the future becomes greater.

Studying development is thus studying the history of *response probabilities*. The response that has been most rewarded in the past is most likely to be included in the current behavior repertoire. Extending this perspective, the environment is a pattern or history of reinforcement contingencies. The most important distinctions among cultures, social settings, and societies are the arrangement of reinforcement contingencies. According to Mead's reports, Samoan teenagers were rewarded (by approval of others, by acknowledgement of conformity to sociocultural norms, and by other means) for cooperation, for submission, for adherence to the group—in general, for fitting in with the behavior of other members of their society. North American teenagers, on the other hand, are typically rewarded for achievement, for efforts to surpass common goals, for lofty aspirations. Skinner would express no surprise whatsoever that two such dissimilar environments with different reinforcement patterns should produce different adolescents. In this manner, individuals are socially conditioned to assume the attitudes, the actions, and the frame of reference of the society and the subculture to which they belong. This, Skinner argues, is the process and the outcome of socialization. It is the microsystem that is all powerful.

The initial efforts to view development from a learning perspective spawned a great deal of research and theory, taking somewhat different courses depending on the particular aspect of development serving as the focus: social development, cognitive development, moral development, and so on. Some theorists, however, attempted to integrate several developmental functions within a single learning framework, and it is to one of these latter researchers that we now turn our attention.

Bandura (1925–   ). Although accepting the learning principles that Skinner had charted, Albert Bandura considered Skinner's model inadequate for a complete understanding of *human* behavior and behavioral development. He proposed, in addition, that learning could and often did take place in the absence of any overt reward or reinforcement. Indeed, while reinforcement might account for the frequency of future responses, how could one explain the origin of a new behavior, the initial acquisition of a response never before enacted and therefore never yet reinforced? Bandura hypothesized additional types of learning to resolve this dilemma: *imitational learning* in which specific behaviors are copied and *modelling* in which people are copied. By observing the behavior of other people (including their expression of attitudes, their interpretations of events, their activities), the individual learns new modes of thought, action, and emotion. Such learning requires no tangible rewards and, in fact, does not necessarily result in any immediate *overt* behavioral change. In other words, Bandura was distinguishing between learning (which might imply only *mental* behavioral change—new interpretations, altered thought patterns, modified expectations) and performance (converting thought into action).

Not only did Bandura propose the possibility of learning in the absence of reinforcement, but he also proposed the existence of alternative forms of reinforcement. Witnessing someone else get reinforced (*vicarious reinforcement*) increased the probability of engaging in behavior for which the *model* was rewarded, and *self-reinforcement* made responses for which individuals rewarded *themselves* more likely in future. Thus, by observing a sibling praised for finding an after-school job (and perhaps more importantly, by noting a subsequently bulging wallet), or by treating oneself to pizza and ice cream whenever one pays a visit to the employment office, the probability of engaging in active efforts to find employment increases.

One further aspect of observational learning requiring attention is the qualities of the model. Characteristics such as age, prestige, appearance, perceived competence, and similarity to the observer all affect the likelihood of imitation. A female high school sophomore may be more *likely*, for example, to model the social behavior of a popular and attractive peer or the study habits of a friendly junior getting A's on compositions in their English class, than she is to model a struggling freshman or absent-minded homeroom teacher. The same is true of negative behavior such as delinquency and suicide.

There are differences across age (as well as sex, status, and subculture) in the optimal characteristics of the model and the relative potency of rewards (e.g., a new stereo versus a backyard treehouse). There are also differences attributable to the context of the modelling experience (e.g., in a climate of warmth and security versus fear and threat) and the relationship of the adolescent to the model (which may help link together this view with the psychodynamic view of identification). However, the principles by which new behaviors are acquired and later performed do not change from childhood to adulthood, and thus there is nothing special about adolescence. Adolescent learning is the same as that of younger children and adults. Because learned behavior is also situationally specific (differentially occurring on the basis of previous reinforcement and current contingencies), there are no universal behavioral patterns typifying *any* particular age or period in life. What has been expected, modelled, and rewarded in one culture may be entirely different in another.

Seen from this perspective, behavior change across age is the result of developmental changes in models and reinforcements. These changes are initiated and arranged by the sociocultural system, according to the same cultural expectations and ideals that Mead and Benedict emphasized. Western cultural conditioning, for example, established the importance of parental and teacher models during early and middle childhood, but is also responsible to some extent for these models being replaced by peers, fictional, and entertainment heroes during the preteen and teen years.

Bandura and his colleagues were most concerned with *social* development when they presented this model of learning. However, they also thought it explained the mechanisms for acquiring *any* overt or covert (i.e., mental) behaviors. Hence, it provides a model for moral development, for career aspirations, for skill learning, and for attitude formation or cognitive structuring as well. This point demonstrates the great explanatory value inherent in Bandura's social learning theory. A limited set of constructs and processes (the model) are used to explain a wide variety of phenomena by employing coordinating defi-

It was headlined in the media as "Teen-Age Suicide in the Sun Belt." However, its implications extend beyond even what these words convey. After the accidental death of a 17-year-old high school student (during a car race with peers), three other adolescents from the same suburban city committed suicide over the course of the subsequent three weeks and there were 12 other suicide attempts by teenagers within that year.

The lessons to be gained from this tragic sequence of events exist on several levels for those concerned with the study of adolescence. A brief glimpse at the background of these events will demonstrate why this is so.

The first suicide victim, a close friend of the teen in the car accident, died by carbon monoxide inhalation in his own car, apparently to the strains of his radio ("Goodbye Cruel World" was the last song on his tape). Six days later, the second victim—unacquainted with either of the other two students—killed himself by the same method, also with the radio playing. The final victim, a ninth grader, shot himself without leaving a note. However, newspaper clippings about both the accident victim and the first suicide were displayed on his bulletin board.

Attention focused on the community context, described by the media in terms of "boredom and restlessness typical of a community with a largely transplanted and homogeneous [upper] middle-class citizenry" (Gelman & Gangelhoff, 1983, p. 70). A sociologist studying the phenomenon focused on the adolescents themselves: "They're dealing with establishing an identity in a place where there aren't any extended families or reference groups. In this kind of community, a peer-group attachment is a validation of yourself. When that is lost, you cease to exist—you die psychologically and socially" (Gelman & Gangelhoff, 1983, p. 74).

But there is a further point to be made that has direct relevance to principles we have been describing in this section under the heading of social learning theory. It is quite obvious that the youths involved were aware of what was probably a great deal of public attention and public sentiment devoted to the tragedy of each previous victim. Indeed, each death was no doubt afforded a considerable degree of drama in its media communication. The overt parallels between these deaths and the subsequent referrals to an epidemic of suicide attempts certainly suggest that principles of modelling may have been of special relevance.

At a period in life when self-identity and peer relationships are major issues and personal truths and idealistic views are dominant, the circumstances surrounding each death could well have presented a most potent model to the youths involved. The possibility that social learning theory principles played an important role in these events suggests the powerful influence that learning may play during this or any other stage in life. In this regard, increasing concern for possibly deleterious effects of media sensationalism, television violence, and easy availability of pornographic materials serves to highlight growing recognition on the part of the public of the potential impact of observational learning.

nitions that delicately balance the abstract with the specific. This balance allows application of learning concepts (modelling, reinforcement, behavior, performance) to circumstances that range from social interaction to career choice. Keep this in mind in later chapters and look for evidence of these principles at work.

The social learning perspective gives precedence to changeability, instability, and specificity in development. The contribution of nature is correspondingly restricted. Variables such as sex, race, health or handicap, activity level, emotionality, and intelligence, all of which appear to possess a genetic component, will in part determine exposure to particular environmental experiences. The availability or scarcity of resources, social encouragement versus criticism, participation in social, educational, political, and religious activities, all depend in part on the individual's characteristics as a biological organism. There remains one final class of developmental theories deserving our attention. These are the cognitive theories.

Cognitive Theories

We presented the foundation for the cognitive theories in Chapter 4 when we discussed cognitive development. Here we consider how they illustrate the characteristics of developmental theories that include more nearly equal roles for nature and nurture. In such a paradigm, both genetic and environmental forces shape development and they are engaged in significant interplay over the entire lifespan. The cognitive theories employ constructs, inferences, and interpretations about this interplay.

Piaget (1896–1980).   Given the developmental issues outlined at the outset of this chapter, it is intriguing to observe both a continuous (termed *stage independent*) and discontinuous (termed *stage dependent*) developmental function incorporated into Piaget's theory of cognitive development.

As we said in Chapter 4, Piaget believed that the development of reasoning and abstract thought resulted from two basic cognitive processes, assimilation and accommodation. Both depend upon physical maturation of the nervous system, on the one hand, and interaction with the physical and social environment, on the other. As the child develops, innate rudimentary cognitive schemes (also called *structures*) restructure environmental input according to their preorganized patterns. This is assimilation. These schemes are themselves gradually modified by discrepancies between their own schematic arrangements and the environmental information. That is accommodation. As time passes, maturation of the neurological system and the increasing capacity to respond to and process environmental input produce new and increasingly sophisticated cognitive schemes.

Consider the case of affiliation with a political party. Initially broad and undifferentiated conceptions of that party are challenged and adjusted by minor pieces of information gleaned from newspapers, television, friends, teachers, and others. Other (congruent) information is directly incorporated into the existing schemes, while information that is highly discrepant with current ideas may be entirely ignored or rejected as biased, uninformed, or inaccurate. Through this cycle of cognitive equilibrium, disequilibrium, and reestablished equilibrium, this political scheme may become highly detailed, internally consistent, and congruent with objective "facts" and subjective feelings.

In contrast to the incremental origin and elaboration of cognitive schemes, more abrupt changes in the overarching quality of these schemes take place during development. In each of the four stages that Piaget described (and we summarized in Chapter 4), the fundamental nature of the thought processes and mental constructs comprising all schemes undergo rapid changes within a brief period of time.

Piaget could and in fact did operationalize the majority of his theoretical constructs and processes. Specifically, he devised tasks designed to assess the extent to which each level of cognitive processing was spontaneously employed by children and teenagers. Chapter 4 mentioned several tasks involving adaption of his principles to empirical tests. Piaget's efforts have resulted in a highly testable theory. However, it is one that still requires us to make inferences from behavior to postulate mental operations and structures such as conservation and schemes. The significant advantages for theory development of being able to test, modify, and retest theoretical constructs and relationships are obvious. Ideally all theories could be subjected to empirical examination as has Piaget's.

The position that Piaget adopted in his theory of cognitive development argues for the uniqueness of adolescence as a period of life. In particular, he proposed that adolescent thought processes and interactions with the environment—their very perceptions of the world around them—are qualitatively different from younger children and to some extent from adults as well. The cognitive processes of the adolescent are distinct from those that are exhibited at other ages. Because development progresses in more general stages, the period of adolescence is a universally identifiable cognitive phenomenon. Although development occurs in a context defined by macrosystems, the biological similarities among all people assure some similarity of functioning across sociocultural settings.

Like Bandura, Piaget professed somewhat less interest in other domains of development, but believed nonetheless that his model accurately described at least some of them (e.g., social and moral development). Partial support for this contention comes from Lawrence Kohlberg, who applied Piagetian cognitive principles to the study of the development of moral reasoning.

Kohlberg (1927-). As we showed in Chapter 4, Kohlberg's approach to moral development represents an extension of cognitive theory, since it views acquisition of certain cognitive processes as a necessary condition for attaining corresponding levels of moral reasoning. It does not guarantee higher order moral reasoning, but is a precondition for their development. Individuals cannot achieve given stages unless they have secured the required degree of cognitive maturity. Thus, adolescence is a crucial time for attaining "higher order" moral thinking. In a manner analogous to Piaget's model of cognitive development, the development of moral reasoning progresses in stages. Although stages may overlap, the process is essentially unidirectional. Kohlberg did not entertain the possibility of much regression in moral thought. There might be some variation from one moral situation to the next, but slippage across an entire stage was not possible. As we noted in Chapter 4, however, the generalizability of Kohlberg's theory is questionable, given its male and Western biases.

One final cognitive theory merits attention. Some call this third approach *humanistic psychology*. Carl Rogers and Abraham Maslow are two of the best known proponents of this view. As humanistic psychologists see things, development concerns people's ideas of themselves and the world. Like Erikson, they emphasize personal identity. Like Piaget, they see the individual growing and maturing into a more fully human person. This implies that there is a positive force at work in human development that energizes this development. People develop well when they uncover and nurture this force; people develop badly when they misunderstand this force, suppress it, or distort it. The process of becoming is one of encountering one's "true self," of forming a better idea of who one is. Adolescence is important because it is in adolescence that the individual begins to be independent enough to figure out who he or she is. In adolescence we are able to begin a quest to discover and nurture our true selves, the beginning of a lifelong process.

It is obvious from these three final theoretical positions that developmentalists can and do range across the entire spectrum of the nature/nurture controversy, some giving more weight to one factor, some proposing a fairly balanced contribution and interaction between the two. This is also true of the question addressing continuity and discontinuity in development. Indeed, we hope that our review of this collection of developmental theories will provide some sense of the continuity across history and across specific content area of all the issues in development discussed earlier, of the various alternatives that have been pursued and adopted up to now, and even of their strengths and limitations as explanations of development in general and adolescent development in particular. What follows is a brief statement in which we strive to bring some unity and some common meaning to our understanding of development.

Toward a Synthesis: A Biologically Sound Cognitive Learning Theory

Every developmental theory discussed in this chapter recognizes *some* role for biological factors in human development. To ignore the contribution of biology is, in our opinion, to deny a fundamental source of individuality *and* to neglect a powerful common force shaping human development. At the same time, to pronounce developmental outcomes as the ultimate product of biology and heredity alone seems to us equally misguided. Our ecological perspective demands that theories of development recognize the interplay of biological, psychological, and social realities. Biology, we suspect, casts its influence on development through three major channels: biological limits, biological agendas, and biological drives.

It is naive to imagine that many if not most of our human characteristics are not subject to some finite limitations. In all probability, physical characteristics, cognitive capacity, emotionality and activity level, are all limited at birth to some finite potential range. That range is, in itself, a characteristic that differentiates one individual from another. Some of us could never learn to play the accordian well. Others could never run the 100 yard dash in less than 12 seconds. Similarly, there is no disputing the fact that some individuals mature more rapidly or more slowly than others, perhaps across the entire lifespan. Finally, particular glands and their related hormones become systematically more active at particular stages in the life cycle, as was demonstrated in Chapter 3 when we discussed the physiology of puberty.

However, the points just made do not by any means rule out the effects of environmental factors. Indeed, they begin to indicate some of the specific ways in which environmental forces have their impact. If biology establishes our underlying makeup (*genotype*), the environment certainly acts to translate this latent code into the visible person (*phenotype*). Furthermore, the specific mechanisms for development may vary somewhat depending upon the particular domain of functioning. Therefore, the interaction between heredity and environment may differ depending upon which aspect of development we are considering. As we examine cognitive development, social development, personality development, and moral development, we find that microsystem influences are paramount in some areas and at certain times, while individual or macrosystem influences are paramount at others.

It would appear that earliest development is by and large a product of the separate influences of both biological and socioenvironmental factors. In other words, features of the environment such as the family structure, socioeconomic status, and early childrearing practices may act directly and *relatively* independently of such factors as physical constitution, intelligence, and gender. Needless to say, we cannot overlook some interactions, as in the case of sex-typed socialization practices, and differences in attitudes and opportunities for the retarded and gifted among different social classes. However, the interactive effects of individual and environmental factors grow increasingly more influential as development progresses and as the complete human ecology comes more directly into play. The impact of social, educational, moral, political, and physical aspects of the environment are qualified by an individual selection process. The developing child, the adolescent, and the adult take more and more active initiative in restructuring the environment, both physically and conceptually. Whereas direct environmental influences on the infant tend to be restricted to the microsystem of the home and family, the growing child and especially the adolescent come in contact with multiple microsystems (school, scouts, peers) and their interrelationships (mesosystems), eventually seeking out those of their own choosing. Thus there is an increasing role for individual characteristics to shape current and future experiences. The values and ideals of the teenager, the emotional reactions and social preferences of the young adult entering the labor market, the cognitive sophistication of the new parent—all of these represent examples of *person variables* that help to determine the kinds of roles, the kinds of situations, and the kinds of experiences that they will encounter. These experiences, in turn, modify the course of development for the individual.

In conclusion, we believe that development is a *mutual* accommodation process between individual biological, socioemotional, and cognitive characteristics on the one hand, and the unique ecological context for that development on the other. Developmentalist Richard Lerner (1982) illuminates the special significance that this position accords to the adolescent period:

> Adolescence is a time when multiple transitions, in the inner-biological, individual-psychological, physical environmental, and sociocultural contexts, occur. Thus, it is a particularly appropriate time to study the relation between a changing person and his or her changing world. Successful adaptation always involves appropriate coordination between our changing selves and our changing contexts. But it is in adolescence, and particularly early adolescence, that such adaptational stresses may be most critical, due to their simultaneity and multidimensionality. (p. 361)

Thus, our understanding of human development may profit from the lessons and insights offered during adolescence. The mechanisms for that understanding are the developmental theories that we construct. So long as we set them within an ecological framework, we will be ready to use them to make sense of adolescent development in all its diversity and commonality.

Ecological Wrap-Up

Organism.   It is human nature to seek order and meaning in the world. This has much to do with the motivation for theory building.

Microsystem.   The microsystems of science exert an important influence in establishing and maintaining paradigms. The kinds of research we do both reflect and influence what our theories look like.

Mesosystems. Good theory seems to thrive on interdisciplinary exchange, for example, when an investigator has one foot in biology and the other in anthropology.

Exosystems. Institutional rewards express paradigms. If the institutions of research are narrow and closed-minded the search for truth suffers.

Macrosystems. Cultural and societal blueprints do much to define what seems "self-evident" and what is "inconceivable." Both shape theory building. These blueprints change in response to changes in the conditions of life as well as in response to the efforts of individuals and institutions to generate new knowledge and communicate that knowledge.

Preview

- *Family* means a stable relationship sanctioned by blood, custom, or law involving responsibility across the generations.

- Studying how families deal with adolescence involves watching what families do, assessing what they would do, and listening to what they say they do.

- The composition and structure of families are changing.

- Separation, divorce, and remarriage affect ever-greater numbers of adolescents, as does maternal employment outside the home.

- Parent/adolescent relations can be classified in several ways, including how much control or authority the parent has and how much affection the parent feels for and shows to the adolescent.

- Adolescent maltreatment affects thousands of families each year, and involves sexual, physical, and psychological abuse and neglect.

- Autonomy is a big issue in parent/adolescent relationships.

*I*n this chapter, we turn to the family life of adolescents. Whether it be adjusting to physical change or facilitating psychological development, the adolescent's family is crucial.

But how do we go about studying adolescents and their families? We saw earlier that *how* we look at things does much to shape *what* we see. Because we all have been part of a particular family we need help in being objective. Feelings and ideas about our own families are so strongly held that they can bias us as we look at other people's families. What is more, our feelings and beliefs about what a family *should* be can influence how we describe and evaluate our own and other families. We must be very attuned to issues of objectivity, bias, completeness, and validity in studying families. Of course we need scientifically legitimate methods for studying all aspects of adolescence, but the issues of adolescents in their families provide a particularly good starting point for our efforts to discover the truth about adolescence. Therefore, we begin this chapter with a discussion of research methods as they apply to studying families, but will return to the themes and terms of this discussion in later chapters.

In our discussion of parent/adolescent relations, we will note a variety of gaps in our knowledge that result from *what* is studied. These include a lack of understanding of the behavioral processes of family life, an appreciation for the reciprocal influences of parent on adolescent and adolescent on parent, and an insufficient number of cross-cultural comparisons. Other gaps or problems exist because of *how* researchers conduct their investigations and *who* they study. Both of these sets of problems limit our confidence in what we know; they call into question the validity of our results.

6

Families and Their Adolescents

A question that all researchers in the social sciences face is "How generalizable are my findings?" or, in nontechnical language, "How much do the conclusions I have reached apply to all parents and adolescents and not simply to the group I have studied?" As we will soon see, this question is particularly relevant to our discussion of parent/adolescent relations because a majority of the findings are based on white, middle-class, two-parent families who probably live in or around a university town. Furthermore, the findings are based on families who are willing to take the time (often over a period of years) to participate in a research project. These statements are not intended to discount the value of the research presented, but to put the findings into a realistic perspective. Certainly some findings based on these easy-to-study families hold up across ethnically, culturally, economically and socially diverse groups. For example, as we reported in Chapter 2, Rohner's studies suggest (1975) that rejection is a universally destructive influence on human development. But our ecological perspective cautions us against expecting that what is true of one group of families (as defined by a particular ecological niche) will be true of other families living in different circumstances with different values. We must always keep our eyes open about *who* was studied as well as who did the studying.

The generalizability of findings may also depend upon the researcher's data collection technique. Researchers use three types of methods for studying parent-child interactions: *naturalistic observations, laboratory analogue studies,* and *interviews* or *surveys.* In choosing a method, investigators must consider which method is most appropriate to their goals and what the method's advantages and drawbacks are.

Naturalistic Observations: Watching What Families Really Do

The process of recording and counting well-defined, naturally occurring behaviors is highly objective. The participants are not asked to recount or recall their attitudes or behaviors. Rather, since we look at what family members *do*, the data are immediate and firsthand.

Additionally, naturalistic observations lend themselves to analyses of interaction. A researcher can identify information on the interchanges between parents and adolescents on the basis of parental acts influencing the adolescent's behaviors, the adolescent's acts stimulating parental behavior, and on the sequences of parent and adolescent behavior, or *reciprocal interactions.*

What *exactly* do you watch, record, and count? Frequently it is difficult to define precisely the behaviors of interest or to obtain reliable data from complex or subtle interchanges. You miss one kind of behavior by paying attention to another. If you record pieces of behavior that are too small, you lose sight of the big picture.

The most common objection to naturalistic observations, however, is that the data may not be representative of what typically occurs between parents and adolescents, since the presence of the observer may affect the behavior. People may consciously or unconsciously misrepresent themselves or their families when they are "on stage." For example, research shows that mothers behave in a warmer, more involved style when they are aware of being observed than when they are unaware that they are being observed (Zegoib, Arnold, & Forehad, 1975).

In addition, if we are to make use of observations of behavior we need to know how typical the situations are that we are observing. If families rarely experience the situations in which we observe them, any conclusions we draw about those families may be misleading. This leads to the second approach, *laboratory analogues.*

Laboratory Analogues: Assessing What Families Would Do

Many researchers have used situations in which an unfamiliar adult in a laboratory behaves in a manner presumed to correspond to important parental behaviors or discipline techniques. The strong points of this experimental situation, or *analogue*, are that the investigator controls what happens (the isolation and manipulation of stimuli), that the investigator can keep out forces external to the family system being studied (control over external stimuli), and that the investigator can therefore be more confident in asserting that one event produced another (greater certainty of identification of cause/effect relationships).

The rigor of the laboratory analogue studies, however, is frequently a problem in itself. As the investigator attempts to generalize the data from the laboratory conditions to the family's natural environment, many questions arise because the experimental analogue differs in two essential respects from its real life equivalent. First, the unfamiliar adults in the laboratory have maximum control over their own behavior. The experimenter/adolescent interaction will lack the normal reciprocity of the parent/adolescent interactions because the experimenter is working from a script and is usually programmed not to let the adolescent direct the situation or stimulate the experimenter to respond apart from the script. Secondly, the adolescent/experimenter relationship is unique. They have no history together. Their patterns of interaction will not depend upon past interactions and emotions that are typical of adolescent's relations with real parents. Laboratory analogues can be very useful in asking highly specific questions, however, often as a prelude to testing the resulting answers in the real world.

Interviews or Surveys: Listening to What Families Say They Do

Probably the most frequently used techniques in the study of adolescents and their families have been interviews and questionnaires. While the interview lacks both the control and immediacy of the other two methods, it is more convenient and less expensive. Because of the *relative* ease of collecting data, data can be collected from a larger sample. Additionally, investigators can sample a much wider range of behaviors or attitudes from a much wider range of people. Observation and laboratory analogue studies usually deal with tens of families, while interview studies deal with hundreds and questionnaire with thousands. Most of the research discussed later in this chapter relies upon interviews and questionnaires.

Although the interview or survey method is the most widely used, it is also the most commonly criticized. The most convincing objections to this method declare that the data are unreliable, inaccurate, and systematically diluted. Parents or the adolescents themselves may be asked to recall details from the past or to rate themselves or other family members on personality or behavioral characteristics, increasing the likelihood of distortion. As Yarrow noted, "mothers' interview responses represent self-description by extremely ego-involved reporters" (p. 217, 1963). We could probably suggest the same thing about fathers and about adolescents as well.

Over the last two decades, several attempts have been made to modify interviews and questionnaires to reduce the degree of distortion. For instance, predictions improve when questions focus on recent events and specific, concrete practices or behaviors rather than general characteristics of family life in the past (Kagan & Moss, 1962; Bell, 1964). Efforts to corroborate data, to compare responses of different parents or groups of parents, or to check reports against observational measures also increase confidence in the validity of self-report measures. Such improvements are significant, and in spite of the limited usefulness of self-report measures, they are still able to tap information that is unavailable through any other method. Interestingly, one recent study comparing maternal, paternal, and adolescent reports on family functioning concludes that adolescents are the most accurate reporters of the three (Sebes, 1983). This bolsters confidence in adolescents as reporters of family problems (Garbarino, Sebes, & Schellenbach, 1984).

Choosing a Method

One problem in choosing a method is deciding who is to be the target of the researcher's efforts. Where researchers are interested in parenting styles, they have usually focused their attention directly on the parent (most often the mother), either asking them about the techniques they use or observing them with their adolescents. However, an adolescent's perception of parental attitudes or behaviors may be more important to development than what the parent is thinking or doing or thinks she or he is doing. A strict parent, for instance, may justify rigid discipline as conducive to the development of a strong moral character. As we shall see, however, the adolescent is more likely to perceive such a parent as someone who is actually suppressing the development of competence.

A recent case study of a single family highlights the need to compare the perceptions of individual family members. In the particular family studied, the parents indicated that they saw some problems, but overall expressed the feeling that the family was basically functioning well. In contrast, the perceptions of two adolescent children differed considerably from each other and from the parent's reports. The 15-year-old female adolescent described her family very negatively, reporting a "chaotic" structure (lacking in rules and boundaries) and "enmeshed" relations. The 12-year-old brother viewed the family in a very positive light. He characterized the family as flexible, with sufficient cohesiveness and freedom (Schellenbach, Sebes, Ford, Garbarino, & Guerney, 1982). Which is true? All are in a way. We must remember that how a family looks to each member is important in understanding how and why members of that family behave the way they do, and how and why the same family can influence each member differently. As far as these adolescents are concerned, they *do not* live in the same family.

These findings are significant because they suggest that past techniques of focusing on a single respondent may not have adequately captured the nature of family dynamics. Measures of the images different family members have of each other and how the family functions may also be important in differentiating problem families from families that are functioning well (Garbarino, Sebes, & Schellenbach, 1984). Some investigators report that dramatic discrepancies between the family member's perceptions may indicate conflict and distress (Gottman, Markham, & Notarius, 1977).

Since none of the methods is sufficiently foolproof in and of itself, many researchers have begun to use multiple measures of parent/adolescent relations. Where there is agreement *(convergence of findings)* resulting from different methods, investigators are more confident that their results are valid.

The importance of these methodological issues will become clearer as we proceed with our analysis of families and their adolescents, remembering always that how you study and who you study affects what you learn about families.

An Introduction to the Meaning of the Family in Human Development

The family is the primary microsystem for human development in North American society, as it is virtually everywhere. It deserves to be called the "headquarters for human development" (Garbarino and Associates, 1982). Again and again we return to the family as a vital influence—be it in educational success, in moral reasoning, in the development of identity, or in adjusting to puberty. Now we turn directly to the family as a context for adolescent development. As we do so we must remember that it is very difficult to understand what life is like for a family member if we can only look from the outside in on a family. This should make us cautious about jumping to conclusions (good *or* bad) about a family, until we have really tried to get an insider's view.

Although what goes on in an adolescent's family is vitally important, it is not the whole story. What goes on *inside* families depends in part upon what is going on *outside* families. Thus, we need to be attuned to mesosystem issues: How congruent is the advice to parents given by church versus that provided by the mass media? Do parents and peers hold basic values in common? For example, it may mean quite one thing for parents to be permissive in the home when all the adolescent's other microsystems are strict, and quite another when the other microsystems are themselves permissive (Bronfenbrenner, 1960). Highly controlling parents may better serve as a source of protection in a socially dangerous environment (e.g., an inner city ghetto or a drug-laden suburb) than in a very safe environment.

Exosystem and macrosystem issues are also crucial in understanding families and adolescent development. For example, the effects of divorce or maternal employment outside the home may depend upon how supportive the community is. Do the community's institutions provide financial assistance to single parents? One frequent consequence of divorce is poverty. Is it normal for a mother to work outside the home in a particular community? If so, it might not have any special psychological connotations—*either* positive (of a working mother being a "pioneer") or negative (of a mother "abandoning" her children).

The issues concerning the individual as a biological and psychological system are likewise important. In many cases the same event (e.g., maternal employment outside the home or divorce) seems to have different effects on males and females as well as on younger versus older youth (recall Elder's study of the Great Depression described in Chapter 2).

Beyond these differences, individual temperament plays a significant role. The same childrearing strategy and techniques that work for one child may not work with another. As we mentioned in Chapter 2, one of the most vivid literary descriptions of this is found in Chaim Potok's novel, *The Chosen* (1967), in which a father who loves his son dearly embarks upon an unorthodox childrearing style (never directly addressing or touching his son) because of the son's highly unusual intellectual abilities (a very high IQ coupled with a photographic memory). Believing his son will not develop sympathy and empathy *(Menschlichkeit)* under normal family conditions because of his extraordinary gifts, the father sees the necessity of a drastic campaign to provide compensatory socialization that many would consider "psychological maltreatment." And, at least as Potok wrote it, it worked.

The Role of the Parent

Being a parent requires flexibility, the ability to adapt general principles (e.g., "be supportive") and techniques (e.g., "reward positive behavior") to the specifics of a particular child or adolescent. As Rogers (1981) points out, the diverse and contradictory nature of research on family relationships cautions us against making specific "how to" prescriptions for parents. While we can (and in this chapter will) say something about general principles, we cannot offer specific prescriptions on how to *guarantee* effective socialization (Farson, 1974). Good parent advice books, consultants, and programs should reflect this (Newson & Newson, 1974), rather than offer a "how to" manual, as many have done in the past (Bronfenbrenner, 1960).

We *can* say, however, that families need a supportive community. To increase the likelihood that families will succeed in adapting to adolescence, we need a community that is rich in social support, both formal support services such as parent education programs and counseling services and informal support services such as social networks, mutual help groups, and positive neighborhoods (Whittaker, Garbarino, and Associates, 1984).

For better or for worse, parents do not *determine* what their adolescents will become. The most caring and wise parents do not always succeed in producing competent, caring, and wise offspring. Likewise, even when children have been abused and neglected by their parents, they do not *necessarily* become socially incompetent, vicious, and uncaring. For all its importance, the family microsystem is not all-determining, and parents cannot always predict the effects of their actions. Peers, the community, the "times in which we live," and the temperament of the individual play big roles.

Having said all that we *still* say that in childhood no other microsystem has greater influence on development than the family. The family meets most of the young child's biological, emotional, and intellectual needs, and interaction with family members constitutes the greatest portion of the child's early experience. However, it is the very essence of development as we defined it in Chapter 2 for the child's world to expand beyond the family to include schools, community organizations, and, most significantly, peers. As adolescents become more actively involved in the wider society, attempt to establish their own independence, and gain a sense of their own unique identities, other influences join, rival, and, in some cases, may even surpass the family's impact on development. The family retains a critical role in enhancing or impeding development, however. Family members may encourage adolescents to discover their potentials, while providing security and affection when appropriate, or they may inhibit psychological growth through insensitive, excessively demanding, or overly restrictive parenting.

No discussion of families will succeed unless it recognizes the special bond between parent and child. To develop well, children need to know that their parents love them intensely and unconditionally. We cannot understand fam-

When I turned thirteen, I was truly excited. I had finally become a teenager. I knew I was entering a real period of growing up and that would be fun. What I didn't anticipate was the difficult and often-times embarrassing situations I would encounter.

My most vivid memories have to do with "falling in (puppy) love" and trying to deal with that. My longest love started when I was fifteen and ended just before I turned eighteen. Definitely a one-sided romance. I tried all I could think of to figure this guy out and get him to notice me. His being 5 years older than me didn't help much. I started writing in a journal periodically from 12–14 but at 15 with the advent of my infatuation with Tony I wrote continually for almost 2 years. Many, many things in my journal are embarrassing now that I look back, but I refuse to throw it away because if I have kids, I want to be able to prove to them that I too have gone through what they will go through during adolescence.

So often I thought I knew so much and fantasized about Tony, and boy, I was sure I knew everything he was thinking. I'd take what I heard about him and dwell on that until I had figured out again just what he was all about.

Needless to say, we never did go out—he never even showed interest. How could he? . . . I was a sophomore in high school and he was a junior in college.

Another memory I have is of a difficult time I went through with my father. When I was 16 we started fighting. Actually, it was my problem, not his. He was merely picking on me, but I hated it, and hated him for doing it. I wrote down my feelings after many of our arguments, but I did throw a few of them away. After I reconciled with Dad, I couldn't bear to keep reading over those bad feelings I had expressed, so I threw them away. The situation finally climaxed with an argument with Dad in which I went out to talk to him (in tears) and he finally did say how much he loved me (and all 5 of my brothers and sisters). I guess that was what I needed to hear. I had never been sure. Now I am and this past year and a half has been a blessing because our relationship has grown so much closer—like a father and daughter should be.

ilies without understanding that to be a parent is to have a special feeling of responsibility. Perhaps the Russian novelist Leo Tolstoy best captured the miracle of seeing a child become an adolescent and then an adult. In his epic *War and Peace* he writes:

> The universal experience of the ages, showing that children grow from the cradle to manhood, did not exist for the Countess. The growth of her son had been for her at every stage as extraordinary as though millions and millions of men had not already developed in the same way. Just as twenty years before it had seemed

unbelievable that the little creature lying under her heart would ever cry, nurse at the breast, or talk, so now she could not believe that this same little creature could be that strange brave officer, that paragon of sons and men, which judging from his letter he now was. (Tolstoy, pp. 291–292)

In this chapter we examine how physiological, psychological, and social changes associated with adolescence affect family relations, and how these relations affect the adolescent's continuing development. Amidst this examination, we must acknowledge that families develop as well. Parents and siblings continue to grow and change. Exosystem and macrosystem events such as social trends and historical events (such as the Great Depression of the 1930s) may intervene to affect the family as a unit (Elder, 1974) and will ultimately have significance for the adolescent's development.

Definitions of Family

Defining the term *family* has proven to be a vexing issue for social scientists. If every family fit some standard—e.g., a nuclear family, comprised a mother and a father who are the natural parents of two or three children—agreeing on an exact definition of family might not be a problem. Difficulties arise, however, when we attempt to reconcile such a definition with the many other social arrangements that many consider to be families: single parents with children, adoptive parents and adopted child, a couple without children, a homosexual couple united in a quasi-official church ceremony called a *covenant* who have adopted a child, or several generations living together under one roof. How can we fit all of these variations within one definition? The systems perspective we outlined in Chapter 2 tells us to organize our thoughts around boundaries (what is inside the family and what is not?), energy, materials, and information (what goes on inside the family?), linkage (with what other microsystems is the family connected?), and dynamic equilibrium (how does the family adjust to

My most vivid memories of adolescence are when I went to Canada, Florida, and Atlantic City with my family. I thoroughly enjoyed the excitement of going on vacation, and treasure those most precious moments.

You see, when my father was on vacation, instead of being all uptight about his extremely stressful job, he would relax, and show my mother, brother, and I his true feelings. The atmosphere was relaxed and filled with pleasureable fun. Rarely was there a squabble. My father and mother took lots of pictures of the good times we had on our vacations when I was a child, and to this day, they're what I think of the most when looking back upon my adolescence.

changes in composition, structure, and external input?). These themes underlie our discussion.

At present, much of the debate over family life arises from efforts to define the family based on who it contains and how they divide the rearing of children. We prefer an approach that recognizes the fact that families are diverse in form, but similar in their function; they are bound together by love, loyalty, caring, and sharing. This is in keeping with the anthropological finding that the membership of families differs cross-culturally. For example, fathers are leaders of families in some cultures, equal to mothers in others, and passive bystanders in others. The point is that cultural standards for family membership, obligations, rights, and behavior vary quite a bit, and we consider this a backdrop for viewing contemporary North American family patterns, particularly since North American society contains many ethnic groups of diverse origins. Consider, for example, that among Hawaiians, marital relationships do not imply the kind of friendship that they do for many Caucasian North Americans (Korbin, 1982). Bott (1971) makes a similar report in her analyses of English lower-class families in contrast to middle-class families.

Definitions of family generally fall into two categories: those that define families on the basis of their function (what they do) and those that concentrate on structure (how the family is organized). George Murdock (1949) was one of the first to develop a functional definition of families. He listed four activities that distinguish families from other social institutions: procreation, sexual relations between married partners, economic cooperation, and the socialization of children. More recently, Ira Reiss (1980) proposed a definition that emphasizes the last item, socialization of children. The family, according to Reiss is ". . . a small kinship-structured group with the key function of nurturant socialization" (p. 29). Reiss's definition, in contrast to Murdock's, would include most of the variations on the nuclear family noted earlier, with the exception of a married couple with no children.

The alternative approach to defining families in terms of their structure focuses on patterns of social organization and the roles existing within the group. In other words, the family is defined as different from other social institutions because of the social roles it contains. A definition proposed by Bell and Vogel (1968) exemplifies this approach: "A family system exists in any society in which the related positions of mother, father, and children are recognized and shared notions" (p.2). Sociologist Talcott Parsons (1949) developed the idea that families depend upon a parental division of labor into two roles: the *expressive* and the *instrumental*. The expressive role serves the family by caring for its emotional life, its need for harmonized feelings. The instrumental role serves the family by arranging its material relations with the outside world, its need for a harmonized balance between resources and expenditures. Parsons saw fathers in the instrumental role and mothers in the expressive role, a view that many critics find to be a simplistic stereotype because mothers and fathers may take on both roles.

For many, a structural definition is preferable because it avoids some of the ambiguities inherent in the functional definition. For instance, a variety of individuals not readily thought of as part of the family, such as teachers, may be engaged in socializing a child. A more precise definition results by specifying a particular organization with specific roles. One researcher holds that only the group composed of a mother, a father, and children may qualify as a family, regardless of whether similar functions are performed by other individuals or groups (Zelditch, 1964). Intrinsic to the roles of mother and father is the notion of nurturing socialization. Indeed, when parents do not provide nurturing socialization and instead are abusive and neglectful, they may be threatened with termination of parental rights and the loss of their family roles.

In our discussion we employ a working definition of family neither purely functional nor totally structural. We view the family as a miniature social organization whose members are related by blood, marriage, or adoption, which has as its function training its younger members for appropriate roles and behaviors in the wider society and meeting the sexual, social, and economic needs of its adult members. In addition to its socialization functions, the family is a significant resource for the adolescent in fulfilling emotional needs, most notably the need for acceptance and security without inhibiting the quest for autonomy and identity.

This discussion of the idea of the family is useful because it helps us see what the families around us have in common. When it becomes a way of degrading cultural and ethnic family variations, it loses its usefulness. We know that families share the functions of bearing and rearing children and providing for the material and psychological needs of its generations, both older and younger. But we also know that the tactics, strategies, and arrangements used by families to achieve these goals differ. This leads us to examine several important ways in which families do differ with respect to children and adolescents: size, composition, and spacing of offspring.

Family Size and Composition

Family structure is significant because it may influence the way in which individuals think of themselves and the way family members relate to one another and the outside world. In particular, family size and the position of individuals in the family (birth order) may influence the course of adolescent development. Generally, research has tried to isolate these two variables and examine their effects separately. Their influence within families, however, is most likely to be combined or interactive. What is more, family size and composition are often related to other factors, such as social class (e.g., lower income families tend to be larger) and religion (e.g., Protestants tend to have fewer children than Catholics). These connections prove to be very important, because social class and religion are powerful influences on many aspects of adolescent development, often overriding the structural aspects of the family. For instance, the second child in a wealthy, Protestant family with two children will develop quite differently from the second child in a poor, Catholic family of six children. Our discussion of the effects of family structure on adolescent development, however, will adhere to the dichotomy that exists in the research literature, which tends to look at family size and composition as if they were really separate factors.

Several decades ago two large scale studies demonstrated an important distinction between large and small families. Bossard and Sanger (1952) and Bossard and Boll (1954) found that large families tend to rely on more authoritarian or restrictive discipline techniques. Research since then has tended to confirm those findings (Richardson, 1981). Moreover, parents of large families tend to be less involved in each child since their attention is more divided. When they do attend to individual children, it is more likely to be for purposes of control. Most people find they can afford to be more indulgent with one or two children but must emphasize control more once they are outnumbered. Parents of children in smaller families give more concentrated warmth and attention, although they are more likely to be overly protective or indulgent.

The results of a recent survey of over six thousand adolescents support these findings. Adolescents from large families (of four or more children) perceived their parents as more controlling and less indulgent (Peterson & Kunz, 1975). Another study found that adolescents from large families experience more conflict with their parents (Edwards & Brauberger, 1973). A related finding suggested that adolescents from these families are more likely to identify with siblings and peers than with their parents (Holtsman & Moore, 1965).

In contrast to their peers in larger families, adolescents in smaller families receive more attention and report fewer conflicts with their parents (Edwards & Brauberger, 1973). This more positive relationship with parents is reflected in greater similarity of attitudes and interests between the generations in smaller families (Douvan & Adelson, 1966). Adolescents from smaller families also have better relations with and report feeling closer to their siblings.

The effects of family size have been noted within the realms of cognitive and personality development as well. Adolescents from small families tend to have higher IQs and do better in school. This is especially true when the children are spaced several years apart (Trotter, 1976). Douvan and Adelson (1966) found that adolescents from small families have greater self-confidence in their relationships with adults, are more frequently involved in groups and organizations beyond their normal school activities, and are more concerned with planning for their educations and future occupations.

These apparent advantages of growing up in a small family seem to derive from the fact that parents are able to spend a greater portion of their time with their children and that there is a larger amount of family resources available to each child. A survey of adolescents in the mid-1970s found that what teenagers value most in a parent is that they spent time with them (Bahr, 1978).

The decline in birthrates during the 1960s and 1970s has meant that adolescents have fewer siblings and therefore *potentially* greater parental availability. Whether or not this potential is fulfilled remains to be seen. Some observers (e.g., Bronfenbrenner, 1970; Wynne, 1977) worry that modern life entices or forces parents and youth to separate themselves from each other increasingly in their occupations and in recreation.

Birth Order

The primary focus of studies on the effects of birth order has been on intellectual achievement, as we said in Chapter 4. This is in the tradition of nineteenth century psychologist Frances Galton (1896) who noted that among Britain's most famous scientists, the greatest portion of them were first-born children. A recent analysis of IQ scores of 400,000 young men showed that first-borns usually have the highest IQs, with second-borns rating second and so on down the line (Belmont & Marolla, 1973). A similar analysis of high school students' scores on the National Merit Scholarship Qualifying Test supported this conclusion. First-borns of both sexes received the highest scores. Similarly, there was a small but noticeable decline in scores for each successive set of later-borns (Breland, 1978). Only children are on the average slightly less intelligent than oldest children, a difference some attribute to the absence of younger siblings for them to teach (Belmont & Marolla, 1973).

In other areas, the effects of birth order have been most evident in the comparison of first-borns with all others. First-borns not only do better on measures of intellectual performance, but *on average* they also have a higher motivation for achievement (Sampson, 1962), they do better in school (Altus, 1965, 1967), they are intellectually more curious and are more competitive (Altus, 1967; Brim, 1956), and there is a greater likelihood that they will attend college (Bayer, 1966).

Except for the decline in intelligence scores with increases in family size, observed birth order effects among later-borns have been less distinct. There is some evidence, however, that while later-born children may not be as intelligent as their older siblings, they may be more socially adept. Walter Toman (1980) hypothesized that since middle children have to relate to both older and younger brothers and sisters, they may experience a greater variety of relationships. Therefore, these children may be better prepared to adopt multiple roles as adults. The youngest child's strengths appear to be in their peer relationships, but perhaps at the expense of the family interactions. Youngest children, when they reach adolescence, have been characterized as more peer-oriented than other family members. However, they tend to have more difficulty communicating with their parents than their older siblings (Peterson & Sharpe, 1972).

As we noted in the opening of this section, the observed effects of birth order and family size are likely to be related to each other and to social class, religion, and ethnicity. Nowhere is this more evident than in the data on intellectual performance. Remember that children from small families receive higher scores than children from large families, and second-borns do better than their later-born siblings. Information on the size of someone's family or their birth order, whether considered separately or as they may interrelate, still does not insure that one can accurately predict their score on an IQ test. There are many other variables that influence performance on intelligence, achievement, and personality measures. For instance, Page and Grandon (1979) provide evidence, based on data from 20,000 participants, that socioeconomic status and ethnic background are more powerful predictors of intelligence than family structure, a finding that bolsters our ecological emphasis on the social context of the family microsystem. They conclude that at least four social factors influence scores on intelligence tests: family size, birth order, socioeconomic level, and ethnicity. The exact role of each differs from situation to situation, but, on average, the highest IQ scores come from first-born whites from small affluent families.

Contemporary American Families

Families today resemble families of earlier generations in many ways. Their primary purpose, on the whole, continues to be socialization and nurturing. But families have lost many of the economic functions common to families of the past. Some argue that the changes are so vast that the family as a social institution must be dying. Others proclaim that the family is simply in a transitional phase to new forms. As we see it, the family is here to stay (Bane, 1976), but is changing its organization and its relationship with the world outside its boundaries.

What are some of the demographic changes that have contributed to the sense that families are on the decline? Many feel that there is a dwindling sense of commitment to the family, as couples tend to have fewer children and the number of years spent rearing children has been greatly compressed. The recent increase in the number of mothers working outside the home, especially among families with children under three years of age who must rely on supplementary child care arrangements, is for many a symptom of the family's (and the economy's) failing health (see Kramer, 1982). Contemporary families also tend to be more mobile. Extended families seem to be an anachronism, as smaller nuclear families move from one community to another, eventually losing contact with other relatives and the support networks of friends and neighbors. Increases in the number of separations, divorces, and remarriages are probably the statistics most frequently cited in support of the notion that the family is breaking down. Finally, alarming increases in the number of cases of child maltreatment that come to the attention of service providers promote the belief that the family is in a crisis (Burgdorf, 1981).

I was the youngest of four children and my oldest brother is 29 years old. I was usually left out. My best friend lived across the street from me and I always used to play with her. Today we are still best friends. As for my brothers, they all live in different parts of the United States. Many things remind me of them, and it makes me wish I could be near them. Now that I have grown up and can do the things they always used to do without me—it makes me want to do those things with them now. As for my family, we always did things together, always went on trips, played sports together, but now everyone went their different way.

Others who are interested in the status of families interpret these data differently, arguing that the family is not in decline. While the family may be changing, there is still a persistent belief in the significance of family life. Survey evidence bears this out (Blake, 1979). Even though families may be geographically separated, this does not justify the assumption that they are isolated. Families moved a good deal in pioneer times too, and today's family members still maintain contact—talking on the telephone, visiting, and offering support when asked (Bane, 1976). Many families *do* have relatives living in the same community, if not the same neighborhood. Those who contend that the family is only in a transitional phase have offered an alternative explanation for the increases in marital dissolutions as well. Marriage as an institution is not being rejected, they argue, but unhappy marital relationships are. People have simply become more willing and able to remove themselves from those relationships that are unhappy, and they may try to establish other relationships that will offer greater personal fulfillment. As evidence, they point to the fact that remarriage rates in this country are almost as high as divorce rates (Cherlin, 1981). The new pattern is often called *serial monogamy*—one spouse at a time, but with the identity of that spouse changing once or more due to divorce or remarriage.

We are not in a position to resolve this issue here. Suffice it to say that commitment to family remains high but that families face many difficult challenges from unsupportive, even hostile cultural and social forces. Of more immediate concern is how three social changes in families influence adolescent development: divorce and remarriage, single parenting, and maternal employment outside of the home.

Separation, Divorce, and Remarriage

Over the last two and a half decades there has been a steady rise in the number of divorces (although this trend abated somewhat in 1982). Whereas families used to be broken up mainly by abandonment or by death of a spouse (Bane, 1976), they now are dissolved by court decree. Recent statistics indicate that two out of every five marriages will end in divorce, but that about three-quarters of those who get divorced eventually remarry (Spanier, 1980). These changes have had a tremendous impact on the meaning of family to many children and adolescents. Growing up and socialization may now occur in a variety of family structures. Forty to 50 percent of the youth in the United States will have experienced both a two-parent *and* a single-parent family (Bureau of the Census, 1980). A large percentage of this group will also experience a third family form: one biological parent, one stepparent, and (perhaps) stepsiblings (Richardson & Pfeiffenberger, 1983).

A more surprising statistic is the number of youth in this country who will experience a second divorce. It has been estimated that 40 percent and possibly as high as 60 percent of the initial 40 percent whose parents divorce and remarry will be faced with the upheaval a second time (Spanier, 1980). While one might have assumed that second marriages should have a better survival rate, this is not the case. Families that have been through one divorce and remarriage must not only contend with those difficulties that may arise in families of first marriages, but are faced with an additional set of stresses in the second and need extra social support to manage (Richardson & Pfeiffenberger, 1983). Stepparents encounter difficulties in establishing themselves as disciplinarians, adjusting to the habits and personalities of stepchildren, and gaining their stepchildren's affection, while not showing favoritism toward their own children. Resolution of these difficulties usually occurs (Burchinal, 1965; Wilson, Zurcher, McAdams, & Curtis, 1975), but requires a period of readjustment on the part of the stepparent and stepchildren alike, and increases the risk of mental health problems (Kalter, 1977; Garbarino, Sebes, & Schellenbach, 1984). Sometimes, however, readjustment never occurs, and the result is yet another divorce. Cherlin (1981) has suggested that much of the stress in second marriages results from the lack of institutional support and clear cultural guidelines or expectations about how these families are supposed to relate to one another. This, he believes, increases the likelihood that these marriages will dissolve. Unfortunately, where emotional attachments have been established to stepparents, stepsiblings, and even stepgrandparents, these must frequently be relinquished because the courts do not award visitation rights to stepparents as a matter of course.

Social scientists have finally begun to produce a body of knowledge about the effects of divorce on children and adolescents. However, the conclusions that we can draw from this work are still tentative and sometimes appear contradictory, particularly on the question of whether the consequences of the divorce are uniformly beneficial or harmful. Chilton and Markle (1972), for instance, found that adolescents may be better off if a divorce means the end of a conflicted, bitter marital relationship. Similarly, in another study comparing children and adolescents from happy but divorced families with those from intact but unhappy families, those from happy, broken homes had better personal adjustment, less stress, fewer psychosomatic illnesses, and less delinquency

(Landis, 1970). These results bolster the general principle that a warm. supportive parent/child relationship transcends structural influences in its importance. But, as we saw in Chapter 2's discussion of microsystem risk, issues of structure and function are important in their own right, and the best developmental results seem to come from setting a warm, supportive parent/child rel..:ionships within the context of a positive marital bond and a socially supportive environment.

In a five-year follow-up of divorced families, Wallerstein and Kelly (1980) found that regardless of the child's age, separation and divorce were initially traumatic experiences. However, as we mentioned in Chapter 4, the manner in which the children reacted to this stress differed for younger and older youth. The younger children tended to be frightened by the separation, fearful about the future, and often blamed themselves for the parental disharmony or for one parent's leaving. Distress in the youngest children was frequently manifested in behavior problems such as bed-wetting or excessive clinging to parents. Young boys appear most likely to show evidence of disturbance (Guibaldi, 1983). Adolescents were more likely to respond without *apparent* emotion as they tried to comprehend the causes of their parent's conflicts. Despite what often appeared to be an absence of reaction, however, many of these adolescents had simply internalized their anger and confusion. Some expressed hostility toward one parent or the other, while others admitted feeling ashamed. Many of the teenagers felt more vulnerable to the emotional demands of their parents. They were more likely than their younger siblings to feel stress when parents leaned on them to take sides in the marital dispute.

Wallerstein and Kelly's follow-up interviews, five years following the divorce, demonstrated that for some of the children and adolescents the harmful effects of the divorce may be long-lasting. One-third of the children in their sample were doing well psychologically, one-third were in the middle range of mental health, and the final third showed evidence of lowered self-esteem, poorer school performance, and less rewarding relationships with peers and others. Overall, it seems children express their distress more directly; adolescents struggle more indirectly.

My most vivid memory of adolescence was one weekend my mother moved away to live in her own apartment. Vivid because it was so sudden. I was fourteen and for some reason all of my brothers and my sister were all out visiting relatives that weekend. I was babysitting for my cousin.

On Sunday we all seemed to arrive home at the same time to an almost barren home—Mom decided to take the furniture with her. Now everytime I think back, I can clearly see the large empty front room and my brothers and sister, all younger than I, sitting on the front room steps in shock.

What factors may help or hinder a child's adjustment following a divorce? The work of Hetherington, Cox, and Cox (1978a, b) and Wallerstein, and Kelly's analyses agree on the significance of at least three factors. First, children seem to adjust better when they have a continuing relationship with both parents following the divorce. When the parents can agree on regular visiting times for the noncustodial parent and avoid confrontations, the child will ultimately have fewer problems. This conforms to research that focuses on parental conflict, not family composition, as the issue. Secondly, children are greatly helped when the parents can keep them out of their disputes and do not encourage them to take sides. Again, conflict is the issue. Finally, if the custodial parent can maintain an orderly household and can be emotionally supportive, then this will help to alleviate many of the child's anxieties and decrease the likelihood of later disturbances.

Studies of the impact of remarriage on children have generally found few differences between the adjustment of children who live with their natural parents and children who live with one natural parent and a stepparent. When differences are observed, the children in the stepparent homes are usually adjusting less well. For instance, in adolescence, Kalter (1977) reported that girls living with their mother and stepfather were over-represented in a sample of outpatients from a psychiatric clinic. Girls aged 12 and over who lived with a stepfather had significantly higher incidences of aggression towards parents and peers, of sexual activity, of drug involvement, and of school-related problems.

Particularly for adolescents, any attempt to evaluate the impact of divorce and separation should consider the other contexts in which adolescents function. The period of adolescence marks the increasing significance of peers who may provide valuable emotional support during a divorce or remarriage experience. Similarly, teachers, coaches and other adults can assume more significant (and perhaps compensatory) roles in the teenager's life. Their support during these difficult transitional periods could make the difference between adjustment and maladjustment. Thus, when considering the impact of divorce on adolescents, we must look to the microsystems beyond the family and to the various mesosystems that link home with other settings such as school and peer group.

The emotional turmoil accompanying a single divorce and compounded in multiple divorces is only one of the consequences of marital dissolution. Separation and divorce result in several other changes that can produce stress. Often a divorce results in a decrease in the family's material standard of living and may send many families below the poverty line (Cherlin, 1981). Maintaining a second household can strain the family's resources to the breaking point. Single mothers may be forced to work to supplement alimony and child support payments or must face relying upon public assistance programs. The fact that many fathers do not live up to their financial obligations compounds the problem.

Single Parents

Single parents experience additional stress as they assume the total responsibility for their children. Based on an extensive study of single parents, Weiss (1979) identified three types of stress: *responsibility overload* refers to the single parent's responsibilities for all the family decisions and child care. *Task overload* is the lack of time for meeting employment, household, and parental demands that are regarded as a full-time job for two adults in a nuclear family. The third stress is *emotional overload,* or the need for and desire to provide emotional support to children, even though one's own emotional resources are under siege. Single parents are often isolated, not receiving social and emotional support from friends, relatives, or neighbors. Consequently, single parents frequently have insufficient physical and emotional energy to meet the demands of their parenting role. These problems are particularly difficult for single parents with young children. In contrast, adolescents often are a source of practical help, emotional support, and comradery for single parents (Weiss, 1979).

Research on single-parent families tends to reflect the fact that over 90% of these families are headed by women. This research holds that observed deficits in emotional or cognitive development or behavior problems in the children of these households were due to the lack of male role models and paternal authority figures (Gurin, Veroff, & Feld, 1960; Nye, 1958), a phenomenon called *father absence.* Recently, however, investigators have suggested that these developmental problems may be more directly related to the day-to-day experiences of these children. What children experience depends in part on the stress that single mothers experience (Lamb, 1976). Herzog and Sudia (1973) have written, "The number of parents in the home is less crucial than the family functioning of the present member—which is harder to assess."

Currently, one child in every five lives with only one parent. It has been estimated that within the next decade, one child in every three may find themselves in this position (U.S. Bureau of the Census, 1980). The distinction between the direct and indirect effects of single parenting and the processes by which a single-parent family affects a child's social and emotional development have yet to be defined. However, although it is not clear *how* single parenting affects development, there are observable differences between these children and those who live with two parents. While many of these differences arise in childhood when most children first experience divorce, they often influence the experience of adolescence.

The available research tells us that single parenthood affects boys more negatively than girls. Boys in mother-headed homes have been found to be more antisocial, impulsive, less self-controlled, and more rebellious against authority figures (Gurin, Veroff & Feld, 1960; Hetherington, Cox & Cox, 1978a, 1978b; Hoffman, 1970; Nye, 1958; Rosenberg, 1965; Santrock, 1975). These attributes, however, are more common in those boys whose fathers are absent because of divorce rather than death. While most of these results are based on samples of younger children, problems were also related to father-absence in adolescence. For example, Suedfeld (1967) found that 45% of the male Peace Corp volunteers who returned home prematurely because of adjustment or conduct problems had been without a father for at least five years prior to their fifteenth birthday. Not all studies report negative results, however. Feldman and Feldman (1979) found no differences in self-concept or in relationships with mothers between adolescent males from father-present and father-absent homes.

The effect of father absence on girls appears to be less marked. One area in which difficulties do arise, however, is in interactions with males. Hetherington (1972) compared three groups of adolescent girls ranging in age from 13 to 17: a group whose father was deceased, a group whose parents were divorced, and a group from homes that were intact. Both groups of girls with fathers absent had no males living in the home. All the girls were observed in a recreation center they attended and while they were being interviewed by a male or female interviewer. Additionally, each participant completed personality inventories and tests designed to measure sex typing.

On the measures of sex typing, and when the interviewer was female, few differences were observed between the three groups. However, observations at the recreation center and when the interviewer was male did reveal differences. Both of the father-absent groups reported feeling anxious around males, but had developed different ways of dealing with their anxiety. Daughters of widows were tense and shy, avoiding contact when possible. In contrast, daughters of divorced women more frequently initiated encounters with males and were more likely to touch the males who were physically near them. The girls in this group began dating at an earlier age and became more sexually active than girls in the other two groups. There was also evidence of more conflict between divorced mothers and their daughters, who tended to view their fathers more negatively than did other girls. The behaviors of the girls from the father-present homes fell between the other two groups on the observational measures.

The effects of familial disruption on the adolescent's development differ from adolescent boys to girls as well. As Hetherington (1972) observed in her work, the severity of the effects may be moderated by the mother's behaviors. Much of the effect of father absence on the adolescent will depend on the mother's own adjustment and her attitudes toward the missing father. In any case, as we said in Chapter 2, a single-parent family presents developmental risks and challenges, with only one adult to manage this vital microsystem.

Maternal Employment

Another shift in our society that has significance for family functioning in adolescence is the increase in the number of mothers who are employed outside the home. In 1980, 62% of mothers with school-age children worked outside the home compared to 1960 when 39% of mothers with children 6 to 17 (U.S. Department of Commerce, Bureau of the Census, 1981) worked outside the home.

My most vivid memories of adolescence involve the constant struggle for popularity with my peers at school. I was always shy. I guess because I wanted to make a good impression and I didn't want to say something stupid. I always seemed to be well-liked and accepted. I had a lot of friends, but only a few really close friends. I always wanted to be outgoing, bubbly, etc., but I just couldn't bring myself to be that way. I had a happy adolescence—I was involved, but still shy. I had a lot of freedom at home. My parents were divorced, and remarried, but I could basically do what I wanted, when I wanted. My parents trusted me and I feel as if I used my judgment wisely. I had your typical junior high school romances. But I tended to be very sentimental—more into long-term relationships. Perhaps this was due to the broken family.

The proportion of working mothers is considerably higher among women who are separated or divorced. It has been estimated that 49% of all married women are working, whereas the comparable figures for separated or divorced women are 59 and 74% respectively (U.S. Bureau of the Census, 1980).

With the sharp increase in women entering the work force, there has been an increase in the research designed to assess the effects of maternal employment on children and adolescents. Once again the conclusions of these studies often seem to be at odds with each other. Some of this work shows a positive relation between maternal employment and children's social and personality adjustment, as well as their school performance (e.g., Gold & Andres, 1978; Hoffman, 1974). Other studies suggest negative effects, e.g., a relationship between maternal employment and antisocial behavior, lower IQ scores, and strains in father/son relationships (Nye, 1958; Rees & Palmer, 1970; Hoffman, 1974). On the whole, however, few studies using adolescent samples have found negative effects (Hoffman, 1979). Most studies that report negative effects find them among middle class *prepubescent* boys.

One reason that research in this area has frequently proved to be contradictory is that a number of factors can affect the outcome. Considerations such as how much a mother works, how much she earns, how long she has worked, whether she works primarily for economic reasons or for personal fulfillment, her husband's attitude about her working, role sharing and satisfaction with child care arrangements can all affect assessment of the influence of mother's working on the adolescent's development. Other factors that researchers generally attempt to control for include income level, gender, educational background, age, family size, and ethnic background. Any attempt to compare and contrast results from this body of research should recognize the factors examined as opposed to those the researcher chose not to include but that may also be influencing the outcome. What researchers *don't* include is often as important as what they do. With these limitations in mind, several general findings emerge concerning the impact of a mother's working on her adolescent offspring.

Early research on maternal employment often started from the assumption that its impact was negative and research sought to confirm that assumption (Bronfenbrenner & Crouter, 1982). Some of the more frequently cited research in this area conducted prior to the 1960s attempted to link maternal employment to juvenile delinquency, for example. Gleuck and Gleuck (1959) made several comparisons between sons of employed and nonemployed mothers within a sample of 500 institutionalized juvenile delinquents and a matched control sample. These researchers found that maternal employment was not associated with delinquency. Rather, delinquency was related to a mother's inability or unwillingness to provide adequate supervision, regardless of her employment status. In a similar study, Nye (1958) also found a relationship between lack of supervision and delinquency. Nye concluded, however, that less supervision may be a function of the mother's employment, which therefore is indirectly related to delinquency. In another study, Rouman (1956) found evidence that both male and female adolescents whose mothers were employed lacked self-reliance and social skills.

More recent research is likely to start with a positive disposition towards maternal employment, and studies completed since the 1960s have obtained more positive results. Two reasons are usually given for these more positive results. First, maternal employment has become a more accepted pattern (Hoffman, 1980), whereas in the 1950s working mothers were seen as somewhat deviant. Secondly, investigators began to improve their methodology by assessing other contributing influences rather than simply comparing children of employed and nonemployed mothers.

In a study of the relationship between maternal employment, adolescent roles, activities, and parental relationships, Propper (1972) found few differences between youth whose mothers were employed and those whose mothers were not employed. She did find that adolescents whose mothers worked had somewhat more responsibility for household chores, but there were no differences in the amount of time spent in social or leisure activities. In the families of working women, reports of disagreements over a wide range of issues were more common. However, the incidence of children needing help with school and personal problems and the degree of closeness to parents were similar between the two groups.

Douvan's (1963) work suggested that maternal employment may have different impacts depending on the family's social class. She observed that lower-class boys whose mothers worked full-time were somewhat more rebellious, less active, and had poorer ego-integration than the lower-class sons of women who were employed part-time and than middle-class sons of women working full- or part-time. Douvan (1963) concluded that full-time maternal employment per se was not responsible for the poorer adjustment of lower-class boys, but rather that the mother's working was a sign of the father's inadequacy as a provider, and hence the father was a poorer role model for his son.

Gold and Andres (1978) conducted a study designed to examine the relation of maternal employment to the development of male and female adolescents of different social backgrounds. These authors had predicted that the 15-year-old sons of employed mothers would have more adjustment and academic problems than the sons of nonemployed mothers. Their data, however, indicated that both sons and daughters were *better* adjusted when the mother was employed. Gold and Andres were able to compare the results of this study with work they had conducted previously with children who were 4 and 10 years old. These authors concluded that maternal employment is a much more salient factor in the development of younger children than in adolescents.

In a study of lower-class adolescent males whose mothers were employed McCord, McCord and Thurber (1963) found that the emotional climate of the home was more highly related to adjustment than to the mother's employment status. If the mother/son relationship was stable, the fact that the mother worked was not significant. When the family's relationships were unstable, the adolescents appeared to be adjusting less well. McCord and colleagues (1963) hypothesized that in an unstable home, maternal employment may be interpreted as rejection, whereas in a stable home it equalizes status between the parents, and thus enhances development of the children.

Studies have also shown that the mother's morale is related to her teenager's development. Employment is valuable to mothers of adolescents because it provides additional stimuli, a sense of competence, and an alternative to the full-time motherhood role that is coming to an end (Hoffman, 1979). Hoffman has theorized that employed mothers with adolescents may be better able to accommodate to the adolescent's needs. She has written that these mothers "are psychologically freer to encourage the child's independence and to communicate confidence in the child" (p. 864). Adolescents require less care than children and are better able to help around the house. Hoffman believes that this added responsibility may be beneficial for adolescents because "they feel they are an integral part of a functioning system, and this adds to their feelings of self-worth and their sense of family" (p. 864).

All in all, comparisons between adolescents whose mothers are employed or not employed result in few differences (Nelson, 1971; Fish, 1970; Baruch, 1972). When differences are observed, maternal employment tends to have its most favorable effects on daughters and most deleterious effects on young sons. Daughters of working mothers have been described as more outgoing, independent, active, and highly motivated, and they receive higher scores on a variety of measures of academic achievement and social adjustment. As Gold and Andres' (1978) work demonstrated, as well as a study by Nelson (1971), *teenage* sons may benefit too (in contrast to younger males). There is evidence of better social and personality adjustment, a greater sense of personal self-worth, and better interpersonal relations, both at home and at school. These contemporary findings parallel Elder's research (1974) on the Great Depression of the 1930s, when many mothers entered the labor force to the psychosocial benefit of their daughters and detriment of their young sons.

Parent/Child Relations

Having looked at the role of structure in the family's influence on adolescent development, we turn to the role of function. The most significant function with regard to adolescence is socialization—how the family influences the adolescent personality, behaviors, and the development of their attitudes, morals, and orientations toward social roles. To examine these processes, researchers and theoreticians have most commonly identified different parenting techniques or characteristics of parent/adolescent interactions and related them to their developmental consequences. Within this approach, therefore, the course of an adolescent's development depends on the type and quality of family interaction. We review this research in light of what has come before, i.e., that social, economic, demographic, and historical context does much to influence the outcome (as well as the origins) of parenting behavior, but that a few general principles seem to have broad general applicability.

As an example of research on parenting with adolescents, Douvan and Adelson (1966) found a strong relationship between parental involvement and adolescent adjustment. Further, both too much or too little involvement inhibited the adolescent's developing sense of autonomy. More specifically, too little parental involvement leads to a sense of insecurity, while parents who are too intrusive produce an exaggerated sense of dependency. Keep in mind that these judgments reflect some important assumptions about what is an appropriate balance of independence and dependence, as we will see in Chapter 7 when we discuss identity.

As is easy to imagine, there are many ways to classify parent/adolescent interactions. Two dimensions receive the most attention in the literature, however: the *control or authority* dimension and the *quality or affection* dimension (Becker, 1964; Conger, 1977; Martin, 1975). We can subdivide both of these still further into more specific subclassifications. The work of three researchers has been particularly influential in identifying these subcategories. The results of their work are interrelated subtypes or models of parenting that seek to represent characteristics of parenting and how they relate as part of a family system.

Once we present the models, we must consider which parenting type best promotes the development of competence. The answer to this question is usually sought by comparing parental characteistics with adolescent characteristics, which include the adolescent's personality or cognitive development, or their specific behaviors in important social contexts. As we compare, we must keep in mind two things. First, the success of a particular childrearing strategy depends partly on what the environment beyond the family microsystem de-

mands and values (Ogbu, 1981). Second, there is rarely a one-to-one correspondence between what parents do and what adolescents become. It seems
that the best parents can do is try to live by some general principles that they
believe in and then be sensitive to the signals that suggest they need to change
their tactics to reach their socialization goals.

Schaefer's "Circumplex"

In 1959 Schaefer proposed a model of parental behaviors that served to organize existing data on the influences of parental practices on child development
and to guide subsequent efforts. Schaefer derived his model of parental behaviors from longitudinal data from the Berkeley Growth Study. Schaefer took
previous observations and ratings from the study and used a statistical procedure called *factor analysis* to determine the general themes in the diverse data.

The results of these procedures were several *factors*, or groups of behavior types, all of which reflect two basic dimensions: *autonomy-control* and
love-hostility. Each distinct parenting style is a different mix of these two dimensions and reflects a point on the autonomy-control dimension *and* simultaneously a point on the love-hostility dimension. Schaefer's hypothetical model
is the basis for Figure 6.1. Extremely unrelated patterns (such as parents who
encourage autonomy versus controlling parents) appear at opposite points on
the *circumplex*. Similar patterns (for instance, neglectful and rejecting parenting) appear close together. Thus, for example, two styles labeled *accepting* and
overindulgent are nearly identical on the *love* dimension but accepting is lower
on the *control* dimension. Likewise, *authoritarian-dictatorial* and *overprotective* are very similar on the *control* dimension, but differ a great deal on the
hostility-love dimension.

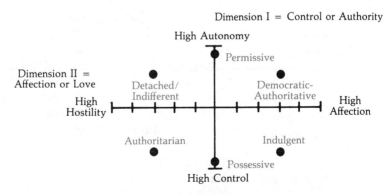

FIGURE 6.1
*A map of parental behavior patterns showing how different combinations of control
and affection result in distinct child-rearing styles (Adapted from "A circumplex model
for maternal behavior" by E. S. Schaefer.* Journal of Abnormal and Social Psychology,
1959, 59, 226–235.)

In order to test the hypothetical model he constructed, Schaefer again used the data from the Berkeley Growth Study. Since many of the children had been observed twice, Schaefer had the advantage of testing the model on children at different ages, as well as exploring the possibility that parents may shift their childrearing styles as children grow up. First, Schaefer looked at the rating of the behaviors of 56 mothers who had children between the ages of 1 month and 3 years. He also analyzed the ratings of 34 mothers' behaviors towards their children between the ages of 9 and 14 years. Both of these analyses provided some support for Schaefer's views concerning the two principal dimensions, but did not support the more specific subtypes. He found that few of the maternal interactions with their infants and toddlers could be described as democratic or cooperative, for example. Within the group of older children and early adolescents, there was virtually no evidence of neglect or indifference. This may imply that infants demand a style that is directive (or permissive) but cannot be part of a democratic approach, while adolescents demand parental response in undeniable ways. It tells us that normal family systems shift and adjust to pursue dynamic equilibrium as members themselves change (e.g., make the transitions from infancy to childhood to adolescence).

When Schaefer compared parental styles across the two age groups, there was evidence of both continuity and change. Variations between the age groups was greater with regard to the control dimension than the love-hostility dimension. The mothers who were rejecting toward their infants tended to also be rejecting towards their older children. The mothers who were permissive or controlling of their infants were not necessarily as permissive or restrictive of the older children (Schaefer & Bayley, 1960, 1963).

Baumrind's Four Styles of Parenting

Working from Schaefer's two-dimensional model, Baumrind (1968, 1978) proposed four general parental types that emerge from different combinations of the degree of control and the quality of affection dimensions. The four types include: authoritarian, indulgent (permissive), authoritative, and neglecting or erratic. Baumrind's approach is probably the best known effort to categorize parental styles. If we bear in mind that it is of uncertain generalizability because it is American and middle class in orientation, we can make good use of it in understanding family relations in adolescence.

Authoritarian Parents

Authoritarian parents are characterized by the two negative extremes of the control and affective dimensions. They are described as being consistently rejecting and restrictive. They assume a rigid set of standards to which they expect their children to conform and by which they judge behavior. Only the parent has input into any decisions and the adolescent is uninformed about the reasons behind any command. Once the parents have "laid down the law," they expect children to comply without question or negotiation. Transgressions are met with harsh discipline.

Characteristics of adolescents raised in authoritarian homes. Love and warmth in the authoritarian home are conditional; they depend upon the adolescent's performance and behavior. The parents have standards that must be met if the adolescent is to feel accepted, and therefore the adolescent feels strong pressure to conform to the parent's demands and expectations. Youth are never listened to and they are free to do only what is demanded and expected of them. They are not accepted as independent individuals and are neither trained nor encouraged to think for themselves.

Baumrind (1975) has characterized authoritarianly raised children as *traditionalists*, i.e., they ordinarily defend the status quo and support the values and opinions of their parents without question. The personalities of these individuals tend to be characterized by rigid, inflexible, and conforming behavior (Becker, 1964). They tend to internalize the anger they have been unable to express against domineering parents and continue this pattern into adulthood (Adorno et al., 1950). However, they are often competent in many important social contexts, because they have been challenged to perform in order to win acceptance from their parents. Though competent, they are likely to miss the joy of life and to withdraw from emotionally expressive intimate relationships.

Permissive-Indulgent Parents

Permissive or indulgent parents place the child's or adolescent's whims and desires before all else. They make few demands, and present themselves as "a resource for the child to use as he wishes, not as an active agent responsible for sharing or altering his ongoing or future behavior" (Baumrind, 1975, p. 256). Discipline, when it occurs, is often inconsistent and unpredictable and is often used only when the child does something that even the permissive parents can-

---

My most vivid memories of adolescence were not the most pleasant memories of my past. During adolescence I was always in trouble with my parents. It seemed like I could never do anything to please them. We fought continuously.

Now that I think back, the reason for all the problems was because my friends' values and my parents' values clashed. My parents were the straight-laced type that ruled with an iron fist. Me, I was your typical little hellion that always wanted her own way.

I used to get into trouble at high school and with the police, but luckily Mom and Dad never knew. As I think back, I'm glad they never found out just how rotten I was. After all, they might not even talk to me today if they did.

not tolerate, which in early childhood may be breaking the television and in adolescence may be breaking the law.

Characteristics of children in permissive homes.   Permissive parents tend to dole out love and affection indiscriminately. Their primary concern seems to be that their offspring like them and that they are happy. They are reluctant to take any action that may cause discomfort and that may deny any wish or desire the child may have.

Baumrind (1967, 1971) has found that permissively-reared children are generally low in self-esteem and self-sufficiency. They have also been found to be self-centered attention seekers who are used to getting their own way. Males tended to show bullying and selfish behavior (low social responsibility) rather than friendly and cooperative behavior (Baumrind, 1971).

However, permissively raised children were not significantly less cooperative than authoritarianly raised children. Also, few parents fell into the permissive category without also being characterized as neglectful. Adolescents raised in permissive homes, with the lack of rules and constraints on their behavior, often are unsure of where they stand and feel insecure and uncertain (Schneiders, 1965).

Erratic-Neglectful Parents

Neglectful parents tend to be inconsistent and erratic in their discipline. There are few definite rules or guidelines, and those that do exist are inconsistently enforced, largely depending on the mood of the parent. Discipline techniques are similar to those of the authoritarian parent with no rationale or concern for the youth's understanding of the reasons behind their punishment or demands. Neglectful parents, like their authoritarian counterparts, can be cold and rejecting. Unlike authoritarian parents, however, their rejection alternates with indifference, whereas authoritarian parents are very involved in order to maintain control and issue directives.

Adolescents in neglectful/erratic homes.   Youth in erratic homes are sometimes loved, sometimes ignored, and sometimes despised and rejected. Expressions of affection, as everything else, flow according to the whim of the parent. Inconsistency is the primary characteristic of the home. These adolescents are often treated unfairly and are often victimized by their parents (Baumrind, 1975). In turn, they often end up victimizing society, expressing their hostility and anger through direct antisocial aggression (Becker, 1964; Martin, 1975). Many delinquent youth come from erratic homes (McCord & McCord, 1964). They have not been taught appropriate social behavior and have not learned how to control their impulses.

Authoritative Styles of Parenting

The authoritative type of parenting has been identified by most writers as optimal, *at least for most children and adolescents who face a middle-class society*

The thing I remember most about adolescence is hating my parents. We fought every day (no exaggeration) and I usually ended up crying in my room. Sometimes my parents picked on me for no reason, but most of the time I gave them good cause to be upset.

When I was thirteen years old I got drunk with a girlfriend. Afterwards, I stumbled home and passed out on the floor where my parents found me. Dad was not pleased! And I was stupid enough to ask him for a cigarette. The punishment for being drunk was nowhere near as bad as the punishment for smoking. In fact, they still haven't let me forget it.

About two months after I got drunk, I had another big fight with my parents. They accused me of smoking in the house (which I didn't do) and I got hysterical and ran away. That night I got picked up by the State Police for walking on the highway. I wouldn't give them my name until they threatened to arrest me. When my parents picked me up my mom cried and my father didn't talk to me. But that's how my parents always were. My father either ignored me or hit me, and my mother always cried. I never got hit too hard, though. Except for the time I called my mother a bitch. Then I got punched. I was so scared my father was going to hit me again—I never saw him so mad.

I have other memories that stand out in my mind, but nothing like those good old family arguments. Those I remember like they happened yesterday.

such as found in North America. This style's flexible use of discipline, combined with consistent positive affection, is most in line with the child's changing developmental needs. Authoritative parents assert their power or place restrictions on behavior, but make an attempt to give some reason and allow independence within those limits. With infants and young children these parents are nurturing and affectionate, but exert control appropriately, enabling the child to develop a sense of self-control. As the child matures, these parents are able to encourage autonomy while continuing to be warm and accepting. Adolescents are given opportunities to disagree, to take responsibility for their behaviors, and to make decisions.

Adolescent characteristics in authoritative homes.   Children in authoritative homes receive love that is unconditional. They are accepted for what they are. Unacceptable *acts,* not *people,* are the target for punishment and punishment is accompanied by rationale that makes it very clear to children and adolescents why they are being punished and what they can *do* to avoid it in the future. They are not made to feel that they personally are unloved because of their actions. They have some notion of why they are expected to do things, not just what they are expected to do. Love and acceptance are always demonstrated and are not withdrawn as a part of punishment.

Baumrind (1975) has described authoritatively reared adolescents as *social agents.* They are self-governing, active, willling to assume the initiative, individualistic, self-reliant, and highly socially responsible. The authoritative home has been characterized as producing stable, nondelinquent behavior in both males and females (Peterson & Becker, 1965). Conger (1977) has emphasized that youth reared in homes where unconditional parental love is given appropriately and where the children receive freedom and independence appropriate to their age, are likely to be more extroverted, socially assertive, independent, creative, friendly, and lacking in hostility towards others and self. In short, the match between the authoritative family and middle-class North American society is nearly perfect.

Elder's Typology of Family Styles

Elder (1963) offers an additional model of parenting types. He analyzed adolescent ratings of their parents rather than analyzing the ratings of independent observers. Elder's approach resembles Schaefer's and Baumrind's conceptualizations in many ways, however. Questionnaires were sent to 7,400 adolescents who were asked to judge how frequently their parents engaged in a variety of behaviors (using a five-point scale from *always* to *never.* By averaging these responses, Elder identified seven modes of childrearing differentiated on the basis of the amount of control the parent exerts:

Autocratic.   Parents make all the decisions concerning the adolescent who is not allowed to express an opinion.

Authoritarian.   Parents make the final decision, but the adolescent has some input in the discussion of the problem.

Democratic.   Parents and adolescents actively interact in decision-making. The adolescents are able to make a decision for themselves, but are subject to the approval or veto of the parent.

Equalitarian.   Parents and adolescents are equally involved in making decisions. These parents are not perceived to be more powerful.

Permissive.   The adolescent is given greater responsibility for making decisions than the parent.

Laissez-faire.   The adolescent can accept or disregard parental authority at will.

Ignoring.   These parents are not involved in any decision-making or discussion of the problem. They are divorced from the role of authority figure.

Elder reports that of the seven types of parenting styles, democratic homes were the most common. This suggests that many families respond positively to the adolescent's developmental need for greater status as a negotiating junior partner in the family. When he broke down the total sample on the basis of parental characteristics, Elder found that fathers are more frequently perceived as autocratic or authoritarian, while mothers were described as more permissive. Furthermore, parents with less education and/or lower incomes were rated as autocratic or authoritarian more frequently. Middle-class and more highly educated parents generally utilized democratic or equalitarian techniques. This seems consistent with Kohn's research described in Chapters 2 and 9, which links the authority style of the father's workplace to his childrearing style at home. It also is consistent with sociological analyses of sex role differences and Gilligan's analysis of male versus female orientations to decision-making, as we presented them in Chapter 4.

When Elder examined adolescent behaviors and personality variables, the results resembled Baumrind's findings. Democratic and equalitarian structures best fostered the emergence of decision-making skills, while autocratic or ignoring parents do not promote this element of social competence. Rosen (1955) found that autocratic and authoritarian families stifle the development of independence, self-reliance, and achievement. In contrast to Baumrind, however, Elder demonstrated that some adolescents whose parents were permissive do well in developing confidence and independence. Finally, adolescents with democratic parents were more likely to report being most satisfied with how their parents were raising them, while those with highly controlling or permissive parents were less satisfied (Bowerman & Elder, 1964; Elder, 1968, 1974).

The parenting styles that are most closely related to the development of competence are those that match the adolescent's needs. Adolescents report a desire to be accepted and loved by their parents without first having to prove themselves or be perfect individuals. They feel uncomfortable and find it difficult to function when they are constantly criticized (Dahlem, 1970). A frequent adolescent complaint is that no one will listen to them. They want their parents to listen to them and understand them in a sympathetic manner (Edwards & Brauburger, 1973). According to adolescents, parents who show interest in their adolescents and are ready to help and support them when it is needed demonstrate a strong level of love and care (Offer, 1969). As we mentioned in Chapter 2, Getzels (1974) refers to this as a *particularistic* as opposed to *universalistic* orientation.

Adolescent Maltreatment

A national survey (Burgdorff, 1982) reveals that adolescents are, if anything, *over*represented as victims of maltreatment (including physical, psychological, and sexual forms of abuse and neglect) when compared with children. Researchers have invoked a variety of factors they believe to be associated with adolescent maltreatment. These may include economic deprivation, social isolation, psychopathology, modeling one's own parents who were abusive *(intergenerational transmission)*, and characteristics of the youth themselves that instigate violence. Research with families at risk for adolescent maltreatment (Garbarino, Sebes, & Schellenbach, 1984) presents a picture of *chaotically-enmeshed* families that are in conflict, that are high on discipline and low on support, that value coercive parental behavior, and in which the adolescent is experiencing significant developmental psychopathology. Stepfamilies in which the adolescent is seriously troubled are at a particularly high risk. Which of these factors is implicated, however, may depend on the history of the family.

Maltreatment in adolescence may either be the continuation of a pattern that began in early childhood or may start when the child becomes a teenager. Cases of long-term abuse tend to be overrepresented in families in lower income brackets, perhaps because of the stresses of poverty. Long-term abusers are also more likely to have been abused themselves as children (Garbarino & Gilliam, 1980).

Abuse that begins in adolescence is not as concentrated in one segment of the population as is long-term child abuse. Some investigators believe that abuse that begins in adolescence may be related to a mismatch between a style of parenting and changes in the developing adolescent. For instance, short-term abuse may be an outcome in families in which the parents have been overly indulgent and expect the child to be dependent and compliant:

> This (pattern) may appear to work in childhood, but that expectation elicits frustration, resistance, and anger in adolescents as they begin to mature. They come to resent being treated like young children when their peers and other adults are telling them they are becoming "young adults." The behavior that characterizes a dependent teenager striving for autonomy is precisely the behavior that will enrage an indulgent parent and lead to cries of "ingratitude!" so often leveled by parents at their teenagers. (Garbarino & Garbarino, 1982, p. 3)

Families characterized by authoritarian patterns of parenting may also be at higher risk for adolescent maltreatment (Garbarino & Gilliam, 1980). As adolescents mature and seek to establish their independence, they are likely to resist intrusive parental control. Parents may then retaliate by escalating their control, which may already involve physical discipline. This confrontation may become maltreatment when normal punishment crosses the line and becomes abusive violence (whether physical or psychological). Obviously, most families avoid these extremes, but the challenges of adolescence to family functioning and punishment are quite real.

The Challenge of Adolescence: Maintaining the Family System in the Face of Adolescent Autonomy

Research on parenting styles and their effects on adolescent development has been the predominant approach to the study of socialization within the family. Child developmentalists and family sociologists alike have not assigned a central role to children and youth in their own socialization and thus have not presented the socialization process in interactional terms, as one of give and take or of mutual influence. Although over the last 30 years there have been social scientists who have argued in favor of studying these reciprocal processes (Sears, 1951; Bell, 1968; Rheingold, 1969; Hartup & Lempers, 1973), until recently their views have had relatively little impact. In the past decade, however, research has been much more attentive to the reciprocal influence between parents and children in family interactions (Lerner & Spanier, 1978). In this section we will review some of the research on changes occurring in adolescents and how these changes may affect family functioning in general and how they relate to parenting styles in particular.

As children develop and move into adolescence, they become concerned with issues of identity (as we will see in Chapter 7) and independence. With physical, cognitive, and social changes, most North American adolescents (particularly males) feel a need to establish an identity separate from their parents (Ausubel, 1977), to relinquish dependency on their parents, and to make independent decisions (Cooper, 1970). As we have seen, especially as it relates to maltreatment, this process may upset family dynamics, as the once-dependent member seeks to renegotiate the terms of the family's governance. Many parents have trouble adjusting to the pattern of self-governance adolescents seek, especially if in the process these adolescents become rebellious, emotional, or hypercritical in their fight for their freedom (Anthony & Benedek, 1970). Ideally, if parents are able to relinquish some of their power and recognize their adolescent's struggle to become a distinct individual, the adolescent's search for autonomy can become an effective basis for the development of a more mature parent/child relationship.

Although attaining autonomy can be difficult in some family structures, it does not always result in open conflict. In fact, when Balswick and Macrides (1975) asked 417 college students whether they had been rebellious as adolescents, only 21% of the males and 23% of the females claimed to have been very rebellious. Sixty-five percent of the males and 58% of the females claimed only slight rebellion. The remainder reported no rebelliousness whatsoever. These findings have the usual drawbacks of self-report data, of course, and it may be that college youth were less or more rebellious in adolescence than those who do not attend college.

So far we have discussed the *need* to achieve autonomy as a general developmental phenomena. Douvan and Adelson (1969) have determined that there are three *goals* guiding the adolescent's search for mature independence: behavioral autonomy, emotional autonomy, and value autonomy.

Behavioral Autonomy

Behavioral autonomy is usually the first of the three goals that adolescents seek to achieve. Much of the potential conflict between adolescents and their parents occurs as the youth begins to become more involved in activities outside of the home, some of which may be unacceptable to the parents. Douvan and Adelson (1969) found that the areas in which adolescents first exert their behavioral autonomy are dating, employment, economic resources, and choice of leisure companions. Table 6.1 shows the increases in each of these domains in a sample of girls ranging in age from 11–18 and a sample of both boys and girls ages 14–16. In examining these data, the most obvious shift is in dating. Also of particular interest is the increase in peer interaction, with a subsequent decrease in the amount of time spent with parents.

The other significant feature of Douvan and Adelson's work is the differences between the sexes in seeking for autonomy. In general, male adolescents desired more independence from parental control, more responsibility for their own decisions and behaviors, and more self-control. Female adolescents, on the other hand, reported that they were more likely to accept parental control and perceived it as reasonable and fair. These findings are consistent with the results of other investigations (Kagan & Moss, 1962; Bardwick & Douvan, 1977). To a large extent, these differences are attributed to the fact that male and female children have been socialized differently. One can only speculate how recent changes in sex role orientations will affect these sex differences.

TABLE 6.1

Indices of behavioral autonomy for girls at eleven and eighteen and for boys and girls aged fourteen to sixteen.

	Change in girls		Girls	Boys
	11 (N = 206)	18 (N = 148)	14–16 (N = 822)	14–16 (N = 1045)
1 Dates or goes steady	4%	94%	72%	59%
2 Has a job outside home	34%	60%	56%	47%
3 Has some independent funds	63%	84%	74%	*
4 Spends most of free time with				
a. friends	22%	46%	32%	*
b. family	68%	44%	56%	*

*The data for boys are incomplete because some questions asked in the study of girls were not included in the boys study.

SOURCE: From *Adolescent development: Readings in research and theory,* by M. Gold and E. Douvan. Boston, Allyn and Bacon, 1969, p. 132. Reprinted by permission.

Steinberg and Hill (1980) conducted an observational study of behavioral autonomy. They found that as children enter adolescence, they seek a greater share of influence in family interactions. In family discussions, for example, they talk and interrupt more. This is a powerful stimulus for family change. Where parents (particularly fathers) cannot adapt gracefully and flexibly to the adolescent's behavioral challenge, the stage is set for conflict.

Emotional Autonomy

Emotional autonomy, as we might expect, suggests the need for adolescents to relinquish or at least alter the close emotional bonds to parents that have been gaining strength since their infancy. Douvan and Adelson define this goal as the degree to which "the adolescent has managed to cast off infantile ties to the family" (p. 130). Some caution is necessary, however, in interpreting this statement, as it is not meant to imply a total rejection of the family as a source of emotional support. For those adolescents who succeed in achieving emotional autonomy, it should be characterized by a *new* relationship with parents not *no* relationship. Also, with emotional autonomy from parents comes emotional dependence on and acceptance of others, especially peers. And, of course, the extent of autonomy may differ between the sexes and across class and ethnic lines.

Emotional autonomy is more difficult to achieve than behavioral autonomy (Gold & Douvan, 1969). For some adolescents, the emotional attachment to parents may never undergo this transition. Some parents may block the achievement of this goal because they are reluctant to "let their child go," and some ethnic heritages encourage them in this. Gold and Douvan observed that indications of behavioral autonomy such as self-reliance in day-to-day activities usually appear earlier than indications of emotional autonomy. Emotional autonomy might be indicated by the ability to use parents as confidantes or express anger towards them without feeling guilty. (On this scale, how many *adults* have achieved such autonomy?) Recall that in Chapter 4 we concluded that adolescence is a time when individuals *can* achieve formal operational thought, although many do not. The same is true of emotional autonomy. It is a considerable task for an adolescent, to be sure. Once again researchers report that female adolescents may rely to a larger extent on their families for emotional support than their male peers. As we shall see in Chapter 7 dependency can be viewed in positive terms as part of feminine identity (Gilligan, 1982). We can also raise the possibility of ethnic differences here. Italian-Americans, for example, place a high value on family loyalty and tend to downgrade emotional autonomy. Autonomy in these families may be interpreted as rejection (Hall, 1983).

Value Autonomy

Value autonomy may occur in adolescence, but it is not usually fully realized until young adulthood (if then), when individuals grapple with issues of educational and occupational goals, and questions related to the establishment of their own family and relationships. Achieving value autonomy is a complex process, involving a balance between family, peer, and other influences. We will give this topic further attention later.

In summary, we can offer several thoughts about the adolescent's need for autonomy and its role in family relationships. Perhaps the major point is the idea that achieving autonomy is not synonymous with cutting all family ties. The degree to which adolescents have to distance themselves from their families will depend on mutual willingness to develop new ways of relating to one another. For some adolescents this may mean a distinct break, while others may find that maintaining the status quo with their parents is the most satisfying relationship. Becoming autonomous is a gradual process of negotiation and accommodation, with different types of autonomy emerging as adolescents move into adulthood and with different goals for different people based on gender and ethnicity.

The Role of Peers in Adolescent Autonomy

The ways adolescents associate with others in their community influences family relations since the family system is linked to the adolescent's other systems. Negotiating terms of the family/peer group mesosystem becomes a high priority item on the agenda of parent/adolescent relations.

Bowerman and Kinch (1959) asked 686 students in grades 4 to 10 to rate the extent to which they identified with their peers and their families, the amount of association with each, and similarity of beliefs and values. Between these grades, there was a noticeable shift across all three areas of family/peer orientation. In the fourth grade, 87.1% of the students were more family- than peer-oriented. By tenth grade, this figure had dropped to 31.6%. The most significant change was in the amount of association, with the least change in identification. This finding agrees with our earlier discussion in suggesting that adolescents are more likely to achieve behavioral autonomy—associating increasingly more with peers—while continuing to identify with and be dependent emotionally on their families. Bowerman and Kinch also observed that when adolescent adjustment within the family was good, their orientation to the family (in terms of association, identification, and similarity of values) remained relatively high. Conversely, when family relationships were marred by conflict or there was little interaction, the orientation to the peer group shifted more dramatically. Adolescents need acceptance from someone. Peers and parents are often two independent sources (Brittain, 1963).

How Does the Family System Adjust?

Many parents may feel rejected by the shift of attention and affection away from them to others (Dreyfus, 1976). During this period, the power and affectional fabric in the family may be torn. This situation is particularly unfortunate because it occurs at a time when adolescents may most need parental support. On their side, parents need adolescent support if the parents are facing mid-life crisis, or *midolescence* (McMorrow, 1977). Sprenkle and Russell (1979) have developed a model of family functioning that seems useful in understanding why families differ in their ability to respond effectively to the challenge of adolescence. This approach views families along two dimensions: *adaptability* and *cohesion*. Extremes of either reduce the family's effectiveness. Too much cohesion is termed *enmeshed*; too little, *detached*. Too much adaptability is *chaotic*; too little is *rigidity*. The value of Olson's approach is evident in a study of families at risk for destructive parent/adolescent relations that found these families to be *chaotically enmeshed* (Garbarino, Sebes, & Schellenbach, 1984).

As teenagers begin to associate more with peers, situations are likely to arise to which they cannot cognitively or emotionally accommodate without help. In these instances, parents are often the best resource for helping to interpret these experiences. When parents step in, help to clarify the experience, and even set limits, often the adolescents are reassured by their support. Many adults remember situations from their youth in which they were secretly relieved that their parents prohibited them from going somewhere or doing something that they *said* they wanted to do but actually were afraid of or uncertain about.

Offer (1969) has described families with adolescents as being in a state of "transitional crisis characterized by confusion." The family reaches a difficult time when there is a need for adjustment and accommodation. There are few clear-cut answers as to how much control parents should seek to maintain and how much freedom to grant the adolescent. Baumrind (1979) contends that in the current climate, in which the rights of youth are emphasized, parents have all the obligations but few rights. She believes that the current emphasis on the rights of children and adolescents leads to narcissistic, selfish behavior in adolescents. Baumrind holds that while adolescents depend upon their parents economically and socially, it is unwise to grant them the full freedom and independence accorded to truly independent individuals. As Baumrind sees it, adolescents lack the natural limits imposed by society that arise from the experience of supporting oneself and, therefore, develop unrealistic expectations concerning the future. This exemplifies how macrosystem influences can shape the family microsystem and how the meaning of specific parental behavior depends upon the context in which it occurs.

How parents respond to the adolescent quest for autonomy depends partly upon the type of family structure present, as defined by the control and affection dimensions. We can consider how families that differ on the control and affection dimensions might be expected to respond to the developmental changes occurring in adolescence.

Conflict of all kinds is found more frequently in authoritarian or permissive homes than in authoritative homes. There is more conflict over spending money, friends, social life and activities outside of the home, and home chores

(Edwards & Brauberger, 1973). The autocratically controlled adolescent is likely to harbor resentfulness toward the parents and is less likely to identify with them (Flacks, 1970). If authoritarian parents are unwilling to adjust to the adolescent's need for independence, attention, and affection and try to maintain their dominance over the adolescent, the adolescent may become either rebellious or dependent (Balswick & Macrides, 1975; Douvan & Adelson, 1969; Nye, 1958; Scheck et al., 1973). Adolescents who are successful in challenging parental authority may become rebellious; adolescents who have experienced severe or unjust discipline without much love and affection may become overtly aggressive and hostile (Weiner, 1970). The adolescent may be driven outside the home for assurance, and this may lead to peer-dependence or delinquency (Martin, 1975; Nye, 1958). On the other hand, if children are completely dominated and have no success in challenging parental authority, they may become meek and conform to the parent's dictates. Both usually show some emotional difficulty (Weiner, 1970) and have trouble proceeding to mature identity, as we will see in Chapter 7.

Permissive parents who cater to every need may engender resentment in the adolescent if they are viewed as being overly-protective or overly-indulgent. Adolescents may resent this babying *(infantilizing)* approach as their contact with the world beyond the family increases. Adolescents sometimes complain that their parents are sticking too close, trying to be their "best friend" (Daly, 1963). Such smothering behavior can produce conflict when the adolescent finally does establish competing relationships, especially sexual ones. The adolescent may also feel confused and resentful at the lack of direction in the home.

Authoritative parents have the best relationships with their adolescents, at least in families in the mainstream of North American, middle-class society (Balswick & Macrides, 1975; Devereux et al., 1969; Scheck, 1973; Baumrind, 1975). They are willing to grant their children sufficient autonomy to develop self-governorship and ego control, but not so much responsibility that it would lead to feelings of omnipotence and social irresponsibility. Their lifelong experience with negotiation and shared control prepares them for adolescence in microsystems away from home as well as in the family.

With the emergence of the period of formal operational thought, many adolescents have the capacity to evaluate parental directions and become increasingly aware of alternatives. Parents are then in the position of having to defend their points of view, a position the authoritative parent has already adopted and become used to. Baumrind (1975) has concluded that parents of adolescents will find the use of power assertion ineffectual: "She (the authoritative mother) makes limited use of power to settle parent/child differences, and then primarily to guard her personal interests or to break a stalemate when the adolescent's objection is based, not on principle, but on pique" (p. 143). Authoritative parents have the advantage during adolescence, because they can "state and defend their own thesis vigorously, and yet will not limit the freedom of the adolescent to express and argue for his antithesis" (Baumrind, 1975, p. 143).

Another significant effect adolescents may have on parents is linked to the different treatment they receive or elicit because of their gender. Parents, especially mothers (Schaefer & Bayley, 1960, 1963), tend to be more flexible with their sons than their daughters (Hart, 1978). Boys are often accorded more room for negotiation than girls, who are allowed less privacy and independence (Duke, 1978).

The greater latitude for boys may explain the results of a study conducted by Adams (1964) of the personal problems of 4,000 adolescents. Adams found that family problems were cited by only 10% of the boys as their most pressing difficulty, while 22% of the girls cited this as their most urgent problem. Studies of runaways indicate that feelings of overcontrol are more likely to be a precipitating factor for girls while boys are more likely to cite undercontrol as a reason for running away (Nye & Edelbrock, 1980).

Transmitting Values

The family has traditionally been regarded as the primary agent for socializing children in their social and political orientations and behaviors. While there is a good deal of research to support this assumption, the evidence is still open to other interpretations, which favor schools, peers, the mass media, and historical events (Acock & Bengston, 1976; Hill et al., 1970; Kandel & Lesser, 1969).

Investigators have generally projected two different images of the transmission of values. As we saw in Chapter 4, some researchers have chosen to focus on the differences or dissimilarities between parents and youth, interpreting their findings in terms of intergenerational conflicts (generation gaps and rebelliousness) (Feuer, 1969). This stance dominated much of the research conducted during the 1960s. Less than a decade later, however, most of these analyses were being criticized as conceptually and methodologically simplistic. Others have argued that intergenerational relations are characterized best by focusing on continuity (Troll, Neugarten, & Kraines, 1969; Thomas, 1971). These researchers have stressed the significance of parents compared with peers as reference points and models for adolescents (Kandel & Lesser, 1969). Yet another set of studies can best be characterized as falling somewhere in between these two opposite views, observing that parents and adolescents share some values, while disagreeing on others. We will explore this further in Chapter 10.

How might one explain these discrepant findings? As is true of most of the research involving families and adolescents, we need to account for multiple variables, including which values and social or behavioral orientations are included in the survey (e.g., clothing styles vs. voting preferences), the nature of the family's interpersonal relations or the family's emotional climate, the degree of similarity between parent and child, the child's and parent's gender, the child's birth order, the family's socioeconomic status, and current historical events or societal trends. Different studies have usually controlled or accounted for these variables to different degrees, which may account for variations in their findings and the interpretations they offer for the results.

Despite the apparent difficulties in studying the intergenerational transmission of values in the family, all is not lost. Lillian Troll and Vern Bengston (1978) summarized the results of a number of studies that they believed to be methodologically sound and that had attempted to account for at least some of these potentially confounding variables. The results of their efforts show both similarities and discrepancies when the value systems of parents are compared with those of their children. For instance, parents and children are most notably similar in religious and political concerns (party affiliation and political beliefs such as humanitarianism, materialism, political participation, and dedication to a cause.) Differences were most evident in orientations toward sex role behavior and life-style characteristics.

The second type of information these investigators extracted from their conglomerate of studies was the effect of social change on the transmission of values across generations. Agreement between parents and children on issues is more likely to result from "their joint exposure to what goes on around them than the results of specific within-family socialization" (Troll & Bengston, 1978, p. 139). When the data are amassed, it seems as though parental influence is greatest when societal trends reinforce particular family values or beliefs. Conversely, it declines when the social tide runs against the parent's position.

Several assumptions regarding gender effects pervade research on family transmission of values. The first is that fathers are more important in determining the intellectual content of their children's values than are mothers. Second, the assumption has been that mothers affect noncognitive aspects of interpersonal characteristics more than fathers. Third, same-gender relationships, that is mother/daughter, father/son, are more similar than cross-sex relationships (mother/son, father/daughter). Finally, daughters are influenced to a greater extent by their parents than are sons. The results of empirical investigations do not always support these suppositions, however.

Several investigations have countered the prevailing view that fathers are the dominant influence in shaping their children's values. The alternative hypothesis holds that mothers have closer ties with their children than do fathers and therefore are more influential. In studies of political party affiliation, some researchers have found that mothers have a greater effect on their children than do fathers (Jennings & Langton, 1969; Acock & Bengston, 1976). In religious socialization, agreement on denominational affiliation between mothers and children tends to be greater than between fathers and children. With the exception of these two findings, however, there is little support for the notion that one parent or another dominates in the transmission of political, religious, sex-role, work, or life-style orientations. Moreover, there were few significant differences in comparing same- versus cross-sex transmission, and sex of the child does *not* appear to be a relevant variable for determining the congruence of

My most vivid memories of my adolescence are those of fun yet hardship. It was hard growing up with two brothers. I was involved in sports and roughhousing most of the time and felt "the girls" were nothing but sissies. I liked to play army and tackle football, go hiking, and climb trees. Life was fun. Then came junior high school. Now was the hardship.

I didn't know how to behave like a girl. It was hard for me to talk to other girls, I wasn't interested in what they were and they definitely did not care about tackle football and climbing trees. I wasn't sure what to do. I wanted to be like the rest of the girls but didn't want my brothers calling me a sissy. My Mom helped make the transition much easier. She never once asked me why I wasn't out with my brothers. She took me shopping to buy "girl's" clothing. She helped me and talked to me about boys and school. She even made my hardship not seem so hard.

parent and child values. Surprisingly, when the quality of family relations (such as closeness) was examined in relation to similarities between generations, the consensus among studies reviewed was that this seems to have *no effect.*

Finally, Troll and Bengston (1978) compared family influence with that of peers and friends. This is an interesting issue, because its outcome may support or challenge the long-standing assumption that parental influence dominates in childhood, giving way to the influence of school and peers in adolescence. The results of Troll and Bengston's composite analysis do *not* lend support to this notion. While they admit that the number of studies they reviewed was small, there were some fairly consistent findings. The influence of peers versus parents seems to depend on the issue of interest, not the phase of the life cycle. Parental influence dominates in areas such as achievement, educational aspirations, and occupational orientations. Peers seem to have their strongest impact in areas such as sexual behavior and drug and alcohol use. However, even here their influence may be moderated by parental attitudes. Troll and Bengston conclude that "in general, peer and parent influence appear complementary rather than oppositional" (p. 146). This is an important point to bring to Chapter 10 when we look at adolescents in the community.

Cross-Cultural Research on Families with Adolescents

The research and theories of familial relationships and adolescent development we have presented so far have been based almost entirely on North American families. Cross-cultural studies in this area are in short supply. One noteworthy investigation highlights some interesting similarities and differences in family interaction and patterns of socialization between North America and another, similar society.

In an extensive survey of high school students, Kandel and Lesser (1969) compared parent/adolescent interaction in the United States and in Denmark. They focused on the degree of independence displayed by youth in these countries and the extent to which family structure encouraged independence. The sample was composed of 1,552 Danish and 2,327 American teenagers who completed questionnaires. Their responses to some of the questions can be seen in Table 6.2.

There is a dramatic difference between the two nations in the areas of parental authority and communication. Parents in the United States either individually or considered jointly are more likely to use the authoritarian pattern of discipline. American families have more rules and are less likely to include the adolescent in decision-making. Danish parents are more democratic and engage their children actively in their decision-making. The more open lines of communication in Danish families are reciprocated by the Danish youth who report being able to discuss their personal problems with their parents.

Fathers tended to be more authoritarian than mothers in both countries, corroborating Elder's (1963) data. Despite the fact that authoritarian styles of parenting dominate in the United States, American mothers are more frequently relied on than any other person for advice. American teenagers also report feeling closer to their mothers and express a desire to be like her.

Another cross-cultural difference that stands out in these data is the different degrees of independence parents encourage. Danish adolescents have a stronger sense of self-reliance, report that they are treated like adults by their parents, and are granted sufficient freedom. In contrast, American adolescents conform to parental rules as long as they are clear and specific.

A look at the differences in background characteristics of the Danish and American participants in the study reminds us that we must be concerned with *who* is studied. Denmark and the United States present contrasting social systems. For example, Americans attend much larger schools and tend to come from bigger communities. Denmark is relatively small and homogeneous and the United States is large and heterogeneous.

Kandel and Lesser imply that differences in adolescent ability to handle independence are at least in part a function of the differential patterns of parenting. Feelings of independence, they write, "are enhanced when parents have few rules, when they provide explanations for their rules, and when they are democratic" (p. 357). If the development of independence is a major task during adolescence, as many would claim, then a democratic form of parenting would be the most conducive to promoting achievement of this task. In conclusion, Kandel and Lesser write, "In the U.S. parents treat their adolescents as children longer than in Denmark. Danish adolescents are expected to be self-governing; American adolescents are not" (p. 358).

TABLE 6.2

Adolescent's perceptions of patterns of interaction with mother and father, by country.

Family Pattern	Interaction with Mother		Interaction with Father		Cross-Cultural Differences*	
	United States	Denmark	United States	Denmark	Mother	Father
Parental Authority						
Authoritarian	43	15	53	31	.001	.001
Democratic	40	61	29	48		
Permissive	17	24	18	21		
Total N	(983)	(950)	(955)	(936)		
Communication						
Percent of Adolescents who feel that parents "always" explain her (his) decisions	30	43	21	33	.001	.001
Total N	(973)	(937)	(954)	(930)		
Reliance						
Percent of Adolescents who depend "very much" or "quite a bit" on parent for advice and guidance	59	54	43	50	.05	.05
Total N	(825)	(852)	(827)	(846)		
Affective Relations Closeness to Parent						
Extremely close	33	21	21	19	.001	.001
Quite close	30	35	29	36		
Moderately close	26	30	27	31		
Not close	11	13	23	14		
Total N	(967)	(944)	(935)	(936)		
Percent of Adolescents who enjoy doing many things with parent	35	35	34	43	ns	.001
Total N	(971)	(941)	(953)	(941)		
Modeling Wanting to be like parent in						
Most ways	42	30	36	36	.001	.001
Many ways	21	40	21	38		
Few ways	37	30	43	26		
Total N	(968)	(941)	(937)	(935)		

*Significance of differences *between* countries for each pattern, as measured by Chi-square.

SOURCE: D. Kandel & A. S. Lesser. Parent-adolescent relationships and adolescent independence in the United States & Denmark. *Journal of Marriage and the Family*, 1969, 31, 348–358. Copyrighted 1969 by the National Council on Family Relations, 1219 University Avenue Southeast, Minneapolis, Minnesota 55414. Reprinted by permission.

Influence of Other Kinship Relations

Parent/adolescent relations have been the focus of our discussion so far. However, parents may be only part of the family system. Siblings and other relatives can also influence the developing adolescent (Lewis & Feiring, 1979). Families come in all shapes and sizes, and the amount of contact with other relatives varies from family to family. It is difficult to make generalizations about the type and amount of influence these various family members will have, but we can offer some information.

Siblings

The results of a survey of adolescents showed that sibling relations during this period are generally positive, with two-thirds of the sample reporting they felt close to their brothers and sisters. Comparatively few adolescents described their relations as negative or hostile. More specifically, siblings who are the same gender are likely to feel the closest. Female siblings feel closer to each other than male siblings. Older siblings prefer younger siblings, and siblings in small families report a stronger emotional tie than is found in larger families (Bowerman & Dobash, 1974).

When adolescents have older siblings, they are likely to use them as role models and confidantes. This type of sibling influence, however, tends to be the greatest in areas in which parents are less likely to be involved, such as peer-oriented activities, physical problems, sexual behavior, and forbidden subjects (Cicerrelli, 1975). Siblings may also influence the adolescent's choice of friends and later the choice of lovers and spouses (Toman, 1980).

No matter how close the siblings, however, there is always the potential for competition or sibling rivalry as each individual competes for parental love and attention within the family system. This is especially likely in families where parents openly pit siblings against one another by making comparisons or by showing greater affection or approval towards one than the other. Although many individuals' feelings of sibling rivalry diminish by the time they reach adolescence, some will be bothered by these feelings throughout their lives (Adams, 1981).

According to a national survey (Straus, Gelles, & Steinmetz, 1980), the level of aggression between siblings in childhood and adolescence is greater than for any other family pairing (e.g., spouse-to-spouse or parent-to-child)— 48% on a severe violence index for siblings versus 14% for parent-to-child. Looking back on their own experiences, most readers will probably agree: hitting is the rule rather than the exception between siblings.

Grandparents

To date, very little attention has been paid to grandparent/grandchild relations in general, let alone in adolescence. The work that has been conducted suggests that three factors may operate to influence these relations: sex, age, and geographic separation.

During my adolescence, I was very obedient towards my mother and never got into any real trouble. I tended to stay away from the booze and drugs. My family situation had a very big influence on how I acted, because my father is not living so I realized that my mother had a dual role—mother and breadwinner. Since my Mom worked, I had responsibilities given to me, such as preparing dinner and looking after the house. I always tried to be a "good girl" so my Mom would have one less thing to worry about.

I often found myself reprimanding my older brother and younger sister when they misbehaved. At one point my sister would say, "You're not my boss, I don't have to listen to you." Then I would go on to explain how we should be considerate of our Mother.

Since I voluntarily accepted responsibility, I tended to be serious most of the time, and my adolescence seemed to reflect that attitude. It wasn't all just fun times and being carefree for me.

As an adolescent I was always the "second" in our family. My older (16 months) sister Kathy got most of the attention and still does. I was usually compared to her and never seemed to meet up to her standards. My father worked most of the time and my mother was always around. She tried to discipline us by yelling and hitting, and apologies always followed. I tried to fit in with the kids on the block but never did. I was somewhat chubby with hair so short I looked like a boy. As I got older I became more quiet and ladylike. In 8th grade I had many friends and seemed to get along with everyone.

Grandparents seem to change their feelings about their grandchildren as the grandchildren develop. Clark (1969) found that grandparents liked their grandchildren better when they were small and attributes this to the fact that as the children got older, they were less interested in the grandparents, and this feeling is reciprocated. Kahana and Kahana (1970) found that children of different ages emphasize different aspects of the grandparent/grandchild relationship. Younger grandchildren thought of the grandparent primarily in terms of their physical characteristics. In preadolescence these researchers noted the emergence of an abstract interpersonal orientation. Furthermore, the youngest children preferred their grandparents for their indulgent qualities, while the older grandchildren reflected emotional distance from their grandparents.

The gender of the grandparent and grandchild also influences the nature of the relationship. Hagestad and Speicher (1981) found that paternal grandfathers were most actively involved with their grandsons who were adolescents or young adults. These grandfathers assumed a role as an advisor, offering information about education, occupations, and money matters. Attempts to influence grandsons in the maternal line were less evident. No information was available on whether this relationship was true of younger grandchildren.

Grandmothers, on the other hand, were less likely to distinguish between grandsons and granddaughters. Furthermore, in addition to discussing issues related to becoming adults, grandmothers were more willing than grandfathers to deal with personal matters regarding family or friends.

Finally, geographic separation is important in the grandparent/grandchild relationship. The effect of separation, as Gilford and Black (1982) discovered, is not simple. When there is opportunity for frequent interpersonal interaction, close bonds are more likely to be established and the grandparents will be more important to the grandchildren independently of the parent. When they live far apart, their relationship depends more upon the grandparent/parent relationship.

Interaction with grandparents may be a significant source of information for the adolescent about family history and history in general. Furthermore, grandparents are significant in learning about our own future physical and emotional development.

Conclusion

The period of adolescence marks the transition from being dependent and childlike to becoming relatively independent and self-governing. In order to achieve autonomy from the family, adolescents increasingly come to rely on other socialization agencies and peers and become less attached to their immediate families. The assumption has been that this shift in attention causes strife and upheaval in families. Proponents of the sturm und drang view of adolescent development characterize the family context as a battleground on which a bitter war is waged against parental restraint, where the opposing sides are unable to speak the same language, much less negotiate a peace plan. In short, this view characterizes parent/adolescent relations not simply as a generation gap, but as a generational abyss (Conger, 1977).

This position, though true in some cases, has generally been overstated. Investigations of adolescent/parent relationships have demonstrated that conflict is not present in all families with adolescents, but rather depends on the nature of the family interactions and the context in which socialization occurs. In families where parents are excessively controlling, restrictive, indulgent, or neglectful, there is a greater likelihood of difficulties arising, in both the interactions between the parents and their adolescents and in other domains of development. Warm, stable parent/adolescent relations, while not devoid of disagreements or dissension, are not likely to present threats to adolescent development.

Our overview of the research suggests that relations with parents, siblings, and other relatives continue to be of central significance to the adolescent's socioemotional and cognitive development. When children are very young, a developmental milestone of great significance is the ability to crawl away from one's parents to explore the environment. Before this can occur, however, children must feel secure in their relationships with their parents. They come to understand that it is safe to venture forth because they trust their mothers or fathers will be there to help should a problem arise. These infants and toddlers have been described as using their parent as a *secure base.*

In some respects, families may function as a secure base during adolescence. When the parent/youth relationship is founded in mutual trust and affection, adolescents develop self-reliance and exhibit competence as they become more active members of society. Adolescent relations with their families are, however, somewhat paradoxical. While adolescence is marked by a decreasing dependency on the family and increasing autonomy, the quality of the family relationships can insure the success or failure of achieving this goal. An important aspect of all this is forming a positive, stable, and realistic identity.

Ecological Wrap-Up

Organism.   It is the changing individual as a biological system (puberty and cognitive maturation) that signals family relationships to begin the transition from parent/child to parent/adolescent relations. Each individual in the family goes about his or her personal agenda and in so doing challenges the family as a system to adapt.

Microsystem.   The family is the primary microsystem for human development. This extends to adolescence when families must come to terms with the consequences of childhood patterns *and* the need to adjust to adolescent realities. While it's impossible to offer a specific prescription for success in parenting with adolescents, it does seem that warm support coupled with negotiated demands is the best way to achieve social competence well-suited to North American middle-class society.

Mesosystem.   The congruence of family with the major microsystems outside the home does much to establish the criteria for assessing and evaluating parental styles. In general, when we consider school and peer group, it appears that what Baumrind calls the authoritative style is effective and wise. It produces and supports the kinds of skills and personality traits that succeed in North American middle-class society.

Exosystem.   The availability of supportive services for families from community institutions is a vital exosystem issue. Parent education and stress-reduction programs are prime examples. The need for such support systems is particularly great when families face special challenges such as divorce, remarriage, and single parenthood.

Macrosystem.   Broad demographic and ideological trends do much to determine whether specific family types and styles are normal and effective. This is why we have limited our analysis to North American middle-class society. Trends toward increasing maternal employment outside the home, divorce and remarriage, small families, and demands for school success do much to set the agenda for families in North America as they adapt to having an adolescent in their midst.

Preview

- Development in adolescence includes identity formation—coming to know *who* you are.

- Erik Erikson's view of identity formation as a succession of stages each with its special challenges dominates our thinking about adolescent identity.

- Males and females tend to approach the task of identity formation somewhat differently: males emphasize who they are as *distinct from* others; females emphasize who they are *in relation to* others.

- Psychological characteristics such as cognitive style and anxiety influence the process of identity formation.

- Family characteristics such as parental childrearing style, ethnicity, and religion also affect identity formation, leading some to search for answers and others to accept the answers first given them by parents.

- Sexual identity is an important facet of overall adolescent identity.

- One way to approach the issue of adolescent identity is to ask what kind of people are best suited to make the world a better place in the future.

As we have learned in earlier chapters, the adolescent is busily amassing new intellectual equipment and putting that equipment to the test in figuring out how the world works. This includes the social as well as the physical world.

Certainly one of the most important aspects of all this concerns figuring out who one is as an individual and as a member of a society, a community, a clan, and a family. Indeed, the very concept of development we are using tells us that developing individuals are enlarging their relationships with the world and their understandings of who they are in that world. Recall Bronfenbrenner's proposition about individual development, as we presented it in Chapter 2.

> The developmental status of the individual is reflected in the substantive variety and structural complexity of the . . . activities which he initiates and maintains in the absence of instigation or direction by others. (Bronfenbrenner, 1979, p. 55)

Development means becoming a competent person, and part of that process is knowing who you are, and where you stand amidst the micro-, meso-, exo-, and macrosystems of life. One of the keys to achieving maturity, according to Charlotte Buhler (1969) and others, is harmonizing the relationship between one's internal and external realities. How does who *I* think I am correspond with what *they* tell me I am? We call this process *identity formation*, and it involves establishing and recognizing a sense of self that is worthwhile and distinct.

Adolescence is the period in life when most of us accomplish much of the work of identity formation. In adolescence, we come up with our first tentative answers to the question "who am I?", answers that we may revise

7

Knowing Who You Are

and update for the rest of our lives. Our answers reflect where we have been, how others define us, and what the society and our culture offers us in the way of alternatives; they reflect the influences of micro-, meso-, exo- and macrosystems. In this chapter we will trace some of those ecological influences and in so doing enlarge our understanding of how *who* the adolescent is affects *what* she or he does.

Like *adolescence* itself, the concept of *identity* has a history. It was not until the 17th and 18th centuries that philosophers were using the term to refer to the psychology of self. British philosophers John Locke and David Hume set out some of the basic issues concerning identity. To this day, we struggle with these same issues in one form or another: Is there a true inner *self* or is the self just the sum total of what we do, think, and feel? Is identity the *discovery* of the true inner self, or a conclusion we reach about ourselves based on how others *define* and *evaluate* us? Do we *find* ourselves or *make* ourselves?

Definitions of Self, Self-Concept, and Identity

To some extent, *self* is a concept we create based on what we are and what we do. It is also something that motivates and guides our behavior. We do some things because of who we are, and we decide who we are because of what we do. Self is an evolving concept, one that we live out in our daily lives, one that arises in the interplay of the individual and social systems. It arises from the human ecology of personality development, and adolescence is its heyday.

As we have said, we define self-concept as the individual's idea of who he or she is, as the answer each person gives to the question, "Who am I?" (Epstein, 1973). It usually is tied to how much people value themselves, or *self-esteem*. As we shall see, self-concept is related to identity, a broader more comprehensive model of how one is similar to and different from others.

The measures used to assess self-concept include interviews, checklists, and projective tests (in which the respondent describes what he or she sees in a set of pictures and the investigator infers things about the person from those descriptions). Many are based on the respondents' assessments of their own self-worth (e.g., Rosenberg, 1965). Another series of measures attempts to tap the structure, function, and quality dimensions of self-concept (Monge, 1973; Mullener & Laird, 1971). Still other methods attempt to measure mental health or well-being and thereby the success of self (Petersen & Kellam, 1977; Gleser, Seligman, Wiget, & Raub, 1977). Damon and Hart contend, however, that none of these self-esteem scales takes into account or *corrects for* developmental changes in self-concept. That is, they believe that as the concept of self changes as part of overall cognitive and social development, the meaning and significance of specific assessments change. This is particularly important for our concerns because adolescence is a time of substantial potential and actual change in self-concept.

The Special Role of Self-Concept in Adolescence

When children enter adolescence, they are individuals with specific conceptions of themselves, the world, and how they should act—all of which need to be adapted to fit the multitude of changes going on inside and outside their bodies. For example, most adolescents have a body-image and a characteristic way of interacting with the world. They also probably have a stable pattern of thinking about how the world works—a cognitive style (which we discussed briefly in Chapter 4). When faced with the vast social, psychological, and physical changes accompanying puberty, all these aspects of the self-concept must respond, adapt, and change. A boy who begins to take on the physical characteristics of a man must figure where the child he was has gone and how to replace that child. A girl who begins to menstruate and develop breasts must adjust to being defined as a sex object by others, and needs to figure out who she now is.

Pubertal Changes

Elkind (1971), McCandless (1970), and Padin, Lerner, and Spiro (1981), among others, have indicated that the physical development of adolescents has a great effect upon psychological functioning, including self-concept. Offer's (1969) study of parents and adolescents indicated that the period between the ages of 12 and 14 was quite difficult in this regard. One attempt to explain the psychological adaptation to puberty focuses upon the way the individual's concept of self and society filters the experience of pubertal changes—the *mediated-effects model* (Petersen & Taylor, 1980). As Petersen and Taylor see it, it may not be the biological events of puberty *per se* that dictate psychological responses, but instead it may be a result of how the adolescent interprets the events (their *subjective* stimulus value). The girl who defines the onset of menstruation as "the curse of womanhood" may incorporate this negative theme into her concept of self, while the girl who sees herself as achieving initiation into "the sisterhood of life" may see the same physiological event more positively.

This links the adolescent experience of puberty to a large body of research on the way people may label changes in psychological states based on what they expect or believe about the cause (Bem, 1974; London & Nisbett, 1974; Schacter & Singer, 1962). This research tells us that when our bodies present us with *physiological* events, we use our minds to give *psychological* meaning to the event. We say, for example, that we are happy, angry, or afraid, depending upon what we know about the cause of the arousal we feel. This model, Petersen and Taylor suggest, implies a sequence in which a change in a physical state brings about the need for self-evaluation in the individual. These evaluative needs then bring about the interpretation of the meaning of the change. Thus, change in the body of the adolescent most likely results in changes in body-image, and possibly of gender identity and self-concept as well

(Blos, 1962; Kestenberg, 1967a, 1967b, 1968; Schonfeld, 1966, 1969; Waterbor, 1972). This makes clear why there is likely to be greater stability in childhood and adulthood, when physical change is slow, more gradual and incremental, as opposed to adolescence (and perhaps old age) when change seems rapid and dramatic.

Individual Differences in Rate of Change

Because of our society's strong emphasis on physical attractiveness as a basis for developing a positive self-concept (particularly for females), the body type that develops as a consequence of differences in the rate of maturation has major implications for social and personal functioning in adolescence. The comments and feedback adolescents get from significant others strongly influence their feelings about themselves and ultimately their assessments of who and how valuable they are as individuals. Do parents and teachers respond to the early maturing girl as "womanly" or as "precociously sexual," to the late maturing boy as "just taking a little extra time" or as "physically retarded?"

This highlights the importance of the adolescent's microsystems (e.g., peers and parents) and macrosystems (e.g., mass media images) in self-concept. Research on adolescent body-image (Bruch, 1943, 1970; Schonfeld, 1966) and the adjustment difficulties of early- and late-maturers (Clausen, 1975; Jones & Mussen, 1958) indicates the importance of both adult and peer evaluations in the way adolescents adjust to their changing bodies (Lerner, 1969; Staffieri, 1967). We mentioned this in Chapter 3, but want to recall it here.

In general, early-maturing boys exhibited a number of advantages over late-maturing boys, including higher peer and adult ratings on physical attractiveness, heterosexual status, self-confidence, and independence. Late maturers were viewed as less attractive, but were rated as higher in sociability, social initiative, and eagerness. In the follow-up study in adulthood, Jones (1965) found that in adulthood the early maturers continued to be socially successful as they had been in adolescence. But he also found some compensation for the late maturers in adulthood, who were described as more exploring, flexible, independent, and humorous.

Jones and Mussen (1958) found a similar pattern for girls and concluded "that late-maturing adolescents of both sexes are characterized by less adequate self-concepts, slightly poorer parent-child relationships, and some tendency for stronger dependency needs" (1958, p. 500). Likewise, Faust (1960) found that for girls, precocious development, while detrimental to prestige during sixth grade, tends to become a real asset during the three succeeding years. The adolescent self emerges from these experiences affected by the reactions of parents, peers, and other significant figures. The point is that the conclusions we draw about self in early adolescence can have life-long consequences, *if* we permit the events of puberty to shape social roles.

Changes in Social Roles

Havighurst (1972) indicated that one important task of adolescence is to establish oneself outward from family to friends to community. In his view, adolescents are first "achieving emotional independence of parents and other adults" (p. 55); second, "achieving new and more mature relations with agemates of both sexes" (p. 45); and third, "desiring and achieving socially responsible behavior" (p. 75).

In order to make this transition smoothly (and thus to gain some sense of self-esteem and competence) adolescents need to decipher what it is that they must do. The range of cultural expectations for the developing person, as Ogbu (1981) aptly points out, varies substantially from culture to culture both in their content and in their explicitness. This was the message in Chapter 2 when we discussed social competence. For adolescents in our culture, it remains somewhat true that they do not wish to belong any longer to the category of children and at the same time know that they will not be readily accepted into the adult group. In this case they have a position similar to what is called in sociology the *marginal man* (Lewis, 1939, p. 881). The marginal man is a person standing on the boundary between two groups, not belonging to

Growing up an only girl and the oldest of three children, I received an above average amount of "protection" from my parents, or so I thought in my teen years.

At the age of fourteen, I was asked to go out for pizza one evening by a very good-looking blond male whom I had adored from afar. I was totally ecstatic about the invitation but my excitement was quickly dampened as my parents refused to let me go out with him. The rule that I could not date until I was fifteen and not anyone out of high school had been previously set down by my father. But since this was not just any guy, I thought that my parents would definitely bend the rules this time. My normal conversation with my parents soon turned to tears as it became clear that they were adamantly sticking to their rules and there was no changing their minds. My futile attempt to persuade them to let me go continued for over an hour and my tears turned to sobs. I told them that most girls would cut off their right arm to go out with this guy but it still did not matter to them. I felt that they were depriving me of one of the best things that would ever happen to me and I pouted for the rest of the evening. I later realized that I really just wanted to go out with him to please my peers. He was considered one of the "hunks" at the time and to go out with him was really something special. This episode seemed so major to me at the time and now is so trivial, but I feel it is a classic example of an adolescent reaction in such a situation.

either and uncertain about his belongingness. If it was true nearly 50 years ago when those words were written, it is probably more true today when the adolescent period of marginality has been extended downward to age 11 and upward to the early 20s. There are precious few ways that 16 year olds can clearly say that they are men or boys, women or girls. Indeed, some observers believe that the lengthy and intense ambiguity of modern adolescence lead youth to have sexual intercourse because it gives them a chance to do *something* really adult.

Being in limbo makes it difficult for adolescents to figure out what is expected of them and what they should expect of themselves, as Bronfenbrenner (1970) has aptly noted:

> A young person can graduate from high school at age 18 never having done a piece of work for anybody else, never having held a baby in his/her arms for more than a minute, never having cared for someone who is old or ill, never having had to comfort the lonely. The result is a generation of helpless misfits who do not know how to live with other human beings. (pp. 35–36)

Identity Formation

Identity formation is the work of the ego in integrating aspects of self into a coherent and distinctive whole (Josselson, 1980). Most theorists believe that it is in infancy that the ego first comes to experience the self as unique and separate from the other (the mother to start with, for most children in most cultures). This process of separating *self* from *other* is called *differentiation.* But it is in adolescence that this rudimentary differentiation assumes profound significance in social relations (Blos, 1962).

Blos saw adolescence as the time to sharpen the boundaries between *self* and *nonself.* Josselson (1980) adds to this the notion that autonomy is the other side of the individuation, the process of becoming a distinct individual. Autonomy here refers to the individual's ability to *operate* as a separate person, to make decisions, act without direct guidance, and display a sense of self-determination. She contends that aspects of the self that have become individuated and autonomous must then be incorporated into identity in the following sequence: individuation/autonomy/identity formation. Thus, as adolescents develop a more stable sense of self, they can then sort through and synthesize childhood identifications and changing physical, social, sexual and emotional selves into one coherent identity.

According to Josselson (1980), however, identity formation goes beyond the tasks of individuation and of reorganization or reintegration of internal experiences (e.g., self-fantasies, emotions). For her, identity formation requires an agreement between one's sense of inner sameness and continuity and the sameness and continuity of how one is defined by other people. She feels that the ego's work on identity formation occurs largely in late adolescence. The middle-adolescent preoccupation with how much to value the self then gives way to the late-adolescent desire to have others value the self or the reasons that one has come to value oneself. Josselson feels, then, that identity resides in mutuality between self and society—a public statement of the self to which the individual intends to be committed. It moves beyond the intimate family to a public presentation in the major microsystems of life as the adolescent proclaims "this is who I am" to teachers, peers, employers, lovers, and others.

According to Lecky (1945), the constructs that make up the self form the core of the personality. As such, self-concept embodies the notion that we actively perceive our self and act in ways that both reflect and change this self-concept. A teenager finds herself thinking or saying "I won't do this. I'm not that kind of girl." In so doing she is acknowledging a self-concept that she is using as a guide for behavior. Self-concept thus presents us with developmental challenges that demand we somehow incorporate the changing world and environment into our changing sense of self. Again we see the self in ecological perspective, as the interplay of individual organism and social systems.

Cooley (1964) offers one hypothesis about how this process works. He refers to the *looking glass self*. As he sees it, we use the responses of others to us as we would use a mirror. Through this interactive, self-inspection process, we establish a self-concept or an idea of how others might see us. The process continues throughout the life course, and each of us contributes to many lives as well as our own, (i.e., while we are busy figuring out how others see us we are also influencing how others see themselves). This dynamic does much to set the agenda for peer relations in adolescence and conforms to the ecological conception of development set out in Chapter 2. Recall that we define microsystems in relation to a *specific* individual, so that individual adolescents are both the focal point of their own micro-, meso- and exosystems, and also participants in the micro-, meso-, and exosystems of others.

Marcia (1980) proposed a way of thinking about identity that we find useful. He views identity "as a self-structure—an internal, self-constructed, dynamic organization of drives, abilities, beliefs, and individual history" (p. 159). This definition suggests a dynamic notion of the self, which also implies that the more developed this structure becomes, the more well-adjusted is the individual. This concurs with Bronfenbrenner's definition of development. But the question we might ask is: how does this development occur?

How we view the process of identity development depends in large measure on how we study that development. All the conceptions of identity formation—Lecky's, Cooley's, Marcia's and the rest—must eventually translate into specific techniques for observing and measuring, into concrete *operational definitions*. Exactly *how* do we detect and assess the looking glass self? Exactly *how* do we determine the elements of Marcia's *self-structure*? We do it by having individuals fill out precoded questionnaires, by asking them open-ended questions and then coding their responses, and by asking them to choose among alternative descriptions of themselves and others that reveal their picture of self. We then compare individuals who differ on traits like age, sex, race, social class, culture, intelligence, parental behavior, and whatever else we think might make a difference. Keep this in mind as we proceed. The essence of a scientific treatment of any topic lies in our efforts to devise concrete, specific techniques for measuring the phenomena of interest. The process of identity development is no exception.

As we pointed out in Chapter 5, the dominant theoretical orientation toward the development of identity comes from the work of Erik Erikson and reflects a strong individualistic ethic. Erikson sees identity formation as the process of differentiating self from others in adolescence (although a reintegration with humankind in old age is also proposed). Identity thus comes from recognition of oneself as an individual first and foremost (from the process of *individuation*). This view is so consistent with the dominant individualistic culture of modern North America that it seems almost self-evident to many of us. But we should recognize that this individualistic approach to identity formation is based in a particular culture, and thus it reflects a macrosystem effect. As we shall see, although Erikson's view seems self-evident for those who embrace the dominant North American perspective on individualism, it is not the only possible view. Collectivist ideologies emphasize integrating self with others and reinforce the idea of becoming a more harmonious part of a larger social whole rather than striving to become a separate, autonomous individual.

Erikson's View of Identity Development

In Erikson's view, identity development is a life-long process beginning with the differentiation of *self* from *other* in infancy and ending with the resolution and integration of *self* and *humankind* in old age. It is the development of a sense of self that is separate from others, a recognition of one's uniqueness, as much a statement of who I am *not* as who I *am*. We will return to this point later, because those who study identity believe that an adolescent who does not work long and hard enough at "who I am *not*" will be too ready to assume parental answers to "who am I" and will thus get sidetracked in achieving a mature identity.

The predecessor of the development of identity in adolescence is the achievement of a sense of industry in middle childhood (Erikson, 1950). According to Marcia (1980), this connection results because vocational commitment is important in identity formation. If children succeed in the tasks of the industry period, they will come to adolescence with confidence in their own worth and a set of skills that will foster the development of a positive identity through the successful selection of a vocation. They will literally know how to go about *making* something of themselves. Adolescence is the crucial period because for the first time the individual possesses the cognitive skills, the physical abilities, and the social permission to construct a workable plan for an adult life and vocation. A successful experience (e.g., selection of a vocation

The most memorable experiences were during my transition from sixth to seventh grade. It seemed as if everything sat at my doorstep but I never walked in the house because of my excellent upbringing and God's protection. Seventh grade—the end of sixth was a time my girl friends were first discovering sex, alcohol, and drugs. They'd tell me all about big trips with the guys and all of the exciting moments of sexual play. I did and didn't understand, but I knew it was wrong so I stayed away but kept the friendship. In seventh grade I was permitted to go to football games, without an older guardian. These football games were filled with alcohol, fights, and backseat excursions. At the time I felt I had it all together but again, never really ever drank, was promiscuous, or even into drugs. The time most traumatic was when my best friend and I went to a treehouse on our block. She had gone there many times to "enjoy" sexual promiscuity; the boys nearly tore her clothes off. When I left I realized the severity of the situation. I went home later, told Dad, and cried. Later I told her if she ever wants people to respect her, she needs to change her ways. Little came of it. Eventually our relationship fell away because we were two different people. My time on the edge of involving myself in "delinquent acts" was over without a scar, or war story to tell. She went on, boys talked, and her name wasn't very reputable. Thank God my parents kept tight reins and taught me to honor my God with "all of my heart." I'm glad I knew who I was.

that one feels good about and does well with) also forms the foundation for continued success in meeting new developmental challenges.

Dominant Stage Models of Identity

As we noted earlier, Erikson's is the dominant stage model of identity formation (1950, 1956, 1959). Most other approaches are defined as amendments or alternatives to it. Therefore, it is essential to understand its basic components. The model rests on eight stages in individual development. These stages of psychosexual development describe the individual's development as a series of *crises* to be encountered and mastered. Marcia (1980) has elaborated the issues of the adolescent period as four different identity statuses defined on the basis of the presence or absence of *crisis* and *commitment* with respect to where one's life is going.

Marcia's (1966) four identity categories are strategies for approaching or avoiding the identity *crisis* of adolescence and are called *identity achievement, foreclosure, identity diffusion,* and *moratorium.* The essential ingredients that differentiate the various categories are the presence or absence of a decision-making period (crisis) and the extent to which an individual has made a commitment to ideology and vocation—realms critical for transition to adulthood (Marcia, 1980).

Identity diffused. Identity diffusion is demonstrated by the lack of commitment to an occupation, to a moral or political stance, and to a religious affiliation. No particular efforts have been made to explore the range of alternatives; no decision has been attempted in choosing among them. Marcia considered this to be the typical status of the preadolescent. The preadolescent may be unsure of future career plans or may seem to be living from day to day. The identity diffused subject is more susceptible to external influence, at least insofar as self-esteem is concerned. In two studies involving the manipulation of self-esteem in college students, Marcia (1966, 1967) discovered that identity diffused youths were significantly more likely to modify their opinions about themselves in response to feedback by the experimenter than were others.

Foreclosure. These individuals have assumed the attitudes, ideals, and goals held by significant others, particularly parents, in their lives. Although they may express convictions and commitments about who they are, there is no personal credo supporting their actions and opinions. They are simply being someone else, usually a parent. Ideological search, conflict of principles, and final personal resolution are all absent. When questioned about their opinions, there is a strong tendency on the part of the foreclosure youth to cite teacher expectations or, more often, parental preferences. Choices are made, actions are taken, and attitudes are expressed on the authority of others, and little initiative is self-inspired. Marcia's studies indicated that these individuals almost invariably score higher on a scale of authoritarianism.

Moratorium. These adolescents are in the throes of their identity crises. In this case, convictions and commitments are absent because there are so many variables currently in the process of being defined, analyzed, compared, and selected. Moratorium is the period of experimentation when new and frequently extreme roles are tried out (radical politics, very conservative religions, religious cults, etc.) and usually rejected in favor of more moderate positions. Although rife with uncertainty, instability, and conflict, youth (or adults, for that

My most vivid memories of adolescence were mainly situated at the beach. The days were full of nothing but sun bathing and swimming. No responsibilities or commitments to anyone except my parents. Life was pretty easy-going, and I was mostly interested in dressing and looking like everyone else, and above all, being attractive to the opposite sex. Long range goals had no place in my life during these times.

matter) who have an opportunity to search, experiment, and compare, will typically discover a meaningful identity for themselves. Marcia reported that approximately 30% of his college student subjects were in this stage, and he claimed it to be a prerequisite for the fourth and final identity development stage, identity achievement.

Identity achieved.   Having considered the alternatives and found an identity that matches past performance, current practices, and future expectations, these individuals achieve a sense of self and a harmony between their particular strengths and shortcomings. They are able to forego both rebelliousness and blind conformity and to commit themselves to positions that, although often similar to their parent's, have nevertheless been scrutinized and now truly belong to the individual, who has learned them and made them uniquely their own. This position covers the full range of social and ideological roles: those concerned with politics, family membership, religion, education, and career. In Marcia's work, they were the students who would not accept *false personality sketches* describing them, and who set more realistic goals for themselves. Having attained a lasting identity, these individuals are now prepared to move ahead to the next stage of psychosocial development by forming a stable, committed, interpersonal relationship.

Several attempts have been made to establish the validity of Marcia's identity statuses by showing that identity achievers have more developed egos (Gregoire, 1976; Marcia, 1966; Simmons, 1970; 1973). Using techniques that call for individuals to describe themselves along a variety of dimensions (e.g., the Ego Identity Incomplete Sentence Blank and the Identity Achievement Scale), these researchers have shown that Marcia's categories are a useful way to describe identity in adolescence, particularly for many males. It may be less fair to use these categories for most females, however, because the categories rest upon the individuation model of identity development and do not highlight the more typically feminine concern with intimacy and interdependence. For females, it seems, identity is more a matter of who one is related to rather than what one is (Gilligan, 1982). This basic difference in males and females leads us to consider the development of sexual identity, because males often seem to believe they need to be sure about who they are before they can risk losing themselves in an intimate relationship. Females, on the other hand, often believe they are more likely to become someone and discover who they are *through* intimate relationships.

Also, some researchers have questioned the validity of identity types in early adolescence (Raphael & Xelowski, 1980). By the end of adolescence, it is probably more significant to ask about being an identity achiever versus an identity forecloser than it is in early adolescence. The key issue is whether an individual achieves identity as a basis for the transition to adulthood, not *how soon* in adolescence he or she does so. We turn next to several factors that seem to influence the timing of identity formation.

Cognitive Style

We defined cognitive style in Chapter 4 as the characteristic way individuals (and cultures) organize and respond to stimuli and intellectual problems. While several researchers have found no differences in the intelligence level of adolescents in the different identity categories (Cross & Allen, 1970; Marcia & Friedman, 1970; Schenkel, 1975), others have reported that when they examined broader cognitive characteristics in conjunction with social skills, there were significant differences among the identity categories (Bob, 1968; Marcia, 1966, 1980). That is, they found some evidence that adolescents find one response to the challenge of identity formation more conducive to their particular cognitive style, irrespective of how intelligent they are. Waterman and Waterman (1974) describe identity achievers as the most reflective and analytical of the four groups.

Examination of several more specific areas of cognitive functioning may shed light on this dimension. Waterman, Geary, and Waterman (1974), for example, reported that those in the identity diffusion and foreclosure categories seemed to be more impulsive (e.g., acted quickly with little thought and with many errors) than those in the other two categories. Complexity is another relevant area. Several researchers examining this area (Kelly, 1955; Kirby, 1977; Tzuriel & Klein, 1977) suggest that, broadly speaking, identity foreclosure adolescents are characterized by cognitive simplicity, achievement and moratorium adolescents by moderate cognitive complexity, and identity diffusion adolescents by the greatest cognitive complexity (Marcia, 1980).

Independence

Most research in the area of independence or self-directedness indicates that identity foreclosure and diffusion adolescents are less independent and self-directed than those in the higher statuses (Andrews, 1973; Orlofsky, Marcia, & Lesser, 1973). Examples of this type of research include studies by Waterman and Waterman (1971) and Neuber and Guenthner (1977). These authors reported that those in the identity foreclosure category tended to want their family's assistance in decision-making, while identity achievers and moratorium adolescents were more independent in making decisions. This carries over to general need for approval and conformity.

Anxiety

Marcia (1967) reported that those in the moratorium category seem to exhibit more anxiety than those in the other statuses. Along these lines, Oshman and Manosevitz (1974) reported that identity foreclosure and moratorium adolescents are characterized by higher anxiety and internal conflict levels when assessed using standard psychological tests. Finally, Stark and Traxler (1974) found that the more advanced the youth in the process of identity formation, the less likely the subject was to score highly on a measure of anxiety.

Coping and Adaptation: Intimacy

In the area of interpersonal communication and intimacy, Orlofsky, Marcia, and Lesser (1973) found that identity achievers and moratorium adolescents were much more likely to have attained intimate relationships. Similarly, Kinsler (1972) found those in the identity diffusion category scored very low on measures of intimacy. These results are consistent with the idea that for those following the masculine path of individuation, it is necessary to achieve an identity before one can risk "losing" oneself in an intimate relationship. Of course, "losing oneself" is not viewed as a risk if one is following a route to identity grounded in interdependence and affiliation as Gilligan (1982) tells us most females are.

Erikson proposed that the development of intimate relationships depends upon the successful establishment of identity. This statement has been supported by several research efforts. Kinsler (1972), for example, reported that identity diffusion youth scored the lowest on measures of intimacy. Similarly, Orlofsky, Marcia, and Lesser (1973), using five levels of intimacy, classified people in varying levels of identity attainment. Identity achievers and moratorium adolescents fell most often into the highest category of intimacy. Those classified as foreclosure and identity diffusion youth, on the other hand, fell most frequently into the category of relationships that were stereotyped. Finally, in the intimacy category termed *isolation*, more of those originally categorized as identity diffusion were found.

These data need to be qualified, however, because of the oft-noted gender differences within the categories of interpersonal relationship development and identity achievement (Marcia, 1980). In 1966, for example, Douvan and Adelson's descriptions of male and female adolescents seemed to indicate that interpersonal intimacy was of greater importance to women. More recently, Josselson, Greenberger and McConochie (1977a, 1977b), in their study of low- and high-maturity males and females, reported that interpersonal relationships were indeed more important to women. After reviewing the results of their recent study on male and female college students, Hodgson and Fischer (1979) similarly conclude that "issues of intimacy are intertwined in female identity development" (p. 49). In Chapter 8 we will consider some of the implications of this difference for sexual relationships in adolescence.

Individual Characteristics
Related to Identity Development

The early research on identity emphasized attempts to connect personality traits and other individual characteristics with differences in how quickly and successfully individuals deal with identity crises in adolescence. Many of these studies suffer from a clear masculine bias. They reflect the masculine model of identity development (and, incredible as it may seem, many deal solely with males in their late teens). However, we can use them as a window on male identity and as a point of potential contrast in understanding female development.

Self-Esteem

Several researchers have found high self-esteem to be more characteristic of some identity statuses than others. Rosenfeld (1972), for example, discovered that college males who were closer to resolving their identity crisis indicated that they felt their real and ideal self were closer (they were more what they wanted to be) than did those in the lower categories. Similarly, Bunt (1968) reported that midadolescent boys in the identity diffuse level exhibited a greater disappointment in their self-perception and their perception of how others saw them than did those in more advanced identity categories. Finally, Breuer (1973) found that identity achievers and those in the moratorium category rated themselves as higher in self-esteem than did those in the other two levels. These results indicate that the more advanced categories are associated with a better image of self.

Self-Understanding

William James divided the self into two parts, the *me* and the *I*. The *me* he described as the sum total of all a person can call his (e.g., material and bodily possessions, social and "spiritual" characteristics) (James, 1892–1961, p. 44). The *I*, according to James, is the "self as knower," or that part of the self that organizes and interprets experience in a purely subjective manner. The self *asks* the question, "Who am I?" Damon and Hart (1982) propose that a stable self-identity derives from a sense of the stability and continuity of the *self-as-knower* (p. 844): "I may change, my body may change, but *I* remain." They then offer a definition of self-understanding as "the totality of a person's conceptions of the 'I' and the 'Me' " (p. 845). This serves as a bridge between cognitive development and the development of self, since the more sophisticated the individual's ability to know things, the more resources they have for understanding self.

Broughton (1978) conducted a study of children's philosophical analyses of knowledge (their *epistemology*). He asked children a number of open-ended questions concerning the self, such as "What is the self?" "What is the mind?" Broughton then probed their responses with a series of follow-up questions. From these reactions, he derived a developmental progression of epistemologies that covers the period from childhood through mid-adulthood.

In early childhood, according to Broughton, the self is understood in a strictly physical sense. The young child thinks that the self is part of the body, usually located in the head. Because of this reasoning, young children offer various ideas that are peculiar to this early stage. For example, the notion that the self is a part of the body often leads youngsters to conclude that even animals and plants have a self (a conclusion that some adults share, although usually in a more sophisticated form), and they often described self in terms of shape, color, or texture. Children at this early stage thus see themselves as different from others because of their physical appearances. According to Broughton, even the volitional aspects of self (i.e., free will) are attributed to physical body parts by children. For example, they may state that the self is in the mind, and that this is where they "decide" to be good or bad.

When the child is approximately eight years old, Broughton's second level of self-knowledge begins to unfold. Children start to roughly discriminate between the mind and body. The fact that children now distinguish between mental and physical characteristics allows them to come to understand the subjective nature of the self. For example, "I am different from others not because I look different, but because I have different ideas, feelings, opinions, behaviors, etc." The self's nature is now defined internally rather than externally. It is seen as composed of psychological rather than physical characteristics.

Using different types of interview procedures, Selman (1980) has attempted to replicate Broughton's developmental progression, examining both the changing understanding of the *I* and the *Me*. Selman posed dilemmas such as: "Eight-year-old Tom is trying to decide what to buy his friend, Mike, for a birthday party. By chance, he meets Mike on the street and learns that Mike is extremely upset because his dog, Pepper, has been lost for two weeks." The story goes on to place Tom in the position of asking whether or not he should buy Mike a new puppy (since Mike said "I never want to look at another dog"). Follow-up questions probe a number of psychological issues revolving around the perspectives of self and others (e.g., "Is there an inside and an outside to a person?"). From children's responses to such dilemmas, Selman outlined three childhood levels of self-awareness.

Selman's first level, "physicalistic conceptions of self," is very similar to Broughton's first level. Children at this level would respond to the above dilemma by denying that a person's statements and behavior can be distinguished from their feelings. They make no distinction, then, between inner, more psychological experience and outer experience. Because children are basically unaware of psychological experience apart from such things as physical characteristics and behaviors, they see and describe themselves in a physical way. According to Selman, then, the self's volitional tendencies are related to various body areas closely related to the functioning of these parts. For example, the young child may say "I am the boss of myself . . . [because] my mouth told my arm and my arm does what my mouth tells it to do" (p. 95).

In late childhood, according to Selman, children begin to note differences between inner and outer states. Now they define the true self as composed of subjective inner states rather than material outer states. In contrast to Broughton, Selman proposes that this developmental change in children's self-knowledge involves two stages or levels. According to Selman, by age six children know that psychological experience is not the same as physical experience. They still believe, however, that psychological and physical experience are consistent, in a sense, with one another. By age eight, the child comes to realize that the self can fool oneself as well as others because of discrepancies between one's own inner experience and one's outer appearance. At this point, he contends the child sees that the self can regulate its own thoughts more directly than others can direct it. This means that one can deceive others by pretending to be something one is not. The child also now becomes aware that the self has better access to its own psychological experience than do other people. The child's growing awareness of the private, subjective nature of the self, according to Selman, causes the child to develop a "reflective understanding that the self is capable of gaining inner strength by having confidence in its own abilities" (p. 100).

From the brief review of these two theories it is apparent that they agree on the basic childhood shift from physical to psychological conceptions of self (Damon & Hart, 1982). Research by Guardo and Bohan (1971) on the cognitive bases for self-identity in 6–9 year olds also supports this shift. Guardo and Bohan's work focused upon children's knowledge of four dimensions of self. *Humanity* has to do with the notion that humans have qualities or characteristics that distinguish them from other life forms. *Sexuality* is the awareness of one's own gender and gender role and behaviors. *Individuality* may be described as the notion that one is unique in the world. *Continuity* pertains to the belief that one is connected with one's own past as well as future self. Guardo and Bohan believe that these dimensions provide a sense that one is a single "being with a unique identity who has been, is, and will be a male (or female) human person separate from and entirely like no other" (p. 1911). They see the self as a psychological construct that has as its main purpose giving one individuality.

It is apparent that the self develops during adolescence and that the individual exhibits an increasing use of psychological and social relational concepts for describing the *I* and *me*. More specifically, the last two levels of Selman's developmental sequence of self-awareness emerge in early and late adolescence. The first adolescent stage (actually Selman's fourth stage) is characterized as the recognition of one's self-awareness. Adolescents now realize that they are able to self-reflect, and this gives them a new monitoring tool, namely their own mental powers of self-awareness. This stage, however, has some limitations, in that the adolescent has not yet obtained a sense of the conscious and unconscious mind. At the second adolescent stage (Selman's fifth and final), adolescents realize that there are mental events that they cannot call into the conscious mind for reflection and examination.

According to Selman, the sequence during adolescence starts with a global notion of the *I* as the controlling, self-reflective component with a somewhat elusive sense that there are some limits to this awareness and control. With entry into the fifth level, adolescents develop an understanding of the conscious and the unconscious and realize that both of these forces influence them. It is in this manner, Damon and Hart (1982) concur, that the adolescent "constructs a unified self-system while still preserving the notion that self-awareness and conscious self-control have their boundaries" (p. 855).

Damon and Hart (1982) offer their own multidimensional conceptualization of a systematic developmental model (see Figure 7.1). We can see that their model addresses the development of four aspects of the self (e.g., physical, active, social, and psychological) along the four components of self-understanding (e.g., continuity, distinctiveness, volition, and self-reflection) from infancy through late adolescence. Damon and Hart (1982) believe that at all ages, children have knowledge of the four constituent self-schemes (e.g., the physical, active, social and psychological self). They go on to say, however, that this knowledge of each self-scheme changes with development. They have represented these changes along the vertical columns of the model's front face. The 16 boxes of the model's front face thus offer brief descriptions of developmental trends.

Along with these developmental trends, within each of the four self schemes, are the *age-related shifts* that favor the physical, active, social and psychological aspects of the self respectively, as the child develops into a teenager (e.g., the color-screened diagonal boxes of the model's front face). According to Damon and Hart (1982), the cubical shape of the model indicates that, during the transition from childhood to adolescence, changes in the understanding of *me* interact with changes in understanding the *I*. This occurs all through the development of self-understanding. Thus, they contend that developmental progression in either seems to inform and foster developmental progression in the other. Through attempts to incorporate these various components of the developing self into our understanding of self-concept, Damon and Hart (1982) have made a useful attempt to establish a recognition of the importance of the notion of self-understanding in future research.

Summary of the Possibilities and Impediments to the Development of Positive Self-Concept

The many influences on self-concept and identity fall into three general categories: *individual (organismic), interpersonal (micro- and mesosystem),* and *societal (exo- and macrosystem).* Examples of individual biology include the finding that early maturing individuals may be rushed into forming an identity and, perhaps, may crystalize their identity prematurely because they appear older than their peers (Simmons & Blyth, 1978; Newcombe, 1979). Examples of psychological factors include self-esteem, independence, anxiety, and coping style. The interpersonal factors relevant to the development of identity and self-concept are the feelings and reactions of significant others (e.g., peers and family). Finally, some of the social factors involved are cultural and ethnic influences on the goals, tone, and structure of day-to-day social experience.

DEVELOPMENT OF SELF-UNDERSTANDING

The "I" dimensions (top faces of cube):

	SELF-CONTINUITY IS ATTRIBUTED TO THE PSYCHOLOGICAL & PHYSICAL PROCESSES THROUGH WHICH THE NATURE OF SELF CONTINUES TO EVOLVE	SELF-CONTINUITY EQUIVALENT TO UNCHANGING PHYSICAL BODY	**CONTINUITY**
DISTINCTNESS ARISES FROM THE SUBJECTIVITY AND PRIVACY OF THE SELF'S EXPERIENCE	DISTINCTNESS DEPENDENT ON BODILY OR NORMAL ATTRIBUTES		**DISTINCTNESS**
ACTIVE SELF-INITIATED MODIFICATION OF CONSCIOUS EXPERIENCE	ONE BODY PART "TELLS" ANOTHER TO DO SOMETHING		**VOLITION**
RECOGNITION OF CONSCIOUS & UNCONSCIOUS PSYCHOLOGICAL PROCESSES	AWARENESS OF BODY FEATURES, TYPICAL ACTIVITIES, AND ACTION CAPABILITIES		**SELF-REFLECTION**

The "me" dimensions (front face of cube):

Developmental Level	PHYSICAL SELF	ACTIVE SELF	SOCIAL SELF	PSYCHOLOGICAL SELF
4. LATE ADOLESCENCE	PHYSICAL ATTRIBUTES REFLECTING VOLITIONAL CHOICES, OR PERSONAL & MORAL STANDARDS	ACTIVE ATTRIBUTES THAT REFLECT CHOICES, PERSONAL OR MORAL STANDARDS	MORAL OR PERSONAL CHOICES CONCERNING SOCIAL RELATIONS OR SOCIAL-PERSONALITY CHARACTERISTICS	BELIEF SYSTEMS, PERSONAL PHILOSOPHY, SELF'S OWN THOUGHT PROCESSES
3. EARLY ADOLESCENCE	PHYSICAL ATTRIBUTES THAT INFLUENCE SOCIAL APPEAL & SOCIAL INTERACTIONS	ACTIVE ATTRIBUTES THAT INFLUENCE SOCIAL APPEAL & SOCIAL INTERACTIONS	SOCIAL-PERSONALITY CHARACTERISTICS	SOCIAL SENSITIVITY, COMMUNICATIVE COMPETENCE, & OTHER PSYCHOLOGICALLY RELATED SOCIAL SKILLS
2. MIDDLE & LATE CHILDHOOD	ACTIVITY-RELATED PHYSICAL ATTRIBUTES	CAPABILITIES RELATIVE TO OTHERS	ACTIVITIES THAT ARE CONSIDERED WITH REFERENCE TO REACTIONS (APPROVAL OR DISAPPROVAL) OF OTHERS	KNOWLEDGE, LEARNED SKILLS, MOTIVATION OR ACTIVITY-RELATED EMOTIONAL STATES
1. INFANCY & EARLY CHILDHOOD	BODILY PROPERTIES OF MATERIAL POSSESSIONS	TYPICAL BEHAVIOR	FACT OF MEMBERSHIP IN PARTICULAR SOCIAL RELATIONS OR GROUPS	MOMENTARY MOODS, FEELINGS, PREFERENCES & AVERSIONS

FIGURE 7.1

Conceptual foundations of the me (physical, active, social, and psychological self-constituents) and the I (continuity, distinctness, volition, and self-reflection) at four developmental levels during childhood and adolescence. (From "The Development of Self-Understanding from Infancy through Adolescence" by L. W. Damon and D. Hart, Child Development, 1982, 53, pp. 841–864. Reprinted by permission of the Society for Research in Child Development.)

302

Within each of these categories, there may be many impediments to the development of a positive self-concept. For example, within the individual realm, physical deviance such as early maturation for girls or late maturation for boys may cause developing adolescents to come to see themselves negatively as compared to others (Jones, 1965; Jones & Bayley, 1950; Jones & Mussen, 1958; Peskin, 1967). Changes in height, weight, complexion, and secondary sex characteristics not only affect how adolescents feel about themselves, but also have significant social impact on the image they present to others (Lerner, 1969). This often can become a vicious cycle of physical deviance, low self-concept, peer and parental evaluation and rejection, and lower self-concept. Finally, in the societal realm, there are also many impediments to self-concept development. Macro- and exosystem threats such as ethnocentric, racist, and sexist institutions (e.g., Ku Klux Klan) may hinder the development of positive self-concept in groups who suffer discrimination. The 1954 U. S. Supreme Court ruling that prohibited racial segregation in schools was based on the belief that discrimination is a clear danger to self-concept and identity.

The Costs and Benefits to Identity of Abstract Thinking in Adolescence

As we showed in Chapter 4, the central intellectual event of adolescence is the dramatic increase in abstract thinking. One major advantage this gives the adolescent is the ability to consider possibilities that are not immediately present (Flavell, 1970; Inhelder & Piaget, 1958; Keating, 1980). It allows adolescents to consider various paths and options available to them (e.g., what kind of job would I like? do I want to go to college? what would it be like if I broke from the traditional way of doing things within my family? etc.). This serves as a self-concept booster, because the adolescent can entertain an endless array of possibilities, then derive ways to achieve these goals and, in so doing, bring the real self closer to the ideal self.

Abstract thinking also gives the adolescent the ability to generate and test hypotheses (Inhelder & Piaget, 1958; Lovell, 1961; Neimark, 1975). This process involves the pondering of the possible as well as the impossible (Keating, 1980). It adds an exciting dimension to the thinking of adolescents, since they can now consider a wide variety of creative hypotheses (e.g., If I do this what would happen? etc.), thus giving them the feeling of being more creative and more in control of their lives.

Finally, a third benefit of abstract thinking in adolescence is the ability to generate strategies to solve problems when they arise (Inhelder & Piaget, 1958; Pitt, 1976; Siegler & Liebert, 1975). In some life situations, this may be the only way to come up with the right or best solution for a situation. An orderly thought process involves planning, foresight, problem definition, development of a strategy, and the ability to implement this strategy and to try alternatives should it fail. This ability equips the adolescents with the tools they need to assume control over their lives.

These formal operational abilities not only enable adolescents to conceptualize their thoughts, but they also permit them to reflect upon the thoughts of others (Elkind, 1971). Thus, with the benefits of being able to think in this more sophisticated manner adolescents also experience the sometimes difficult realization that others do not see them in quite the way they would like. Adolescent adaptation of the self-concept thus hinges on their own view of themselves as well as the sometimes painful views of others. We find an illustration of this notion in the work of Lerner and his colleagues (Lerner & Karabenick, 1974; Lerner, Orlos, & Knapp, 1976). These researchers found that physical attractiveness was strongly related to self-concept: the more attractive adolescents *thought* they were to others, the higher their self-esteem. The realization that the thoughts of others can be a problem for the adolescent leads us to ask: What are the costs of abstract thinking?

The first major cost may be an inability or unwillingness to reach closure on identity issues. When adolescents get caught up in generating and considering possibilities, they can become paralyzed with indecision. No solution is perfect, so adolescents may go overboard in considering hypothetical identities as they search for the elusive, perfect ideal self.

A second cost is that overreliance on abstract thinking in identity formation may lead to the insensitivity to day-to-day emotional realities of social experiences. Males may be especially vulnerable to this sort of overabstraction (Gilligan, 1982). Females, because of their greater orientation to interpersonal relationships rather than abstract concepts of the autonomous self, may be protected from this danger. However, as we saw in Chapter 4 (the excerpt from Ellen Goodman), females may be more prone to excessive interpersonal empathy that paralyzes them in indecision. One message our ecological perspective sends us is that all human paths have their distinctive costs and benefits.

Having laid out the very plausible and common sensical grounds for believing that achieving formal operations and attaining identity are related, we can take a look at the evidence. Several attempts have been made to study the relationship of formal operational thinking to identity, but the results have been contradictory and yield only qualified support for this very plausible link.

Berzonsky, Weiner, and Raphael (1975) and Cauble (1976), for example, studied undergraduate females and males and discovered that these two constructs did not overlap (i.e., adolescents did *not* seem to use formal operational thinking to solve their identity crisis). On the other hand, Wagner (1976) did find a relationship between formal operational thinking and identity resolution.

More recently, others have attempted similar studies of the relationship between formal operational thinking and identity status with more convergent findings. Leadbetter and Dionne (1981), for example, studied 92 males aged 17–20 who were identified as being in one of Marcia's four identity categories. Results supported the hypothesis that individuals in the higher categories

Adolescence is now a collage of dissociated impressions focusing on school, my neighborhood, and my family. No one image stands out in contrast to the rest, but in thinking it over, I momentarily re-experience a few very personal impressions and reactions. One, in particular, seems particularly appropriate in this context. The locale is a crowded, hot, deafening lunchroom. I'm nearing the end of my high school years and have become more lax about preparing a lunch in the early hours before school or, at my most organized, the evening before. So I carry my steaming tray of brownish chow mein toward my small group of close friends and classmates.

As I scramble around wooden chairs and over piles of books heaped on the floor, I notice a group of girls laughing and joking together at the end of one of those interminably long cafeteria tables. These students are, at first glance, very alien to me with their cheap and sometimes gaudy summer outfits, their pale faces and arms (no Florida tans among this set), and their slick hairstyles—typically either elaborate or neglected. They are boisterous, for the most part, and I can feel confident that they are not discussing their anxiety over upcoming A. P. exams, the homework for Chemistry class, or the debate about tragic heroes in Honors English.

And then, with a start and a sudden sense of shame, I realize that these are my former companions—long neglected—from my first year in high school. I remember my confusion and loneliness that first year, lost in the masses that periodically ebbed and flowed through the tiled halls. These girls were my first refuge, a little island of companionship in an overwhelming ocean of unfamiliar faces. And now I see how much our courses have diverged as they settled among the ranks of the uninterested—taking the lower level classes and more applied subjects, swapping details now over recent or prospective dates, concerned with jobs rather than careers, and fitting school around an already hectic schedule of part-time employment.

It was with embarrassment that I witnessed, in those moments, how the well-off, the well-educated, the achievement-oriented family background provided the easy "leg up" the academic ladder. It was with regret that I observed how those without the ready advantages were shifted to the lower ranks like so many pebbles in some murky pond water. And it was with shame that I recognized my own complicity with this system that subtly but inexorably separated out the strata of social classes and dictated so much what the character of our later lives would be.

—Joan Vondra

(achievement and moratorium) exhibit a more sophisticated use of formal operational thinking.

Rowe and Marcia (1980) found that mastering formal operations permitted but did not guarantee post-conventional thought and identity achievement. Based on these findings from their admittedly small (N = 26) sample of late adolescents, Rowe and Marcia (1980) suggest that future research needs to address the relationship of social perspective taking in identity development, thus attempting a link between cognitive and psychosocial developmental theory.

Social Characteristics Related to Identity and Self-Concept

As we have suggested throughout this chapter, personal and social identity arises from the successive perceptions and conclusions developing individuals form about themselves. Children and adolescents develop these successive views of self as they function in all their microsystems: home, peer group, church, school, and neighborhood. As Dreikurs (1953) has pointed out, children first see themselves within the context of their families and thus through the eyes of parents and siblings. This directs our attention to the child-rearing patterns that may affect the development of identity.

Although many things occurred during this trying time of growing up, I guess what is foremost in my mind is how I struggled to attain my own identity, and to become noticed despite the fact I was the "baby" of the family. My brother, six years older than myself, and my sister who is eight years older than me always did things together so, of course, their circle of friends were the same people. However, when little sister wanted to be part of their group and do the things the big kids were doing, it was "get lost." For years I tried to become one of them and be as close as they were. However, they had other ideas; I was still the baby of the family, their little sister. After a while I accepted the fact and resigned myself to being their kid sister. However, as I became involved in my own life with my own friends and activities, I forgot about the problem I had; well not actually, I still hurt. However, I accepted it.

Now though I am happy to say that since we have become older, we have grown closer. The relationship that I struggled for and longed for so much during adolescence all came naturally these past few years. I'm still considered the baby and their little sister, but they also realize I have grown up and they never seem to remember me doing it. Now we can have memories to look back on in future years to come.

Family Influences on Identity Development

Several researchers have studied the different types of parenting practices and patterns related to the attainment of the mature identity. Using both parental and adolescent reports, Jordan (1971) found several parental patterns to be characteristic of the different identity categories. Members of the families of identity achievers unanimously reported positive relationships with each other. Adolescents in the moratorium status level, on the other hand, reported having ambivalent relationships with their parents. Identity diffusion adolescents reported experiencing a sense of rejection and detachment from their parents, especially their fathers. Finally, identity foreclosure adolescents described their parents as accepting and encouraging while the parents saw themselves as child-oriented and very protective (Jordan, 1971). All these results seem to make sense in light of what each identity status implies.

Others have reported results that add to and support these findings (Donovan, 1975; Matteson, 1974; Schilling, 1975). For example, Matteson (1974) found families with forclosure adolescents to be extremely task-oriented and father-dominated. Such families discouraged affective expression. When examining families of identity-diffused adolescents, Matteson found that fathers tended to be inactive and detached (thus confirming Jordan's view of these families as ambivalent).

Finally, Enright, Lapsley, Drivas, and Fehr (1980) conducted two studies that examined parental influences on autonomy and identity development. Using a measure of autonomy, of identity, and of the adolescent's perception of parenting style, they reported two interesting findings. First, across both studies, they found that gender-role socialization was very influential in the development of autonomy: more traditional strict sex–typing is associated with foreclosure. Secondly, the father's use of democracy was a significant influence on advanced identity formation.

Thus, it *appears* that family experiences play a large role in the formation of identity (Marcia, 1980). Positive but traditionally authoritarian families tend to produce identity foreclosure youth. Positive, expressive, and flexible families tend to produce identity achievers. Conflicted and negativistic families tend to produce identity diffusion or moratorium adolescents. However, we must keep in mind that this research does not demonstrate cause and effect, only correlation. The studies report that the same youth who are identity foreclosers come from families that are positive but authoritarian. But we cannot be sure from that finding alone that it is that aspect of the family that produces or causes the identity forclosure adolescent. Both could result from some other factor. We should exercise this kind of caution in interpreting the meaning of correlational studies so that we do not jump to conclusions and exceed the strength of the evidence. Of course these correlational relationships indeed may turn out to be true causal relationships. But proving that is the task of further research, particularly research that follows youth over a long period of time *(longitudinal research)* and that is designed to rule out other factors as the real cause of identity differences.

Establishing Sexual Identity

From the time we are born, we learn that people have definitions of us and expectations for how people of our gender behave. As Manaster (1977) points out, parents ask two questions about their newborn babies: "Is it healthy?" and "Is it a boy or girl?" Without denying the importance of the former, we can say with confidence that the answer to the latter question (gender) dictates much of what is to follow in the socialization process.

Biology and Society: What Does It Mean to Be Male or Female?

We begin, of course, with biological gender. Determining biological gender is a somewhat simple task (except in those rare cases where genital organs do not conform to the normal pattern for one's chromosomal gender). Labeling someone as having a masculine or feminine gender *role*, however, is quite a different story. By gender role, we are referring to the process of psychological gender differentiation whereby boys and girls grow to become similar to their same-gender adult counterparts in behavior, attitudes, and feelings. Most of the major theories discussed in Chapter 5 have something to say about psychological gender differentiation. We start, however, with the excellent integrative view proposed by Maccoby and Jacklin (1974):

> We believe that the processes of direct reinforcement and simple imitation are clearly involved in the acquisition of sex-typed behavior, but that they are not sufficient to account for the developmental changes that occur in sex-typing . . . (a child must also) "develop concepts of "masculinity" and "femininity," and when he has understood what his own sex is, he attempts to match his behavior to his conception . . . . The generalizations he constructs do not represent acts of imitation, but are organizations of information distilled from a wide variety of sources, a child's sex-role concepts are limited in the same way the rest of his concepts are, by the level of cognitive skills he has developed. Therefore the child undergoes reasonably orderly age-related changes in the subtlety of his thought about sex-typing, just as he does with respect to other topics. Consequently, his actions in adopting sex-typed behavior, and in treating others according to sex-role stereotypes, also change in ways that parallel his conceptual growth. (1974, pp. 365–366)

Excellent as this statement by Eleanor Maccoby and Carol Jacklin is, it is interesting to note that by today's standards, exclusively using the male pronouns (twelve times!) in this short section would lead some readers to label the language sexist. Some believe that accepting the long-standing convention of using the male pronouns to refer to both sexes perpetuates the masculine bias in thinking, speaking, and acting about human development.

Freudian theory emphasizes that sex differentiation occurs through a process of imitation and identification. The basic idea is that children unwittingly choose a gender model to emulate, most often the same-sex parent. For Freud, personality in general and gender identity in particular develop from the inside out. Freud placed great emphasis on the role of intrapsychic forces (conscious and unconscious thoughts, wishes, and impulses). He proposed that the essence of personality lay in what the child thinks, desires, and feels. To understand how a child develops gender-role identity, then, one must understand the child's feelings and fantasies. Of particular importance here is Freud's concept of castration anxiety, the result of a combination of intense feelings and the somewhat tenuous grasp of reality characteristic of young children.

In Freud's theory, gender identity for boys is achieved through the resolution of the Oedipus complex. The typical resolution is for the child to renounce his sexual feelings for his mother and to identify with the father. The Oedipus complex completes early psychosexual development for boys and was seen by Freud as the prime determinant of adult gender and sexuality. Girls are somewhat of a puzzle in the Freudian perspective. They seem to parallel boys in being worried about inciting the jealousy of the same-sex parent, but resolve their problem by becoming like the mother (so the father will love them too and will protect them from their mother).

In contrast, social learning theory suggests that parents and family, as well as other members of society, positively or negatively reinforce the learning of one gender-role over another. In this framework, girls receive rewards for acting in feminine ways and boys are given approval for behaving in a masculine manner. Working within a learning theory framework, Kagan and Moss (1962, 1964) suggest that gender-role development involves not only reinforcement and punishment, but an ongoing process of self-monitoring. They view children as constantly scanning the social environment for information concerning what is expected of them. Children then compare their behavior with the adult and social expectations they perceive in the environment. If the match is close, they receive positive reinforcement and this serves to motivate continued scanning and appropriate behavior. In sum, reward and punishment depend upon how the child behaves, showing the degree of congruence between two sets of information, one from the social world and the other from the self. Cognitive abilities and skills thus come to play an important part in the maintenance of gender role identity. Kagan expands the use of the learning theory framework to set the stage for the introduction of the *cognitive-developmental* theory.

Adherents to the cognitive-developmental view propose that the child *first* comes to recognize itself as a boy or girl, assigns itself a gender, and *then* begins to conceptualize and categorize behaviors and activities as gender appropriate.

Kohlberg (1966) makes cognition central in his discussion of gender-role identity. He sees cognition and the stages of cognitive development as the factors responsible for gender-role identity. Kohlberg begins by portraying the developing child as a curious and enterprising creature whose first conceptualization of gender role will be crude, perhaps even faulty. As children develop their understanding and cognitive abilities, their concepts of gender role become enriched and broadened. Thus, Kohlberg contends that boys and girls do not learn appropriate gender roles because their behavior is differentially reinforced. Rather, he posits, they first grasp the idea that gender type is an essential characteristic of the self and *then* are attracted to and find gratification in sex-appropriate activities as these are consonant with their developing sense of self.

All three conventional theories (Freudian, social learning, and cognitive-developmental) tell us that the basic accomplishment of gender identity is well advanced before adolescence (by age five in most theories) and continues to develop within this period. Perhaps the strongest statement of this view has come from the work of John Money and Anne Erhart (1972). Their research has emphasized individuals who have some contradiction between the biological aspects of their identity (e.g., genital appearance) and the social and psychological aspects of their identity (e.g., how others label them or how they think of themselves). As Money and Erhart see it, there are two critical periods when sexual identity forms. The years 1 through 3 are critical in that the child is learning to differentiate the basic physiological differences between the sexes as well as the differences linked to social conventions (e.g., clothing and hair style). The sexual identity formed by age 4 sticks, and efforts to change it are very disruptive.

Adolescence is, however, also a critical period for living out the social and psychological implications of gender. The adolescent is open to reconceptualizing sexual identity and its implications, as we shall see in the next chapter where we deal directly with sexuality and intimacy. It is also a time when real and supposed gender differences affect life-long decisions concerning vocational and educational development.

Beliefs and Myths about Sex Differences

Gender roles are changing in North American society, and individuals are granted more freedom in defining the attitudes, beliefs, values, and behavior that describe them as sexual beings. Even so, many prescriptions still exist in the media, in religion, in the job market and workplace, in fashions, and even in laws. The big issue is the extent to which differences in gender roles derive from biological sex differences. It seems the best answer is that biological factors *may* point males and females in different directions, although they do not *determine* the final course in any great detail. Diamond (1978), for example, contends that biological factors such as hormone balance set the boundaries for our sexual responses and for what we are as sexual beings. However, within these boundaries, social experience creates most of the variation among individuals and between groups. Maccoby and Jacklin (1974) propose that it is the combination of biological gender, the child's sex-role concepts, level of cognitive skills (at varying ages), and finally, the reinforcement obtained from others that shapes the gender role. The human ecology has often seemed unified in differentiating masculine and feminine roles, even though different cultures may assign different characteristics to each.

Whatever explanation we use for the development of the gender role, it is clear that gender-role identity is fixed prior to adolescence. The question we pose at this point is: To what extent are sex-typing and stereotypes empirical realities? In other words, to what extent are the perceived differences between males and females biological, social, or nonexistent? In an attempt to discount some of the commonly held untruths about gender differences, Maccoby and Jacklin (1974) examined the biological, psychological, and social factors that they thought might contribute to sex differences. They then categorized their findings into three groups: beliefs about sex differences that were totally unsupported, those that remained somewhat equivocal, and those that they felt were firmly established.

Table 7.1 contains sample beliefs that fall into these three categories. We should also note that research done in the years since Maccoby and Jacklin compiled their list has called into question some of their conclusions and reinforced others. For example, Lips and Colwill (1978) reported that females were more aggressive than males in family-conflict situations, but survey research on domestic violence shows that males are more physically destructive in such family conflict situations (Straus, Gelles, & Steinmetz, 1980). On the matter of being influenceable, Eagly and Carli (1981) report that most studies do show females as being more sensitive in this regard, a finding that Adams and Gullotta (1983) attribute to their greater emphatic skills and orientations. Finally, Fischer (1981) concludes that adolescent females do develop and sustain more intimate friendships. Thus we see that the debate over sex differences continues, with some differences holding up to scrutiny (although their origins may remain unclear and debatable), while others are exposed as insubstantial, exaggerated, or simply the product of biased observation.

Overview of Alternatives to Traditional Gender-Role Development Theories

Sandra Bem (1974) suggests an alternative to conceptualizing ones' self as either totally masculine or feminine. Bem contends that femininity and masculinity are two *separate* dimensions. Thus, people can be both feminine and masculine to varying degrees. As she sees it, people who score high on both of these dimensions (i.e., who are *androgynous)* are more flexible in their gender role and thus have more options (behavioral responses, activities, jobs) open to them. Since these people seem to have access to a more diverse array of behavioral responses, they may match behaviors to the particular requirements of specific

TABLE 7.1
Review of research on sex-role stereotypes or sex differences.

Unfounded Beliefs	Beliefs Open to Question	Well-Supported Beliefs
that girls are more social than boys	the belief that girls are: more fearful, timid, anxious, compliant, show more nurturance & maternal behavior	that girls have greater verbal ability than boys
that girls are more "suggestable" than boys		that boys have greater visual-spatial ability
that girls have lower self-esteem		that boys have greater mathematical ability
that girls are better at rote learning & simple repetitive tasks that require high-level cognitive processing and the inhibition of previously learned responses	the belief that boys are more competitive and dominant	that males are more aggressive than females
that boys are more "analytic"		
that girls are more affected by heredity, boys by environment		
that girls lack achievement motivation		
that girls are auditory, boys visual		

situations rather than adhering to traditionally acceptable behaviors and having a more limited repertoire. With a greater range of behaviors comes greater social competence, and thus, according to the model we presented in Chapter 2, more fully *human* development.

Block (1973) similarly argues that the ultimate goal in the development of a sexual identity should not be the development of masculinity or femininity *per se.* She contends that sexual identity should mean rather "the earning of a sense of self in which there is a recognition of gender secure enough to permit the individual to manifest human qualities our society, until now, has labelled as unmanly or unwomanly." Block goes on to argue that "both a redefinition of conventional sex-role and a revamping of socialization practices are required if our societal goal is to encourage individuation and personal maturity for our young." (1973, p. 526)

Even though the effects of macrosystem developments such as the Industrial Revolution and the Women's Movement have been felt in varying levels of our society, the myths and stereotypes involving the roles of men and women seem to continue. These beliefs are perpetuated by exosystem institutions such as the mass media and advertising (e.g., girls are sexy, fresh, and cute; boys are macho, rugged, and handsome). The microsystems of childhood and adolescence often reinforce sex-typing. Family context and parental values (e.g., buying gender-related toys, rewarding masculine or feminine behaviors, etc.), peer pressures (e.g., behaving as the crowd prescribes in order to be accepted and popular), and the general socialization practices inherent in our schools and churches follow suit (Burke & Tully, 1977). The following studies illustrate the maintenance of this trend.

Rosenkrantz and colleagues (1968) examined gender-role stereotypes and self-concepts in late adolescence. They discovered that the traits that were valued for males and females differed. Females tended to value gentleness, loquaciousness, sensitivity, neatness, strong need for security, and the expression of tender feelings. The sterotypic traits valued by men, however, were aggressiveness, independence, emotional detachment, objectivity, strong competitiveness, and adventurousness. These results seemed to indicate that, despite the changing status of women in the 1960s, both women and men tended to express beliefs that were associated with traditionally masculine and feminine stereotypes. Carlson (1971) reported similar results, indicating that women tend to endorse cooperative and interpersonal concerns, while men consistently exhibit attitudes that favor competition and individualism. As we will see later, this difference may mean that femininity is more needed in the complex modern world than masculinity, which may be out-of-date.

Ahlgren and Johnson (1979) used a sample of school children from the midwest United States to illustrate this difference. They found that males showed consistently more positive attitudes than girls toward competition. These attitudes occurred in grades 2–12 but were largest in grades 8–10. This is particularly interesting because many investigators have pinpointed early adolescence as the time when most cultural issues involving adolescence, such as peer orientation, are at their peak. Thus, early adolescence may be the time when individuals struggling to answer "Who am I?" are most prone to grab for the simplest answers their culture can give them: "You are a boy, do this." "You are a girl, do this."

Along these same lines, in more recent research from the 1970s, Ponzo and Strowig (1973) studied the gender-role identity of high-school boys and girls using an adjective checklist to examine these boys' and girls' conceptions of appropriate behavior. These authors reported finding sets of 65 objectives for males and 59 for females that they contended indicated traditional gender-role stereotypes. They noted, however, that there did appear to be a trend towards a more androgynous or at least blended gender role-identity among these students.

Block (1973) conducted an integrative analysis relevant to our study of sex-role identity and values. She examined the conception of gender roles cross-culturally (in Norway, Sweden, Denmark, Finland, England, and the

U. S.). She used Bakan's (1966) differentiation between *agency* and *communion*, as basic modes by which people operate in the world.

> Agency is concerned with the organism as an individual and manifests itself in self-protection, self-assertion, and self-expansion. Communion is descriptive of the individual organism as it exists in some larger organism of which it is a part and manifests itself in the sense of being at one with other organisms. (Block, p. 515)

We can hear Gilligan's two gender voices here—the masculine speaks of agency, the feminine of communion. Block saw evidence to support this expectation in the data.

The male and female college students that Block sampled provided descriptions of their ideal self and thus, provided a projection of the values of their culture. The findings support the contention that there is a certain amount of cross-cultural stability in masculine-feminine ideals (see Block, 1973, pp. 518–519). Block concludes that for girls there is an emphasis in the interpersonal, communal characteristics while for males the emphasis is on individuation.

In Block's (1973) study, American males were distinguished from men of other countries by their greater emphasis on adjectives such as *self-confident, assertive, shrewd*, and *competitive*. American women also differed significantly from women of other cultures in their ideal image by incorporating adjectives such as *practical, self-confident, assertive, ambitious*, and *shrewd*. These findings may indicate that the American macrosystem cuts across gender lines in some respects (at least when Americans are contrasted with Europeans). In this sense, we North Americans may be moving towards a more androgynous society. Later we will ask if these are the values and characteristics we wish males and females to share.

Collective Orientations to Identity

Before proceeding, we should take some time to examine alternatives to the individualistic ethic inherent in most North American approaches to identity. These macrosystem alternatives suggest a different perspective on self and identity, as William Glasser suggests in his book *The Identity Society*.

One of these alternative views is actually a critique of our attempts to foster the development of an independent identity in Western society. Rotenberg (1977) has outlined this view, and proposes that the individualism characteristic of the North American macrosystem produces a sense of separateness that is akin to alienation. Along these same lines, Blauner (1964) argues that this macrosystem produces complex modern organizations and bureaucracies (exosystems) that foster the development of alienated individuals. Rotenberg claims that the intentional development of independence and autonomy in the family and in the community has a negative corollary—isolation and power-lessness. As he sees it, the development of a healthy, positive identity, from the dominant North American perspective, fosters a sort of self-centeredness that emphasizes individual freedom strongly and views dependence as an undesir-able sign of failure.

An interesting contrast to the individualistic view is the notion of desired dependency (*amai*) that is cultivated in Japan by the family, by the mental health field, and in organizations. Family and institutions foster and institu-tionalize dependence (Doi, 1973). Along these lines, DeVos (1973) points out that in traditional Japan, achievement motivation refers to the realization of self as embedded in affiliation, nurturing, and familial obligations. Thus, one does not work to get personal satisfaction or to improve one's sense of self, but to help and align oneself with the company, with fellow workers, and with family. Modernization has challenged this orientation in contemporary Japan (McGrath, 1983).

Bronfenbrenner (1970) presents a similar view in his contrast of child-rearing in the United States and in the Soviet Union. Observing across various ecological systems (e.g., the classroom, school, family, neighborhood and larg-er community), Bronfenbrenner notes that it is the joint influence of all of these that forms the personality and identity of the child. He goes on to point out that whereas the Soviet system promotes a strongly *social* identity, several North American institutions have created and perpetuated the age-segregated (and thereby often amoral or antisocial) world in which many North American children live and grow. In the course of contrasting these two societies, he of-fers several strategies by which our culture could foster the development of a

My most vivid memory of adolescence was when I was sixteen, and we played some Canadian hockey teams in our Christmas tournament. The hockey games were thrilling, exciting experiences for me. I got to meet different people from another country. It was truly a growing experience. Each player housed one of the Canadian boys and you got to show them all around, taking them to a movie, telling them about your home town—it was a big thrill! We were the first team ever from our area in our age group to ever beat a Ted Reeves Canadian team. In game one, we lost 3–2, the winning goal was scored with only 45 seconds left. It was a heart breaker to lose, I couldn't sleep that whole night. The next day I was so pumped full of adrenaline our team was ready. We dominated and coasted to a 6–0 victory. But that night each one of us had to take one of the Canadian boys home, it was so hard to be friendly after we lost that first game. My parents were great and saved the day at home. I learned so much from meeting and associating with the Canadian players and people who came down for our tournament, a vivid memory indeed.

more caring, altruistic generation without sacrificing the sense of personal identity we cherish. In such a system personal identity would have a strongly prosocial orientation at its core.

Consciousness III is a term introduced by Reich (1970) to describe the 60s generation who, he felt, were beginning to react to the impoverishment and irrationality inherent in the North American socioeconomic and political systems. He describes this group of youth as the product of two interacting forces: the *promise of life* offered by our current system and the *threat* of a nuclear holocaust. He contended that the 60s generation would not settle for the stifling and lonely life engendered by the "Corporate State" and would opt instead for the restoration of the nonmaterial elements of human existence. Reich agrees with Bronfenbrenner and Rotenberg that North American methods of raising children to fit into an alienating society creates "automation-like" individuals who are stifled by their sameness and lack of creativity. He appears to diverge from Bronfenbrenner and Rotenberg, however, in the solutions he offers. Reich not only encourages the development of a more altruistic, mutually beneficial and caring society, but further suggests that what is needed is the self-searching of one's own potential and uniqueness. This view seems to go full circle back to Erikson's individualistic view and recalls Rotenberg's criticisms of American culture. Reich seems to be proposing *more* rather than *less* individualism as the solution, while Rotenberg and Bronfenbrenner see this as the road to more alienation.

Starting from a different perspective, Carol Gilligan (1982) offers an approach to the development of identity that may be most akin to the ideals Rotenberg had in mind. Gilligan observes that females tend to diverge from the masculine model of individuation and present an alternative path to identity (for which, she observes, they are downgraded by male-dominated theories and institutions). Marcia (1980) represents the masculine view in saying that the development of a sense of identity is a precursor to intimacy. Gilligan turns this around and argues that for females, intimacy is the *foundation* for identity. Perhaps one way to meet Rotenberg's goals would be to promote this feminine route to identity among males.

All this leads to several questions about the best way to go about establishing a personal and social self. As we pointed out in Chapter 2 when we discussed social competence, the development of a sense of self is most successful and adaptive when it allows one to function at the highest level possible within the principal contexts of one's life. People should realize who they are, what they can do, and what they want individually, but should also incorporate the very important components that allow them to interact in harmony with others and to feel connected. This issue, the proper mix of interdependence and autonomy in identity, runs through all our discussions of this topic. It is particularly important when we ask what kind of adolescents are needed to meet the social challenges of the twenty-first century (Garbarino, 1982).

Religion

As adolescents develop their sense of self, they begin to question childhood beliefs and move towards forming a personalized set of morals, values, and religious beliefs. Wagner (1978) aptly described this process as "a period of revolt against authority of all kinds including the family, the school and religion" (p. 350). During this period, adolescents are inclined to develop or to attach themselves to a life philosophy, world view, or a set of guiding morals and values that may seem nonnegotiable as much to reassure themselves as to thwart adults (Conger, 1977). Both moral and cognitive development play important roles in the search for life values. As general cognitive abilities allow and encourage abstract thought, adolescent religious beliefs tend to become less literal and more uncertain.

How widespread is this process of religious doubting? Some studies, for example, Allport (1950, 1961), have shown that two-thirds of all adolescents rebel against the religious teachings of their childhood. However, a similar proportion acknowledge that religion plays a large role in their lives (Boyer, 1959).

Attempts have been made to delineate a developmental progression in attitudes towards religious beliefs. Harms (1944), for example, identified three stages in the religious development of children: *the fairy-tale stage*, *the realistic stage*, and *the individualistic stage*. The third stage occurs in late adolescence, and it is then that adolescents must select from among the various religious beliefs (including those held in childhood) the set that they can best incorporate into their developing identity.

For some, this incorporative process occurs gradually (Clark, 1929). For others, an identifiable moment of conversion exists (Ernsberger, 1974). Clark (1929) differentiated between *definite crisis* conversion, which is more typical of conversion in later adolescence, and *gradual growth* conversion, which is the culmination of a gradual process and is more likely less intense and more likely to occur in early adolescence.

There appears to be some consensus that within religious conversion experiences there is an identifiable moment of decision (Ernsberger, 1974). Ernsberger defines this moment of conversion as:

> . . . the ability to recall the occasion when one became more vitally committed to previously held religious beliefs or the ability to attribute one's religious commitment to a distinct point in one's life at which one made definite decisions in favor of some religion (p. 2)

Manaster (1977) looked comparatively at three religious surveys: one by the strongly conversion-oriented fundamentalist-evangelical National Sunday School Association, a confederation of sect-type churches (Zuck & Getz, 1968), a second done by three Lutheran dominations (Strommen, 1972), and the third by the United Presbyterian Church (Klever, Woods, & Chapman, 1971). Of significance here is his finding that youth who had gone through a conversion showed steadier growth and steadfastness in their faith and beliefs through the high school years. It appears, then, that for those who have this type of intensive experience, beliefs become a very strong, perhaps rigid and unwavering part of identity. The data also indicate that within fundamentalist sects there is strong pressure from the total religious community as well as from parents to have such a conversion experience.

Innumerable religious cults have surfaced in North America since the 1960s. Although their visibility seems to wax and wane (Lanier, 1982), their seductive effect on youth remains constant. These teachings, with their promise

---

Adolescence for me was a great transition period. Having always been a tomboy in my younger years, it was a big shock for everyone when I turned into a young lady at the age of 13. After starting to wear make-up and getting my hair cut, many older guys started paying attention to me.

Everyone thought that I really had my act together—cheerleading, good grades, many dates, fairly wealthy family—but what they didn't see was a fake. I was always trying to be someone else and got very involved with the social life—party scene. But even that was a phony way of having a good time because it never lasted—it was only temporal.

At the age of 16 some friends invited me to a home Bible study—not a cult. I really didn't want to go and yet I did. They kept asking every week so finally one week I thought I'd go. Well, when I arrived there, I never expected what I saw—a real genuine love and kindness in everyone. It was so different from the church in which I was brought up. After the study—which was so touching—I met the leader. He asked me if I was saved. I said, "What do you mean, saved from what?" He said saved from hell. I said, "What do you mean?" He proceeded to explain when you're saved, you know without a doubt if you're going to heaven when you die. He said you've got to do three things to be saved. First, believe you can't earn your way to heaven—you don't get there by just being a good person. But believe that we're all sinners and the punishment for our sin is hell. That's what we deserve. But God didn't want to send man to hell. He had compassion on man. So He became flesh in the form of Jesus and when He died on the cross—He took the physical punishment for us—for what we deserve in hell for our sins. He paid the price for us—so we can't earn our way by doing "good" things. Second, sincerely ask forgiveness for my sins. Third, ask Christ to come into my life and willfully choose to turn from sin in order to follow Him. (When we make the decision and effort, He gives us the grace and power not to sin.)

Since Christ has become first in my life, I've never had such an inner joy and peace. Nothing in the world can substitute for it.

of clear moral choice may be perceived by young people as an easy way to establish some order among their incongruous beliefs and lives or as an alternative to the stuffy, superficial beliefs of their parents. The trade-off is often a loss of personal identity as they are consumed by the cult mentality. Several authors (Sargent, 1971, 1975; Schein, 1971; Stoner & Parke, 1979) have discussed how cults use coerciveness and enslavement in the conversion process.

A first step in the cultification or "brainwashing" process is the promising of simple answers to all of life's questions. As one former cult member remembers:

> I just met a couple of people from their bus team and was very intrigued by them. . . . I had never heard of "cult" or "brainwashing" at that point. I had a mixed reaction. First, I felt somewhat amused by the literature they gave me, which seemed to be fairly childish and juvenile. They were proposing to answer the profound questions of life in a series of three or four lectures, and here I had spent three years trying to understand the questions. But then, on the other hand, there was this really powerful devotion and commitment in the young woman who handed me the literature and struck up a conversation with me. (From Dellinger, 1980)

As this man became more and more brainwashed, the pressure increased to the point that he was required to attend a 100-day leadership workshop. This camp, which operated on a rigid schedule, was designed to physically, emotionally, and mentally break the person's will to resist. During this time, a constant stream of input overwhelms the convert. As this man described it:

> ultimately, you become so fatigued and your emotions are so strongly accentuated that they set off to the side any kind of rational thinking process. You become an absorber of feelings and attitudes and behavior patterns rather than an alert adult responding to a community that is offering something which you can take or leave.

The steps in this process, according to Singer (in Dellinger, 1980) are: A) separation from friends and family; B) a focus on past deviant behavior; and C) convergence to the idea of total commitment. Singer feels that parents who inform their children early about the dangers of religious cults and who themselves are well informed may prevent this brainwashing process. As we shall see in Chapter 8, this is a prescription for preventing sexual problems as well.

Ethnicity

Much of the early research on the development of identity among different races and cultures involved attempts to compare blacks and whites. Such research has many problems since it is based upon the reports of individuals and it is often hard to know exactly how to interpret the results. Individuals may try to put up a good front and describe themselves more positively than they really think they are, for example. Also, it is often difficult to know with whom individuals are comparing themselves and what standards they are applying. With those cautions in mind, we can take a look at research on self-concept that compares different ethnic and racial groups.

Much of this research consistently indicated that blacks had lower self-concept scores. However, more recent research indicates that blacks, Mexican-Americans, and Puerto Rican children and adolescents report *equal if not higher senses of identity and self-esteem* than do other (more "advantaged") children (Powell & Fuller, 1970; Soares & Soares, 1971; Trowbridge, 1970). Powell and Fuller (1970) tested 617 school-aged students and found *higher* self-concept scores for black students in all–black schools. Black males had higher self-concept scores than white boys regardless of the racial composition of the school. Soares and Soares (1971) in their study of elementary children and high school children found that the disadvantaged view themselves more positively and attribute more positive views of themselves to others (i.e., their class-mates, teachers and parents) than do the advantaged and that elementary school children have more positive self-images than secondary school students (in comparison to elementary school children, both disadvantaged and advantaged high school students showed a diminishing self-image). Trowbridge (1970) found that regardless of whether schools were more or less equally integrated or were more white or more black in population, and regardless of socioeconomic status (SES) or neighborhood, disadvantaged boys and girls had consistently higher self-concepts than advantaged children.

Frazier and DeBlassie (1982) recently compared the self-concept and academic performance of Mexican-American (MAS) and non-Mexican-American late adolescents. The findings of this study indicate that, *given equal levels of academic ability*, MAS and non-MAS adolescents do not report discrepant self-concepts in terms of either academic success or self-esteem. This seems to parallel the myths of gender stereotypes. Long-held notions about the development of identity and self-concept among blacks and other races and ethnic groups do not always stand up to rigorous study. A generation of ethnic and racial awareness programs seems to have advanced their goal of promoting pride and self-esteem among minority groups, particularly when comparisons are made between groups equal intellectually. The continuing problems of economic deprivation and academic difficulties, however, testify to the fact that the social conditions facing minority groups still exist and will not be as easy to remedy. The issue of cultural pride and a sense of validity is vital, however.

Ethnic and racial pride based on success *within* a subgroup has both costs and benefits for developing adolescents. An obvious benefit is that their cultural roles are more clearly defined by the subgroup and that they know what they must do during adolescence to become an adult. In these usually tightly knit neighborhoods, there is also a sense of closeness and interdependence among neighbors. Thus, young people can gain support and learn strategies for approaching life, all of which make establishing a positive sense of self somewhat easier. There is a sense of rootedness and acceptance. However, as Rosenberg (1965, p. 56) writes, "there is no indication that the distribution of self-acceptance in a group is related to the social prestige of that group in American society." Thus, there may be a negative reality in the social environment beyond the neighborhood with which adolescents must eventually come to terms if they are to succeed in the larger society. The beliefs, values, morals, and behaviors that are learned in the neighborhood may not be ones that are accepted by society at large. This may compound the problem of developing mainstream social competence.

Keil (1966), Liebow (1967), and Ellison (1964), among others, have attempted to describe, explain, and validate the patterns and roles of black culture in response to the typical view that black culture does not exist except as a deviation from "middle-class white culture" (Howard & Scott, 1980). In his book *Urban Blues* Keil (1966) demonstrated the existence of a unique black culture, the core concept of which is *soul*. Keil proposed that the fact that blacks have been treated as outcasts has almost hidden the fact that they *have* a culture. He argues that social scientists neglected the fact that there exists a special domain of black culture that has proved and preserved black humanity. Leibow's (1967) and Ellison's (1964) work in conjunction with Keil's served to shift the description of Afro-American behavior away from those aspects that could be construed as deviations from white middle-class norms to attributes that are positive components of black culture and identity.

According to Howard and Scott (1980), Mexican-Americans differ in this respect in an important way. Whereas blacks were seen as being cultureless, Mexican-Americans were seen as having a damaging culture (Ramirez & Castaneda, 1974:

> The "damaging-culture" assumption as it has been applied to Mexican-Americans has consistently led to the conclusion that the culture of Mexican-Americans socializes individuals to become lazy, resigned, passive, fatalistic, nongoal-oriented, docile, shy, infantile, criminally prone, irrational, emotional, authoritarian, unreliable, limited in cognitive ability, untrustworthy, lax. . . and nonachievement-oriented. (Ramirez & Castaneda, 1974, p. 9)

Ramirez and Castaneda go on to attribute the presumed learning difficulties of Mexican-American children to value conflicts. They claim that Mexican-American children experience difficulties in the school because the schools do not recognize or incorporate components of their culture in the teaching process (Tharp [1973] makes the same point for Hawaiians). According to Ramirez and Castaneda:

> The sociocultural system of traditional Mexican-American culture is composed of four major value clusters: (1) identification with family, community, and ethnic groups; (2) personalization of interpersonal relationships; (3) status and role definition in family and community; and (4) Mexican Catholic ideology. (1974, p. 56)

According to these authors the schools are most likely to incorporate middle-class American values such as the sense of a separate identity and individual, competitive achievement (Ramirez & Castaneda, 1974). This is quite similar to the argument presented by Rotenberg earlier in this chapter. Both argue for the recognition and possible incorporation of features from other cultures into American institutions.

Failing to recognize the validity of alternative cultural themes causes individual adolescents psychic conflict and creates social conflict in the community. Whether the issue be genetic deficiency (Jensen, 1969), cultural deprivation (Tulkin, 1972) or "sociogenic brain damage" (Montagu, 1972; Valentine & Valentine, 1975), this view leads to the tendency to stereotype the ethnic poor as lazy and slow with little motivation to change, rather than focusing on why subgroups are different and how institutions might better approach their educational, economic, and social development. Teaching two languages, studying the minority group cultures, and adopting a more group-centered orientation rather than stressing individual achievement could all be considered better approaches for dealing with diverse ethnic groups. Tharp (1973) and his colleagues report success using such approaches in dealing with native Hawaiian youth.

Macrosystem Issues in Identity

Any discussion of ethnic and cultural differences highlights the more fundamental question of "What kind of people does the world need?" There is growing recognition that the world is approaching a decisive economic and environmental crisis (Daly, 1980). With this recognition comes the need for more harmonious, cooperative social relationships and institutions that reduce wasteful exploitation of physical and social resources in order to achieve a society that can endure and enhance human quality (Brown, 1981). Such a society needs individuals to define themselves in new ways that deemphasize materialism, competition, and aggressiveness in favor of spiritual development and cooperation (Garbarino, 1979, in press). We need to ask whether we are encouraging adolescents to develop the kind of identity we need people to have in a sustainable society. Without a realistic sense of the possibilities and limitations of the human role in the world, discussions of fulfilling individual potential sound hollow.

A related issue is whether or not we should accept and encourage differences between males and females in the development of identity. As we have noted, although much has been written about the notion of androgyny, it has yet to be widely accepted by most institutions or individuals, although there do appear to be trends in this direction (Bem, 1974; Block, 1973). Do we want to encourage females to become more masculine, males to become more feminine, or both? Some say we need most to encourage each adolescent to transcend gender roles entirely and simply become what they are best suited individually to become. In any case, one may then ask, "How can we foster the skills necessary for the development of a sound identity during adolescence?" One approach has been to teach these skills in the context of the schools.

Identity and Enhancement of Self-Concept

Among the various training programs currently available, several have attempted to foster the development of identity as well as a positive sense of self. Among these are values clarification (Casteel & Doyle, 1974; Simon et al., 1972), identity education (Weinstein & Fantini, 1970), the classroom meeting model (Glasser, 1969), the role-playing model (Shaftel & Shaftel, 1967), positive self-statement training (Hauserman, Miller, & Bond, 1976), and Valett's (1977) humanistic education approach. The overriding theme of all these programs is that they teach students the skills they will need to develop personal identity and positive self-concept and they encourage the practicing of these skills in the real-life setting of the school, which is an important arena for the transition or socialization into adulthood (Garbarino, 1978). Although each of these programs may be beneficial to the developing adolescent and thus deserves our exploration, we will take a closer look at only a few exemplary programs to gain a sense of understanding of the goals of these approaches.

One of these programs (Weinstein & Fantini, 1970) is especially relevant here because it attempts to provide the student with a curriculum that incorporates affective, cognitive, and interpersonal concerns. This program attempts to bridge several important contexts in which the developing adolescent must learn to function. To do this, it focuses on three themes: the development of a strong and positive sense of self, the desire to explore the possibilities open to one's self and to choose wisely among alternatives, and the development of strong affiliation with and understanding of others in the social environment.

Thus, the broad goals for identity education according to Weinstein and Fantini's program are a positive identity, sense of self-determination, and a sense of relatedness. These constitute the development of a sound personal and social identity. The first step of this program is to assess the needs of the adolescent: developmental age, economic status, community type (urban or rural), and cultural, racial, ethnic, and gender identifications. Once the characteristics of the group are identified, their individual and collective concerns are addressed (e.g., self-perceptions, value systems, and concern for how others perceive them). In this way, the educational process incorporates and deals with these important factors by reflecting and identifying problems in such group exercises as role playing, exploration, and problem solving.

Valett's (1977) approach similarly suggests the use of materials, resources, and activities that work toward the development of the total person. The author discusses five life stages and presents a curriculum guide for affective education. The stages begin with understanding basic human needs and move toward the development of personal and social identity and maturity. A guide is provided that consists of goals, objectives, and learning activities appropriate for students in varying developmental stages, thus helping them to deal effectively and adaptively with the challenges of each.

Finally, the Shaftels (1967) have designed a model of teaching that details a rationale and teaching process for "enactment." They believe that role playing, since it gives adolescents an opportunity to try out various roles, can improve their adolescent's self-concept. The teacher can develop situations in which "undervalued" adolescents can perform skills not usually noticed by their peers, thus providing these children with a different status and a potential for a more positive identity.

These approaches do have several shortcomings, however (Lockwood, 1978). The only way to know if current programs are effective is to systematically evaluate students before and after they participate and compare them to identical students who have not had the training (control groups). Such experimental control is often difficult to achieve. There is a general murkiness in the literature that evaluates results (Frank, 1979; Borkovec & Bower, 1980), and this stems from the many problems that naturally occur in this type of research (Campbell & Stanley, 1963). The studies do not clearly show who improved and why. They sometimes show arbitrary relationships between program process and the measurement instruments and reveal unclear specifications of program components and lack of feedback on how to make the program better.

Second, while the programs and procedures mentioned above appear to have much potential, the program designs have seldom been viewed in a truly developmental framework. Efforts to study and exploit developmental differences are not evident in these programs, nor in the general literature on the promotion of social development in children (Furman, 1980). A careful examination of the developmental literature can provide important, empirically derived questions for research as well as guidelines for programming (see Urbain & Kendall, 1980 for review). Future research on the enhancement of the self-concept and identity development (especially during adolescence) would do well to first adopt a framework such as Damon and Hart's (1982). (See Figure 7.1.)

From this point, it would be possible to identify the important components of the broader concept of self-understanding, recognizing that individuals will have limits as to how much they can learn, depending upon their cognitive, social, and physical stage of development. Those interested in research in this area may then look for measures of social cognition, understanding of self, identity status, self-concept, and any other facets they feel are important in assessing the level of identity development at the specific stage of the group being studied. Identity is important, and whatever we can do to facilitate the development of socially appropriate and psychologically sound identity among youth will be a significant contribution to our general goal of reducing social risk and increasing sociocultural opportunity. We will see this clearly as we discuss sexuality in Chapter 8.

Ecological Wrap-Up

Organism.   Identity and self-concept depend in part upon the development of the ability to think abstractly and to reason about oneself (to engage in *introspection*). Physical characteristics (e.g., physical attractiveness and timing of puberty) provide positive and negative stimuli in this process. They provide information to use in drawing conclusions about the self, in large part because they elicit reactions from others that provide evidence for the individual to use in cognitively processing the question, "Who am I?"

Microsystem.   Social validation of self, how others respond to the individual and the tentative conclusions about self drawn by that individual, is critical in the development of self-concept and identity. Family, peers, and school reinforce positive or negative self-concept and encourage or discourage the openness required to proceed through the process of identity development to reach the stage of identity achievement.

Mesosystem.   *Severe* discrepancies between home and neighborhood, on the one hand, and school, on the other, are a threat to self-concept and identity development. Among these are cases in which ethnic identity is threatened when one's home language differs from the language used at school. This is a national issue as the numbers of French and Spanish-speaking youth grow to significant proportions in more and more areas of the North American continent.

Exosystems.   The politics of culture—what values are rewarded institutionally—does much to determine the simplicity or difficulty of the path youth must follow to combine positive self-concept and productive identity. As an illustration, if schools enforce rigid and traditional sex roles they will create strain for atypical males and females. If schools allow a wide range of characteristics for both sexes, they will reduce the strain encountered by the male who wishes to pursue a traditionally feminine path and for the female who seeks a more characteristically masculine route to self-concept.

Macrosystem.   The overarching historical, cultural, and economic context should serve as a guide to answering "What kind of people do we need as we enter the twenty-first century?" Our answers have important implications for efforts to assess, evaluate, and facilitate identity development. For example, if the world needs more empathic, socially harmonious individuals to deal with environmental and economic challenges, we may want to encourage a more traditionally feminine identity in males and females while downplaying the traditional masculine themes of aggression and dominance.

Preview

- Sexuality is not simply a biological phenomenon.
- The meaning of sex depends upon its social, cultural, and psychological context.
- Sexuality and intimacy are linked in a mature person.
- Intimacy includes both physical and emotional closeness.
- Dating provides a structured way to develop appropriate attitudes and behaviors concerning both sexuality and intimacy.
- Sexual values have shifted to favor "permissiveness with affection" in ever-larger numbers of young people.
- Effective contraception is a serious issue for adolescents, their parents, and their communities.
- Sexually transmitted diseases are a major concern in considering adolescent sexuality.
- One task in adolescence is sorting out issues of sexual orientation, and it is a very important time in the life of a homosexual.
- Sex education can increase responsible sexual behavior and more psychologically satisfying relationships.

*S*exuality is not simply a biological phenomenon. In adolescence, or in any
other phase of life for that matter, a constellation of factors contributes to sexuality. There
are many ways to become, act, and feel sexual, and an individual's particular path depends on a wide variety of psychological, social, and cultural forces. It is shaped by
individual, microsystem, mesosystem, exosystem, and macrosystem forces.

As advice columnist Ann Landers is fond of
pointing out, the most important sex organ is
the brain. How we think, feel, and believe
about sex determines its impact. Thus, the individual's understanding of sexuality develops
in conjunction with cognition, self-concept,
and emotional sophistication, and issues in
these areas play a crucial role in sexuality (Jorgensen, 1981, 1982). We should try to keep
this developmental perspective in mind
throughout our discussion in this chapter.
Adolescence is a crucial time in the life course
for developing ideas and feelings about sex in
much the same way it is for ideas and feelings
about politics, gravity, history, love, morality,
and identity. Sexuality includes a broad range
of behaviors, feelings, preferences, and values.
Our main purpose in this chapter, therefore, is
to present sexuality in all its biological, psychological, and social dimensions.

In addition to recognizing the complexity of
sexuality, two other points are important in
understanding the information we present in
this chapter. First, sexuality is an integral part
of identity (Jorgensen, 1983). It interacts with
all aspects of the self and helps define who we
are. The physical components of sexuality
identify us as male or female and contribute to
our sense of masculinity or femininity. Our
sexual roles and values affect how we define
ourselves socially and guide our conduct in interpersonal situations.

8

Sexuality and Intimacy in Adolescence

A second important point is that sexuality is a fluid, dynamic set of characteristics; it constantly develops. This means that developing a sense of sexuality does not terminate in adolescence, but continues throughout life in interaction with biological, psychological, social, and cultural influences. While sexuality is a life-long process, we emphasize puberty as a phenomenon critical to sexual development and sexuality as critical in the process of adolescent identity formation. In addition, adolescence is the time when most (but not all) cultures expect individuals to become sexually active.

Each aspect of the human ecology contributes to the adolescent's developing sexuality. For example, at the level of microsystem, peers or parents may begin to treat adolescents as sexually active beings, whether they are or not. Similarly, at the exosystem level, institutional authorities, such as school boards, may construct and impose rules to regulate or control what they perceive to be normal adolescent sexual behavior. At the macrosystem level, society's beliefs about the rights of adolescents versus parents in contraceptive decision-making—may greatly affect the sexual activities of individual adolescents.

Viewing sexuality as a developmental process leads us to question the notion of sexual maturity in adolescence. Perhaps adolescence is best thought of as a time of sexual unfolding (Sarrel & Sarrel, 1979). This unfolding entails the complex agenda of growing up: an evolving sense of the body, the recognition of what is erotically pleasing, the ability to overcome or moderate guilt and inhibitions associated with sexual thoughts and behavior, the ability to assume sexual responsibility for oneself, one's partner, and society (through using contraception and avoiding sexual exploitation), a growing awareness of being a sexual person and the place of sex in one's life, and finally, the ability to experience eroticism as *one* aspect of intimacy with another person.

This last component of sexual unfolding relates to the second concern of this chapter—*intimacy*. We discuss this concept in greater detail later. Often people discuss adolescent sexual development only in terms of sexual behavior and sexual attitudes, usually within the context for the two person relationship, or the *interpersonal dyad*. What is sometimes not made clear is that adolescence is a time for developing intimate relationships in a variety of contexts. Not all of these close associations are sexual, and for the ones that are, sexual behavior is only one part of the relationship. Indeed, finding the proper place for sexuality in intimacy (and vice versa) seems to be one of the tough issues facing adolescents, one that often continues well into adulthood as men and women deal with the possible sexual overtones of being friends, associates, or coworkers.

In the first part of this chapter we consider theoretical perspectives on adolescent sexuality, the development of adolescent sexual and intimate relationships, sexual attitudes and behaviors, considerations of intimacy in sexual encounters, and the acquisition of sexual knowledge and the developing capacity for intimacy. The second part of the chapter is issue-oriented, and follows a case study format to better illustrate everyday concerns of adolescents and contemporary community conflicts over adolescent sexuality.

Theoretical Perspectives

As we discussed in Chapter 5, theory guides the way we think about and study phenomena. Although there are many theories regarding sexuality, we will consider briefly a few of the major ones as a background for examining specific issues concerning adolescent sexuality.

Freud and Psychoanalytic Theory's View of Sexuality

Freud's psychoanalytic theory has exerted a powerful influence on how most North Americans view sexuality. Freud believed sexual energy (libido) was one of the key forces in human life and maintained that it is even unconsciously apparent in such nonsexual behaviors as art and music. Recall that Freud saw the personality as being divided into three major parts: the id, ego, and superego. To illustrate simplistically the operation of id, ego, and superego in a sexual situation, consider an adolescent female on a date with her boyfriend. They are watching a sexually suggestive scene in a movie theater. The female's id says, "I want to begin petting right here and now!" Ego intervenes and says, "We can't do it now because there are people all around us. Let's wait until we leave the theater and are alone." Superego says, "I shouldn't engage in petting at all because nice girls don't do those sorts of things." What actually happens depends on the relative strengths of the girl's id, ego, and superego and the operation of these same forces in the boy.

Freud also believed that individuals pass through stages of what he called *psychosexual development*. Each stage highlights a different aspect of sensual feeling. In infancy and early childhood, the child as Freud saw it goes through an *oral stage* where pleasure is derived from sucking. The *anal phase* follows, in which the major focus is on the pleasure of elimination. Around age 3 to 6 years, the *phallic stage* predominates. The boy's interest focuses on his penis while the girl suffers from penis envy (a concept that many today find hard to accept and dismiss as a figment of Freud's sexist imagination). The *latency stage* (also discounted today) follows and lasts until adolescence. In this phase the sexual impulses are repressed until urges are reawakened in the *genital stage* of adolescence. Here, sexual urges become more specifically genital, and sexuality becomes less self-directed and more oriented towards others.

Although Freud succeeded in bringing sex out of the closet (and shocking his readers in the Victorian era), his theory has evoked widespread attention, lavish praise, *and* storms of criticism. His concepts are hard to evaluate empirically, as we noted in Chapter 5. Also controversial is the fact that Freud saw the female as biologically inferior because of her lack of a penis and believed that female sexuality is passive. In addition, as many people see it, psychoanalytic theory fails to give sufficient recognition to the importance of the environment and learning.

Learning Theory's View of Sexuality

It is quite apparent that we learn much of what we call human sexual behavior; we do not act completely by instinct. According to operant learning principles, reinforcement of a particular behavior tends to increase the frequency of that behavior. For instance, if an adolescent male has a successful sexual encounter on a first date with a girl, he may tend to be very forward on initial dates with other girls. As another example, a girl may learn that giving in sexually to boys increases her chance of weekend dates. Thus, the likelihood of more dates reinforces this behavior.

Another operant principle involves learning through association. McGuire, Carlisle, and Young (1965) discuss how this extends to sexuality. For example, if a young female's first coital experience is painful or psychologically uncomfortable, she will probably want to have sex infrequently or not at all because she associates it with some sort of negative feeling. Many believe it is through similar association that people develop and maintain a link between sex and violence, an association perpetuated by the mass media.

Social learning theory (Bandura & Walters, 1963) is based on the principles of operant conditioning, but it recognizes how much social interactions influence the learning process. According to social learning theory, the processes of imitation and identification play key roles in how we acquire our sexualities. For instance, these processes are useful in explaining the development of gender sexual identity. Children may copy the actions of their same-sexed parents and thus learn behaviors appropriate to their gender. In turn, societal approval may reinforce gender-specific behaviors. Thus, parents and institutions form a partnership in producing identity.

The mass media often provide models for adolescents. Provocative ads featuring young fashion models might suggest the value of wearing tight-fitting jeans to adolescent girls. Or a boy might see a movie in which the hero's domineering technique seems to "turn women on" and so try to use this technique with his own dates (Hyde, 1982).

Sociological Theory's View of Sexuality

Sociologists tend to think of sexual behavior as but one specific form of general social behavior embedded in the context of society. Sociologists see numerous cultural forces (such as norms) that affect sexual interactions. Norms are rules for behavior that are understood by people within a culture and that guide them. North Americans have many norms regarding sexual behavior, such as those that discourage homosexual behavior and premarital sex. On the other hand, our norms validate sexual behavior between married people (so much so, of course, that sexual unavailability is grounds for divorce). Tracing change in cultural systems (overall norms concerning privacy, power, gender, responsibility, etc.) illuminates values that affect the development of sexual behavior. We will return to this macrosystem issue later.

The process of socialization conveys cultural forces to the individual in the microsystem. As we have said, in early childhood, parents are the chief socializing agents. As children approach adolescence, other influences, including nonparental adults, peers, schools, and the mass media, increasingly contribute to socialization. Part of socialization involves learning roles, of which sexual roles are an important part. Gender roles, for example, have much to do with how we behave sexually. For example, traditionally, the male, not the female, is supposed to initiate sexual activity.

Gender roles do not tell the whole story, however. People behave differently even within the same general culture and do so partly because they have different *scripts* (Gagnon & Simon, 1973). Scripts are learned rules of sexual behavior that consist of directions for what we will do and plans of action for how, when, where, and with whom we will do it. Scripts refer to the fact that much of our sexual behavior is programmed rather than totally spontaneous. Adolescents learn the scripts that guide their first, fumbling attempts at sex not usually from experience, but from fragments they have picked up from others in conversation, in "man-to-man" talks, in church, in "girl talk," watching television, in books, and elsewhere. We will return to this notion in our discussion of interpersonal scripts guiding adolescent intimate and sexual interaction. Here we can say that scripts imply a cognitive/developmental theory of sexuality that emphasizes how ideas about sexuality evolve (much as other socially- and physically-oriented ideas develop).

Cultural Perspectives

Most of us familiar with North American views of sexual behavior dimly recognize that these are not the only perspectives. Anthropologists have discovered that there are wide cultural variations in sexual behavior and attitudes. Considering this variety helps to put our own cultural standards in perspective because in matters of sexuality most of us tend to assume that our way is *the* way and other ways are crazy, immoral, or both (see the box on p. 332 and 333).

Generally speaking, cultural customs and values vary along a continuum, with sexual repressiveness at one end, and sexual permissiveness at the other. Two examples of these extremes are Inis Beag, a restrictive society, and Mangaia, a permissive society (Marshall & Suggs, 1971). In Inis Beag (a small island off the coast of Ireland), the people seem to have no knowledge of a number of sexual activities such as French kissing, oral stimulation of the breast, or hand stimulation of genital areas. Sex education is practically nonexistent. There is no idea of the physiological significance of menstruation and a woman is even considered dangerous at this time. The islanders abhor nudity and believe intercourse is hard on one's health. Premarital sex is unknown. In marital

The Nacirema

The Nacirema are a North American group living in the territory between the Canadian Cree and the Yaqui of Mexico. The Nacirema culture is characterized by a highly developed market economy which has evolved in a rich natural habitat. While much of the people's time is devoted to economic pursuits, a large part of the fruits of these labors and a considerable portion of the day are spent in ritual activity. The focus of this activity is the human body, the appearance of which looms dominant concerning the ethos of the people. While such a concern is certainly not unusual, its ceremonial aspects and associated philosophy are unique.

The Nacirema have an almost pathological horror of and fascination with the mouth, the condition of which is believed to have a supernatural influence on all social relationships. The daily body ritual performed by everyone is a mouth-rite. Despite the fact that these people are so punctilious about care of the mouth, this rite involves a practice which strikes the uninitiated stranger as revolting. The ritual consists of inserting a small bundle of hog hairs into the mouth, along with certain magical powders, and then moving the bundle in a highly formalized series of gestures. Were it not for this ritual of the mouth, they believe that their teeth would fall out, their gums bleed, their jaws shrink, their friends desert them, and their lovers reject them.

Most of the Nacirema population shows definite masochistic tendencies in their daily body rituals. For example, one distinctive part of the daily body ritual is performed only by men. This part of the rite involves scraping and lacerating the surface of the face with a sharp instrument. Special women's rites are performed only four times during each lunar month, but what they lack in frequency is made up in barbarity. As part of this ceremony, women bake their heads in small ovens for about an hour.

In addition to such body rituals, mention must be made of certain practices which have their base in native esthetics but which depend upon the pervasive aversion to the natural body and its functions. There are ritual fasts

sex, foreplay is generally limited to kissing and rough fondling of the buttocks. The husband always initiates the activity, takes the man-on-top position, and female orgasm is unknown.

Compare the Inis Beag to the people of Mangaia (an island in the South Pacific). Sex, in Mangaia, is thought of as primarily for pleasure. The Mangaian boy is told of masturbation at age 7. At age 13, he undergoes a penile incision ritual that initiates him into manhood. The performer of the incision gives him sexual instruction on various techniques to stimulate his partner, and the youth is taught the value of bringing his partner to orgasm several times before he has his own orgasm. Two weeks after the operation, the boy has into make fat people thin and ceremonial feasts to make thin people fat. Still other rites are used to make women's breasts larger if they are small, and smaller if they are large. General dissatisfaction with breast shape is symbolized in the fact that the ideal form is virtually outside the range of human variation. A few women afflicted with almost inhuman hyper-mammary development are so idolized that they make a handsome living by simply going from village to village and permitting the natives to stare at them for a fee.

Reference can be made to the fact that excretory functions are ritualized, routinized, and relegated to secrecy. Natural reproductive functions are similarly distorted. Intercourse is taboo as a topic and scheduled as an act. Efforts are made to avoid pregnancy by the use of magical materials or by limiting intercourse to certain phases of the moon. Conception is actually very infrequent. When pregnant, women dress so as to hide their condition. Childbirth takes place in secret, without friends or relatives to assist, and the majority of women do not nurse their infants.

Many of us probably find the beliefs and practices of the Nacirema unusual, if not barbaric, by American standards. But we should be careful not to judge the activities, values, and beliefs of other societies by our own cultural standards. Many of us are immersed in our own culture and fail to realize that much of our behavior may appear very strange to people of other cultures. Various aspects of the American culture can seem quite unusual when viewed from another perspective. *(Reprinted by permission of the American Anthropological Association from* American Anthropologist, 58 *(3): 503–507, 1956.)*

By the way, this article was written for an audience of Americans ("Nacirema" spelled backwards) about Americans and their strange, ritualistic ways! How have things changed since the 1950s when this was written?

For a complete account of the Nacirema, see the original article, Horace Miner's "Body Ritual Among the Nacirema." It is an eye-opening treat.

tercourse with an experienced woman who provides him with practice in various acts and positions. She also trains him to refrain from orgasm. After this, the Mangaian boy seeks out girls with whom to have intercourse every night. The emphasis is always on bringing his partner to orgasm.

The Mangaian girl receives sexual instruction from an older woman. The average girl will have three or four successive boyfriends when she is between the ages of 13 and 20. Some boys may have 10 or more girlfriends. Mangaian parents encourage their daughters to have sexual experiences with several men. They want her to find a congenial marriage partner. At age 18, the Mangaians typically report having intercourse every night, with three orgasms per night.

Adolescent pregnancy is very common as a result and well-accepted as a normal event.

Before focusing upon North American sexuality, it is illustrative to view sex in the Soviet Union as another example of a repressive society. Although sex is an especially taboo topic in the U.S.S.R., Mikhail Stern (1980) provided some information based on his experiences as a physician there. The state has taken on the role of moral overseer and has attempted officially to discourage sex. Young unmarried people who are seen kissing in public may have their pictures posted in a village square. According to Stern, marital sex is brutal and grim. For men, sex is seen as a performance, an indication of strength and masculinity. A Soviet medical journal offered the opinion that the ideal duration of the sexual act was two minutes. Things may be changing somewhat. The Soviets have begun to initiate sex education in the schools as part of an effort to cope with the increasing rate of out-of-wedlock births and the rising divorce rate.

How does the North American culture stand on the repressive/permissive continuum? Thirty years ago, our society was seen as a relatively restrictive one (Ford & Beach, 1951). However, sexual behavior and attitudes among North Americans seem to be becoming relatively permissive. Miller and Simon (1980) link our sexual standards and attitudes to the fact that we are an industrial society. They hold that contemporary industrial societies view adolescence as a change in social status, with puberty representing the end of childhood. However, adolescents are not seen as mature in every respect. According to Miller and Simon (1980), "What is unique in the experience of industrial societies is that young people are defined as sexually mature while simultaneously being defined as socially and psychologically immature" (p. 383). Thus, adolescents receive mixed messages from society, a situation that no doubt adds to their confusion concerning sexuality.

The Nature of Intimacy

Sexual behavior and the formation of intimate relationships are both important tasks in adolescence. However, sexuality and intimacy are not the same thing. North Americans, especially females, are socialized to expect these concepts to go hand in hand. Frustration, confusion, and hurt can result when such expectations are not met. The newness of adolescent feelings and their social confusion can combine with other aspects to make this a particularly vulnerable time in the life course.

There are actually two major dimensions of intimacy: physical and emotional (Neutens, 1980). Sexual intimacy can be simply physical intimacy and may be very empty when it is not also emotionally intimate. As Jacobs (1978) suggests, sex can even be used to ward off emotional intimacy. An overemphasis on the physical aspects of a relationship can preclude the exploration of other levels of the relationship. In this way, sex may not reinforce and extend emotional intimacy, but rather may displace it.

A second dimension of intimacy is the attempt to explore another's thoughts and feelings (sometimes with little success). Strengths of a person's character are displayed, but weaknesses are concealed. Nonintimate areas are the focus of conversation and the individual avoids self-disclosure, and hence, vulnerability. *Authentic* or *feeling* intimacy involves self-disclosure and an exchange of feelings *(reciprocity)*. It refers to an intense personal relationship developed only after gradual progression into deep self-disclosure (Neutens, 1980). Intimate relationships are not necessarily physically sexual, just as sexual relationships are sometimes not intimate (with prostitution being a clear but by no means exclusive example). Learning this distinction is important in defining interpersonal relationships, and the process begins in adolescence and continues as a vital aspect of becoming mature in adulthood.

Intimacy is related to love, and love becomes more differentiated through the processes of assimilation and accommodation. At its core is a strong positive feeling, a sense of caring, a warmth. In adolescence the individual learns to conceptualize love as a set of relationships, differentiated by the object of their affections—love for parent, love for siblings, romantic love, etc. Intimacy provides the vehicle through which adolescents develop a more mature understanding of their capacity to love.

An adolescent's first sexual encounters may not be authentically intimate—some may not even want them to be, preferring to "get it over" without

---

I sat alone, in the corner of the smoke-filled room, wondering what the hell I was doing there. I was really thinking more than that though. I was really wondering why I always ended up in these situations—where I felt I didn't fit in. I knew why. I guess I had these friends who had more of a tendency to live life in the fast lane—all older, more experienced. I looked around the room, carefully observing what was going on. There was the usual pot smoking and drinking. Even I had a drink clutched in my hand, trying to drink it and look cool. There were even some guys doing quaaludes. That was something I had never seen before and knew I was terrified of. Jane was one of the gang, smoking, drinking and having a good time. Jill had left with a guy. I sat, occasionally talking to someone. It all seemed so empty and meaningless. The talk, I mean. Well, I decided I was going to be an outsider no longer. I went and got another drink and joined Jane. I was pouring and a guy approached. His name was Brian. We talked and talked. I really thought I found someone normal, someone like me. We started kissing and stuff. Well, turns out he only wanted someone for a quick lay. Would I ever learn?

getting involved. The quality of a relationship is important in determining how the youth experiences sexual episodes. Although this is true throughout life, it may be especially important for individuals who are engaging in sexual behaviors for the first time. Knowing a person in a warm, close way may help alleviate feelings of awkwardness and ineptitude. Fortunately, although there is considerable variability in adolescent sexuality, sex often occurs in the context of such intimacy (Lerner & Spanier, 1980). Therefore, before discussing adolescent sexual attitudes and behaviors, it is worth examining how close relationships evolve.

Dating begins at a younger age now than it did in previous decades, especially in middle class families (Conger, 1977). It is difficult to talk about specific ages because of different definitions of dating and changing trends. Dating in North America, in contrast to much of Europe, is not perceived as courting behavior, especially in early and middle adolescent years. North American adolescents see dating as a convenient and satisfying social relationship in its own right. Much of the formal dating of the past has been replaced by informal socializing, often within a group context. It is common for youths to attend parties, extracurricular activities, and movies as groups rather than as couples. Dating is less supervised than in the past and less sexist in terms of who asks and who pays (Rogers, 1981, p. 310).

Libby (1976) has described two ways in which relationships develop. The traditional one is the "primrose path of dating." The contemporary sequence is referred to as "branching paths of getting together." These scripts are two types of sequences rather than actual dichotomies, and there is probably some switching from one style to another. While people still develop relationships along the traditional sequence, researchers believe that contemporary sequences are even more common (see Table 8.1).

Among older youth, dating serves the purpose of courtship. Until then, dating serves a number of useful functions (Rogers, 1981). It provides recreational opportunities and experiences in socializing with opposite-sex peers. This

TABLE 8.1
Social scripts for sexual relationships.

	Primrose Path of Dating	Branching Paths of Getting Together
Fifth to sixth grade	Engaging in structured heterosexual activities (spin-the-bottle type of activities); having one boyfriend or girlfriend.	Engaging in unstructured activities of mutual interest with friends of both sexes; not emphasizing relationships with one member of the other sex.
Seventh to ninth grade	Having group dates and dating with parents as chaperone figures (parents drive car, etc.); sneaking around with other sex; conforming to peer expectations.	Continuing nonpossessive, egalitarian activities with friends of both sexes, with no dichotomy between sexual and nonsexual relationships.

TABLE 8.1 (continued)

	Primrose Path of Dating	Branching Paths of Getting Together
High school	Having double dates or single dates in cars, with exclusive expectations after dating a person a few times (going with one person or "going steady").	"Getting together" rather than having dates, with females initiating relationships, paying, and driving the car as often as males do.
After high school	Working and/or going to college, with continued monogamous dating or dating more than one person or marrying monogamously. (These relationships tend to be characterized by static, rigid role expectations for females and males.) Viewing the level of physical intimacy as the basis for sexual morality and sex as a form of economic ownership and a way of meeting one's personal security needs. (The partners tend to have an expectation of exclusivity, especially if living together, but there may be "cheating" on the side.) Blaming each other when unhappiness occurs, rather than questioning the form of the relationship. Breaking up, tolerating an unhappy relationship or marriage, or living happily ever after in a sexually and/or emotionally exclusive monogamous marriage. Repairing, perhaps with a repeat of the above. Becoming disillusioned with "primrose path" relationships; searching for the "good life," but experiencing confusion as to how to find it.	Working and/or going to college, with a range of options: singlehood, living together, marriage, a network of relationships, swinging, group marriage, communal living. (These relationships tend to be characterized by a process of on-going, friendly negotiations.) Valuing touching and sensuality in mutually agreed-upon situations, with friendship and common interests serving as the basis for decisions about whether to have sex and/or whether to be sexually open or exclusive. (The partners may view outside relationships as supportive rather than threatening.) Viewing the relationship as a continuing process of change rather than a static set of promises. Encouraging personal and mutual growth, seeing the relationship as open ended, or experiencing breaking up or divorce without anger. Repairing or mutually agreeing to change in a continuing relationship.

NOTE: It is not uncommon for persons socialized in the traditional script to decide later to take on different roles and to adopt one of the emerging alternatives to the monogamous image or changing one's reality . . . so some switching back and forth between scripts prior to and after marriage(s) is common. These scripts are to ideal types on a continuum rather than actual dichotomies. However, many people still fit the traditional extreme of the "primrose path."

SOURCE: From *Sexuality Today and Tomorrow* by S. Gordon and S. W. Libby. Copyright © 1976 by Wadsworth Publishing Company, Inc. Reprinted by permission of Wadsworth Health Sciences, Monterey, California 93940.

promotes the acquisition of the social and interpersonal skills needed to associate with members of the opposite sex. Dating is also a means of achieving social status and prestige. Dating desirable members of one's group raises one's prestige. Additionally, dating provides opportunities for sexual experimentation.

My most vivid memory of adolescence is when I finally could tell all my friends I had been kissed by a boy. I went out bowling on my very first date. I remember taking two and a half hours to get ready. What should I wear? How should I fix my hair? Did I have too much make-up on?—I was very nervous. Finally, the doorbell rang. It was my man of the hour. I introduced him to my Mom and Dad. I could feel my voice quivering. "Calm down" I told myself, but the harder I tried, the worse it got. Finally, it was time to leave. Of course, Mom said to be home early. We did the usual first date things, went bowling, got some hamburgers and fries afterwards. I just remembered another reason for my nervousness; I had only bowled twice in my life. Two new experiences in one evening—could I handle this? But then came the moment for the really big moment, my first kiss. He walked me to my front door—of course the porch light was on, and we had the usual conversation—I had a good time. We both stood there for a while not knowing exactly what to say or do. Then all of a sudden his lips were against mine.

Boy did I have a story to tell all my friends the next day.

The things that I remember most about my adolescent years was the way I would get so worked up over girls but be too shy to ever really get to know them. It seems to me that I would fall in love every other week with a different girl. I realize now that what I was feeling was not really love but something else. What, I'm not really sure. Even though it wasn't love, I remember it being a very powerful emotion and would constantly put me in a "high" or a "low." These highs and lows are some of the experiences I remember most.

My first kiss is a vivid memory of my adolescence. Standing at my front door; the porch light on, a screen door barely open and the car running in the driveway, we said goodnight and I almost let go of the door when smack, our lips met. Down the front steps and out into the darkness he ran while I slowly stepped into my house. As I closed the door it hit me, we kissed, we actually kissed on the lips! Star struck, surprised but very happy, I smiled and leaned back against the front door. Immediately I tried to repeat the whole incident in my mind to make sure it had happened and then to be sure and plant every last second of my very first kiss in my memory bank.

Going steady remains a popular way to establish interpersonal intimacy. Research from the 1960s showed that up to a third of teenagers were going steady with someone at any given time (Poffenberger, 1964) and this proportion has remained stable in recent decades (Hansen, 1977). One survey, the Gallup Youth Survey (The Philadelphia Inquirer, November 17, 1977), indicated that most parents approve of going steady (only 8% disapproved).

Going steady encourages the development of romantic intimacy. Adolescent romance provides experience in relating intimately as a total person outside of the family context. In romantic love relationships, young people learn how to express and receive affection and learn the pleasures and problems of maintaining close relationships. This experience can help an adolescent move from the self-centered and relatively nonsexual interpersonal love relations of childhood to the intimate sexual love relations of adulthood (DeLora & Warren, 1977).

Couples who are going steady or who are otherwise emotionally committed are more likely to integrate sexual behavior with feelings of love and respect. They are likely to feel and believe that being in love legitimizes sexual activities and decreases guilt, and this feeling promotes sexual learning in a more comfortable context. Adults who fear teenage promiscuity should be reassured somewhat by the frequency with which adolescents confine sex to caring relationships.

There are also disadvantages to dating and going steady. The pressure for peer acceptance and popularity may cause adolescents to begin dating too early, before they are comfortable with their own sense of self, before they have achieved and learned about same-sex friendships, and before they are cogni-

---

My most vivid memory from around the ages 13-14 was wanting a boyfriend. I can still remember seeing all (well, maybe not all) my friends standing in the halls at school with their boyfriends holding hands and sneaking a kiss here and there. I was so jealous of them.

I got my first real boyfriend when I was 15. We were acutally going steady. We held hands, talked for hours on the phone, and made out in dark corners during the Friday night dances. It was great. It lasted about a total of 3 weeks. I think we sort of grew bored with each other and let it drift apart.

After my first romance, I didn't find anyone I was really madly in love with. I didn't know what was wrong. Most of my friends had steadies and were going out for months.

Another vivid memory from my adolescence was that I was so preoccupied with how I looked and dressed. I would spend hours combing my hair until it was just right even if it meant being late for school. I made sure I had the same clothes as my friends and classmates and never wore anything different. I had to be sure I was one of the crowd.

tively and emotionally mature enough to handle and understand dating as a training ground for intimacy. Dating and going steady at a very early age can also encourage sexual behavior before the partners are emotionally prepared for it (Atwater, 1983; Jorgensen, 1983). Also, Johnson and Leslie (1982) report that the more deeply involved a couple becomes in their relationship, the smaller and less intimate their friendship and kin networks become.

The formation of boy/girl relationships, or *heterosexual dyads*, depends on developmental, psychological, and social factors. Characteristics of heterosexual relationships change and become more involved as adolescents become more socially and physically mature (Feinstein & Ardon, 1973). At any developmental level, physical attraction is certainly influential. Value and attitude similarity is also important and adolescents tend to date individuals from their own crowd, from their own social reference group. We must not underestimate the role of friends and relatives as influences in the formation of dyads. Relationships do not form in a social vacuum, yet little research attention has been given to the importance of significant others in the formation and maintenance of heterosexual dyads (Lewis, 1975). Sororities, fraternities, and other organized social groups are one way adults seek to channel youth into paths that will be *socially* acceptable, and that will expose them to "the right kind of people."

Dyadic interaction arises in part out of positive social rewards and interaction with significant others (Lewis, 1975). Friends and relatives can promote an adolescent relationship by responding to the couple as a social unit, by inviting them to social events as a pair, for example. Thus, friends and relatives can function as filters that select, reinforce, and sustain some pairings in preference to others. Coombs (1962) believes that parents are active in this process because they have a vested interest in what happens to their children and to the family traditions those children represent.

Ryder, Kafka, and Olson (1971) outlined the roles played by peers in the formation of dyads. Friends often initiate first meetings between two people and may provide further opportunities for their early interactions by, for example, inviting them to parties together. Even more so, friends support the developing relationship in a number of ways. They offer protective situations and convenient excuses for the couple to get together. For example, Joan may receive parental permission to visit Mary at Mary's house while "forgetting" to mention to her parents that Joan's boyfriend Tom will also be at Mary's house. Friends also encourage relationships through supportive conversation and advice.

Besides the immediate social environment, macrosystem and exosystem changes affect adolescent dating and relationship development. Cultural values and institutional policies affect who is eligible as a prospective date. For example, in most of North America racial barriers have long existed that prohibited cross-racial dating. Those who violate these unwritten rules risk peer rejection that may include threats and even physical assault and adult intervention. Racial barriers are diminishing in many areas, particularly in the wake of successful school desegregation programs (Dickinson, 1975). Dating activities of whites and blacks are themselves becoming more similar. Blacks are changing more than whites and in the direction of white patterns.

An important psychosocial factor affecting adolescent sexuality and intimacy is sex-role development. We considered sex-role development in Chapter 7, but mention it here because norms of gender-appropriate behavior are probably among the most powerful factors influencing sexual conduct (Miller & Simon, 1980). It is necessary to make a distinction between gender *identity* and gender *role* at the outset. As psychologists and sociologists use the term, gender identity refers to the *internal,* personal sense of being male or female. Gender role, on the other hand, refers to learning and performing the *socially* accepted characteristics and behavior of a given gender.

Males and females follow different scripts for interpersonal sexuality. The traditional female has been characterized by expressiveness, emotional commitment, and passivity. Males have been reinforced for inexpressiveness, independence, and assertiveness. These role differences contain biological and cultural elements that are translated into the scripts individuals learn to follow in interpersonal relations and sexual interaction. For example, the male is viewed as the initiator of sexual activity and the society is more permissive about his sexual behavior.

Carns (1973) described differences in male and female motivations for their first sexual encounter. For young males, the rewards are the pleasure of the act itself and the recognition of its achievement by self and others. Young females, however, usually engage in sexual relatioins for the promise of emotional involvement and the security of commitment to and from their partners, with its attendant value as social currency. Zelnick and B. Shah (1983) report evidence reaffirming the validity of Carn's analysis.

My adolescence holds some very vivid memories. The most memorable were the onset of high school and all of its activities and the discovery of the opposite sex. It was my freshman year in high school and I was working on the stage crew of our school musical. We were building sets, putting up lights, working the curtains. And most of all, meeting that certain someone. We were just friends, working with each other on the same set. One day I remember well. It was later in the afternoon and for some reason, we were there pretty much alone. And then it happened. He came from behind me, put his arms around me and placed a very delicate kiss on my lips. I think it was then that I fell for him. He was a senior and I was a freshman. We went out a few times after that and I was in seventh heaven. But I guess senioritis got too much for him and our little romance was over. I was very sad but it was very special memory for me to recollect—my first real kiss from my first real love.

I was about 13 years old, she was about 12. We had been seeing each other all summer long. We rode bikes, swam, and played together. Our contact went no further than hand holding up until a certain evening in late August.

The day had been exceptionally hot so we spent the day swimming at the local pool. We came out to see each other after supper. We hung around with the rest of the neighborhood kids until the sun went down. Then came 9:00 p.m. when we both had to head for home. I walked her to the front of her house and stopped. She looked especially nice in the dimly lit street and I remembered how she had looked in her bathing suit earlier in the day. I began to talk but was too nervous to make much sense. She came closer and I had trouble deciding what to do with my hands so I put them behind my back. She asked what was wrong. I said "nothing" but she knew better. She put her arms around me, got on her tipped-toes and closed her eyes. She kissed me on the lips very gently. I kissed her back and she opened her mouth. I felt something wet and warm enter my mouth as she drew me closer. She massaged my back and shoulders and stroked my hair while continuing her kiss. I hugged her tighter and felt myself starting to get an erection. I was very embarrassed because I didn't know that it was natural. I pulled out of the kiss and said "goodnight" and walked home. Then I realized that my heart was pounding like a puppy's heart. I continued to see her and repeated the experience many times.

These rigid gender role expectations linger today, blocking adolescent ability to express needs and be open and intimate with others. However, Miller and Simon (1980) discuss evidence that indicates a trend towards greater similarities, or *gender convergence.* In this day and age, there appears to be increasing sexual experimentation among girls and increasing emotional involvement among boys.

Sexual Attitudes and Behaviors

Before discussing adolescent attitudes and actions regarding sexuality, we must recognize that attitudes and behaviors are not the same. According to McCary and McCary (1982), inconsistency between sexual attitudes and behavior is characteristic of North American culture. Several factors contribute to this inconsistency. First, sexuality is still something of a taboo topic in our society, and we convey this message through socialization. Most parents still do not talk openly about sex with their children and adolescents (Davis & Harris, 1982). Children may grow up with very rigid attitudes toward sex acquired from their parents or religion. When interpersonal sexual interests emerge in adolescence, behaviors may follow that are inconsistent with former attitudes. For example, a girl may believe that it is proper to remain a virgin until marriage. Yet, she may engage in sexual relations before that time, perhaps out of love, fear of rejection and being unpopular, or curiosity. The inconsistency between her attitudes and behaviors will no doubt produce feelings of guilt, or, at the very least, confusion.

We need to point out here that engaging in inconsistent behavior does not necessarily mean that attitudinal change will follow. A study by Ball and Logan (1970) illustrates this point. They interviewed a number of delinquent adolescent girls who were sexually active. The girls were asked about their feelings concerning their behavior. Of all the girls participating, 91% believed their behavior to be wrong, yet they maintained their activities. The bewilderment and confusion surrounding such inconsistency must be especially difficult for young, cognitively and emotionally immature adolescents.

Behavioral and attitudinal disagreement may manifest itself in another way for youth. Adolescents have a need for peer acceptance and approval. Their desire to fit in might lead them to adopt or espouse liberal attitudes that do not in fact guide their behavior. When it seems sophisticated to sound sexually active, adolescents may overstate their level of activity as well as their belief in liberal sexual attitudes. When it seems wise to downplay their sexual activity and beliefs (e.g., in front of parents or teachers), they may *under-report* them. Some youth may overstate their level of sexual activity to researchers (recall Derek Freemen's criticism of Margaret Mead's work on this score), while others may downplay their sex lives to such researchers. We will return to this topic when discussing the question of whether or not there has been an adolescent sexual revolution.

Adult expectations for sexual maturity increase the complexity of the interaction between adolescent and society. However, biological maturity does not always coincide with psychosocial maturity, and a cultural readiness to expect and regulate adolescent sexuality can leave the teenager confused, perhaps feeling that if they are *not* sexually active they are socially retarded. Adolescence is a time for personal and interpersonal exploration as well as sexual experimentation. Society's emphasis on the latter does little to help an adolescent who is trying to learn about and integrate both.

Adolescents are certainly aware of many of the mixed messages that come their way. On the one hand, the media promotes adolescent sexuality by using young actors, actresses, and models dressed in provocative fashions. On the other hand, parents try to restrict activity or limit opportunities for sexual engagement by curfews and other limitations. Both messages convey the expectation of adolescent sexuality, but they differ in their approval. Adolescents must not only weigh these messages, but must do so against the background of an overall changing cultural context of sexuality.

A New Sexual Ethic?

The feminist movement and the emergence of singlehood and cohabitation as acceptable life-styles, as well as other social forces, have caused the norms of previous decades to wither. As early as 1968, Farnsworth described our cultural tendency toward a "new morality," characterized by sex after the establishment of friendship and love, no exploitation of sexual partners, fidelity and consideration of others, and an overall ethical orientation to sexuality.

Reiss (1981) refers to a new sexual ideology he has labeled *modern-naturalistic*. This ideology recognizes *body-centered* sexuality but emphasizes *person-oriented* sexuality. Reiss claims that it is characterized by egalitarian gender roles, a positive valuing of both body- and person-centered sex, and the view that one's sexual emotions are both strong and manageable. The modern-naturalistic outlook affirms the major goals of sexuality as physical pleasure and psychological intimacy. In addition, it involves an acceptance without guilt of a variety of sexual behaviors that do not involve force or fraud.

If such cultural ideologies are truly forming, what is the effect on adolescents? Many individuals have spoken about a sexual revolution among youth. In determining whether a sexual revolution is occurring with adolescents we must examine three levels of change (Elias, 1978). The first involves the mass media. Commercial products, programs, advertising, music, and performances project the image of a sexy society. Youths are depicted in these various roles more now than ever before.

The second level of analysis is attitudinal and involves feelings and opinions expressed by adolescents. There seems to be a revolution in sexual openness and liberal thinking in public. However, frankness of public dialogue is not automatically accompanied by frankness in intimate relations. Attitudinal and behavioral inconsistencies continue. Behavior is the third level and refers to the forms of sexual activities in which adolescents engage.

The controversy over the existence of a sexual revolution revolves around two issues. The first is the distinction between *revolution* and *evolution*. Revolution supposes a sudden increase in adolescent sexual behavior. This incease has been equated with promiscuity, which has the connotation of indiscriminant sexual relations. While survey data do indicate an increase in behavior, the data do not necessarily mean that adolescents are more promiscuous. They may be more sexually active, but confine their activity to serious relationships, as we shall see. Evolution implies gradual change regarding sexuality. In fact, significant changes in human mores, behavior, laws, and social institutions usually do occur gradually, and it may be more accurate to describe these gradual changes as evolutionary rather than revolutionary (McCary & McCary, 1982).

The second issue bearing upon the existence of changes in adolescent sexuality is whether one is observing attitudes or behaviors. In the 1970s, two major studies were published on the sexual behavior and attitudes of American teenagers. In 1973, Robert Sorensen collected data from over 400 adolescents between the ages of 13 and 19 from both questionnaires and interviews. In 1979, Aaron Hass measured sexual attitudes and behaviors of over 600 15-year-olds and 18-year-olds. All answered a questionnaire, and 60 were interviewed. Most of our standards for comparing information on adolescents' sexual attitudes and behavior come from these two studies. It is important, however, to read the results with caution. As in any investigation, the data from each of these studies come from one limited sample. Although an effort is made in research to choose a sample that is representative of the population, there is never a guarantee that this is accomplished. Also, there is always the problem of respondents consciously distorting their behavior and attitudes or unconsciously misremembering what they do or believe. These two considerations make it risky to generalize research results. Therefore, we must exercise caution in interpreting trends based on one or two studies as is the case here.

There are many similarities in the results reported by Sorensen and Hass. Interestingly, when these data are compared with results for adults, teenagers in the 1970s appeared *more conservative* than *single* adults, especially in their views of extramarital relationships and their choice of sex partners. Perhaps the most significant change has been the growing liberalization of sexual attitudes and less adherence to the double standard (i.e., establishing one set of rules for males and another for females). The surveys indicate a rise in the numbers of females having sexual intercourse but not to levels that exceed that of males. It appears, then, that attitudes and behaviors of males and females have been converging, but that significant differences remain. Females are still held to a stricter sexual norm. For example, Robinson and Jedlicka (1982) report that when asked if they thought someone who had sexual intercourse with many people was "immoral," both male and female college students said yes if the person was a woman rather than a man. The authors do note, however, that overall, females were much less likely to define a person with many sexual encounters as "immoral" in 1980 than they were in 1965 (while males remained unchanged in their attitudes over that period).

Any effort to describe general trends in adolescent sexual behavior can be misleading if it does not emphasize the wide range of behaviors as well. Some adolescents abstain completely. Others are best described as sexual adventurers, who perhaps do conform to the older term *promiscuous* in that they frequently engage in sexual intercourse with many people and do so on a relatively casual basis. In considering the psychology of adolescent sexuality, it is important to know the individual pattern of behavior as well as what the average teenager is doing.

Survey data on adolescent sexual behavior by Zelnik and Kantner (1977; 1980) indicate an increase in the prevalence of coitus among adolescents. However, this behavior was not rated as promiscuous because the number of partners for most youth remains small. Rather, the increase in sexual intercourse seemed to mirror characteristic willingness to act upon the intimate feelings of an ongoing relationship. In short, sex was characterized by what Ira Reiss

(1967) labeled "permissiveness with affection." Whereas in the past many youth who felt strongly about someone with whom they were engaged in an ongoing relationship would have refrained from sexual intercourse, now youth are more apt to consummate their relationship sexually.

Reiss (1967) provided important data on sexual attitudes that suggest that teenagers recognize the relationship between sexual relations and interpersonal involvement. Results of his study, and those by Sorensen (1973) and Hass (1979), indicate that while a majority of adolescent males and females approve of premarital sexual intercourse, they do not approve of it indiscriminately. The new norm is that sex is acceptable within a loving and affectionate relationship. Promiscuity and exploitation are considered unacceptable and are usually socially punished by youth in peer settings by ostracism. Zelnick and Shah (1983) report that a majority of females define their relationship with their first sex partner as either "engaged" or "going steady." A majority of males defined the relationship as either "engaged," "going steady," or "dating." This shows both that intimacy is very important in relationships and that males continue to require a less committed relationship before engaging in sexual intercourse.

We should note that at this point these changing attitudes have not meant an end to sexual coercion. Many females report being pressured into sex. In a survey of female college students, Kanin and Parcell (1977) found that half reported sexual aggression in dating situations, with one-fourth of the incidents involving forcible intercourse. *Acquaintance or date rape* remains the most common (and least commonly reported) form of rape.

Chilman (1980) draws a parallel between adolescent behavior and serial monogamy among adults. The majority of adolescents value a commitment to a loving, monogamous relationship, although the relationships themselves tend to be temporary. Lerner and Spanier (1980) make an important additional point. They, too, observe the permissiveness-with-affection standard. However, they believe that the level of commitment necessary for affection has been lowered in recent years. Adolescents may rationalize sexual permissiveness under the guise of a relationship that, in fact, does not have a particularly high level of commitment.

Finally, Dreyer (1982) has remarked on socioeconomic, ethnic, and gender influences in adolescents' sexual attitudes. Permissiveness was traditionally associated with higher educational levels *or* lower socioeconomic levels (i.e., the high-school educated middle class was least permissive), greater age, greater sexual experience, being male, and being black. However, the studies of the 1970s indicate that these associations are no longer as strong as in the past. The general increase in acceptance of sexual behavior for adolescents has superseded such sociological characteristics.

In summary, new cultural sexual ideologies reflect North America's evolution into a permissive but not promiscuous macrosystem. Changes in adolescent sexuality mirror this evolution, with the predominant change being a liberation of attitudes.

Sexual Encounters

The Continuum of Sexual Encounters

Earlier in this chapter, we introduced the notion of sexual scripts. Recall that scripts are the learned etiquette of sexual behavior. It appears that there is a rather predictable script, or chain of events, leading up to the point at which a couple has intercourse for the first time.

Jemail and Geer (1977) attempted to identify the sequence of sexual behaviors that is scripted for males and females in a heterosexual relationship in our culture. Participants were given 25 sentences, each describing an event in a heterosexual interaction. They were asked to rearrange the sentences in a sequence that was "most sexually arousing" and "the most likely to occur." There was a high degree of agreement among both males and females about what the sequence should be. The standard sequence was kissing, hand stimulation of the breast, hand stimulation of the genitals, mouth-genital stimulation, intercourse, and orgasm. These results suggest that there are culturally defined sequences of behaviors that we all have learned, much as the notion of script suggests. This is so ingrained that it would appear quite shocking if a couple engaged in oral-genital stimulation before kissing. The fact that encounters with prostitutes often take this path testifies to the impersonal nature of such encounters.

Current (1977) had young males and females respond to items on a heterosexual behavior scale and results were obtained similar to those of Jemail and Geer (1977). His data support the hypothesis that male and female sexual experiences are cumulative and follow a fixed pattern. However, one gender difference was found. Females were more apt than males to perform oral-genital activities before engaging in sexual intercourse.

Survey Data on Sexual Encounters

Studies of premarital sexual intercourse among adolescents indicate that over the last 50 years there has been an increase in adolescent sexual activity, particularly among white, middle-class females, who traditionally reported much lower rates than blacks and males (Dreyer, 1982). The percentage *reporting* premarital intercourse more than tripled from 1925 to 1973, and increased 30% between 1971 and 1976 (see Figure 8.1). Keep in mind here as elsewhere in this chapter that self-reports about sexuality seem particularly prone to distortion, given the strong feelings, attitudes, and values involved. Recent studies indicate that rates for females have continued to rise during the 1970s so that in 1979, approximately 44% of all high school girls and 74% of all college women reported premarital coitus with the percentages higher for each age within these

FIGURE 8.1

Sexual and contraceptive experience, showing percent of never-married women aged 15–19 who have had intercourse by age for 1971, 1976, 1979. (Zelnick and Kantner, 1980)

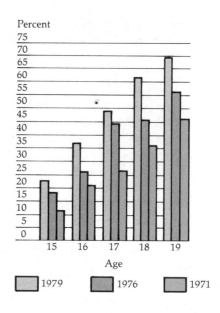

two groups, as shown in Figure 8.1. Rates for males have also increased since the 1920s. However, these changes are less dramatic, since male rates have been much higher than female rates until recently. In 1979, about 56% of 17-year-old males and 81% of 21-year-old males reported ever having sexual intercourse (Zelnick & Kantner, 1980).

Zelnik and Kantner (1977; 1980) conducted extensive surveys of the sexual behaviors of adolescent females. Interesting trends emerge when we compare their 1971, 1976, and 1979 results. Age of first intercourse dropped by a few months (Zelnick & Kantner, 1980) to 16.2 years for females, a small but significant change.

Sorensen's (1973) data show that over one-half of all teens have had sexual intercourse before the age of 16, with girls waiting somewhat longer than boys. Studies of black adolescents are fewer in number than those of whites but seem to indicate, as do Finkel and Finkel's (1975) data, that blacks begin sexual activity earlier than whites. Dreyer (1982) cites several studies (e.g., Chilman, 1979) showing that while about 30% of white boys and girls are sexually active by age 15–16, 90% of black boys and 50% of black girls have engaged in coitus by that age. Remember that data on attitudes, however, show the races to be converging.

The Alan Guttmacher Institute (1981) summarized data on the prevalence of sexual activity based on 100 studies. Since 1970, the number of adolescents who have engaged in sexual intercourse has increased by two-thirds. Today, only about one in five males and less than one in three females report *not* having experienced sexual intercourse by age 19. We should bear this in mind in thinking about sex education and family planning programs in schools and churches. Parents who grew up before these changes took place need to appreciate them as they give advice about adolescent sexuality.

Other data concerning adolescent sexual encounters deal with frequency and number of partners. This information is important in qualifying the inference of promiscuity that some draw from data reporting dramatic increases in rates and prevalence. According to Zelnik and Kantner (1977), frequency of teenage intercourse is sporadic, at least with females. Less than 3 in 10 girls have intercourse as much as three times in one month. In terms of numbers of partners, there was an increase from 1971 to 1976 (see Figure 8.2). However, 80% of sexually experienced adolescents never have more than three partners and most of these only have one partner.

An earlier Guttmacher report (1976) presented data that show an increase in pregnancies, and this has been most dramatic for young teens who are less than 16 years of age. Considering all adolescent females, 4 out of 10 will become pregnant at least once during their teens. Although this is a projected ratio, we must be prepared to deal with it and will discuss it in Chapter 13.

Factors Associated with Sexual Encounters

Dreyer (1982) reviewed studies describing factors associated with premarital intercourse. He reports that several psychological and sociological variables correlate with adolescent sexual behavior, although causal relationships cannot be specified. For both males and females, the following sociological factors appear to be associated with a greater likelihood of premarital sexual activity: exposure to permissive sex norms of the larger society, association with sexually active peers, having lower socioeconomic status, being a member of a racial minority, being poor, using drugs and alcohol, and having friends with sexually permissive attitudes.

FIGURE 8.2
Sexual and contraceptive experience, showing percent of sexually experienced never-married women aged 15–19 by number of partners ever, 1976 and 1971. (Zelnick and Kantner, 1977)

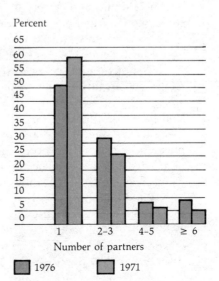

There are also several psychological factors that correlate with adolescent sexual behavior. These include low educational aspirations and achievement, deviant attitudes, poor relationships with parents, going steady and being in love, and having risk-taking attitudes.

It is interesting that so many variables are related to adolescent sexuality when it was earlier reported that adolescent *attitudes* of sexuality have superseded many of these characteristics. It seems that knowing a person's race, educational level, age or sex is of little help in predicting sexual attitudes. But it does much to predict behavior.

Situational factors also appear to play a role in sexual encounters. The opportunity must present itself, most typically in a private setting. The backseat of the car appears to be a setting of the past. Most sexual intercourse (particularly among younger teens) occurs in one of the partner's homes, most often the female's (Jorgensen, 1983). This is because in a large percentage of families, both parents are working and adolescents can count on them being out of the house at regular times.

Preparing for Sexual Encounters

Contraceptive use.   Given the recent advances in contraceptive technology and changes in social, educational, and legal stances regarding the availability of contraception, we might have expected major reductions in adolescent pregnancy during the 1970s. And indeed, a smaller percentage of sexually active adolescents get pregnant. High rates of adolescent pregnancy confirm that a large portion of the sexually active adolescent population is not using contraception effectively, however (Bolton, 1980; Baldwin, 1982; Zelnik & Kantner, 1983; Zabin & Clark, 1982).

Studies in the early 1970s (Bauman & Wilson, 1974; Presser, 1974; Sorensen, 1973) indicate that only 45% of sexually active teenagers used any type of contraceptive technique at the time of their first intercourse and that only 50% of college students and 20% of high school students reported any consistent use of birth control (Kantner & Zelnik, 1972).

The picture has changed somewhat since the early 1970s, but the *overall* adolescent pregnancy rate is still on the rise due to the fact that more females are sexually active. Zelnik and Kantner (1978) and others (Forrest, Hermalin & Hanshaw, 1981; Zabin, 1981) estimate that programs that provide contraceptive services appear to have prevented more than half a million adolescent pregnancies that would occur each year. In fact, contraceptive practice among unmarried teenage women improved significantly between 1971 and 1976 (see Figure 8.3), up 53% for whites and 76% for blacks.

We should note here that research and programming dealing with adolescent contraception focuses mainly on females (Clark, Zabin, & Hardy, 1984).This reflects both the fact that it is the female who risks pregnancy and the double standard that demands less responsible sexual behavior of males than of females. Some studies have directly studied male contraceptive atti-

FIGURE 8.3

Adolescent pregnancy, showing percent of sexually experienced never-married women aged 15-19 who used contraception at last intercourse, by age, 1976 and 1971. (From Zelnick and Kantner, 1977)

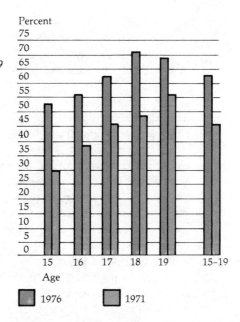

1976   1971

tudes and behavior (Finkel & Finkel, 1975; Hendricks, 1982; Vadies & Hale, 1978). They reported a mixed picture. Some males do have a strong sense of responsibility for contraception; others do not. Zelnick and Kantner's (1980) survey data indicate that the use of condoms and withdrawal (the two techniques that require the greatest assumption of responsibility by the male partner) rank second and third (after the pill) as the most likely method of contraception used by adolescents, being reported as the "most recent" method used in sexual intercourse involving 15–19-year-old females, with 23% reporting their partners used condoms and 19% withdrawal (vs. 41% using the pill).

Changes in the types of contraceptives being used played a big role in this (Zelnick & Kantner, 1977). Many more young women used the pill and intrauterine device (IUD) in 1967 than in 1971. However, Zelnick & Kantner's (1980) more recent data show a decline in the use of the more effective methods (particularly the pill) and an increase in reliance on the more ineffective methods, particularly withdrawal. The reasons for this are unclear, but seem to include publicity about health risks of the pill and the fact that more very young adolescents, who do not have easy access to other, more reliable, forms of birth control, are sexually active

There is usually a gap between age at first intercourse and age at first use of contraception. Half wait 6 months or more and only 14% used contraception the first time they had intercourse (Zabin & Clark, 1981). There does not appear to be any evidence that this gap is narrowing. However, the older teenagers are at the time of first intercourse, the more likely it is that they will begin to use contraception at the same time they begin to have sex (Zelnick &

Kantner, 1977). Perhaps older adolescents are mature enough to recognize and reason about responsibility. This may be attributable in part to the cognitive maturation that goes on in adolescence, as we showed in Chapter 4, as well as other differences between those who begin sexual activity early compared to those who delay it.

The lag between age of first intercourse and age of first contraceptive use is a significant problem (Zabin, Zelnick, & Kantner, 1979; Zabin & Clark, 1981) and also appears to be related to how guilty adolescents are about their sexual activity (Rains, 1971). In a sample of sexually experienced college women, Allgeier, Przybyla, and Thompson (1977) found that females with a lot of guilt about sex took longer to begin contraceptive use after first intercourse (lag of 15.7 months) than did females with little guilt (lag of 3.5 months). Allgeier and her colleagues reasoned that if sex is a source of guilt, then acquiring contraception prior to engaging in intercourse may be experienced by those high in sex guilt as tantamount to "planning their sin," and thus something to put off as long as possible.

Very young adolescents or individuals high in sex guilt are not likely to admit that they may continue to have sexual activity and, in turn, may not use a reliable form of birth control or may not use it regularly (Rains, 1971; Lindemann, 1974; Herold & Godwin, 1981). Zelnik and Kantner (1977) found that the more committed to sex a young woman is, the more sophisticated her initial use of contraception. Interestingly, there was not a correlation to age at first use of contraception nor to a resulting pregnancy. As evidence of the importance of commitment, the longer the relationship lasts, the evidence indicates that the greater the chance for consistent and effective contraceptive use.

An intimate and involved relationship appears to be a major influence in contraceptive use for adolescents. The commitment to contraceptive responsibility appears to be a developmental process that grows as a relationship grows. Miller (1980) proposes four hypothesized stages couples go through in accepting the responsibility of becoming sexually active. First, the couple is sexually active but limits their activities to petting. Second, the couple begins having intercourse, but without contraceptive protection. The third stage in responsibility development involves a missed or delayed menstrual period. Miller believes that this triggers responsible behavior (in the normal progression). There can be two outcomes at this stage. If the girl's period comes, the couple may pull back into false security or the couple may acknowledge the danger. However, after this stage, the couple is still ambivalent about being sexually active and there is no consistent use of birth control. The final stage is when the relationship develops into a sense of commitment and involvement, followed by the consistent use of reliable birth control. Whether or not a couple proceeds through these stages depends upon the adolescent's maturity of cognitive level, sexual attitudes, and development of the relationship. In discussing the barriers to contraceptive use, we will examine how such factors influence responsible sexual behavior.

Barriers to contraceptive use.   The high rate of teenage pregnancy that exists despite the availabilitiy of contraceptive materials and services suggests that a combination of psychological and social factors is impeding adolescent contraceptive use. Sociological studies of group characteristics focus on females, and show a statistical relationship to risk-taking in sexual encounters (Chilman, 1979). Females bear most of the burden of pregnancy and have traditionally been forced to assume responsibility for ensuring contraception takes place (even if it is to take the form of males using condoms). Thus, research has examined factors impinging upon female contraceptive use. According to Chilman's review, poor, inconsistent, or nonuse of contraceptives by sexually active adolescent females is related to the following social characteristics:

1   Being younger than age 18. Young women are less likely to accept their sexual activity and to prepare for it than are older women.
2   Being single. Married women are much more likely to use contraceptives than are single women.
3   Not being in a steady, committed, dating relationship. Women who are involved with a man over a long period of time are much more likely to use contraceptives than are women who are not so involved.
4   Having intercourse sporadically. Regular intercourse leads to expecting and planning for such activity.
5   Being a fundamentalist Protestant. Women who espouse fundamentalist beliefs are more likely to deny that they are involved in sexual activity and are unlikely to admit such behavior to themselves by using contraceptives.
6   Being from a lower socioeconomic status family. Where costs may be a real factor and attitudes about sex less contraceptively-oriented, contraceptive use is diminished.
7   Desiring a pregnancy.
8   Being black or Hispanic, among whom rates are higher.
9   Not being a college student. College youth receive greater exposure to contraceptive ideology, have greater access, and more resources generally.
10 Not having had a pregnancy experience. Women who have had a previous pregnancy are much more likely to use contraceptives than are women who have never been pregnant.

Oskamp and Mindick (1981) provided a similar review of the personality and attitudinal factors related to contraceptive nonuse, but one that has greater applicability to males as well as females. Included are:

1   Viewing oneself as not sexually active; the failure to accept one's sexuality and the adult responsibility that sexual activity connotes.

2   Being poorly socialized; having incomplete learning or acceptance of the norms of society; being deviant and irresponsible.

3   Having poor cognitive skills; poor coping skills, being unable to solve problems, being slow to acquire useful knowledge, not having enough knowledge of birth control and reproduction. Importantly, intelligence as measured by IQ tests is *not* related to lack of contraceptive use.

4   Not having a future orientation; not being planful and reflective about one's life and actions, not being in control of one's impulses.

5   Being neurotic, anxious, and having poor social adjustment; having a high level of sex guilt, not being able to express oneself well or to communicate well with one's partner. The implication of social competence for adolescent sexuality is underscored here.

6   Having negative attitudes and intentions about contraception; being fearful, mistrustful, or ignorant about contraceptives.

7   Having a poor sense of personal efficacy; feeling incompetent, having an external locus of control or reinforcement, being passive, and expressing learned helplessness.

Related to Oskamp and Mindick's (1981) last characteristic is a belief in stereotypic sex roles. Many females view males as expecting or demanding intercourse (and, of course, may be accurate in this perception), and this persuades them to go along, even without protection from pregnancy (Luker, 1975; Scales, 1977; Jorgensen, King, and Torrey, 1980). Witness the finding reported earlier that 1 in 8 college women reported that they had been coerced into sexual intercourse in a dating situation (Kanin & Parcell, 1977). Despite changes in attitudes toward equality between the sexes, there are still feelings that the male should take the initiative in sexual relations and the female in contraception. In a sense, girls may feel that they damage their self-concept as attractive, desirable, "good" girls when they take the initiative in planning for intercourse, expecially in tenuous relationships. Kantner and Zelnik (1972) discovered that young adolescent girls relied more on their male partners for contraceptive protection. This is still common, as the data on condoms and withdrawal cited earlier indicate (Zelnick & Kantner, 1980).

Oskamp and Mindick (1981) mentioned the relationship of poor cognitive skills to lack of contraceptive use. Lower levels of cognitive development may also impede the use of birth control and the success of sex education programs. Recall from Chapters 4 and 6 the discussion of adolescent egocentrism that occurs in the process of attaining formal operational thought. Cvetkovich, Grote, Bjoresth, and Sarkissian (1975) have applied Elkind's (1967) notions of *imaginary audience* and *personal fable* to adolescent sexuality and contraceptive behavior. The imaginary audience consists of the adolescent's anticipations of the reactions of others to him or her. Adolescents assume others are as preoccupied with them as they are with themselves. As we mentioned earlier, adolescents may not be ready to accept their sexuality. To prepare by using contraceptives is to admit to themselves and the *audience* a willingness to accept sexuality. A study by Fisher, Fisher, and Byrne (1977) illustrates this type of egocentrism. They investigated the reactions of adolescent males to purchasing contraceptives and found that a sizeable proportion of their sample believed that the pharmacist would have a negative view of them. Many adult males will remember the anxiety they felt purchasing their first condoms, and mass media portray this situation humorously.

If adolescents fail to differentiate self-concerns from the concerns of others, they also commit a complementary error by over-differentiating their uniqueness in a *personal fable*. As a barrier to contraception, one fable encompasses the belief that pregnancy is unlikely or impossible for them. In Sorensen's (1973) study of adolescents, 46% of the girls who had sex during the preceding month without using contraception agreed with the statement, "If a girl truly doesn't want to have a baby, she won't get pregnant even though she may have sex without taking any birth control precautions!" Kantner and Zelnik (1973) found that 56% of the 15–19-year-old girls in their sample did not use contraception at last intercourse because they did not believe that they could become pregnant (although, of course, if they were using the rhythm method there might be some basis for their belief). This failure to use contraception stems in part from the girls' misinformation about ovulation and contraception, of course, as well as their personal fables. Cvetkovich, Grote, Bjorsetin, and Sarkissian (1975) report that many adolescents do not understand the probabilities of conception, especially the fact that it can happen each time that they have intercourse regardless of the number of times they have it. We must keep in mind the Zelnick and Kantner (1980) data that reports that only 34% of sexually active 15–19-year-old females said they *always* used contraception (much of it being ineffective methods) and 27% said they *never* used contraception.

Finally, the connection between *knowing* about effective contraception and *using* it is not as strong as we might hope and expect (Chilman, 1979). This does not suggest that education is useless. However, engaging in intercourse and using or not using contraceptives are not primarily intellectual processes, and this has implications for sex education, as we shall see. This fact is clearly seen in the first-hand accounts of teenagers talking about pregnancy. Many have at least some knowledge about contraception, but most don't seem well-prepared to practice it consistently and effectively.

Consequences of Sexual Encounters

Pregnancy and abortion.   The failure to use contraception often results in pregnancy. If one had no knowledge of an adolescent's contraceptive behavior, the best predictor of premarital pregnancy is the duration of exposure, that is, the difference between the age at first intercourse and current age (Zelnik,

Kantner, & Ford, 1981). Social variables such as social status, religion, and family stability are of little importance in predicting the occurrence of premarital pregnancy, once the length of ongoing sexual activity is taken into account.

We will consider adolescent childbearing in a later chapter (13), but we will discuss the alternative of abortion here. According to Baldwin (1976), the abortion rate for teenagers rose by more than 60% between 1972 and 1975, following legalization by the U.S. Supreme Court, while the rate for girls under age 15 doubled during the same time. Overall, there are about one million teenage pregnancies per year, of which about 45% are aborted, 10% result in miscarriages or stillbirths, and 45% are born live (U.S. Department of Health and Human Services, 1980). These data demonstrate that the use of abortion as a response to adolescent contraceptive failure remains high (Baldwin, 1982).

Contrary to stereotype, abortion does not appear to be a lower-class phenomenon, nor is it exclusive to those with negative personal characteristics, such as irresponsibility. In fact, Dreyer (1982) reviewed studies of females who seek abortions and found that many use contraception (albeit ineffectively or sporadically in many cases) and have high educational and occupational aspirations. They typically come from stable middle-class or higher socioeconomic backgrounds. They also possess feelings of control over their lives and see themselves as competent people. Thus, abortion does not appear to follow automatically from any disadvantaged status; and personal characteristics may not be a major factor at all. Rather, the decision to have an abortion may better reflect a complex process of moral thinking on the female's part (Gilligan, 1982).

Few studies of the psychological effects of abortions upon women exist. Of those that do, there is little evidence that abortion has serious harmful psychological effects on the adolescents who have them. (Dreyer, 1982). The majority report feelings of relief. The most frequently reported negative feelings are those of mournfulness and guilt, felt more by females who are Roman Catholic, younger, of lower socioeconomic backgrounds, and who feel that abortion is being forced upon them (Evans, Selstad, & Welcher, 1976).

Sexually transmitted diseases.   Veneral diseases have become serious health hazards for the young. The greatest incidence of venereal disease is among the 20–24-year-old group, followed by the 15–19-year-old group (NIAID, 1981). The rate of syphilis among adolescents has not risen in the last 25 years. However, gonorrhea rates have tripled since 1956, with the greatest increase being among young women (Center for Disease Control, 1979). Although gonorrhea is readily treatable by antibiotics, many adolescents do not seek treatment because they fail to recognize the symptoms. This is especially true among women, who today are more sexually active at younger ages when they are less likely to be aware of symptoms. As many as two out of three women infected with gonorrhea are not aware of it; and this explains the dramatic growth of the disease in the population of women. Untreated gonorrhea results in inflamation of the Fallopian tubes, infertility, birth malformations, or menstrual disorders (NIAID, 1981). In men, gonorrhea is the single most frequent cause of sterility (Gordon, 1973).

Syphilis is less common than gonorrhea, but is more serious. Syphilis generally shows up in three stages. The first sign is the presence of a sore at the place of contact, from a week to several months after contact with the infected person. The sore disappears within a month and is replaced with other symptoms such as rashes. Soon all symptoms disappear while the disease progresses into an advanced stage, in which it can cause such serious damage as paralysis, heart disease, blindness, and even death (Gordon, 1973).

Another venereal disease that is running rampant in America is herpes simplex virus II, commonly known as venereal or genital herpes. Over 20 million Americans have it, and as many as half a million more may be contracting herpes each year (NIAID, 1981). Herpes is a virus characterized by blistery sores on and around the genital area, sometimes accompanied by headache, fever, muscle aches, and swollen glands. Although symptoms will disappear, the disease does not (and symptoms occur in irregular cycles). Regardless of whether it is dormant or active, the herpes virus always remains in the body. At the present time, it is incurable and highly contagious while in the active state.

In addition to intermittent discomfort, genital herpes can lead to serious complications. Newborn infants exposed to herpes sores (during an active phase of the disease) in the birth canal can suffer brain damage or death. Furthermore, women infected with herpes are eight times more likely to have cervical cancer than women not infected (Harvard Medical School Health Letter, 1981).

The psychological effects of herpes may be more devastating than its medical symptoms. In a survey of herpes sufferers conducted by the Herpes Resource Center, 53% of the respondents said they had consciously avoided potentially intimate situations, even during periods of latency; 35% had experienced impotence or a reduced sex drive; 40% had trouble at work; and 84% had encountered periodic depression (*Mademoiselle*, September, 1982). On the positive side, concern about herpes may have reduced casual sexual contacts, and this has been associated with reduced incidence of gonorrhea and syphilis in 1982 (Center for Disease Control, 1983).

Society is responding to the herpes epidemic in a number of ways, including research devoted to developing a vaccine and/or a cure, the distribution of brochures, media coverage, and even a dating service for those who have herpes. Although the average age of herpes sufferers is 33, it is only a matter of time before the adolescent population is seriously affected, especially since sexual behavior has been increasing among the young. Perhaps the tendency to limit sexual activity to close, intimate relationships will help to keep the disease at bay. Table 8.2 summarizes the most important venereal diseases.

TABLE 8.2
Sexually transmitted diseases.

Disease	Transmission	Symptoms	Diagnosis	Treatment
Gonorrhea ("the clap," "the drip")	Most common sexually transmitted disease in U.S. Highest incidence among 20–24 yr. olds; second highest among 15–19 yr. olds. Transmitted by genital, oral, or anal contact with infected person. Infants can contact gonorrhea by passing through birth canal of infected mother. May cause blindness in infants unless eyes are treated with silver nitrate.	*Females* 80% do not show symptoms and go untreated; site of infection is cervix. When disease is contracted, vulva becomes red and irritated 2–7 days after infection; frequent urination with pain; yellow-green puslike discharge may result. If untreated, infection may pass to reproductive organs in abdominal cavity; can reduce chances of pregnancy. *Males* Symptoms occur 3–5 days following infection. Discharge is at first thin and clear, then turns thick, yellow-green, and puslike; burning and sometimes blood with urination. Symptoms may subside in few weeks. If untreated, infection will spread and may cause sterility.	*Two tests* Gram strain—reliable when symptoms are present; culture—reliable when symptoms are not present.	Easily treated with penicillin, or tetracycline if allergic to penicillin.
Syphillis	Genital, oral, or anal contact with infected person. Infected mother can transmit to fetus and cause miscarriage, stillbirth, or congenital syphillis. Fetus will probably not be harmed if mother is treated before fourth	Four-stage process: *Primary* Chancre appears within 2–4 weeks at site of infection—external genitalia, cervix, vaginal walls, rectum, breasts, mouth, or hands. Sore is painless and disappears in few weeks. *Secondary* Few weeks to 6 months after chancre disap-	External exam during primary stage. Blood tests are used but can't get results until a month after infection; blood tests are only 75% accurate so they are usually repeated once each month for 4 months.	Easily treated with penicillin, or tetracycline if allergic to penicillin.

		raised bumps that are first red, then darken; not painful or itchy; can break and ooze thick liquid. Might have coldlike symptoms (fever, sore throat). Hair might fall out. Extremely contagious in this stage. Symptoms disappear within several weeks. *Latent* Absence of symptoms for 1–40 years or more. Disease burrows in circulatory system, central nervous system, and bones. *Tertiary* Large ulcer on internal organs, skin, and muscle tissue; can be treated successfully. More dangerous when it attacks cardiovascular or central nervous systems. Then it can lead to paralysis, mental deterioration, and death.	No known cure. Can prevent transmission to offspring by caesarean deliveries. Can help prevent transmission to others by sexual abstinence and use of condoms.
Genital herpes (herpes simplex virus, type 2)	Potential for becoming more widespread than gonorrhea. Transmitted by genital, oral, or anal contact with infected person, especially when disease is not dormant. If mother has active infection, can pass to newborn and cause neurological damage.	Small red bumps in genital area, thighs, and buttocks 2–8 days after contact; develop into painful blisters that burst and pour out millions of infectious particles. Disease most contagious at this point. Fever and burning urination. In 10 days, sores heal and disease becomes dormant but does not go away. Returns without warning during stress, menstruation, and changes in temperature. Herpes is linked to cervical cancer in women. Psychological stigma can be more painful than symptoms.	

TABLE 8.2 (continued)

Disease	Transmission	Symptoms	Diagnosis	Treatment
Pubic lice ("crabs")	Sexually transmitted but *also* from contact with infested towel, sheet or toilet seat. Lice only survive 24 hrs. without human host.	Itchy pubic area caused by lice big as head of pin. They attach to base of hairs and feed off host's blood. Lice live maximum of 1 month, but they lay many eggs.		Kwell cream, lotion, or shampoo.
Scabies	Transmission similar to pubic lice.	Itchy genital and surrounding areas due to microorganisms that burrow into skin and lay eggs.		Kwell cream, lotion, or shampoo.

Variations in Sexual Orientation

Most of the information in this chapter has focused on typical heterosexual relations. Equally important, although not socially normative, is the development and expression of *homosexuality* and *ambisexuality*. Homosexuality refers to sexual relations with members of the same gender. Ambisexuality, also called bisexuality, refers to sexual relations with members of both genders. The term ambisexuality is more accurately descriptive than bisexuality since the prefix *bi* implies a 50/50 split in preference for males and females, when this is not always the case.

In determining whether one is a homosexual, the above definitions are far too simple. They refer to homosexual and ambisexual *behavior* but not necessarily to one's *identification* as a homosexual or ambisexual. A prevalent notion is that homosexual and heterosexual are two separate and distinct categories. However, people may engage in homosexual behaviors for a variety of reasons without feeling that they *are* homosexuals. For example, Kinsey and his asssociates (1953) found that while only about 2% of subjects were exclusively homosexual, the number of people who have had at least some homosexual experience ranges from 13% for females to 37% for males. Likewise, it is important to specify that the range of behaviors included in the terms *homosexual experience* and *homosexual activity* can be quite broad. That range runs from affectionate nongenital touching (e.g., hugs and caresses) to genitally-focused activities leading to orgasm. Much of the homosexual activity reported by relatively large numbers of adolescents is at the lower end of this sexual continuum.

The distinction between occasional or *transient* homosexual activity and homosexual identification is especially critical in adolescence. Homosexual activity is fairly common in adolescence, but is not indicative of later sexual preference. In their classic study (using a sample of undetermined generalizability), Kinsey and his colleagues (1948) found that about two-thirds of all males have a homosexual experience before age 15. Such behavior, however, did not appear to be a predictor of adult homosexual behavior. More recently, Hass (1979) found that approximately 10% of teenagers have had homosexual experiences, most of which occurred in preadolescence.

The motivation to engage in homosexual activity in the pre- and early adolescent years results from curiosity, exploration, and experimentation. These are the years in which same-sex friendships are predominant, and sexual exploration may occur within these close peer relations because the participants are in a comfortable social setting.

The few good studies of homosexual behavior among adolescents reveal three consistent findings. First, homosexual contacts are most frequent before age 15 and are more likely to be experienced by boys than by girls (Hass, 1979; Hunt, 1974; Kinsey et al., 1948; Kinsey et al., 1953; Sorensen, 1973). Second, acceptance of homosexual relationships by adolescents is widespread, although more so among higher socioeconomic status youth and among older adolescents. Almost 70% of 16- to 19-year-olds accept sexual relationships between two girls and slightly less that that accept such behaviors between two boys. In general, boys are more accepting of female homosexuality than they are of male homosexuality, while girls accept both equally (Hass, 1979). Third, despite these liberal attitudes, less than 15% of boys and 10% of girls report having had any homosexual encounters during adolescence, and only 3% of the boys and 2% of the girls report participating in an ongoing homosexual relationship (Chilman, 1979; Hass, 1979). It is interesting to note that while other types of sexual behaviors have shown an increase in the last 30 years, the incidence and rate of adolescent homosexuality seem to have remained the same or even decreased (Chilman, 1979; Hunt, 1974).

It can be somewhat misleading to discuss homosexual identification in adolescence. Remember that most individuals in this phase of life are still forming their identities. As part of a person's overall identity, sexuality is in the formation stage, too. Since the process of sexual unfolding means many changes, sexual orientation may change as well. Nevertheless, adult homosexuals indicate they had some recognition of homosexual orientation in their adolescent years. Thus, while homosexual behavior does not guarantee homosexual orientation, adult homosexuals do seem to come from the much larger pool of adolescents with some homosexual experiences.

There are differences between the way that females and males react to homosexual identification. For females, there is often a gap between recognition that one may be a lesbian and acting on that suspicion; attempts at heterosexual sex are tried first (Schafer, 1976). For males, on the other hand, homosexual activity begins earlier, often to the exclusion of any heterosexual contact (Nass, Libby, & Fisher, 1981). Compared to females, however, males report far greater difficulties in developing a homosexual identity (Blumstein & Schwartz, 1977). The reason may be that masculinity is made a major element in males' feelings of self-worth in our society. Because many people define homosexuality as impaired masculinity, it threatens the self-esteem of those who practice it. For females there is less threat to self-esteem.

It is not fully understood why a person becomes heterosexual, homosexual, or ambisexual. Many theories emphasize the relationship with parents. They suggest that homosexuality can result from poor identification with the same-sexed parent or a poor, aloof relationship with the same-sexed parent. However, a significant number of homosexuals have enjoyed satisfactory relationships with their parents, whereas many heterosexuals had disturbed parent/child relationships. This suggests that the development of sexual object preference is more complex than is often thought, and may include inborn predispositions in some cases. Research is not clear about how males and females decide which sex will become the focus of sexual interest. Lerner and Spanier (1980) suggest that socialization influences during childhood and adolescence interact with hereditary or biological factors to direct one's sexual orientation. As in most cases, such an interactionist view makes sense.

How Does It Feel? What Does It Mean?

Many of the preceding sections report data on rates and prevalence of adolescent sexual encounters. What is perhaps equally important, from the perspective of individual development, is the *meaning* adolescents attach to sexual behaviors. Most research deals with the facts of who, what, where, and how often, but the big issues of how it feels and what it means go relatively unstudied (Jorgensen, 1983). Recall that our definition of development emphasizes just such a subjective, competence-oriented approach. Sorensen (1973) attempted to explore adolescent feelings about sexuality. Most generally, he found that the majority of teens felt their sex lives to be normal and satisfying. Also, although boys conform more to peer pressure in the sexual realm than do girls, sex is not rated as the most important teen activity by either gender. This is encouraging, because if we are to have a sexually sensible society, we must be comfortable with sexuality and see it as a *part* of life.

Adolescent self-stimulation serves as an introduction to the more general topic of feelings about sex. Although few studies have addressed the topic of masturbation in adolescence, those that do indicate a lessening of traditional prohibitions against masturbation and an increase over the last 20 years in the percentages of teenagers who both accept and practice masturbation. When the adolescents in Sorensen's (1973) study were asked about masturbation, over 90% of both sexes reported masturbating by the age of 15. In fact, more girls than boys had masturbated by the age of 10. Hass' (1979) more recent study indicated that about 70% of boys and 45% of girls masturbated by age 15 and that among 16- to 19-year-olds, more than two-thirds of the boys and half of the girls masturbated once a week or more. Diepold and Young (1979) reported figures of 90% for 18-year-old males and 50% of 18-year-old females. Some sex counselors have built upon this to encourage teenagers to pet to orgasm as a substitute for intercourse (Hamilton, 1978). The traditional criticism of this as "nothing but mutual masturbation" is deflated by normalizing attitudes about masturbation in general. That is, as masturbation itself has gained increasing acceptance as a normal and healthy sexual act, "petting to mutual orgasm" is also being more widely accepted.

According to Hass (1979), sexually active adolescents tend to masturbate more than those who are less sexually active. However, boys involved in an ongoing sexual relationship tend to forego masturbation, while girls involved in an ongoing relationship increase their rate of masturbation (perhaps to achieve the orgasms not experienced during intercourse and generally to augment sexual satisfaction that is often low in their relations with adolescent males).

Although prohibitive attitudes have lessened in recent years, about one-half of adolescents continue to have feelings of guilt or anxiety regarding masturbation (Sorensen, 1973). Furthermore, Sorensen noted that of all sexual behaviors considered, teenagers had the most difficulty in discussing masturbation; this activity evoked the most reticence and embarrassment. Apparently, many teenagers still have misgivings about achieving pleasure through self-stimulation, even if they practice it. Part of this may be because of the absence of a close, loving partner that as we noted earlier legitimizes sexual behaviors in the minds of many adolescents (and *does* seem to liberate girls to masturbate).

Gender differences emerge when adolescents articulate their reactions to their first experience with intercourse. Generally, males have a more positive reaction than females. Many of the girls in Sorensen's (1973) study felt pressured into intercourse and were uncertain about the effects it would have on their relationship. Although most of Sorensen's adolescents were glad they had engaged in intercourse and felt it had strengthened their relationship, three times as many girls as boys wished they had waited until they were older before having their first coital experience. Nearly half (46%) of the males and one quarter (26%) of the females reported feeling "excited." While 17% of the males said they felt "afraid," fully 63% of the females reported this feeling. Nearly half the males (43%) said they felt "satisfied," as opposed to only one fifth (20%) of the females. More than a third of the females felt "worried" or "guilty" (as opposed to less than 10% of the males).

Females tend to be more accurate in interpreting their partner's reactions to intercourse (Sorensen, 1973). Males, on the other hand, misread their partners reactions, usually assuming that the experience is more positive than it actually is. This, again, may be due to females' emphasis on the romantic aspects of sexual encounters. Girls may be more sensitive to emotions, including their partner's. Males may be more egocentric and less empathic. Despite this gender difference, Hass' (1979) study indicates that the majority of adolescents do not feel that physical pleasure is the most important aspect of sex. Affection, love, and closeness are the main reasons given for sexual intercourse. So, although girls are more apt than boys to link love and intimacy with sex, slightly more than half of the sampled boys agreed with this concept, at least *in principle*. In fact, they may be more motivated by physical pleasure and "conquest" than they admit.

Sexual Knowledge: What and From Where?

Most authorities and much of the general public (75% according to recent polls) believe that sex education in some form should be initiated in early childhood (Richardson & Cranston, 1981). When adolescence arrives, sex education becomes especially important to individual development and social competence. Sex education involves much more than reproductive instruction, however, particularly for teenagers. Rather, sex education should seek to teach youth to understand and accept themselves as people with sexual feelings and reproductive capacities. It should include learning how to interact with others in a competent, responsible, healthy, and meaningful way. Its goal should be to achieve a balance between social responsibility, on the one hand, and personal freedom and growth, on the other (Lerner & Spanier, 1980, p. 319).

There is an ongoing debate over who should be responsible for sex instruction (parents? teachers? specialists? generalists?) and the effects of sex education (increased sexual activity? less guilt? more responsibility?). We start from the recognition that sexual knowledge can come both from informal networks and from formal sources.

Informal Sources

Although the home would seem to be a natural setting for instructing children about sex, adolescents report that they receive relatively little sex instruction from their parents (Atwater, 1983). Some surveys tell us that young people are dissatisfied with the sex information available at home, but would really prefer their parents to be the primary source (Bennet & Dickinson, 1980; Sorensen, 1973). In Sorensen's (1973) study, over half the boys and two-thirds of the girls expressed a desire to learn more about sex from their parents. Despite this, more than two-thirds of these same adolescents said that their parents did not talk openly about sexual matters to them. Davis and Harris (1982) report that females are more likely than males to receive information from parents. When parents do give sex instruction, it is often limited almost exclusively to facts of menstruation and pregnancy (McCary & McCary, 1982). Fox and Inazu (1980) found that only one-third of the mothers they studied discussed intercourse or birth control with their 14–15-year-old daughters. And most of what they did say was negative, and tended to interfere with sexual satisfaction (Darling & Hicks, 1982). However, Fox (1980) reports that when mothers and daughters do discuss intercourse and contraception openly, this communication is particularly influential in preventing adolescent pregnancy. Explanations of this parental reluctance focus on parental inhibitions as the stumbling block (Dickinson, 1978).

Most of the information adolescents obtain regarding sex comes from peers (Thornburg, 1981). Some research (e.g., Dickinson, 1978) even suggests an increasing reliance on peers. Unfortunately, peers, the least reliable source, are the primary sources of information concerning masturbation, intercourse, and homosexuality, and this information is the least accurate. Parents, school, and literature provided the information about the topics rated most accurate (e.g., menstruation and venereal disease) (Thornburg, 1972).

According to Hunt's (1974) survey, only 10% of adolescents rated siblings as primary sources of sex information and only 10% rated other adults as a primary source. Davis and Harris (1982) report that less than half of the adolescents they surveyed even mentioned siblings or doctors or nurses as sources of information about sex. According to McCary and McCary (1982), other adults are not very accurate sources. Clinical psychologists, the clergy, professional counselors, social workers, and even physicians are not trained to disseminate sexual information. Lloyd (1980) acknowledges that only one-third of the medical schools provide organized course material in the reproductive sciences.

Finally, it appears that the media and reading material supplement sexual information learned from peers (Adam & Gullotta, 1983). Davis and Hunt's (1982) survey indicates that reading is a primary source of information, second only to peers. Although reading the *correct* literature can supply accurate information about sexuality, most information presented through the media must be carefully critiqued. The popular media often offer distorted impressions and link sex with violence. If adolescents carry inflated, media-fed expectations of eternal romance, passionate fireworks, and multiple orgasms, their future experiences may lead to disillusionment and distress. On the other hand, also distressing and potentially debilitating is the paralyzing guilt that can result from moralistic, rigid, antisex propaganda. Much of the fictional literature on sex available to adolescents errs in one of these two directions. The nonfiction is generally much better, as is evident in contemporary informational and advice publications. Hamilton's *Sex With Love: A Guide for Young People* (1978) has received good reviews (Adams & Gullotta, 1983). Ira Gordon's *You Would If You Loved Me* (1978) is another good choice. Most Planned Parenthood chapters maintain a well-stocked library of such publications.

Formal Sources

Since many children are not given thorough and reliable sexual information in the home, and peers are shown to be unreliable sources, strides have been taken to provide quality sex education through the schools. Polls reveal that about 75% of parents support the idea of sex education in the schools (Richardson & Cranston, 1981). As recently as 1975, however, only one-third of high school teachers taught anything about reproduction, intercourse, or abortion; less than that discussed birth control (Guttmacher, 1976). Many barriers remain today, as debates over back to basics, the mission of schooling, and allocation of resources for training and teacher preparation continue (Scales, 1981; Kenney & Alexander, 1980).

The lack of sex education programs in schools might seem surprising in light of the 75% majority of parents who approve of it, at least *in principle*. In addition, adolescents themselves are strongly in favor of expanded and improved sex education courses (Hunt, 1970; Sorensen, 1973; Rubenstein, 1976; Yarber, 1979). However, the minority who are opposed to sex education are so influential that they have been successful in blocking comprehensive sex education programs in many school districts (Thornburg, 1982; Orr, 1982; Kirby, Alter, & Scales, 1979).

Clawar (1977) reviewed six major areas of resistance to sex education. One is concern over the teacher's qualifications. The second concern is over what should be taught and how. Third, parents worry about the teacher's values. Even the context for presenting factual information is probably affected by the teacher's own attitudes. This is especially problematic in schools where students come from a wide variety of backgrounds. The fourth problem involves the sex educator's age. Some parents fear that a young teacher may not be mature enough to teach sexuality responsibly. The educator's personal characteristics are clearly important to parents of adolescents.

The last two areas of resistance center on the acquisition of sexual knowledge itself. Some parents worry that such information will speed their child's transition to adult status and blame sex education programs for contributing to children slipping out of parental control. Sex education serves as a convenient target for parents who are reluctant to recognize that their children are growing up biologically and socially. Finally, an outspoken minority believes that sexual information will lead to premature and promiscuous sex. This, however, does not appear to be true.

The Effects of Sexual Knowledge

Evidence does not support the contention that sex education encourages adolescent sexual behavior, particularly irresponsible sexual behavior (Zelnick & Kim, 1982). Over 1,000 college students were interviewed about their sexual behavior and where they obtained their sexual knowledge (Spanier, 1976, 1977). Results indicated that sex education in schools had little effect on premarital sexual activity.

The impact of educational programs in any liberal direction seems to be on attitudes rather than behaviors. Kilmann, Wanlass, Sabalis, and Sullivan (1981) reviewed the impact of sex education and concluded that such programs result in increased sexual knowledge and more liberal sexual attitudes. However, these attitudes must be considered in context. For one thing, many of the studies done on the effects of sex education involve college students or upper division secondary school students; few involve junior high or middle school pupils. Also, most studies deal with changes in expressed attitudes and values. Their relation to actual sexual behavior thus remains untested in most cases.

A study by Luttman and Parcel (1979) indicated that although students who participate in sex education develop more permissive and accepting attitudes toward the idea of sexual behavior in committed relationships, they develop *less* tolerant attitudes of sexual behavior in casual or exploitive relationships. Most adults should be pleased by this second outcome, even if they have trouble accepting the first. One might conclude that sex education promotes factual information, understanding, awareness, and comfort with the idea of sexuality, but does so within the context of social competence, respect, and responsibility. For instance, one study indicated that sex instruction in schools was correlated with a 50% decrease in the incidence of gonorrhea in a year's time (Levine, 1970). Furthermore, after exposure to discussions regarding birth control, adolescents of both sexes demonstrated greater use of contraceptives (Scharff et al., 1980). There is no evidence that sex education encourages sexual encounters but when sexual activity does occur, informational programs appear to promote responsible sexuality.

Long-term effects of school sex education have been examined by Schaeffer (1967). In comparing female students of sex education to girls who were not exposed to sex education programs, Schaeffer found that the former students had fewer out-of-wedlock births, more successful marriages, and took better care of their children. Thornburg (1982) confirms these results.

Finally, Gordon (1977) emphasizes the importance of developing sexual competence, the idea that sexuality is an area of a person's life in which he or she can be knowledgeable, responsible, and capable. Competence in the sexual sphere can be a contributing factor to a healthy psychological make-up, as much as it depends upon overall competence (Jorgensen, 1981). McCary and McCary (1982) argue (admittedly without conclusive evidence) that adequate sex education contributes positively to general psychological adjustment. This makes sense when one considers that learning the facts about sex and learning to feel natural and comfortable about the topic may help adolescents cope effectively with their own emerging sexual feelings. This process should then contribute to sexual competence, evident in healthy, interpersonal sexual expression.

It should be clear by now that we are convinced of the need for sex education in the schools as part of a broad community approach. Churches, youth groups, and other community agencies, as well as females must participate if adolescents are to be well-prepared for responsible and satisfying sexuality (Kirby, Alter, & Scales, 1979; Jorgensen, 1981; Scales & Kirby, 1981). No one institution is going to resolve all the issues adolescents face as they become sexually active. But sex education in the schools can help, particularly if it conforms to the principles laid down by Thornburg (1982):

1   Give students basic accurate factual information on *all* the key aspects of sexuality—from masturbation to intercourse, from homosexuality to venereal disease, from pregnancy to abortion.
2   Explore the emotional issues adolescents face as they seek to harmonize the voices of self, peers, parents and the mass media.
3   Examine the specific physical problems that derive from individual differences in attractiveness and sexual function.
4   Assist adolescents in developing a code of ethics that tries to meet personal needs and respect community standards.
5   Encourage self-awareness to increase the power to make and implement sexual decisions.

Certainly this is a tall order for any educational program, particularly in light of the school's failure to teach some of the academic basics to all students.

Issues in Adolescent Sexuality and Intimacy

In just one chapter it is not possible to describe all the real-life situations that involve adolescent sexuality and intimacy. Yet it is important to acquire a sense of how this area affects individuals and their social systems on a variety of levels, including personal decision-making, social policy, and social change. In addition, it is interesting to note the different ways in which such a highly personal behavior such as sexuality can become a public issue.

Three issues involving adolescent sexuality illustrate these points. They are: Should adolescents be sexually active? Should contraception be available to adolescents without parental consent? Is childhood being sexualized through mass media and marketing? We discuss several other issues, including adolescent prostitution and sexual abuse in Chapter 11.

Issue 1: Should Adolescents Be Sexually Active?

It is difficult and unrealistic to offer one general answer to this question. Regardless of biological maturity, adolescent psychological and social maturity levels differ, as we saw in Chapters 3, 4, and 6. One 16-year-old adolescent may be ready for and able to cope with sexual behavior while another may not be based on ability to reason morally and their sense of self. Many times, however, teenagers do become sexually active before they are ready to evaluate the situation and handle the consequences. However, some (e.g., Sussex, 1978) believe that adolescents are capable of coming to reasonable decisions regarding their sexual behavior if they are helped to look at the issues involved.

Sussex presents four questions adolescent girls should ask themselves before engaging in sexual activity. The same questions can also be asked of boys. The first is, "Is there any chance of pregnancy?" If the answer is yes, the decision not to engage in sexual behavior should, of course, be made and the rest of the questions are skipped. If contraception is available or if for some other reason the risk of pregnancy is considerably lessened, the next question is asked: "Will I lose my reputation?" The answer to this requires knowledge of how one's partner is viewing the situation, the degree of trust involved, and how much they both respect the privacy of their encounter. If there is some certainty that reputations will be preserved, the next question is considered: "Will I be humiliated or exploited?" Again, this requires a judgment of confidence in the other person involved and a feeling of personal understanding and comfort in the encounter. If the answer is no, the final question is asked: "Will I feel guilty?"

The problem with these questions is two-fold. First, Sussex's chain of questions implies a rational process and the answers must be considered in abstract form. The cognitive sophistication of adolescents varies and some may not be cognitively mature enough to consider the implications of the answers. Sussex does state that adolescents should be helped to consider the questions. But who will be the helper? Many young people do not confide in their parents about sexual decisions, and it would take an exceptional parent to be totally objective about their child's sexual decisions.

Second, it is not possible to answer Sussex's questions definitively. In many cases, the answers are not available until after the fact (even *long* after the fact). How does one really know whether guilt feelings will emerge until after engaging in the behavior in question? It is one thing to imagine feelings and quite another to experience them.

We might add that adolescents should consider other questions before sexual activity. For example, what is the risk of contracting a venereal disease? What will be the effects on my partner and this relationship? Clearly, asking these questions brings us back to the topics of moral reasoning we covered in Chapter 4. Decisions about sex challenge the moral judgment of the adolescent to the limit. Is it little wonder that most adults worry that youth in early adolescence are ill-equipped to give informed consent for sexual intercourse? Can most 14- and 15-year-olds reason effectively about something so socially complex and psychologically powerful as sexual involvement? It does suggest that if they are to be making decisions about sexual intercourse (particularly in the sex-charged climate created and reinforced by the mass media), adolescents will need all the help they can get from adults.

Opportunity and risk have been examined in other areas of adolescent development and are present, too, in sexuality. The risks are perhaps more obvious than the opportunities. However, outcomes of sexual activity *can* be the growth of a relationship, the enhancement of self-awareness, a sense of competence, and enjoyment. Sometimes risks can become opportunities for learning and growth. Consider how the following aspects of sexual encounters can be opportunities for development:

Expectations and disappointments.   Although sexual encounters may not be as exciting and romantic as adolescents fantasize, this early realization may benefit the growth of future relationships and help to place them within a realistic framework.

A pregnancy scare.   Encountering the personal reality of an apparent pregnancy can help adolescents realize the importance of contraception and may better guarantee contraceptive use in future encounters.

Learning to interact with another person.   Sexual activity can teach an individual to be sensitive to another person. Couples can examine each other's attitudes and feelings and this can help teach them to be giving, to compromise sometimes, and to achieve a balance between personal wants and desires.

Understanding sexuality.   Inasmuch as experience can be the best teacher, young people can learn about sexual behaviors and feelings through encounters with another person. This knowledge can prepare individuals for future sexual situations.

It appears that with the potential for opportunities and risks, adolescents must be encouraged to perform a sort of cost-benefit analysis before engaging in sexual relations. One of the benefits of sexual education is the opportunity for youths to learn to think in these terms, and to practice doing so in a supportive, informal context. Sex education thus becomes a crucial microsystem for the adolescent, and the mesosytems between sex education, peers, and parents are themselves important issues.

Issue 2: Should Contraceptive Information and Technology Be Available to Adolescents without Parental Knowledge and Consent?

The 1980s have seen a political struggle unfold about whether parents must be informed when their adolescents receive contraceptive services. For a few years, the federal government tried to deny funds to birth control agencies and physicians that did not inform the parents. In 1983, the government dropped their efforts to accomplish this goal through executive action in response to being blocked by the courts, but the issue remains alive. Opponents labeled the proposal to require notification the *squeal rule* and claim that it would prevent many teenagers from using birth control. Supporters say it is simply a reaffirmation of the basic rights of parents to know what treatment their children are receiving and that it will promote parent-child communication about the child's sexual behavior

The following statements represent the stances taken by various members of society on the question of parental notification. After considering these perspectives, consider your own position and be able to defend it.

Adolescent: I don't think parents should be told if a teenager makes an appointment and gets birth control. It's an invasion of privacy! People should just be glad that teenagers are willing to do something about preventing pregnancy. If my parents knew that I was having sex, they would never let me out of the house! They just don't understand that I'm not a little kid anymore. If I thought that they could find out that I'm on the pill, I would stop going to Family Planning. And then I'm not sure what I would do.

Parent #1:   I think parents have a right to know what is happening with their child. Parents are legally responsible for their children as long as they are minors. But regardless, we care about our kids and how can we possibly be of any help to them if we are kept in the dark about their lives? They are reluctant to tell us anything but they could sure benefit from our advice.

Parent #2:   I don't feel a need to be involved in my teenagers' sex lives unless they ask me to. We have always talked about sexual matters openly in our home and have supplied as much information as possible about sexuality. Although it always hurts a little to watch your kids pull away from you as they grow up, I feel it is a necessary process on the road to self-sufficient adulthood. We are here to help them be responsible for themselves. I trust the relationship I have with my children and am confident in their ability and willingness to make appropriate decisions, including approaching us for guidance without fear of negative reactions.

Politician #1: I am in favor of informing parents of their children's activities whenever possible. The family is the primary socializing force in our society and how can it operate if parents remain unaware of their children's behaviors? How can children be guided? I believe that it would be antifamily *not* to pass the law requiring parental notification of birth control use. The foundation of our society is family life, and we need to take whatever measures necessary to encourage and preserve it.

Politician #2: I believe that our democratic society is based on constitutional rights. The right to privacy is foremost. It would be setting a bad example to take this right away from young people who will be our future leaders. Also, it would be an attempt to undermine our democratic ideals that could have national and international ramifications.

Doctor #1: There are certain medical risks with most forms of birth control. It is for this simple reason that parents should be notified of any prescription or device their child may be using.

Doctor #2: If adolescents are aware that their parents will be notified of their contraceptive use, they will not feel as free to obtain birth control. This can result in increased pregnancies and this presents biological risks for young mothers and poor prenatal care for the fetus or a rise in abortion that has its own medical hazards.

Social Scientist: Contraceptive information and technology should be available to adolescents without parental knowledge. As developing individuals, a sense of freedom and personal responsibility is important to adolescents' sense of maturity and preparation for adult roles. Learning about sexuality is important to the teenager's emerging identity. The child must be given this room to grow. Taking away the privacy to act in a sexually responsible way is an attempt to thwart the growth process.

Family Planning Worker: Many people think that if adolescents don't use birth control, they won't be sexually active. This is wrong. The data make it clear that they are likely to maintain their sexual activity even without birth control. Indeed, most adolescents seek contraceptive services *after* they have been having intercourse over a period of several months. Therefore, it is our responsibility to see that contraception is made available to them. In most of our cases, adolescents request confidentiality. If the parental notification law is passed, teenagers will be less likely to seek birth control. Statistics on pregnancy rates and abortions continue to show an increase and will become higher without birth control use. Our organization does not haphazardly distribute contraceptives. Our clients undergo a medical examination and talk with trained counselors to decide the best contraceptive method for them. The safety and reliability of contraceptives, if used properly, is quite high. We do everything possible to ensure understanding and proper use of the methods with our clients.

Issue 3: Is Childhood Being Sexualized through Mass Media and Marketing?

The sexually suggestive nature of advertising and the media has always been a point of discussion and controversy. At the present time, advertisers are using young, sexually provocative models, usually females, to sell their products. A case in point is a commercial using the young model, Brooke Shields, to advertise designer jeans. Some of these commercials were aired on television and then taken off because of their overtly sexual poses and suggestive dialogue. It is a popular feeling that adolescents and even younger children are being portrayed in ad campaigns as sexual beings, and are thus being exploited in order to sell products, as a form of low-grade pornography. Many are dismayed at what this says about the priorities of business in our society.

Should childhood be protected from sexualization? What is the effect on youth who pay attention to commercial campaigns? Do adolescents want to be identified as "sexy" or as "experimenting with adult roles?" Regardless of the motive, tight jeans and make-up are popular and are being worn at earlier ages for many reasons, including commercial advertising. But aren't adolescents sexual beings? After all, this entire chapter has focused on adolescent sexuality.

There appear to be at least two issues involved in answering this question, which coincidentally, are also involved in adolescent pornography. In both sexually-oriented marketing and pornography, the objective is exploiting sexuality to sell products. This generally works against the presentation of sex as a natural and responsible activity. The second criticism is the age groups involved. Children and adolescents are just beginning to comprehend sexuality and to recognize and deal with sexual feelings. Using sex for purposes other than personal and interpersonal intimacy and awareness may confuse the meaning of sexuality for pre- and early adolescents. The only other difference between adolescent sexual marketing and adolescent pornography, besides the fact that marketing is more subliminal, is the fact that marketing has received sociocultural acceptance, if not encouragement, whereas pornography has been met with condemnation. Of course pornography is tied into a network of criminal activity. However, the question our society must address is whether sexually suggestive advertising is just a subliminal form of pornography and, in fact, whether it legitimatizes pornography.

Conclusion

We have discussed sexuality as a developmental process that becomes an integral part of our identities. We focused on adolescence as an important early phase of this process and presented statistics that indicate that teenage sexual behavior occurs more prevalently and at earlier ages. Yet, we found that adolescents are not simply more promiscuous, but that they adhere strongly to the permissiveness-with-affection philosophy and tend to have sexual intercourse only within ongoing relationships.

What can we expect in future years? Since sexuality is particularly dependent upon biology, we would guess that adolescent sexual behavior would parallel the secular trend in physical maturation. In other words, sexuality is a function of maturity more that it is of chronological age. Although adolescents are physically maturing at younger ages, biological sexual maturity is still a phenomenon of adolescence rather than childhood. Therefore, we would expect some age boundaries for the onset of sexual behavior. Sexuality is also a function of psychological and social maturity, however. So, although sexual activity *can* begin at virtually any age and most likely *will* be a product of physical maturation, it *should* begin only when individuals have acquired a sense of responsibility and an understanding of the consequences. We feel sex education is a valuable aid in furthering adolescent awareness and growth.

Another important consideration for the future is sexual equality for males and females. There is evidence that adolescent attitudes and behaviors are converging. Our greater societal emphasis on androgyny should help support and promote this similarity. However, discrepant sex role socialization is still prevalent and double standards continue to appear in different guises in various sectors of life. In addition to these constraints, equalitiy in sexuality will always be limited by biological considerations. For example, females, because they can get pregnant and males cannot, must accept the ultimate consequences of using or not using contraception. Reliable contraception and an increasing number of males using condoms are helping to reduce this risk. However, thorough competence is a lot to expect of teenagers who are simultaneously dealing with many other developmental issues. Thus, sexuality and equality are especially precarious in adolescence.

Since the data indicate that adolescents are losing their virginities at earlier ages, the future of chastity is questionable (recall that we reported earlier that 1 in 5 males and 1 in 3 females is still a virgin by age 18). However, we have already seen that the alternative to chastity is not simple promiscuity. As Yankelovich (1981) states, American culture may be moving toward a new ethic of commitment that reduces exploitation and emphasizes the search for closer and more responsible ties to others. Perhaps in the future we should seek ways to help adolescents understand sexuality within the contexts of intimacy and relationship development. One way to accomplish this is to emphasize the development of personal moral codes. Cognitively-oriented moral development is a critical influence in choice of personal sexual standards. The Jurichs (1974) found that those standards that demand greater role-taking and decision-making were associated with high moral maturity. Those college students who endorsed permissiveness with affection had higher moral maturity scores than those who endorsed permissiveness without affection. Similarly, D'Augelli and Cross (1975) found that sexual behaviors, as well as standards, are tied to moral reasoning. The way people reason about their relationship structures their decision-making. D'Augelli and D'Augelli (1977) stress the importance of individually-ascribed and dyadically-conceived meaning of sexual behaviors in reasoning about relationships. Being able to consider both individual and interpersonal components in sexuality implies that the individual has personal and social competence, a developmental theme emphasized throughout our discussions.

Finally, although we must acknowledge the risks of sexual behavior, we view sexuality as a developmental challenge that stimulates psychological growth. We have continually emphasized that adolescents learn through interpersonal encounters. Prescott's (1975) cross-cultural studies indicate that body pleasure, gained from the intimacy of touching, is crucial to the healthy development of personalities. Prescott studied 49 contemporary societies and found that the beneficial effects of infant physical affection can be negated by the repression of physical and sexual pleasure in adolescent life. Likewise, infant affectional deprivation can be compensated for by sexually pleasurable experiences in adolescence.

Bell (1974) summed up the importance of adolescent sexual experience for North American youth in terms of three tasks:

1 Establishing one's self-identity, particularly as a sexual person who is capable of relationship intimacy.
2 Developing the skills for monitoring intimate relationships; learning the communicational skills involved in an intimate relationship.
3 Establishing the autonomy of one's own moral values and responsibilities independent of parents. Sexual experiences and the decision-making that goes with them are vital for internalizing a value system that draws on parents, family, and society, but is adapted and personal.

In conclusion, the overarching task for adolescents in the sexual arena is integrating sexual behavior and intimacy with overall identity. An earlier chapter focused more specifically on the development of identity in adolescence and considered several other components important in identity formation. The following chapter will address yet another: academic and vocational development.

Ecological Wrap-Up

Organism.   Physical development of the organism, such as the ability to conceive, is important to sexuality and intimacy. However, sexuality and intimacy are fundamentally subjective phenomena. Their meaning is not built into the acts and physical sensations, but comes from the individual's psychological response.

Microsystem. The dynamics of sexuality and intimacy require establishing or participating in such new microsystems as dating, love, and going steady. These ecological transitions are challenging. Preparation for sexuality and intimacy derives largely from modeling and instruction at home, in school, and in peer groups. These microsystems support and influence individual behavior in the sexual domain.

Mesosystem. Contradictory messages from microsystems about sex and intimacy can be a significant source of social risk for adolescents. This may include a situation where peers reward sexual activity and parents punish it.

Exosystems. Sexuality is highly politicized. Decisions about sex education, contraception, and pregnancy are made by community institutions. The controversey over the squeal rule, sex education in the schools, community response to venereal disease, and treatment of pregnant teenagers, all illustrate this.

Macrosystem. Perhaps more than any other aspect of human development, sexuality is a cultural phenomenon. Almost all variations on the theme of human sexuality are normal in one culture or another. Also, broad forces are at work in North America to exploit sexuality and inhibit intimacy. These include mass media presentations that associate sex and violence and that portray young adolescents in a sexually suggestive light.

Preview

- School and work combine to shape the transition into adulthood.
- Schools are often seen as vehicles for social change or for personal advancement.
- High schools sort out adolescents, directing some towards college, some towards work.
- School success represents a combination of cognitive and social competencies.
- When an individual leaves school has a lot to do with future prospects for employment and financial success.
- Career development should be the process of matching individual characteristics to job characteristics and having access to jobs that match the individual's desires, expectations, and needs.
- Family background, particularly social class and ethnicity, is an important influence on vocational development.
- Changes in the career orientation of females may require changes in conventional thinking about vocational development.
- Peers are an important influence on vocational development.
- Part-time work during adolescence is very common and can undermine development if it involves too many hours and takes place in settings that do not teach important skills.

The school provides a context for many of the experiences and processes that distinguish adolescence from other periods in life. It is the most important microsystem after the family. As we shall see in this chapter, *what* adolescents learn and *how* they respond to the educational system affect career plans, occupational choice, and economic success. As we have seen in Chapters 4 and 7, the ability to consider possibilities and alternatives, as well as the desire to formulate an identity, all emerge during adolescence. These emerging abilities and desires, combined with suggestions, expectations, and pressures from adults, stimulate adolescents to try to plan the future and to consider what their place will be in that future. These considerations, as well as the emerging realization that the future is just around the corner, make adolescence a critical period in the process of vocational development.

As 18-year-old Judy wakes up, her thoughts immediately turn to the impending physics test. She knows that an *A* on this test will increase her chances of being accepted into the premed program at her father's prestigious alma mater. Her parents would be elated, and she would be on her way. For her chosen career, college education is essential. Across town, Tom awakes with a start. He realizes that the sounds that awoke him are from his father returning from work. As Tom tries to slip back into sleep, he vows never to work the midnight shift. But then, what *will* he do? Three months until graduation, and he has no plans beyond finishing high school. College is definitely out. His grades are okay, but school never seemed to offer him much. What they wanted him to learn didn't seem that important. He has plenty of friends, and has had plenty of laughs, but these days are ending. Maybe Mr. Griner will give him a job at the shoe store if his father can't get him in at the plant.

9

Adolescents in Schools and at Work

Obviously, adolescents are not always as preoccupied with thoughts of school and career decisions as are Judy and Tom. But Judy and Tom do demonstrate the intricate link between school and work in adolescence. While this link is not always readily apparent, it is deeply embedded in the meaning of adolescence for individuals, for families, and for society.

For society, the school provides a necessary *safe-keeping* function. It serves to contain a large portion of the population that is not yet ready or needed for adulthood roles. More importantly, however, the school provides society with a way (albeit not always the most fair or effective way) of preparing and *selecting* adolescents for adulthood roles. Through the school, society imparts values and attitudes, and encourages behaviors and activities that are essential for the maintenance of the social order. Again, because adolescence is a prime time for self-definition, it is a critical period for this process of social definition.

The links between school and work in adolescence are complex indeed. In this chapter we will examine these links, as well as the problems that result when these links break down. We also will address some current issues involving schools, vocational development, and employment, while recognizing many contemporary vocational and educational issues have long historical traditions and deep roots in the evolution of the North American macrosystem.

Schools and Education

In the 20th century, the secondary school has come to rival the family as the dominant microsystem for adolescents. Most youth under the age of 16 are enrolled in school, as are more than three-fourths of the 16-, 17-, and 18-year-olds. Many adolescents spend more of their waking hours at school because of extracurricular activities. The nature of the school experience—its short- and long-term effects—is a vital issue for everyone in society.

The School's Image

Throughout our history, schools have been seen as the solution to or the cause of society's problems. This was perhaps most true during the 1960s when leaders and the general public were buoyantly optimistic about changes in the school. To create what he called the "Great Society," President Johnson focused on the schools. In July 1964, he stated: "If we are learning anything from our experiences, we are learning that it is time for us to go to work, and the first work of these times and the first work of our society is education" (Perkinson, 1977, p. 211). The schools were designated as both the vehicles and the battlegrounds for eradicating poverty and ignorance. Racial injustice, for example, would be wiped out by integrating the schools. Cultural impoverishment would be fought with academic enrichment programs at all age levels (Bronfenbrenner, 1974). The Elementary and Secondary Education Act of 1965 supplied the nation's schools with over 4 billion dollars for 1965 alone (Perkinson, 1977). The

1960s gave the schools a new positive image as agents of social change in the wake of the late 1950s, when the fact that the Soviet Union won the first round of the space race by orbiting a satellite suggested that American education was failing. The tone in American education became decidedly upbeat.

With the 1970s came a decline of the school's positive image. It became apparent that schools did little and probably could do only little to erase social inequalities. For example, James Coleman (1966) had reported that there was a significant gap between black and white children in measures of achievement as early as the first grade, and that this gap *widened* as the children progressed through school. While he found that children from disadvantaged backgrounds did somewhat better in predominantly middle-class schools than in predominantly lower-class schools, Coleman's report indicated that schools had little power in overcoming differences in family background. By the 1970s, Coleman's conclusions were being listened to and amplified. Jencks (1972) had a similar message: schools could not help the poor escape from poverty. The educational programs that stemmed from the reform movement of the 1960s did little to alter the educational system. According to Silberman (1970), ". . . the reform movement has produced innumerable changes, and yet the schools themselves are largely unchanged." One commentator (Hodgson, 1973) referred to the attitude of the 70s as "The Retreat from Education."

The 1980s did little to alter the increasingly bleak image of education as social reform. Just as the 1950s saw the technological achievements of the Soviet Union as an indictment of North American schools, in the 1980s the economic achievements of the Japanese (backed up by their hard-driving educational system) were seen as a testimony to a poor educational system. In 1983 the National Commission on Excellence in Education brought the issue to a head with a wide-ranging critique of the intellectual and social mediocrity in the schools. The result was a movement that was based on improving education through greater discipline, more goal-directed teaching, and more attention to incentives for students and teachers alike. The debate continues over just how much power the school has to improve student performance. The best answer seems to be "more than the harshest critics tell us, but less than optimistic boosters would have us believe" (see Levine et al., 1971 and Wallberg & Rasher, 1977, for reviews of this issue).

This movement took place in the context of a vocal "back to the basics" movement that emphasized more attention to fundamental academic preparation, more discipline, and more performance-based testing, both for students (such as tests of basic competence required for graduation) and teachers (such as merit raises based on student achievement). To some, this movement seems to be our last great hope for reversing the ineffectual reforms of the 1960s; to others, it seems a reactionary attempt to return to the narrow, rigid, stultifying approach of the 1950s.

In many ways, our thinking about education in the United States has come to a standstill. The public's doubts and fears grow in a climate marked by disruption, violence, and apathy. Educators are beset by conflicting advice, recommendations, mandates, and demands. The consensus necessary to sustain coherent and informed action is absent. Morale is low in many schools across the country. Education is increasingly cut off from a firm theoretical base, from coherent social policy, and from a mutually satisfying relationship with its employees and clients (Garbarino & Asp, 1981).

We should, however, not be too hasty in condemning or despairing over schools. In the past four centuries, the schools have been given a variety of special functions to serve youth individually and the society at large. If success means achieving these functions 100% of the time, then the schools have failed miserably, just as has every other human microsystem. But we must keep in mind that most adolescents still go to school most of the time, and that most schools are teaching students math, English, science, social studies, home economics, and all the other subjects we value, as well as providing extracurricular activities in which much important nonacademic learning takes place. In addition, remember that the school is only one of the several microsystems embedded in the overarching macrosystem, a system that undergoes continuous change. It is unrealistic to place the entire burden of social change on the schools. We need to decide what we can hope for and expect from schools for adolescents and develop some goals for the educational system.

What are the goals of education? Now as ever, people differ on this matter. Pounds and Bryner (1973) outline six of the current major philosophies regarding the goals of education:

1   *Perennialism.*   The main goal is the development of the intellect.
2   *Essentialism.*   The main goal is to pass on the time-tested elements of the society's heritage that are essential to social advancement (e.g., reading, writing, computation).
3   *Social realism.*   The main goal is to develop individuals for effective social living, to teach people to do better what they would do anyway.
4   *Experimentalism.*   The main goal is to develop critically-minded individuals with the ability to refine the social heritage and to improve society.
5   *Reconstructionism.*   The main goal is to develop individuals for a new society based on the best solutions to present conditions and trends.
6   *Educational Laissez Faire.*   The main goal is to encourage the fullest development of the individual.

These philosophies wax and wane throughout history; sometimes one is dominant, only to be displaced as conditions change. Perhaps the best way to ascertain the goal of education in the schools is to consider what the schools emphasize. Schools in our society emphasize academic achievement (the ability to get good grades) and social adjustment (the ability to get along with others).

Good grades are rewarded by the schools, parents, and society at large. Why is this so?

Anyone Can Go To College

One reason for the emphasis on grades is the way the school system is set up. Basically, the educational system in the United States is a single-track system, characterized by assigning students to one general pathway from the first to the last year of school. All students continue along the same path until they leave school, whether they exit by dropping out or by graduating. This single-track system contrasts with the European multiple-track system in which children start out together at the elementary level, but are soon separated into different tracks such as vocational/technical schools, teacher's college preparation schools, and university preparation schools (Havighurst & Neugarten, 1977). In practice, the American schools are not purely a single-track system either, of course. Different tracks *do* appear beginning in junior high school, if not before. The tracks are not as clear-cut as they are in Europe, and it is possible for the adolescent to switch tracks. Entering the vocational track in the tenth grade would not preclude the possibility of entering college, however much it may reduce the chances of that happening. We should remember, too, that there are many kinds of post-high school educational institutions in our educational system, of which trade, technical, and professional schools are but a few examples.

In the American system it is possible, in theory, for anyone to go on to college, provided the individual has high enough grades and is able to score adequately on entrance exams. This system is one of *contest mobility*, in which outcomes are thought to depend on a continuing series of direct competitions. The educational system does not attempt to select directly the student's eventual socioeconomic status. The British school system, in contrast, has favored selecting children early for identification as elites, an approach that is characterized as a system of *sponsored mobility* (Turner, 1961). British youth are placed in either high-status grammar schools or lower-status secondary modern schools at about age eleven. After this selection, which is based on tested academic ability, British youth are educated *and* socialized towards their eventual socioeconomic level. In contrast, American schools attempt to give *everyone* the chance for higher education (or at least try to convey this impression), and the criterion for advancement is academic ability as measured by grades. British schools select certain students for higher education and then socialize them for their future role. Once the selection occurs, grades are no longer the criterion for advancement.

Current Issues in the Schools

Several problems and issues confront today's schools. We consider several of these to illustrate that they are interrelated in their causes and consequences.

Declining Academic Competence

Many experts view the Scholastic Aptitude Test (SAT) as a significant indicator of academic competence. The national average for SAT scores reached their peak in 1963. Between 1963 and 1980, mathematics scores dropped significantly from an average of 502 to an average of 466 (a drop of 36 points) and verbal scores dropped by a whopping 54 points, from 478 to 424. There have been other indicators of declining academic competence, and these reached a crisis in 1983 when the National Commission on Excellence in Education blasted America's schools as bastions of mediocrity. Colleges across the country report substantially decreased competence in writing and reading among entering students. The National Assessment of Educational Progress (NCES, 1975) reported that a national comparison of science achievement scores revealed a decline in competence between the late 1960s and 1970s.

While this represents a national phenomenon, with declines across all social groups (Bronfenbrenner, 1975), it is concentrated most heavily among poor students, both urban and rural. For example, Goldberg (1971) reported that the percentage of functionally illiterate ninth grade students was 70% in socioeconomically deprived areas of New York City, compared with 21% in other areas of the city.

Why has this happened? Are adolescents becoming poorer students? Are educational standards slipping? Are teachers performing poorly? Or, is the academic climate of the entire social system declining? All of these are possibilities, but we must remember that the mid-1960s represented a high point in American social history. These years saw the peak of the post-World War II socioeconomic blossoming that brought unprecedented affluence and educational development to a broad cross-section of U.S. citizens. Hopes were high; progressivism was in the ascendancy. By the mid 1960s, the schools were doing a better job of educating all students, especially minority group and lower-class students, than were the schools of only a generation earlier (Silberman, 1970). The retrenchment economy of the 1970s inflicted a mortal wound on progressivism and social development, however. Since that time, academic competence and schools in general have seemed to decline, reaching a stable but lower level in the early 1980s. We see this in the problem of school crime and behavioral disruption (Safe School Study, 1978).

Declining Standards of Social Conduct

Discipline problems in the schools are probably as old as formal education itself. Discipline was a major problem in schools of the 18th and 19th centuries as we saw Chapter 1. However, what we are now witnessing in the schools is much worse than ordinary classroom disruption and insubordination. There are several indicators that schools have become increasingly out of control or downright dangerous. While lack of discipline was rated as the number one problem facing schools in ten of the eleven years (1969–1980) of the Gallup poll of parents' views of schools, the 1975 poll brought first evidence of a new top ten concern—crime, including vandalism, theft, and assault (Gallup, 1980). A report filed with the U.S. Senate indicates that in 1974 there were at least 70,000 serious assaults on teachers in U.S. schools and that $500 million worth of damage was done by vandals (U.S. Senate Subcommittee on the Judiciary, 1975). A report compiled for the U.S. Department of Health, Education, and Welfare indicated that 50% of all assaults on 12–15-year-olds occur in schools and that 33% of all large city junior high school students report being afraid to enter three or more areas within their schools (Baker & Rubel, 1980). A poll of teachers conducted by the National Education Association (NEA, 1980) revealed that during the 1978-79 school year 110,000 teachers (1 out of 20) were assaulted by students on school grounds and that another 10,000 were attacked by students off school grounds. This was a 57% increase from the previous year. Furthermore, the poll showed that 10% of the respondents were afraid of being attacked while in school, and 25% reported that they had had personal property stolen and/or damaged at school.

Schools have tightened up in response. Whereas in 1966 U.S. schools employed a *total* of only 25 security guards, in 1976, there were about 25,000 (Ban & Ciminillo, 1977). Polls indicate that parents want the schools to re-

Probably the most vivid incident I can recall from adolescence occurred while in the seventh grade. I had encountered virtually no problems all through my elementary years. I had no real pressures with my friends or for grades. Life was very easy for me. Well, upon entering seventh grade, everyone moves to a different building. New teachers and faces abounded. One particular teacher was my science teacher, Mr. Briehl. Boy, is he a vivid memory! The man was notorious around school as strict and hardnosed. I remember he used to wear mirrored glasses so no one could see where he was looking. Well, the big thing for girls those days was to smoke in the bathroom, which of course they were not supposed to do. So Mr. Briehl decided those of us who didn't participate in this action should stand up for our rights. So we began posting signs saying please do not use this bathroom for smoking. Well, one day we were all there replacing our mutilated signs and a group of about 5 girls (our opposition) walked in. Somehow I was targeted as the person they should "bitchout" or rough up as an example. Well I wouldn't argue back so I got slapped.
However, I just turned and walked out the door leaving my other friends with a bad case of slack jaw. None of us had ever encountered anything like this before. Anyway, I went and got Mr. Briehl and eventually the girl was suspended. I was quite upset and of course word travelled quickly around school. This made many of the events the rest of that year quite trying and I feared the stigma would follow me. But I did survive and went on to lead a fairly happy and untraumatic adolescence.

spond with stricter security. In a 1975 Gallup Poll, 57% of the parents responding said that, if given the choice, they would send their children "to a special public school that has strict discipline, including a dress code, and that puts emphasis on the three R's" (p. 231). All this complicates the lives of well-behaved adolescents, who may be caught in the cross fire between parents and administrators on the one hand, and criminal and disruptive peers, on the other.

Decreasing Morale, Commitment, and Involvement

Among teachers, morale has slipped. In both 1965 and 1970, a nationwide survey asked teachers: "In general, how would you compare teaching as a profession today and five years ago?" In 1965, 70.2% replied that teaching was getting better, and in 1970, 34% said the same. Correspondingly, the percentage of those who said it was getting worse rose from 13.1% in 1965 to 29.6% in 1970 (Silberman, 1970). Furthermore, 26% of the teachers responding in 1965 were no longer teaching in 1970. Teacher opinion has held constant through the 1970s into the 1980s.

For the students, the decline in morale, commitment, and involvement seem to have taken the form of increased alienation. A 1972 study of a national sample of high school seniors indicated that nearly 40% stated that not feeling "part of school" had interfered "somewhat" or "a great deal" with their school education (National Center for Educational Statistics, 1975). The problem of alienation is as much a social problem as it is a school problem. A poor match between social climate and individual characteristics seems to breed alienation and antisocial behavior. This becomes more of a problem as institutions become larger and more impersonal as we saw in Chapter 1 when we discussed school size.

Cultural Lag

Cultural lag is the gap between changes in the broader social context (macrosystem) and changes in the social institutions (exosystems and microsystems). Usually, the latter follow far behind the former. As Pounds and Bryner (1973) point out, once the schools became a major institution, it was inevitable that a cultural lag would appear. This pattern is especially apparent when social change occurs very quickly, which seems to be the case today.

Moreover, cultural lag is further accentuated when youth-oriented institutions are involved, most notably the schools. Pounds and Bryner (1973) put it this way: "Because the school is dealing with the youthful and immature, society is very careful to have it teach only the tested and tried. There is a fear, culturally originating when society is prone to instability and new ideas tend to upset the stability, that the young might take up the new ideas too quickly or go off on some tangent that would be detrimental to society" (p. 561). Thus, schools find it very difficult to keep up with the rapidly changing times. Students change quickly but the community wants schools to put the brakes on.

Although social change can and does occur through the schools, it will generally occur slower than its proponents desire.

How do students feel about school?   We have touched on some of the issues and problems that confront today's schools and affect today's adolescent students. We will discuss other issues of this type as we proceed with our analysis. Here we need to balance our problem orientation with the fact that most students find school a positive experience much of the time. They find the school experience at least as humane and supportive as they do the rest of their lives. Most adolescents adapt and make it through secondary school with many positive experiences (Flanagan, 1978).

Research from the 1960s revealed that many students wanted more student participation in making decisions, 58% in one study (Harris, 1971). Research in the 1970s reaffirmed this theme and went further to show that many students wanted greater access to activities (National Association of Secondary School Principals, 1974). A Gallup poll of *parents* in the late 1970s (Gallup, 1978) found that about 60% of the parents thought their children enjoyed school "very much." A ten-year follow-up of high school students who were asked to evaluate their school experience from the perspective of a decade in the real world found that most thought the school had been a generally humane and safe place that offered an opportunity to learn for those who wanted to take advantage of it (Flanagan, 1978; Garbarino & Asp, 1981).

School Success

Given our emphasis on social competence, it should come as no surprise that we are interested in knowing something about the meaning of school success and failure. What is competence in the school as a microsystem? How does such success translate into success in the workplace and beyond?

Academic Excellence

Perhaps it seems self-evident that school success is determined by academic excellence. The conventional *official* American concept is that the school is a setting dedicated primarily to cognitive development and the acquisition of knowledge and intellectual skills, in short, to academic excellence. It might logically follow that excellent grades mean school success, and less-than-excellent grades mean some degree of school failure.

Whether we define school success as success outside and beyond school, or in terms of success within the school context, academic excellence does not seem to be a very good measure of school success. We can start with the weak link between academic excellence and life success. David McClelland (1973) reviewed the issue of grades and testing. He demonstrated that while aptitude tests predict grades in school (and a positive though modest correlation exists between IQ and grades), neither aptitude tests nor grades are very powerful predictors of success in future careers or in life in general, however that success is measured. For example, Berg (1970) summarized the relevant literature and concluded that grades in school are not related to vocational success as a factory worker, bank teller, or air traffic controller. Furthermore, even for such jobs as scientific researcher, better grades in college are not related to superior job performance (Taylor, Smith, & Ghiselin, 1963). In other words, students with high grades in school are generally no more successful in vocational life after school than are those with average *(but passing)* grades. This is a key point. Getting *passing* grades is essential to staying in school. And getting high grades may offer adolescents more choices of *where* to continue their education beyond high school. But the net effect of grades within the passing range is small.

Furthermore, within the larger social context of the school, academic excellence does not do much to help the adolescent win respect, friendship, prestige, and status in the eyes of peers (in most schools at any rate). In fact, as Coleman (1961) reported, and others have reaffirmed, academic excellence is likely to elicit a *negative* social response from peers in many schools unless it is linked to some other, more negotiable characteristic, such as athletic prowess or extracurricular social leadership. It is presumably for this reason, among

---

I entered adolescence around the age of twelve. The age period from 12 to 17 holds several vivid memories for me, some good, some bad. Some of my earliest memories stem from my very first year in junior high school. Just like any other child, what I wanted most was acceptance in my peer group. I was an exceptional student, and since I attended a rather progressive junior high, most of my peers were also rather brilliant students. However, I had great difficulty fitting in with this crowd, for they seemed to me to be rather cruel and snobbish to the students in the lower sections. Thus, it was that I discovered at this time that there was an "in" clique, and you were either in it, or you were persecuted for whatever faults you had, whether it be lack of money, good looks, latest styles of clothing, athletic ability, or other "essential" criteria. I discovered that I did not fit well into this clique, or any other, and had simply learned to live with all of them. As the class progressively grew older, the cliques developed names. There were the "Academics," the "Jocks," the "Vo-Techs" (often classed as Deads (Heads?) regardless of whether it was true or not) and the Business students.

This sociology both disgusted and fascinated me. Although I was never a member of any particular group, I got along well with members from all of them.

others, that in Coleman's (1961) studies of high school students, grades reveal only a moderate relationship to intellectual *ability*, as measured by intelligence tests. This gap between intellectual ability and grades seems to indicate that rather than focusing on getting high grades, the interest, time, effort, and resources of students go elsewhere for the most part (and that teachers use criteria beyond intellectual ability in grading performance).

Since academic performance fails to relate strongly to important factors of life success outside the immediate school setting, to play a vital role in the social system of students, or to elicit student efforts commensurate with their ability, it does not appear to be the principal component of school success. This is not to say that academic excellence has nothing to do with school success. Indeed, excellent grades open many more doors to future opportunities than do mediocre grades (although having a wealthy family often does more). Nevertheless, academic excellence does not by itself mean school success, particularly in the current era when mass education is a reality, and success cannot be defined by the standards and values appropriate to elite education (where academic excellence *may* be more feasible even if it is generally supplanted by other interests).

Social Status

If the adult-defined *official* institutional meaning of school success (i.e., grades) is found wanting, perhaps we should let the students themselves define school success. This makes sense: to understand why people succeed in schools, we need to know what *they* judge success to be. According to students, school success seems to be defined in terms of peer social status. As Coleman (1961) stated: "The fundamental competition in a high school is neither for grades, nor for athletic achievement, nor for any other such activity. It is a competition for recognition and respect—the elements of which status is composed—in the eyes of one's fellows and the opposite sex" (p. 143). And we might add that some studies of teachers report that *they* value things like prosocial behavior, athletic and artistic accomplishments, and good personality more than they do grades. This tells us something about the *hidden curriculum* (as opposed to *official curriculum*) of the school and lends credence to our inclination to question academic excellence as the criterion of school success (Garbarino & Asp, 1981).

Using social status as the major criterion for defining school success is alluring, since it speaks directly to the need for understanding the school setting in terms of the participants, as well as the need to focus on the interaction patterns within and outside the school (Epstein & Karweit, 1983). With this in mind, what does it take to gain recognition and respect, and hence succeed? According to Coleman's classic study (1961), athletics (for boys) and extracurricular social activities (for girls) are important criteria for school success, but personality counts most. Other studies report similar results. Cawelti (1968) found that among predominantly college-bound students in a suburban high school, 54% wanted to be remembered for popularity, 28% for leadership in activities, and 18% for academic achievement. Synder's (1972) study of how high school juniors rank the importance of an individual's characteristics revealed personal qualities in first place (60.6% of the boys and 89.3% of the girls felt this was most important); material possessions second; academic achievement third (35.9% of boys and 23.6% of girls); activities/athletics fourth; and the right friends fifth. The recent upsurge of female participation in sports seems to have changed the sources of status and prestige for females, and we can expect that future research will reflect these changes.

Friesen (1968) conducted a similar survey among 15,000 students in 19 Canadian high schools. He focused on the way students ranked the importance of academic achievement, athletics, and popularity. When the students were asked to rank them according to which was the most satisfying in school, males tended to rank athletics first, popularity second, and academics third. For females the rankings were popularity, academics, and athletics. These results are in accord with those reported above. However, when the students were asked which value was of greatest enduring importance *for the future*, the order of *both* males and females was first academics, then popularity, and finally athletics. Whether Friesen's results mean that Canadian adolescents value academics more than U.S. adolescents or reflect a difference in the way the questions were asked, is not known. However, Friesen did report that fewer Canadian students valued athletics and popularity over academics than did the students in Coleman's study, at least when asked to respond hypothetically about the future (where their answers might be most influenced by what they believe is the most socially desirable answer).

All things considered, however, peer social status may not be the best choice for an overall index of school success. It does not relate directly enough to the cognitive goals, purposes, and functions of the school. Furthermore, as Friesen's (1968) study exemplifies, peer social status may not be durable. On the other hand, Hanks and Eckland (1978) reported that greater involvement in high school extracurricular activities led to greater involvement in the adult community (including voting) when the former students reached age 30. If academic excellence is inappropriate because it tends to ignore social competence—indeed, the entire social system—then peer social status is likewise incomplete because it focuses too exclusively on nonacademic factors. We need a different measure of school success, one that incorporates the positive elements of academic excellence and peer social status.

Educational Attainment

Educational attainment (the number of years of schooling completed) involves the development of academic skills, social relations, and educational interest sufficient to produce continued participation in formal educational settings. Hence, it appears to be a strong candidate for selection as the most appropriate index of school success. Looked at in the most positive light, it implies an acceptance of the broad goals of schooling. Looked at in the most cynical manner, it indicates ability and willingness to work the system, an aspect of social competence that has application to a wide range of microsystems, both within and outside the school context.

Educational attainment is positively and strongly associated with socio-economic life success in a way that simple academic excellence is not. It also offers a more realistic and more durable index than does simple peer social status. The attainment of adequate educational progress—that is, grades sufficient to ensure promotion and opportunity for further educational participation—is positively related to peer social status in the school (for most peer groups) and is negatively related to juvenile delinquency and social pathologies of all sorts (in most youth populations). In short, educational attainment is associated with cognitive and social developments leading to life success. As Christopher Jencks (1979) stated in an update of his earlier work on inequality and education, "The best readily observable predictor of a young man's eventual status or earnings is the amount of schooling he has had" (p. 228). What is more, unemployment rates are significantly related to educational attainment: those with more education are less likely to be unemployed (Garbarino, 1984).

If we define school success as educational attainment, we can see clearly the difference between the implications of school success and failure as being the difference between the schooled versus the unschooled. For one thing, school success means higher status job opportunities and more money. School failure—not obtaining a degree, specifically a high school degree—means greater chances of unemployment, lower status jobs, and less money. Educational attainment provides credentials. School success confers more powerful credentials with which to secure higher status jobs almost independently of the individual's personal competence. School success does not necessarily mean "better skilled" in the narrow sense. Indeed, often what is specifically learned in school has little to do with what is needed in the work setting. Rather, academic credentials document that an individual has displayed as much social competence as the school requires and thus is a good prospect for success in work settings. The opposite may be true for school failure. By school failure, we refer mainly to not completing high school. It is increasingly true that a high school diploma is a prerequisite for basic participation in society at large. This leads us to consider the clearest form of school failure, *dropping out.*

Dropping Out or Leaving Early?

History tells us that in the 1930s, only 42% of those who were enrolled in the fifth grade actually completed high school, and a mere 15% went on to college. By the 1980s, these figures were more like 80% and 45%. Overall at least 16% of all youth drop out before they complete high school (U.S. Bureau of the Census, 1981). Thus, in the 1930s persons who did not complete high school were part of the majority, today they are part of a relatively small minority. As members of a minority who have failed one of the major tests of adolescence, economic, psychological, and social dropouts are subject to a variety of limitations imposed by themselves and by society.

We consider dropping out of high school as the primary issue for two reasons. First, because high school dropouts are a minority they are much more clearly a social problem than college dropouts. In contrast, only a minority of youth graduate from college four years after age 18. Second, while few students who withdraw from high school return (although some do complete high school equivalency exams), many who withdraw from college do return (Golladay & Noell, 1978; Timmons, 1977). Thus, dropping out of high school is likely to be a much more permanent condition. We ask several questions about high school dropouts:

- Why do adolescents drop out?
- Has the historical shrinking of the size of the dropout population (from 58% to 15% of those who were enrolled as far as 5th grade) been a sociocultural benefit or cost?
- How can we prevent dropping out?

Why Do Students Drop Out?

We can start by saying that dropping out is much more a social-psychological than an intellectual problem. Elliott, Voss, and Wendling (1966), for example, reported that as many as three-fourths of those who drop out of school demonstrate cognitive skills adequate to do "passing or superior work." Social class plays a large role. Whereas only 4% of the affluent intellectually capable students dropped out, the figure for the low-income group was 20% and for the poor was 71%, where both were intellectually capable. The overall rates of dropping out reflect a similar overrepresentation of low-income youth (Atwater, 1983).

Nonetheless, dropouts are usually marginal students and are often troubled (Howard & Anderson, 1978). Frequently they have a spotty if not completely failure-ridden academic record (Ahrendt, 1970; Thornburg, 1973; Jones, 1977). They often show poor performance on standardized assessments of academic achievement and aptitude and self-concept (Bachman, O'Malley & Johnson, 1979; Ahlstrom & Havighurst, 1971; Jones, 1977; Thornburg, 1971, 1974). Youth at high risk for dropping out often have negative perceptions of school (Ahlstrom & Havighurst, 1971; Thornburg, 1971; Honigstein & Thornburg, 1980). As Lloyd (1978) points out, early reading problems (usually evident by third grade) seem to set in motion the negative dynamics that result in dropping out of school in adolescence. Those at greatest risk for dropping out are those whose friends have already dropped out (Adams & Gullotta, 1983).

Pregnancy and childbirth figure prominently in dropping out—for girls because they either are excluded or cannot meet simultaneously child care, income-producing work, and educational responsibilities; for boys because they must earn money to support a child. The pressures of low income mean that adolescent pregnancy is more likely to mean dropping out for the poor. The Children's Defense Fund's report *Children Out of School in America* (1974) found that many schools deliberately excluded pregnant adolescent women. What is more, they found that schools excluded most of the students who were not in school though legally required to be there (i.e., those under 16 years of age) directly by expelling them for disciplinary problems or indirectly because of conditions for attendance the students could not meet (e.g., fees that poor students could not afford or activity requirements that handicapped youth could not perform). Much has been accomplished in removing these stimuli for dropping out since the early 1970s, but the problem of institutionally-precipitated dropping out continues to exist.

We will deal with juvenile delinquency in Chapter 11, but here we note that dropping out and delinquency are related. It seems that delinquent youth are at high risk for dropping out, but that once they drop out their rate of delinquency decreases, perhaps because they do not have the frustrations of being a marginal student (Gold, 1973); certainly they do not have the school as a convenient social setting in which to meet other delinquent peers and initiate delinquent activities.

Is the Historical Increase in the Proportion of Students Finishing High School a Sociocultural Benefit or Cost?

In answering this question we find ourselves in the classic position of the two-handed psychologist: "On the one hand. . . , but on the other hand. . . " On the one hand, we believe education is a good thing and know that the available research demonstrates many benefits associated with experiencing and completing secondary school.

But on the other hand, we worry about the overall social effect. Perhaps our high schools have become so difficult to govern and our student bodies so difficult to educate because our classrooms contain a substantial proportion of students who would have been able to leave school *honorably* and to find adequate work in an earlier era, but who now are pressured to remain in school by counselors, parents, the job market, and their own understanding of the world. There is evidence that we have experienced something of a "credentials inflation" in which the same job now requires more schooling than it did 40 years ago. Thus, college graduates are often able to enter the vocational system at the position where high school graduates did before, while high school grads enter the job market at the position where dropouts did before.

In this connection, it is interesting to note that the British have used the term *early leaver* instead of *dropout* in their system, in which about 75% of the students leave school before age 17 (in contrast with about 15% of American youths). *Early leaver* and the more recent term, *school disengagement*, have a much more positive connotation than dropout. Is British society any the worse for their high rate of early leaving? (Note that in recent decades the British system has been moving closer to the American in establishing the expectation of being in school until after age 17.) Is American society dramatically better for our high rate of high school completion? Or, is the American situation a cultural mistake, because so many of the 17-year-olds in school don't gain or contribute much to the quality of the school (and would just as soon not be there if they could stay out without incurring socioeconomic penalties) and because it defines those who do leave early as failures?

Would we be better off with lower expectations for school success (after all, basic skills are learned well before age 16 if they are learned at all in school)? It may be a moot point because the expectation of high school graduation has become unalterably embedded into adolescent, parental, professional, political, and cultural norms, that is, into the adolescent's individual micro-, meso-, exo- and macrosystems. Perhaps the wisest course is to do all we can to ensure that all (or nearly all) adolescents meet the critical criterion of school success defined by high school graduation. Perhaps we can also be wary of allowing credentials inflation to work its way up through the educational system to the point at which a college degree becomes a universal expectation (and thus dramatically less useful as a way to differentiate among youths). Among some groups (most notably affluent, well-educated families) this has already happened, and it may be one reason that so many colleges and universities are struggling with the problems of basic academic competence, intellectual motivation, and control that are so well known to secondary schools. Interestingly, early leaving from college *as yet* has little of the stigma associated with dropping out of high school. It much more closely resembles early leaving from high school in the 1930s. We might bear in mind that according to some calculations concerning the work force, 75–80% of the new job opportunities in the 1980s will be in areas *requiring* only a high school diploma (Garbarino & Asp, 1981).

How Successful Are Efforts to Prevent Students from Dropping Out?

We noted in Chapter 1 that smaller schools (on average) have lower dropout rates. Also, most special schools or programs within schools that seem to succeed in preventing dropping out among high-risk, marginal students are small, presumably because they can provide the personalized feedback and the elicitation of participation in undermanned settings. A second pragmatic influence on dropping out addresses the fact that for females, pregnancy and childbirth are highest on the list of causes. Revoking policies that mandate or permit expulsion on the grounds of pregnancy is a helpful programmatic step which was taken by many schools during the 1970s. Providing help so that teenage parents can stay in school is the next order of business here.

A third pragmatic effort centers around alternative programs that attempt to kindle and reinforce new interest in schooling, that can be successful in remediating deficient academic skills, that can facilitate the meeting of child care and economic obligations, and that can generally find a way to embed high-risk marginal students into the school so that social magnetism will hold them there.

Several alternative educational options are available to adolescents. These alternative options include: greater options within the existing school; greater interaction between individual students and teachers; more student responsibility for learning; greater emphasis on the individual needs of the student; and less emphasis on traditional class hours and textbooks (Deal, 1975; Pearman & Plisho, 1979; Rogers, 1969; Thornburg, 1982).

A good student/teacher relationship tends to promote a personal climate that reduces many of the negative outcomes associated with institutionalized learning (Fantini, 1973). One way to capitalize upon this is to create highly personalized and individualized learning experiences through, for example, creating contracts between students and teachers for specific performance and reward contingencies (Sulzer-Azaroff & Mayer, 1977).

Alexander and Hines (1966) studied independent study programs and found the following patterns:

1   Independent study privileges or option: independent study is optional, but encouraged by scheduled time, for students.

2   Individually programmed independent study: each member of a special needs group is *guided* individually in planning and conducting a program related to his or her needs.

3   Job-oriented independent study: the focus is on individual preparation for a specific job or career, which may range from a semi-skilled occupation to college level academic research.

4   Seminars based on independent study: independent study students get together in scheduled small groups to discuss their projects or research.

5   *Quest* programs for development of special aptitudes: activities for students working almost completely on their own in the exploration and refinement of special aptitudes and interests not related to vocational choices.

These programs have neither taken over the educational system (as their proponents hoped) nor been discarded as useless novelties (as their critics expected), but have become a modest but stable part of the system (Raywid, 1981; Case, 1981).

Perhaps the most significant of the alternative options are aimed at the high-risk student. Such students usually end up in the general curriculum or drop out. Thornburg (1971) investigated the effectiveness of a special dropout prevention project in holding high-risk students in school and changing their attitudes toward school. The study took place in a rural Arizona high school where 45% of all freshman entering each year were potential dropouts. Of those potential dropouts, 165 were left in regular classes (control groups), 120 were placed in vocational-educational programs, and 45 were placed in the special program consisting of team-taught English and math courses. The program was continued through the adolescent's high school years (in the 10th grade, the special program focused on English and biology, 11th grade on English and history, and 12th grade on social studies). At the end of their senior year, the following drop out rates were found: control group: 12%; vocational-educational group: 18%; special program group: 9.3%. In addition, and more importantly, the special program was especially effective in reducing the drop-out rate among minority group students (i.e., Mexican Americans, Native Americans, and blacks) who otherwise had the highest drop out rate (Thornburg, 1974).

Characteristics of the School Context

Up until this point, we have discussed the school as a constant. Of course, differences among schools as microsystems and exosystems produce different experiences for adolescents. In this section, we will consider several of these characteristics.

Types of Schools

The social class of schools.   Many studies report that the socioeconomic status of the school's families influences the students' educational experience and aspirations. For example, Levine, Mitchell, and Havighurst (1971) studied high school seniors in 55 schools in the Kansas City metropolitan area. They classified these high schools on the basis of student background, SES, school size, and whether it was under public or private control. After analyzing the information, they identified six types of schools:

1 Middle class: 44% of fathers being college graduates.
2 Socially comprehensive: wide distribution of family SES.
3 Working class (white): 41% of fathers employed in manual occupation.
4 Working class (black): as above, but with a predominantly black student body.
5 Small public: less than 100 high school seniors, usually rural, and similar in social status to working class schools.
6 Catholic and other private schools: social status similar to socially comprehensive schools.

These investigators asked the seniors if they intended to go to college. The results show both the socioeconomic type of school and the socioeconomic background of the student influence college plans. Social class is a very important influence in North American education. Upper-class students from the middle-class school were most likely to go to college (87% did so). But even lower-class kids in the middle-class school went to college (70% did so). School context effects were greatest for lower-class students, who were more than twice as likely to go in the middle-class school than in the working-class white school. Upper-class students had high college attendance rates regardless of school.

Schools for early adolescents.   When we think of different types of schools, we can also distinguish schools according to the grade levels they serve. In the historical overview presented in the appendix to Chapter 1, we pointed out that the junior high school emerged around the beginning of the 20th century because early adolescence was being increasingly recognized as a special phase in the life course and to deal with the process in which adolescents would be selected to enter different types of classes (Perkinson, 1977). However, it was not until the early 1950s that the junior high school became a prominent organizational feature of the school system. Prior to this, students usually attended elementary school through eighth grade and then went on to high school.

With the proliferation of junior high schools came a more standard marker for the lower boundary of adolescence (Elder, 1980). Moving from sixth to seventh grade took on new meaning. For example, whereas the previous progression from first to eighth grade was fairly continuous with respect to the curriculum, there was now a marked difference in the curriculum faced by elementary and junior high school students. The junior high school required new academic and social competencies, and these serve to mark early adolescence as a critical transition period. While few students with poor elementary school performance improve in junior high school, many who have done well previously do less well in junior high. For example, Armstrong (1964) reported that 45% of the students with good elementary school records produced fair to poor work in junior high school. Furthermore, very few of the students with poor elementary school grades improved in junior high school. Thus, it appears that the junior high school is a significant point in the weeding out process.

What is it about junior high school that causes this phenomenon? For one thing, the junior high school is more similar to the high school than to the elementary school in many ways. These include a more abstract curriculum and more formalized extracurricular activities. In addition, junior high school heightens the importance of social competence in school success. For example, Finger and Silverman (1966) conducted a study of academic performance in junior high school. They related performance to prior academic proficiency and to the social components of being a good student in its various senses. Their data show that at every level of elementary school achievement (using better grades as the index), students whose academic performance in junior high school was worse than in elementary school were those students with significantly lower scores on measures of persistence, self-control, and deliberateness. These data suggest that the students who are not holding their own in junior

The first biggest change I remember in my adolescence was the transition from elementary school to high school. When you're in the 6th grade you feel like a top dog, the first time you really feel old. Then all of a sudden you're in high school, 7th grade, down at the bottom of the ladder again. Shortly after that I moved to a new area, new school, etc. It was terribly hard at that time, I was 13. Friends are very important at that age. I was basically pretty shy too. I didn't really have such a bad adolescence; I have a great family which I feel is an important part of growing up. There were always difficult times when you think everyone is out to get you, but when I look back I feel pretty lucky. Peer pressure is hard at that age. It's hard to be individual. I was terrified of embarrassment.

high school are those who do not have improved attitudes about school work, and this may tell us something about their attitudes towards work in general.

Reform movements of the 1960s criticized the junior high school for its inability to deal adequately with the special needs of early adolescents (Lipsitz, 1979). Out of these criticisms came the middle school movement. The middle school was to be a new educational entity that would replace what the critics of the junior high school saw as its developmentally unsound, discipline-bound, and high school-mimicking character. In theory, middle schools would be quite different from junior high schools. They would be less formal, more geared to the young student's need for emotional support, and more "child-oriented" (rather than adolescence-focused). However, today, the middle school and junior high school appear very similar. For example, Brooks and Edwards (1978) conducted a survey to ascertain the state of the middle school. They reported few differences in terms of curriculum orientation, teacher-student interaction, and extra-curricular activities between middle schools and junior high schools.

Ability Grouping and Curricula

Although the American school system is basically a single track system, students are grouped frequently according to ability and curriculum. Ability grouping *(tracking)* involves placing together students who are of the same general tested academic ability. Such grouping can occur for a single course (e.g., students with high scientific abilities) or in a comprehensive manner across all subject matters, in which case it is likely to overlap with curriculum grouping, in which students with different post-graduation goals (e.g., college versus technical trades) are separated. Since about 1965, ability grouping has been criticized extensively for three reasons: ability tests tend to favor middle-class students, ability tests serve to segregate students by social class and race, and segregated experience works against the best interest of many students, both in the high and low tracks. In some areas the practice of ability grouping has been ruled illegal by the courts, and some school boards (mainly in the larger cities) have abandoned or reduced the practice (Havighurst & Neugarten, 1977).

Rosenbaum (1975) studied the impact of ability grouping on intellectual development. Whereas most studies of ability grouping are difficult to interpret due to the mixing *(confounding)* of race and social class with ability groupings, Rosenbaum's study is relatively unambiguous because it dealt with a rather homogenous population. The high school under study consisted of white, lower-middle or working class students. Tracking was across all subjects (i.e., comprehensive) and potent (e.g., whereas over 80 percent of the college-track students went on to college, fewer than five percent of the noncollege-track students did so). Rosenbaum found that across the high school years the intellectual competence (IQ) of the students declined within the three lower ability groupings while it increased among the upper two. Furthermore, the variation in IQ scores increased in the upper two and decreased among the lower three groupings; scores in the upper two groups spread out more while scores in the lower three groups moved closer together. Thus, the upper settings were *differentiating* while the lower were *homogenizing*. For example, the average IQ in the highest grouping *increased* from the eighth to tenth grade (from 123 to 127). And the figure representing how spread out the scores were (the *variance*) increased from 23 to 48. The average IQ score *declined* in the lower noncollege track from 97 to 93, while the spread (variance) declined from 87 to 78. We do not know exactly how the students felt about tracking, but based on our experience we suspect it rigidifies the social class and ethnic barriers that exist in many schools.

The traditional curriculum options for high school students include: college preparatory, vocational, and general. In some cases, there is a fourth option, the commercial curriculum, which focuses on business and secretarial courses. While these options usually exist within a single high school, sometimes in large city and consolidated rural school systems, high schools specialize in one of the options—e.g., college prep high schools, trade or technical schools, and arts academies (Havighurst & Neugarten, 1977). Although it is usually not until the tenth grade that students decide upon a curriculum option, their options can usually be predicted long before that in light of the academic weeding out that goes on in junior high school.

The college preparatory option is ordinarily the most prestigious curriculum and contains about half of the students (Rice, 1981), most of the ones who go on to post-secondary education. Its main goal is to prepare the student for college, and the program seeks to offer courses required for college entrance, such as foreign languages and advanced math (e.g., algebra, trigonometry). Generally, this option is the domain of the middle and upper class students.

The vocational option attempts to provide students with marketable skills for employment. For the most part, this option consists of some general academic course work, augmented by specialized training, and in some cases, on-the-job experience. Instructors either work in or have past work experience in the specialty they teach, and there are often formal and informal ties with businesses in the community. This is a good option for students who already have a good idea of what they want to do. Lower-class students predominate in vocational programs.

The general option is probably the most ineffectual curriculum. Its main goal is to provide general education that may be useful for some unspecified job or for post-high school training. Students in this option tend to include those who could not make it in either of the other two options and those who are not committed to college or a specific vocation. Such students have a difficult time getting into college because the curriculum does not include foreign languages or advanced math and a difficult time getting jobs because the program does not teach specific marketable skills. Most high school drop-outs and unemployed youth come from this general option, in which lower SES students predominate (Rice, 1981).

Curriculum grouping (i.e., assigning students to classes on the basis of their overall program) is, in practice, a form of ability grouping because students in the upper ability groups end up together for their required courses (such as English, math, science, and social studies) while students from the lower ability groups (who are in the noncollege curriculum) end up together in their required classes. Thus, it often receives the same criticism that ability grouping receives, especially because of social class and race issues. Furthermore, opponents of curriculum grouping claim that noncollege prep students view themselves negatively and have limited future prospects. Advocates of curriculum grouping argue that those within similar groupings profit from being able to advance at a pace appropriate to their abilities (Alexander, Cook, & McDill, 1978). As is always the case, there are costs and benefits.

Teachers

What makes a good teacher? Of course, we need to ask first what *is* a good teacher? Is it one who follows a specific instructional approach? One whose students score well on standardized achievement tests? One who is well-liked by students? One whose students develop a love for learning? One whose students behave themselves in public and at home? Most would agree that some combination is the best answer. As we are using the term here, a good teacher is one who engenders competence as we discussed and defined it in Chapter 2. A good teacher helps students learn how to succeed academically and socially and helps develop long lasting positive effects for students facing sociocultural risks.

Research suggests that good teachers have high expectations for themselves and their students (Coombs et al., 1974). These teachers employ a variety of techniques, depending on the students' needs, backgrounds, and their own resources, but their goal is always to help each student achieve success. This is not to imply that content, knowledge, and competence in various instructional techniques are unimportant. While competence is essential, it alone does not distinguish good teachers from the rest of their colleagues. Teachers who have a positive attitude about themselves and their students and who demonstrate this positive orientation through modeling and reinforcement set themselves apart from those with similar levels of knowledge and instructional skill. This is important because given the very social-psychological nature of school success, the assumption and expectation that students can and will succeed can do much to advance that goal in practice.

Of course no one fits the description of the good teacher all the time, and many teachers never do. In addition, as schools get larger, teachers interact with more and more students on increasingly more superficial levels. Currently, the average secondary school teacher instructs or is otherwise directly responsible for about 120–150 students per day. The teacher is often overwhelmed and may retreat to bureaucratic formalities and purposeful separation. As Gump (1977) stated, most teachers relate to their students "in a universalistic, not individualistic, fashion, responding less to their emotional needs and more to the necessity for them to become task and achievement oriented" (p. 153).

Certainly, the problems that schools face today are not exclusively the fault of teachers, but good teachers can make a difference, especially with marginal students. Whiteside and Merriman (1976) asked high school dropouts about *good* and *bad* teachers. Self-confidence emerged as the most important attribute of a good teacher. The students found that self-confident teachers did not belittle others to feel secure.

Athletics

As we indicated earlier, part of school success is peer social status. Extracurricular activities are one way to build prosocial behavior patterns in school and thus contribute to school success. For the academically-marginal student, such activities may be essential to maintaining motivation and standards of conduct.

Athletics continue to be especially significant for peer social status (e.g., Coleman, 1961; Snyder, 1972). Therefore, one unfortunate outcome of increased school size is the increased competition and the overall decrease in varsity participation of students with average abilities. This may benefit the stars and the audience as quality of performance increases, but it adversely affects the marginal students who could probably use the recognition and involvement the most.

Athletic participation also seems to have a positive impact on academic matters. Rehberg (1969) reviewed the relevant literature, added some of his own thoughts, and offered five possible explanations for the link between educational goals and sports:

1   Athletics facilitate association with achievement-oriented peers.
2   There is transfer from the traits developed through athletic achievement to academic achievement. Athletic participation seems to have an incremental effect on grades and educational expectations.
3   Aspiration and self-esteem are a function of internalized appraisals from significant others. Athletic competence tends to elicit positive appraisal from significant others, hence, it may serve to enhance self-esteem and raise educational performance and expectations.
4   Athletes may find themselves under pressure to present a consistent nondeviant image among scholastic performances, educational goals, and athletic ability. This pressure is intensified by the greater visibility and prestige connected with athletics.
5   By being more conspicuous in and valuable to the school and the community, athletes may receive scholastic and career counseling and encouragement that is of superior quality and quantity to that received by academically comparable nonathletes.

Participation in athletics also allows the adolescent to come into contact with a potentially significant adult influence—the coach. Snyder (1972) studied 270 high school basketball teams in an effort to determine the impact of the coach on the adolescent's educational plans. Coaches emerged as the third most influential person on future educational plans, surpassed only by parents. Adolescents from lower-class families were more strongly influenced by their coaches than those from higher class families. In fact, the coach's advice on whether and where to attend college was about as influential on educational plans as was the adolescent's socioeconomic background.

One final note. Sports and its virtues are no longer the exclusive domain of males. Whereas the closest that most adolescent females used to get to athletics was cheerleading, they are now participating directly. Participation in sports is beginning to have a similar impact on both males and females. More and more females are competing in high prestige varsity sports (and earning collegiate scholarships), as well as participating in informal sports settings with both male and female peers.

The Family and the Academic Environment

As we noted in Chapter 7, value conflicts involving home and school often threaten the process of identity development. Ramierez and Costaneda (1974) pointed out, for example, that Mexican-American youth are often encouraged to favor interdependence at home, while at school, competitive individualism is stressed. Cultural differences such as these diminish the higher one goes on the socioeconomic level. Middle-class individuals across ethnic or cultural lines are often more alike than are lower-class individuals across the same lines (Almond & Verba, 1965), although some ethnic and cultural differences remain as one ascends the social class ladder (Howard & Scott, 1980). In assessing the school/home mesosystem, we must be particularly attuned to value conflicts linked to differences in socioeconomic status.

One of the facts of life for adolescents in schools is that SES and family background play a major role in their school success. Scores on intelligence tests, educational attainment, educational aspirations and expectations, grades, and peer status all tend to be higher (on average) the higher one goes on the social class ladder. As we noted previously, Coleman (1966) and Jencks (1972) report that the schools often have relatively little power in overcoming background influences on school success. SES is associated with many factors that serve to enhance or limit adolescent educational progress, including role models, resources for college, educational values, and direct parental influences.

However, when attempting to understand how the family influences the adolescent's education, it is important to look beyond SES and into family processes that characteristically are linked to school success. These characteristics serve as the basis for competence in the schools. In Getzel's (1974) terms, these characteristics include both what the individual believes the people around him or her value *(value codes)* and how they express themselves, analyze the world, and use printed material *(language codes)*, and include the following:

1 Fluency in conceptual language.
2 A hypothesis-oriented style of personal inquiry.
3 Positive orientation to written materials.
4 Willingness and ability to delay gratification based on the authority of adult requests.
5 Ease in manipulating symbols.

The absence of these characteristics constitutes what some have called a *cultural deficit,* but a more precise and more rigorous analysis suggests the term *cultural difference* as a more appropriate label for the phenomenon (Tulkin, 1972). The issue is the match between the culture of the school and the culture of a youth's family, peer group, and neighborhood. It is thus a mesosystem issue, as we showed in Chapter 2.

The academic culture tends to be rooted in value codes of adults that are associated with middle-class experiences, resources, and goals. But the connection is not inevitable. The real issue is one of values rather than income. Thus, it is very much a cultural phenomenon, rather than simply an appendage to social class. When we consider the family's academic culture independently of SES, we find that it is more powerful as a predictor of students' school success than is SES alone.

To illustrate this, consider a study of two Jewish middle-class groups, one Ashkenazic and the other Sephardic (Gross, 1967). The former group places a high value on intellectual development through verbally mediated interaction and conceptual language; in short, it strives to optimize the academic culture. The latter group downgrades academic development and the academic culture in general. The differences between the children from these two groups, with respect to the academic culture, are as great as between any different SES groups. The Ashkenazic children are competent in the school setting (and its related standardized testing situations), whereas the Sephardic children (despite their affluence) do poorly. Nevertheless, because of their access to commercial opportunities and training in commercial competence, the Sephardic children can expect to replicate their parents' economic success. Social class and cultural values are separable and distinct here. Each tends to reproduce itself, so the affluent make money while the academically sophisticated do well in school. Some groups (like the Ashkenazic community) tend to have both. Others (like the Sephardic) tend to have only one (money, in this case). Still others may have neither.

The family can influence the adolescent's educational experience in a number of other ways. One such way is family structure—size, birth order, sibling spacing, and family intactness. For example, Zajonc (1976; Zajonc & Markus, 1975) conducted research and put forth a model suggesting that the ability of the family microsystem to stimulate intellectual development decreases with family size, but only if the spacing between the children is small. As the spacing increases, the negative intellectual effect of a large family decreases. This phenomenon, which was found to hold among both Dutch adolescents (Zajonc & Markus, 1975) and American adolescents (Zajonc, 1976), suggests that as sibling spacing increases, the relationship between older and younger siblings becomes more that a teacher/student than a rivalrous relationship (the *confluence model*, as it is called). Beyond the issues of academic culture raised in this chapter, most forms of family disruption (divorce, abuse, etc.) are associated with decreased school success (on average).

Conclusion

Our review of adolescent schooling makes it clear that the big issue is how success and failure in schools relates to success and failure outside of school, both during adolescence and on into adulthood.

Careers and Work

Our society is very work-oriented. What we *are* is often defined by what type of work we *do.* But why do we work? What purposes does work serve? First, from a macrosystem viewpoint, work is necessary for the continuation of society. Work transforms resources into goods and services. From the exosystem perspective, work is one way of allocating resources to satisfy human needs. From the perspective of the microsystem, people work to gather necessary resources. This much is obvious, but beyond these reasons people work for a variety of psychological reasons, such as feeling a part of the broader system of society, having something to do, or having a purpose in life (Morse & Weiss, 1968). When people don't work, their psychological needs go unfulfilled. In short, the need to work is very strong and is a basic characteristic of the human individual. But what does this need have to do with adolescence?

The Timing of Adolescence in the Development of Work Roles

Upon leaving high school, most adolescents either enter the paid labor force, begin to manage a household, or postpone full-time work to start some form of career preparation. Some adolescents have begun working long before leaving high school. Regardless of the specifics of sequence and timing, however, adolescence is a major time for career decisions for *both* developmental and social reasons. As Vondracek and Lerner (1982) state:

> Clearly, for its continued survival, society needs individuals to engage in those specific behaviors requisite for the maintenance and perpetuation of the social context . . . The adolescent is already moving toward reorganization as a consequence of his/her changes and for the first time in the life span possesses the physical and cognitive attributes needed for choosing and playing an adult role and for making vocational role or career choices; therefore, the essential developmental task of adolescence may be a cost-efficient, appropriately-timed societal "demand" (p. 978).

The Process of Choosing a Career: Theoretical Perspectives

Several approaches have been proposed to explain and describe how people make career decisions, and most give considerable attention to adolescence. Here we will consider two. The first emphasizes individual traits and the second, developmental issues.

The Individual Traits Approach

According to this approach, people choose jobs that are congruent with their various personality characteristics. John Holland has been most influential in this area. Holland (1973) maintains that people view the world of work in terms of occupational stereotypes, and the process of choosing an occupation involves projecting a preferred life-style onto these occupational stereotypes and finding the one that matches best.

Holland outlined six general personality types and six corresponding work environments. Briefly, they are:

1 realistic: orientation towards concreteness and physical skills (e.g., farmers, truck drivers);

2   investigative: orientation towards intellectual thought and under-
    standing (e.g., chemists, biologists);
3   social: orientation towards interpersonal relations and providing in-
    structional services (e.g., teachers, clinical psychologists);
4   conventional: orientation towards structure, rules, and identifying
    with power (e.g., bookkeepers, bank tellers);
5   enterprising: orientation towards manipulation, domination, and as-
    piring to power (e.g., salesman, politician); and
6   artistic: orientation towards self-expression and physical skills (e.g.,
    musicians, artists).

If a person has several orientations, either one will emerge as dominant or the person will vaccilate among the several orientations (or perhaps find an occupation that combines several orientations). Once they choose and enter a job environment, people must continually adjust to this environment. If this adjustment is too difficult, the person may move on to a different, more congruent environment.

Holland's theory is useful in underlining the role of personality characteristics in choosing a job. In general, research has supported the notion that individuals of similar orientation are in similar job environments (Osipow, 1973). However, this approach does not tell us how individual orientations develop. In addition, it does not consider the possibility that people change orientations or that job environments change (Osipow, 1973). Finally, it doesn't focus at all on the broader social forces that shape occupational choice.

The Developmental Approach

The developmental approach emphasizes how the process of making career choices changes in accordance with other developmental changes, particularly in cognitive sophistication. Prior events and internal processes receive primary consideration. This approach is generally congruent with the thinking of Piaget and Erikson (discussed in Chapters 4, 5, and 7), and like their models, focuses on describing stages of development. Havighurst's (1964) notion of developmental tasks often forms the core of a developmental approach. Recall that developmental tasks are tasks arising during specific periods of life that individuals must confront in order to move forward. Successful completion of one task leads to satisfaction and success with later tasks, while failure leads to dissatisfaction, disapproval, and difficulty with later tasks. Havighurst (1964) examined the work-related developmental tasks for adolescents and identified two tasks. Between the ages of 10 and 15, the major task is to acquire basic habits of industry. This involves learning to organize time and energy to get work done, and putting work ahead of play when necessary. Between the ages of 15 and 25, the major task is to acquire an identity as a worker in the occupational structure. This entails choosing and preparing for an occupation and obtaining work experience. Other theorists have offered more detailed accounts of these developmental tasks (e.g., Ginzberg et al., 1951; Super, 1953; Super et al., 1963).

Conclusions, Weaknesses, and Recent Developments

The process of choosing a career is complicated, and (according to most theorists) is not a one-time decision. Several aspects of the person are important, the personality component (as in the case of Holland's analysis of why some jobs are more attractive to one type of person than another), the developmental and decision-making components (as in the case of Ginzberg's approach), and the self-concept components (as in the case of Super's efforts to link vocational development to the more general processes of identity formation). Together, these theories have outlined the social-psychological events and processes that occur in choosing a career.

Realistically, however, the process of vocational development is also a product of external events and processes. It reflects the meso-, exo-, and macrosystems (Super, 1980; Schein, 1978; Vondracek, Lerner, & Schulenberg, 1983). To illustrate this in the extreme, Osuji (1976) found that adolescents in Nigeria commit themselves to a career much earlier than do adolescents in Western countries. He attributed this finding to factors in the Nigerian social-economic context, such as technological and economic underdevelopment, limited job opportunities, and strong extended family obligation (e.g., the cultivation of elite relatives as employment liaisons). Closer to home, Elder's (1974) study of the Great Depression of the 1930s showed the serious effects of a deflated job market. The demographic data we cited in Chapter 1 also show that personal decisions are conditioned by social context.

So far, we have only discussed the process of choosing a career. Now we examine what careers adolescents actually do choose and what factors are associated with the choices made.

Vocational Choice

Out of the thousands of vocations available to adolescents, how do they limit themselves to one or at most, a few vocational choices? As we have seen, the choices they make result from a long process. Many vocations go unconsidered, sometimes realistically, sometimes unrealistically and sometimes out of ignorance of the alternatives. Some receive brief consideration but are dismissed. Only a few receive intensive consideration. The social and economic context limits the types of vocations to which adolescents are exposed.

Thus far, we have used the terms *vocation, career,* and *occupation* interchangeably. Such interchangeability reflects the way theorists and researchers have used the terms. Distinctions have been made, but are neither generally agreed upon nor frequently followed. Basically, all three terms refer to type of employment, and we will continue to use the terms interchangeably in this chapter. We can, however, subdivide vocational choice into vocational aspirations (i.e., the vocation that one would like to have) and vocational expectations (i.e., the vocation that one expects to have).

We also evaluate vocations on the basis of occupational status. Occupational status refers to the socially prescribed status of a given vocation and forms the basis for the social differences we have cited throughout this text. The occupational status hierarchy in this country, which classifies occupations according to such factors as money, job attributes, psychological rewards, necessary education, and power, generally becomes common knowledge to adolescents during high school (Gunn, 1964). It should come as no surprise that families play a large role in shaping the way occupational status enters the process of career development, both as an influence on what individuals aspire to and how likely individuals are to realize those aspirations.

Individual Factors

So that we do not lose the individual adolescent in this discussion, we should consider the role of individual attributes on adolescent vocational choices. For most adolescents, the vocational choices they make are ultimately *their* decisions.

To begin, intelligence may be associated with differences in adolescent vocational choice. For example, the higher adolescents score on an intelligence test, the better able they are to make realistic vocational choices (Gribbons & Lohner, 1966; Dilley, 1965). However, as we said earlier, scores on intelligence tests may not have much to do with life success, particularly career success. Of course, if we look to school performance and the ability to take tests, socially competent people have a better chance of entering and doing well in college and subsequently attaining higher occupational statuses. And, some vocations do require a higher level of intelligence than do others. When it comes to success in the world of work, high intelligence may be required for some jobs, but it is not by itself enough to guarantee entrance or success.

Obviously, what adolescents are interested in and have ability for will influence their vocational choice. If adolescents have no interest in fixing cars, it is doubtful that they will become mechanics. Or, if adolescents have little musical ability, they probably will not chose to be musicians. In accord with Super's self-concept theory, people generally try to enter jobs that are consistent with their self-concept, including their interests and abilities. However, as is the case with intelligence, while interests and abilities may be necessary for choosing certain vocations, they are not sufficient. Interests and abilities do not always correlate. For example, Ewens (1970) reports that in only about one-fourth of the high school students is there a medium to high relationship between interests and abilities. This means that most students face the problem of settling for a career that is not their first choice (by interest) but for which they are suited (by competence).

Motivation and other personality characteristics are perhaps the most powerful of the individual factors related to adolescent vocational choices. Adolescents are oriented towards vocations that are consistent with their dominant personality characteristics. For example, Holland (1963) reports that adolescents with scientific vocational interests are likely to perceive themselves as analytical, curious, hard-headed, imaginative, quiet, reserved, and scholarly, while those with artistic vocational interests are likely to perceive themselves as introspective, intuitive, disorderly, imaginative, original, sensitive, unconventional, and impractical. In addition, Burnstein (1963) found that students with low levels of anxiety, little fear of failure, and a strong need for achievement tended to aspire to high-status occupations while those with high levels of anxiety, great fear of failure, and weak need for achievement tended to aspire to low-status occupations.

Explanations of sex differences in vocational choices have proceeded from differences in sex-role orientations. Rigorous competition and success in the world of work has an aggressive connotation that is more in keeping with the traditionally masculine sex-role orientation. Matina Horner (1970) proposed the concept of *fear of success* to explain why females have tended to be less motivated towards achievement in the world of work. In the main, this concept suggests that for a female, success in a competitive situation, especially in a work-related and typically masculine situation, would be viewed by others and by herself as unfeminine. As a result, she fears success. Slowly, however, this is changing. Being unfeminine or unmasculine no longer carries the social stigma it used to. As Vondracek and Lerner (1982) state: "If adolescents are to attain adaptive development in relation to this changing context, they should adopt vocational roles that transcend the traditionally sex-role stereotyped vocational distinctions extant in earlier historical eras. Adaptive development should be associated with more egalitarian development" (p. 992). Hence, sex-role orientation may lose its differentiating power in the future.

Another individual factor that is susceptible to changes in the macrosystem is work values. What spurs adolescents into employment will surely influence their vocational choices. As a result of the social upheaval of the 1960s, there appeared to be a new work ethic requiring that work "be of greater significance to the individual and of greater value to society" (Havighurst & Gottlieb, 1975, p. 160). Harris (1971) reported results gathered from a representative national survey of adolescents. The most important factors in choosing a job were (in order of importance): enjoyable work, pride in job, pleasant working conditions, and creative satisfaction. The least important factors were: short hours, recognition by society, and achieving status. Seventy percent stated that they would not "work for a company that causes substantial pollution." *Presumably,* an adolescent with such a value would avoid employment with some industries and seek out work with others. However, times continue to change, and in these days of increasing conservatism and high unemployment, the new work ethic may be diminishing. Indeed, surveys by Yankelovitch (1981) through the 1970s documented an increasing shift to instrumental concerns (employability, income, security) as society experienced economic deterioration and unemployment.

The Family

There are several ways in which families may influence the vocational choices of adolescents. These influences can range from the direct (such as strong encouragement from parents) to the indirect (such as the size of the family). Most studies that have investigated the role of the family in vocational development look at one, or at most, a few of these associations. However, in viewing the family as a microsystem, it is important to focus on the interrelationships of conditions within the family, as well as relationships between the family and the social systems outside its boundaries. With this in mind, we can look at how differences in families are associated with differences in vocational choice.

Location of the family in the broader socioeconomic context.   As used here, the "location of the family in the broader socioeconomic context" refers to a family's socioeconomic status. Occupational status is one of the major determinants of SES, and therefore occupational status tends to continue across generations. For example, a doctor's son is much more likely to become a doctor, and a garbage collector's son a garbage collector. In summarizing the relevant research, Gottlieb and Ramsey (1964) indicated that about two-thirds of males choose an occupation in either their father's status category or in the status category directly above their father's. There are several reasons why this occurs. As Schulenberg, Vondracek, and Crouter (1984) state: "If one were permitted only a single variable with which to predict an individual's occupational status, it would surely be the SES of the individual's family of orientation. As a measurement construct, SES usually incorporates one or more of the following: paternal and maternal educational attainment, family income, and paternal (and sometimes maternal) occupational status. All of the factors, as well as such corresponding factors as values, opportunities and parental encouragement serve to enhance or to delimit an individual's potential occupational status" (p. 11). This is not to say that the adolescent will be stuck with his family's status level since in North America upward and downward occupational status mobility across generations does occur. Each generation must reaffirm its position: status is achieved, not ascribed. Nonetheless, the best single predictor of the status an adolescent will achieve is the family of origin's socioeconomic status.

The relationship between family SES on the status of adolescent occupational choices seems to work in two ways. The first concerns the opportunities the family offers for education and training (Schulenberg et al., 1984). For example, with a 1961 national sample of over 20,000 males between the ages of 20 and 64, Blau and Duncan (1967) found that the higher the father's occupational status, the more education the son received, and subsequently, the higher the son's occupational status. In general, those adolescents of higher SES background have greater opportunity because they have greater financial resources with which to attend college than do those with lower SES background. Even among those who attend college, those adolescents with higher SES background may still have greater educational opportunities. In a representative sample of college students, Karabel and Astin (1975) found that students with low SES backgrounds tend to be in colleges with lower admission standards, and students with high SES background tend to be in highly selective colleges *even when differences in the students' academic abilities are accounted for.* Furthermore, McLaughlin, Hunt, and Montgomery (1976) found that among high school females, those with lower SES backgrounds were more inclined to attend community or technical colleges, while those with higher SES backgrounds were more inclined to attend four-year colleges. Hence, it appears that adolescents of higher SES families generally have greater educational opportunities, and consequently higher status occupational choices. In addition, there are other opportunities more available to higher SES youth that influence adolescent occupational choice. These include such opportunities as role models, occupational knowledge, and informal and kinship networks.

However, as important as differences in opportunities may be in selecting a vocation, they do not fully explain the selection process. As Schulenberg and his colleagues (1984) see it: "it is difficult to envision an individual acting upon the presented opportunities without having the inclination to do so. This inclination has roots in family processes—specifically socialization practices" (p. 7). Hence, the second way family SES may be associated with adolescent vocational choice is through socialization practices. Researchers report that SES differences exist in vocational socialization practices, just as they do with respect to academic socialization, as we showed earlier.

John Ogbu's (1981) discussion of the development of human competence from a cultural ecological perspective is relevant here (Ogbu was discussed earlier in Chapter 2). According to Ogbu (1981): "Child rearing in the family and similar micro settings in the early years of life and subsequent socialization of adolescents are geared toward the development of instrumental competencies required for adult economic, political, and social roles. These cultural imperatives vary from one cultural group to another as do the required competencies" (p. 413). In other words, and for our purposes here, parents attempt to pass along the competencies that *they* view as essential for success in their work place to their children. As we reported in Chapter 2, Kohn (1969) used data collected from a nationwide sample of working adults during 1956–1964 to demonstrate the link between type of employment and views about child-rearing. He found that those in middle-class occupations, where occupational success tends to depend upon self-direction, tended to value self-direction in their children. Those in working class occupations, where occupational success depends upon conformity to authority, tended to value conformity in their children. Presumably, this means that as parents behave differently, they employ different socialization practices among the two groups. As a result, middle-class adolescents may seek and be more appropriate for employment in which self-direction is important, and working-class children may seek and be more suited to employment in which conformity is important.

It is important to note that we are speaking in general terms. Adolescents can and often do break out of patterns that seem to be natural to their family background. However, the general pattern is for occupational status to be transmitted across generations. Working class youth may have vocational hopes or goals (aspirations) as high as middle class youth, but their vocational *expectations* tend to be lower. For example, among 71 working-class and 73 middle-class high school seniors, Caro (1966) found that both groups of students preferred higher status occupations, even though this pattern was stronger for the middle-class students. When it came to expectations, however, middle class students were more likely to *expect* a higher status occupation than were working-class students. In addition, while both groups saw college as a means to increasing occupational status, the working class youth showed only a slight preference for college over work after high school.

Family structure.   Family configuration (size, sibling spacing, and birth order, and single parentness) is also related to the occupational choices adolescents make. When we take into account SES, males from larger families tend to have lower educational expectations, attain less education, and subsequently tend to have lower occupational status. In large families (five or more children) youngest sons attain more education than oldest sons. In smaller families (four or less children), there is a slight trend for oldest sons to attain more education. However, when we account for differences in both SES *and* educational attainment, there is little difference in the occupational status of males from large and small families (e.g., Blau & Duncan, 1967). So it seems that large families can provide the same opportunities and incentives *if* all other things are equal (which, of course, they rarely are).

In larger families the opportunities presented by parental resources may be more limited, and socialization practices may be different in comparison to smaller families. For example, Schenk and Emerich (1976) found that, when asked about college education, high school males from larger families saw their parents as being less supportive and less able to be supportive (because of limits on their time) than did those from smaller families. Large families seem to put a strain on parental resources in many ways. This includes time (which must be shared among more compelling relationships) and money (it costs 1.67 times as much to raise two children as it does one according to Olson [1983]).

One of the most studied aspects of family structure related to vocational choices is birth order differences. Studies have sought to demonstrate that since first-borns tend to be more organizing, controlling, and directing, and later-borns tend to be more sociable, sympathetic, and empathic, siblings make different vocational choices consistent with these birth order-related traits. However, in reviewing the literature, Gandy (1974) indicates that the findings have been inconsistent, contradictory, and plagued with methodological errors. Gandy explains that several other factors operating in families serve to cancel out birth order differences in vocational choices when comparing different families. That is, being second born in a rich, well-educated small family is more desirable than being first born in a poor, large, poorly educated family, when it comes to career prospects. However, birth order differences may be found when looking *within* specific families. For example, Verger (1968) found that within three-sibling families, the vocational choice of the first and third siblings were more similar than those of the first and second siblings. He explains the results on the basis of sibling alliances and rivalries. For example, the second sibling is "picked on" by the first sibling, and the third sibling is "picked on" by the second sibling and "defended " by the first sibling. This brings the first and third together and isolates the second.

The rise in single-parent households leads us to wonder if it is a significant influence on adolescent vocational choices. Blau and Duncan (1967) found that, after taking into account family SES, males from single parent households (regardless of which parent departed or the manner in which the parent departed) tended to attain less education and consequently had jobs of lower occupational status than did males from two parent households. Rosenthal (1979) also studied seventh, eighth, and ninth graders from single-parent and two-parent households. He found that vocational aspirations and vocational maturity were lower in adolescents from households in which the father was absent. However, Biller (1971) indicates that father's absence in childhood has been associated with high occupational success in adulthood in some cases. Considering this contradicting evidence, as well as the several variable aspects of single-parentness (e.g., which parent is lacking, the financial and supportive resources available to the single parent, age of child when one parent departs), we need to know more about the conditions under which the absence of a parent has negative effects upon vocational development.

Parental influences. Parents can have both a direct and indirect impact on adolescent vocational choices. First of all, adolescents often follow in their parent's occupational footsteps. For example, Werts (1968) indicated that 43.6% of physician's sons choose medicine as their vocation, and 27.7% of lawyer's sons choose law as their vocation. Also, family businesses are frequently passed along from parent to child. In addition, parents sometimes provide apprenticeship training for adolescents. Gottlieb and Ramsey (1964) reported that 95% of the male adolescents who chose farming as their vocation were sons of farmers. Such evidence points towards parents serving as positive role models, but parents can also serve as negative role models. In a longitudinal sample of 101 male adolescents (measured when 15 and 25 years old), Bell (1969) found that vocational adjustment (e.g., job satisfaction and fulfillment of original adolescent vocational goals) at age 25 was: highest among those who indicated (at age 15) their fathers as strong positive role models, next highest among those who indicated their fathers as strong negative role models (i.e., what *not* to do and be), and lowest among those who indicated their fathers as weak or nonexistent role models.

Parental motivation influences the adolescent's vocational choice. For example, Douvan and Adelson (1969) found that high school students tended to have higher aspirations when their parents had high educational and occupational aspirations for them and rewarded good school work. This pattern existed even after accounting for differences in SES and IQ. Furthermore, this pattern was stronger when students scored high on personality measures of authoritarianism and conformity. Parents sometimes come right out and direct adolescents into specific vocational paths. These directions and orders can be reinforced through such techniques as withholding money for college unless the adolescent chooses the right major. They may have many unintended negative side effects, however, in the form of resentment and resistance on the adolescent's part.

As we suggested earlier, when we considered the topic of family SES, the family can be quite subtle in its influence on adolescent's vocational choices. While parental employment can influence the occupational status of the adolescent's choices, it can also influence the style of work characteristic of an adolescent's vocational choices. This has been well-documented by Mortimer (1974, 1975, 1976). Style also refers to the social richness of the job, what it offers in the way of intellectual and other personal challenges, whether it offers work that is rewarding in its own right (intrinsic rewards) or only worth doing because one gets paid for doing so (extrinsic rewards). This side of work is labeled its *nonvertical job characteristics* (Mortimer, 1974).

In a longitudinal sample of college males studied during 1962–1967, Mortimer found that if students did not choose their father's occupation (which most did), they chose occupations that had nonvertical job characteristics similar to their father's occupation. Among college seniors, Mortimer (1975) found that sons from professional families were more concerned about the intrinsic values and less concerned about the extrinsic values, while the opposite was true of sons from families where the father was employed in a white-collar business setting. Furthermore, this pattern occurred more often when the student reported a close father-son relationship *and* when father's occupational status was high (Mortimer, 1975, 1976). Powerful models are more powerful influences. Finally, in a ten-year follow-up, Mortimer and Kumka (1982) indicated that the patterns observed earlier persisted.

The Vocational Choices of Females

Until recently, the study of vocational development was the study of males (whether explicitly, by having only male subjects in research, or implicitly by basing norms on male patterns). The participation of women in the labor force is rapidly changing. For example, between 1970 and 1980, the number of 20- to 30-year-old females in the labor force increased 85%, while the overall number of young people rose only slighty. What is more, recent polls show that most young women would prefer to work outside the home rather than stay at home full-time to raise children. Our knowledge is only beginning to catch up with these changes in the role of women in the world of work.

Several studies have identified a strong link between family SES and high *educational* aspirations and expectations for females. However, when it comes to *vocational* aspirations and expectations, the strength of this link diminishes (e.g., Hauser, 1971; Marini & Greenberger, 1978). Whether a female chooses to work does not appear to be associated with family SES (Almquist & Angrist, 1970; Bielby, 1978). However, it does appear that females from higher SES backgrounds tend to choose less traditionally feminine vocations. For example, Burlin (1976) found that females from high SES backgrounds were more likely to plan careers in science and less likely to plan to be housewives or office workers.

The most significant family factor associated with female vocational development involves maternal employment outside the home. In their review of this literature, Huston-Stein and Higgins-Trenk (1978) concluded: "The most consistent and well documented correlate of career orientation and departure from traditional feminine roles is maternal employment during childhood and adolescence" (pp. 279–280). Maternal employment has also been linked to vocational choices of higher status (Almquist & Angrist, 1970; Banducci, 1967) as well as more nontraditional vocational choices (Almquist & Angrist, 1970; Tangri, 1972). Explanations of these phenomena generally portray the employed mother as a significant role model. If a mother is employed, then the daughter can observe and learn from a "working model."

However, the fact that a mother works outside the home does not guarantee that the daughter will. There are several other factors that must be considered. For example, a daughter is more likely to follow her mother's role, regardless of whether she is employed, if the mother appears satisfied with her role (Altman & Grossman, 1971). In addition, the father has been shown to be influential in the daughter's vocational choice. As Weitz (1977) indicated, the father's influence is

> . . . complementary to maternal influence . . . for two reasons: (1) it can directly affect career choice through non-traditional socialization practices and through exposure to career fields, perhaps the father's own; and (2) it indirectly provides a counter-model for the cultural "male attitude," reassuring the girl that she has not priced herself out of the marriage market by choosing a career. (p. 145)

Ridgeway (1978) found that female college students' career goals were related to fathers' negative view of the housewife role. Also, in studying females in male-dominated occupations (i.e., lawyers, physicians, managers) and in female-dominated occupations (i.e., social workers and nurses), Tenzer (1977) found that although both groups tended to identify more with their mothers than fathers, the former group (in male-dominated occupations) perceived their fathers as stressing what we defined in Chapter 6 as instrumental values and behaviors more than expressive values and behaviors, while the opposite was true for the latter group. Thus, it appears that both parents have a significant impact on whether a daughter works, and what type of employment she seeks. Fathers can be very influential. If they show an interest and ability in demonstrating emotional competence and not just managerial competence, they can liberate their daughters for careers that might otherwise *seem* closed to those young women.

We have focused on family SES, family structure, and parental behavior as factors associated with adolescent vocational development. Family is important, but we should remember two things. First, when viewing the family's influence on an adolescent's vocational choices, it is important to look at the interaction among family members. Just looking at background characteristics such as SES or educational attainment does not tell the whole story. Secondly, the family exerts a major force on an adolescent's vocational choices, but its power is limited by many other contextual factors. Vocational development, like all aspects of development, results from the interaction of systems at all levels in the human ecology.

Minorities and the Occupational Structure

Until recently, to begin and to advance through the occupational structure in this country has been almost the exclusive domain of white males. In their 1961 national sample, Blau and Duncan (1967) observed that the more education a black male attained, the greater the occupational status gap between him and white males of similar educational attainment. In other words, the more education a black male received, the less equal he was to his white male counterparts. Furthermore, among black males, background SES did *not* correlate with educational or occupational status attainment (as in the usual white pattern). These findings suggest that blacks encounter a different sorting process than whites. One interpretation is that blacks are judged solely on their merits (and background characteristics are not used). A more plausible explanation in light of what we know about racial discrimination, is that blacks experience blanket discrimination that suppresses achievement generally. This interpretation receives support from the finding that educational attainment relates less to income differences among blacks than among whites.

This was the picture prior to the civil rights movement of the 1960s and subsequent equal opportunity legislation. In some ways, it has not changed. Hauser and Featherman (1974) concluded that as of 1972, discriminatory practices were still responsible for much of the racial differences in occupational status attainment. Nevertheless, the occupational structure facing today's black adolescents is more conducive to their advancement than it was 20 years ago.

In general, researchers report that minority group adolescents do *not* have lower status occupational choices than majority group adolescents when we take into account SES. For example, Leifer and Lessor (1976) reviewed the research and concluded that among children of similar SES and ability levels, black children tended to have *higher* vocational aspirations than white children. Also, Dillard and Perrin (1980) found no differences among white, Puerto Rican, and black high school students in vocational maturity and vocational expectations. However, both the Puerto Rican and black students had higher vocational aspirations than the white students. (This seems consistent with the findings concerning self-concept presented in Chapter 7.) Whether these higher aspirations of minority students will serve to strengthen their movement upward on the SES ladder or serve to set them up for greater frustration depends upon the payoffs of the occupational structure. This issue has been evident among females, who though not a majority group when it comes to numbers, have held an inferior position in the vocational system (Marini, 1978) and earn, on average, 60% of what males earn. We will learn in time if the positive feelings associated with genuine new opportunities outweigh the frustration of dealing with unfulfilled expectations.

Peer Influences

Lower-class adolescents with middle-class friends generally have higher status vocational choices than lower-class adolescents without middle-class friends. This pattern has been explained by what Simpson (1962) calls *anticipatory socialization*. Anticipatory socialization refers to the situation in which the lower class adolescent is exposed to the values, interests, behavior patterns, and goals of his higher class friends. In effect, the lower class adolescent is socialized into middle-class patterns, including high status vocational choices in anticipation of experiencing that higher status. The opposite has also been found to be true for middle-class boys with working-class friends, who tend to have lower vocational and educational aspirations than their middle-class counterparts (Simpson, 1962; Bell, 1963). One could reasonably ask: do adolescents seek out friends with similar goals, or do they change their goals to fit the goals of their friends?

One way researchers have sought to answer this question has been to compare parental influences with peer influences. For example, Kandel and Lesser (1969) studied the congruence of male and female adolescents' educational plans with the aspirations of their parents and peers. They found that a mother's aspirations for her children were about twice as often in agreement with the adolescent's aspirations as were the aspirations of the adolescent's best friends. In addition, 57% of the adolescents had aspirations that were congruent with those of their parents *and* friends. Of those who were in agreement with their parents, 76% of them were in agreement with their friends, while of those who were not in agreement with their parents, 59% were in agreement with their friends. Furthermore, when an adolescent's parents wanted him or

her to go on to college, 65% of the time that adolescent's best friend also wanted to go to college. When an adolescent's parents had no college plans for their
children, 66% of the time that adolescent's best friend also had no college
plans. Hence, as Kandel and Lesser (1969) concluded, friends serve mainly to
reinforce pre-existing family plans when it comes to educational aspirations.

In another study, Simpson (1962) classified the occupational goals of
working- and middle-class high school males as high or low in both parental
and peer influences. He found that parental influence was stronger than peer
influence in reference to high status aspirations in *both* groups of students.
Also, in the working class group, students were most likely to aspire to high
status occupations if they were influenced in this direction by both parents and
peers (71.4%), and least likely to have such aspirations if neither parents nor
their peers influence them in this direction (25.6%). In addition, when middle-
class students were not subjected to either peer or parental influences towards
high status aspirations, only 30.1% of them had high aspirations. Hence, it appears that the vocational choices adolescents make are influenced by peers, and
this influence mainly operates to reinforce pre-existing and concurrent patterns.
It also says that the continuity across generations in middle-class families does
not happen automatically (unencouraged middle-class students are only a little
more likely than lower class youth to have high aspirations—30.1% versus
25.6%). It takes parental or peer encouragement.

Summary and Conclusions

In this section we have considered the social and individual factors associated
with adolescent vocational choices, specifically the family, the occupational
structure, peers, and individual influences. It is important to note that not one
of these factors, taken by itself, can fully explain how the adolescent chooses
and enters a vocation. We must consider all these factors and go still further.
First, we must understand the macrosystem and exosystem issues of employment opportunities. Second, we must return to the school as a microsystem for
vocational development.

Employment Opportunities

Developing a vocational interest does not mean that one can choose to follow
it. The macrosystem sets limits and restricts options. The rise of technology
and industrialization resulted in an overall decline in the need for unskilled laborers and farmers and an overall increase in the need for white collar workers. This pattern will probably continue, at least for the next decades in North
America. Correspondingly, the educational level of the average worker has increased and will continue to increase. For example, Johnston (1973) reports
that between the early 1970s and 1990, the proportion of the civilian labor
force with four or more years of college will increase from 14.5% to 23.8%,
while the proportion of those with eight or less years of formal education will

decline from 19.1% to 6.1%. However, since the late 1960s and early 1970s, increased education has not led to the occupational payoffs and employment opportunities many expected.

During the 1970s, with a slow-moving recession, greatly reduced governmental support for education, research, and social services, and with previous overproduction in many professional, scientific, and technical fields, many highly educated and specialized workers found themselves either unemployed or employed in lower-level jobs than their credentials would predict (Conger, 1973). A *credentials inflation* occurred in which a college degree bought less and less. The 1980s have brought little relief. During 1982, the economy (as measured by Gross National Product) declined a total of 1.8%, the worst decline since 1942. In addition, the unemployment rate reached a 42-year high of 10.8% in December of 1982, and experts predicted that the unemployment rate for the mid 1980s will continue to be at least 7%, well above what most consider full employment, between 4 and 5% (*New York Times*, January 19, 1983).

Adolescents at Work

Thus far we have focused on adolescents and their future employment. Next we will take a look at employment *during* adolescence.

Employment Characteristics

According to Steinberg, Greenberger, Garduque, Ruggiero, and Vaux (1982): "Proportionally more American teenagers are employed in part-time jobs today than at any other time in the past 40 years, and those youngsters who are employed work for greater amounts of time each week than did previous counterparts . . . By the time they graduate from high school, nearly 80% of adolescents will have had formal work experience" (p. 385). Most adolescent work is part-time work, but some do work full-time. Rosenfeld and Grover (1972) reported that during the early 1970s, about 37% of the males and 27% of the females aged 16 to 21 worked full-time, with most of these being post-secondary school employment.

The types of jobs and hours of employment for adolescents are restricted by law. Thornburg (1982) summarized the current federal child-labor laws:

1   Age 17 and above: any type of employment, unlimited hours.
2   Age 16: any type of employment except those declared to be hazardous by the Secretary of Labor.
3   Age 14–15: any type of nonmanufacturing, nonmining, nonhazardous employment, with following limits: 3 hours per school day, 8 hours per nonschool day, 18 hours per school week, 40 hours per nonschool week, only between hours of 7:00 A.M. and 7:00 P.M. (9:00 P.M. during summer).

4   Below 14: employment limited to: newspaper delivery; acting or per-
    forming in television, movies, radio, and theatrical productions; for
    parents in solely owned nonfarm businesses.

Of course, not everyone adheres to the law. Currently, adolescents are required to receive at least minimum wage. Recently, there have been attempts to
change some of these laws by lowering age limits, increasing hours, and decreasing the minimum wage for adolescents (see the box below).

Change Adolescent Work Laws?

On July 16, 1982, the Labor Department proposed the following regulatory changes concerning the employment of 14- and 15-year-
olds: increase the maximum number of hours
per week that they could work during the
school year from 18 hours to 24 hours, allow
them to work until 9:00 P.M. on school nights,
broaden the types of jobs they can hold that
currently are the domain of individuals 16 and
over, and pay them a subminimum wage.
These proposed changes caused quite an up-
roar. The Department of Labor advocated for
the changes in an effort to make employing
14- and 15-year-olds more appealing. Other
groups such as the AFL-CIO, National Child
Labor Committee, and the PTA, advocated
against such changes. Some of the chief complaints about the regulatory changes centered
around the adverse effects on adolescent development and school performance, as well as
about the infringement on older employees'
jobs (e.g., if a 15-year-old can be paid less
than an 18-year-old for performing the same
job, who do you think will get the job?)
(Greenberger, 1982).
   On January 12, 1983, President Reagan

proposed a reduction in the minimum wage
for teenagers. The proposal received approval
from his Cabinet council. Basically, it was proposed that 16–20-year-olds could be paid
$2.50 per hour (85 cents less than current
minimum wage) during the summer months
only. As with the above proposals, this proposal caused debate. Those for the proposal
argued that it would curb the high youth unemployment during the summer by making
employment possible for as many as 500,000
teenagers. Those against the proposal (including the AFL-CIO) argued that it would encourage the replacement of adult employees with
teenagers (N.Y. Times, 1/13/83).
   These proposals must be viewed in terms of
the costs and benefits, specifically for whom it
is a cost and for whom it is a benefit. Clearly,
businesses would benefit financially, but they
would have to deal with younger and less experienced employees. But would the adolescent benefit? Maybe, and maybe not. How
about the older employees? Probably not. If
you were in a position to approve or disapprove these proposals, what would you do?

Adolescents work in a variety of low level and temporary jobs, often on a temporary basis. For example, among 212 first-time working tenth and eleventh grade students, Steinberg and his colleagues (1982) found that the most common jobs were food service (34.9%), manual labor (14.4%), retail sales (12.9%), cleaning (9.6%), clerical work (9.1%), operatives and skilled labor (7.3%), and child care (4.9%).

In general, among industrialized nations, adolescent employment is most common in the United States. Ruebans, Harrison, and Rupp (1981) report that during 1978–79, when over two-thirds of all the American 16- and 17-year-old students were in the labor force, comparable youth labor force participation was much lower in other countries: Canadian youth, 37%; Swedish youth, 20%; Japanese youth, less than 2%.

Correspondingly, adolescent unemployment is a phenomenon most characteristic of the United States (because unemployment is based on the number of people actively seeking work). Adolescent unemployment, especially among minorities, has become a major national concern. According to data from the U.S. Labor Department, the growth of employment opportunities for blacks has lagged far behind whites (Newman, 1979). The employment-population growth ratio is lowest among nonwhite males and highest among white females. Table 9.1 depicts the unemployment rate according to age, sex, and race. As we will see in a later section, unemployment is especially a problem for high school dropouts.

Effects of Adolescent Employment

Given that so many adolescents work, how does the experience influence them? Some commonly held assumptions about adolescent work are that it creates a sense of responsibility, gives adolescents a positive socialization experi-

TABLE 9.1

Percent of labor force unemployed by age, race, and sex (1980).

Age & Race	Male	Female
All Workers (Aged 16–65 and over)	6.9	7.4
16–19 yrs.	18.2	17.2
20–24 yrs.	12.5	10.3
White (Aged 16–65 and over)	6.1	6.5
16–19 yrs.	16.2	14.8
20–24 yrs.	11.1	8.5
Other Races (Aged 16–65 and over)	13.3	13.1
16–19 yrs.	34.9	36.8
20–24 yrs.	22.4	21.9

SOURCE: Adapted from U.S. Bureau of the Census, Statistical Abstract of the United States: 1981 (102 edition). Washington, D.C.: U.S. Government Printing Office, 1981.

ence for future employment, and keeps adolescents out of trouble. In some cases, these assumptions may prove to be true, especially when considering work experience that resembles job training or apprenticeship. However, as Steinberg, Greenberger, and their colleagues have shown, most adolescent work does not seem to fit the picture painted by our hopeful assumptions.

These researchers studied the costs and benefits of early work experience to adolescent development. They conducted a longitudinal study of 3,100 tenth and eleventh grade students in Orange County, California, starting in 1978, gathering information from students before and after they began working. This allowed them to assess the impact of work on these adolescents.

Work was associated with greater personal responsibility, but not social responsibility. Working adolescents reported high levels of punctuality, dependability, and self-reliance on the job (Greenberger & Steinberg, 1981; Steinberg et al., 1982). In addition, adolescent workers scored higher than nonworkers on tests of self-reliance and indices of ability to complete a job successfully, and take pride in doing so (Steinberg, Greenberger, Vaux, & Ruggiero, 1981). However, working did not appear to enhance *social* responsibility; it did not cause adolescents to be more committed to the welfare of others or more tolerant of individual and cultural differences (Greenberger & Steinberg, 1981; Steinberg et al., 1982).

Adolescent workers were more negative in their attitudes toward working than their nonworking peers. Many of the working adolescents became more cynical about the intrinsic value of work (Steinberg et al., 1982). Furthermore, working increased the use of marijuana and cigarettes (Steinberg et al.,1982), and this was *not* due solely to increased incomes (Greenberger, Steinberg, & Vaux, 1981). The more an adolescent worked, the greater the likelihood of marijuana use.

In general, it appeared that working diminished involvement in nonwork microsystems activities and relationships such as school, friends, and (especially for females) the family (Steinberg et al., 1982). While this may have some positive implications in that it helps the individual move away from childhood and into the world of adulthood, Steinberg and his colleagues (1982) point out that working 20 to 25 hours per week may cause the adolescent to miss out on important socialization and learning experiences that occur in other microsystems. Remember that these adolescents were employed in low-level jobs. Whether the results of this study are representative of all adolescent workers is uncertain. The results do tell us that adolescent work as most youth experience it has many developmental costs, and despite its benefits and opportunities *can* become a developmental risk.

Summary and Conclusion

In this section, we have focused on adolescent vocational development and work. We noted that choosing a career is a long and complicated process. Several factors go into adolescent vocational choices, ranging from individual factors, such as personality characteristics, to contextual factors, such as the family's SES. The choices adolescents make are often a reflection of their past as well as a projection of their future. Obviously, deciding on a vocation is a major task for adolescents. Adolescent employment plays an ambiguous role because it usually involves low skill, dead-end jobs.

Reciprocity between Schools and Careers

We have noted the strong link between schools and careers through our discussions in this chapter. Given that one of the major functions of the schools is to prepare adolescents for adulthood, and given that a major component of adulthood is work, the nature of the link between schools and careers is a critical issue. At times, this link is quite direct, for example in the case of guidance counseling and work-study programs. The latter are especially important for adolescents on the verge of dropping out. Overall, however, the link is one of schools giving their stamp of approval in the form of degrees and certificates—*credentialization.*

The Issue of Credentialization

The rise of credentialization as a goal of schools began around the turn of this century. Previously, academic credentials had little to do with job opportunities. Now, academic credentials have everything to do with job opportunities. In the contemporary United States, high school graduation has become almost a prerequisite for full personhood. Correspondingly, as Jencks (1972) reported, the major determinant of occupational prestige is amount of education. It is no accident that in this country, SES is primarily determined by type of occupation and educational level.

Credentials = Jobs.   As Squires (1979) indicates, the supply of workers with a given level of education often determines what the educational requirements for a job will be. If the supply of labor is tight in a certain area, then educational requirements will be lowered. Of course, however, there are few areas today where the supply of labor is tight. As we indicated previously, more and more people are obtaining degrees, hence employers can afford to have ever higher educational requirements and still have a large labor pool to choose from. Often, educational credentials are used to reduce the number of job candidates an employer needs to consider.

During the 1980s, 75%–80% of the new job opportunities are in areas requiring only a high school diploma (Garbarino & Asp, 1981). However, that which is *required* is not the same as that which is *desired* by employers. Some jobs that were once the domain of the noncollege-educated are now the domain of the college-educated. Squires (1979) reports the findings of the *Recruiting Trends Survey 1974–75* sponsored by the Michigan State University Placement Services that deals with this issue.

The survey was conducted with representatives of 220 businesses, industries, government agencies, and educational institutions that employ new college graduates, and focused upon responses to this question: "If you had a job opening that required only a high school diploma, would you hire a college graduate if he or she were willing to work for the same wage?" Some 35% of the respondents said they would give preference to a high school graduate; 23.2% would hire either without preference; 22.2% would not hire a college graduate; and 19.5% would give preference to a college graduate. When the representatives were asked if a candidate with a master's or Ph.D. would be hired for a position that required only a bachelor's degree, the responses were as follows: 56.8% would give all equal consideration; 27.6% would hire a bachelor's candidate only; and 10.6% would give preference to a master's candidate. These figures may not seem all that unfair. However, as Squires (1979) points out, many of the respondents probably offered responses that they considered to be socially desirable, thus disguising their actual preference for those surpassing the minimum educational requirements.

No Credentials = No Jobs.   The counterpart of this is that those without educational credentials will lose out on many jobs. The plight of high school dropouts is the focal point for this discussion, to augment what we said earlier in this chapter. The problem is far worse for minorities. When they drop out, the door into the occupational door becomes very hard to open. Unemployment for dropouts was about 7% greater for black males and Hispanic males and 14% greater for white males, in contrast to high school graduates. The gap was even greater for females: 35% for blacks, 28% for Hispanics, and 21% for whites. Hourly wages were about $.50 per hour lower.

As might be expected, the situation gets worse as the dropout gets older. Stevenson (1978) cites evidence from a national 10-year longitudinal survey of 10,000 males and females indicating that unemployed adolescent dropouts are far more likely to be unemployed years later as young adults than their graduating counterparts. New, young, uncredentialed workers are usually less demanding. The older ones are expendable. In addition, if they do become employed as young adults, their earnings are only approximately half that of the average for their race and sex. In a system that is becoming more apt to hire a college graduate over a high school graduate, high school dropouts have few places.

Thus the overall trend is that greater school success (educational attainment) confers more powerful credentials and generally higher status jobs and more money. When speaking of income differentials and school success or failure, we should distinguish between raw dollars and income as defining an ecological niche. To illustrate, we need only to look to the U.S. Department of Labor's Bureau of Labor Statistics (1980) that publishes sample budgets (for a family of four) to live at several levels of socioeconomic viability. While these sample budgets are crude and somewhat arbitrary, they do allow us to demonstrate the link between school success/failure and certain socioeconomic ecologies. According to the Bureau's budgets in the mid 1980s, a family of four needs an income of about $25,000 to attain what were termed a comfortable intermediate-budget lifestyle. Incomes between $9,000 and $14,000 represent *struggling (lower budget);* an income below about $9,000 represents *poverty.* Table 9.2 presents the relationship of educational attainment to presence in different socioeconomic ecologies.

The racial difference that Table 9.2 portrays merits further comment. Jaffee, Adams, and Meyers (1968) studied the discrepancy between white and black income for individuals with the same level of educational attainment. They computed a *dissimilarity index* that reveals the degree to which there is

TABLE 9.2

Percentage in different socioeconomic ecologies, by educational attainment.

Educational Attainment	Socioeconomic Ecology Gross Categories			
	Struggling or Poverty		Comfortable or Affluent	
	Whites (%)	Blacks (%)	Whites (%)	Blacks (%)
1–7 years Elementary school	82.2	84.0	17.8	10.3
8 years	75.6	84.3	24.4	15.7
9–11 years High school	67.6	81.8	32.4	18.2
12 years	51.8	69.4	48.2	30.6
13–15 years College	44.2	65.3	55.8	34.7
16 years	25.7	36.9	74.3	63.4

Educational Attainment	Detailed Breakdown							
	Poverty		Struggling		Comfortable		Affluent	
	Whites (%)	Blacks (%)	Whites (%)	Blacks (%)	Whites (%)	Blacks (%)	Whites (%)	Blacks (%)
1–7 years Elementary school	36.3	51.6	45.9	38.1	11.3	5.8	6.5	4.5
8 years	27.8	41.1	47.8	43.2	13.9	10.5	10.5	5.2
9–11 years High school	18.3	32.5	49.3	49.3	19.4	11.5	13.0	16.7
12 years	9.9	26.6	41.9	42.8	24.9	21.2	23.3	9.4
13–15 years College	7.2	20.4	37.0	44.9	27.0	18.4	28.8	16.3
16 years	3.3	5.0	22.4	31.9	24.0	27.0	50.3	36.1

SOURCE: Reprinted by permission of the publisher, from *Successful Schools and Competent Students* by James Garbarino and C. Elliott Asp. (Lexington, Mass.: Lexington Books, D.C. Heath and Company, copyright 1981, D.C. Heath and Co.)

an imbalance between the value of educational attainment in producing access to jobs. The focus of this study was the *vocational gap* between whites and blacks who had the same level of education. In examining recent trends in this index, Jaffee and his associates found that the gap was closing and that educational attainment was becoming more equally available. Racial differences in educational attainment have come to account for more and more of the actual employment gap, and vocational barriers based on direct racial discrimination have been reduced.

But Does It Work?

The real question becomes whether *credentialized* means *qualified*. In a way, the answer is no. As Squires (1979) states: "The majority of workers in the United States have not learned the skills required on their jobs in formal educational or training institutions, despite the tremendous expansion of those institutions" (p. 102). Basically the increase in skills required to do most jobs has not been commensurate with the increase in the necessary corresponding credentials. Being more credentialized does not necessarily mean being better skilled, at least in the technological sense. Neither does it necessarily mean being able to perform the job better. Squires (1979) summarizes the relevant literature and indicates that there is little evidence to support a direct positive relationship between job performance and educational attainment. Hence, when comparing workers in a similar job, the more highly educated are *not* more qualified in terms of skills or performance.

Having a high school or college diploma is not so much an indication of what one knows as it is an indication of what social situations one has mastered and what one has tolerated. In this sense, credentialized does mean qualified. The diploma shows that one can function and compete successfully in a bureaucratic and institutionalized microsystem similar to the microsystems offered by most jobs. Sometimes, employers are not even interested in what the candidate's degree is in.

This is not to say that the whole credentialization system is based solely on the ability to conform and perform. We are referring to general patterns, and there certainly are many types of educational credentials that *do* indicate knowledge and technical skills necessary for certain jobs. Without a high school diploma, adolescents are saying that they will not or cannot comply with the occupational system. Indeed, viewed in this manner, the link between school and work is quite strong, and even appropriate.

But the school/work link has weakened somewhat under the burden of increased credentialization. We are in a time of *credential inflation*. The degree obtained today is not worth as much as the same degree obtained in the past. The market has become flooded with college graduates and the college degree is no longer an automatic ticket to success. Many college graduates are underemployed or unemployed. But before we despair of the value of college education, consider the following statement by Neal Rosenthal (1973) from the Bureau of Labor Statistics: ". . . It is unlikely that the unemployment rate of college graduates will be affected significantly. . . Problems for college graduates will more likely be underemployment and job dissatisfaction, resulting from increased occupational mobility . . . Workers with less than a college education will have less chance of advancing to professional positions" (pp. 24–25).

Ecological Wrap-Up

Organism.   The quality of the individual, intellectual and otherwise, is relevant to academic and vocational development mostly at the extremes. An unusually talented individual can transcend the probabilities established by social context and institutional policy. A seriously deficient individual can confound efforts to move it through the educational system. But by and large, where an individual of normal ability ends up is a matter of social influence.

Microsystem.   The microsystems of family, peers, school, and workplace all interact, but also exert independent influence on academic and vocational development. The key is providing models of success and reinforcing behavior consistent with those models. Family influences are at the top of the list, although highly motivated and talented teachers can create influential classrooms. Coaches can do the same in their settings outside the classroom.

Mesosystem.   As ever, the issue is whether microsystems are acting in concert or in opposition. Research identifies negative mesosystems as significant retardants of both academic and vocational development.

Exosystem.   Decisions about educational policy and practice affect marginal students particularly. The same is true in the world of work, where decisions to reduce labor-intensive, low-credential jobs are the big issue in economic policymaking, and the vulnerable group overlaps significantly with the academically marginal. The dropout is a social problem largely because of changes in the environment of work.

Macrosystem.   Basic values and norms about prestige, education, work, justice, and economics set the stage for academic and vocational development. Events at this level demonstrate the power of the human ecology to reach into individual lives and microsystems, as when broad economic shifts affect vocational socialization and academic maturation. History accounts for much of the variation in possibilities and probabilities that shape the choices recommended and made by individuals of different genders, races, and social classes.

Preview

■ As children grow up, the range and complexity of their environments increase.

■ The growing range of the adolescent increases the direct importance of the community in day-to-day life.

■ Chief among the community influences on an adolescent's life is the peer group.

■ Conformity to peers is an important feature of adolescent life, particularly in early and middle adolescence.

■ Peer adjustment is an important predictor of life success.

■ In adolescence, friendships come to resemble adult friendships more than childhood friendships.

■ Females tend to have more intimate and exclusive friendships than males.

■ Adolescents gain some of their community status through their purchasing power, based upon their high level of discretionary spending.

■ The opportunities offered youth for employment, schooling, and reaction by the community affect the way adolescents feel about the community and how they behave towards it.

*A*s children grow up, the range and complexity of their environments increase. They participate in more microsystems and initiate more mesosystems. As they reach adolescence they begin to spend more time away from the family and in the community, usually in the company of peers. One source of the growing complexity of the adolescent's social environment is the changing demands and expectations they experience. The community expects the adolescent to be more mature and responsible, yet in many cases, the community is not ready or willing to grant adolescents the freedom to take responsibility for their own actions (Melton, 1983). Adolescents remain legal minors long after many of them have become lovers, workers, citizens, and even parents.

As we said in Chapter 2, social competence includes the ability to establish and maintain mutually satisfying relationships with adults and peers (O'Malley, 1977). Adolescence demands substantial improvement in the ability to do so, not only for maintaining social order in the community, but for personal development and fulfillment as well (Greenberger & Sorensen, 1974; Weinstein, 1969). Calling an individual *socially mature* means that we believe he or she is competent to function in socially acceptable activities. Adolescents need to know what to do and say in formal as well as informal situations to achieve this social maturity.

The way in which a community deals with its adolescents (the opportunities and risks it offers, the attitudes it displays towards its young people, and the general context for development it provides for its members) is a major factor in their development. What goes on in the community interacts with what happens in the family to shape the experience of adolescence. We saw this in Chapter 9 as a mesosystem issue (school—home).

10

Beyond The Family: Peer Group And Community

The community where adolescents live is the place where they will try out what they have learned in their families and in the community of peers. While there are many definitions of community, for our purposes we think of it as a collection of micro-, meso-, and exosystems held together economically in a specific place, a place where people love, work, and play. The community is the geographic context in which the activities of life take place (Garbarino, 1982).

As children become adolescents, their community becomes increasingly influential in their lives in direct ways because they begin to experience more and more of it first-hand. What were formerly exosystems become microsystems as the adolescent participates directly in more and more settings.

> It seems to make little difference to young children where they live. They take their parents, their homes, and their communities rather for granted, do not question them, and seldom seek to transcend or move beyond them. Their "cognitive organization" according to Piaget does not include the idea of community. At adolescence, however, the average United States child, particularly the urban majority child, moves from his neighborhood—the narrow segment of his community—to a junior high school for which his neighborhood elementary school is only one of several feeders. Two or three years later, he is likely to encounter an even broader spectrum of his community as he goes on to high school for which, in turn, his junior high school is only one of several feeders.
>
> As he makes these moves, the adolescent is likely (perhaps more likely if he is white) to encounter children who have grown up very differently from him, who are of a different color and religion, whose parents have different educational backgrounds and values or much more or much less money than his parents and other parents in his childhood neighborhood possess. At the same time he begins to make these discoveries, he is more and more often exposed on his own to the different faces of the community. He travels alone or with a few friends. He shops on his own. He begins to act in his own right, and he is reacted to as an individual who is responsible for its own behavior (McCandless, 1970, p. 178).

Communities influence adolescents directly as they define what skills and behaviors are needed for adulthood. Of course, adolescents and their families must make their own arrangements to acquire the means to gain these competencies. But communities do much to set the agenda for the transition to adulthood. Communities outline appropriate behavior for adolescents and set up rules designed to encourage or enforce such behavior. In a more indirect manner, communities figure in adolescent development because they affect the primary social systems of adolescence.

> Next to his family and his school, the community influences an adolescent-
> . . . perhaps more so than any other factor, since the community's organization, rules, and provisions for growth and development dictate much of the shape and

function both of an adolescent's family and of his educational institutions (McCandless, 1970, p. 178).

Those who study peer relations come from a variety of backgrounds. Many are social psychologists who emphasize the way characteristics of the individual interact with the characteristics of the immediate setting in shaping peer relations. They focus on the operation of social forces. Others try to see how human peer relations resemble peer relations among other primates such as gorillas and chimpanzees. Here the focus is likely to be on how peers arrange themselves according to a pecking order—a "hierarchy of dominance and submission." These investigators are likely to seek hypotheses and explanations in genetically-based dispositions and are called *ethologists*. Others adapt a sociological approach, and emphasize the role of big social forces such as social class, race, gender, and ethnic identity in determining who associates with whom, as well as who leads and who follows. Still others concentrate on how the individual's level of cognitive sophistication affects the way he or she sees, evaluates, and acts in social exchanges. This "social cognition" approach emphasizes the similarities between the way children and youth approach the social environment and the way they approach the physical environment.

Adolescents in the Community of Peers

Most of our stereotypes and images of adolescents involve groups of them. Groups hanging out at the local drive-in or streetcorner. Gangs of teenage hoodlums roaming dark alleys and subways. Packs of Valley Girls cruising the

I remember when I thought that going to the mall every Friday night and "hanging out" on the benches was the thing to do. Anyone who was someone would be sitting on those benches or walking past the stores. A few of my girlfriends and I would start planning whose parents were going to do the driving to the mall by at least lunch time on Friday. We usually arrived at the mall around 6:30 on Friday night and upon arrival we would walk through all the stores just to see which of our other peers were there. After walking around and doing a little shopping we then found a bench to sit on and gossip, giggle, or watch the other shoppers walking by. While sitting on the bench we usually met all of our other friends. When we grew tired of sitting on the bench we then moved into the pizza palace where we each ordered a slice of plain pizza and a large Tab™. After our feast it was then time to return home and we would call someone's mother to come and pick us up. The next Monday at school in the halls before first period the topic of conversation would be who we saw at the mall last Friday night.

There isn't one particular memory of my adolescence that sticks with me. I just remember running around in "gangs" trying to find things to do. The guys were always in one group, and the girls were in another. Sometimes we'd do things together but I mostly remember driving around trying to find where the guys were.

We'd go to sports events and when they were over we'd leave and go for pizza. Before we could drive our parents would drop us off and pick us up. Once we got our licenses, however, we'd spend a good part of the night "cruising" around looking for people.

The main topic of discussion during these years was always who was going out with who, who liked who, and why so and so wouldn't go out with someone.

When I think back, I realize what really worthless hours we spent trying to find things to do or guys to do them with.

shopping centers. Kids off to the beach, the lake, or the woods for parties. Even when they are not in bunches they still maintain contact, often by spending hours on the phone to friends.

Although most of these images portray a narrow view of middle-class America, groups of young people do become more visible and noticed as they become adolescents, often because their physical growth and changes in behavior put them further away from the control once wielded by adults.

In addition to the family, the peer group provides a context for a sense of self to take shape and be tested against social realities. In the peer group, adolescents develop social skills for dealing with equals, and learn to apply the tactics and rules they have learned at home about how to compete and cooperate, often in the face of, or even in defiance of parental or other adult authority. The peer group provides support and understanding when it seems that parents "just don't understand" or otherwise cannot provide what the adolescent needs. It also provides an opportunity to have fun, be free, explore, and test abilities and skills. But it is also in the peer group that problems that may affect later interpersonal functioning and general adjustment often become clearly apparent. Children become members of society through their place in the local community and, on a more basic level, by first becoming members in the community of peers. It is in the community of peers that children learn to love, work, and play with peers who have their own goals, motives and desires, yet are bound together by similar expectations and demands placed on them by parents and other adults in the community.

In extreme circumstances, the peer group may entirely take the place of child/parent or other child/adult relationships. Anna Freud and Sophie Dann (1951) found in studying bands of concentration camp children after World

My most vivid memories of adolescence included establishing friendships with school peers. I worried about whether or not I was considered "one of the crowd." I felt I was very easy to get along with and had no problems establishing a friendship with my peers. But the friendship with school peers led into attention to the opposite sex. This was harder to deal with, for it did not meet my parents' approval. I felt as if I was being sheltered and kept tied "underneath my mother's apron strings." "You'll understand yourself some day when you have kids," is the response I'd get from my mother. "What did your mother say?" "What did your father say?" were common responses when I wanted to go out with my friends.

War II that the children referred only to each other for support, attention, or authority. Their experience with adults had been cut off so traumatically that they became their own parents and guardians. Many parents of teenagers may feel that their children have become like this, but, as we have discussed, children *do* absorb the values and advice of their parents, and usually grow up more like them than not.

One of the basic assumptions that developmental psychologists have brought to the study of adolescence is that the quality of parent/child relationships in childhood sets the stage for competent functioning in adolescence and adulthood. But, as we have seen in Chapter 2, there are other important socializing contexts and relationships that can have influential effects throughout the course of life. With increasing frequency, researchers and theorists are acknowledging that peers have a major influence on children and adolescents, providing functional experiences that could enhance or undermine the development of social competence and psychosocial maturity. But how significant *are* peer relations in adolescence? And, what role do peer relations play in developing skills necessary for successful social functioning?

Fitting In: The Adolescent Peer Group

Fitting in, being part of a group, being acknowledged and accepted, being like everyone else (or at least not being different)—all become particularly important as the child enters adolescence. At a time when a well-defined concept of self is just forming, what other people think of an adolescent (or how the adolescent *thinks* they think of him or her) and how they treat the adolescent become important messages in the process of building a coherent sense of self and ultimately of identity. The peer group sets standards of behaviors, rules, and customs by which individuals are measured, and by which they measure others. It also provides models and opportunities for developing the traits that cause one to be an accepted (or, in some cases, highly regarded) member of the group. The causes, correlates, and consequences of fitting in are important topics for research.

The process of fitting in takes place in response to the developing nature of peer relations. Dunphy (1963) did some of the classic work on this topic. His map of the relationships found among adolescents showed a developmental trend. In early adolescence isolated groups of boys and groups of girls run parallel to each other but have little direct interaction. Eventually these same-sex groups interact to form heterosexual crowds. Couples form within the group, and the high status couples form an elite. These elite couples serve as models for others in the group. By late adolescence, interaction is tight within couples and much looser among couples. The peer group thus provides a bridge into heterosexual interaction.

When I think of my adolescent years I am reminded of "the gang." We used to do everything together—go to the movies, play softball 'till it got very dark, go to the football games and sit in the same two bleachers, or just sit and talk. The fun and special aspect of the gang was that it was made up of both boys and girls at a time in our lives when we liked each other, but hadn't yet passed into the stage where we dated. Then, gradually the girls and boys began going in separate directions and all of us girls had our crushes and you would meet the boy you liked at a movie (because your parents had to drop you off) or you'd be on Cloud 9 because he asked you to slow dance at the Record Hop (which you always bought a new shirt for). Usually after one week or sometimes sooner you were "going together" and you'd meet him in the hall at school or sit near him in class—but not too close or his friends would harass him. Usually the romances only lasted for a few weeks, until you decided you had a bigger crush on someone else, or until your friends told you to drop him for some stupid reason, or your parents didn't want you to be going out with a boy seriously because you were too young. They may not have lasted long, but they really were fun!! For one incident in particular that I remember, I was going with a boy named Kevin when I was in 9th grade and we were at a football game together and he went over to the visitor's side with another boy to see some girl. At first I didn't mind, but my friends convinced me that it was a really awful thing for him to do, so when he came back over I had a few of my girlfriends tell him that I wanted to break up with him. Now when I think about it, I can't believe how immature I was for not even talking to him myself. He was one of the first boys I ever liked and I didn't know how to handle the situation—or even how to talk about it with him. It was easier for me to let my friends do the dirty work. I just feel like I wasn't fair to him—for years after high school and even now, when I see him occasionally we talk and have patched things up, but I still feel foolish when I remember 9th grade.

Savin-Williams (1976) has studied the formation and structure of these peer groups among a sample of normal middle-class boys at a summer camp. This allowed him to observe group processes in a kind of social vacuum. He found that a very clear dominance hierarchy was established by the third day. Savin-Williams' observations were very similar to the boys' own perceptions of who was tough and who the leaders were. This early structure lasted for the entire camp session (five weeks). While peer hierarchies in the real world may differ somewhat from what Savin-Williams found, it is clear that dominance hierarchies play an important role in male adolescent peer groups.

Of course, the most vivid aspect of fitting in is what some have called *the cult of conformity* (Rogers, 1981; Sebald, 1981). Looking back on adolescence, many adults vividly remember the pressures to conform and their emotional and behavioral responses. This memory may include regrets (e.g., cutting off relations with an interesting individual who was defined as out of it by one's friends), amusement (e.g., suffering through ironing one's hair twice a week to keep it smooth and straight), or pain (e.g., having to swallow one's pride and give in to the group on a matter of principle for fear of being cut off and isolated). Conformity *can* be a prosocial force, of course. It raises the academic aspirations of some adolescents (Atwater, 1983) and can actually be part of the treatment program in dealing with delinquency and other behavioral problems

---

My late junior high and early senior high years were full of many different experiences of growing up. My most vivid memory was the "peer pressure" which seemed to control most of my social life. At this age I felt I had to do what all the other kids were doing to be accepted. If I went to a party where all the kids were drinking—I drank, too, not because I really wanted to but because of the weird looks I would get if I didn't.

At this stage of my life, I'm fully free of the "peer pressure" and do what I want or don't want to do regardless of what others think.

My most vivid memories of adolescence are from my family's move from Long Island to New Jersey. I was happy where we were, but I understood that we had to move. I was upset that I had to leave my friends, but I was looking forward to making new friends and meeting new people.

Unfortunately, the move was much harder on me than I thought it would be. The kids in school were snobbish and they all had their cliques. The cliques did not take well to newcomers. It was easy to be "friends" with the individuals from the cliques in classes, but they wouldn't "allow" you into their clique outside of school. For nearly two years I had very few friends in school and rarely did anything with the kids from school. I was never so unhappy. I was always wanting to talk to kids my age and have friends like I saw everyone else did, but it never worked out that way.

My most vivid memory of adolescence was my insecurity. I spent the prime of my adolescence in an all-girl high school in Connecticut. Many of the girls I attended school with were very wealthy and very snobby. If you weren't in with them, forget it. They had a way to make you feel very clumsy and stupid. I never felt comfortable around them and was afraid to answer questions in class, for fear they'd laugh if it was the wrong answer. They just made me feel very self-conscious. That is one of the main reasons I came to a big university—to be "just a member." I didn't like the cliques, but here there are so many kinds of people, it's easy to make friends and just be yourself.

(Feldman & Wodarski, 1974). But when we speak of conformity we are usually concerned about the induction of antisocial or shoddy behavior (Haney & Gold, 1977).

The classic developmental study of conformity conducted by Costanzo (1970) lays out the issue for us. His results showed that conformity rises through childhood to reach a peak at 12–13 years of age, then gradually subsides. As we might expect, the power of conformity varies from situation to situation and from person to person along some patterned lines (Atwater, 1983). The more intellectually sophisticated youth are, the less conforming they are (Polory, 1980). The more self-confident and in possession of a mature identity the adolescent is, the less conforming he or she is (Costanzo, 1970; Iacovetta, 1975). Traditionally feminine females are more likely to conform than less traditional females (Bem, 1975; Eagly & Carli, 1981; Feldman, 1972), particularly in sex-typed issues (Sistrunk & McDavid, 1971), but they resist pressure toward misconduct better (Bixenstine et al., 1976). Beyond conformity, however, lies another aspect of fitting in, namely how well an adolescent matches the microsystems presented by the social environment.

What seems to be important is not merely how an individual looks or acts, but *how these features match the expectancies and values of the relevant social environment.* Lerner (1982), for example, reports that adolescents whose temperamental characteristics fit that of the school environment, whatever that environment encourages, tend to have better peer relations, have higher self-esteem, and show better adjustment across different settings. How well adolescents do in different settings, however, depends largely on how similar or different expectancies are between these settings. Thus, for example, a quiet brainy teenager may do better in a special science and math high school located in a major urban area than in a small rural high school. Better adjustment in the peer context, as measured by number of friends, may not necessarily mean better adjustment in the classroom, as measured by classroom behavior or achievement scores.

Susceptibility to conformity is related to how others perceive individuals and how they perceive themselves. Conformity can result when an individual

Adolescence for me was a time of constant rebellion, not only with my parents and elders, but my peers also. I tried to be as different from everyone else without going so far that I was labeled "weird." Some of my most vivid memories are of parties. I never drank alcohol while my friends indulged (since then I still don't); contrary to what everyone says about peer pressure, I felt none. I really have become to think that is just a teenage cop-out for doing things they really want to do, but know are wrong. I honestly don't like the taste of alcohol, but more than that, not drinking made me unique. It was the topic of many conversations and almost an ice breaker at times to be able to laugh with the guy serving drinks when I ask for a coke. Later in high school many kids (mostly only when alone with me) told me they really respected me for not drinking and wished they could do the same.

Because beer parties and other things that high school students sneak are always the topic of conversation and help kids socialize, etc., my not drinking was something everyone knew about. But I didn't mind. I was "different."

is very sensitive to the needs of others and places those needs ahead of their own. Conformity can be an attempt to gain the approval of more powerful individuals or to avoid incurring their disapproval. Those who are unlikely to conform may *either* be very secure in their self-image and position within a group or feel disconnected with that group and housing an allegiance to another reference group.

Thus those who are of low status in a group are more likely to conform than are high status group members (Harvey & Rutherford, 1960), while those who have higher self-esteem and feelings of competence are less likely to conform to peers (Gelfand, 1962; Landsbaum & Willis, 1971). Most groups and organizations require some measure of conformity if they are to function at all, but excessive conformity can be a problem as well.

Popularity and Social Acceptance

Fitting in means being accepted by peers, and adolescents are almost constantly around peers in school. They have to function in groups, or at least in the company of others. Like adults, they are members of both voluntary and involuntary communities of peers. Some thrive in the social environment and are active, outgoing, and popular. For others, it can be a painful and lonely time.

The most commonly used measure of social adjustment has been how well-accepted or rejected individuals are by a relevant peer group, most often their school class. *Sociometric status*, as it is called, is measured often by asking members of a class to nominate someone who they feel fits some criteria, such as "is your best friend," "you like to work with," "people can talk to when they have problems," and so on. Its most frequent use, however, is to see how popular each individual in a class is (i.e., how many positive nominations they receive).

Early studies sought to identify personality characteristics that were associated with popularity. Kuhlen and Lee (1943) compared personality characteristics of "most popular" with "least popular" children in grades 6, 9, and 12 in a rural area and found that popularity was linked to the traits of friendliness, cheerfulness, enthusiasm, enjoying jokes, and initiating games and activities. Gronlund and Anderson (1957) found basically the same traits to be important for seventh and eighth graders in an urban city. "Good looks" were also mentioned as being important, along with being "active in games" for boys. Wheeler (1961) likewise found traits of cheerfulness, good looks, physique, and sociability to be important to popularity. In addition, boys often mentioned athletic ability.

In more recent research, other studies have generally found that social status, prestige, and popularity are linked to the display of admired qualities or characteristics. These include physical appearance, material possessions, athletic and academic achievement, and participation in activities (Rice, 1981).

Often studies have attempted to identify other aspects of behavior that predict popularity or unpopularity. Observational research with younger children shows that popularity is related to personal characteristics, such as ap-

Part of my most vivid memories of adolescence include being amazed by the change in my friends and also myself. Body appearance changing, voices changing, morals (or lack of) changing. I felt how I was gradually gaining freedom from my parents and would purposely not be home for hours on end. The one thing that really bothered me was how corrupt the world is. I had a hard time watching so called friends "stab" each other in the back. So, I became a hermit from the onset of adolescence. As a classical/jazz flutist, I spent hours in a room playing beautiful melodies of the great masters that were far above the quality of most people I knew. The type of love I sought was hard to find. I ended up at an early age, 12, befriending a jazz teacher—one who had the same ideals as I.

On a less serious side I was called a prankster—drawing pictures of the "teach"—pulling over all kinds of things on them all like total B.S. I even wrote a pamphlet "The Art of Courtly Bull"—(Art of Courtly Love—satire). I loved to sit back and watch the world evolve around me—I'm a bit ahead of my age group for doing so. So many engaged in what was called "relationships"—consisting of sex & sex & sex. I desired to know and love everyone—eventually a young man. Now those who engaged in quick sexual relationships are married, pregnant, and on the way to divorce. Frankly, I wonder if I had much of an adolescence.

pearance and having an uncommon name, to environmental factors, such as opportunity for participation, and to social skills, how individuals interact with others and the basic skills required for positive encounters (Asher, Oden, & Gottman, 1977).

An important aspect of social competence is dealing with people. Ideally, adolescents should be able to establish and maintain good interpersonal relations and interact with others in socially acceptable ways. Social acceptance by peers may be an important indicator of interpersonal functioning. However, what is socially acceptable may differ from setting to setting, and for adolescents particularly, from school to school. For example, in some schools academic achievement earns peer acceptance and being sexually active does not, whereas in other schools the reverse is true.

While being popular or well-liked by others may be of great concern to adolescents and may have social consequences, what may be of greater importance for healthy psychosocial development is the quality of relationship with at least one friend. Isolation, not the absence of popularity, is the critical issue. Friendship is a two-way street; it requires mutual choice and reciprocity of affect and behavior. Thus, it implies a high level of interaction between individuals, a feature not necessarily captured by measures of popularity. Friendship is mutual; popularity or admiration may be one-sided. Harry Stack Sullivan outlined this model of social development in his classic *The Interpersonal Theory of Psychiatry* more than three decades ago, and it continues to be a valid description.

Friendship as Relationship

Although being a friend may mean different things to people of different ages, gender, and cultural backgrounds, friendships have certain general features that distinguish them from other relationships. In contrast to popularity or admiration, friendship implies *reciprocity of choice* and some level of *mutuality.* The way these choices are mutually expressed reflects two major components of friendship: the feelings of liking or attraction between two people *(affect)* and behavior (how people treat each other, the kinds of activities they participate in, and the way they act in the presence of each other).

Among adults, friendship is but one form of close relationship. According to Huston and Burgess (1979), when people involved in a relationship become closer,

1 They interact more often, for longer periods of time, and in a widening array of settings.
2 They attempt to restore proximity when separated and feel comforted when proximity is regained.
3 They open up to each other in the sense that they disclose secrets and share physical intimacies.

4   They become less inhibited, more willing to share positive and nega-
    tive feelings, and praise and criticize each other.
5   They develop their own communication system, and become more
    efficient in using it.
6   They increase their ability to map and anticipate each other's views
    of social reality.
7   They begin to synchronize their goals and behaviors, and develop
    subtle interaction patterns. (p. 8)

As we shall see, younger children display many of these features in ways
that may be quite different from the way adults do. It is in adolescence that
friendships begin to resemble adult friendships, and issues of interpersonal
trust, loyalty, and intimacy appear to become dominant. Like most aspects of
social and psychological experience, friendship matures in adolescence.

Who Becomes Friends?

In reviewing studies addressing factors in friendship selection, Horrocks (1969)
comments:

> Despite the cultural and technological changes of the past half-century, adoles-
> cents' reasons for selecting their most intimate peer associates remain virtually un-
> changed. The nature of the context in which interpersonal transactions take place
> and the specific activities indulged in do change or are modified, but today's teen-
> ager continues to use the same criteria of personal preference or of fortuitous cir-
> cumstances that determined the friendship selection of his parents and even of his
> grandparents. (p. 287)

The Demographics of "Fortuitous Circumstances"

Throughout childhood and adolescence, children interact most often with others who are like them, who are of the same age, sex, and (usually, in North
America, at least) race. Not surprisingly, friendships are more likely to develop
between individuals who are similar in these characteristics (Hallinan, 1979;
D. M. Kandel, 1978; Tuma & Hallinan, 1979). In addition, friends tend to be
in the same school grade and come from families of similar socioeconomic status (Hartup, 1979).

A major factor in friendship selection is the availability of particular potential friends or the degree of opportunity for social contact with particular
individuals. Physical proximity *(propinquity)* is perhaps the most influential
factor. Friends are chosen (at least initially) from a pool of peers who share the
same social environment. In adolescence, friends probably go to the same
school, live relatively close together, come from the same community (or from
one that is nearby and similar), and are similar in ethnic and socioeconomic
factors. Living in a particular neighborhood and attending a particular school

My most vivid memory of adolescence is when my family moved from New Jersey to Pennsylvania. I thought it was the end of the world, that I'd never meet any new friends and would certainly lose the old ones. The most vivid thing I remember about this time is a going away party given in our honor. I remember this the most because I was very upset, not about leaving, but because no one seemed to pay any attention to me at the party. My friends seemed to ignore me, my parents were too busy with their friends, so I sat alone on the steps. I don't know if I was imagining all of this or not. Maybe I was just overly sensitive at this time. All I know is that I was miserable and hurt by this experience.

limits the kinds of people available to socialize with, the conditions and situations in which these interactions will take place, and the range of activities and opportunities that are available for peers to participate in together. Thus, characteristics of neighborhoods and schools do much to channel the choice of individual friends.

Ziegler (1980) studied 12- to 15-year-olds in schools of four neighborhoods in Toronto. All the neighborhoods were urban, predominantly working class, and otherwise comparable, except for the distribution and proportion of ethnic groups. The schools differed in their ethnic diversity. While studies in the United States show significant racial cleavage on measures of friendships, Ziegler found that friendly contact was related to the degree of ethnic diversity in a particular school. Inter-ethnic friendships were more common in ethnically diverse schools, and for each of the three ethnic groups (Anglo-, Italian-, and Chinese-Canadian), friendship outside of the ethnic group was 13–35% greater if the group was numerically subordinate rather than dominant. That is, minorities were more likely to make friends outside their group than were majorities.

Similarity

What aspects of personal preference are important in friendship selection? Besides sharing similar demographic characteristics, friends tend to be similar in some aspects of personality and social behavior. Generally, adolescent friends tend to be similar in academic attitudes, achievement, and aspirations. They tend to like the same kinds of music, have similar taste in clothes, and enjoy the same kinds of leisure time activities. They also tend to be similar in whether or not they use alcohol or drugs frequently (Berndt, 1982; D. B. Kandel, 1978).

Because most studies measure attitudes and attributes of individuals who are already friends, any similarity or resemblance found between friends could be explained in two ways. One is that individuals who share relevant similarities become friends *because* of their similarities. This implies that similarity operates mainly in the selection process. Or, as Huston and Burgess (1979) point

My sophomore year in high school in Hawaii we'd go down to the beach and drink a half-gallon of Spañada by the edge of the breakwater. Occasionally the waves would come crashing over the wall and get us soaked. Sometimes we'd get some other kind of wine, usually Boone's Farm Strawberry Hill or Annie Green Springs. A little later we switched to beer. The first beer I ever had was an Oly. We only drank Oly or Bud. Only weirdos drank anything else.

A new kid joined our class, a haole (white) boy from Minnesota. He pissed us off by showing off in class, by speaking proper English, and by just being haole. We nicknamed him Trog and verbally abused him as much as we could.

My junior year I hung around with a bunch of guys and girls but my best friend was Kitsu, who lived a few houses away. We'd go cruising in his blue-on-burgundy '54 Chevy with the Hurst-shifter and dash-mounted Sun tachometer. Our favorite pasttime was to tailgate on moonless nights with the headlights off.

I got to like Trog—he was OK for a haole. You had to give him credit for taking all the garbage that we dumped on him and still keep on trying to be our friend. He stopped showing off how smart he was in class, and began to get into trouble like the rest of us. He even tried talking in our "pidgin" dialect to be like us. He sounded pretty funny but we quit teasing him about it. We let him drink with us.

My senior year I was on the newspaper staff. Our copy had to be approved by both our advisor and the school principal before it was printed. An article on sex education was censored by our advisor. We made up a dummy copy without the article and had it approved by our advisor and the principal. Then we replaced the censored article in the copy and had it printed. All hell broke loose, but the freedom of the press had been maintained!

I fell in love with a girl I had known as a friend for many years. It happened in one night. We were at the beach taking pictures of the sunset for our yearbook cover. We made the shots and stayed and talked. We took a walk across the sand. The moon was full, the offshore breezes balmy, and it seemed only natural that all of my hormones began to surge with the tides. Overnight it seemed as if my life was perfect and would be complete for the rest of my days.

Trog became one of my best friends. I began to appreciate and respect his wit and intelligence. And I admired his spunk. It wasn't easy for him, being the only haole in a bunch of "local" guys, but he proved himself. He went away to the University of Redlands, and everytime Elton John's song "Daniel" played on the radio, I'd think of him and cry.

out, partners in a relationship may socialize each other so that friends become more similar through the course of a relationship, reflecting a process of mutual social influence. More than likely, both processes operate in friendship selection: likes attract likes and then become more alike.

What may be important is not *actual* similarity, but how similar friends perceive themselves to be. Davitz (1955), for example, studied friendship in summer camps and found that best friends were perceived as being more similar in activity preferences than were nonfriends. Even when there were no apparent differences in actual similarity between individuals and friends versus nonfriends, best friends were *perceived* as being more similar than they actually were.

Davitz's study points to another question: What are the essential features on which adolescents base selection? Werner and Parmlee (1979) found that similarity between friends in their preferences for leisure time activities was a better indicator of friendship than either perceived or actual attitude similarity of the personality of the friend. As far as friendship goes, what friends *do* is the vital aspect of the relationship. Studies of conceptions of friendship show that participation in common activities remains an important aspect of friendship from early childhood through adulthood. It is basic to relationships and is necessary before participants can make any judgments of affect.

D. B. Kandel (1978) followed a sample of ninth through twelfth graders over a school year. Comparisons of new, stable, and dissolved friendships at the beginning and at the end of the year showed that selection and social influence played nearly equal roles in explaining similarity between friends. Kandel found that adolescents tended to choose as friends those who were similar in their use (or nonuse) of drugs, in their academic interests, in their further educational aspirations, and in their participation in peer activities. Although there might be initial differences, individuals who remained friends eventually resolved these differences, resembling each other more and more over the course of the year. Relationships in which initial differences were not resolved usually dissolved by the end of the year. Epstein (cited in Berndt, 1982) also found that

---

I guess my most memorable experiences as a youth probably took place during my sophomore year in high school. A few of my friends did a lot of drinking and this particular summer was no different. We started out by getting a couple six packs, as juveniles will do, and we decided to try and pick up a few female companions for the evening. The idea was whomever didn't get a girl that evening had to chug a six pack. Well without going into much detail, I never thought six beers would taste so awful. Oh those high school days sure were fun.

This is not a vivid experience, but it is a long term experience of my high school years.

I am from a small, middle-class, conservative and isolated town. My family is not originally from this town, so we are still outsiders after 13 years. There is a good, but small State College so many people are born, educated, and die without having to leave the area.

My family, and me especially, are different from the norm, and as a result I experienced many problems and inner conflicts as an adolescent.

I qualified as a social elite. My dad was a professor, so our social status was high, and I was intelligent. I was always in the A sections, honors courses, band, drama, you get the picture. The only difference was the way I thought. I was brought up not to conform whereas all my peers were.

The problems started when I began to associate with a girl, Lisa, who was not "in" the group. She was neither smart nor upper-middle class. My friends would not accept her because of this and for the first time I was exposed bluntly to middle-class snobbery. She wasn't from the "right" family and, therefore, would never be one of them. Because of this I changed. I spent a year trying to change them but that was similar to banging my head against a brick wall. What hurt and puzzled me the most was as individuals they would accept Lisa and we'd have a great time, but they would then go back to the group and reject her.

Halfway through my junior year I did what many people thought was crazy. I rejected my social standing and my old "friends." I lowered my status in order to keep a friend. I even went extreme and skipped my senior year, totally rejecting what they thought was most important.

I might have been leaving a cult. These social elites became defensive. I guess it threatened them because here I was rejecting what they'd been told all their lives was what to work for. A strong rivalry started between an old "best" friend and Lisa and I. Even the school system gave me problems. They didn't want me to leave early, saying my senior year would be the best in my life. My band instructor ignored me on the street. I was in fact "excommunicated."

I must say I have never regretted my decision. These people will someday be successful, live in nice houses, with two cars and a picket fence, but they still won't think or act on their own. They will be sheltered and be like all the other middle-class families in other towns and suburbs.

In a way I was a rebel and I saw how tight the "elite" groups are. I also saw how scared they were about losing their comfortable positions in society. It made for an interesting adolescence for me anyway.

friends in grades five, six, eight, and eleven became more similar to each other over the course of a year on measures of self-reliance, school attitudes, college plans, grades, and academic achievement.

Selection and social influence may thus operate together in determining the who's and why's of friendship during adolescence. Even in contexts of mutual influence, however, there is also room for individual growth:

> Adolescents select friends who are similar to themselves on certain characteristics, but because friends differ on other characteristics, there is still room for further similarity to develop through social influence. Friends also could become less similar over time because differences in their rates of development or changes in other aspects of the social environments. For these reasons, friendships always involve a blend of similarity and complementarity. (Berndt, 1982, p. 1255)

The Nature of Adolescent Friendships

What are adolescent friendships like? One way to find out is to ask adolescents. In asking questions like, "What makes someone a close friend," or "How do you show someone that you are a friend," researchers are interested in finding out how people understand friendship and how it is expressed: "How a child organizes thoughts about what to anticipate and value in a peer and how this evolves over time" (Bigelow & LaGaipa, 1980). Although the specific research approaches vary, the results have shown remarkable consistency in charting developmental patterns in conceptions of friendship and social cognition in general (Selman, 1980).

Selman (1980) highlights the importance of *social perspective-taking*, understanding the "intrinsic psychological characteristics and capacities of individuals." The ability to conceptualize others as distinct personalities with characteristics that overlap with but are different from our own is crucial. This is part of *social* cognition. Recall again Aristotle's conception of humans as the *social* animals (Chapter 2).

According to Selman, conceptions of self and interpersonal relations themselves undergo parallel changes in stage-like sequences. In so doing they reflect the "deeper" structural changes involved in the development of social perspective-taking, the common thread underlying social understanding. As the ability to take perspectives develops, there is a growing capacity for self-reflection, introspection, for taking the *third person* perspective essential for self-analysis. The youth can reflect on reflections, be aware that self-deception is possible, and recognize that there may be unconscious motives or causes of behavior. Likewise, conceptions and expectations for friendships undergo developmental changes (Bigelow & LaGaipa, 1980; Selman, 1980) that reflect the ability to know what it is like to be in another's shoes, and the understanding that certain actions can affect both the internal state of the other and the quality and meaning of the relationship as well (Youniss, 1980). This development

Selman's Stage of Interpersonal Conceptions

Children's understanding of friendship—their reasoning about it, their conceptions and theories about what it is and how it works—is dramatically different from that of adults. Of course, many people are aware that children see the world differently. What is not so obvious is that the differences are not just based on misunderstandings or lack of information. Children have their own original theories for interpreting the events in their lives, theories that change as they grow up. They "know" a lot about friendship. It's simply not the same as what we adults know.

In describing children's unchanging theories of friendship, our work ultimately addresses how these theories relate to children's social interactions.

We have found that children's understanding of friendship does develop in a relatively universal and orderly sequence of stages, each characterized by a distinct, formal structure of thought, which does parallel stages in their thinking about relationships with others in general. More specifically, we have identified five separate stages in their thinking about friendship (the ages are rough guidelines):

Stage 0 (ages three to seven): This is the stage of Momentary Playmateship. The child has difficulty distinguishing between a physical action, such as grabbing a toy, and the psychological intention behind this action. He cannot distinguish between his viewpoint and those of others. Friends are valued for their material and physical attributes, and defined by proximity. As one child told us, "He is my friend." Why? "He has a giant Superman doll and a real swing set."

Stage 1 (ages four to nine): At this stage, the child can differentiate between his own perspective and those of others. However, he does not yet understand that dealing with others involves give-and-take between people. This is the stage of One-Way Assistance. In a "good" friendship, one party does what the other party wants one to. Assessments of friendship deal with the viewpoint, needs, or satisfaction of only one party. Said one child, "She is not my friend anymore." Why? "She wouldn't go with me when I wanted her to."

Stage 2 (ages six to 12): The child has the ability to see interpersonal perspectives as reciprocal, each person taking into account the other's perspective. This is the stage of Two-Way Fair-Weather Cooperation. Conceptions

of empathy is critical for success in the role of parent. Impaired capacity for empathy is linked to child abuse (Bavolek et al., 1979).

Developmental Trends in Conceptions of Friendship

Descriptions of the nature of friendship and the values and expectations individuals hold for friends follow a developmental progression that parallels changes in cognitive abilities. This is not too surprising, since the method of inquiry used to study friendship requires verbal expression. As children get older, of friendship include a concern for what each person thinks about the other; it is much more a two-way street. Friendship is not seen as working unless both friends participate. However, the limitation of this stage is that the child still sees the basic purpose of friendship as serving many separate self-interests, rather than mutual interests. "We are friends," said one youngster. "She likes me and I like her. We do things for each other."

Stage 3 (ages nine to 15): Not only can the child take the other's point of view, but by now he or she can also step outside the friendship and take a generalized third-person perspective on it. This is the stage of Intimate, Mutually Shared Relationships. With the ability to take a third-person perspective, the child can view friendship as an ongoing, systematic relationship. There is a shift from seeing friendship as reciprocal cooperation for each person's self-interests to seeing it as collaboration with others for mutual and common interests. Friends share more than secrets, agreements, or plans. Friends share feelings, help each other to resolve personal and interpersonal conflicts, and help each other solve personal problems. The reasoning at this stage can also limit young people's thinking, because close friendship is viewed as an exclusive, intimate, and rather possessive connection. An example, "He is my best friend. We can tell each other things we can't tell anyone else; we understand each other's feelings. We can help each other when we are needed."

Stage 4 (age 12 and older): This is the stage of Autonomous Interdependent Friendships. The individual sees relationships as complex and often overlapping systems. In a friendship, the adolescent or adult is aware that people have many needs and that in a good friendship each partner gives strong emotional and psychological support to the other, but also allows the friend to develop independent relationships. Respecting needs for both dependency and autonomy is seen as being essential to friendship. According to one child, "One thing about a good friendship is that it's a real commitment, a risk you have to take. You have to be able to support and trust and give, but you have to be able to let go, too."

(From Selman, R.L., & Selman, A.P. Children's ideas about friendship: A new theory. *Psychology Today*, October, 1979.)

their descriptions of peers become more diverse and differentiated, as well as more abstract. They move from using words to describe physical attributes and observable features, to elaborating on internal states and psychological characteristics (Livesley & Bromley, 1973; Peevers & Secord, 1973). As children get older, they have different explanations about the meaning of friendship. These explanations might be acquired through socialization, but there are developmental constraints on the child's ability to understand, operationalize, and articulate these explanations.

Going to the first high school dance. . . All the couples who were going out were making out on the bleachers. Girls who were single were standing around in small groups discussing which boy they would like to dance with. After about a half hour, some boys would get enough courage to ask the girls. Some boys would stand around (near the door) and talk about football or cars. Eventually, some boy who I really wouldn't pick as my first choice, would walk up and ask me to dance. I always said yes because I thought it would be better to at least be dancing than standing around so everyone would know no one asked me. After the dance I would always go home and tell my parents I had a great time.

Children's conceptions of friendship come to resemble adult conceptions as they approach adolescence. In early childhood, friendships are based primarily on the availability of another child as a playmate and on participation in common activities. In early adolescence, friendship comes to involve the sharing of thoughts and feelings, and terms like *trust, loyalty,* and *sharing secrets* become common. Friendships become *intimate* in the sense of that term as we developed it in Chapter 8.

Dunphy (1963) proposed a five-stage model worth noting here. In Stage 1 (as early adolescence begins) unisex groups predominate. Each group may have 3–9 members and groups sometimes interact with each other. Mainly, however, they hang out and talk as separate microsystems. In Stage 2 the groups increase the level of contact as mesosystems increase. In Stage 3 the unisex groups begin to break down as their leaders become involved in heterosexual relationships. In Stage 4 the groups fully integrate, and in Stage 5 couples replace individuals in groups as the major format for social life.

Gender Differences in Adolescent Friendships

Researchers report consistent differences in patterns of friendship among boys and girls. Adolescent boys and girls tend to expect different things from friendship, have different concerns about friendship, and seem to express friendship in different ways. For example, girls seem to have more intimate and exclusive friendships than boys (Berndt, 1982).

When asked of their expectations for friends, girls more often mention intimate sharing of thoughts and feelings than do boys (Berndt, 1982; Bigelow & LaGaipa, 1980; Douvan & Adelson, 1969). These themes of sensitivity and empathy were hardly mentioned by 14- to 16-year-old boys studied by Douvan and Adelson (1969). Boys in their study more often mentioned common pursuits, gang activities, and the need for help when in trouble. In general "girls want friends to be loyal, trustworthy, and reliable sources of emotional support; boys want friends to be amiable, cooperative, and able to control aggressive impulses. The support boys want is against concrete trouble, especially conflicts with authority, whereas girls want help with their own emotional crises" (Smart & Smart, 1978, p. 130).

Accordingly, adolescent boys and girls express different concerns and anxieties over friendship. Girls express greater concern over faithlessness and greater anxiety about rejection (Berndt, 1982). Coleman (1974) found that girls at ages 11, 13, 15, and 17 all showed more anxiety about friendships in small groups than boys in each age group. Girls more often described negative themes such as tensions, jealousies, and conflicts among close friends. In most cases, these conflicts centered around rejection or exclusion from a friendship. Douvan and Adelson (1969) found that boys tended to focus on quarrels and outright disputes over property, leisure time activities, and girlfriends. These differences can influence the experience of all forms of social activity, as the accounts of athletics in the vignettes below suggest.

Girls also seem to be more exclusive in their relationships, a pattern that appears in early and middle childhood. During this time, girls are apt to spend more time in *intensive* relationships with a few peers, while boys' relationships are more *extensive* and include a wider range and number of peers (e.g., Waldrop & Halverson, 1975). When given a situation where one can help or share

---

My most vivid adolescent memories basically revolve around sport. During this time my mind was focused on that day's athletic activity. In early adolescence, it centered around many sports—baseball, football, basketball, and hockey. But as I reached later adolescence, I centered on one specific sport: ice hockey. I also recall the budding of a social life, first experiences with beer, girls, etc. But I seemed to put all these other factors into a perspective that hockey would come first. I remember going to Europe to play internationally, and having foreign teams come here, with players staying in my home and living our lifestyle, as I had done there. I remember best the friends I've made through ice hockey: the teammates, coaches, and parents.

During my adolescence I never had much to worry about. I would go to school to learn, play sports, and socialize. I remember always hanging around a big crowd of girls. Talking on the phone was the main focal point of my day for many years. Having my own phone was a must.

Playing sports was always fun for me. Having my family come to watch me always made me happy and proud. Senior year, when I became captain of the field hockey team, was really exciting. But, a big brawl with the coach at the end destroyed everything. I lost confidence in myself and was troubled for awhile. It reflected in my grades, too. She really hurt me a lot and I wouldn't have wished that on anyone.

Some of my most vivid memories of adolescence are those of my athletic career. (Those were the good memories anyway.) How I struggled and sweat through each of the workouts to be a good highjumper. I had always dreamed of taking a high school record and winning a championship. Not only did I get my record (they closed my school a year later, so it's everlasting), but I won the league championship and I won the district championship, and finally placed 4th at state.

Other vivid memories are those of being down at the shore in the summer with my boyfriend. I enjoy the beach and the waves and gazing out at the horizon. The most vivid memory of the beach was the nighttime when my boyfriend and I laid on a blanket and stared out at the moonlit water. I can still picture it and that was two years ago.

I've also got vivid memories of wild high school parties and video arcades. It seemed that was what I lived for (I now know better). I remember how each time I walked into my favorite arcade that a bizzare fiasco would always result. It usually ended up in some kind of scrape with the local police. (Don't get me wrong. I was always a good kid, if you do recall my first paragraph on this page!!)

with a close friend or some other classmate, girls say they would share with and help a close friend more than any other classmate. Boys, on the other hand, claimed they would treat friends and other classmates the same (Berndt, 1982). Of course, whether boys are really so objective and impersonal is doubtful. In another study, 14- and 15-year-olds in a group of friends were observed to see how they would react to a newcomer attempting to join the group. Girls were less welcoming, took longer to allow the newcomer to join the conversation, and were more likely than boys to express negative or rejecting attitudes (Sones & Feshbach, 1971).

Of course, we do not know if boys really feel less intensely about friendship. They may simply not acknowledge their feelings as well as girls. Gilligan's (1982) approach (as outlined in earlier chapters) suggests the differences may be real. Females may be more selective and exclusive because once they define a relationship, they commit more of their personal resources to it. Males may be less exclusive because each friendship costs them less in the way of psychological investment. Certainly this hypothesis parallels what those who look for the biological bases of social behavior (*sociobiologists*) refer to as the natural differences between females and males in investment (Trivers, 1972). Whether it be children or lovers, say the sociobiologists, males invest less in more individuals while females make a greater investment in fewer individuals. All this may also be related to what Gilligan identifies as the masculine effort to appear rational and objective, while the female is more openly concerned with the feelings of those for whom she cares for.

Identity and Intimacy through Interaction

The interactions that occur in the context of friendships between same-sex friends during childhood and adolescence have been implicated as important factors in the development of self and identity and as a prerequisite condition for the development and practice of love and intimacy in heterosexual relationships (Erickson, 1959; Mead, 1934; Sullivan, 1953). The intensity of friendships among girls may prepare them better for intimacy and love than do the shallower friendships of boys who stress objectivity and autonomy (Gilligan, 1982).

Interaction and Identity

According to Erickson (1959), affiliation with peers provides many of the essential experiences and opportunities for self-definition required for the formation of identity (see Chapter 7). Successfully achieving identity has implications for subsequent social development because the next developmental task is one of "intimacy versus isolation and includes the establishment of a mutually trusting love relationship in which partners must know themselves first (identity) before merging in a mature way with another (intimacy)" (Grotevant, Thorbecke, & Meyer, 1982).

Studies have demonstrated some connections between peer interaction, identity, and intimacy, but the direction of effects is not simple or clear. For example, Kacerguis and Adams (1980) found that individuals who had achieved a coherent sense of identity had relationships that were more intimate than those who were at other, less mature identity states. It is not clear from this type of study, however, whether knowledge of self precedes or follows knowledge of others. It is likely that intimate relations aid in the development of identity. It is hard to know, however, because measures of identity (most notably Marcia's, see Chapter 7) focus on "crisis and commitment" as it applies primarily to occupational and vocational choice and aspirations. There may be other components of identity (such as an ideology of interpersonal relations—an idea of who and what one's friends should be) that are more clearly related to actual interpersonal functioning. It would be possible for adolescents to exhibit "intimate" behaviors in the search for self, but that "prior processes of exploring and making a commitment to an ideology of interpersonal relations is an important aspect of adolescent identity and probably a presursor of truly intimate relations" (Grotevant, Thorbecke, & Meyer, 1982).

Several studies suggest that friendships and other relationships may be more salient for identity formation in women than in men. In these studies women tended to focus on who they were in terms of their relations to other people, while men define themselves with respect to issues of competence and "what they would become" in terms of future vocations (Hodgson & Fischer, 1979; Josselson et al., 1977b). Gilligan (1982) has worked out the implications of this difference for mental health in adulthood (see Chapter 7).

Fischer (1981) studied the pairs *(dyadic relationships)* of 357 students in high school and college between the ages of 15 and 20. These friendship pairs were categorized into four groups on the basis of how the relationship was rated according to two factors: *intimacy,* (which included ease of communication, attachment, and affection), and *friendship,* (which concerned mutual activities with a special other person). Participants were asked to select someone who was closest to them, and to rate their relationship on the basis of ease of communication, sharing confidence, empathy, egocentrism, closeness, distance, seeing the other as a unique person, and voluntary dependence. The categories of relationship style were: *integrated* (high in intimacy and friendship), *intimate* (high intimate, low friendship), *friendly* (low intimate, high friendship), and *uninvolved* (low on both intimacy and friendship). There were more women than men at both ages (high school and college) who had integrated or intimate relationships. The proportion of women who had these types of relationships increased during college and applied to friendships with both males and females. Men's relationship style changed little with age; their friendships with other males remaining relatively uninvolved. Friendships with females, however, were more likely to be integrated or intimate than relationships with other men at both ages.

Sullivan (1953) proposed that relations with same-sex chums gives rise to the capacity for intimate relations. The results of Fischer's studies show that men are more willing to disclose themselves and their feelings to female partners than to male partners. This suggests that learning *how* to be intimate depends largely on experiences with females and the practice of intimate behaviors that females encourage. It suggests that male adolescents profit from microsystems that contain female peers, because males are less likely to help each other learn to share feelings effectively.

Self-Concept

The development of the concept of self is interwoven with the development of understanding others, with the growing ability of the child to "take the role of the other" (Shrauger & Schoeneman, 1979). According to Piaget, it is social interaction that brings about cognitive growth, particularly the ability to decenter and establish the self as separate from others.

Relations with peers, unlike those with parents or other adults, are based on reciprocal processes and are characterized by the parties being on equal footing, at least in contrast to adults (Youniss & Volpe, 1978). The essential feature is that individuals develop a notion of general procedures or rules of behavior when interacting with others. Two people bring their own ideas about exchange, and in order to combine relations, they must reach agreements that will guide them in subsequent interactions. With peers on an equal footing, there is a process in which the two individuals discover procedures for interaction by creating them through reciprocal exchange and cooperation *(co-con-*

struction). In effect, they collaborate to construct or agree upon a mutually shared notion of social meaning:

> Development then pertains to discovering exchanges, conceptualizing them as interpersonal relations, and continuing to organize relations with respect to each other and to their application to social reality (Youniss & Volpe, 1978, p. 5).

Adolescent peer relations are the principal context for these experiences.

These processes, according to Youniss, make children more sensitive to others and are the main sources of mutuality—the primary features of chumships that, as Sullivan proposed, serve as the basis for interpersonal affection and love. The ability to co-construct, to discover and conceptualize relations and exchanges, has been linked to underlying processes that arise with growing social cognitive ability. As we noted earlier, one of these processes includes developing understanding of how people's points of view are related and coordinated (Selman, 1980).

Peer Relations and Social Adjustment

There is accumulating evidence that children with poor peer relations are at risk for developing a variety of adjustment problems during adolescence and young adulthood. Researchers report that the inability to establish and maintain good peer relations is an important factor in predicting neurotic and psychotic disturbances (Cowen et al., 1973; Kohn & Clausen, 1955; Mednick & Schulsinger, 1970), as well as conduct disorders and delinquency (Conger & Miller, 1966; Conger et al., 1966; Roff, Sells, & Golden, 1972).

Janes and her colleagues (1979) found that teacher ratings of boys' "failure to get along with peers" during adolescence predicted a wide variety of maladaptive adult behaviors, including trouble with the law, poor school achievement and dropping out, having problems at work, and psychiatric hospitalization for boys referred to a child guidance clinic. These boys were also rated high in bad conduct or *acting out behaviors* that included disobedience, lying, stealing, and fighting. The results indicate that those identified as "not getting along" were not the shy and withdrawn, "but a subset of troublemakers teachers had many complaints about." Being a troublemaker by itself did not necessarily mean later problems, but being a troublemaker who *also* alienated peers meant almost certain trouble later in life. This may be relevant to understanding youth from socioeconomically deprived or ethnic minority backgrounds who have trouble in school but succeed in their peer group.

Other longitudinal studies have shown that except for extreme cases of childhood neuroses that require long-term treatment, most shy or withdrawn children do *not* seem to develop problems that come to the attention of community agencies. The prognosis is different for those who are rejected (as opposed to neglected), particularly if they are aggressive and exhibit antisocial behavior in more than one setting (see Chapter 11). These individuals (primarily boys) are likely to continue on a troubled trajectory through young adulthood, resulting in criminal records, and have a high probability of exhibiting other coping problems as well (Loeber, 1982; Robins, 1978).

Werner and Smith (1982) found that one factor that characterized resilient adolescents exposed to high risk conditions yet free of serious coping problems (as compared with peers who *did* develop such problems) was the ability to draw on support from friends during times of stress. Not only were friends *available*, but resilient individuals seemed to be able to elicit positive social attention from their social environment. Personal and social development are intertwined; the same people both amass social capital and have the skills necessary to spend it wisely.

It is difficult to determine how much personal attributes cause variations in peer relations versus how much peer relations cause variation in personal attributes. It is most likely that both are occurring simultaneously. Those who are good at relating to peers will have more opportunities and support for developing further expertise in social functioning. Those who are not so good at it often do not have the opportunity to engage in relationships in which they can develop these skills. The socially and psychologically rich get richer and the socially and psychologically poor get poorer, particularly in adolescence.

What Does It Take To Make and Keep Friends?
Lack of friends or peer rejection in adolescence may have very different causes and consequences than rejection in early childhood. For adolescents, a lack of friendships may indicate that they are at risk for less than adequate and effective functioning in that:

1 They may lack the skills, characteristics, or attributes required for making friends of their own age.
2 The lack of friends may prevent or make difficult to obtain experiences within a relationship needed to develop these skills that are important for general social functioning and psychological adjustment.

As we noted in Chapter 2, Weinstein (1969) has proposed that we think of interpersonal competence as being made up of three major components. Deficits in each area predict problems in social relations. The first is the ability to "take the place of the other," to be able to predict the effect that one's actions will have on the other. The second is the availability of a wide repertoire of alternative lines of action. Finally, one must have the *intra*personal resources to implement action in particular situations. These intrapersonal resources refer to aspects of a person's personality (e.g., motivation, locus of control, self-esteem) that may prevent or predict particular ways of doing things. Thus, one could assess the situation, know what to do (or what should be done) but be unable to carry off action for some reason having to do with personality.

As we saw before, youth of different ages have different conceptions of interpersonal relations, and this seems to be related to differences in basic social cognitive processes (Selman, 1980). Selman found that youth with poor peer relations seemed to be delayed in the development of skill in social perspective-taking. Likewise, Chandler (1973) found differences between delinquent and normal boys on their abilities to "take the role of the other."

Suttles (1970) and Fine (1981) have argued that cultural information relevant to the problems of growing up is transmitted through friendship ties, be it in dyads or in groups. According to Fine (1981) relationships with peers:

> . . . provide the child with a stock of knowledge and repertoire of behavior useful for encounters with other peers. Children acquire information from many sources—the media, schools, religious organizations, and their families—all adult-dominated institutions. In contemporary American society, adults typically share an ideology that prescribes what children should and should not know. There are several topic areas in which children are interested but that they cannot learn about from adults: the practice of sex, informal rules of institutions (how to *really* succeed in school), the art of making negative evaluations (insults), and how to have excitement and adventure (pranks, mischief, and illegal behavior) (p. 44).

Without the experience and instruction from peers, individuals may have a more difficult time learning appropriate or acceptable ways of dealing with common situations.

The Life-Long Significance of Friendship

Friendships can have both direct and indirect effects on the development of social competence. First, having companionship and affection increases adolescent self-esteem and feelings of satisfaction. Second, friendships provide a context for learning skills that make adolescents more competent in dealing with themselves and others. Having successful interactions with friends enhances the adolescent's sense of competence and esteem. The skills and attributes developed in these relations (such as high self-esteem) may aid in the quality of functioning in other social settings. Lastly, having friends who can be counted on in time of need as a personal resource may foster a sense of security and confidence to engage in opportunities that have potential for substantial payoffs, although they entail risk.

In a national survey investigating the quality of life of Americans, the number of friends a person had was found to have substantial direct and indirect influences on how satisfied a person was with his or her life (Campbell, Converse, & Rodgers, 1976). Campbell and his colleagues hypothesized that feelings of personal competence are an important factor in predicting feelings of well-being. They confirmed this relationship in their study. The actual number of friends was among the best predictors of feelings of competence, particularly in men under 35. Additionally, the number of friends had the biggest direct effect on life satisfaction as compared to other resources such as health, income, and education, especially in older individuals. According to Campbell and his colleagues, there seems to be a developmental relationship between direct and indirect effects of friendship:

> Among the young, feelings of personal competence are still being established, and an adequate network of friendships appears to be quite important for the outcome. At this age level, a fair portion of the impact of friendships upon the sense of well-being is in fact mediated by enhanced feelings of personal competence when friends are abundant. (Campbell, Converse, & Rodgers, 1976, p. 373)

Friendships and peer relations are the contexts in which adolescents develop many skills and attitudes that contribute to social competence. They may carry the skills they develop and use in relationships with peers into other relationships such as marriage and parenthood and into other settings within the larger social environment as they enter more and more microsystems. Being able to establish and maintain positive social relationships is important for personal well-being and for fostering a supportive social network that may be an important resource in adapting to stressful social conditions such as poverty and discrimination, in adjusting to sudden unpredictable events (e.g., divorce, sudden illness), and for dealing with stresses that accompany *normative* changes (e.g., transitions from high school to college).

The relationship between friendship and the development of socially competent behavior is one of complex, reciprocally interrelated effects, where friendships are both product and producer of socially competent behavior. The lack of friends during adolescence may have different causes and consequences when compared to the lack of friends in early childhood. Because the ability to establish and maintain friends involves more adult skills and expectations for friendship, the lack of friends during adolescence may indicate that adolescents may be lacking or deficient in certain skills and attributes necessary for interpersonal functioning that may affect their general level of social and emotional functioning in the social environment. It may also indicate that without friends, the person may not be able to get the experiences required to develop these skills, indicating potential risk for *future* functioning.

The competencies that the community of peers values and reinforces depend upon what conditions of life are like in the broader community in which they live (Ogbu, 1981). Being tough may score points in one neighborhood while being smart is the ticket in another. The meaning attached to particular behaviors depends upon the nature of the interrelationships between microsystems (family, peers, school) within a given community context. When these different mesosystems value particular life outcomes and behaviors, the microsystems that make up these mesosystems will reinforce the development of the same set of competencies. This is a strong, developmentally enhancing mesosystem. When there is discontinuity or discrepancy *between* microsystem contexts (between the home and the school, for example), there may be conflicts in the definition of competency and in how much people value particular behaviors; what is considered competent in one context may undermine the performance of behaviors that are considered competent in another. One study of a lower-income, inner city population (Cauce, Felner, & Primavera, 1982) found that number of friends and perceived support was significantly related to self-esteem, but *negatively* related to academic performance (see the box below). Among white middle class populations, these variables are more often *positively* related to each other, and, in several studies, indicators of social functioning

A na M. Cauce, Robert D. Felner, and Judith Primavera did a study examining "the structure of social support and its relationship to adjustment for adolescents from high-stress lower socioeconomic class inner-city backgrounds." Previous study had shown that social support (in the range of interpersonal relationships a person has) mediates the consequences of certain life crises, contributes to a person's ability to withstand stress, and enhances general adjustment and feelings of well-being. Children and adolescents from lower socioeconomic levels and minority backgrounds are frequently considered "at risk" for developing maladaptive behavior due to higher levels of stress.

Two hundred and fifty 9th and 11th graders were randomly selected from the inner city public high schools in a northeastern city that serve predominantly lower income minority students. Sixty-seven percent of the subjects were black, 22% white, and 10% Hispanic. Three sets of measures were collected: *school performance* as noted by grade point average (GPA), *self-concept*, and *social support*. For the social support measure, students were asked to rate how helpful a number of different individuals (e.g., parents, teachers, friend,

clergy) were to them. Individuals who provide support could be seen as falling into three groups: *family*, consisting of parents and other relatives; *formal support*, which included counselors, teachers, and clergy; and *informal support*, made up of friends and "other adults."

In examining the relationship between social support and academic adjustment and self-concept, the authors found that while family and formal support did not affect GPA and absences, informal support did. Informal support, however, had a *negative* relationship to academic adjustment: higher levels of informal support was related to lower GPA's and greater absenteeism.

In this inner-city population, higher levels of informal support, while associated with positive peer self-concept and adjustment in one microsystem (peers) was also related to poorer adjustment in another (school).

If the two mesosystems have differing values regarding education, some discrepancy will result. As conformity is important during early adolescence, it is not surprising that those who have much contact with peers will adopt peers' values—values that may prevent academic achievement in school.

and peer relations are better predictors of school performance than indicators of cognitive functioning.

This leads us back to the community as a social context. How individuals experience adolescence depends a great deal on where and with whom they experience adolescence.

Adolescents and the Community

In the remainder of this chapter we will examine the role of the community in adolescent development. Of particular interest is the way the expanding peer network characteristic of adolescence shapes the community and in turn how the community shapes peer relations. The following questions serve as the focal points of our discussion.

1   How does the community change for children as they become adolescents?
2   How does the community actually influence development (at least what are some ways in which we think it works)?
3   What are the (community) variables that affect community influence on adolescent development?
4   How do adolescents and their communities get along (what are the major issues in that relationship)?

The Transition from Childhood to Adolescence: How the Turf Changes

As children become adolescents they engage in more and more encounters with the community outside and beyond the family. Several aspects of this change have developmental implications. First, adolescents, as opposed to children, must deal with increasingly complex community institutions. This may teach them both respect for such institutions and a measure of cynicism. Second, at adolescence, the peer group expands and becomes more diverse and influential. Third, the community of peers that arises at adolescence becomes a force to be reckoned with in the minds of many adults. Therefore, the community views the adolescent with more concern than it does the child. As we showed in Chapters 1 and 9, the school is the prime example of the increased size and complexity of community institutions with which the adolescent must deal.

Curricular and extracurricular activities in secondary schools are taken seriously. In sports, for example, the level of competition is high, and participation is restricted to a small percentage of the total student body. Even junior high school teams are supported by cheerleaders and pep clubs, and many of these groups have selective membership policies themselves. Along the same lines, even social events become more serious. School dances and other similar activities have an orientation to couples, and there is more pressure to be popular, have a girl/boy friend, and to be seen at social functions. The strategic interactions described by Elkind (1980) (see Chapters 4 and 8) blossom.

Like the schools, other institutions in the community, such as recreation programs and service organizations, present the adolescent with a more complex and demanding set of roles and responsibilities. For instance, recreational activities for adolescents are generally less fun-oriented, and more competitive, organized, and structured than those available to children. Sandlot ball games give way to Little League; League playoffs and city championships replace neighborhood victories. Arts and crafts classes emphasizing exploration and enjoyment defer to serious study, exhibitions, and contests.

Other community settings treat adolescents differently as well. As we saw in Chapter 9, the economic system sees teenagers as both consumers and as part of the (part-time) work force. Adolescents constitute a major consumer group and American business is certainly aware of that, as evidenced by the great number of commercials in the mass media designed to grab a share of the adolescent market. Teenagers spend millions of dollars each year on records and clothes, making up a significant proportion of the total national expenditures of these items. Adolescents also spend their money on more substantial items. For example, one study showed that even in a rural Maine community, over 50% of the eleventh graders owned a camera, 22% had a car, 85% a radio, 58% a record player, 31% a T.V. set, and 76% owned a watch (Rice, 1981).

In order to get the money to run their cars and buy their stereos, many adolescents find jobs, as we saw in Chapter 9 and will review here. In fact, according to the U.S. Bureau of Labor Statistics, about 50–55% of the 16- to 19-year-old males and 45% of the same aged females are part of the civilian work force (Rice, 1981). These figures include both full- and part-time workers, but even those youngsters who work part-time work a lot. According to U.S. Labor Department (1980), of the adolescents who work part-time, over 60% of the males and 50% of the females work 15 hours a week or more. Similarly, Steinberg (1982) reports that over 80% of the high school students in their study of the effect of work on young people were employed at least part-time. It is apparent that the economic aspects of the community play a larger and more complex role in the life of the adolescent than in the child's.

Now that we have seen how the turf changes, we can examine some ways in which these changes might actually affect adolescent development.

The Community as an Influence on Adolescent Development

As we consider the community as a force in development, it is important to keep in mind that diversity plays a role amidst the regularities imposed by the macrosystem. Young people spend their lives in specified contexts, in schools and neighborhoods within communities (Elder, 1975). Diversity is the norm, both within and among communities. For instance, schools for early adolescents (junior highs and middle schools) may be organized in much the same way across the country and may appear almost identical within a single community. However, there is a great deal of variation between such schools in their size, available resources, social climate, quality of school life, curriculum, and parental involvement and support (Epstein & McPartland, 1976; Garbarino & Asp, 1981; Garms, Gutherie, & Pierce, 1978). Also, these variables may interact with other community characteristics. Thus, a youngster attending a junior high with an enrollment of 1200 in a very rural area will most likely have a different school experience than an urban counterpart who goes to a school of the same size.

The *diversity rule* holds for neighborhoods as well. For example, Garbarino and Crouter (1978) in studying child abuse, looked at neighborhoods in the same city that appeared very much alike on the surface (similar SES characteristics) but had vastly different maltreatment rates. They found that differences between the neighborhoods in the strength of social support networks or social links was strongly associated with the differences in the rates of child maltreatment. Such differences may not be visible in official socioeconomic and demographic characterizations of communities, but can make a large difference in the nature of the developmental context that the community provides.

A few final notes about diversity are in order. In trying to understand community effects on adolescent development, we need to remember that individual youngsters respond in different ways to the same environment. A small school may be stifling and restrictive for one adolescent, and warm and supportive for another. Also, school size or any other physical variable may not be as important as the combination of adults and adolescents in a certain community context. An institution that may appear large and impersonal on the surface may be staffed by adults who overcome the difficulties inherent in its basic structure, thereby creating a warm and supportive atmosphere for adolescents. In addition, some young people may get enough nurturing at home to override the effects of community institutions, except for provision of some services (e.g., educational credentials). In short, it is the interaction of the adolescent's unique characteristics with environmental stresses and opportunities that defines the quality of the community as a context for development. Adolescents are active in shaping their own development.

With that in mind, how does the community influence development? As we mentioned earlier, this occurs both directly and indirectly. Direct community influence exists in several ways. First, the community offers opportunities to its adolescents (McCandless, 1970). For example, Cloward and Ohlin (1960) examined the opportunities various communities made available to youngsters, and they found that a community is a positive force in adolescents' lives to the extent that it offers what Cloward and Ohlin term *legitimate opportunities* to its young people. A community is unsuccessful in promoting healthy development to the degree that it makes *illegitimate opportunities* available. Legitimate opportunity is the chance to succeed in socially approved roles, while illegitimate opportunity is the chance to be competent in socially undesirable or even unlawful pursuits. According to these researchers, juvenile delinquency arises in part from an excess of illegitimate opportunities, but is even more a result of a lack of legitimate opportunities. They feel that adolescents will use legitimate opportunities rather than illegitimate ones if the former are available. In fact, Cloward and Ohlin believe that young people will pursue illegitimate opportunities (such as delinquency) *only* when the community provides too few avenues to be competent in socially desirable activities. They argue that deviant behavior is likely to occur when there is a large discrepancy between aspirations considered desirable and attainable by the community and the legitimate means by which adolescents can realize those aspirations.

This idea of discrepancies between goals and the means to attain them and their effects on human behavior has been the subject of theoretical treatments by sociologists Durkheim (1951) and Merton (1961). Durkheim viewed society as providing norms (models of adult behavior). This encouraged the formulation of goals on the part of the individual. In turn, goal formulation led to the development of ambition and drive to reach these goals. If this ambition can be channeled into legitimate avenues for success (socially approved ways of attaining goals), then individuals will feel a sense of control over their lives and have no need to engage in deviant behavior. However, when societal conditions are such that goals are no longer regulated and become fuzzy (and thus unattainable), then a sense of powerlessness or anomie results. Such conditions often are present in societies undergoing modernization and economic expansion as well as in times of economic decline (McCandless, 1970). In Durkheim's view, if industrial societies are to survive they need to promote the development of ambition and a strong orientation towards success, but at the same time must provide clear norms and legitimate avenues to success in order to prevent alienation and deviant behavior.

While Merton's thinking is similar to Durkheim's, he places more emphasis on the discrepancies between what society says an individual's goals should be and the means that the society provides for individuals (and groups) to reach these goals. For Merton, it is not the lack of norms that causes anomie and deviant behavior, but the lack of legitimate ways of reaching socially approved and valued goals. Incidentally, Merton predicts that low social status and poverty will lead to greater alienation.

Merton's and Durkheim's ideas provide us with one example of how to analyze and understand the role a community might play in adolescent development. However, community influence on development can operate in more tangible and localized ways as well. Each social system or context within a community, such as the school or some neighborhood organization, offers risks and opportunities to the adolescent. But the community as a whole may also directly affect adolescents. For instance, in attempting to control or protect adolescents, a community may enact curfew laws or special ordinances, such as those restricting young peoples' access to video game arcades during school hours. While these are more mundane than the abstract notions of Durkheim and Merton, this type of exosystem influence on adolescent interaction patterns can have a great impact on adolescent life.

In a less direct manner, communities affect adolescent development by influencing the primary social systems where young people live (their microsystems). Unemployment and prosperity influence family life. Zoning laws or school board mandates can affect the availability of social services and can even alter the quality of life in a neighborhood. Many of the actions or influences have little or nothing to do with adolescents *per se*. In fact, many times the people who are making decisions do not even consider the impact of such action on young people. A community's attitude toward birth control or marriage or a zoning law prohibiting the operation of liquor stores in certain areas do reveal a concern for adolescents, although this concern is often negative in the sense that it tries to control adolescents without understanding their needs.

In summary, then, we have seen that the community can influence adolescent development both directly and indirectly on a number of levels. This influence may operate through societal norms for success or concrete rules for adolescent behavior set up by a community. It may be the result of action on the part of the community that is aimed directly at adolescents, or as a by-product of steps taken to deal with other problems or issues.

What Are the Important Variables?

Sociocultural factors.   Social class is important because it seems to manifest itself in all of the adolescent's microsystems. Schools in low-income areas, for instance, typically have fewer resources than schools in high-income districts, as well as lower achievement scores, graduation rates, and percentages of students going on to college (Garbarino & Asp, 1981). However, some schools in very poor areas that qualify for special federal or state aid possess the resources and equipment of their much wealthier counterparts. In fact, in recent years it is the schools in moderately poor and working class neighborhoods that get the short end of the educational stick because the wealthier schools can take care of their own and the very poor get lots of extra help.

School facilities, equipment, and resources are not the only differences between poor and rich schools, however. Often there is a major difference in personnel too. Not only do schools in poor neighborhoods usually have larger class sizes, but they typically have less experienced staffs as well. For example, a study in Oakland, California, found that schools in poorer areas were staffed by a large percentage of younger, less experienced teachers while schools in higher income areas had more experienced personnel. Some of this was caused by a transfer policy that gave first choice of assignment to the most senior teachers. However, this policy was amended in the early 1970s in an effort to more uniformly distribute personnel. Whether or not this situation was beneficial, detrimental, or even made a difference in the quality of education provided is open to question, although many in Oakland felt it was a slap in the face to lower-income kids and families. What is important is that we understand that SES is associated with a number of school characteristics, and these go beyond just physical facilities.

SES is also related to family and neighborhood differences, including family stability, rates of abuse and neglect, or even values. For example, in a book that we discussed in Chapter 2, *Class and Conformity*, Melvin Kohn (1977) describes the differences in childrearing practices and parental expectations of children's behavior between working and middle-class families. Working class families, according to Kohn, want their children to be obedient, follow the rules, and conform, while middle-class parents want their kids to be creative, questioning, and nonconforming. This may be an important influence on the social climate of the schools and peer groups of adolescents.

Neighborhoods may differ along the same lines. Social competence varies from neighborhood to neighborhood. Recreational and employment opportunities differ between lower and higher SES communities. Also, the institutions within communities may give different messages to children from different SES backgrounds. For example, a child from a working class family with one set of expectations for school behavior may attend an upper middle-class school that demands a different set of behaviors. This may also be true for adolescents who are part of racial or ethnic minorities. They may be told to behave in one way at home and another at school and may also experience different value systems that promote different life goals, definitions of success, and meanings of social competence. This is particularly true in areas where an ethnic group does not constitute a large enough proportion of the community's population to gain and hold political and policy-making power.

Demographic and geographic factors.   Here we are referring to the location, size, and the demographic characteristics of the population in a community. Community influence on the adolescent experience involves factors such as whether the community is rural or urban, has a large percentage of young people in the population or is populated mostly by adults, is located in the southwest or the northeast regions of the continent.

For adolescents growing up in rural areas or small cities, the school may be the focal point of the community for both parents and young people alike (Peshkin, 1978) (see the box on p. 464–465). However, for suburban kids the shopping center or mall may be the hub of activity. In the same vein, a community with a large percentage of young people in the population will be likely to provide a wider variety of recreational and educational activities for adolescents than a community where most people are unmarried, childless, or past child-rearing age.

In his book *Growing Up American*, Alan Peshkin describes the result of several years of research on the experience of growing up in a small midwestern town. Peshkin actually lived there (he calls the town Mansfield) while he was making his observations. His work is in the tradition of the community investigations of Hollingshead (1961) and Havighurst (1962), but draws from the qualitative studies of schooling exemplified by Cusick (1973) and others (e.g., Jackson, 1969) as well.

In this excerpt from the book, Peshkin is describing the fundamental role the school (particularly high school athletics) plays in this community. The high school draws Mansfield together and serves to give the community definition, maybe even a reason for being.

> Approach Mansfield from any direction on any one of five Friday nights in fall and you will see, even while still a considerable distance away, a bright glow illuminating the dark sky. The closer you move toward Mansfield the sharper the glow appears until its source emerges—football lights. They stand like giants at attention guarding the school district's football field and the very small town adjacent to it. Football games are the focus of community concern on these five autumn evenings; they are played at night to accommodate the team's numerous fans. Many are college students who return home for the weekend to see these games, their presence a tribute to their loyalty to Mansfield and evidence of their preference for nearby postsecondary schools. People say Mansfield is a football town, and they are right. No other activity elicits the same degree of devotion and support. In two recent years, paid attendance for five games was 4,342 and 4,666. If we consider these figures beside the total school district population of approximately 2,100, and discount about 20 percent of the crowd as supporters of the visiting team, we are still left with more than 40 percent of all local persons standing and sitting under the Friday night lights, being seen, running with friends around the refreshment stand, strolling on the track that encircles the field, and even watching the game.
>
> The football sideline is the most attractive place in town these Friday nights, its attraction enhanced if the team wins. More than just an athletic event, a football game is a significant social occasion, during which a variety of personal and communal needs and feelings are satisfied and reinforced. The football games provide unsurpassed opportunity for recreation and social interaction and for promoting and expressing community pride and loyalty. On these five nights, more than at any other time, the school can be seen as the heart of Mansfield.
>
> . . . Mansfielders do not claim to live in paradise—indeed, some might object strenuously to this religious allusion—but it is clear that many hold strong positive feelings about their school and community. Many others, of course, hold strong negative feelings. The experience of

History.   Here we refer to the rate of change and amount of stability in the community. We are interested in questions such as: Is the population increasing or decreasing drastically? Have there been shifts in employment opportunities (new plants opening or old ones closing down)? Have there been any recent, large changes in the make-up of the population (fewer children, more elderly, a large influx of some ethnic group)?

growing up in a small, cohesive community is felt deeply, for better or for worse. In any event, this study has focused on those with positive views who feel they belong in Mansfield. Belonging is a powerful, precious sentiment, an invariable attribute of community; it moves people to strongly defensive behavior and supports the feeling that even beyond one's family one is not alone. Mansfield provides this sense of belonging.

Mansfield's ethos, "the guiding belief. . .the spirit that motivates the ideas . . .or practices of a people" (Webster), has been formed partly in response to the realities of small-town rural life and partly in reaction to the predominance of urban society. It incorporates the conviction that people live a good life in small towns, and that Mansfielders are more at home in Mansfield than somewhere outside the community. Other beliefs, generated by contrasting urban and rural life, characterize Mansfield as a preferred place where people are safer and more secure, uncrowded, better looked after, friendlier, independent, and God-fearing. Tim Browne believes that people in bigger places "don't give a damn how you are." Believing that people give a damn is central to Mansfield's ethos; it unites school district residents. Mansfield High School is central in an outlook which claims uniqueness for Mansfield only as one of a class of unique places—rural communities—although Mansfield may be unique in itself for persons like Nancy Parker, third-generation native, who acknowledges, "I belong here as I would no place else."

The Nancy Parkers of Mansfield form an important part of the high school's support community, but this is more than a school-related group, a conglomerate of people with the school alone as a unifying factor. It is a community in sociological as well as geographical terms. That is, within a given area its people share common interests and loyalties, not through singularities of language, race, or religion, but through shared outlook, history, occupations, institutions, and purposes. It is a community with integrity and identity. Its small, white, fairly stable, mixed blue collar-farmer population is the group whose property is taxed, whose children attend the school, who buy the cakes at bake sales, who attend Homecoming parades, and who elect the school board. Not just textbook stuff, its history is carried forward by living people whose tastes and values emerge from this history to influence the present. Although those tastes and values are moderated by the forceful messages of the nation's media, they continue to instill in each new generation visions of a safe, secure Mansfield.

Generally similar communities are found in some suburbs and cities as well as in other small towns. The residents believe their school belongs to them and that the well-being of their community is tied to their school.

(Reprinted by permission from *Growing Up American* by Allan Peshkin. Copyright © 1978 by University of Chicago Press. All rights reserved.)

In recent years, we have seen a lot of action along these lines in communities across the continent. For example, changes in the age composition of the population have led to declining school enrollments and caused many school closings. Thus, many youngsters now attend larger schools further away from home than did their older brothers and sisters. Also, the depressed state of the economy across the continent, particularly in unemployment hot spots, has led to reductions in youth services and job prospects. As well, the large and sudden influx of immigrants into some communities has changed the environments in which young people from these areas grow up. For example, the relocation of groups of Vietnamese and Cambodian refugees to various cities and towns across the continent, and the large number of Haitians and Cubans who arrived in southern Florida in the late 1970s and early 1980s have changed the character of their new communities. The *sudden* increases in population experienced by some communities, both large cities and small towns, particularly in the Rocky Mountain states and the Southwest as a result of the economic boom in energy development, similarly alters the social context in which youth experience adolescence.

However, these macrosystem phenomena are not the whole story. Businesses close or move to new locations as a result of exosystem decisions, as well as in response to some national economic crisis. Some communities felt the effect of declining school enrollment long before the decline of the post-war baby boom. But whether or not a community's history results from local events or national trends, the direction and rate of change are important influences on adolescence, influences that we will return to in Chapter 13. Community characteristics are often highly correlated with one another. Social class and ethnicity are highly related to other population characteristics and geographic location, as well as community history. The adolescent faces a community as a package of influences. Thus, the community context in which adolescent development takes place depends upon the combination or interrelation of a particular community's characteristics. It makes more sense to look at issues in the relationship between adolescents and their communities on the basis of how these issues arise and how different communities handle them.

Adolescents in the Community

As we have seen, a community has a different relationship with its adolescents from the one it has with its children. Most communities want to maximize the developmental opportunities and minimize the social risks for both children and adolescents. However, when it comes to adolescents, the community is also concerned with protecting itself, minimizing the risks to other members of the community posed by the adolescents. This often results in conflict between adolescents and communities, conflict that centers around the issues of protection versus suppression and nurturing and support versus control. The community views the peer group as a powerful force and wants to channel it in a positive direction, while at the same time allowing youngsters enough freedom so that they can develop a sense of responsibility and gain the social competencies needed to function successfully in the adult world. Why is the community concerned with protecting itself from its adolescents? One reason is the heavily negative stereotypes people hold of adolescents (as we saw in Chapter 1). A second is that when adolescents are delinquent, they tend to do so in ways that can harm themselves and others.

Ecological Wrap-Up

Organism.   Physical and cognitive development put more power in the hands of the individual. This makes the individual adolescent a force to be reckoned with in the community. When adolescents band together as peer groups they become a potent stimulus for community response. Those exchanges are governed, in part, by the competence of adolescents *in* peer groups, e.g., their ability to empathize and resist the social psychology of conformity.

Microsystem.   One of the big community issues in adolescence is controlling microsystems, particularly peer groups. These peer microsystems are complex social and psychological entities in which prestige, popularity, and influence work on individual self-concepts. The results often have life-long significance.

Mesosystem.   School/home and peer group/home mesosystems do much to influence the issues faced by the community in responding to its adolescents. When these mesosystems are conflict-ridden there is likely to be troubled and troubling adolescent behavior.

Exosystem.   Community influences are determined by the decisions made by institutions such as big businesses or governmental agencies. Thus, the ideology guiding these institutions is vital, particularly with respect to its orientation towards adolescents.

Macrosystem.   Community variation occurs within the context of macrosystem blueprints, of course. For example, small towns in modern industrialized societies offer many of the same opportunities as big cities. In preindustrial societies the gap is usually much bigger. Some societies permit more local autonomy than others. Thus, for example, schools are a local and state matter in the United States but nationally uniform in England. Just as mesosystems do much to establish the community's agenda vis-à-vis adolescents, so does the macrosystem. It contributes the values, stereotypes, and broad policies that form the guidelines within which adolescents and their communities negotiate their relationship.

Preview

■ Serious disturbance in adolescence often leads to difficulties in adulthood, particularly if the problem is one of disturbed thinking and acting rather than feeling.

■ Delinquency is a major adolescent adjustment problem that has many causes and affects many youth.

■ Runaways are vulnerable to victimization and exploitation on the streets, particularly if they have personal adjustment problems, have experienced severe family conflict, or have been the victim of abuse at home.

■ Juvenile prostitution is a serious problem and is tied into other adolescent problems, particularly drug misuse and sexual abuse.

■ Drinking and other drug use seems to have leveled off, but is still at a seriously high level.

■ Suicide is a leading cause of adolescent deaths.

■ Eating disorders such as anorexia nervosa and bulimia are critical problems in adolescence.

■ Major approaches to assessing adolescent adjustment problems, mental illness, and behavioral problems include the American Psychiatric Association's Diagnostic and Statistical Manual, and problem checklists designed to provide profiles of troubled youth.

A s we noted in Chapter 1, there is great public and professional confusion over what is a normal adolescent. The mass media emphasizes adolescent problems, as do professionals who provide human services. Both reinforce negative stereotypes of youth and both do so partly because both professional helpers and reporters tend to see only troubled and troubling adolescents. The good news about youth is that most are psychologically and socially well-adjusted (even during the challenging years of adolescence). The bad news is that some youth really are troubled and troubling. In this chapter we examine the psychological and social adjustment problems that do affect adolescents. In Chapter 12 we will look at intervention; how peers, parents, and other adults can help troubled adolescents cope with their problems. In this chapter we confine our attention to the problems themselves.

We look at these adjustment problems from our ecological perspective. Thus, we begin with organismic factors that predispose youth to abnormal development (to *pathology*) or to antisocial behavior. We do so, however, with the recognition that the significance of these organismic factors derives in part from the microsystems in which they are expressed. What is more, we recognize that some microsystems themselves produce pathology (and are thus *pathogenic* microsystems) or encourage behavior that results in social problems (e.g., excessive alcohol consumption). For example, a cold, rejecting family may produce a depressed and hostile adolescent and a family that misuses alcohol can model and reinforce problem drinking. Furthermore, the other systems in the ecology of youth may instigate, precipitate, and exacerbate psychological and

11

Adjustment Problems in Adolescence

social adjustment problems. For example, an unsympathetic school can precipitate delinquency in a lower-class youth from an ethnic or racial minority (mesosystem). Likewise, the institutions (exosystems) of the sex industry (pornography and prostitution) can exploit vulnerable youth who run away from home. Finally, cultural patterns (macrosystem) that worship thinness may contribute to the problem of self-imposed starvation in teenage girls *(anorexia nervosa)* as well as to problems of low self-esteem generally among the many girls who cannot fit the ideal body type. Also, a culture that legitimates "a pill for every ailment" may increase the magnitude and severity of all forms of substance abuse.

We begin with an effort to sort out psychopathology from the normal problems of development, those problems that children and youth commonly experience and that tend to clear up (or naturally get cleared up). These normal problems stand in contrast to abnormal problems that predict a long-term pattern of serious developmental dysfunction. We can examine this distinction in terms of two basic types of problems, those that are mainly *internalized* and those that are *externalized*. The former tend to make the young person *feel* and develop badly (and include many forms of incompetent and self-destructive behavior); the latter tend to make the young person *act* badly (and include many forms of antisocial behavior). Both normal and abnormal problems can be internalized or externalized. However, in many cases the externalized problems are more likely to stimulate some sort of intervention, intervention that *either* helps resolve the problem or makes it worse.

Growing up I was a shy, quiet, and very confused young girl. I was very unsure of myself and spent a lot of time by myself. I remember feeling a lot of pressure because I didn't feel I belonged anywhere. My parents were extremely strict and gave me very little freedom. I wasn't allowed to go out very often so I spent a lot of time alone in my room. I had a hard time making friends at school and so, even there I spent a lot of time alone. I was terrified of being rejected by people so I kept quiet and to myself. I guess I remember my adolescent years best as a time of loneliness.

The thing that I remember most vividly would have to be the night my friends and I got caught by the police. We were all 13–15 and had pushed the car out of the garage around 2 a.m. Sandy was to be the driver so we all piled in while she took the wheel. We drove around for two hours and were on our way home when the state police pulled us over. He asked to see our ID's and when we couldn't show any we were taken to the barracks and our parents had to come and get us.

We found out later that we were stopped because the trooper thought we all looked too small to be out that late and driving a car.

When I was going through adolescence I felt it was a traumatic experience. My brothers and sisters were a few years older than me and I thought they were always "picking" on me. I threw a lot of temper tantrums. I would get upset because it was the four of them against me. I felt that even my parents were on their side. During adolescence, I grew up more as an individual than a group oriented child. Quite often, I would get the feeling that people were against me and would be very defensive. Whatever, I would play in a group, however. I was alright as long as I was an important member in that group. Although, as soon as I realized I wasn't important, I didn't want to play or thought to myself, maybe we should do something else that I could contribute more to. It always seemed to be my older sister who would come and take this "confidence" or feeling of authority away from me.

The first thing that springs to mind are sexual fantasies. There are times when these fantasies consume the better part of a day. They can involve friends, famous people, or even strangers I pass on the street. They're always vivid and explicit, but I don't think of them as X-rated. They always seem to have a teenage innocence, not to mention quite a bit of romanticism.

Another non-specific remembrance of adolescence is the disappearance of simplicity. Suddenly, the clothes I wore, the way my hair was cut, the way I talked all mattered a great deal, unlike my preadolescent years. Also, relationships with people became much more complex.

Do adolescents who experience psychological problems grow out of them? The data bearing on this question reveal some interesting patterns. In the Symptomatic Adolescent Research Project, Masterson (1967, 1968) studied 12- to 18-year-old male and female patients being seen at a private psychiatric facility (the Payne Whitney Clinic). He and his colleagues examined case records, conducted interviews, evaluated questionnaires, and visited patients' homes in order to study the symptom patterns. The patient sample was matched (by age, sex, race, grade, religion, and school type) to 101 persons in a control group who had never been psychologically evaluated or seen in psychotherapy. Seventy-two of the original 101 patients were interviewed at 2½- and 5-year follow-ups (Masterson, 1967b). In these follow-up interviews, patients were rated for minimal, mild, moderate, and severe psychological impairment. More than half of the patients had received treatment of one sort or another after the initial interview, but despite this, 62% of the patient sample exhibited moderate or severe impairment at the 5-year follow-up (more later on which ones did and which did not). In evaluating his findings, Masterson (1967) writes:

> Adolescence was but a way station in a long history of psychiatric illness that began in childhood and followed its own inexorable course—a course only temporarily colored by the developmental stage of adolescence. The decisive influence was psychiatric illness, not "adolescent turmoil". (p. 1343)
>
> The poor clinical outcome, together with the persistence of underlying conflicts and persistence of underlying conflicts and pathologic character traits, strongly indicate that the growth process if left to its own devices does not "iron out" adolescent difficulties. (p. 1344)

Masterson goes on to say that the adolescent may show fewer symptoms, but we should not be satisfied with this since:

> . . . the persistence of these conflicts makes them vulnerable to a variety of environmental stresses while at the same time the pathologic character traits impair their flexibility to respond to stress. Rather than growing out of their difficulties they have found ways to adjust to them, which, while enabling them to function better, at the same time leave them vulnerable to future stress. (p. 1343)

In Masterson's view then, serious psychological problems in adolescence often extend into adulthood. They make adolescents vulnerable to normal and abnormal stress in adolescent microsystems.

Some studies suggest, however, that certain kinds of problems in childhood and adolescence are better predictors of later adult maladjustment than other kinds of problems. Difficulties in areas related to cognitive functioning (deficient school performance, confused or disordered thought processes, impaired ability to make moral judgments) and antisocial behaviors (arson, vandalism, stealing, assaultiveness) predict adult disturbance with much greater accuracy than emotional, or what have been termed *neurotic* problems (shyness, dependency, nervousness, anxiety, depression) (Robins, 1966, 1972, 1979; Cass & Thomas, 1979). For example, Masterson himself (1972) found that 91% of the adolescent neurotics (who were plagued by troublesome feelings but were not antisocial) were unimpaired as adults, but that *all* those with seriously distorted views of the world and behavior motivated by antisocial personalities *(sociopaths)* were still moderately or severely impaired in adulthood. So it matters whether the problem is mainly one of how one *feels* versus mainly of how one *thinks* and *acts*, with the latter presenting a poorer prognosis.

In a hospitalized sample, Annesley (1961) found that two to five years after admission, only 19% of the seriously disturbed had recovered and 23% improved. For those diagnosed as exhibiting antisocial behavior disorders, 38% had recovered and 22% had improved. Among this group, outcomes of those who exhibited *multiple* antisocial behaviors (e.g., stealing, violence, *and* truancy) were worst, while those who showed a singular, isolated antisocial behavior of whatever kind had much better outcomes. Neurotics fared best, with 40-55% recovered and 24-50% improved. Warren (1965) found similar results.

In addition to the *kind* of problem considered, the *severity* of a problem and the frequency with which it occurs have been shown to be relevant as an indicator of possible psychopathology in children and adolescents (Rutter, Tizard, & Whitmore, 1970; Rutter, Graham, Chadwick, & Yule, 1976). The number of problems the child is experiencing also appears to be a valid indicator of later psychopathology. The more symptoms children exhibit, the more likely they will later be diagnosed as suffering from some form of clinical psychopathology (Rutter, Tizard, & Whitmore, 1970; Robins & Wish, 1977; Robins, 1979). This suggests that exhibiting one problem is relatively normal, while exhibiting several is not. This will be something to remember in Chapter 12 when we discuss intervention because it tells us that professionals must pay special attention to the multiproblem youth.

Another important dimension to consider is the age-appropriateness of a behavior, because it helps us predict whether or not a problem is likely to have long-term consequences. Longitudinal studies provide us with information on what kinds of behavior tend to occur at what age. The Berkeley Growth Study (Macfarlane, Allen, & Honzik, 1954) is an example of such a study. Every third child born in Berkeley, California, for an 18-month period was assessed annually to detect the presence of 39 symptoms of psychopathology. This study provided information about what kinds of symptoms tend to occur at what age. This is important, for, as Weiner (1982) points out, if a six-year-old complains of poor appetite, it does not have the same meaning as it does in a 14-year-old. We find from the study that 40% of six-year-old girls complain of poor appetite, whereas among 14-year-olds, this is an uncommon complaint. Therefore, we may be unconcerned about the six-year-old noneater, but the 14-year-old noneater may be showing signs of depression, or perhaps some kind of eating disorder (such as anorexia nervosa, a problem that has received widespread public attention in recent years).

We see then that whether or not problems in adolescence predict problems in adulthood depends on many factors. Some kinds of problems seem to carry over into adulthood, while others do not. The important point, however, is that we cannot assume that the disturbances of the teenager are just a phase. Serious problems experienced during adolescence, particularly if they are numerous, are to be taken very seriously, and sometimes require the help of a professional (our topic in Chapter 12).

Delinquency

We saw in the previous section that age is an important factor in evaluating the appropriateness of problematic behavior. The consideration of age in judging behavior has been institutionalized by American society in the way it deals with juvenile misbehavior.

The United States established a juvenile justice system at the turn of the twentieth century. Before this time, criminal action by a child over the age of seven was punished in the same manner as an adult perpetrator. The juvenile justice system was established in response to the belief that children were dependent, not yet responsible for their actions, and in need of special guidance and nurturing, not punishment. Rather than being considered a *criminal*, the child who committed a crime was termed a *juvenile delinquent*.

In addition to juvenile delinquents, society has come to recognize another group of misbehaviors as *status offenses*. Status offenders have not broken any criminal laws that apply to adults, but they have demonstrated *wayward or incorrigible* behaviors such as running away from home, using tobacco or alcohol, or engaging in sexual intercourse. These behaviors are illegal *only* because the individuals performing them are under age, dependent, and not considered responsible for themselves. Therefore, the important difference between a juvenile delinquent and a status offender is that a juvenile delinquent violates laws that apply to everyone (adult or minor), while a status offender violates laws that apply only to his or her particular age bracket.

Now that we have defined juvenile delinquency, we can ask the usual questions: Who are they? Why do they do it?

These are difficult questions because the answers depend in large part on how we gather the data. Remember that in analyzing family relations in Chapter 6 we also observed that what you conclude about adolescence depends in large part on how and where you look; what methods and sampling techniques you use. The same is true here as well. There are two main sources for data on crime. The first source of data on delinquency comes from the official sources. The two most extensive of these are the Uniform Crime Report (UCR), and the National Crime Panel (NCP). The UCR is compiled by the Federal Bureau of Investigation, and reflects the record keeping of law enforcement agencies, which makes it liable to bias and distortion based upon local policies and practices, a real problem according to a Police Foundation study (Burnham, 1984). The NCP is a survey of households and businesses that is undertaken every six months, and is based on a national probability sample. More than 130,000 individuals are surveyed by the NCP each year. This survey is conducted by the United States Bureau of Census, under the sponsorship of the U.S. Department of Justice.

The second main source is self-report surveys of crime, such as the National Surveys of Youth. These confidential surveys ask people whether they have engaged in certain specific illegal activities. As might be expected, these two sources do not always agree. The discrepancy becomes quite large when dealing with the question of who commits delinquent acts.

We present findings from self-report and official sources to outline the current picture of delinquency from two perspectives. We then present a brief discussion of the difference between self-report and official data in the hope of clearing up some of the confusion created by the conflicting sources of data. We should note, however, that the methodological issues concerning self-report vs. official sources are complex, and experts in the field are still trying to resolve them. There are problems of whether the measures actually assess what they claim to assess, as well as whether they do so in a way that yields the same results each time they are used.

Self-Report Studies

One advantage of self-report studies is that they include individuals who may engage in delinquent activity but do not come to the attention of law-enforcement agencies. Thus, in theory, this approach provides a perspective on delinquency that is unbiased by official law enforcement policies, prejudice, and record-keeping techniques. This is important, because policies and practices differ from place to place, as well as from time to time.

The 1972 National Survey of Youth interviewed a representative sample of 1,395 American youth between the ages of 11 and 18 in 40 geographical areas around the United States (Gold & Reimer, 1975). The youth were interviewed by a young adult of the same sex as the respondent. They were given 17 cards, each of which described a particular delinquent act (e.g., property destruction, carrying a concealed weapon, theft, etc.), and asked to sort the items into three piles which indicate whether they had committed the act "never," "once," or "more than once" within the last three years. They were assured of the anonymity and confidentiality of the interview and urged not to respond if they could not be completely honest.

It was found that 18-year-old boys and girls admitted to having committed nearly five times more nontrivial delinquent acts than 11-year-olds report (it should be noted that although the question sampled the previous three years to the present for each age group, 81% of the reported acts had been committed in the previous year).

Although there is a fairly stable rise in the overall frequency of delinquent acts from ages 11 to 18, the largest jump in the rate was found to occur between the ages of 14 and 15. This fact is especially interesting when we consider the severity of the crimes. The investigators classified crimes according to their seriousness using scales developed by Sellin and Wolfgang (1964) and found that for both males and females, the highest peak of seriousness occurs at the age of 15 (although the males tend to commit much more serious acts overall).

While there is a significant sex difference in the findings, no differences in delinquent behavior by race or class were found. The issue of race and class differences in delinquency research is a complex one, and we will return to it in our discussion comparing self-report with official statistics (which *do* show social class differences).

The largest self-report study of delinquency to date is the 1977 National Youth Survey (Elliot & Ageton, 1980). This study interviews the same people over a long period *(longitudinal panel design)* and includes a cross-section of households in the continental United States. The sample originally included 2,375 youths, aged 11–17 in 1976. Seventy-three percent of the original sample (N = 1,726) agreed to participate in the study, and completed the 1977 interviews. The investigators report that their findings with regard to the age and sex distribution of the delinquent behavior of their sample agree with other large scale self-report studies, such as the 1972 survey reported above, and others (Hirschi, 1969; Williams & Gold, 1972; Illinois Institute for Juvenile Research, 1973; Gold & Reimer, 1975; Elliot & Voss, 1974). Males report more, and more serious delinquent acts, and the peak for delinquency comes at age 15.

Elliot and Ageton (1980) do differ from the previous self-report studies in reporting class and race differences in self-reported offenses. For race, they found a black/white differential in total offenses of nearly 2:1. For predatory crimes, this ratio increased to over 2:1. They found significant but less extreme class differences in self-reported delinquency. Lower-class youth reported more delinquent behavior than working- or middle-class youth. On the dimension of predatory crimes against persons, the lower- to middle-class differential is 3:1.

In this study of self-reported delinquency then, the investigators found that delinquent behavior was more frequent among racial minorities and lower-class youth. We will return to this study and the issue of class and race differences after a brief look at the official statistics on delinquency.

Uniform Crime Reports

In his foreword to the 1981 edition of the Uniform Crime Reports, William Webster, the director of the Federal Bureau of Investigation writes:

> An issue of great concern is youthful criminal involvement. In spite of various changes in the realm of criminal activity, one element has remained constant—the age group that tends to be arrest prone. Those individuals between the ages of 16 and 24 are arrested with greater frequency than any other segment of the population. Short-term studies reveal that the peak age for violent crime arrests is 18 and for property crime arrests, the age of 16 . . .

In the percent distribution of total arrests, a peak is reached at 5.8 for 18-year-olds. Looking at the category of violent crime, 18-year-olds lead all single year age groups, with 26,815 arrests, or 5.8% of the total. In property crime, 13- to 14-year-olds lead every other age category by far with 163,644 total arrests for a percentage of 8.9 of the total. Breaking property crime down into its component elements of burglary, larceny-theft, motor vehicle theft, and arson, larceny-theft and arson primarily differentiate the 13- to 14-year-olds from other age groups. While we are all relatively familiar with the definition of arson (setting fires), it may help us to understand the nature of the delinquent behavior of the 13- to 14-year-old if we are certain of the definition of *larceny-theft*. The *UCR* defines this category as:

> . . . the taking, carrying, leading, or riding away of property from the possession or constructive possession of another. It includes crimes such as shoplifting, pocket-picking, purse-snatching, thefts from motor vehicles, thefts of motor vehicle parts and accessories, bicycle thefts, etc., in which no use of force, violence, or fraud occurs.

Notice also that this age group is involved in a significant percentage of violent crime (3.5% of total arrests). In short, youth involvement in crime is a very serious problem.

While the official data are in agreement with the self-report studies on the variable of age, this agreement breaks down on the variable of race. The data show that blacks account for 24.3% of all arrests of persons under the age of 18. According to the 1981 U.S. Bureau of Census Report, approximately 14% of persons under 19 are black. In terms of *overall arrests* then, blacks are somewhat overrepresented. Looking at the violent crime category, we see that 53.4% of arrests of persons under 18 are black. This is about four times their proportional representation in the population. In the past, many have concluded that the official data on race reflect the biases of law-enforcement agencies, and that in fact blacks are not involved in more crime, they just tend to be arrested more frequently because they are black. This argument derives support from the fact that self-report instruments traditionally do not reflect this overrepresentation of blacks. We can see why the issue of the discrepancy between perspectives is such a crucial one, and why much has been made of the 1977 National Youth Survey's findings (Elliot & Ageton, 1980), a point we will return to shortly.

The National Crime Survey—The Perspective of Crime Victims

The last source of data we consider here is the National Crime Survey (NCR) described earlier. This study reports crime from the *victim's* point of view. We should note that the accuracy of the results of this report depend completely on the accuracy of the victim's perceptions of the offender. The victim does have the opportunity to respond that they "do not know" if they are unsure of a characteristic of the offender, however.

In averaging the results of the surveys conducted during the years 1973–1977, Hindelang (1981) reports black males have the highest incidence of offending in personal crimes (rape, robbery, assault, and larceny from the person). White males have the second highest rate, black females the third, and white females the lowest rate. The black-to-white ratio for incidence rates of offending for males is 5:1, and the peak age for offending is the 18-20 group.

Violent offenses are a sum of rapes, aggravated assaults, and simple assaults; *theft offenses* are a sum of robberies and larcenies. The peak age for violent offenses is again 18-20 for males, with black male rates over three times that of whites. The greatest racial difference in incidence rates is found for theft offenses, where black male incidence rates are 11 to 20 times that of the next highest group. Hindelang (1981) demonstrates that the NCS data closely parallel the UCR data for 1976 on the robbery dimension.

Self-Report Data Vs. Official Arrest Records

Self-report measures of delinquency have generally presented a picture of the incidence and distribution of delinquency that contrasted with official arrest records. Both of these types of studies have shown significant age and sex differences, but the difference is much smaller with self-report measures than with official arrest data (Williams & Gold, 1972; Gold & Reimer, 1975; Elliot & Voss, 1974; Illinois Institute for Juvenile Research, 1973; Bachman et al., 1970, 1971; 1978). As we suggested earlier, however, the main focus of debate has been that self-report studies generally minimize differences in delinquent behavior by class or race, while official reports accentuate them (Gold & Reimer, 1975; Elliott & Voss, 1974; Williams & Gold, 1972; Hirschi, 1969; Bachman et al., 1970, 1971, 1978; Illinois Institute for Juvenile Research, 1973). Investigations using police and court data find significant differences by both class and race (Wolfgang et al., 1972; Williams & Gold, 1972; Gordon, 1976; Short & Nye, 1957).

The discrepancy concerning race and class seems to be due to the fact that self-report measures tend to emphasize less serious crimes than the Uniform Crime Reports, and whites tend to report more involvement in the less serious offenses while blacks tend to report less frequent, more serious offenses (Hindelang, Hirschi, & Weis, 1979). Thus, in the self-report data, frequency and seriousness tend to balance each other out. There is also some corroborating evidence gained from checking to see if those on the books for offenses self-reported those offenses when asked to as part of a research study (what is called a *reverse record check*). Black male offenders *fail* to self-report official offenses at a rate about three times greater than whites—57% vs. 20% for serious offenses (Hindelang, Hirschi, & Weis, 1981). This helps resolve the apparent contradictions.

As reported earlier, Elliot and Ageton (1980) *did* find race and class differences in self-reported delinquency in their study, results closely paralleling official *UCR* data. They conclude that three factors led to their bridging the gap between *UCR* and self-report study results: A) their items were picked more carefully, and fully represented the offense areas in question, B) their response sets reflected the total frequency range of committing an action, being less limited than previous studies that provided response categories such as "never" or "more than once," and C) previous studies using only summary measures obscured important differences in the type and seriousness of offenses. In fact, when they reanalyzed their data using the traditional rather limited response sets used in previous self-report studies, they found no significant differences along racial or class lines, and were thus in agreement with the traditional self-report studies. We conclude from this that "normal" delinquent acts are dispersed widely across the population, but that among racial minorities (most notably blacks), these normal antisocial acts are more likely to grow into a pattern of serious criminal activity. Why? The ecology of race documents the syndrome of limited opportunities and social discrimination that is fertile ground for antisocial behaviors.

What is more, recent research and analysis by Hindelang, Hirschi, and Weis (1979) suggests that it is race and ethnic differences that account for what have long appeared as social class differences. If the data are examined separately for males and females of all different races and ethnic groups, it appears that there are no real differences among social class groupings *within* those breakdowns. But keep in mind, of course, that there are big social class differences between racial groups in North America, so race and social class are often linked together.

Elliot and Voss (1974) report an analysis that appears to demonstrate that the lowest SES class group in the study has about 4.5 times the number of police contacts than their highest SES group per 100 self-reported offenses. Hindelang and his colleagues (1979) show that this relationship is confounded by sex and ethnicity, and a true picture of the data is obtained when the data are separated by these variables. A reanalysis of the original data separately for males and females within different ethnic groups produced *no* significant effects of social class on the police contact ratios.

As we stated earlier, the debate goes on concerning the discrepancy between self-report and official sources of delinquency, and we cannot present the final word. The picture of delinquency that appears to be emerging from all data perspectives, however, is that crimes against property tend to be committed by 15-year-olds more often than any other age group, that crimes against persons are committed most often by 18-year-olds, and that poor blacks are involved in delinquency at a higher rate than affluent whites.

Theories of Delinquency

Now that we have some idea of the prevalence and incidence of delinquency in the United States (*who* does it), we consider *why*. Weiner (1982) has identified several types of delinquency that emerge from studies of the causes of misbehavior: *sociological delinquency, characterological delinquency, neurotic delinquency.* This categorization scheme helps us sort out different classes of causes. The minute we ask *why* we should recall that each of the major theories we discussed in Chapter 5 will have its own answers. Behavioral theories emphasize the modeling and reinforcement effects of delinquent peers and adults. Psychodynamic theories emphasize unresolved parent/child authority issues, aggressive impulses, and fantasy. Cognitive-developmental theories focus upon primitive moral analysis.

Sociological Delinquency

Sociological delinquency is defined as illegal behavior that is encouraged by membership in a gang or group that endorses antisocial norms for conduct, and it thus reflects an anthropological and social learning view. In the *Diagnostic and Statistical Manual of Mental Disorders*, Third Edition, known as DSM-III (American Psychiatric Association, 1980), this kind of delinquent behavior would be diagnosed as a *socialized conduct disorder*, either of the aggressive or the nonaggressive type. The key point is that these youth engage in delinquent behavior with others as part of a well-defined group experience, as opposed to committing these acts on their own. As Jenkins (1955, 1957) has described it, delinquency occurs in an organized, premeditated manner as a means of affirming the values and solidarity of the group. These youth do not experience psychological distress as a result of this behavior if they are truly socialized into the group's antisocial norms. They have many friends (the group members), and feel accepted and secure (Empey, 1969; Friedman, Mann, & Friedman, 1975; Glaser, 1965; Quay, 1979; Short, 1974).

It is important to note that while these children may gain security and acceptance from this gang membership in the short run, the reader will recall that research shows that exhibiting antisocial conduct disorders during adolescence is a strong predictor of later adult maladjustment. It is possible for experiences that feel good psychologically at the time they occur to have psychologically negative effects because of the *social* consequences (something to keep in mind later when we consider sexual abuse). Follow-up studies have shown that poor outcomes are associated with antisocial youth to a much greater degree than for neurotic youth (those exhibiting tics, speech difficulties, shyness, fears, oversensitiveness, nervousness, irritability, tantrums, and insomnia) (Quay & Werry, 1972). In follow-up studies conducted in Dallas (Michael, Morris, & Soroker, 1957; Michael, 1957) and St. Louis (Robins, 1966), when antisocial youth became adults they showed more psychiatric hospitalization, more job difficulties, problems with the law, with families, and with social relationships than did neurotics. So, while socialized delinquents may not experience psychological distress as youngsters, this mode of behavior does *not* appear to continue to serve them well as adults. Remember that our ecological perspective tells us to look beyond the microsystem at one point in time.

Characterological Delinquency

Individuals displaying characterological delinquency tend to be loners and have been called *asocial, antisocial, psychopathic,* and *sociopathic personalities*. They do not show regard for the rights of others and seem unable or unwilling to control their behavior. They trust no one, and engage in social interaction only to further their own ends through the manipulation of others. They tend to act out of impulse and calculating selfish desire, rather than by group pressure of peer acceptance as does the sociological delinquent. Such delinquent behavior may reflect deficiency in moral development, adverse social learning in the family microsystem, and even personal deficits in personality traits such as empathy. The psychoanalytic theorist would see a weak superego.

This behavior is diagnosed in the 1980 American Psychiatric Association's Diagnostic and Statistical Manual (DSM-III) as an *undersocialized conduct disorder,* either of the aggressive or nonagressive type. After the age of 18, this behavior fits the DSM-III diagnosis of *antisocial personality disorder.*

Neurotic Delinquency

While the first two patterns of delinquency are of a chronic, recurring nature, neurotic delinquency is out of character for the individual and has been called *acute, anxious, accidental,* and *situationally provided* delinquency (Genshaft, 1980; Hare & Cox, 1978; Smiley, 1977; Weiner, 1975, 1982). Neurotic delinquency occurs as an expression of psychosocial problems or concerns the individual is experiencing, rather than as a deliberate attempt to break the law for the antisocial and personal gain aspects of such behavior. Those who know these individuals are often surprised to learn that these normally very well-behaved youngsters are suddenly engaging in illegal activities. It is easy to see that the psychoanalytic perspective would interpret such behavior as a reflection of improper balance among the id, ego, and superego.

These individuals seem to act in this manner to satisfy unmet needs for attention, affection, admiration, and assistance in helping to solve personal problems. They are unable or unwilling to communicate these needs in a more direct manner, and resort to delinquent behaviors that they are certain will lead to their drawing attention to themselves. These tendencies are neurotic in that they are maladaptive indirect means for meeting psychological needs. Getting arrested as a result of feeling lonely and neglected is not very adaptive, for example, when more adaptive means for seeking help exist.

The Adolescent Runaway

Running away to and, more significantly, running away in America has traditionally grown out of a mixture of youthful expectations and the hope for a better life away from home as well as out of frustrations and despair over current life circumstances. (Liebertoff, 1980, pp. 151–152)

Yeah, I ran. I ran to get away from that house and the people in it. I wanted to be on my own without all the hassles . . . Yeah right, so I ended up on the street. No job because I was too young; no place to stay because I didn't have any money. So when this dude approached me I went with him . . . You know the rest of the story. (a 15-year-old runaway)

Running away from home has a long tradition in America. It played an important role in the settlement of the Western frontier and is immortalized in Mark Twain's classic *Huck Finn.* As romantic as it sounds, running away has become a significant social issue in the United States. While traditional reasons for leaving home may continue to motivate young people to hit the road, the social stakes are higher and the challenges greater for today's runaway. The prolonged period of adolescence as a moratorium from adultlike responsibilities such as work has destroyed many of the legitimate economic roles into which runaway youth once could fit. In an earlier era, when full-time, unskilled and uncredentialized work was the norm for adolescents, a runaway youth could readily fit into a new community. Now, there are few legitimate work roles for the runaway adolescent, and this pushes some adolescents into socially illegitimate and dangerous economic activities such as prostitution, robbery, the drug trade, and other forms of hustling. Like high school dropouts, runaways have become social deviants since their place in the social order has been displaced by changes in the economic and educational systems. Along with these social changes, a general aging of the population has pushed the entrance into adulthood further and further away from the typical 16-year-old runaway and nonrunaway alike.

But, let us remember that the greater economic opportunities for runaways in earlier times did not mean that there were no social risks for the runaways of the 19th and early 20th centuries. The neglect and predatory exploitation that characterizes the plight of many runaways today existed in earlier times as well. In his excellent historical review, Libertoff (1980) cites the observations of George Matsell, a 19th century police official in New York City (as reported in Bremmer, 1970, p. 755):

> . . . a large proportion of these juvenile vagrants are in the daily practice of pilfering whatever offers and begging where they cannot steal . . . The female portion of the youngest class, those who have only seen some eight or twelve summers, are addicted to immoralities of the most loathsome descriptions.

They are still there, of course, and the "loathsome immoralities" are institutionalized in major urban centers where illicit sex and drug industries and their exploitative subsidiaries are located.

What is a runaway? And, how many are there? These two questions are the obvious starting point for our discussion. The number depends, of course, on the precise definition used in accounting them. In 1976, the *National Statistical Survey on Runaway Youth* conducted by Opinion Research Corporation reported that there were about 733,000 youth aged 10–17 who were absent from home at least overnight without parental permission (Nye & Edelbrock, 1980). Only when the definition of running away as "absent without parental permission for two hours or more" was used did the figure reach one million. To complicate the picture even further, the *National Statistical Survey* reported that in nearly half the cases of 10- to 17-year-olds absent from home without permission, the parents knew where the AWOL youth had gone, expected them to return, and thus did not define the incident as running away. In our discussion we will reserve the term *runaway* for youth who leave home without permission, are gone at least one night, and intend to remove themselves from the parents' awareness and control (cf., Nye & Edelbrock, 1980). These issues are very important from the social worker's perspective in properly diagnosing the meaning and significance of running away.

According to the *National Statistical Survey*, runaways come from across our society, but the likelihood that a family will produce a runaway bears some relation to its socioeconomic and demographic character. Low-income families and, to some extent, upper-income families have more than their share of runaways. Middle-income families have the lowest rate. Likewise, very small families (one parent, one child) and very large families (six or more children) have higher rates than medium-sized families. Overall, about 3% of American families produce an adolescent runaway in a given year. Overall, about 12% of America's youth run away by the time they are 18 years old, and age 16 seems to be the peak year for running away (with about 31% being that age). The rate is about the same for males and females; for anglos and blacks; for white collar and blue collar. In their review of this evidence, Nye and Edelbrock (1980) comment on the fact that these national figures depart somewhat from the caseloads of agencies that serve runaways. The served clients tend to be younger and are somewhat more likely to be female. They also note that the *National Statistical Survey* reports some significant regional differences, with lower rates in the Northeast (1.5%) and Southeast (2.1%) and higher rates in the Northwest (5.0%) and West-Midwest (4.1%). This can be a significant factor for those responsible for community-based programs. The picture is especially complex for those who work in areas such as New York and San Francisco that experience significant runaway immigration, as youth from other regions join the pool of "indigenous" runaways. Of course, these runaway meccas face special problems and have special service needs. In New York City, for example, officials estimate that "some 20,000 to 30,000 runaway youth are wandering the street" and unofficial estimates put the numbers much higher (Children's Defense Fund, 1981). As a result, intensive programs exist in major metropolitan areas that can serve as laboratories or research and demonstration projects for developing and evaluating services for runaways. In New York, for example, the Group Live In Experience (GLIE) has been in the business of identifying and meeting needs for service since 1968. Of course, smaller communities may find it difficult to translate such metropolitan-oriented programs to the often substantially different needs they face when dealing with local runaways.

We will have more to say later about how far runaways typically travel, but let us note here that according to the *National Statistical Survey*, only 18% of them travel more than 50 miles from home and 70% had returned home within a week of their departure. This is an important piece of information because it helps to normalize the problem. For most adolescents, most of the time, running away from home is best thought of as an episode. It may grow out of a chronic personal or family problem but the running incident itself is typically a short-term phenomenon. Of course, it may set in motion a long-term process of conflict and/or reorganization in parent/child relations once it is over. Nonetheless, when we consider the magnitude of the runaway problem we must always remember that most running away is, in a sense, self-correcting.

It is clear from survey research and case studies that running away means different things for different people. Like most behaviors, it can result *from* diverse circumstances and result *in* a variety of consequences. Given our problem-orientation, we think it is appropriate to look at running away as both the effect and cause of adolescent troubles.

Running away is an effect of adolescent troubles when it results from problems in the youth's day-to-day existence. Research demonstrates that these problems take three principal forms: *personal maladjustment, family conflict,* and *parental mistreatment.* All three are significant causes of running away, and they can interact with each other in negative ways.

Personal Maladjustment

A substantial minority of runaways are characterized by personal maladjustment of one sort or another in varying degrees. In one empirically grounded study, Edelbrock (1980) used the Child Behavior Checklist in matched samples of children and youth—1300 referred to mental health services *(disturbed)* and 1300 not referred *(normal).* He found that the difference between the disturbed and normal groups was most evident in adolescent girls, some 30% of the disturbed group had run away in the previous year versus about 2% of the normal female adolescents. For males, the disturbed vs. normal comparison was not nearly so significant, 10% vs. about 1%. Overall, running away was associated with five problem behaviors—truancy, use of alcohol or drugs, screaming, and suicidal talk and attempted suicide. As Edelbrock points out, however, ". . . these behaviors are not necessarily *predictive* of running away" (p. 218), since the study did not assess the children and youth systematically before they ran away. The results do indicate that, as a group, runaways are more likely to exhibit a pattern of disturbed social functioning. One additional important conclusion emerged from Edelbrock's study. Although disturbed youth are much, much more likely to run away, most runaways are not disturbed. The low rate among the normal population produces greater numbers of runners than the high rate among the disturbed youth population, because most youth fall into the normal category and relatively few into the disturbed group.

Some runaways exhibit little if any indication of personal maladjustment. These normal runaways, as we shall see later, usually do not go too far from home and soon return of their own accord. However, as we shall also see, these normal runaways may become victims of the web of exploitation and hardship into which a substantial number of runaways fall.

As noted earlier, the runaway population is most characterized by brief runs, relatively close to home. There is evidence of substantial personal maladjustment among those who run far and stay away a long time, however. The evidence comes from a variety of studies of diverse methodological rigor, but includes findings of less favorable self-concepts, poorer interpersonal relationships, greater defensiveness, depression, and feelings of powerlessness and failure (Brennan, et al., 1978; D'Angelo, 1974; Jenkins, 1978; Shellow, et al., 1967; Wolk & Brandon, 1977). These indications of personal maladjustment are not the whole story, of course. We must recognize that family conflict involving otherwise psychologically normal youth can produce running away.

Family Conflict

Behaviorally oriented researchers and clinicians have made an important contribution to our understanding of family dynamics by documenting and explicating how what seem to be innocuous behavioral interactions can build up into full-blown pathological patterns of family conflict. Parents and children can become entrapped in coercive, conflictual behavior patterns through a gradual process of escalating reinforcements (Patterson, 1976). Some families permit minor conflicts to evolve into major confrontations. In some situations, disputes over issues like dinner time, hairstyle, and curfews can divert attention from more basic commitments of love and regard and result in a running incident (Kimball, 1970).

An interesting sex difference has been reported concerning the family context of runaways. In Wolk and Brandon's study of runaways' perceptions of self and parents (1977), they report that runaway girls indicate excessive control as a critical issue while runaway boys indicate inadequate control as an issue. This coincides with the general impression gained from youth that overcontrol is usually more of a problem for females. It may tie in with the finding that teenage boys with single parents and teenage girls with stepparents are at greatest risk for mental health referrals (Kalter, 1977). The former is more likely to be an undercontrol situation while the latter is more likely to bring to the fore the issue of overcontrol.

Most runaways in this category engage in a short run and a relatively quick return. Much more serious seem to be incidents of running that are a response to parental mistreatment.

Parental Mistreatment

Evidence continues to accumulate documenting the role of parental mistreatment in producing running away from home. For youth exposed to chronic mistreatment at the hands of parents or guardians, running away from home may constitute a "healthy and adaptive response to an impossible situation" (Silbert & Pines, 1981). What is more, some runaways are actually "throwaways," in the sense that they are rejected by their parents and forced into the streets.

Several studies have linked parental mistreatment to running away from home, particularly in cases where the adolescent goes far and stays away a long time (Garbarino & Gilliam, 1980). An H. E. W. report estimated that mistreatment figured in one-third to one-half the cases of running away served by agencies. Houten and Golembiewski (1976) concluded that more than 80% of all serious runaways flee serious family problems, particularly abuse and alcoholism. Others who have looked at the situation concur in the conclusion that parental mistreatment is a significant cause of running away (e.g., Ambrosius, 1971; D'Angelo, 1979; Libertoff, 1976). The only existing national study of abused adolescents (Fisher, et al., 1982) found conclusive evidence of this link.

Clearly, all three causes of running can interact. Personal maladjustment, family conflict, and parental mistreatment can become a self-reinforcing, vicious cycle. Victim can become victimizer (Garbarino, 1980), and the effects of damaging family interaction can produce deficits in social competence that precipitate still more conflict. Running away is often bound up in this cycle. All of these causes have a bearing on running itself as a cause of adolescent troubles.

The Risks of Running Away

As we move from considering running away as an *effect* of adolescent troubles to running away as a *cause* of adolescent troubles, we encounter a pattern of developmentally disastrous victimization. Naturally, the personal maladjustment, family conflict, and parental mistreatment that often precipitate running also make the adolescent specially vulnerable to the risks that running away itself produces. The deficits in social competence and self-esteem highlighted earlier as correlates of running will tend to make an adolescent particularly vulnerable to the psychosocial threats of life on the streets. Runaway adolescents who do not return home quickly have inadequate financial resources to meet their basic needs because of their poor prospects for legitimate employment. Thus, they are candidates for recruitment into the illicit economy—dealing drugs, larceny, hustling, prostitution, and pornography. We should certainly consider the role larger society plays in all of this: Our society encourages these illicit activities by both tolerating and directly supporting them.

The proportion of female to male runaways has shifted recently. The 1970s saw the number of female runaways surpass the number of male runaways. The Department of Health, Education and Welfare reported that 68% of all runaways are female (Sarri, 1976). According to the Uniform Crime Reports (1981), 145,301 juveniles were arrested in 1981 as runaways in the United States. Of these, 67,304 were male, and 77,997 were female, with 15-year-olds being the most common for both sexes. Wooden (1976) estimates that about 600,000 youth run away each year.

The link between running away and prostitution has been most clearly demonstrated, but we assume that the results for illicit sex parallel those for drugs and related activities. Silbert and Pines (1981) have reviewed the available evidence and conducted their own study. The conclusion they offer is that the runaway/prostitution link is a clear causal connection. Adolescent runaways cannot meet basic economic needs on the street. They eventually choose or fall into one of three courses: get off the street, steal what they need, or sell what they have. Silbert and Pines report that nearly all the juvenile female prostitutes they interviewed were runaways and nearly 90% cited "needed money, was hungry" as "the main reason for their initial involvement in prostitution." Of course, there are adults who are ready, willing, and able to facilitate this entry into "the life."

Pimps are known to cruise bus stations and runaway hangouts looking for recruits. Once having identified the runaway youth, these predatory adults (perhaps through their adolescent representatives) will offer housing, food, cash, and perhaps even emotional support as a way of engaging the youth for future service. Any runaway youth can be taken in this way, but disturbed youth are particularly vulnerable. Of special concern are adolescents who have a history of having been sexually abused. These adolescents seem most readily channeled into the runaway-prostitution system (cf., Crowley, 1977; Meyerding, 1977). Silbert and Pines (1981) indicate that 60% of the runaway-prostitutes in their sample reported sexual abuse at home prior to running away. Involvement in the sex industry generally brings with it a vicious cycle of victimization—rape, assault, incarceration, and other degrading experiences. And, although most research has focused on female runaways in the sex business, experts generally agree that many male runaways face the same pattern of exploitation and victimization (Meyerding, 1977). Several recent infamous cases have involved male runaways in homosexual victimization and murder. How can the professional helper offer assistance to the runaway? We will have more to say about how the professional helper can offer assistance to the runaway in Chapter 12, but we can consider some of the issues here.

Help for Runaways

We have tried to show that the motives for running away from home differ significantly among adolescents. Some youth are psychologically normal and leave home seeking adventure. Others are suffering from serious personal maladjustment and leave home driven by their inner turmoil. Still others are fleeing conflict or mistreatment. Once on the road, differences in motivation continue to be a significant factor. Although any adolescent on the run can be victimized by predatory elements, run afoul of the law (perhaps through the very act of being AWOL from the family), and otherwise become embroiled in trouble, we believe those who leave home *because* of trouble are most likely to become involved *in* trouble. Furthermore, these youth may be most difficult to serve, to return home, and to restore to the family. It is for this reason that we believe issues of diagnosis and typology are so very important in dealing with adolescent runaways.

Several investigators have suggested dichotomous classification of runaways. It is always appealing to say, "there are two kinds of people in the world: those who X and those who Y." Such dichotomies may even be sufficient for the purpose of a particular agency or professional. For example, a number of professionals and researchers are most concerned with distinguishing between those who go far and stay away a long time and those who stay near home and return home quickly (e.g., Haupt & Offord, 1972; Houten & Golembrewski, 1976). A related interest is in contrasting those who run away once and return permanently and those who run away repeatedly. Indeed, a follow-up study by Olson, Liebow, Mannin and Shore (1980) found that repeaters showed much higher levels of personal and social dysfunction as young adults than did one time runaways. The repeaters were characterized by academic and vocational failure coupled with court involvement. They also appeared to have had disrupted family relationships even before they ran that became worse when they returned (or were returned). This suggests that professionals should be especially concerned about adolescents who run more than once. Nye and Edelbrock (1980) have incorporated this concern into their treatment typology. They focus on the degree of alienation and ambivalence between youth and parents and suggest alternative counseling orientations. It appears that many runaways are able to reintegrate themselves into their families after the dramatic act of running away. As we shall see later, however, one important area for professional activity may be in preparing families to accomplish this process of reintegration.

Other dichotomies used to characterize runaways are *running from* vs. *running to* (Homer, 1973), terms that are analogous to Berger and Schmidt's (1958) *reactive runaway* vs. *spontaneous runaway* and Tsunt's (1966) *escapist runaway* vs. *romantic adventurer.* Professionals may find these dichotomies useful. Another classification with much appeal is Scientific Analysis Corporation's (1976) designation of runaways who are *sick, bad,* or *free,* i.e., disturbed, delinquent, or adventure-seeking. This trichotomy is useful in highlighting the diversity of needs and resources among the runaway group, as well as cautioning against a simplistic view of runaways as uniformly *reasonable, noble,* or *victimized.* Brennan and his colleagues (1978; 1980) have produced the most sophisticated typology of runaways. Based on a variety of statistical clustering techniques, Brennan and his group used interview data gathered from 183 runaways to generate seven types of runaways in two broad categories. Once they had statistically grouped the cases, they examined the characteristics of each type to give it a label.

Class 1:   Not Highly Delinquent, Nonalienated Runaways

Type 1:   Young, overcontrolled escapists
Type 2:   Middle-class loners
Type 3:   Unbonded, peer-oriented runaways

Class 2:   Delinquent, Alienated Runaways

Type 4:   Rejected, peer-oriented runaways
Type 5:   Rebellious and constrained middle-class dropout girls
Type 6:   Normless, rejected, unrestrained youth
Type 7:   Rejected push-outs

In their efforts to assess the validity of these categories, Brennan and his colleagues (1978) have found differences among them in specific aspects of the running syndrome. For example, they report that Type 1 runaways were most likely to return home within a day and stay close to home, Type 5 youth were most serious about actually planning a long-term break, and Type 7 adolescents were most likely to be repeaters and to elicit minimal parental interest upon their return (Brennan et al., 1980). The Brennan typology may be particularly useful for agencies planning a large-scale institutional response to runaways and who therefore need a sophisticated system of classification. For the individual professional or small agency, the simpler dichotomies or trichotomies may suffice to highlight important issues in assessment and case management.

Ideally, agencies and individual professionals will be able to match their service to the specific needs of each individual runaway using the most sophisticated and elaborated diagnostic categories available. In fact, however, only the grossest discriminations are often possible because of limited information (e.g., the absence of a family contact), legal restrictions (e.g., confidentiality, "innocent until proven guilty" and "least restrictive alternative" mandates), and scarcity of resources (e.g., having only a small fraction of the residential facilities needed). Therefore, practitioners will need to adapt and simplify the typologies to meet their needs and resources.

We should note here that all the typologies discussed earlier deal with running away from home. This, of course, is our principal concern. Just as most discussions of child maltreatment focus on abuse and neglect in the family context, most discussions of running away are limited to running away from parents. However, a second form of both maltreatment and running away concerns institutions. Running away is one of the more difficult problems faced by many residential facilities. In fact, the runaway rate is one of the commonly used indicators of program operation used by those charged with the responsibility of managing such institutions. For example, the "Teaching Family Program" at Boys Town in Nebraska reports a decline in the facility's runaway rate (from a monthly average of 7.3% to just 1.5%) as testimony to the program's success (Watson, et al., 1980). Running from foster home placements is a related and vexing problem where troubled adolescents are concerned (Friedman, 1978).

Summary

Running away from home is not a new phenomenon, but contemporary society makes it especially risky. The costs to the adolescents, to their families, and to society are substantial. The link between running away and illicit activity is now well established, particularly for repeaters, of whom roughly half admit illicit activities such as theft, according to survey data (Brennan et al., 1978). The link between running away and the sex industry is particularly disturbing.

The causes of running are multiple and often benign, particularly for the majority of runaways who do not go far and who return home relatively quickly. However, those who run away to escape overwhelming personal and family trouble are a serious social problem. Their troubles tend to be exacerbated and multiplied by life on the run and on the streets. They require intensive and sustained intervention by sensitive professionals who are willing and able to handle these troubled and often troublesome youth.

Juvenile Prostitution

Although much has been written on the subject of prostitution, surprisingly little has been written specifically on adolescent prostitution, male or female. Most of the research is based upon samples of females, but researchers are beginning to examine male prostitution. We do know that teenage prostitution is not a recent development or one limited to North America; it has been found in many times and places. Nineteenth century England saw widespread adolescent prostitution as industrialization that upset the socioeconomic fabric of society (Baizerman, Thompson & Stafford-White, 1979). There does seem to have been an upsurge of adolescent prostitution linked to the runaway problem in recent decades in North America, however. Society's tolerance of adolescent prostitution (and indeed of the sex industry in general) combines with adverse family dynamics to produce a widespread problem not likely to disappear or be solved easily (Brown, 1979). Data from the Uniform Crime Reports reveal that in comparison to 1972, there was a 125.5% increase from 1971–1981 for individuals *above* 18, but for teenagers *below* 18, there was a *160.8%* increase in prostitution (Uniform Crime Reports, 1981).

Female Juvenile Prostitutes

The Delancey Street Foundation conducted a study of 200 street prostitutes in San Francisco (Silbert & Pines, 1981). These individuals were contacted "through the streets," as opposed to through "official sources" such as the police, which are subject to institutional policy biases. Of these 200 prostitutes, almost 60% were 16 and under, and some were 10 and 11 years old. Of the total 200, 78% reported beginning prostitution as a juvenile, and 68% reported being 16 or younger when they began.

It is clear that adolescent prostitution is a serious and ubiquitous problem, and deserves more attention than it has received. Juvenile prostitutes are apparently the rule rather than the exception, and policy has not been adjusted adequately, both by those who favor a punitive approach and by those who prefer to define prostitution as a *victimless crime.*

Why do they do it? Prostitution may be "the oldest profession," but the evidence shows that for juveniles it is a dangerous and developmentally debilitating pattern of victimization. While there are several aspects of the lives of young prostitutes that seem important in understanding their behavior, none is more consistently implicated in the research than feelings of alienation from their families. Studies by Kagan (1969), Greenwald (1970), Gray (1973), and James (1976) have revealed home situations characterized by divorce, parental separation, rejection, and abuse. Why do some young people respond to negative home situations by becoming prostitutes, while others do not? Greenwald (1970) studied 20 prostitutes and found that most came from broken homes, but that most also had engaged in a pleasurable sexual experience at an early age with an adult male for which they were rewarded in some way. Greenwald (1970) proposed that the experience of the pleasurable sexual experience with an adult outside of the home in the context of an unrewarding and perhaps punishing home environment may result in the young girl becoming vulnerable to the psychological rewards of prostitution.

In her study of 17 adolescent prostitutes, Gray (1973) found that the average age of the white girl's first sexual encounter was 12.9, while for blacks it was about two years earlier. She also found that by adolescence, all of the girls felt like there was nothing for them at home. Parental ties and family attachment had grown weak, due to the lack of communication, intimacy, supervision, expression of affection, or attention given to the girls by their parents. One of the girls in the Gray (1973) study who was placed in a foster home by her mother expressed it this way:

> I tried to communicate with my mother . . . I wrote down exactly how I felt and I mailed them but she wouldn't write down her feelings in letters. Even when we talked, she didn't have any interest in what I wanted to talk about . . . what I suppose about her now is that she really—that at the time—she didn't really want me and my sister (p. 405).

The picture is one of lonely, dejected girls who feel unloved (at best) at home, and who, in fact, are sometimes abused. Kagan (1969) studied 36 teenage prostitutes in California and found that over half of them felt socially isolated, feeling no real attachment to either parents or peers. The teenage prostitute is likely to have quit school after having experienced repeated failures (Gray, 1973). The values of education have no meaning for her and this may add to the young girl's experience of rejection and social isolation at home.

What are these lonely dejected youth with little schooling to do on their own? If the girl views herself as sexually promiscuous either because of accusations or sexual abuse at home or by schools, she may see herself as a *slut* or *whore* despite overt attempts to rationalize these feelings (James, 1976; Jackman, O'Toole, & Geis, 1963). Thus, the adolescent girl, identifying with socially stigmatized labels, and feeling rejected, may resort to prostitution to support herself. She seems to figure that if she is already paying the psychological price of stigmatization, she might as well play the role.

We must remember just how young these girls are. Many are 12, 13, 14, or 15. They are often quite naive and are ripe for the lines of seduction offered to them from pimps who profess their love for them and their desire to shelter and take care of them. One of the youngest girls (age 13) in Gray's (1973) study spoke of her relationship with her pimp:

> He told me that this wasn't for the money; he really liked me. He told me that he couldn't really hurt me unless I did something he already told me about and I go out and disrespect him. He said we were meant to be together. That made me feel pretty good; so it was love too. He said, "You not only make money for me, you're making it for the two of us." And that really made me feel good. I had what I wanted then. I had him. And really, that's all I wanted but at first I couldn't understand the game because I figured it like this: Why did I have to give him all the money? And he had all his main ladies over my head. I couldn't stand this. I wanted to be number one. But I was with him with love all the time, but I didn't know that he was too. So then, after that, I started going out steady. (p. 415)

As Gray (1973) observes, the social reinforcement this girl received by feeling loved by the pimp outweighed the unpleasantness of giving him all the money. This passage demonstrates quite poignantly the desperation of this girl, her need to feel loved, and the great lengths she will go to in order to feel loved and accepted. Many teenagers who become prostitutes may have this same need for acceptance and intimacy, and this need may play a critical role in the process of socialization to prostitution.

The obvious financial rewards for engaging in prostitution are a major reason mentioned by prostitutes of all ages for their behavior (Gray, 1973; Jackman et al., 1963; Pomeroy, 1965; Hayes, 1974; Brown, 1979). Runaways who are poorly educated have few options and are particularly susceptible to the promise of financial rewards since their employment history tends to be rather sparse and unfulfilling. Some investigators have suggested that the type of jobs many prostitutes have held in the past may have helped them decide to prostitute themselves. Usually they are low-paying, low-skill jobs such as waitressing (James, 1976), go-go dancing (Hayes, 1974), and department store clerking (Rosen & Davidson, 1977). As Brown (1979) has observed, flirtatiousness is encouraged in all of these jobs and because of this, they may encourage the step to the higher-paying enterprise of prostitution. The extra money allows teenagers to acquire the possessions so desirable to them. The research is replete with teenage prostitutes speaking of their desire for clothes and adventure as a motivating force for their behavior. They see and meet prostitutes their age who have things they want and are tempted, by example, to become prostitutes themselves.

Often adolescents view prostitution as a way to escape the boredom and uselessness they feel at home and in school. The girls speak of their desire to experience excitement and a fast-paced social and sexual life that does not exist in the suburbs or rural areas (Pomeroy, 1965; Gebhard, 1969; Jackman et al., 1963; Gray, 1973). James (1976) concludes that prostitutes view being a housewife as the ultimate in boredom and constriction and actively try to avoid such a role. As we have suggested, their personal experience of what home life is like may not have been very attractive. None of the teenage prostitutes in Gray's (1973) study reported having the future goal of being a wife and mother, and none reported being attached to a steady boyfriend. Most reported they had a slim chance of a happy marriage.

The composite image we are left with is of a socially isolated, dejected, unhappy individual who wants to escape a dreary and depressive (possibly abusive) life for the excitement of the big city and the independence that comes with it. The individual quite probably has a negative self-image, has strong needs for affection, and possesses few, if any, job skills. While prostitution may not be on their minds when they leave home, they find it an easy way out when they meet other prostitutes or pimps who convince them of the ease of action. Or, they may be swayed to engage in prostitution by receiving social reinforcement (affection) for such behaviors by pimps and prostitutes who befriend them. There is another way runaways become involved in prostitution, one that is much more sinister and frightening.

Wooden (1976) reports that the average runaway has enough money for three days. This fact is well-known by unscrupulous individuals who look to recruit runaway girls for prostitution. Wooden relates the following incident as described by a teenage prostitute:

> When I got off the bus from Philadelphia, my feet hadn't even hit the ground before these two girls approached me. They knew a place where kids crashed until they could find work. We got into this big shiny car, and another girl shoved something under my nose. I woke up tied down to a bed; a bunch of blacks did a train on me (gang rape). They kept it up all night. They shot me up with scag for a week. After that nothing seemed real. At thirteen, I was a mainlining hooker, working for the street pimps. (p. 86)

Thus, we see that not all adolescent prostitution begins in a voluntary manner. The risks to the young runaway girl in the big city are many, and involuntary commitment to a kind of modern slave trade is a definite, horrifying possibility. Very little is known about these underground organizations, and there is no telling how many young girls have been subjected to such brutal treatment.

Prostitution itself is by no means a safe trade, even if one engages in it voluntarily. Results of the extensive interviews conducted through the Delancey Street Foundation (Silbert & Pines, 1981) in which 60% of the sample was under age 16 reveal many hazards. Of the sample, 78% reported being victimized by forced perversion (an average of 16.6 times for each woman); 70% reported customer rape or going beyond the contract (an average of 31.3 times); 74% reported nonpayment (average 5.2 times); 45% reported being robbed (average 3.6 times); 65% were victims of violence, being physically beaten by the customer, most of the time for no apparent or expressed reason (average 9.2 times); and 49% reported an unfair split of the money with pimps (an average of 35.5 times). These women often blame themselves for their victimization, and feel there is nothing they can do about it. They report they have no options. Thus, these individuals find themselves trapped in a situation where they have little recourse but to keep going. Despite the danger, they proceed in their "profession" because they feel they have no alternatives.

Male Juvenile Prostitutes

There is little information available on male juvenile prostitution (referring here to homosexual prostitution, which by all accounts is the bulk of the problem). Allen (1980) reports that his survey of the Cumulative Medical Index for the past ten years shows that only 10 out of 100 published papers on prostitution refer to males. The Institute for Sexual Research at the University of Indiana (Kinsey Institute) prepared a bibliography on male prostitution in which only 14 English language articles are listed. Psychosocial studies on male prostitution in the United States are relatively rare (MacNamara, 1965; Ginsburg, 1967; Deisher et al., 1969; Gandy & Deisher, 1970; Russel, 1971; Coombs, 1974; Caukins & Coombs, 1976; Allen, 1980). The relative paucity of research in this area is surprising since some experts believe that there may be as many male as female prostitutes (Kinsey, Pomeroy, & Martin, 1948).

Male prostitution is defined as the exchange of money for sexual activities between males. Male prostitutes are likely to be between 14 and 24 years old, unemployed, *usually not* strictly homosexual, with a spotty work history, from a disadvantaged socioeconomic background, below the national average in education level achieved, and from a home characterized by poor parental role models, marital discord, violence, lack of love and affection, and rejection (Allen, 1980; Caukins & Coombs, 1976; Coombs, 1974).

Allen (1980) interviewed 128 male prostitutes in a three-year period between 1974 and 1977, with the aid of a male prostitute who helped make contacts and to verify some of the interview data. A method of referral was developed in which interviewees contacted friends who later participated in the interviews. This study is the largest of its kind to date, and its findings clarify and expand earlier studies of a similar but smaller scope. About the only common characteristic Allen (1980) found among his diverse sample was that these individuals all accepted money for sexual activities. He did, however classify them into four groups.

Group 1 consists of full-time professionals who practice their trade either in the street or through hustling in the bars. The individuals usually portray a very masculine image and may have girlfriends and/or wives whom they support with their activities. They are usually drifters, however, without social attachments. They live for the present, perhaps moving with the warm weather, saving no money, and making no plans for the future. They typically hang out in the poor sections of town and make about $15 to $25 a customer, though they may brag about making much more. These individuals tend to be very young (between 14–18 in this sample), and to be school dropouts. Runaways make up a large portion of this group. Street hustling is considered the lowest form of male prostitution, and so within the subculture, these individuals command little respect. This group is mainly comprised of kids just hitting town and trying to make some money. The older males who stay in this group tend to be just average-looking. Some individuals return to this kind of prostitution when they get older and are no longer able to make it in the more prestigious modes. They become pitiable figures who have little education or job skills and no options available to them (Caukins & Coombs, 1976).

The second group who are also full-time professionals are the *call boys* or *kept boys.* Call boys work through some sort of service or on their own; they are distinguished by their availability to a customer through phone contact. A time and meeting place is worked out, and the call boy meets his client. Call boys are generally more physically attractive than the street or bar hustlers and are also more diverse in their sexual repertoire. They tend to do almost anything the client desires, as long as the client is willing to pay accordingly. They are also used as dates or companions.

Kept boys are much like the female mistress. They are supported by an individual (usually an older male) in exchange for sex. They may live with their benefactor or have the rent on an apartment paid for them. They might do chores around the house. They may live a rather luxurious life, but have no independence.

Like the street and bar hustler, call boys and kept boys tend to have levels of education below the national average and to have few if any job skills. In Allen's (1980) sample, this group tended to have more schooling than the street or bar hustler and tended to be about a year older (average age of 17.6 as opposed to 16.6), in part because it often takes a while to work up to this status.

The third group is composed of part-time prostitutes who have other areas of their life in which they are active. This group largely uses prostitution as a means of supplementing their incomes. Their mode of operation can vary: they usually are street or bar hustlers, but they can also be on call for a few select clients, or work for a pimp. They may be students supplementing their income or work only when they need extra money for a specific event or activity (concert, holiday, etc.). Allen (1980) reports they sometimes work to make money for a date with a girlfriend or boyfriend. This group tends to be about the same age as street and bar hustlers (mean age 16.7 in Allen's [1980] sample). These individuals seem to tend toward more normal levels of education and generally appear better adjusted than any of the other groups.

Group 4 are also part-time prostitutes, but these individuals are part of a peer-delinquent culture. They may pick up a homosexual only to rob him, beat him up, threaten him, or blackmail him. This violent activity can solidify status within the gang culture by proving to one's peers one's masculinity and fearlessness. These individuals may actually be homosexual and may engage in some homosexual activity, but deny it and beat up gays to convince themselves as well as others of their heterosexual persuasion. These individuals tend to be the youngest of all the groups (mean age 15.8 in Allen's [1980] sample), and to have about the same level of schooling as group 3, the part-time hustlers.

Probably the most distinguishing feature of male prostitutes in general is the lack of a stable, intact family upbringing. This finding is identical to the finding for female prostitutes. In Allen's (1980) sample, only 18 out of 98 subjects had an intact family, defined as a family with both parents present and reasonably functional in their role (providing at least some affection, limit-setting, support, and structure). As one might expect, group 3 (part-time nondelinquents) had the highest percentage of intact families (27%) while group 1 (full-time street and bar hustlers) had the lowest (4%). Even in intact families, subjects generally described a home atmosphere lacking warmth and caring, lacking structure (overpermissive), and abusive physically. Only about one-quarter of the fathers and one-half of the mothers of these families were present and effective. About 14% of the fathers were considered ineffective because of alcoholism, while 4% were considered abusive. About one-third of the entire sample were runaways, with *all* of the runaways reporting either absent or ineffective fathers. Runaways accounted for 70% of the membership of groups 1 and 2 (the full-time prostitutes), while only 2 out of the 48 individuals in group 3 (about 1%) were runaways.

Concerning self-described sexual orientation, using Kinsey's classification (Kinsey et al., 1948), Allen (1980) found that most individuals considered themselves bisexual, with group 2 (call boys and kept boys) the most homosexual, and group 3 the next highest. Group 4 was the only group to characterize themselves more heterosexual than bisexual. Group 1 was solidly bisexual.

Male prostitutes tend to be from broken homes, to have a relatively low level of education, and to be bisexual. The absence of the father in the home appears to be an important factor. Many of the street and bar hustlers are runaways who are in desperate need of money and have few or no job skills or work experience. Many of these individuals have low self-esteem and have a high need for the warmth and acceptance they did not find at home. Often, they appear to have given up and become social isolates who are unwilling or unable to develop social attachments. A certain comraderie and sense of community is found within the profession, however.

Male prostitutes often protect each other from robbery and nonpayment. Often, street and bar hustlers will team up and rent rooms or apartments together. There is a definite subculture in which they can feel comfortable. Some part-time prostitutes in the Allen (1980) study in group 3 mentioned that they are not very sexually active or in need of money, but enjoy the acceptance and togetherness they find in the subculture that they find lacking in school or at home. While meeting some psychological needs, the cost to these individuals is high, however.

Venereal disease is one risk (and the recent AIDS crisis a related one), but the lack of vocational development and independence seem the most tragic aspects of the male prostitute's life. They never establish skills they need to survive as independent adults. The ability to plan for the future is not developed, and these individuals may spend their later years in poverty. As Butts (1947) has pointed out, and Caukins and Coombs (1976) have reiterated, our society is very willing to spend money on punishing these individuals, but seems hardly motivated to prevent prostitution or rehabilitate existing prostitutes. The young male prostitute who spends his youth quickly finds himself impoverished in later life, and the prognosis for normal adjustment as an adult is not good.

We have been referring, in a rather vague way, to physical and sexual abuse in the home as an important factor in the background of adolescent prostitutes—male and female. Weber (1977) reports that a study of adolescent prostitutes in the Minneapolis area found that 75% of them were incest victims. While not all children who are abused become prostitutes, abuse itself is an important negative experience which affects psychological adjustment.

Physical, Psychological, and Sexual Abuse

In Chapter 6 we introduced the topic of adolescent maltreatment. According to a national survey (Burgdorf, 1982), the incidence of maltreatment for adolescents equals or exceeds that for younger age groups. Physical abuse is a big part of the problem as we saw in Chapters 1 and 6. Neglect (including encouraging the teenager to leave home, as we saw earlier when we discussed runaways) is also a major problem. Much of the maltreatment adolescents experience is psychological—i.e., being *rejected, terrorized, isolated*, or *mis-socialized* (Hart, 1983). All these forms of maltreatment exist separately, but they often overlap in cases of sexual abuse.

The National Center on Child Abuse and Neglect is specific in its definition of sexual abuse. Sexual abuse involves:

> . . . contacts or interactions between a . . . minor . . . and an adult when the child is being used for the sexual stimulation of the perpetrator or another person when the perpetrator is in a position of power and control over the victim (National Center on Child Abuse and Neglect, 1978, p. 2).

Sexual abuse includes forced intercourse, genital fondling, and exhibitionism (Peters, 1976; Sarafino, 1979). The term rape is usually restricted to the act of sexual intercourse forced upon an unwilling individual, male or female. Physical force, violence, or the threat of violence is involved in rape, while the sexual abuse of the child by the adult may not involve violence—the implicit authority of the adult and the trust in the adult by the child are enough to secure the child's compliance. It is the exploitation of this trust and authority of the adult that lies at the heart of the crime of sexual abuse (Finkelhor, 1979; Garbarino & Gilliam, 1980).

Rape and sexual abuse are frequently perpetrated by people familiar to the victim. DeFrancis (1969) found in his study that 30% of the offenders were relatives, and 45% were acquaintances of the victims. While rape is usually restricted to one circumscribed incident, sexual abuse tends to involve repeated incidents (Finkelhor, 1979). Children may be the victims of sexual abuse for ten years before they let anyone know about it. This is especially true if the abuse is by a family member *(incest)*. Sometimes this is because children do not realize anything is wrong until they get older and are told by the authority figure not to tell anyone. Other times they either know or have a sense that it is wrong, but they are too ashamed or scared to tell anyone about it. It is their own private terror.

Incest is one form of sexual abuse and is defined generally as sexual involvement between two family members, but specific definitions vary. The problem of defining incest is well-illustrated by the range of definitions employed from state to state. The definition varies from "sexual penetration with an ancestor or descendant or brother or sister (whole or half-blood) or uncle, aunt, nephew, or niece by blood" in Alaskan state law, to "a person over 18 who engages in sexual intercourse or deviant sexual conduct with another person who knows the other person is parent, step-parent, child, stepchild, grandparent, grandchild, sibling, aunt, uncle, niece or nephew" in Indiana law (Herman, 1981). Definitions are changing. The trend is for a broader definition, which includes sexual acts other than intercourse. We are concerned with the social and psychological consequences of such behavior within families, not just the biological or genetic repercussions. For this reason, we share the view that sexual acts other than intercourse be included in the definition of incest. Incest may thus be understood as a category of sexual abuse.

Physical and sexual abuse differ in many important ways. Physical abuse may be defined as the inappropriate and developmentally damaging use of force by a parent, a guardian, or other authoritative person (Garbarino & Gilliam, 1980). It is not so much the physical injury that is important as the manner or intent behind the injury. For instance, a broken arm suffered in a football game, while physically painful, may be a source of pride in the young adolescent. A broken arm inflicted by one's father ordinarily has an entirely different meaning.

Physical abuse does not *necessarily* occur during an incident of sexual abuse. In his study on child sexual abuse, DeFrancis (1969) found that only 11% of sexual abuse cases involved direct physical abuse. This is because there is a lack of need for physical coercion in many cases. Physical abuse results in physical pain, whereas in sexual abuse, the pain is frequently restricted to the realm of the psychological (at least among adolescents who are physically mature). In fact, feelings of pleasure that are sometimes experienced during sexual abuse later can cause much more psychological suffering, including guilt. Society is much more permissive of physical abuse than sexual abuse.

Many people approve of the use of physical punishment for disciplining children. However, parents who use physical force as the sole means of shaping the behavior of their children may find they need to increase the level of force applied as the child grows older to achieve the same effect (Garbarino & Gilliam, 1980). This creates a potentially dangerous situation, as the level of violence may escalate until the adolescent is seriously injured, runs away, or strikes back, perhaps injuring the parent (recall the case of "parricide" described in Chapter 1). Increasing the level of violence as the child grows older is a poor way to adjust to the growth of the child. A much more effective approach is to recognize the other areas of growth in adolescence as well, and to make use of the newly forming intellectual and cognitive capacities of these youth by negotiating solutions to behavioral problems. Fortunately, most parents tend to use force less as the child enters adolescence (Gelles, 1978).

Incidence and Related Statistics

It is very difficult to obtain an accurate estimate of the incidence of physical and sexual abuse in the United States. Estimates for physical abuse put the number at about one million (if a very broad definition is used). Sarafino (1979) estimates that there are about 336,200 cases of sexual abuse every year in the United States, some of which are the same cases counted in the physical abuse totals. The National Center on Child Abuse and Neglect estimates that there are at least 100,000 cases of sexual abuse each year. One review concludes that one girl in every four in the United States will be sexually abused before she is 18, *although most of these incidents will be relatively minor,* such as cases of exhibitionism (Weber, 1977). However one estimates the prevalence rate, it is clear that sexual abuse is a problem of major proportion in the United States.

A study by the American Humane Association conducted in New York City in 1967 found that the ratio of girls sexually assaulted to boys is 10:1. However, more recent reports tell us that many more male victims go unreported. This study also found that ¾ of all sexual molestations were committed by someone known to the victim. In 34% of the cases, the offense took place in the home (DeFrancis, 1969). Meiselman (1978) reports that the father-daughter dyad constitutes more than 70% of the cases of sexual abuse. Despite discrepancies in the exact figures, it is clear that incest is a major part of the sexual abuse problem.

Incest and the Human Ecology of Justice

We have defined incest as sexual abuse that occurs in the home. While sexual abuse in general is underreported, incest is especially underreported. Not only are there issues for the victim and family that make it difficult to report, there is evidence that authorities are reluctant to acknowledge incest. In a study of the sexual abuse of children in Minneapolis, the investigators found an inordinate number of cases of *indecent liberties* reported and few cases of incest (Jaffe, Dynneson, & tenBensel, 1975). *Indecent liberties* defines a wide spectrum of activities such as genital exhibition, rectal stimulation, masturbation, physical advances, and the use of obscene language. Closer investigation revealed that there were numerous incidents of incest that the police classified as indecent liberties. As the investigators state, the police "often resort to filing charges under the heading of indecent liberties, when conviction is easier and may be obtained without family members having to give testimony about incest" (Jaffee et al., 1975 as cited in Sarafino, 1979). As Sarafino (1979) points out, district attorneys interested in maintaining a high conviction rate prefer the "indecent liberties" category to incest. So it is apparent that authorities contribute to the underreporting of the crime by misclassifying it. Kinsey and his colleagues (1953) found that one in 16 of the 8,000 white, middle-class women in their survey reported sexual contact with an adult relative during childhood. Finkelhor's research (1979) suggests comparable figures. In almost all cases, the incident remained a secret.

Incest is often much harder for victims to deal with than sexual abuse by a stranger outside of the home. There are several reasons for this. While abuse by a stranger usually involves only one incident, incest often involves a series of activities over a long period of time. It is a relationship, not a single circumscribed event. The average incestuous affair has a duration of 3½ years (Meiselman, 1978). Finkelhor (1979) reports that one girl in his sample was sexually abused by her father from the age of 4 to the age of 15. The incestuous affair is difficult to terminate. Usually daughters do not report the incest, but end the relationship either through marriage or by running away (Meiselman, 1978). As we reported earlier, many of those who escape by running away end up becoming prostitutes.

Another reason incest is difficult to deal with is that there is a lack of a supportive social network for the victim. Who can she tell? As far as parents are concerned, only the mother is available. The mothers in families in which incest occurs (hereafter referred to as *incest mothers*) have been the subject of much speculation and investigation. Theories abound concerning them. One traditional view accuses them of collusion with the father to produce the incestuous situation. These women are seen as cold, withdrawn, depressed, and unable to provide nurturing for the father or the daughter. Desiring to shirk their maternal responsibilities, in this view, they encourage or groom the daughter to become the mother of the household. It is thought that the incest relationship is a source of relief for them (Kaufman, Peck, & Taqiuri, 1954). The incest mother has also been described as passive, dependent, infantile, and masochistic (Courmier, Kennedy, & Saugovicz, 1962). Browning and Boatman (1977) studied 14 incest mothers and found that 9 out of the 14 were clinically depressed, and two were anxious. It seems fair to say that any mother is going to suffer psychologically when she finds there is incest in the home. It is difficult to say for certain what the mother was like before the incest occurred. There may be an interactive effect: she is depressed and withdraws from the husband, then becomes more depressed when he turns sexually to the daughter.

One very prevalent type of incestuous father is the nice guy who will do anything to help anyone, suggesting that he has a high need for acceptance. The mother may be unwilling or unable to provide for his emotional needs, so he may turn to the daughter for his source of love and affection. So many different patterns have been reported in the literature that it is fair to say that there is no clear picture of the incestuous family. Large scale, longitudinal research is necessary to unravel this mystery. Thus, it is difficult to say for certain what the mother's role is in the incestuous family. The point to be made here is that it is not easy for the daughter to turn to the mother for support or for the mother to seize upon a productive course of action.

Denial is often a mechanism employed by the family to mitigate the horrors of incest. Researchers and clinicians report frequently that when daughters do try to tell their mothers and other family members about the incest, they are not believed or taken seriously. Certainly this is understandable. It would be hard to imagine what could threaten family cohesiveness more than incest. Loyalty to the family member, fear of public embarrassment, fear of losing the family income (a real issue if the perpetrator is imprisoned)—all of these are powerful factors that operate against facing the reality of the situation. In many cases the daughter does not attempt to tell the mother, because the mother has put up with a lot of abuse herself and the daughter has learned not to expect any protection from her (Herman & Hirschman, 1977). The mother may feel powerless to do anything about it; she may fear being beaten and may feel a sense of guilt or complicity in the affair herself. Just not knowing what to do, where to go, or what will happen, may be enough to encourage the family to ignore the situation. At times, the daughter is blamed for the problem and made the family scapegoat. Incest affects the members most directly involved, but it is also a family issue, and the dynamics involved are complex.

One caution to keep in mind is that since incest is highly underreported, and only families that have come to the attention of service agencies provide us with information, the data may be biased. It may be that most families that discover incest deal with it effectively on their own. But it is just as possible that they do not. Herman and Hirschman (1977) suggest that it is only the disorganized families who "lack the resources to preserve secrecy" that come to the attention of social agencies. This argument is analogous to the one presented earlier, in which we saw that since only troubled adolescents came to the attention of service agencies for years, professionals had a distorted view of the world of the teenager that helped perpetuate the myth of storm and stress. We must be careful to recognize the limitations of our data, lest we misrepresent the family dynamics surrounding incest.

Just as the family has trouble facing incest, the same appears true for society. One film on the topic is called "The Victim Nobody Believes." While the incidence of sexual abuse approximates that of physical abuse, society has paid much more attention to the battered child and virtually ignored sexual abuse. Every state has laws specifically requiring the reporting of physical abuse, but as late as the mid 1970s nearly half of the states did not specifically mention sexual abuse in their mandatory reporting laws (Weber, 1977). Physical punishment is an accepted form of discipline in North American society. The striking of another can even be understood as an expression of concern and caring in the family context. The point is that physical abuse is at the extreme end of the continuum of an accepted mode of behavior; we can all identify with it. But sexual abuse is abhorrent to society. Cases of sexual abuse, like all sexual matters (see Chapter 8), are hushed up. It seems likely that the sexual abuse situation will not improve until our society is ready to deal with the problem directly and openly and provide easily accessible help for sexual abuse victims.

The Effects of Sexual Abuse

It is hard to say with conviction what the consequences of sexual abuse are to the victim. A lot may depend on the age of the victim when the abuse occurs. Finkelhor (1979) provides an excellent summary of the ongoing debate in the research concerning the consequences to victims. Two major positions exist. One argues that many frightening things happen to children that do not affect them later on and having the genitals fondled or encountering an exhibitionist is just one of them. Kinsey (1953) argued that "it is difficult to understand why a child, except for its cultural conditioning, should be disturbed at seeing the genitalia of other persons" (p. 121). Several surveys and case studies have shown children to be relatively unaffected by these encounters, unless adults make a big deal of it (Gagnon, 1965; Bender & Grugett, 1952; Burton, 1968; Yorukoclu & Kemph, 1969).

The other side argues that hospital emergency rooms are frequently visited by children who have been sexually abused, and they appear to exhibit the same symptoms of disturbance as do adult rape victims (Burgess & Holnstrom, 1974). As Finkelhor reports, there is confusion, crying, depression, and later the guilt, shame, and awareness of stigma in these children just as there is in adults who have been sexually assaulted.

Reports from psychotherapists indicate that large numbers of their clients have been victims of sexual abuse as children (Herman & Hirschman, 1977; Swift, 1977) and that many of them are depressed (Henderson, 1972; Molnar & Cameron, 1975). Kaufman and his colleagues (1954) studied 11 female incest victims ranging in age from 10 to 17 and found that all of these girls suffered from guilt and depression. Two had become promiscuous, and one ran away.

Sloane and Karpinsky (1942) studied five incestuous families in rural Pennsylvania, in an area where such behavior was generally tolerated to a greater extent by the "locals" than in other parts of the country. They concluded that:

> Indulgence in incest in the post-adolescent period leads to serious repercussions in the girl, even in an environment in which the moral standards are relaxed . . . In

addition to the individual variations, however, one common manifestation appears to be the tendency to act out conflicts by indulging in promiscuous relationships . . .

The apparent relationship between incest and promiscuity is also supported in a more recent report by Benward and Denson-Gerber (1975). It merits repeating that in a recent study of adolescent prostitutes in the Minneapolis area, 75% of them were found to be incest victims (Weber, 1977). We can see a clear pattern: the girl is sexually abused by her father, is unable to escape the situation, decides to run away, has low self-esteem and a distorted view of her sexual identity and of sex itself, needs to support herself, and decides to sell sex.

Victims report feeling different and distant from ordinary people. They feel isolated and socially inadequate. Therapists complain that it is difficult to establish relationships with them. The girls frequently report a coping strategy of passive resistance to their fathers by pretending "this isn't really happening." Such denial of reality and distancing themselves from the world served them well as a defense against the shame, guilt, and anger they felt during the incestuous relationship, but after it is all over, this pattern is not easily broken.

The sense of distance and isolation which these women experienced was uniformly painful, and they made repeated, often desperate efforts to overcome it. Frequently, the result was a pattern of many brief unsatisfactory sexual contacts. Those relationships which did become more intense and lasting were fraught with difficulty (Herman & Hirschman, 1977, p. 750).

Here we find another reason why victims of incest are prone to engage in prostitution.

The victim of sexual abuse suffers a severe emotional trauma. The bruises and scars do not show outwardly as they do in physical abuse, but they are plain to the victim on the inside. It is difficult for the victim to face the reality of sexual abuse, and it is difficult for society as well. Many of the problem behaviors exhibited by these victims affect all of society. Divorce, running away, prostitution, drug abuse—all of these have ties to the maladjustment of the sexually abused youth. There is some evidence of society recognizing this problem—e.g., police departments around the country are setting up special abuse units to deal with these victims in a sensitive manner. Many of the general strategies for intervention we will discuss in Chapter 12 have a role to play.

Substance Abuse

There is a clear connection between sexual abuse and the misuse of drugs and alcohol (substance abuse). A family therapist in Minneapolis reports that of the more than 500 cases he has treated for adolescent drug addiction, about 70% were involved in some kind of family sexual abuse (Weber, 1977). Odyssey House, a residential drug treatment program with offices in several states, reports that 44% of its cases have a history of family sexual abuse (Weber, 1977). Drugs may serve as another means to escape the reality of sexual abuse. It has been widely reported that many prostitutes also abuse drugs. But these are special subgroups of adolescents. The problem of substance abuse is wide ranging and multifaceted.

Although there are compelling reasons for using the general term substance abuse, we recognize that in North America alcohol is viewed as more acceptable than other drugs. Because drinking has such a respectable reputation, it is easy to forget that alcohol *is* a drug, a very addictive drug at that. Adams and Gullotta (1983) highlight this in their review of "substance abuse minimization." They remind us that in the 19th century the use of many drugs, including opium and cocaine, was widespread and accepted in North America. The 20th century brought a change.

> Although Western society continued into this century the profitable export and sale of narcotics to underdeveloped nations, concern over the use of these drugs increased at home. By 1916, with the passage of the Harrison Narcotics Act, this nation joined the rest of modern industrialized society in restricting usage by its populace. In the United States this fever of sobriety extended beyond the powders extracted and refined from plants to the juices of fruits and the fermentation of grains . . . . Prohibition. Judging from Madison Avenue Ads, this short-lived experiment seems not to have been very successful. (p. 410)

We start from this recognition, that alcohol is part of the substance abuse issue but has a privileged social position. Thus, we look first at drug abuse and then at alcohol misuse.

Drug Abuse

Hundreds of surveys and studies of drug abuse have been conducted in the past 20 years, but it is often difficult to combine and generalize from their findings. The first difficulty is with the definition of drug abuse. When does drug *use* become *abuse*? There are many definitions of the term. Some emphasize physical dependence, others psychological dependence. Some focus on the presence of specific negative consequences while others require only feelings of distress or the risk of future harm. Confusion surrounding the term drug abuse has been so great that The National Commission on Marijuana and Drug Abuse recommended doing away with the term and focusing instead on how to use drugs appropriately rather than destructively (Farnsworth, 1974).

There are also problems with the term *drug addict.* There are two major perspectives on this issue: the medical and the psychological. The medical view emphasizes addiction as a disease and focuses on the presence of physiological symptoms of withdrawal when the drug is no longer taken. Jessor and Jessor (1975) have emphasized that adolescents may not show symptoms of physical dependence and destruction because these symptoms take time to develop.

Therefore, the medical view may be less appropriate for adolescents than it is for adults.

Some practitioners have criticized the medical disease model of addiction for fostering a sense of helplessness on the part of the addict. Since addiction is viewed as a disease, the sense of personal responsibility is taken away from the addict, leading to a passive acceptance of addiction.

Psychological dependence emphasizes the feelings of the individual. Adolescents may not have cirrhosis of the liver, but they may be just as dependent on drugs to create a world in which they feel comfortable. What is more, they may feel depressed, anxious, angry, and even suicidal when it is withdrawn.

A common misconception is that most of today's youth are on drugs. We spoke earlier of the stereotype of the teenager as a drug abuser who wants to get high and do nothing else. While much has been written in the popular press to promulgate such a view, it is an exaggeration. Because of the large number of studies on drug use, which ask different kinds of questions, sample different groups, and yield contradictory findings, it is difficult to summarize the data accurately. For this reason, we have decided to focus on one survey (probably the best one for our purposes) rather than try to make sense of diverse findings in this brief review. The largest and most representative national survey was commissioned by the National Institute on Drug Abuse (Johnston, Bachman, & O'Malley, 1980). This survey samples high school seniors each spring in 125 to 130 public and private high schools throughout the United States. The survey began in 1975, and information is available for each year through 1980. The sample size for each year varies a little, but the average for the five years is 17,169.

Here are the highlights of the findings. In 1980, *daily* marijuana use dropped from 10.3% to 9.1%, after years of continuous increase. For the first time since the study began, the proportion of students who feel that friends would disapprove of marijuana smoking increased (from 66% to 72%). The 1980 data also reveal a slight decrease in annual marijuana use (down 3%). In 1979 and 1980, seniors reported a drop in how "high" they got, and in how long they stayed high. In addition, daily cigarette smoking also dropped from 25% to 21% in 1980. Both of these findings seem to reflect greater concerns about health.

The annual prevalence (defined as use of the drug in the past year but not in the past month) of the dangerous hallucinogen PCP dropped from 7.0% to 4.4% in 1980. Cocaine and heroin use remained stable in 1980. Inhalant use (ranging from glue sniffing to solvents to nitrous oxide) after increasing continually from 1975 through 1979, declined a little in 1980.

Now for the bad news. The overall number of seniors reporting the use of some kind of illicit drug other than marijuana continued to rise in 1980 from 28% to 30%. This rise is attributed to an increase in the use of stimulants (primarily amphetamines, especially cocaine). Stimulants are second only to marijuana in the prevalence of illicit drug use. The annual prevalence is now more than 1 in 5. The increase was greatest among females, the noncollege bound, and those in the North Central and Southern regions. There are some interesting changes in the patterns of stimulant use—partly in response to changing regulations, such as the decision to greatly limit amphetamine diet pills in the late 1970s. While stimulant use continues to go up, the proportion of users who usually get "very high" to "moderately high" has dropped (from 60% in 1975 to 40% in 1980). The drop from 1979 to 1980 was 9%. This is most probably related to the shift in the reasons given for amphetamine use. While 62% reported using speed "to feel good or get high" in 1976, only 48% reported this reason in 1980. More seniors are now giving reasons such as "to help me lose weight" and "to get through the day" than before. The number giving the reason "to get more energy" has remained the same. It may be significant to note that while stimulant use had been about the same for both sexes since 1975, the annual prevalence was 19% for males and 22% for females in 1980. This represents a 4% increase in annual prevalence for females from 18% in 1979 to 22% in 1980. One wonders if the reason "to lose weight" accounts for this. Perhaps there is a link between anorexia nervosa and the use of amphetamines. With the incidence of anorexia nervosa continuing to rise, as we shall see shortly, the use of amphetamines by females "to help me lose weight" may rise also. This may signal the beginning of a major new female drug abuse problem.

The use of quaaludes (methaquaalude) rose from an annual prevalence of 5.9% in 1979 to 7.2% in 1980. There was, however, a sharp drop in the duration of the high. The increase occurred mostly in males and the college bound. Barbiturate use also continued to decline. In recent years attention has focused on *lookalikes,* capsules and pills that resemble the desired illegal drugs but actually contain legal but dangerous levels of caffeine, phenylpropanolamine, and other substances that give the user a kick. The report draws the following conclusion: Overall, drug use among high school students remains widespread. Nearly two-thirds of the age group (65%) have used an *illicit* drug, and nearly two out of every five (39%) have used an *illicit drug other than marijuana* (Johnston et al., 1980, p. 9).

Data on drug use are disturbing. However, when we examine surveys there is some cause for reassurance. The percentage of students reporting use in the past month is rather low. This is not the pattern of a drug addict, but of the occasional, recreational user. This is important, because those who use drugs for social and experimental purposes are much more similar to their nondrug using peers than they are to drug abusers (Weiner, 1982; Amini, Salasnek, & Burke, 1976; Wieder & Kaplan, 1969). What is more, most teenagers have never used most drugs. For each drug considered (except marijuana, alcohol, and tobacco) about 80% have not tried it.

While it is true that this sample *does not* include high school dropouts, it is fairly clear that not every teenager is high all the time, and in fact, most never are. Furthermore, we should also state that these data represent the worst case in terms of age. Drug use increases with age, so that we may expect high school seniors to give us close to the upper limit on adolescent drug use. Over-all drug use (including alcohol) starts to decline in the early twenties (U.S. Department of Health and Human Services, 1980).

Alcohol Misuse

We cannot begin to understand alcohol misuse unless we understand overall alcohol use. United States per capita alcohol use is nearly three gallons of pure ethanol per person on average. No other drug (alcohol is a depressant) is so accepted. And yet, no other form of drug misuse causes such widespread medical and social damage. More than 10% of *all* deaths each year are related to alcohol. The economic costs of alcohol misuse and alcoholism in 1975 were estimated at more than 40 billion dollars (DeLuca, 1981). Of course, these costs exist in the context of many tens of millions of alcohol consumers. Most people drink, but drink without seriously damaging themselves or others. This is the context in which we must understand adolescent alcohol use and misuse. Despite the 25,000 alcohol-related deaths per year on the highways, despite the *millions* of days of work and school lost to alcohol, despite the billions of dollars alcohol costs society, it has a tenacious hold on the macrosystem.

Nearly 90% of high school seniors report alcohol consumption within the past year (Johnston, Bachman, & O'Malley, 1980). Forty-five percent have gotten drunk once or more, and more than 20% get drunk frequently. As Kandel and Faust (1975) report, alcohol is virtually always the first drug in the career of a drug abuser. Its availability and widespread social acceptability ensure this. This means that social drinking provides the entry point for alcohol misuse, although for most youth it is simply the entry point for a life of moderate social drinking marred only by a few occasional bouts of drunkenness.

Those who become problem-drinkers usually do so in response to a pattern of psychological and social problems. The standard composite picture emphasizes peer-dependence, social incompetence, and depression (Adams & Gullotta, 1983). There are also grounds for believing that some individuals are physiologically prone to alcohol misuse because their bodies cannot process alcohol adequately. They have what amounts to an allergic reaction to alcohol that makes anything but problem drinking a near impossibility. Given the cultural support (if not outright pressure) for drinking, it is hardly surprising that many of these alcohol-sensitive individuals end up as problem drinkers.

Substance abuse, like delinquency, tells us to be most concerned about those adolescents who develop a patterned, chronic problem. The occasional delinquent act or experimentation with drugs is much more normal and does not predict life-long troubles. Most such experiments need not have permanent consequences.

Suicide

Suicide among adolescents has received a great deal of attention in the popular press with good reason. The award-winning novel (and later film), *Ordinary*

People (1976) did much to stimulate public interest. Suicide is now the third leading cause of death among teenagers in the United States (at 7.6 per 100,000), behind accidents (57.4 per 100,000) and homicides (9.6 per 100,000) (Vital Statistics of the United States, 1979). But the actual number of adolescents committing suicide is not all that high. Of the 26,832 known suicides in 1976, 6.9% (1,719) were committed by persons under 19 (Vital Statistics of the United States, 1979). However, within the past ten years the suicide rate for teenagers has almost doubled, and some deaths recorded as accidents are actually suicides. Among the major industrialized nations in 1978, the United States was fourth in the suicide rate for persons between the ages of 15–24, behind Austria, Germany, and Switzerland (Statistical Abstracts of the United States, 1980).

While 6.9% of suicides are actually committed by adolescents, they account for 12% of the total number of *recorded* attempts (Weiner, 1982). It has been estimated that the ratio of suicide attempts to successes among adolescents is 50:1 or even 100:1 (Jacobinzer, 1965; McAnarney, 1975; Seiden, 1969; Stengel, 1964), while for adults it is about 8:1 (Weiner, 1982). This would mean that there are an astounding number of attempts in this age group each year—more than 100,000!

There is a marked sex difference in suicide rates, with more males actually committing suicide but more females attempting it. The suicide rate in 1978 for white males in the 15–24 age group was 10.1 per 100,000. For white females it was 5.0 per 100,000. Males who are members of minority groups (primarily blacks in the United States) show an especially high incidence of suicide (14.8 per 100,000 in 1978, as compared to 3.2 per 100,000 for minority females).

This sex difference is not well understood. Societal pressure on males to repress their emotions may be a factor. Attempted suicide may be seen as being less masculine than completed suicide; thus males would use suicide less as a call for help than females might (Lester, 1979). Another reason offered is the difference in methods chosen.

Methods of Suicide

Methods used to commit suicide vary from self-inflicted gun shots to taking pills. Males tend to use more violent and sure-fire means. The methods used breakdown as follows: firearms and explosives (males, 58%; females, 41%); hanging (males, 20%; females, 7%); poison (males, 7%; females, 36%); gas (males, 8%; females, 5%); others (males, 7%; females, 11%) (Weiner, 1982).

The biggest difference between the sexes occurs in the firearms and poisoning category—methods that differ considerably in their effectiveness, as well as along the active/passive dimension. This may reflect a cultural effect: sex-typed female behavior tends to be more passive and submissive, and male behavior more active and aggressive. Researchers and clinicians believe that the seriousness of the attempt is reflected in the method used. If one shoots oneself in the head and lives, the attempt has been judged to be a lot more serious than if one takes an overdose of aspirin or some other mildly toxic drug. Attempts to assess the psychological intent of suicide and to predict a successful suicide met with little success until investigators included medical lethality in their analyses. Apparently, if the person has an accurate understanding of how lethal the act is likely to be, suicidal intent becomes a more accurate predictor of danger to self (Beck, Beck, & Kovacs, 1975).

No matter how nonserious a suicidal attempt may seem, however, the commission of a suicidal gesture is *not* a normal part of adolescence and should be taken very seriously (Weiner, 1982). Such an attempt is a sign of some kind of disturbance that merits careful professional evaluation. Individuals who attempt suicide by means that have little chance for rescue are at greater risk than those who do leave a chance for rescue open. A sudden attempt with no precursors such as leaving notes, making threats, or giving away valued possessions has a better prognosis than well-planned attempts that are marked by a strong desire to die (Beck, Kovacs, & Weissman, 1979). Again, we cannot emphasize too strongly that suicidal gestures or even threats should be taken as serious signs of a problem that requires attention.

Attempts to predict who will attempt or commit suicide have not met with much success. Not surprisingly, depression has been identified to be the most salient psychological characteristic involved in the suicide of 15- to 19-year-olds (Weiner, 1975). Often the suicidal adolescent feels "no one cares," that "there is no one to talk to," and "no one wants to listen" (Weiner, 1982). These adolescents do not expect things to improve, so hopelessness and despair lead to ending it all. It is essential to respond to this call for help—to listen and communicate. Such a call may come from profound disturbance (e.g., chronic depression) as well as situational crisis (an anxiety attack). Whatever its origins, it calls upon us to understand the broad spectrum of psychological malfunctioning. This leads us to consider systems for classifying psychopathology.

Classification of Psychopathology

While it may seem obvious that professionals need to classify psychological problems, clinicians and researchers continue to debate whether an individual exhibiting symptoms of psychopathology should be diagnosed at all. Some feel that any diagnosis reflects the preconceptions and value judgments of society and the particular biases of the diagnostician rather than any objective appraisal of the individual in question. Furthermore, these critics object that the diagnosis is a label that explains nothing, but results in damage to the individual's self-concept and self-esteem that may perpetuate and exacerbate the individual's problems. The stigma associated with a label of *psychopathology* may also influence the way others behave toward the individual, and thus serve in various ways to maintain the level of maladaptation. These issues are particularly critical in the formative years of an individual's identity. Adolescents who receive a diagnostic label may view themselves as mentally ill, and thus create a possibly self-fulfilling prophesy in which the adolescent plays this role with little expectation for improvement.

Defenders of the practice of diagnosis state that certain behaviors or symptoms of a disorder occur in "clusters" or syndromes, that there are particular patterns that can be identified as manifestations of psychopathology. Such categorization of behavior occurs naturally: when we say, "I'm feeling depressed," we know that means we are sad in mood, may feel tired, don't particularly feel like socializing, and are otherwise down. This being the case, why not categorize the package of feelings as psychopathology?

There are three major benefits to diagnosis. First, it helps in specifying a treatment plan. From past experience, clinicians know which treatment tends to work with a particular disorder or syndrome.

Second, clinicians can communicate among themselves concerning a case in fairly specific terms in a short amount of time. Specificity and uniformity are important; strict guidelines ensure that when clinician A diagnoses a person as having a major depressive disorder, clinician B knows what he is talking about. There is no question concerning whether what clinician A means by *depressed* is the same thing as what clinician B means.

Third, categorization facilitates further research efforts in the syndrome or disorder. By specifically classifying the disorder, we are able to study the associated conditions of the disorder, which may help in determining causes and treatments. Without specific classification, we cannot be sure of what we are studying or trying to explain. Different disorders have different dynamics, and the lack of homogeneity of group samples confuses the clinical picture and hinders progress in the understanding of these dynamics.

DSM-III

The most widely used diagnostic system of psychopathology in the United States is the previously mentioned third edition of the *Diagnostic and Statistical Manual of Mental Disorders* (DSM-III), published by the American Psychiatric Association in 1980 (American Psychiatric Association, 1980).

The DSM-III system is based on observations of behavior made by clinicians. Disorders are classified in very specific terms. These categories represent points on a continuum of behavior, and not simply unrelated elements:

> Although this manual provides a classification of mental disorders, there is no satisfactory definition that specifies precise boundaries for the concept of "mental disorder" . . . In DSM-III there is no assumption that each mental disorder is a discrete entity with sharp boundaries (discontinuity) between it and other mental disorders, as well as between it and No Mental Disorder. (DSM-III, pp. 5–6)

The ultimate goal is to make the distinctions clinically useful, not to resolve philosophical issues concerning subtle distinctions in behavior. Nonetheless, the DSM does convey efforts on the part of those espousing different developmental theories to influence the discussion of how psychopathology arises. The issue of labeling an individual is also addressed in DSM-III:

> A common misconception is that a classification of mental disorders classifies individuals, when actually what are being classified are disorders that individuals have. For this reason, the text of DSM-III avoids the use of such phrases as "a schizophrenic" or "an alcoholic," and instead uses the more accurate, but admittedly more wordy "an individual with Schizophrenia" or "an individual with Alcohol Dependence." (p. 6)

It is clear then that the purpose of DSM-III is to diagnose disorders, not individuals. Its purpose is to facilitate research, treatment, and communications.

DSM-III is a descriptive document. It usually does not go into theories concerning the origins *(etiology)* of disorders, since these are not well understood (and this is a controversial issue in many cases). Including statements about etiology tends to confuse matters and highlight conflicts among different schools of thought. DSM's purpose is to provide concrete, behavioral, well-specified categories of behavior that either describe an individual or do not. This leads to a minimum of confusion, and better agreement between different clinicians on which diagnosis to apply to the disorder of an individual *(interrater reliability)*, even if they then disagree on *why* a person is experiencing a problem and *how* to treat him or her.

The advent of DSM-III has been particularly important for diagnosing disorders in adolescence and childhood. One section of the manual is entitled "Disorders Usually First Evident in Infancy, Childhood, or Adolescence." This section contains 49 specific diagnoses under the general headings of mental retardation, attention deficit disorder, conduct disorder, anxiety disorders, eating disorders, stereotyped movement disorders, developmental disorders, and other kinds of disorders. The rest of DSM-III is also applicable to adolescents, but these 49 are considered especially relevant to youth.

One of the major problems in the psychiatric diagnosis of adolescents in the past has been the widespread use of the now-outmoded DSM-*II* category of *transient situational disorder.* Transient situational disorder is defined as a limited reaction to pressing current stressors in an otherwise psychologically stable individual who has neither current nor future dispositions to diagnosable psychopathology. Research suggests that clinicians are prone to diagnosing patients as having transient situational rather than other more serious kinds of disorders possibly because of the common stereotype that most adolescents experience turmoil.

This would be fine were the stereotype true, but as we have seen, it is not. Weiner and Del Gaudio (1973) analyzed a follow-up of psychiatric case register data from Monroe County, New York, of 723 adolescents who had appeared in the registry on two or more occasions over a three-year period. They found that 27.1% of the diagnoses for this group of adolescents were transient situational disorder. This stands in contrast to the finding that only 6% of adult patients seen in outpatient clinics were given this diagnosis (Outpatient Psychiatric Service, 1969). As Weiner and Del Gaudio see it, while youth may perhaps react more to situational stress, this diagnosis is over-used and inaccurate in many cases. They point to the data. Looking across all of the diagnostic contacts of the same individuals (a new diagnosis is made at each readmission), situational disorder has the least amount of agreement between contacts (only 14.9%) of all the diagnoses made. More than 11% of the teenagers receiving this diagnosis were subsequently considered schizophrenic. If these adolescents were correctly diagnosed as having transient situational disorder, a *limited* reaction that does not suggest future dispositions to diagnosable psychopathology, then how did they later develop schizophrenia? In addition, 51.9% of patients receiving a diagnosis of situational disorder received subsequent psychiatric treatment. Moreover, Weiner and Del Gaudio cite the findings by Rosen and his colleagues that adolescents diagnosed as having situational disorders are treated just as often as those whose diagnosis is personality disorder or neurosis. For all of these reasons, Weiner and Del Gaudio conclude that the diagnosis of transient situational disorder is often misapplied to and over-used with adolescent patients. As we have emphasized before, a pattern of problems experienced during adolescence is to be taken seriously; they are not "just a phase" the teenager is going through.

The need for very specific diagnostic categories is great when dealing with adolescents. Broad, general categories such as transient situational disorder are not of much help. This is because adolescents *do* go through a period of uncertainty during which they try to fit their values and goals into their futures as adults. For example, trouble establishing identity *may* indicate the onset of schizophrenic patterns. Depression *may* be related to learned helplessness. Extreme egocentrism *may* degenerate into actual psychopathology.

As we have seen, however, this period is not necessarily a time of overwhelming confusion in which adolescents are severely disturbed. There is a need to determine whether their problem is a clinical, psychopathological disorder, or just a normal period of uncertainty. This is where specific diagnostic criteria are useful. There is some evidence that DSM-III is specific enough to be of use to clinicians working with adolescents. Strober, Green, and Carlson (1981) analyzed the inter-rater reliability of two highly trained, experienced diagnosticians using DSM-III to evaluate 100 consecutive first admissions of adolescents to the Neuropsychiatric Institute of the University of California at Los Angeles (UCLA). They found inter-rater agreement between the two raters for 73 of the 96 patients included in their report, which is especially impressive since they used 13 syndrome categories in their evaluations. This study, although quite limited by the use of just two raters, shows that DSM-III can be useful for diagnosing adolescent disturbance across a wide variety of syndromes. The reliability obtained is similar to that found in diagnosing adult disturbance (see Appendix F of DSM-III, American Psychiatric Association, 1980; Spitzer, Endicott, & Robins, 1978).

Empirically Derived Classification

While DSM-III is designed to provide a systematic, reliable, and valid diagnosis of mental disorders, it nevertheless has its roots in clinical inference and impressions. Essentially, it represents many mental health professionals putting together their experience, knowledge, and observations into one systematic manual. Empirically derived classification schemes begin in an entirely different manner. They begin with objective, empirical data. Systematic observations are made of behavior with an assessment instrument, often a behavior checklist, in which the observer records the occurrence of specific behaviors. They then combine all of this information into a single data base. Statistical procedures are applied to this data base to highlight *clusters* of behavior, that is, behaviors that occur in the presence of each other. These clusters are empirically derived syndromes because there is little or no inference at all, just behavior and statistical processing.

Achenbach (1978; see also Edelbroch & Achenbach, 1980) collected data on children and youth using his Child Behavior Checklist (a questionnaire to be filled out by parents or parent surrogates that contains 118 behavior problem items). He collected data on 450 boys, and from this data, nine behavior clusters emerged. The first cluster, for example, was comprised of the following observed behaviors: auditory hallucinations, visual hallucinations, fears, fears of school, clings to adults, anxious, nightmares, public masturbation, shy, and timid. This cluster falls within a category *internalizers*. Achenbach (1978) determined that in addition to internalizers, children and youth could be called *externalizers*, and *mixed*. Internalizers are those who exhibit self-destructive or inner-directed problems. The externalizer category includes antisocial behaviors and "acting out." The mixed category included the cluster labeled social withdrawal.

Due to its reliance on strict behavioral data, the empirical approach is very useful for reliably categorizing individuals. Achenbach's procedure is being used in many research projects—e.g., to study and intervene in adolescent maltreatment (Garbarino, Sebes, & Schellenbach, 1984). Its utility for planning treatment has yet to be tested conclusively.

Now that we know the symptoms of some of the clinical concerns of adolescence and how the disorders are diagnosed, we can look at the disorders in a bit more depth.

Depression

Mental health researchers estimate that 25% of the people born in the United States will suffer from depression at some point during their lifetime, and that 6% of the United States population is depressed at any one time (Weissman &

Myers, 1977). Studies of children and adolescents have found between 20% and 30% of this age group to show definite *signs* of depression at some point (Albert & Beck, 1975; Lefkowitz, 1977; Rutter, Graham, Chadwick, & Yule, 1976). In terms of clinically recognized depression, however, the prevalence in children and youth seems to be from ¼ to ½ the rate found in adults, with the incidence increasing with age (Weiner, 1982). It is unclear whether this is a result of youth not being classified as depressed because of their age or of youth actually being less depressed than adults. Depression is more common among females than males, on the order of 2:1 in adulthood.

In late adolescence, many youth have developed cognitively to the point where they closely resemble adults, and are capable of having and *expressing* the self-doubts, low self-esteem, and hopelessness often found in depression. At age 15 or 16, they may also express their depression indirectly, through the behaviors such as drug abuse, suicide, sexual promiscuity, and general alienation. These behaviors may be caused by other factors, however, and should not be considered an absolute expression of underlying depression (Weiner, 1982).

The causes of depression are unclear. There is some strong evidence for a genetic or temperamental component in the disorder, and some researchers now believe it is linked to chemical imbalances in the brain that lead to a breakdown of neural transmissions. In identical twin studies, the average co-incidence (where one has it so does the other) of depression is 69.2%, while in nonidentical twin studies, an average of just 13.3% co-incidence has been observed (Gershon, Bunney, Leckman, Van Eerdewegh, & De Bauche, 1976). This pattern is supported by studies of identical twins reared apart (Price, 1968), thus controlling to some degree certain social and familial factors.

There are several contemporary psychological models of depression. Lewinsohn (1974a; 1974b) presents a behavioral model emphasizing a loss or lack of "response-contingent reinforcements," meaning that depressed people do not act in ways that elicit reward from their environment. For example, a lack of social skills leading to a dearth of positive social interaction would contribute to depression.

Seligman (1974, 1975) describes depression as a form of "learned helplessness," where one believes that one has no control over one's life. This model

My most vivid memory of my adolescence is when I was one of the twenty finalists in County Junior Miss Pageant. I was a senior in high school.

In my senior year of high school I decided that it was going to be my last year of high school so I was going to make the best of it and join some groups and get involved. The first thing I did was join ASTRA, a group for girls. The next thing I did was enter in "Almost Anything Goes," that is where the juniors, freshmen, and seniors of our school competed against each other in various activities from egg tossing to tug-of-war. I also joined the dance marathon. The major thing I did that year, though, was send my application for Junior Miss. I did not know it at the time, but this was going to end up being something that was going to have an effect on the rest of my life.

When you sent in your application you got a letter in the mail welcoming you; they also told you that you were going to have two cuts to decide on twenty girls to compete in the actual pageant. The first cut was an interview. I passed that and proceeded to pass the last cut, talent. All of a sudden, I found myself a Junior Miss contestant. I was very excited because nothing like this had ever happened to me.

The next four months were hard work, learning steps for the show, putting together my talent for the talent part, learning how to poise myself while walking on stage. There was a lot to do and I put a full one hundred percent into it. This put a big strain on me because, being a senior, I had a lot of things to think about. I had been accepted at college and started the day after graduation. I was making my decision about what I planned on majoring in in college and if I wanted to work while going to college. I was making all the major decisions every senior in high school has to make about the rest of their life. But, with me, things were looking great, I was a finalist in Junior Miss, an accepted student at college, I really felt good about myself. That is, until the night of the pageant.

The whole night was like a dream come true, I felt like someone important because, out of the fifty-three girls who sent in applications, I had made it to the top twenty. I had no hopes of becoming Junior Miss, just making it that far made me feel as though I was someone and that I really was just as good as the next person. But, when it came time to pick the winners of the pageant, talent, poise, physical fitness runners-up and Junior Miss, I found myself hoping, just a little, that I might win. Then, it was time to pick the next Junior Miss. All of a sudden, the announcer called my number, we all had numbers one to twenty. My number was seventeen, I couldn't believe it, I don't think I could ever have been more happy than I was at that very second. I say one second because that is all it lasted; the announcer had made a mistake. The number the announcer wanted to call was number seven, ten numbers away. When the announcer made the correction, I was devastated, the first thing I thought was "How could they have humiliated me like that in front of all these people?" But, I had no idea at the time how it would affect the rest of my life.

I find now that I am very insecure about things that are very important to me. I am also not as outgoing as I used to be, I tend not to get involved in anything. I guess I'm most afraid of something like that happening to me again. That happened almost four years ago, and at times it seems like yesterday.

That is my most vivid memory of my adolescence; it's not a very happy one, but it's a memory that I will not soon forget.

grows out of laboratory research with animals, in which animals receiving punishment (shock) no matter what they do to avoid it exhibit behavior that closely resembles the symptoms of depression.

Beck (1970, 1971, 1974) presents a model of depression based on three cognitive patterns: negative view of the world, negative view of the self, negative view of the future. This triad is maintained through various forms of cognitive distortion, so that one sees confirmatory evidence of these views all around. Individuals learn these patterns from childhood, and are therefore particularly vulnerable to loss and stress, reacting to such events with depression.

Schizophrenia

Schizophrenia refers to severe disruption of an individual's thought process, self-concept, motivation to communicate, or appropriateness of feelings about relationships. It is usually what people mean when they use the colloquial term *crazy*. It has been estimated that between one and two out of every 100 people in the United States will suffer from schizophrenia at some point in their lives. It is frequently a chronic condition, with 40% to 60% of first admissions to hospitals being readmitted within two years of their release.

The term schizophrenia was coined by the Swiss psychiatrist, Eugen Bleuler. Bleuler commented "the adolescent age period seems to offer a particular disposition to this disease" (Bleuler, 1911, p. 340, as cited in Weiner, 1982). Research since then has supported this observation (Arieti, 1974; Holzman & Grinker, 1974; Spitzer, Andreasen, & Endicott, 1978). Studies have shown that schizophrenia is diagnosed in 25% to 30% of adolescents admitted to public mental hospitals, in approximately 15% of those admitted to psychiatirc units of general hospitals, and 6% to 8% of those treated in outpatient clinics. This makes schizophrenia the most frequently assigned diagnosis in public mental health hospitals, and near the top (second and third) in the other institutions. Only transient situational disorder in boys and transient situational disorder and depressive disorder in girls are more frequently assigned in general hospitals and outpatient clinics (Rosen, Bahn, Shellow, & Bower, 1965; Strober, Green, & Carlson, 1981; Weiner & Del Gaudio, 1973). With the displacement of transient situational disorder in DSM-III, this may change and some will be diagnosed as having more serious conditions (e.g., schizophrenia) while others are treated as having less serious adjustment problems.

It is often difficult to detect schizophrenia in the adolescent. Clinical studies have shown that only 30% to 40% of schizophrenic adolescents present initial symptoms that are clearly indicative of the disorder, such as breakdowns in the ability to think clearly, to act appropriately in social settings, and to perceive reality in conventional terms (Weiner, 1982). The two behavioral patterns of the adolescent prior to diagnosis are signs of schizophrenia overlaid with emotional disturbances, primarily depression, and signs of schizophrenia with conduct disorder problems, such as truancy, stealing, fighting, and running away (Feinstein & Miller, 1979; Hudgens, 1974; Masterson, 1967).

Guidelines reviewed by Weiner (1982) help to distinguish the young schizophrenic from nonschizophrenic youth. One is the persistence of the schizophrenia symptoms. The longer the specific symptoms (such as thought disorder) remain, while other symptoms fluctuate or remit (such as depression), the more likely is a schizophrenic diagnosis. Another dimension is the extent to which the adolescent progresses and is involved with the demands of developmental tasks. Such tasks include the development of a sense of independence from parents, coming to grips with sexuality, *real* enjoyment of social interaction and the making of friends (not just going through the motions), and concern with life goals. Youth who make no progress in these areas, or just seem to "ignore" them—never having it occur to them that they will one day have to be on their own, for example—may be showing early signs of schizophrenia. These are only guidelines, however, and refer just as much to the style of how adolescents behave, as to what they actually do.

Outcome studies of schizophrenia have shown that approximately 25% of adolescents hospitalized for schizophrenia recover completely. About 25% improve substantially, but have lingering symptoms or periodic relapses, and 50% show little or no progress—requiring continuing residential care. Schizophrenic adults do somewhat better, with 50% recovering completely, 25% achieving substantial improvement, and 25% remaining hospitalized (Weiner, 1982).

Individuals who develop the disorder early tend to have a poorer prognosis: the later one develops it, the better the prognosis. Other favorable prognostic factors are a sudden onset in response to a specific highly stressful event, as opposed to a gradual development of the symptoms with no clear precipitating event; no schizophrenic relatives; previous evidence of adjustment (good school work, social interaction, normal affect); and initial symptoms characterized by confusion, distress, and moodiness.

There are many other areas to be covered in this complex disorder, and we refer the interested reader to Weiner's excellent discussion (1982, Chapter 6) of schizophrenia during adolescence.

Eating Disorders

Anorexia nervosa and *bulimia* are the most common eating disorders in the United States (excluding obesity). Both are dramatic and serious disorders.

Anorexia Nervosa

The DSM-III diagnostic criteria for anorexia are:

1 Intense fear of becoming obese, which does not diminish as weight loss progresses

2   Disturbance of body image, e.g., claiming to "feel fat" even when emaciated
3   Weight loss of at least 25% of original body weight or, if under 18 years of age, weight loss from original body weight plus projected weight gain expected from growth charts may be combined to make the 25%
4   Refusal to maintain body weight over minimal normal weight for age and height
5   No known physical illness that would account for the weight loss; e.g., amenorrhea in women (DSM-III, p. 69)

There are no reliable incidence studies of this disorder in the general population at present. The major problem is a lack of standardization of the diagnostic criteria for the disorder. It has been commonly observed that anorexia occurs most frequently in well-educated, adolescent females. Incidence rates of the severe disorder have been observed to be about 1% (Crisp & Toms, 1972; Nylander, 1971). Crisp and Toms (1972) have estimated that one out of every 15 cases is male. The disorder has been found to be more common in private schools, implying a social class factor, that it is more common among more affluent adolescents (Crisp, Palmer, & Kalucy, 1976).

There is great variability in the psychological profiles of anorectics, but some common features have been identified. Anorectics tend to feel inadequate, mediocre, and inferior to those around them. They frequently feel ineffective, and not in control of their own lives. All energy is directed at covering up these flaws, and to projecting an image of an ideal or perfect person. Cultural values enter here, as the ideal woman is currrently one who possesses a thin, slim-hipped figure (Schwartz, Thompson, & Johnson, 1982). Issues of control are often involved. It has been frequently suggested that self-denial of food may be the ultimate expression of control for the individual, and thus that youth resort to this strategy in an effort to reduce feelings of ineffectiveness and powerlessness, e.g., in contending with domineering, achievement-oriented parents.

Bulimia

Bulimia is an eating disorder primarily characterized by the ingestion of astounding amounts of food (binging). It is sometimes followed by self-induced vomiting. The DSM-III criteria for the disorder are:

1   Recurrent episodes of binge eating (rapid consumption of a large amount of food in a discrete period of time, usually less than two hours).
2   At least three of the following:
    A   consumption of high-caloric, easily ingested food during a binge

B inconspicuous eating during a binge

C termination of such eating episodes by abdominal pain, sleep, or self-induced vomiting

D repeated attempts to lose weight by severely restricting diets, self-induced vomiting, or use of laxatives or diuretics

E frequent weight fluctuations greater than ten pounds due to alternating binges and fasts

3 Awareness that the eating pattern is abnormal and fear of not being able to stop eating voluntarily.

4 Depressed mood and self-deprecating thoughts following eating binges.

5 The bulimic episodes are not due to anorexia nervosa or any known physical disorder.

Bulimia and anorexia nervosa are often observed to occur together, although by DSM-III standards this would mean that the condition is not bulimia. In bulimia, the apparently ravenous hunger, which does exist in the anorectic, breaks through and the individual binges. Estimates of the presence of bulimia in anorectics (variously termed bulimia nervosa or bulimarexia) vary from 10% on upward (Sinoway, 1982; Bruch, 1976; Casper, Halmi, Goldberg, Eckert, & Davis, 1979; Garfinkel et al., 1977a; 1977b; Halmi, 1974; Hsu, Harding, & Crisp, 1979) depending largely upon the diagnostic criteria. Most female adolescents report having had the fear that they will begin to eat uncontrollably. Many young women are extremely concerned about being thin.

Estimates of the prevalence of bulimia alone vary. There have been few systematic research efforts in this area to date. Sinoway (1982), in a study of 1,172 college freshman women found that 25% of the sample identified themselves as binge eaters, eating large amounts of food and feeling fearful that they may be unable to control this behavior. Fourteen percent of her sample met the criteria for binging and then employing methods other than vomiting, (purging, fasting, and dieting) to rid their body of food. Hawkins and Clement (1980) found 79% of women in their sample of university students identified themselves as binge eaters (on a questionnaire) and 49% of the males also identified themselves as bingers. Only 9 women of the entire sample reported in engaging in self-induced vomiting after a binge.

Halmi and his colleagues (1981) found a 13% incidence of bulimia as defined by DSM-III in their sample of 355 college students. Eighty-seven percent of these were female, and 13% were male. This prevalence seems alarmingly high; it is clear that bulimia is a common problem on college campuses.

It appears that bulimics as a group show a psychological profile similar to the anorectics, but at a less intense level. They are better adjusted than anorectics, being less obsessional, anxious, and concerned with control and independence. Bulimic women have been found to be overly concerned with rejection by males, gauging their self-esteem by the approval they receive from the opposite sex. Their family history tends to be one of reward for compliance, especially in regard to good behavior and physical attractiveness, and punishment for expressions of independence and assertiveness (Boskind-Lodahl, 1976). They tend to view themselves as fat, even though most are of normal weight or just above normal weight, and to blame themselves for their problems (Sinoway, 1982; Boskind-Lodahl & Sirlin, 1977; Russell, 1979). They show the same high need for perfection and achievement as do anorectics.

Anorexia nervosa and bulimia are serious problems for today's teenagers, and it is hoped that research into these areas will become more systematic, employing well-defined and consistent criteria. It is encouraging that research in these areas is becoming much better methodologically.

In this connection, we can see the importance of good diagnostic criteria for the understanding of a particular disorder. We have variable findings in this area that present a confusing picture because of the use of nonuniform diagnostic criteria. As we have seen throughout this chapter, our ability to assess and respond to a problem depends to a great extent on how we define that problem, whether it is juvenile delinquency or bulimia. In any case, it is clear that adolescents experience significant and serious social and psychological disturbances. This leads us to consider human services for adolescents in our next chapter.

Ecological Wrap-Up

Organism.   Some individuals are biologically primed for psychopathology or other personal and social problems (such as alcohol misuse). This fact accentuates the importance of a supportive and responsive social environment.

Microsystem.   Family dynamics play a pivotol role in the etiology of personal and social problems. Some families are pathogenic. However, parents are not necessarily to blame for adolescent troubles. Adolescents are active shapers of their own experience. What is more, other microsystems such as peer group and school play important roles in promoting mental health or increasing the odds of pathology.

Mesosystem.   The greatest risk for disturbed development comes from situations in which there is a powerfully pathogenic mesosystem—e.g., when both home and peer group reward delinquent behavior.

Exosystem.   Institutional forces play an important role in adolescent troubles by tolerating or even profiting from them. The clearest example is the sex industry that feeds upon troubled youth ripe for exploitation. Similarly the juvenile justice system can play a role by the degree to which it is rehabilitative versus punitive in orientation.

Macrosystem. The blueprints of society can exacerbate some adolescent problems. For example, the formula *thin equals sexy* seems to increase the risk of anorexia among vulnerable adolescents. Similarly, the tolerance of alcohol and even pressure to drink increase the risk of adolescents developing alcohol abuse problems.

Preview

- Human services include face-to-face contact, direct and indirect contact (microsystems), and institutional resources (exosystems) that help adolescents succeed in life.

- Human services include formal organizations (such as schools) and informal relationships (such as friends).

- General ethical standards guide human service professionals, and adolescents present special ethical challenges.

- Human services can be preventive or remedial in orientation.

- Psychological intervention can include individual and group therapy and may aim at feelings, ideas, and/or behavior.

- Exemplary treatment programs exist to deal with drug abuse, alcohol problems, running away, juvenile delinquency, abuse and neglect, pregnancy, prostitution, and suicide, and combine nurturing and control to provide a social support system.

The purpose of this chapter is to examine the ways that professionals can intervene in the lives of adolescents in response to the kinds of problems we discussed in Chapter 11. Some forms of intervention are specific to a particular problem (e.g., substituting methadone for heroin addiction), but most forms (such as peer mutual help groups) apply to a broad class of problems faced by adolescents. Therefore, we look at the various types of interventions with an eye towards assessing their common purposes, targets, and methods. Specifically, we highlight the special issues that affect delivery of human services to adolescents, including confidentiality, privacy, and informed consent. We also discuss the broader political context of services to adolescents—the macrosystem of intervention. As we see it, the many types of services delivered to adolescents are grouped into two primary modes of service delivery: preventive and rehabilitative (remedial).

12

Human Services for Adolescents

General Issues in Human Services

In general, most people seek professional services when they feel a discrepancy between the way in which they perceive themselves and the way that they would rather be. We refer to the former as a *dysfunctional state* and the future goal after change has occurred a *developmental objective* (Urban & Vondracek, 1977). For example, a 15-year-old girl may discover that she is not going to graduate unless she brings up her grades. The discrepancy is that she is failing her courses when she wants to be passing. The goal is to raise her grades to a level that will enable her to pass. To achieve this goal, she may implement several types of action: study each evening rather than waiting until the day before the exam, seek help from teachers, guidance counselors, or parents for remedial aids, adjust her goals to a lower level, or take part in a remedial education program. Each of these alternatives may assist her in achieving her goal, and each may use different levels of technical assistance from professionals, resources or learning materials. Community support may be necessary to provide programmed assistance or raise personal investment or motivation on the part of the student. Intervention may involve many different professionals including teachers, psychologists, social workers, and lawyers.

Human development intervention is defined as planning and deliberately entering into the developmental course of individuals and families (Urban & Vondracek, 1977). This occurs over a period of time, and requires resources to devise, carry out, and evaluate activities directed toward facilitating and promoting development. It is also important to note that the values of society are involved in any decision to seek intervention. At times, these values come into play in the initial choice to seek professional assistance, since adolescents are not always given this choice. In some cases adjudicated delinquents or minors are ordered to seek intervention by the courts.

Our ecological perspective tells us that we may classify human services into two broad areas. The first serves the most immediate settings of adolescents and families (microsystems) and includes such services as counseling programs in high schools and programs and agencies that work directly with families. The second occurs at the broader level—the exosystem (e.g., the workplace of parents) or the macrosystem that includes the ideology and social policy that organize the world of the adolescent. Community services that operate through the exosystem of the adolescent include "primary community services" (Urban & Vondracek, 1977) such as public education, recreation, religion, transportation, communication or housing. On a broader level, social policy, legislation, research, the political milieu, education, and research will affect adolescents and their families. For example, legislation that reduces financial support to mental health services may force local child and youth services to abolish alternative education programs to adolescents.

The *timing* of the intervention refers to the onset or initiation of service delivery in the course of achieving developmental tasks. Intervention may occur before a problem develops. Sex education, for example, is an intervention program designed in part to prevent the occurrence of teenage pregnancy. But intervention may also occur following the development of a problem, such as in support services for unmarried adolescent mothers.

A related characteristic is the *purpose* of the intervention. There are three basic goals of intervention efforts. *Remedial* programs aim to correct a prob-

---

Carol and Bobbie were the toughest challenges I faced as a junior high teacher. Carol was a tough cookie in many ways. She talked back to teachers and sometimes got in fights with other girls. But she cried the day we took the whole ninth grade to see Romeo and Juliet. *Bobbie was something of a young hood. He was floundering academically, having been held back a grade already. He talked tough and hung out with a group of kids who were always in trouble. His father was a heavy drinker who had trouble holding down a steady job. His mother was a dreamy sort of woman, never quite all there. Carol's mother was an alcoholic; her father was nowhere to be found.*

Carol and Bobbie were always being sent to the Vice-Principal's office for goofing off in class, for being late, and for just about everything else kids could do without being in "real" trouble (i.e., getting expelled or picked up by the police). But there was something sweet about Carol and Bobbie, down under their tough exterior. I liked them, and they loved each other. Over the course of that year, I tried all the tricks of the trade to help Carol and Bobbie do better in school. I tutored them. I tried to persuade them to stay out of trouble. I tried to set up a system of rewards for doing their school work. I even invited them over to dinner one night after school (which was against school policy). We talked about their future. They had big plans. So did I.

One day in school I intervened in a fight and ended up being threatened by a group of tough punks who backed me into a corner. Bobbie showed up in the nick of time and rescued me. One day Carol came back from Art class with a birthday card for me. On more than one occasion I intervened on their behalf with the Vice-Principal (and I stretched the truth a bit to do so). So it went, with me trying to help and the two of them teetering on the edge. In June they graduated from the junior high school and went on to 10th grade.

I saw Carol the following fall. She was three months pregnant and Bobbie had just been sent to the State Training School for breaking into a hardware store. I hadn't heard the terms "ecology of human development" or "sociocultural risk and opportunity" yet then. But I felt defeated by so many forces outside my control that were dragging these two basically nice kids down the drain.

—James Garbarino, Ph.D
Teacher

lem already in existence. A program that places abused adolescents in group homes, for example, attempts to reduce the negative effects of the abusive home by putting the adolescent in a different environment. *Rehabilitative* programs aim to alleviate the surrounding conditions of the dysfunction. One example is hospitalizing heroin-addicted adolescents and placing them on methadone to alleviate the symptoms of drug withdrawal. Note that this intervention does nothing to train the body to survive without the social contexts associated with heroin use. It simply makes life bearable without it. Skills training and psychological support are necessary to build a life-style without drug dependence. Finally, *prevention* has as its goal creating conditions that will reduce the likelihood that a dysfunction will occur. A public awareness campaign that details the negative effects of drug abuse would attempt to discourage use of drugs among adolescents prior to the development of a problem. The effectiveness of preventive programs can be and often is much higher than remedial programs, although often difficult to prove. It is harder to reverse a dysfunction process than to stop it before it begins, but it is easier to measure improvement in an already identified problem than to detect a lower incidence of the problem in the first place. Several researchers see the goal of prevention as arranging conditions to maximize positive and constructive development of individuals and families (Carkhuff & Berenson, 1967) in order to provide individuals with tools to solve their own problems.

Intervention programs also differ in their scope. They may be either *single-purpose* (e.g., drug abuse programs) or *comprehensive* (social skills building programs), and they may be *direct* or *indirect*. Two methods of direct approach include individual or group approaches (e.g., psychotherapy, financial training, or academic counseling) that foster communication skills and a sense of belonging. Intervention that occurs within the context of a group provides an important vehicle for feedback from significant others to the adolescent. Adolescent service delivery may also take place indirectly through intervention in the exosystem. This kind of intervention seeks to change the conditions in an environment that will, in turn, affect the adolescent. A good example is a program that stimulates housing developments that provide recreational facilities for adolescents.

We also can classify standard methods of service delivery on the basis of their sponsorship. Public services include community services that are provided equally to all residents. Public education, public health services, and adolescent protective services are examples. Private sector services are of two types: profit and nonprofit. Nonprofit services are those that are funded by private organizations such as the Girl Scouts or Boy Scouts or the Catholic Youth Organization. Private-for-profit services include physicians, clinical psychologists, or any interventionist involved in private practice with adolescents as clients.

Finally, adolescent services may be classified as being *formal* and *bureaucratically created* (such as the school system) or *informal* and *spontaneously formed* such as self-help groups (e.g., Al-Anon). Informal groups provide social support during transition points or stressful periods in the lives of adolescents (Whittaker, Garbarino, & Associates, 1984).

Generally, the informal social support group evolved from the rationale advanced by Caplan (1974), Cassel (1974), and Cobb (1976), who have documented the importance of primary group support in helping people cope with stress related to emotional disorder. Mental health professionals refer to the health-protective benefits of these social support groups as a *buffer* (Caplan, 1974). The persons involved need not be close family. They may be individuals who function as "natural helpers" in the microsystem of the adolescent, including neighbors, peers, teachers, other relatives, and colleagues. They are usually the first level of helpers sought by an adolescent.

When formal programs adopt a social support approach they typically include one or more of the following strategies: personal network intervention or sustaining strength of bonds that already exist; volunteer linking of lay helpers within the community; mutual aid networks such as Weight Watchers or Al-Anon; neighborhood helpers or the identification of central figures in a neighborhood to whom persons turn naturally for help; community improvement. All of these efforts can provide a wide range of resources that can provide emotional support and practical assistance (Froland, Pancoast, Chapman, 1981).

Caplan (1974) sees the role of informal support groups as providing an enduring pattern of ties that significantly helps maintain the psychological and physical well-being of the individual. Individuals need only be valued by the adolescent in order to be effective in providing feedback or functioning as standards or models with whom the adolescent will compare her- or himself (Festinger, 1954). For adolescents who are unsure of their identity and highly impressionable, engaging in the process of social validation *(mirroring)* is central to the development of a sense of self. This capitalizes upon the imaginary audience. From Caplan's point of view, the very value of social suppport is, in fact, the feedback that others provide:

> . . . the harmful effects of absent or confusing feedback in a general population may be reduced in the case of those individuals who are effectively embedded in their own smaller networks which provide them with consistent communications of what is expected of them, support and assistance with tasks, evaluations of their performance, and appropriate rewards. (p. 4)

Thus, informal sources of support have the potential to significantly augment the power of professionals in providing specific types of help and support.

Special Issues in Services for Adolescents

Four issues in the macrosystem influence human services for adolescents: the legal status of the adolescent, the negative cultural image of the adolescent, the meshing of the need for service with a political milieu that does not value human services, and the community ideology concerning responses to adolescent problems.

Legal Ramifications of Intervention

Because human intervention has the potential to change human lives, there is a great need for the professional to respect the personal rights of clients. Ethical standards and legal guidelines have been developed by professional organizations, legislators, and consumer groups to standardize practices in human service delivery. In all human service delivery three ethical issues are paramount: confidentiality, privacy, and informed consent (Urban & Vondracek, 1977).

Confidentiality. The right to protection of personal information that is given to professionals by individuals in the process of seeking help is called *confidentiality*. This means that an unwritten agreement exists between professional and client implying that the client is honest in providing information and the professional assures the client that all such information will never be revealed (with the implicit exception of suicidal or criminal behavior). Such a contract of confidentiality fosters trust between client and professional in the therapeutic relationship. One problem that confronts the professional interventionist is judging when to act upon confidential information. This situation usually arises when clients provide information that could lead to endangering the safety of other persons or themselves. For example, a client may divulge that a parent has been sexually abusive. The professional is bound by confidentiality, but is also obligated to intervene in all abuse incidents. The professional might ask: What evidence is there to believe this accusation? Is the adolescent in immediate danger?

Privacy. Professionals must assure the client that only that personal information that is necessary for successful intervention will be requested. This is another area in which professional judgment is required to assess the kind and depth of information necessary. The common guideline is that only the information directly related to the problem is necessary. For example, it is unlikely (but not impossible) that information about sexual conduct would be relevant in the case of an adolescent seeking counseling for academic problems.

Informed consent. The third issue, *informed consent*, involves the process by which clients (or research participants) are informed of all aspects of the intervention procedures and provide consent for participation. Informed consent serves as a contract that informs clients of all details and assures them of confidentiality and privacy. There are, however, forms of treatment and psychopathology in which fully informed consent is not feasible (e.g., a psychotic delinquent). The point is that the professional be as honest and truthful as possible about what is going to happen as part of the intervention.

Decision-making and the court system.   It is in the treatment of adolescents that these fundamental rights become difficult to interpret. Because of the ambiguous legal status of adolescents, it is often difficult for the professional to know how to meet a legal obligation to intervene while maintaining the privacy of the family. In most states, any individual under the age of 18 is legally considered a minor, except in special circumstances (e.g., a 16-year-old mother is legally allowed the right to make more decisions than a non-mother of the same age). As such, the minor is considered incapable of entering contractual agreements such as social services, marriage, rent, or financial loans (although this is beginning to change in some areas). The parents are considered sole authority over all rights of the adolescent unless a court grants legal emancipation. It is reasonable to assume that parents will provide proper socialization and protect the welfare of their children. However, in reality, some parents are known to neglect the needs of their children through lack of knowledge, insufficient resources, or their own psychological dysfunction. Parents are also known to abuse their children physically and emotionally. Do such parents forfeit their right to make decisions for their children?

The problem for the professional involves the trade-off between protecting the privacy and authority of the family versus providing necessary intervention to minors who are incapable of obtaining services for themselves. Parental rights may be terminated only when one of the following conditions has been documented: parental abandonment or parental deprivation in the form of neglect that results in physical, emotional or mental harm to the child. These conditions are often exceedingly difficult to prove. Although all states have mandatory reporting laws for cases of suspected abuse, court intervention in cases involving adolescents is rare. Furthermore, minors are legally restrained from obtaining or accepting services without written consent of the parents in most circumstances.

Service providers are obligated to provide services to adolescents who are not receiving adequate parental care, but professionals are also legally at risk if they do not stay within societal guidelines. For example, professionals may provide an initial interview in case of an emergency, but counseling cannot continue for more than 24 hours without written parental consent (U.R.S.A., 1980). Further medical care, therapy, or education may not be provided except in suicidal or other emergency cases. In addition, there are other decisions that are difficult given the ambiguous nature of the legal status of the adolescent. The right of the adolescent to obtain contraception without parental consent is one such issue. Another area for concern is involvement in establishing therapeutic goals (Melton, 1981). Another difficult question is: Should adolescents have control over their records?

A few states now have laws that permit minors to enter into psychotherapy without parental consent (Melton, 1981). A study conducted to determine the impact of such a law reported that *all* minors using this legal right were adolescents. Common sensitive problems for which adolescents sought help independent of parent consent were abuse and neglect, pregnancy, sexual abuse, drug abuse, and contraception. We know that some adolescents in need of services do not receive them because they cannot obtain parental consent and find service agencies unwilling to accept the risks of proceeding without it.

I first met Susan after she was admitted to the inpatient psychiatric unit where I worked. She had "totaled" the family jeep and walked away with barely a scratch. The suicide note was vague and rambling, likely due to her drug usage. Her parents expressed the usual: shock, disbelief, and a willingness to do whatever was advised. The first meeting made me uncomfortable: Sue's mother stated that it wasn't intentional, just an accident caused by her daughter's allergy pills. Susan was silent in front of her parents, but to staff spoke of wanting to die for a long time. Her father was confused, not knowing whether to believe what he knew to be true or to go along with his wife and believe what was easier to believe.

Over the course of several weeks, Susan expressed a new interest in school and peers. Her parents were pressing for her discharge. All agreed on continuing family involvement in treatment in the outpatient department. Once away from the hospital Susan said that she did not want to continue with treatment. Her parents stated that difficulties with work schedules could not be worked out. Besides, they said, all was well at home once again. Phone calls expressing concern were at first politely and then more strongly rebuffed. Susan's mother complained of harassment, her father was in the middle once again.

The day before Susan climbed into the loft in the barn, a neighbor who had known of her hospitalization called the mental health department expressing concern over Susan's odd, druggy behavior. The staff felt frustrated, hoping that the neighbor's concern, redirected to the family, would help.

Susan had never in her life felt so betrayed by her father. Her anger intensified as he scolded her for smoking dope. She ran from him determined that he would be the one to find her. As she climbed up the ladder in the barn, she checked to make certain that no one saw her. Once in the loft she made two deep cuts, one in each wrist and then picked up her father's hand gun: this time she would be sure. They kept her alive mechanically—breathing and heart beating for two days while looking for someone in need of donor organs. With her parents' consent, they removed her corneas and unhooked her from the machine.

William Tolan, Ph.D
Pediatric Clinical Psychologist

One of the major problems in emergency service delivery arises in cases of maltreatment and running away. Although child protective service agencies are mandated to provide services, court intervention within the 24-hour legal limit of counseling is rare. Similarly, youths may not remain in any emergency service for more than 24 hours without notification of the parents or guardian. The alternatives for the adolescent and professionals caught in this situation without parental consent are: to obtain a court order of emancipation from parents documented by abuse or neglect; immediate placement in foster home; or to obtain a status offense citation in order to permit the probation department to petition the court for custody of the adolescent. In the courtroom, the adolescent often masks abuse and neglect, making these behaviors difficult to prove.

Because court intervention is rare, abused adolescents are more often labeled as status offenders or delinquents because both are easier to uphold in court and appear to be more expedient than proving abuse and neglect on the part of the parent. However, this form of plea bargaining entails many costs to the adolescent and to the community. Indeed, services to status offenders sometimes seem to be threatening and even abusive.

A study by Cohn and Andrews (1978) found that one-third of all adolescents cited for status offenses were, in fact, cases of abuse and neglect. Status offense often serves as a form of social control that appears harmless or even positive, but is susceptible to being misused to the detriment of adolescents, particularly the poor and the ethnic or racial minority youth (Piven, 1979). One study conducted by the Massachusetts Advocacy Center (MAC, 1980) reports that of 103 detained juveniles on one day, only 18 were awaiting trial. The remaining number were being detained for status offenses or for their own protection, without receiving mental and physical health care, social services, education, or training and rehabilitation. What is needed is a more efficient way to process the large numbers of adolescents who enter the detention system, and a system that is more client-oriented.

The relationship of human service professionals to the court system is primarily one of defining intervention strategies for court clients and providing direct services to youths. Zinn (1980) makes the point that the role of the professional involves less knowledge of psychopathology than understanding of social and institutional norms of expected behavior. The practice of treating youth and adults differently for the same crimes is largely limited to the United States. As we pointed out in Chapter 11, the origin of this practice is in a 19th century concern for homeless children and the belief that children should not be punished for wrongdoing but rather assisted in developing in socially constructive ways.

It appears that there are three groups of delinquent adolescents, each of which requires different kinds of services: those who commit isolated and trivial antisocial acts; those whose acts reflect developmental problems; and those who manifest chronic antisocial conduct. Most delinquency falls into the first category (which includes school truancy and property offense, but very few reports of violence toward individuals). In fact, many occasions of delinquency include vandalism and burglary attempts that never come to the attention of police (Schwartz, 1978). One study found that almost all adolescent males had committed a delinquent act (Offer & Offer, 1975). This means that the potential for discriminatory legal action is great: everyone is vulnerable but only some are prosecuted.

The Negative Image of Adolescence

The problems that the legal system has in dealing with adolescents is compounded further by the poor public image of adolescents. These negative stereotypes, as we have seen, portray youth as rebellious, indignant, disrespectful to adults, and aggressive. Adults already holding this negative stereotype may be further impressed by the fact that the adolescent may appear to dress sloppily or observe poor grooming habits as a gesture of defiance against adults (Garbarino & Gilliam, 1980). In addition, as we have seen, adolescents tend to be involved in groups of their peers and this, too, is threatening to adults. This image of the adolescent lends credence to another stereotype—that adolescents are troubled and troublesome. While many adults may find it easy to picture the *child* as victim, they may find it much more difficult to picture a tall and powerful adolescent as a victim. Therefore, adolescents frequently have difficulty in obtaining a sympathetic ear, and their own natural behavior may contribute to the public's unsympathetic attitude toward them.

Parental attitudes.   As we have seen, the rapid developmental changes of adolescence are very demanding of parents and families. Parents must accommodate the physical and social changes of the adolescent within the family system. For many parents, this stressful period overlaps with a personal identity crisis—what McMorrow (1977) has labeled *midolescence.*

Middle-age may stimulate adults to evaluate their own lives, to examine their own productivity in work and fulfillment in family and personal matters. Frequently, adults find that their lives have fallen short of their original goals. This disillusionment, combined perhaps with physical signs of age, may lead the adult to direct depression or anger toward the adolescent whose future and physical stamina are blooming. In addition, the adolescent's new found autonomy may cause the parents to feel anxiety over separation from their children. Full-time mothers, particularly, may feel that their job has been terminated. All of these issues may create conflict and may even undermine the sympathy of professional helpers. Parents may respond with stronger discipline or more restrictive rules in order to maintain family equilibrium. Adolescents may then resist this additional control and professional mediation may need to focus on resolving an escalating crisis.

Ideology and Community Response

The current ideological milieu downgrades the status of adolescents and advocates greater use of power to control adolescents. Groups of parents have even formed a national organization to assert control, and support parents in taking control. Called Toughlove, this organization seeks "to bring change into the lives of young persons who are *"impossible/incorrigible/uncontrollable/addicted/physically or verbally abusive/in trouble in school/in trouble with the law/destroying the family"* (York et al. 1982). Although it may be helpful to provide support to parents of teenagers, this philosophy may exaggerate existing negative stereotypes of the adolescent. The deliberate use of emotionally-laden words implying that the adolescent is responsible for "destroying the family" or for being "addicted" or "abusive" may contribute to a situation in which punitive parents feel justified in taking extreme actions against the adolescent. Although we recognize that adolescence is a difficult time for everyone involved, adolescents can hardly be solely responsible for destroying the family.

Perhaps it would be useful to look to our community institutions and the efficacy of the legal system in generating and correcting social problems. The following statement made for the American Psychological Association raises these issues (Alexander, 1982):

> At a time when many parents are laying down the law with their teenagers, some psychologists are worried that such a "toughlove" approach may actually produce more disobedience, rebelliousness, and unhappiness for many families.
>
> "Handing down a set of rules and firmly enforcing them works well for young children," Dr. Alexander said, "but that same strategy might create terrific problems for an adolescent. You've got to change approaches as your youngster grows."
>
> "A teenager needs more independence, so you need to negotiate the rules and the consequences and allow more flexibility within those limits. But once you agree on the rules, then you can be just as firm and in control as always."
>
> The trouble is that when parents are faced with a disobedient, irresponsible teenager, they often adopt the opposite strategy, observed Dr. Alexander.
>
> "What is preferable, I think, is to negotiate the rules by expressing your needs—not telling the kid what to do—and by allowing the youngster some choice within acceptable limits."
>
> "Let's take the curfew, for example," continues Dr. Alexander. "You can say, 'I need to know where you are at night, and I worry when you are out late. These are my needs. What are yours?' "
>
> "After listening, you might say, 'Before you had to be in at 9:00 no matter what. I understand you are older now, and you get something going with your friends and you don't want to come home right away. So I propose an 11:00 curfew on Friday and Saturday, and we'll make that an average time—if you are out until 11:30 one night you have to be in by 10:30 the next night. But midnight is the absolute latest. How about that policy?' "
>
> "Once you agree on the rules, you need to negotiate what happens if they are violated. If they are, you must firmly implement the agreed-upon discipline—

early curfew, work detail, loss of telephone or car privileges, whatever you have decided."

We need community systems that see the adolescent as a positive force, not as a victimizer. We need to monitor and reinforce positive behavior (Caplan, 1974; Caplan & Killiea, 1976) rather than support increased force and physical punishment. The following section will examine community human services as preventive programs to enhance positive development.

Models of Human Services for Adolescents

We review our ecological framework here briefly to remind us that intervention may occur at any of the five systems levels: organism, micro, meso, exo, and macro. We can place intervention with the organism when we work directly upon the characteristics of the individual adolescent through counseling, psychotherapy, or skill-building. This kind of intervention is required in most cases where developmental risk stems from some problem of genetic (e.g., physical handicap) or microsystem origin. As we have seen, one risk for adolescents derives from parents who severely and inappropriately restrict adolescent opportunities to experience microsystems beyond the family microsystem. The adolescent may be at risk for emotional abuse, manifest in several conditions (Garbarino & Vondra, 1983): A) *terrorizing* the adolescent and thereby producing seriously impaired competence in social relationships including low self-esteem, a consistent pattern of negative affect, and a serious inability to respond appropriately to the normal behavior of adults; B) *rejecting* the adolescent by refusing to provide normal care, by punishing normal behavior or by consistently humiliating the adolescent; C) *isolating* the adolescent from normal social relationships; and D) *mis-socializing* the adolescent by teaching or encouraging inappropriate or antisocial behavior or values. Each of these involves emotional maltreatment in the *family* microsystem, and it tells us that one form of intervention would be exposing adolescents to new microsystems that can complement and even compensate for malfunctioning families.

The mesosystem is the link between the immediate microsystems the adolescent experiences. For example, the degree of parental participation in school-sponsored activities or youth groups affects the richness of these connections. If the family isolates itself from the activities of the larger community of which it is a part, the adolescent may be at risk for developmental damage. The development of the adolescent is heavily influenced by both the *number* of links among school, church, peer group, and family and also by the *level* of involvement or depth of these links. So, the stronger and more diverse the links among these spheres of functioning, the greater the opportunity for adolescent growth. Intervention at this level seeks to prevent disorders by improving these links through social support or community involvements; intervention attempts to create and enhance mesosystems.

Involvement of families in the community is often influenced by work demands or local institutional constraints. These influences are described as exosystems for the adolescent but as mesosystems for the adults since they affect the lives of adolescents indirectly. For example, if parents are extremely stressed by conditions at work and this prevents them from spending much time with their adolescents, then the adolescent may be less likely to receive the quality attention and supervision necessary for promoting healthy development. This phenomenon is common in a society where both parents (or the only parent) in most families works to meet economic demands and personal fulfillment. Intervention might try to alter the work patterns of adults as well as create new microsystems for adolescents that provide for supervision and quality attention.

Local government may indirectly affect conditions in which the adolescent must function in several ways. For example, local funding agencies may allocate money in such a way that youth services (e.g., recreational programs or sports events) or much needed social programs will be initiated or maintained. Intervention at this level may take the form of advocating for youth services. Institutional decisions often reflect the ideologies held by the larger culture, and we call this the influence of the macrosystem.

The macrosystem is the "cultural blueprint" that underlies the structure of institutions that make up the society. Any norms or attitudes that permeate the society have the potential for influencing adolescents. The devaluation of children and youth in our society influences the support given to youth development services. Norms and attitudes of the larger society concerning violence toward children, economic policies that result in a high rate of youth unemployment, increased acceptance of divorce—all of these can undermine youth development. Intervention at the macro-level involves efforts at broad social reform, such as mass media campaigns against domestic violence.

Remedial and Preventive Models of Human Service

The remedial model has long dominated the field of adolescent services. Consider as an example the way most adolescents enter the social service system. Typically, the first step includes identifying the specific dysfunctions that impair adolescent functioning in some area of daily life such as interpersonal relationships, school achievement, or physical health. At that point, the adolescent is referred to a professional (e.g., school psychologist, social worker, physician, or nurse) and an evaluation occurs. Finally, the evaluating professional suggests a plan for treatment. This plan might be limited to psychological or social services, or it might include a package of services that complement each other, such as medical evaluation, psychological services, school services, and legal action.

Trying to remedy diagnosed problems has been the major method of service delivery for adolescents. There are, however, several problems with this approach. The potential failures of the system fall into three categories: failure to enter the system at the right time, inability to meet need for service, and in-effectiveness of treatment (Cowen & Gesten, 1978).

The intervention treatment system may fail first in that there may be a stigma for entering treatment at all. This may result in adolescents, who are particularly conscious of social validation as a developmental issue, avoiding professional assistance in the first place.

Second, there are insufficient resources to meet the overwhelming need for professional remedial services. As early as the 1960s, two main reasons were cited for this deficiency. There exists a significant gap between the need for services and availability of professionals to provide them (Albee, 1963), and psychotherapy has yet to establish itself as most effective in treating ado-lescent problems (Eysenck, 1961). Indeed, Eisenberg (1962) asserts the gravity of the first problem:

> The limitations of present therapeutic models doom us to training caregivers at a rate that ever lags behind the growing legions of the ill . . . society can ill afford today's precious over-specialization in which trainers may learn one method . . . but a method that ever lags behind the demands placed upon it. (p. 825)

Furthermore, there is geographically inequitable distribution of services that favors urban areas. Consequently, adolescents in rural areas may be underserved or isolated from needed services.

The current human service system breaks down at three steps in service delivery: identification of a particular malfunction in the adolescent; assess-ment of etiology and seriousness; intervention to change the identified dysfunc-tion (Sarason, 1971). At each stage the breakdown may come because of an inappropriate conception of the problem. One such inappropriate conception is often referred to as the *medical model.*

The medical model assumes that psychological problems may be treated using the same strategies that are used in treating physical problems. However, psychological problems usually are more interconnected and are a result of a variety of influences on the individual. Given this complicated network of in-fluences, it is exceedingly difficult to identify one specific cause of the problem. There is really no germ on which to blame the problem of social psychological dysfunction as there often is in the case of physical disease.

In general, we need an overall shift from the *reactive* approach of the medical model to one that aims to create conditions that will prevent disorders from developing (a more *proactive* approach). A report by the Surgeon Gener-al's Report on Health Promotion and Disease Prevention (1979) has supported prevention as the most fundamental movement in health care:

> There are three overwhelming reasons why a strong new emphasis on preven-tion—at all levels of government and by all our citizens—is essential. . . . Preven-tion saves lives. . . . Prevention improves the quality of life. . . . Finally, it can save dollars in the long-run.

The strategies that communities have used in prevention flow from a conceptual approach that is both broader and well-defined.

Bloom (1979) discusses conceptual developments that have influenced the field. First, there has been a shift from searching for a specific set of factors that are associated with dysfunctional behavior to a broader view that incorporates stressful life events that may place the individual at risk for psychological problems. That is, intervention has begun to recognize the importance of the context of events for psychological disorder. For the adolescent confronting many significant life changes associated with the developmental stage of adolescence, this is a significant factor. Indeed, a body of literature has documented the relationship of stress and psychological adjustment in both adolescents (Garbarino, Sebes, & Schellenbach, 1984) and adults (Holmes & Rahe, 1967).

Second, Bloom (1979) suggests that there has been a corresponding shift from preventing specific disorders to promoting health—a more positive approach. He defines health promotion as a

> variety of non-specific practices; for example, the provision of crisis intervention services or social supports during times of stress which may have a positive effect on health in general and may, in'fact, prevent a variety of forms of behavior disorders. Community mental health approaches imply a positive emphasis on restoration, early detection of disorders, and consultation, all of which use resources of the community to build new areas of competence, as opposed to repairing "casualties" of the mental health system.

Indeed, the overarching and unifying theme of our approach to intervention with adolescents is the development of social skills.

Formal and Informal Services

According to Cowen and Gesten (1978), the two systems with the greatest impact on the adolescent are the family and the school. Success in school depends largely on the ability to acquire skills and competencies, and a failure to do so defines the individual's failure within the system. For the adolescent, the school world constitutes a major portion of life. Garbarino and Asp (1981) outline three major factors which contribute to an adolescent's success: prior mastery of basic skills; social forces within the school that influence the adolescent including social structure and cohesion among individuals; and linking present school activities to the future in concrete ways.

Adolescent peer groups can guide activities toward prosocial as well as antisocial goals. Adults then may be in a position to positively reinforce those prosocial activities. As Caplan (1974) has suggested, it may be the school as a support system that promotes the development of basic skills. Adolescents involved in extracurricular activities have greater opportunities to become involved in a number of more varied activities and to gain new experiences and competencies that help to clarify and structure the formation of identity. The more activities in which a student is involved, the greater the sense of commitment to the school, to peers, and, symbolically, to the community.

As we saw in Chapter 1, small schools provide an opportunity to create demands for participation in the environment (Garbarino, 1980). A smaller setting also provides a reasonable environment for close observation of students by adults, thus increasing accountability on both sides of the relationship. It also provides a setting in which social competence may prosper in many areas including intellectual development, sports, or vocational development. This makes policy changes favoring small schools an important form of exosystem intervention.

Indeed, a small group setting may be the very environment to foster specific social competencies, even among marginal adolescents. Gold (1969) has written that it is *marginality* or feelings of lack of cohesion (arising from exclusion from group processes) that are related to antisocial behavior of juvenile delinquents. Large schools appear to contribute to negative character development by exacerbating such marginality and producing greater anonymity among students, creating conditions in which adolescents may find it easier to experiment with antisocial behaviors. The key is to arrange the microsystems of adolescence so that they encourage prosocial behavior.

The following case study provides an illustration of the potential impact of small group processes on adolescents:

> Tommy was four years of age, retarded, unable to speak and very antisocial in his behavior. His common method of interaction was highly aggressive, usually characterized by hitting, kicking, or biting for attention. He was the child of abusive parents—father addicted to narcotic drugs, mother an alcoholic, which caused the physical and mental deficiencies in the child at birth. Yet Thomas (Tommy) played in the streets of a metropolitan ghetto until it was well past sundown.
>
> Sometimes he would run wildly away from the immediate area surrounding his home; he was known to dash into the streets and this was particularly dangerous for a deaf, mute, and unsocialized child. Interestingly, the people who served as protectors of Tommy were also the gang of adolescent neighborhood hoodlums. Although the local stores were terrorized by the boys, they consistently acted as safeguards for the four-year-old child, supervising his play from their gathering place in the park. Whenever Tommy would get lost, his parents never bothered to search for him because they knew the boys from the neighborhood gang would bring the child to their doorstep before the night was over. The entire local area was dotted with friends of the group, so there was virtually no place that the child could wander where he would be unsafe.

This is an example of how a group may function to reinforce prosocial behavior directed at a member of the neighborhood. Strong loyalties developed among group members that produced both prosocial behaviors (directed inward toward the group members and selected individuals, such as Tommy) *and* antisocial behaviors (directed outward toward the society and its structures, such as local businesses and school). It is important to note that such groups are more likely to be prosocial if such goals are modeled and reinforced by adults who are valued by the adolescents. This can occur very effectively in more formal and informal settings within the community, as discussed in the next section.

Community-based formal support systems.   The new emphasis on building competencies rather than repairing problems also finds expression in programs that use community resources to reach adolescents. In the ecological framework, the integration of the adolescent into the community creates more microsystems and more nurturing mesosystems, and thus more opportunities for developing competence and growth. Frequently, this process occurs through participation in community organizations such as scouts, YMCA, church youth groups, and sports teams. All of these present informal opportunities to become involved in meaningful activities that tap competencies in a variety of areas that school may not. Participation in these groups exposes adolescents to a group approach directed toward prosocial goals in society.

This approach has served as the model for several innovative efforts in community mental health. One such effort was the Residential Youth Center (Goldenberg, 1971), which provided a model of how to implement such a community program with inner-city youth. The program was a significant departure from traditional therapy in that the founder assumed that disadvantaged inner-city youths could be better served in a residential setting separate from their homes. On this basis, the Residential Youth Center was established as a short-term care facility. Unique to the setting was the provision that the responsibilities for the group were shared over all professional levels among the staff members. Similarly, all staff members shared household duties as well. The residential program included personal counseling, vocational training, education, and maintenance of the household duties. Average duration of stay of adolescents aged 16–21 was approximately five months. Program evaluation revealed that the residents who were involved in the program had significantly higher employment rates, better work attendance, more income, and fewer incarcerations compared to a control group of similar, nonprogram adolescents.

Another example of a community psychology program with inner-city youth is the Howard University Institute for Youth Studies (Fishman, Denham, Levine, & Shatz, 1969). This program sought to train adolescents in basic general skills of problem-solving, deficits in which seem to underlie more specific dysfunctions in social competence. The emphasis was on skill-training and specific job-related skills. Evaluations of the program showed gains for participants in increased job stability and reduced rates of delinquent behavior among 100 inner city youth.

Blackhawk Cottage—part of a larger residential center for adjudicated delinquents—scheduled a roller skating party with a girls' cottage from the same institution. Since the boys would be host for the activity, they met in their management group to plan the evening, including music, games, and refreshments. One of the members, Jerry, was considerably less mature and sophisticated than the rest of the group. He was more impulsive, gregarious, and at times provocative. During the planning session, a concern arose as to how Jerry would "come across" at the party—whether he would "act funny" or dress properly. Several members chorused that Jerry should stay back in the cottage, despite the entreaty from the group leader that this was a total group activity. Jerry responded in two ways to this mounting criticism—by acting humorously (playing the buffoon) and, finally, with anger. Eventually he stormed angrily from the roc n. The other members seemed to greet his exit with a mixture of guilt ("We sure took care of him") and relief ("Now let's get on with the planning"). As group leader, I briefly looked for Jerry to rejoin the group, but he had gone to his room sobbing and refused to come out. I returned to the group and, after expressing disappointment in the group's behavior, called an end to the planning meeting and scheduled a special group session to discuss the incident with Jerry after supper.

The focus of the group had clearly shifted from the task of planning to some basic issues concerning the group's way of handling one of its members. I sought Jerry out and supported his coming to the evening session to explore the problem, which, in his case, was long standing. The focus of the meeting was on developing positive ways of providing criticism—so that Jerry can get a handle on what he does that upsets the group. Additionally, I explored why these kinds of concerns—about dress, behavior, and appearances—occurred in the first place and how they might relate to some larger concerns of the group, which they conveniently laid on Jerry.

Jim Whittaker PhD
Social Worker

Informal Support Systems and Their Relation to Formal Support Systems

A more informal method of reaching adolescents in the community uses existing networks of peers and adults who interact with the adolescents each day. This method is a primary outgrowth of preventive community mental health programs and taps paraprofessionals and lay people in the community as helpers. Indeed, these individuals are often the first sources of help to whom troubled adolescents may turn. For example, it is much more likely for an abused adolescent to confide in a trusted teacher or a neighbor rather than a stranger (this is often true of adults as well). This system has been used to reach an ever-increasing number of individuals in both urban (Collins & Pancoast, 1976) and rural settings (Danish & D'Augelli, 1980).

Although different forms of service to adolescents are usually described separately, our ecological framework reminds us that it is the links among all of these settings that must be considered in caring for the troubled adolescent. A continuum of care should exist, including family-centered services, foster home care, and specialized group homes (Hawkins & Weis, 1980). Further, to provide the best possible conditions for family development, informal supports such as relatives, churches, and neighbors need to collaborate with public services such as social agencies or community programs.

Community links are any mechanisms that join or connect a child or youth service to its sources of community support (Whittaker, 1980). Resource families in a residential treatment center for abused adolescents and foster grandparents in treatment programs for status offenders are two examples of community links. All of these efforts attempt to integrate disturbed adolescents and their families into the normal community while using competencies and natural supports that exist in that community.

Whittaker (1980) emphasizes that quality links among the social networks of a problem family may also be the target for intervention. This intervention may take place both in the service setting and in the youth's family. Services for adolescents must tend toward "the least restrictive environment." To do this, Rhodes (1970) suggests that "we need to increase the adaptive capacity of communities not just of adolescents themselves."

Rehabilitative Approaches

Traditional treatment services have been restorative in nature. In contrast to a preventive model, this approach rarely emphasized the construction of new skills for the client. Rather, therapy focused on repairing skills or strengths that the individual already had. The goal of the therapist's action is returning the dysfunctional adolescent to a more normal path of development.

Some of the special issues of adolescence contribute to the complexity of adolescent treatment. Often, the resolution of identity crisis, concerns about body image, and the independence-dependence struggle become important issues in the therapeutic process. In contrast to most adults, most adolescents are engaged in a transitional lifestyle in which interests and relationships are highly variable and unstable. Adolescents are also legally and financially dependent on parents, which may present further treatment complications and ethical considerations for the therapist. In addition, adolescents are rarely the initiators of therapy, and therefore frequently resist making the initial personal investment necessary for therapy to progress. Finally, psychological problems of the adolescent are often clouded by the effects of drugs or severe mood swings.

Any rehabilitative service must conform to the court decision (Wyatt v. Stuckey, 1972) that established that intervention for youth must be guided by the principle of *least restrictive treatment*. In treatment settings, this principle means that the therapist must attempt to use a minimally intrusive approach, such as seeing the patient on an outpatient basis, before resorting to more intrusive elements, such as residential treatment.

Therapeutic Approaches

Dyadic counseling.   Dyadic counseling is the most common traditional method of treatment for adolescents. The therapist in the novel and film *Ordinary People* (1976) presented a model demonstration of dyadic therapy, which usually takes the form of verbal psychotherapy. This may present problems for a confused adolescent who may find it difficult to express feelings in words. What is more, the adolescent may not be cognitively up to the level of the therapy.

The initial contact with the therapist plays an important role in establishing the motivation for the client involved in therapy. For the adolescent, the initiation of therapy may be a particularly troublesome issue. There are three possible sources of referral for the adolescent—self, family, and community institution. The ideal situation is one in which the adolescent initiates therapy because of a self-perceived personal need, because this demonstrates that the adolescent is invested in the therapeutic process. If the referral is initiated by a family or institution (e.g., school, court), the adolescent is likely to be highly resistant. For example, the family may view the adolescent as *the* problem and as such, the focus of all dysfunction within the family microsystem. The adolescent may interpret parental action to initiate therapy as rejection or as symbolizing the family's feeling of hopelessness about the adolescent. In these circumstances, it may be helpful for the therapist and adolescent to create a *precontract negotiation* in which they set down the goals of therapy and the methods to be used. This shifts responsibility from parents as initiators of therapy to adolescent as participant in defining the therapeutic relationship.

Once therapy has begun, the therapist may highlight specific issues in the progression of the relationship from initiation to final termination. The overall model of therapy for adolescents is characteristically open and direct, as opposed to an adult-oriented psychodynamic technique that is usually more formal and indirect. Indeed, to free any resistance, the therapist may encourage the adolescent to share themselves by showing hobbies or using various projective techniques in which the adolescent tells the therapist what he or she sees in ambiguous pictures or stories. The therapeutic techniques should be flexible to prevent the adolescent from losing motivation to continue. The task of the therapist is to strengthen the ego in areas of existing competence and to eliminate destructive impulses that deteriorate developing strengths.

The therapist who demonstrates sincerity and caring for the adolescent has the best chance for developing a good therapeutic relationship. The therapist should adopt a nonjudgmental stance that does not criticize the values held by the adolescent even as it tries to modify the behavior those values produce. Therapists should also aim their language at the level of the adolescent. Finally, the therapist must be flexible, (e.g., scheduling appointments after school) and encourage activities that help the adolescents build their competence.

Three issues that place a special burden for the therapeutic relationship are managing acting-out behaviors, potential manipulativeness, and polarization. Setting firm limits and helping the adolescent integrate thought into the process of acting out destructive feelings help produce greater autonomy for the adolescent. *Polarization* is the common tactic of playing sides between two or more authority figures. The therapist may prevent this problem by ensuring that no miscommunication occurs among all the parties involved. Adolescents will then find themselves reassured within the boundaries of the therapeutic relationship, and this may reduce the desire to test limits. Consistency, honesty, and predictability help the adolescent form boundaries for behavior.

Toward the conclusion of successful therapy, the adolescent will begin to become involved in a greater number of activities and show deeper relationships with peers and improved family relationships. As these less formal types of support and validation occur, the adolescent will decrease dependence on the formal support of the therapeutic relationship. Self-concept will be enhanced and academic functioning improved.

Angela had always done everything her parents had asked of her. Fourteen years old now, she was considerate, well-mannered, a hard worker and outstanding student, pretty, out-going, and modest, too. Although she sometimes seemed a little jealous of her five-year-old sister, her parents could find nothing else to fault her for. Her father, a university professor, and her mother, a former beauty queen and herself the holder of a graduate degree, seemingly had all their wishes fulfilled in Angela.

What happened then, when the family went for a sabbatical tour of the Middle East? A diet that Angela had begun with some friends for Lent achieved her goal of losing ten pounds by May. She was a trim 105 pounds, five feet two inches, just beginning to show breast buds, and ready for swimsuit season. But the habits of picky eating, fussing with food preparation, and sometimes not eating a meal at all didn't go away. By June, when the family was to leave, she weighed 96 pounds.

Despite their concern, and hoping Angela would respond to their threats of not taking her unless she "started eating right," the family departed. Foreign food and irregular schedules allowed Angela to get away with disobeying her parents' increasingly desperate rules about eating. She now looked unhealthy, her clothes hung on her, and she was always cold, despite the fact that it was summer. The family returned to the United States several weeks earlier than planned. The family physician hospitalized Angela in an intermediate care psychiatric hospital. She weighed 76 pounds, menstruation had ceased, and Angela denied that anything was the matter.

Treatment in the hospital was strictly behavioral. Angela had to eat certain foods, or lose privileges such as watching T.V., going for a walk, telephoning a friend. She was weighed daily, and got extra privileges for every half pound she gained. Individual and group psychotherapy were tried, but like most anorectics, she disagreed that she had any problems. At the end of seven weeks, Angela was discharged. She weighed 96 pounds and had agreed to a contract: if she weighed less than 95 pounds, her parents would return her to the hospital. She still saw herself as "fat," and wished that she would be allowed to lose weight.

In October, Angela returned to school, and she also began individual therapy. She was not interested in talking about her problems, but she soon began disclosing things about her family life that had been making her very unhappy and that she had felt helpless to change. Her father was away from home, or there but busy most of the time, and she felt very distant from him. Her mother was anxious about her daughter's popularity, and, indeed, Angela had not yet dated. She was especially concerned about her daughter's appearance; as it turned out, Angela's mother was the one who was always on a diet, trying to lose the pounds that made a once slender beauty rather plump. In this as well as other areas, the mother's high intelligence and high aspirations for her daughter came across to Angela as her mother's attempts to control her. Food was one area where these struggles were particularly fierce. And finally, Angela admitted that she was really very jealous of her sister, feeling that the younger girl got all the attention and approval Angela once had.

It took several months of individual work before Angela felt ready to have her family join the therapy sessions. Getting the feelings expressed that she had been harboring so long was a major effort. For their part, Angela's parents were genuinely surprised that they had caused her such pain, and found it particularly hard to see in what ways they had been "controlling" her. They were able and willing to make some changes; in other areas, Angela had to face the fact that she would have to accept them as they were. Perhaps most helpful during this phase of treatment was the family's agreement not to restrict, comment on, or in any way "control" Angela's eating behavior, so long as she kept her weight above 95 pounds. Despite insights she gained during this time, and despite her new-found "control" of herself, she still thought she was "fat." But she had at least learned to disregard this perception, and tensions over food and other areas of contention soon diminished considerably.

The next, and final stage of Angela's treatment, was group therapy. She became a member of an adolescent girls therapy group that met weekly. She began talking about her anorexia to the girls, describing how she chose her foods and why, telling how it felt to perceive herself as fat no matter what the mirror reflected. The group ate dinner together once each month; Angela *always brought her contribution, but never partook of anything. She was different in other ways, too: she always carried piles of books and was an A + student; she had no interest in boys and had not been to any boy-girl parties. The group was curious about her, but Angela also found that they accepted her. No one tried to make her different from the way she wanted to be.*

Perhaps because of this, perhaps because of the reduced tensions at home, Angela began to change. She no longer had stacks of books with her when she came to group, nor used the few minutes before it started to read. She attended, and even hosted, a boy-girl party. Eating and appearance became less and less frequent topics of her conversation. She still saw herself as fat, but she acknowledged that other people didn't. Anyhow, she now found it more interesting to talk about boys and parties, teachers and college.

The group disbanded at the end of summer. Angela, her family and the therapist all agreed that now was a good time to try ending therapy. No significant problems occurred. Angela still ate oddly, but she began to gain weight. By winter she was beginning to look plump, and a little like her mother. She also began to look more and more womanly. Although some of her old fears (of being fat) seemed now to be close to coming true, Angela was not particularly distressed. She found the subjects of colleges and boys (who were attracted by her pink prettiness, and not in the least dissuaded by her plumpness) more interesting than food. Her grades remained high, but she also took time to make friends, and by spring reported (still embarrassedly) that she had a boyfriend.

Although Angela is not yet through all the stressful points that could cause a recurrence of her anorexia, she has some tools now with which to combat it. She has learned to control herself and to get away from other's control of her in an assertive manner. She has learned that family members are not the only ones whose approval feels good. She has overcome her fears of boys and dating, which will hopefully continue to generalize when she gets to later stages of sexual behavior. And she has learned to disregard what she thinks the mirror tells her, which is all right; for even though she's plump, she's a far prettier and healthier girl than the one she used to be.

Nancy R. Chiswick, Ph.D.
Clinical Psychologist

Group therapy.   Although dyadic counseling remains a common model of treatment for adolescents, group therapy is a popular alternative or complement. The group setting offers the opportunity to receive support and validation for individual feelings from a group. Group sessions offer a chance for the leaders to help participants gain knowledge, skills, and work through dynamic psychological issues. Two different variations of group therapy merit consideration: (1) group therapy and peer helping with professional leaders (Feldman &

Wodarski, 1975; Garbarino & Jacobsen, 1978; Longberg, Bickerstaff, & Fishbach, 1981); (2) group counseling that trains parents as therapists (Guerney & Guerney, 1969).

Group psychotherapy with professional leaders may be particularly effective with adolescents who are strongly influenced by peers. Briefly, the group process involves five phases: revealing one's own story to the group *(cartharsis);* testing professionals on issues of confidentiality and maintenance of group limits; group identity formation; resistance; and clarification of personal problems. Professional leaders who strive to provide lively groups using varied formats of discussion will have the greatest success.

One example of peer helping is the Youth Helping Youth program directed at helping abused adolescents gain interpersonal and social skills (Longberg, Bickerstaff, & Fishback, 1981). The goal of the program is to provide a supportive atmosphere in which abused adolescents can learn effective interpersonal and problem-solving skills, including self-esteem, recognizing and understanding feelings of oneself and others, and responding to criticism. The groups meet in six consecutive weekly meetings, approximately 90 minutes long. Characteristically, the group gets acquainted in the first few sessions, then becomes productive in dealing with content and psychological issues, and finally begins the process of moving out on their own as the group draws to a close. Each session consists of an opening, a content-oriented skill-training time, practice, application to real-world situations, and closing.

An illustrative program that emphasizes indirect intervention for adolescents is the Parent-Adolescent Relationship Development program developed by Bernard and Louise Guerney (1969). This program incorporates both knowledge and skill. It seeks to

> . . . impart knowledge and interpersonal skills to parents in dealing with their children that will help them create an optimal growth pattern in their respective families. Further, it seeks to train parents in such a way so as to make the knowledge and skill a part of their permanent behavioral repertoires so that consolidation of therapeutic gains and growth do not stop with the end of the treatment program. (L. Guerney, 1976, p. 70)

Group leaders are trained in the use of techniques that are didactic *(informative)*, dynamic *(reflective)*, and reinforcing *(behavioral)*. Attempts are made to generalize newly acquired interpersonal skills to the home setting. Parents can be involved on the basis of expressed interest based upon a common problem (e.g., forming a step-family or running away).

Another kind of group intervention lead by professionals takes place in a residential setting and focuses on teaching specific social skills by using behavior modification techniques. One such program has been implemented at Father Flanagan's Boys Town by a group of therapist/investigators (Maloney, Fixen, & Maloney, 1979). These therapists suggest that it may be unrealistic to expect that *all* the problematic behaviors of the adolescent be reformed. Rather, they suggest that a more effective approach is to select the behaviors that are most critical for therapy and competent functioning and focus on these for treatment.

Behavioral Methods

Four behavioral techniques have proved particularly effective in changing behaviors. These include contingent positive attention, behavioral contracting, implementation of a token economy, and training in prosocial behaviors.

The first technique involves giving positive attention to prosocial behaviors. The specific underlying goals of this approach are designating a clear-cut group of behaviors to be encouraged, providing guidelines to others regarding the occurrence of appropriate and inappropriate behaviors, and developing rules for ignoring antisocial behaviors. In a classroom study using this approach, Hall, Lund, and Jackson (1968) found that teachers were able to decrease nonstudy behaviors of disruptive students and increase prosocial and study behaviors. Since attention is a potent factor influencing adolescent behavior, we should note that negative attention (such as reprimands) can reinforce and thus increase inappropriate behavior. The tough issue, of course, is how much to ignore to extinguish bad behavior without losing control over the situation.

Behavioral contracting is an agreement between an adolescent and adult that provides explicit guidelines for expected behavior. Five elements of an effective behavioral contract are: detailed privileges that both parties expect to earn as a result of fulfilling the contract; detailed responsibilities for appropriate behavior; sanctions for failing to meet responsibilities; a bonus clause that assures positive reinforcement for compliance; and a feedback mechanism. Behavior contracting has been successfully implemented with juvenile delinquents (Jayaratne, Stuart, & Tyrodi, 1974) and in correctional institutions (Musante, 1975). The behavioral contract is a particularly advanced therapeutic technique because it addresses the issue of control, since both client and therapist share in responsibility. The more completely the therapist can control the adolescent's environment the more powerful the contract.

The *token economy*, originally developed by Ayllon and Azrin (1968) for treatment of hospitalized psychiatric patients, has also been effective in dealing with youthful problematic behavior. It is based on the principles of the behavioral contract but is expanded for use with a group of individuals. Typically, the token economy allows the adolescent to earn points for behaving in socially appropriate ways and to lose points for behaving in antisocial ways. Accumulated points are used to obtain tangible rewards in the form of privileges or gifts. One example of the token economy with adolescents is the teaching-family model (Phillips, Phillips, Fixen, & Wolf, 1974). In this model, using point losses to decrease the occurrence of verbal aggression was more successful than verbal correction by authorities. An important issue facing programs such as this is how well they generalize to real life situations.

The final method involves the training of prosocial behaviors. While other approaches attempt to deal with behaviors that already were present in the behavioral repertoire, this approach seeks to provide the conditions for the adolescent to acquire new skills. Techniques often used in skill training are *prompting, fading,* and *shaping.* Prompting provides a condition that will increase the probability that a new behavior is performed. Fading is a process in which the condition or stimulus is gradually and systematically reduced so that the behavior remains but the stimulus is removed, *weaning* from the original stimulus. Shaping gives systematic positive reinforcements to parts of the entire complex behavior until the whole behavior is consistently established.

One area of social skill deficiency that has received attention is shyness. Zimbardo and his colleagues (1974) studied ways to overcome shyness. Zimbardo reports that most young people report being shy at some point, with adolescence being an especially critical point. He and his group report success in remediating serious shyness by: absorbing the adolescent in a task that submerges self-consciousness (e.g., a game); teaching and practicing specific social skills as they bear on specific troublesome situations; assertiveness training; explaining how widespread shyness is and reinforcing the idea that the adolescent will grow out of it.

Residential Treatment

Home-based intervention is not the whole story, of course. Some youth are best served in residential facilities. In the case of runaways, for example, some period of out-of-home services may be a necessary first step in the direction of stable independent living or reunion with parents.

Programmatic Service Needs of Adolescent Runaways

The problem of runaway adolescents in our society has become more important as the complexity of modern society has increased. As we have seen in Chapter 11, runaways who hit the streets of large cities with little money and no friends often become involved in illegal, dangerous, and immoral activities such as drug traffic, pornography, and prostitution in order to meet immediate practical needs. They present a serious challenge to human service delivery systems.

As Chapter 11 told us, one important distinction between troubled adolescents who run away as compared to normal adolescents who run away is the duration of time spent away from home. Those who attempt to reach a place far from home and stay away for a long time tend to exhibit a greater number of more severe psychological problems. Serving these adolescents is very difficult because they are characterized by less favorable self-concepts, poorer interpersonal relationships, higher incidence of depression, feelings of failure, loss of control, and less motivation to seek help (Brennan, Huizinga, & Elliott, 1978; D'Angelo, 1974; Wolk & Brandon, 1977).

In a study using the Child Behavior Checklist, Edelbrock (1980) compared a sample of youth referred to mental health service to those adolescents who were not referred. Among the samples, 30% of the referred sample had run away during the previous year in contrast to about 2% of those who had not been referred. Overall, the problem of running away seemed to be associated with five areas of dysfunction on the Child Behavior Checklist: truancy, alcohol and drug abuse, screaming, attempted suicide, and suicidal talk.

Many runaway youth are products of disturbed family functioning and may, indeed, use running away as an escape from a troubled home. Approximately 80% of long-term runaway adolescents are escaping serious problems such as drug or alcohol abuse in the family (Houten & Golembiewski, 1976). Indeed, about one third of runaway adolescents who report to social service agencies have histories of maltreatment and blatant parental rejection. Many of the effects of abuse—low self-esteem, poor social skills, few bonds or enduring interpersonal relationships—make the runaway adolescent more vulnerable on the streets and more difficult to manage in a program setting. While these traits make adolescents more eager to form new relationships with anyone who appears to offer emotional support, it also makes them suspicious of parental figures represented by social service agencies. As we pointed out in Chapter 11,

---

The short, slightly built, twelve-year-old came strutting in the door with all the confidence of an experienced thirty-year-old. This was Freddy's fourth foster care placement in less than a year. Two years earlier, over the course of six months, Fred had stolen a bicycle, thrown rocks at a car, received stolen goods and, in the company of a friend, stolen a motorcycle. His mother, unable to tend to her own disorganized life, was incapable of providing Fred with either the loving attention or consistent discipline he needed.

In a series of scattered responses to these incidents, the local Juvenile Court had found Fred delinquent, referred him to an intensive diagnostic center, returned him to his mother's home under the supervision of the county Children's Services, changed his legal status from delinquent to dependent, placed him in a foster home and finally referred him to our specialized, family-centered foster care home.

In the home, "Fearless" as he was called by the other boys, continued to demonstrate the types of behavior that had led to difficulties in other placements. Although now able to sustain an activity, he displayed many residual traits associated with an earlier diagnosis of hyperactivity. Fred had difficulty organizing his efforts and completing tasks. Simple one- and two-step instructions and constant supervision were required. Fred was easily distracted and, more seriously, made snap decisions without thought of consequences.

His adjustment to school was more positive. Fred was assigned to a special class with nine other children. More sociable and more creative than his classmates, Fred quickly became the "teacher's pet." As a result, he was able to receive a great deal of individual attention.

With the end of the school year, Fred sought other sources for the stimulation and attention that he craved. With the staff of the home, he vied for a favored position as the baby of the family. In pitiful attempts to gain attention from the older boys in the house, he alternated reckless acts of bravado with assorted activities to incite their wrath. He seemed to get a gratifying emotional "high" from any attention, whether positive or negative. When reality threatened his highly charged, fantasy-laden world, he would withdraw, blocking the history of sadness in his life.

Neither his behaviors, nor his perceptions of self were age appropriate. While he liked to think of himself as a capable adult, his needs, cognitive level, and behaviors were those of a young child.

The confrontation between fantasy and reality and between the two age inappropriate styles came with an important marker event—his thirteenth birthday. After months of planning, Fred made a visit home for a special family birthday party. Fred found, however, only a birthday card, and promises. Many of his childhood possessions were gone. In defense of his frustrated child-self, Fred denied his disappointment and overcompensated by acting out.

Over the course of ten days, Fred ran away three times, being gone for two or three days at a time. He was often located hundreds of miles from home. Exhibiting no sense of possible consequences, the diminuitive waif managed to obtain several rides hitchhiking. His size and blind courage earned him "stowaway" status on buses and trains. He later related how several people had given him money. His emotions and his actions were out of control. As a result, the county Children's Services agency placed Fred temporarily in a more restrictive setting. Following several more incidents of running away, the exasperated staff at the county Children's Services agency asked Fred to tell them what they should do with him.

In characteristic style, Fred chose the fantasy of a happy and secure existence with his mother, unable or unwilling to comprehend that his mother was not able to meet that dream.

At home, Fred's life lacked the affirmation and consistency he needed. He ruled his own life by impulse. Soon Fred was back in court. This time he was returned to delinquent status and placed in a juvenile detention facility to await a new round of placements. At last report, Fred had run again; an out-of-control teen running from reality, in search of a self.

Robert Gibson, ACSW
Clinical Social Worker

many of these adolescents fall into the hands of prostitution networks who offer them a place to stay, money, and emotional support. A large proportion of these adolescents have been sexually abused in their homes (Silbert & Pines, 1981).

The first and foremost service need of the runaway is protection (Garbarino & Garbarino, 1983). One way to afford runaways protection is to provide them with short-term economic support so that they will be less likely to turn to illicit and illegal forms of financial support, such as prostitution and pornography. Runaway houses provide both immediate protection from victimization of adolescents on the streets, as well as shelter and food.

Once the adolescent has entered a treatment facility, it is possible to assess the precipitating factors in the adolescent and in the family. Friedman (1978) asserts the need for family treatment and preparation for the return of the adolescent. Such treatment may be crucial to reintegrating the adolescent into the family. Successful resolution of family conflict at this stage may prevent a repeated incident.

The reintegration does not stop at the family level, however. The alienated adolescent will need to restore functioning in the neighborhood, school, and community. This is where coordination of community services with school and family becomes crucial (Whittaker, 1980).

Peers may also serve to prevent runaway incidents by providing support prior to the incident. The National Runaway Hotline (1-800-621-4000) also provides advice to the prospective runaway. During the incident, peers may refer runaways to shelters or treatment centers. Finally, peers may participate in self-help groups that provide direct services to runaways. One illustrative example is the social skills training orientation of the Youth Helping Youth program mentioned earlier (Longberg, Bickerstaff, & Feshback, 1981).

Substance Abuse

Substance abuse is one of the major social problems confronting professionals dealing with adolescents. Data from a 1980 survey of high school seniors (Johnston, Bachman and O'Malley, 1980) indicate that while many adolescents have tried illicit substances, relatively few continue to use them, and only a very small minority are frequent users. For example, about 9% said they had used marijuana daily in the previous 30 days and 6% reported having used alcohol daily in that time period. The figures for some of the more well known illicit substances were: inhalants .1%, hallucinogens .1%, cocaine .2%, heroin less than .1%, stimulants .7%, and sedatives .2%. The comparable data for having used the substance in the previous 30 days was 34% for marijuana, 72% for alcohol, 1.4% for inhalants, 37% for hallucinogens, 1.4% for cocaine, .2% for heroin, 12% for stimulants, and 4.8% for sedatives.

All these substances can be harmful. Solvents and the hallucinogen PCP have been singled out for special warning by some observers because they can be very physically harmful in the short run (Adams and Gullotta, 1983). Since *most* adolescents are involved with *most* drugs only in the short run (with marijuana, alcohol, and heroin being exceptions in that initial use is strongly related to chronic use), this short run effect makes these drugs stand out. But dealing with them is probably best done within a general approach to controlling substance abuse (with the addition of the necessity for an immediate effort to stop their use to prevent their harmful short-term physical effects, such as poisoning). The same general approach, outlined below, makes sense for adolescents dependent upon valium, quaaludes, and the rest of the commonly used illicit substances.

Here we consider only specific therapeutic responses to three major types of substance abuse—heroin, alcohol, and marijuana abuse—emphasizing the goals for treatment of addiction, treatment procedures, and probable outcomes for adolescents.

The initial stage of addiction is psychological dependence, the mental stage in which adolescents begin to perceive themselves as functioning at a satisfactory level only when involved with a drug. This stage may progress to an actual physical addiction (the bodily need for the drug), which involves both physical and psychological dependence such that maintaining appropriate doses of the drug is a primary concern since removing the drug results in a potentially dangerous psychophysical withdrawal syndrome.

In general, attitudes toward adolescents and drugs inhibit the effectiveness of treatment strategies. One such attitude is the idea that the victim is to blame for the drug problem (Ryan, 1976). This view may even be prevalent among professional staff.

There are other factors bound up in the very nature of drug abuse itself that contribute to the difficulty of treating drug dependent adolescents. As we shall note later, the psychological problems and low self-esteem of the adolescent drug abuser may be the root cause of the dependence on drugs. Furthermore, drug abusers are often associated with a subculture that rejects conformity to mainstream values, and they thereby align themselves with a deviant group. Helpers must be aware and sensitive to the value system of the adolescent, particularly when it differs from mainstream values. Finally, drug abusers may be particularly resistant to therapy, since they may return to drug use. Medical professionals often view drug abuse as a physical problem that can be cured when the individual is symptom-free. However, it is not that simple. The web of psychological and social factors (friends, lifestyle) that bind the adolescent to drugs is much more lasting, with widespread effects on the adolescent's functioning.

The most general model of intervention involves an initial entrance stage, a withdrawal stage, a support and competence building stage, and a reintegration into the community. The first step to progress in treatment is to remove the adolescent from his environment and begin the withdrawal process. It is

David S. is a 17-year-old white single male who was referred to drug abuse counselling by his parents. He was attending a local private high school when he was found with marijuana in his possession and was expelled. Arrangements were made with the school for him to complete his required courses during the summer so that he could attend college that fall.

During the initial interview with David, he admitted to marijuana use several times every day, weekly LSD and quaalude use, and occasional use of cocaine. He was also using alcohol to excess on the weekends. He was very open about his situation and admitted that he had a problem with drug abuse. All of his friends were involved with drugs and he had acquired a strong reputation as a heavy drug user. His parents expressed dismay about his drug use and were unsure if he should go away to college next fall. They felt that if David was on his own, his drug use would increase and interfere with his education.

It was decided that David would be seen individually twice a week. Family conferences with David and his parents would be held once per month. The initial focus of treatment was to get David to stop using drugs and to then help David recognize how drug use was interfering with his self stated goals.

We began treatment by establishing a basic treatment plan. This plan included: 1) A progressive series of commitments on David's part to reduce and eventually eliminate his drug use, 2) keeping a daily log of all thoughts and feelings regarding his drug use, 3) outlining exactly what type of behavior was expected of him and how this related to his being allowed to go away to college in the fall, 4) the development of a more positive attitude toward the education process. I would assign him homework assignments in the form of doing reports on topics of interest to him. He would receive no other reward than the good feelings associated with a positive learning experience.

During the first two months of treatment, David eliminated his use of LSD, quaalude and cocaine with little difficulty but continued using marijuana, and his alcohol consumption increased. He was requested to refrain from any drug use for one day, then two days and so on until he was able to go for a week with no drug use. He had difficulty doing this and would offer justification for his drug use. He was not able to understand that any drug use would result in a rapid escalation of the quantities of drugs he would consume. He would cite examples of people he knew who would smoke marijuana and drink and seemed to not have any associated problems. I would often have to refocus the attention back onto his own personal pattern of abuse. He would get angry and resist the idea that he couldn't use drugs "recreationally." During this period of time our relationship was growing and David began to see me as an older brother whom he didn't want to disappoint. We would spend time discussing philosophy, music, art, and poetry. We worked on looking at the world as an infinitely interesting place which could be more enjoyed without the use of drugs. David was asked to do things he had always done when he was using drugs and to compare the experiences. He gradually began to appreciate the experience of being straight and how much more he remembered about his experiences. I was particularly encouraged when David reported that he had attended a rock concert, not used any drugs, and enjoyed himself immensely.

As the Fall semester approached, we began to discuss the possibility of David going off to college. He felt confident that he was ready and wanted to go. David was still smoking pot occasionally and drinking on the weekends. I had some real reservations about his ability to maintain this reduced drug use once he was away from treatment and his home. He agreed to try to not use any drugs or alcohol for the next 30 days and if he could do this, he would go off to college. His parents agreed to this plan. At this point, I felt confident that David would be honest about his drug use and accurately report any slip-ups. He was able to keep this commitment and left for college. He was to continue counseling at a program in the town the college was located in and keep in contact with me.

Approximately two months later I received a call from David's father who reported that David had been suspended from school for a semester and would be coming in to see me again. David reported that he had gotten drunk, "borrowed" someone's bicycle and was caught by campus security.

At our first session David was embarrassed and expressed feelings that he had let me and his parents down. He had begun smoking pot and drinking about two weeks after he arrived at school. He was confused about how he could want something so badly, i.e., being drug free, and yet continue using drugs. It was obvious that David had been staying straight not for himself but for me and his parents. He continued in treatment for the next four months. We worked mostly on internalizing what he had learned during his previous treatment experience. He was able to stay away from all drugs during this time period and developed a more realistic view of himself and his drug abuse patterns. We also had David participate in an adolescent group lead by two other therapists. He became the client group leader and a role model for some of the other group members.

He eventually returned to college and six months later is not using any drugs or alcohol. He is participating in the soccer team and is a member of several campus clubs.

John Garbarino
Drug Counselor

best to treat patients in family groups so that support from the immediate environment is available to make re-entry into the community easier.

Frequently, drug use is a replacement for ego defenses, and when deprived of the drug the adolescent feels inadequate, has poor self-esteem, exhibits difficulty in maintaining relationships, and may be withdrawn. Group therapy with peers may assist the adolescent in gaining new interpersonal skills and finding social validation from others with similar problems.

The behavior modification treatment approach to intervention begins with positive reinforcement for non-drug-related behavior following withdrawal. Procedures such as exposing the adolescent gradually to some stimuli associated with drugs *(systematic desensitization)* may be useful in reducing anxiety in the stage between withdrawal and re-entry into drug-free society. At this point, the goal of therapy is to provide realistic, attractive alternatives to the drug-dependent lifestyle. Additionally, the adolescent may find validation for identity within the peer group setting.

Another therapeutic mode is the *community model* in which adolescents live with peers while receiving treatment. Adolescent drug abusers live in a self-regulated community and are protected from isolation that may occur in hospital treatment settings. These are exemplary models of treatment for drug abusers.

Treatment of Heroin Dependence

Physical dependence on heroin (the principal illegal narcotic) is usually manifest by variable symptoms that appear four to six hours following the last administration of the drug. These symptoms include a craving for the drug, anxiety, restlessness, yawning, and perspiration. If narcotics are not taken, a peak of these symptoms occurs at two to three days, with disappearance only after seven to ten days have passed. This period is often very painful and terrifying without appropriate medical and psychological support.

The chief form of medical support is detoxification by methadone treatment for at least a two week period. Methadone is a synthetic narcotic drug similar to morphine. Its side effects and withdrawal symptoms are less severe than morphine, which makes it suitable as a transitional addiction. In a methadone maintenance program, treatment begins with a minimum dose and continues until the adolescent attains total withdrawal from heroin. It is not uncommon for a treatment plan to last two years.

Physical dependence is only one aspect, however, and clinical care and rehabilitative training need to be directed toward facilitating re-entry into society. Frequently, vocational training is helpful in easing the transition to the drug-free lifestyle, both because it provides new skills and because it encourages drug-free relationships.

Alcohol Dependence

A more common form of drug abuse among adolescents involves physical and psychological dependence on alcohol. Alcohol is popular among adolescents, in part, because it is inexpensive compared to other mood-altering drugs, and because it is accessible. The use of alcohol is also often directly or indirectly supported by the parents. Parents may drink themselves, thereby validating alcohol use by the adolescent. Parents may also be less concerned about alcohol use by their children because they feel it is a better alternative than other forms of drugs.

Alcohol abuse can be identified by physical symptoms following a bout of heavy drinking: depression, anxiety, and inability to sleep—the symptoms commonly referred to as the *hangover*. In the early stages of alcohol dependence, these symptoms reinforce social insecurities that are already present in the adolescent and may delay help-seeking on the adolescent's part. For the seriously dependent adolescent, severe physical symptoms appear within 24 hours after drinking is stopped, and include headache, nausea, diarrhea, nervous agitation, depression, and inability to sleep. After 72–96 hours, confusion, disorientation, delusions and impaired psychomotor functioning appear in the form of *delerium tremens* (the DT's). In some severe cases, grand mal seizures may occur, and brain damage may result.

There are many alternatives for treatment of the adolescent alcohol abuser. An important part of the treatment program is identifying physical health problems associated with problem drinking—e.g., nutritional deficits and liver and stomach damage. However, it may be exceedingly difficult to obtain an accurate medical history from the adolescent. Therapists, parents, and peers should be nonjudgmental, realistic, and encouraging in dealing with alcohol-dependent adolescents. Physical medication may be used, including mild sedatives (such as benzodiazepine) to combat agitation and inability to sleep. An electrolyte imbalance may need to be treated as a result of dehydration, and potassium treatment is appropriate to prevent growth disorders. Vitamin therapy using large doses of B vitamins is also useful for alcohol abusers.

Long-term treatment for psychological dependence is similar to those models described for other drug addictions. Individual therapy aimed at changing self-image and gaining interpersonal skills may be helpful in reducing need for alcohol. Group and family therapy provide crucial support in the microsystem for the reforming alcoholic. Drug treatment with disufirum (antabuse) may be particularly useful in combination with any of these. Antabuse produces the immediate, aversive physical reactions of nausea, vomiting, and flushing when combined with alcohol in the body. These aversive reactions become associated with alcohol, and thus decrease desire for alcohol as the adolescent continues to experience the symptoms. Alcoholics Anonymous is another effective treatment that uses peer group influence. Many groups aimed at helping alcoholics are often active in developing special programs for adolescents.

Marijuana Use

Although research suggests that marijuana is not addictive, heavy and frequent use may interfere with daily functioning. When adolescents find that the effects of marijuana inhibit school achievement or social functioning, then the drug contributes to dysfunction. Perhaps it is advisable to focus on the adverse psychological effects of heavy use of this drug, since there is much disagreement about how harmful marijuana is when used occasionally and recreationally (much as there is controversy over alcohol in this regard). Treatment for adolescents who are abusing marijuana typically involves efforts to resocialize the youth into a more active and independent life-style, and to increase participation in socially-approved activities. It thus falls within the general social skills building models we discussed earlier.

Juvenile Delinquency

An extensive review of intervention efforts for antisocial adolescents would be impossible because there have been thousands of attempts to deal with such problems. However, a few of the major approaches merit our attention. Keep in mind that the variety of techniques we discussed earlier apply to delinquency as well. However, the special issues, such as illegality of actions, coercive environment, genuine danger to staff in some circumstances, and political pressure to protect the community, complicate the task.

Internalized social norms and the prospect of getting in trouble normally control most antisocial behavior among most adolescents. Specialized classrooms, probation in a juvenile court system, and commitment to a group home for delinquent youths are examples of responses commonly provided by our social system when prevention fails. However, these measures are often ineffective in rehabilitating antisocial behavior once it is established as a pattern.

The behavior modification techniques discussed earlier are promising for the treatment of juvenile delinquency because they focus on socially incompetent and antisocial behavior, seeking to control these patterns while replacing them with more positive behavioral patterns. The teaching-family model was successful in lowering the number of repeat offenders, accomplishing higher grades, and reducing truancy and police and court contacts over a two-year follow-up period, particularly when compared to a program that placed boys on probation (Phillips, Phillips, Fixen, & Wolf, 1974). Much more extensive research is needed for future planning of services for delinquent adolescents, however.

Another treatment option worth noting is Outward Bound, a program that has many forms, all of which emphasize wilderness experience as a way of dealing with troubled youth. Outward Bound in New York City (sponsored by Return to Employment and Learning or R.E.A.L.) takes youths from inner cities who have been convicted of two or more felonies and attempts to train them in skills that would be effective in the working world. Adolescents in this program are taken on a wilderness trip to upstate New York during which they are taught new skills, including cooperation and trust in one's partners, in order to survive in the wilderness setting. They learn to maintain motivation for achieving goals (such as scaling a cliff) that require sustained commitments of time and physical energy rather than giving up in frustration as often happens in the real world. Training emphasizes self-sufficiency, perseverance, and mutual cooperation. The advantages of this type of program are numerous, particularly for the most difficult cases. Evaluation of these new programs will permit social services to develop more innovative programs for delinquent youths.

Abuse and Neglect

The problem of abuse is often the underlying factor for a number of serious problems that occur later in life. Abuse has been correlated with delinquency, criminal behavior, abusive parenting styles, and severe personality disorders (Helfer & Kempe, 1982). Recently, child abuse has been defined for the public as one of the most serious social problems in North America. Yet, despite the public awareness and concern for abuse toward younger children, the negative public view of teenagers seems to blunt concern for adolescent victims (Garbarino & Gilliam, 1980). The National Incidence Study (Bergdorf, 1981) devised a methodology that compiled both cases of adolescent abuse reported to protective service agencies and cases of adolescent abuse embedded in referrals to other service agencies such as police and probation departments, teachers and guidance counselors, and neighborhood sources.

As we noted earlier, the study revealed that the incidence of adolescent abuse equals or exceeds that of abuse toward young children (Bergdorf, 1981). Further, many of the adolescent cases do not receive services because the social system fails to define the problem as abuse. Rather, these adolescents are treated for academic problems, delinquency, or other conditions that focus on the adolescent as the problem.

Based on data from the National Incidence Study, we know that protective services for the abused adolescent handle only a small proportion of actual abused cases. Further, the power of protective services is often limited by the inability to document cases of neglect, sexual abuse, and emotional abuse. When a protective service does intervene as a control mechanism, it is often difficult to re-train abusive parents. Removing adolescents from an abusive home and placing them in foster homes or other care facilities is often difficult because of the limited number of placements for adolescents (they are large, loud, expensive to feed, and likely to require special handling). Intervention is often more effective when directed toward support and skills training of the adolescent rather than the family system.

Local community institutions can be brought to a greater awareness of the magnitude and severity of the problem of abused adolescents. If local communities are more vigilant in acting as advocates for adolescents in violent home situations, the sense of isolation common to abused adolescents might be dissipated. Community interest in providing support for troubled families is also an effective deterrent to abuse (Whittaker, 1980).

Adolescent Pregnancy

Services for adolescent pregnancy have changed considerably since the 1950's, when most schools and communities did little more than banish pregnant girls. Since it has been determined that pregnancy is not associated with any single characteristic such as income, background, race, education, or psychological problems, social service agencies have begun to develop comprehensive multi-disciplinary programs for pregnant adolescents. These programs are designed to intervene in the immediate crisis of the pregnancy as well as in the long-term effects, and include hospital-based programs, school programs, and national preventive programs. Counseling programs aimed at girls who have abortions or who give their babies up for adoption exist, but most recent attention has focused on improving the outlook for girls who keep their babies and raise them alone. One reason for this is that the likelihood of this happening (as opposed to either getting married or giving up the baby for adoption) has increased markedly in the last decade (Furstenbern, Lincoln, and Menken, 1981).

Early intervention efforts were based in hospitals because of concern for medical risk among adolescent mothers. The Young Mothers Program of the Yale-New Haven Medical Center, for example, continues to provide prenatal care, as well as counseling for nutrition, labor and delivery, and general health care. The program also attempts to train participants for their new social roles as mothers (Johnson, Walters, McKenny, 1979). Similar programs provide medical assistance, contraceptive services, and discussion groups dealing with topics such as physiology, peer and family relationships, and sexual behaviors (Furstenberg, 1977). Evaluation of these programs shows that adolescents deliver healthier infants with higher birth weights and lower incidence of medical complications, prematurity, and fewer fetal deaths compared to non-participants.

While these programs appear effective in reducing medical risk, attention also needs to be given to social and psychological problems of the adolescent. One attempt to provide such services comes from school-based programs. An exemplary program was conducted at the Edgar Allan Poe school in Baltimore. The program is comprehensive, offering basic education, guidance counseling, and job counseling as well as the health and social counseling emphasized in previous programs. This program also reported medical gains (lower rates of infant mortality and higher birth weights).

Previous efforts at training in contraception have not proved to be consistently effective in preventing further pregnancies. One innovative attempt (Schenke, Gilchrist, & Small, 1979) discovered that the problem was related to two factors: the newly evolving physical maturation of the adolescent that is not yet integrated into the whole self, and the interpersonal nature of sexual activity. More specifically, it was found that adolescents who became pregnant a second time were distinguished from those who did not by lower sensitivity, less verbal disclosure, lower empathy, a lack of control, and less cognitive clarity (Campbell & Barnlund, 1977). The intervention program employed a cognitive-behavioral approach that provided not only the information necessary for controlling pregnancy, but training in the skills of making effective decisions and implementing them. This program represents a more sophisticated approach to comprehensive service delivery.

Other intervention programs are directed at improving the mother-child relationship. For example, many experts believe that adolescent mothers have inappropriate expectations concerning their infants. They expect them to do more than is normal at any given age, such as be toilet trained at six months (Epstein, 1980). This demands a program that helps train mothers in appropriate developmental expectations for their infants in cognitive and social areas. Other programs (Field, 1980), called *infant stimulation programs*, attempt to boost the development of high-risk infants. Parent education has been successfully integrated as a part of well-baby check-ups in physician's offices (Welcher, 1980).

All of these attempt to provide support for adolescent parenthood. Other important efforts involve career and job training for adolescent mothers, local and state-supported day care, and staff advocates that maintain and direct the adolescent mother in a network of support services. We will discuss teenage pregnancy and parenthood as part of the transition to adulthood further in Chapter 13.

Eating Disorders

There is little agreement regarding appropriate methods of intervention in bulimia and anorexia cases. Medical treatment is often necessary for physical symptoms associated with the frequent vomiting associated with bulimia and anorexia, such as stomach ulcers, severe headaches, rectal bleeding, and malnutrition (Russell, 1979; Young, 1979). For the serious emotional problems of guilt and shame associated with binging and starving behavior, many treatment approaches have been recommended, including behavioral modification, family therapy, cognitively-oriented counseling, and chemotherapy (Bruch, 1973; Minuchin, Baker, Rosman, Liebman, Milman, & Todd, 1975; Orleans & Barnett, 1980). There is no evidence that any one approach is more effective than others in treating bulimia and anorexia. More research is needed, particularly to decrease the relapse rate, which remains high (White & Boskind-White, 1980).

Minuchin and his colleagues (1975) developed one useful approach to the problem of anorexia. The major premise of the approach is focusing on the sick child within the family microsystem rather than the individual anorectic patient, as the target for intervention. The system model predicts that the psychopathology of the anorectic is maintained by feedback from the family. This assumes that certain types of family organization are closely related to developing and maintaining psychosomatic symptoms, and that adolescent psychosomatic symptoms play a major role in maintaining family stability. That is, at times of stress or transition within the family, family interactions may trigger the onset of psychosomatic symptoms, and symptoms function as social psychological mechanisms that regulate and stabilize family interactions.

The family model suggests three postulates. First, the adolescent is physiologically vulnerable (that is, a specific organic dysfunction [anorexia] is present). Second, the child's family has the following four interactional characteristics: enmeshment, overprotectiveness, rigidity, and lack of conflict resolution. Third, the sick child plays an important role in permitting the family to avoid overt conflict, and this role serves as a reinforcer for symptoms (it works at producing a semblance of family harmony).

In a research study designed to assess treatment outcome of family therapy based on this model (Minuchin, Baker, Rosman, Liebman, Milman, & Todd, 1975), Minuchin's group intervened with 25 anorectic patients and their families. The anorectic group had suffered an average weight loss of 30% of total body weight. Evaluation of outcome for anorectic patients was based on weight gain, with data about behavior used to detail the process of effects. Therapeutic intervention was aimed at changing the family context that maintains the pathology. The program obtained the following results: in families involved in the program from four months to one year with a minimum of follow-up of one year, of 25 subjects, 21 were recovered on the basis of medical criteria (3 dropped the program and 1 received a "fair" prognosis). In clinical assessments, which included evaluation of social, school, and family adjustment, all were recovered. It appears that a model that takes into account the transactions in the family microsystem is a promising method of intervention. Minuchin underscores the need to modify the family *system* of the dysfunctional adolescent as the way to sustained remission rather than intervention that focuses exclusively on the individual adolescent.

A similar approach to therapy with adolescents effective with other eating disorders is called *nurturant-authoritative psychotherapy* (Levenkron, 1982). This model also attempts to deal with underlying family dynamics of the disorder. In these families, children have often been given *too much* independence and responsibility. Thus, one goal of therapy is to allow the adolescent to experience support and direction from the therapist. In contrast to the traditional neutral posture of the therapist, the nurturant-authoritative therapist provides strength and nurturing. In eating disorders, the patient has often been rewarded for *not* needing support or direction, and this control becomes associated with control over eating behavior. In providing a balance of these two postures, the nurturant-authoritative therapist allows adolescents to release themselves from obsession. Although no large-scale evaluations have been conducted, preliminary results suggest this approach is effective in some cases.

Juvenile Prostitution

A report by the Youth Development Bureau (1982) states:

> There is no single type of program or approach that is most effective in serving adolescent prostitutes. The population is receiving assistance from diverse agencies, including runaway programs, traditional community-based agencies, gay service agencies, and medical clinics.

One example of an agency that provides assistance to juvenile prostitutes is Covenant House in New York City. Covenant House serves both male and female prostitutes. It provides community education, in addition to direct services and residential shelter in a program called "Under 21."

Community-based programs, such as Central City Hospitality House in San Francisco, offer a range of services including streetwork, referrals, casework, counseling, emergency food and shelter, job development, crisis intervention, and a community-based newsletter. The success of this program is attributed to its comprehensive approach and coordination with the juvenile justice system.

Medical clinics serve the health needs of street youth, offering drug counseling and detoxification services, venereal disease screening, and nutritional care. These are often the entry-point into the helping system for youth involved in prostitution and include examples such as the Red Door Clinic in Minneapolis, The Door in New York, and The Bridge in Boston. All are comprehensive youth service centers that permit entry on a very wide range of terms with a specific plan for intervention evolving according to the adolescent's specific needs.

Adolescent Suicide

Experts agree that intervention is needed whenever an adolescent seems to be slipping into isolation and depression, particularly if there is talk of suicide. Preventing suicide is largely a matter of restoring relationships or forming new ones that enhance the adolescent's connections with life. If suicide attempters do not perceive a change in relationships, they are likely to make additional attempts, often with greater prospects of success.

Evidence indicates that suicidal adolescents have a high incidence of parent or sibling loss because of separations, deaths, or divorce. (Barter, Swaback, & Todd, 1968). One focus of intervention then often includes assistance in successfully completing the process of mourning.

Family relationships in suicide cases often appear to have been characterized by unstable, conflict-ridden, and rejecting attitudes (Schrut, 1968). Furthermore, family problems or quarrels with parents are frequently cited as the precipitating incidents in adolescent suicide attempts (Ijaz, 1968). Certainly, the effects of an unpredictable environment may be magnified by the normal insecurities of adolescence, and, in turn, these disruptions may trigger a deep-seated feeling of rejection by the family. The adolescent experiences a lack of belongingness and support so essential to advance development and produce confidence in mastering the environment. Peer-oriented mutual help groups can serve to stabilize the high-risk adolescent and prevent social isolation and depression from deepening.

Lacking the support of the family, the peer group may become even more important than would normally be expected. Suicidal adolescents may lack the support they need in this area, often because of the social stigma that surrounds suicide. In follow-up studies of adolescents who had been hospitalized for suicide attempts, the rate of peer contacts for those who continued to exhibit suicidal behavior tended to be significantly lower than for those who discontinued the suicidal behavior (Barter, Swaback, & Todd, 1968; Stanley & Barter, 1970). Blaine and Carmen (1968) affirm that suicide is most likely to occur at a time when adolescents are badly in need of support that is unavailable to them, often because of their own distancing behaviors. Social skills training is in order.

The precipitating circumstances of the suicide attempts also document the role of the lack of social support. Schrut (1968) found that the precipitating events for adolescent girls were most often rejections from boyfriends or lovers. Another source of immediate crisis is the school, usually involving the adolescent's failure to meet parental standards of achievement in academics, sports, or social activities. The negative effects of these failures, especially in view of the importance of the peer group for adolescents, seem to undermine the developing self in a debilitating fashion.

Given this picture of the situation, it is important to address the internal resources of the adolescent to cope with the potentially devastating experience. For the suicidal adolescent, the outlook is grim. Evidence indicates that the adolescent is most often in a state of depression prior to the suicide (Growo, Schwartz, Grinder, & Lorenson, 1970). The habitual style of coping with emotional conflict may be different for the suicidal adolescent. In a study that compared adolescents who had attempted suicide to delinquent girls matched on age, IQ, and socioeconomic status who did not (Doroff, 1969), it was found that suicide attempters had a high degree of internalization of external conflicts as compared to delinquents, who acted out their conflicts. The subjects were also rated on the presence of 30 psychological and social variables. Results indicated that the suicidal adolescents displayed high degrees of depression, anxiety, and withdrawal. Inability to trust in any social relationship, combined with the personal lack of inner resources to cope with the problem precipitate the utter sense of hopelessness that precedes a suicide attempt. Gould (1965) supports this notion in his assessment of suicidal adolescents as characterized by a sense of impulsivity, an ego identity in the state of flux, and feelings of loneliness and impotence in mastering the environment. The suicide attempt may be interpreted as a final way of asserting power over the social environment. From the outside it may be seen as a permanent solution to a temporary problem, but from the inside it may seem like the only way out of an intolerable situation.

In view of the evidence, it seems the suicidal adolescent often begins in a family having trouble communicating and in establishing trusting, supportive relationships. This, in itself, may tend to inhibit the development of healthy social relationships and a positive concept of self. As these children move into the uncertain area of adolescence, they also experience failure to develop meaningful relationships with peers. Finally, those troubled adolescents turn inward and do not find the ego strength necessary to cope with emotional trauma. The focus for intervention must be on building up personal and social resources, generating some positive momentum to the youth's life.

Jacobs and Teicher (1967) provide a comprehensive conceptual framework for understanding the notion of adolescent suicide. They view each event as an isolated occurrence, but within the context of the biography of the individual adolescent. In comparing a sample of 50 suicidal adolescents to a control group of 32 adolescents matched on age, race, sex, and family income, Jacobs and Teicher found that it was not the presence or absence of certain events but the progression and psychological effects of those events on the adolescent's self-concept that differentiated the suicide attempters from the control group. The authors describe the progression of life events of the suicidal adolescents as follows:

1   A long-standing history of problems (from childhood to the onset of adolescence).
2   A period of escalation of problems (since the onset of adolescence and in excess of those normally associated with adolescence).
3   The final phase, characterized by the chain reaction dissolution of any remaining meaningful social relationships in the weeks and days preceding the suicide attempt.

Results from the two groups indicate that both suicide attempters and controls often came from broken homes. The difference was in the time the separation occurred. The controls had experienced a stable home life during the five years before the onset of adolescence. In contrast, suicidal adolescents had experienced the separation during the stressful and uncertain time of adolescence. Furthermore, this loss and the resulting depression were part of a long-term process for the adolescent suicide attempter, rather than just a short-term crisis. Finally, the process culminates in a period of intense escalation of alienation and isolation followed by a perceived loss of social relationships just prior to suicide that leaves the adolescent completely alone. Turning inward, the ego and internal resources are also in a state of confusion, incapable of coping with the magnitude of the situation. For these adolescents, suicide represents a solution to the problem of living in a world that seems to have fallen apart around them with no sense of having the social skills necessary to rebuild that world. Intervention can occur at any stage in the negative progression, but the further down this road the adolescent has traveled, the more difficult the task (but ironically, the easier to recognize the existence of a serious problem). In this way the suicide problem exemplifies the challenge of providing human services for adolescents. Early intervention is usually more promising, but less readily justified since often there are not dramatic and unequivocal signs of dysfunction.

Ecological Wrap-Up

Organism.   One major aspect of human services to adolescents involves building up the internal resources of individuals, either in a preventive or rehabilitative context. This includes their self-esteem. It also includes training in important social skills such as dealing with criticism, saying *no* in a noninflammatory manner, and listening to others.

Microsystem.   A second major thrust for interaction lies in establishing and enhancing supportive relationships within important microsystems. The dyadic therapy or counseling microsystem dominates intervention, although behavior modification and group approaches are also strong.

Mesosystem.   One of the key intervention issues is how to generalize skills and attitudes learned in the intervention context (e.g., the residential treatment facility or mutual help group) to other microsystems (e.g., home, school, peer groups). This highlights the mesosystem issues of intervention. Many intervention programs that have succeeded in their artificial microsystem have not carried over to the real world microsystems.

Exosystems.   The actual process of intervention depends in large part on the level of support provided to and the nature of the constraints imposed upon direct services for adolescents by powerful institutions (e.g., courts, school boards, local government). Funding is always a problem, and except when they cause public trouble (e.g., crime) adolescents are likely to be a low priority.

Mesosystems.   The constitutional definition of the adolescent's rights is a significant constraint on intervention. Individual practitioners and agencies operate in a highly charged emotional climate when they deal with adolescent clients. The pressures to control adolescents are intense.

Preview

- The modernization of North American society has produced more widespread and prolonged experience of adolescence.

- Modernization has also pushed the major transitions to adulthood into the early 20s for many individuals who may be part of a post-adolescent period in the life-course called *youth*.

- History expresses itself in the experiences common to those born at specific times.

- Youth has led the way in modifying tradititonal values towards work, marriage, sex, and affluence.

- Colleges and universities are the dominant institutions shaping and supporting youth.

- Society faces increasing polarization as some adolescents enter youth and delay parenthood, while others prematurely become parents and/or marry.

- In modern North American society early marriage (in adolescence) is associated with low satisfaction and instability.

Our treatment of adolescent social development in earlier chapters emphasized the transition from childhood *into* adolescence and focused on the range and diversity of adolescent lives. We tried to make clear that adolescence itself is socially created and defined. By nature, adolescence is the time between childhood and adulthood. Yet we cannot think of what these terms mean without reference to a particular society and culture, to the specific macrosystem of a particular adolescence. What adolescents do, how they become adults, and how long the transition takes all differ from one society to another and from one historical period to another. In this chapter we will examine the passage into *adulthood,* and the importance of social and historical considerations in understanding the events and processes of this transition. This will take us back to some of the topics we covered earlier, but here we will focus on how adolescence influences adulthood. In particular, we will focus on the years *after* high school, which today include a variety of activities, from college and military service to marriage, work, and parenting. We will refer to the years between the end of high school and full participation in adulthood (roughly the ages 18–24) as the period of *youth.*

13

The Transition to Adulthood: Youth and History

Adolescence and History:
A Community Case Study

In Chapter 1 we outlined the social history of North America as it shaped the meaning and experience of adolescence. The agrarian era was a time of large families, and intergenerational and cross-age contact was a part of daily life between parents and children (Demos & Demos, 1969). Industrialization altered the social fabric of life for youth people (Kett, 1977).

A case study of the effects of industrialization on the lives of young people in 19th century Canada shows that major changes come to pass in a fairly short time (Katz & Davey, 1978). The study compares census data from 1851, 1861, and 1871 in Hamilton, Ontario, a city that grew from a commercial harbor of 14,000 inhabitants in 1851 to a growing industrial center of 26,000 people in 1871.

In 1851, the status of Hamilton teenagers could best be described as *semi-autonomous* (Katz & Davey, 1978, p. 92). Because there were no established institutions, adolescents planned for their future as best they could among family, school, and vocational training. In order to ease their family's burden, many left their parents' home and boarded out with other families to perform work or learn a trade. For example, in 1851, 34% of male and 28% of female 16-year-olds boarded out. Only 28% of teenagers aged 13–16 were in school. Idleness was common: 55% of boys and 71% of girls were not at work, school, or boarding-out.

By 1861, a depression had curtailed the city's economic progress as a seaport, but advances in education were remarkable. The percentage of 13–16-year-olds in school rose to 52%. Boarding-out decreased dramatically for boys and slightly among girls. Young people were more likely to be in school and living with their parents in 1861 than in 1851.

Industrial growth between 1861 and 1871 clearly affected the lives of teenagers. Education was not extended beyond 1861 levels. In fact, the creation of large numbers of industrial jobs drew both boys and girls *from* school, boarding-out, and idleness into the work force. Interestingly, class distinctions emerged, as the sons of white-collar workers began to stay in school at levels beyond the sons of working-class fathers and to marry later than working-class sons married. Thus, the trend toward teenagers living at home and increasing their schooling can be seen as marking the beginning of adolescence as we know it in the 20th century. Katz and Davey (1978) concluded that: "Adolescence may be defined as a phase of institutionalized dependency that came to characterize the experience of youth in the 19th century" (p. 117).

The growing commitment to education at this time came at no small price. Teenagers at the end of the 19th century still made a substantial contribution to the family economy. In 1870s Massachusetts, for example, children between the ages 10–19 provided one-fourth of family income, one-third in families in which the father was unskilled (Kett, 1977). Most families based the decision to keep even one child in school on the hope that it would lead to a better job for that privileged child, possibly in the professions or the growing white-collar jobs in business. They hoped such an investment would pay off for the chosen child and for the entire family in improved status and income.

The growing importance of schooling for teenagers around the end of the last century was influential in the development of three major institutional changes concerning adolescents: compulsory education, child-labor laws, and separate legal status for juvenile offenders (Bakan, 1975). Although state laws differed for all three, in the early 20th century, there was an unmistakable legal trend towards distinguishing adolescents from adults and keeping adolescents in separate educational and judicial institutions.

The teenage years, of course, have only gained in strength since 1900 as a recognized part of the life span distinct from childhood and adulthood. The trends toward urban and industrial development have continued to decrease the value of manual labor, and education has expanded accordingly. The story is dramatic: in 1900, 6.4% of the 17-year-olds graduated from high school; in 1940 the figure was 50.8% (Kett, 1977), and the percent graduating in 1980 was about 85% (Garbarino & Asp, 1981). By 1920, the Lynds described the high school in their Middletown study this way: "The high school, with its athletics, sororities and fraternities, dances and parties, and other 'extracurricular activities,' is a fairly complete social cosmos in itself, and about this city within a city the social life of the intermediate generation centers" (Lynd & Lynd, 1929, p. 211).

Thus, adolescence has become institutionalized in this century as technology and affluence have spread. High school is the main environment for teenagers, and a greater percentage than ever continue their education into college. College has become the new stepping stone to better jobs, as a high school education once had been. What are some of the causes and consequences of this continuing trend toward increased education and further postponement of adult roles? How much has the end of adolescence changed?

The Meaning of Youth as a Period in the Life Course

Social and economic change in the 20th century affects people in virtually all walks of life. An increasingly technological post-industrial society requires educated workers rather than unskilled laborers. Today's economy does not need young people, except in low-paid, unskilled jobs such as golf caddy, fast-food employee, and babysitter. Thus, the number of years of training needed before entering the work force has increased for the average adolescent.

The term *youth* has been used to describe this new kind of post-adolescent. If we think of the period of youth as involving three main transitions (leaving the parental home, establishing economic independence, and forming a family), this period includes many of today's 18–24 year olds (although some may complete these transitions before or after this age period). According to Keniston (1970), the harbingers of this new stage of life are affluent middle- and upper-middle class, urban and suburban college students. While physically and mentally adults, these youth are not accepted by society as adult, nor are they themselves ready to be accepted as adults (Eisenstadt, 1972). Under circumstances similar to those that caused the rise of adolescence a century earlier, the period of youth has emerged as a new, independent psychological stage following adolescence (Keniston, 1974).

Keniston defines and recognizes youth by specific issues that flow from adolescence and from the completion of the identity formation processes discussed by Erikson (see Chapter 7). Although they may have established personal identity, what remains undefined for youth are questions concerning the relations between individual and society: vocation, life-style, commitments, and roles. Their advanced education encourages independent thinking and idealism, while affluence minimizes the need for an early entrance into the work force. What is more, Keniston speculates that youth are more likely than others to be at the highest levels of moral development as defined by Kohlberg's schema (see Chapter 4), and thus to evaluate adult roles and values from a highly principled ethical perspective (Keniston, 1974). Thus, Keniston viewed youth as ambivalent, detached observers of the adult world, alternatively testing the waters and then retreating to the safe harbor of college or other sanctuaries. His speculations suggest that the phenomenon of youth is an extension of Erikson's idea of psychosocial *moratorium* (1968) into what had formerly been adult years.

Others have attempted to formalize their speculations and observations into a more systematic statement about the key features of youth as a distinct period in the life course. Robert Havighurst (1975) has proposed the following objectives for youth as an agenda for development:

Objectives for self-development

1 Cognitive and noncognitive skills necessary for economic independence and for occupational competence.
2 Capability for effective management of one's own affairs.
3 Capability to engage in intense concentrated involvement in an activity.
4 Capability as a consumer, not only of goods, but more significantly of the cultural riches of civilization.

Objectives of social relations

5 Experience with persons differing in social class, subculture, and age.
6 Experience of having others dependent on one's actions.

7 Experience of interdependent activities directed toward collective goals. (From Havighurst, 1975)

What Is Adulthood?

Adulthood is one of those common terms we use all the time, but which is surprisingly difficult to define specifically. The word naturally suggests associations with maturity, independence, and responsibility. It may be easier to ar-

---

On the western coast of Italy, just North of Naples, a small town is nestled in the hills over-looking the sea. The town, known as Sorrento, has been a favored vacation spot for Italians over the centuries. The phrase, torna a Sorrento, *which translates into return to Sorrento, characterizes the lure of this small fishing town for those that have visited once, fallen in love with the area, and continue to return to Sorrento whenever possible.*

On the coast of Maine is another small town that is also known as Sorrento. For as long as I can remember I have spent my summer vacations in Sorrento. As a child, the end of school meant it was time to say good-bye to my friends and pack my bags for the trip North. I was off to see my grandparents who lived in Sorrento, along with my sister, my brothers, and a gaggle of cousins. It was like summer camp as there were different outdoor activities and projects, the only difference was that I was related to everybody in sight. Summers were wonderful during this time, but by the middle of August I would begin to anxiously anticipate the return home. I would be preoccupied by such major concerns as who would be my new teacher? Was my hamster still alive? Would all of my friends look different?

By the time I was an adolescent I began to recognize how important Sorrento and the summers I spent there were to me. It seemed like a corny thought at the time, but I realized that Sorrento was my "roots," it was home. I loved spending that time with my family, but I also began to see how much I loved the sea, the rocks, the sound of a fog horn early in the morning, bonfires on an island in the middle of the bay, and the little things, periwinkles, Queen-Anne's lace, and blueberries. By the time I was 16 I dreaded the end of summer and the imminent return to school in September. I would gather up smooth stones, shells and driftwood to take back along with the photographs I had taken that would be stored in a scrap book and serve as reminders of the past summer and the pleasures of future summers.

The fact that Sorrento, its people and treasures, are part of my identity was recognized in adolescence. Now, I simply take for granted that I will always "torna a Sorrento."

—Wendy Gamble

rive at a definition if we break down the idea of adulthood into components. First, there is physical adulthood. As we said in Chapter 3, maturation is generally completed by age 16, and by 18 has occurred for most young people. Physical maturity is a condition *necessary* for a general definition of adulthood, but alone is not *sufficient* to tell us a person has become an adult. Second, relative cognitive maturity seems essential for adulthood. Yet like physical maturity, cognitive development in the sense of the ability to reason and integrate knowledge (formal operational thought as we called it in Chapter 4) is present in some young people by the mid-teens, and never present at all in some 50-year-olds. It is another contributing, but not sufficient requirement of adulthood.

The psychological differences between adolescents and adults are often thought to lie on the continuum of maturity, however difficult it is to define. Maturity involves a number of related elements: realism, compassion, autonomy, and responsibility (Jersild, Brook, & Brook, 1978). We might add the element of sheer experience. Even those who are not cognitively or affectively advanced can have a basis for making mature decisions simply by recalling what has happened before and using those memories as a guide. The discussion in Chapter 7 on identity formation sheds some light on this concept of maturity. Marcia (1980) operationalized identity as certainty with regard to occupational choice and commitment to certain values, beliefs, and ways of living. Maturity is a state of stability, a resolution of conflict and doubt about self-definition (Pellegrino, 1981). A mature person can face life, can summon up the courage and determination to take care of him or herself and others, and can take responsibility for one's actions. Although varying widely among people of *all* ages, maturity is another necessary, but not in itself a sufficient, condition for the attainment of adulthood.

The macrosystem also differentiates between adolescence and adulthood, and these differences get expressed in laws and customs. Most societies have clear ideas about the conditions necessary for adulthood. Our society has chosen age as a marker, and sets age limits by creating laws that control the rights and responsibilities of adult status. Depending upon the jurisdiction, one may start to drink, drive, marry, vote, serve in the military, sign contracts, and be liable for imprisonment in adult jails at various ages between 16 and 21. The fact that these milestones differ from place to place and across history suggests that legal criteria alone should not form the basis of a definition of adulthood, but rather should be regarded as another necessary, but not sufficient, condition of adult status. We think it is the meeting of all these conditions in the context of performing key roles that defines adulthood.

Adults occupy roles distinct from adolescents. In fact, the microsystems of the two stages are generally complementary. Adolescents spend the bulk of their time with their parents and siblings (in their *family of origin*) and in school. Adults, by contrast, are commonly working, living independently from parents, perhaps in a different family, a *family of procreation*, formed by marriage or long-term cohabitation. The age at which an individual becomes independent differs from person to person, and depends, in part, on time and place. In most circumstances, however, the enactment of adult roles is a necessary condition of adulthood, and when combined with physical, mental, legal, and emotional maturity, is sufficient qualification for a young person to earn adult status. An adult, then, is someone who is physically, mentally, culturally, and emotionally mature, and who is involved in responsible work and family roles. Obviously, individuals must earn adult status, and although the criteria vary, there is a good degree of social consensus about when someone has attained adulthood.

Since adult roles are the key to the concept of adulthood, they warrant a closer look. As we mentioned earlier, responsibility is the critical aspect of these roles. More than the collection of physical and emotional characteristics that emerge in late adolescence, adulthood is a set of interlocking *roles* defining and assigning the responsibilities of day-to-day life. Most adults play three key roles: worker, citizen, and family member (spouse and/or parent). The quality of life for adults, and indeed the entire society depends upon the responsible performance of these roles.

As worker, an adult joins the productive ranks and becomes part of the process of sustaining self and community with the goods and services necessary for life. *Most* jobs provide *some* feeling of accomplishment and knowledge that one is contributing to society. Thus, working has two important functions: providing the economic means to an independent life, and granting the status and self-respect associated with contributing to the public good. We developed this theme in Chapter 9.

The role of citizen is a more general extension of the work role into the wider social and political affairs of society. Virtually all societies enforce a distinction between those who may contribute to the public debate and government and those who are too young. The voting age in the United States is the main entry point into full citizenship (although the U. S. Constitution sets higher age restrictions for holding national office). Like the role of worker, citizenship is both a right and a responsibility; a democratic system requires the participation of citizens in a wide range of activities, from the most local to the most global. One of the primary functions of education is to prepare young people to take up the responsibilities of citizenship thoughtfully and conscientiously.

It is in their role of spouse and parent in the family microsystem that adults enact the idea of responsibility in its most personal terms. By its very nature, marriage is a commitment to another, a far different state from the freedom and independence of dating, which most people experience in their teens. Every marriage requires sacrifice and compromise, as two lives and personalities join to carry out a shared agenda. This is not easy, as the high divorce rate indicates. Yet marriage continues to be a goal for the vast majority of young people (Yankelovich, 1974).

The responsibility of marriage is dwarfed by the amount and the degree of care required to raise a child. In parenthood, all the aspects of the adult role unite in the most giving and demanding relationship any person will enter into. Support for parenthood comes first from the marital union as a microsystem, second from friends and relatives in mesosystems, and third from the larger and more distant medical, legal, educational and social institutions of the exosystems and macrosystem that the parents, as citizens and workers, help to sustain.

Adults, in their families, jobs, and communities contribute to the well-being of themselves and those around them. They are engaged in activities recognized and accepted as responsible, and are treated with the full status of adults. It should be clear from this discussion than an issue central to the transition from adolescence to adulthood is the assumption of adult roles. Levinson (1978) writes of this period:

> During his twenties, a young man ordinarily forms a preliminary adult identity. . . . Early adulthood is the time to pay his dues and make his essential contribution to the survival of the species: begetting and raising children, maintaining a marriage and family, giving his labor to the economy and welfare of the "tribe"—that part of the species in which he is most fully involved. With luck, he has the sense of doing something for himself as well as others, of both satisfying his own needs and contributing to his society. (p.22)

Although written about men, this description speaks to modern women who are likely to be involved in the labor force outside the home.

Cohort and Generation

In the preceding historical discussion we sought to convey the magnitude of the changes affecting youth over the past century. An ecological perspective emphasizes the importance of social context in determining the kind of life developing individuals lead, and when studied over many decades at once, the undeniable effect of history on lives becomes clear. This opens a set of methodological issues that go beyond what we discussed in Chapter 6.

From an historical perspective we see that one important characteristic about individuals is their date of birth. When people are born tells us something about the experiences they are likely to encounter. Like other variables, we can use date of birth to categorize groups of people. The term that is used for a group of people who experience a common event in a given time period is *cohort.* Cohort is used most commonly to refer to people born in a given year (or years), a *birth cohort*, although when we talk of the *Class of 1987*, we are referring to a *school cohort.* The concept of birth cohort coincides with one meaning of the term generation, in the sense that one speaks of the *Depression* or the *1960s* generation. Generation has another meaning as well: the three generations of grandparent, parent, and child within a family. We can resolve this confusion in the term generation by using the term *cohort* to refer to the macrosystem phenomenon of shared history *across families,* and *generation* for the constellation of members *within families* (Hagestad, 1981).

Now that we have a sense of what a cohort is, how important is it? Were people to live forever we would not have to worry about the transmission of roles and values. Yet the natural, inevitable process of aging means that there will always be older people leaving the population and younger people who need to be educated and socialized to enter into adult roles. And, as we pointed out in Chapter 1, demographic data tell us the relative size of these two groups can change from decade to decade. In the 1980s and 1990s, for example, it is the relative size of the elderly group that is growing while the number of youth remains about the same.

The shared experience of passing from childhood to adulthood at the same time gives birth cohort a particular identity, in addition to the several ethnic, social class, gender, and religious identities they may have. The epilogue that follows this chapter presents a case study of just this phenomenon. Major events like wars, depressions, and rapid social change separate cohorts into those that lived through a certain time of history and those who came before and after.

The concept of cohort is especially important during youth. At the time when people are establishing personal, occupational, and family identities, they are particularly affected by the state of the society around them, and so will share the experience of adapting to particular economic, cultural, and social conditions. Furthermore, youth is a time of openness, comraderie, and strong peer involvement, and this natural same-age interaction strengthens cohort unity. Of course, not everyone in a cohort will experience the same social circumstances; numerous subcultures will have differing relations to society. Yet within regional, social class, ethnic, and cultural groups, cohort differences are still important.

The size of a cohort will also be an important influence on the opportunities that its members will find as they enter adulthood. In general, the more people born at a given time, the more they must compete with each other for a place in society. For example, in the depths of the Great Depression, it was a hardship to raise children and the birthrate dropped. The average family had only 2.1 children, and there were only 2.3 million births a year (Wachter, 1982). This small cohort reached adulthood in the early 1950s, when the economy was growing strongly. As a result, it was possible for young parents to plan large families, and for mothers to stay home and raise their children. At its peak in 1957, this *baby boom* had an average family size of 3.8 children, with four million babies born that year. This large cohort came of age in the 1970s, as economic growth slowed markedly. The baby boom children grew up with high expectations and are finding it hard to meet them. It is harder to afford large families, and in the 1970s a *baby bust* occurred. In 1976 the average family had 1.8 children, and 3.1 million births were recorded. This *bust* may set the stage for yet another upcoming *boom* in the future, but it depends on the interaction of cohort size and economic opportunities, and so is difficult to predict (Wachter, 1982).

Karl Mannheim, one of the first modern social scientists to recognize the importance of cohort in the study of social change, made clear that the extent to which cohort membership becomes a significant force in society depends on the existence of shared experiences or ideas which gives members of a cohort a shared *spirit* or style (Mannheim, 1928). Such a spirit is the basis of youth movements and peer groups, because young people come to see themselves as linked more to other youth than to their elders and established social patterns. Ryder writes about this relationship:

> In an epoch of change, each person is dominated by his birth date. He derives his philosophy from his historical world, the subculture of his cohort. The community of date equips each cohort with its own experience of time, its own style, and its own truth. (Ryder, 1965, p. 855)

Youth, because they are on the verge of establishing adult commitments, are particularly affected by social conditions (Keniston, 1963). Particularly in times of rapid social change, the reactions of youth in their personal and collective lives can make clear and immediate the meaning of the circumstances surrounding them. It is primarily the privileged middle- and upper-middle class college students and others outside of adult roles who most epitomize the spirit of the moment because they are more independent of restricting commitments and free to articulate life-styles and cultural expressions, be it the *progressivism* of the 1960s or the *economic pragmatism* of the 1980s. Light and Laufer (1975) put it this way:

> Social and historical forces most greatly affect the talented and unfettered of a generation during their formative years. For this reason, able students attending college away from home are an important barometer of the climate of a generation. Free from parental bonds and the burden of a job, aware and sensitive, and clustered together in large numbers, they often articulate the values and qualities of their time for their generation and to some extent for the rest of society. (pp. 93–94)

As political events unify a cohort group, so can shared cultural experiences. Some of the most noticeable of cohort differences are tastes in clothes, music, dating, and recreation. Partly because of technological innovation and partly because of the mysterious swings of popular tastes, a cohort can be distinguished forever by such rallying points as a particular dance step, song, or style of dress. Often a parents' fond recollections of things "in my day" colors their whole adult life, providing the standards and heroes by which they judge later experiences and people, including their own adolescents. It is in adolescence and youth that many life-long tastes and interests form. These experiences can unite people who share them and take on special significance over the rest of life.

Youth and Social Change

Using the concept of cohort as a link between adolescent and youth development and society, we can better appreciate the complex relationship between youth and social change. As our brief look at history made clear, the lives of youth differ significantly from one social and historical context to another. Mannheim and others have emphasized the important role youth can play in *bringing about* social change as well. Thus, the relationship between youth and social change can be viewed from both directions, with youth being *affected* by and themselves *effecting* social change.

There are several reasons for this interaction that follow from what we have said already about youth and society. According to Lambert (1972), there are three main considerations in the youth-social change dynamic. First, the succession of cohorts into the social system is itself a natural impetus for social change, because youth of a cohort group bring with them their own ideas and experiences. For example, some researchers claim that younger workers have different attitudes and expectations about their jobs than older workers. Howard and Wilson (1982), for example, report that new employees of AT&T in the 1970s were much less interested in moving up to leadership positions in the corporation and more oriented toward life-style issues than were their counterparts from the 1950s. As these younger workers continue to replace older, retiring workers, norms about the meaning and value of work will come to increasingly reflect the views of the younger (and eventually more numerous) workers.

Second, cognitive and moral development, together with a stable sense of identity, favor the elaboration of "political-cultural consciousness" (Lambert, 1972, p. 24) between the ages of 18 and 26, when the individual can reflect thoughtfully and responsibly about the world before experience solidifies his or her ideas into dogma. Thus, it is during the period of youth that sociocultural beliefs and attitudes are formed and stabilized, making this period important for life-long political and cultural attitudes.

Third, the collection of social-cultural forces that composes the human ecosystem will be important for the development of political-cultural consciousness, and social change will separate cohorts into discontinuous, even possibly opposing, ways of thinking about and acting in society. For example, Lambert, expressing ideas shared by Margaret Mead (1970) and others, claims that 1945 was a watershed year that brought the dawn of the *Atomic Age*, America's peak of world leadership, computers, widespread affluence, and technological triumphs. Those who came of age after these events take them for granted; those older can never quite accept them.

The Life-Course Perspective

In recent years a conceptual framework for studying the links between a person's age (and developmental stage) and time has arisen, the *life-course perspective*. As explained by Glen Elder (1980), the life-course perspective looks at three distinct levels of analysis: *individual lifetime* as measured by age and stage of development, *social time* as measured by the roles one fills and their meaning in a given society, and the *historical time* period and events one lives through. The life-course perspective is a way of studying the pathways people follow through their lives and how those pathways are influenced by social norms and historical change. Individuals are the focus, but they can be categorized by such social markers as gender, social class, region, and, of course, cohort. Elder (1974), for example, studied children born just before the Great Depression (see Chapter 2), and contrasted the different life experiences of boys and girls of different social classes who had different experiences during the Depression. The life-course perspective can be used to study differences within one cohort as well as variations among cohorts.

While sounding very abstract, this perspective has some very concrete applications. For example the 1960s was a period when youth rose to become a catalyst for widespread social change. An examination of the 1960s, focusing on the youth movement and considering the importance of cohort, social, and historical circumstances, will serve to tie together the close interrelations between youth and social context.

As we saw in Chapter 1, the 1960s marked the maturation of the largest cohort group in American history, the post-World War II baby boom. Between 1947 and 1958, there was a dramatic increase in births, along with widespread affluence and large-scale bureaucracies and institutions. The middle class expanded dramatically, as suburbs mushroomed around cities throughout the country (Wynne, 1977).

An emerging social and cultural mood coalesced among those who reached college age in the 1960s, a mood that valued social justice, idealism, and personal fulfillment (Yankelovich, 1974). The civil rights movement captured the imagination of many young people who sought to extend the opportunities they themselves had enjoyed to others less fortunate.

The Vietnam War, more than any other historical event, distinguished the 1960s. Because it so directly concerned youth who were called upon to fight what many young people saw as an immoral war, Vietnam provided the spark that lit a fire in the youth of this time, and that created, in Mannheim's terms, the *generation unit* of shared values and purpose.

For the most part, however, the activism of youth in the 1960s was confined to a small proportion of youth. Studies suggested that student activists tended to come from liberal activist families and thus to represent more family continuity than antagonism (Flacks, 1971). Whatever their background, youth focused on what they saw as the contradictions of American society at that

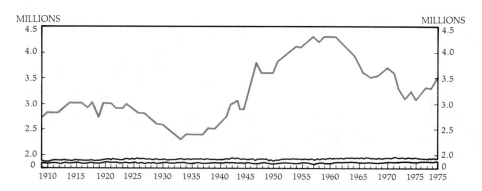

FIGURE 13.1

Annual Births in the U.S.: 1909–1979. (SOURCE: *Population Bulletin*, Vol. 35, No. 1, 1980, "America's Baby Boom Generation: The Fateful Bulge".)

time and were successful in shaping public debate. Many of the trends and ideas of the 1960s have become increasingly accepted since then, while others have faded. The period remains important as a time when a large number of young people united into a social and cultural force of major proportions, when age became a social marker ("Don't trust anyone over 30"), and when many of the aspects of youth as a discrete stage of life erupted into prominence, even if most young people were only part-time participants in the *youth culture.*

The Role of Work
in the Transition to Adulthood

As we said earlier in this chapter, the adoption of adult roles is really the main transition necessary to become recognized as an adult. Working is an essential aspect of this shift in roles. In the context of marriage, working in the home is a recognized adult role, but a marriage in which neither spouse works and that is economically dependent on others is not seen by many as performing the basic functions of adulthood. Work, perhaps even more than marriage, is central to adulthood.

The vast majority of youth want to work and consider work a central goal of adult life (Yankelovich, 1974). They recognize that work defines who one is in society. In our mobile and competitive world, what matters most is what you can do in the working world, not who your parents are or what you did in school. Work provides a social yardstick of achievement and success and entering the world of work brings with it a set of peers, a track for possible advancement, and social identity. Work is important both as a means to contribute productively to the social good as well as for providing the economic and social means to adult status in society. The late economist E. F. Schumacher described three functions of work:

> "1) to give a person a chance to utilize and develop his faculties; 2) to enable him to overcome his inborn egocentricity by joining with other people in a common task; and 3) to bring forth the goods and services needed by all of us for a decent existence." (1979, p. 118)

From the point of view of the transition to adulthood, we will be considering the first two of Schumacher's items and will examine the ways in which work helps to change an adolescent into an adult.

As we saw in Chapter 9, for a large proportion of youth, part-time work experience has been part of their experience since age 16 or younger. During summers and after school many adolescents get their first exposure to the working world and to the responsibility of having a paying job. Sometimes these part-time jobs even lead eventually to full-time employment. While in high school, the student must begin to consider vocational choices, relying on school and work experiences for indications of interests, capabilities and ambition.

The first major decision to be made concerns *when* to enter full-time work, a question that usually translates as when to terminate education. In 1981, roughly 85% of America's adolescents graduate from high school (Garbarino & Asp, 1981). Once out of high school, the next major decision is whether or not to continue education, and if so, what type of schooling to obtain. As we said in Chapter 9, many personal and social factors influence these decisions. Currently, about half the high school graduates enter some sort of higher education, with approximately 25% of all youths eventually earning a college degree (Garbarino & Asp, 1981). Thus, the process of entering into full-time work begins at 16 for a few youth, and continues until age 24, when over 80% are out of school, with the majority working or in the armed services. Obviously the kinds of work youth enter into and the paths leading to those jobs vary tremendously. Yet there are some general qualities that apply to the process of entering the work force for all strata.

Regardless of age and type of job, full-time work plays a vital role in marking the beginning of adult responsibility and accomplishment. Economic independence, even for those youths still living with their parents, brings a measure of recognition and respect beyond the purchasing power of the wages themselves. Working people can take care of themselves, and this fact goes a long way toward the social definition (and self definition) of people as adult—capable, mature, independent, responsible.

Working brings with it a direct confrontation with reality. It involves meeting and working with a variety of people, often from different backgrounds and creates a series of pressures that may be different from personal goals and interests. Thus, the entrance into the workplace is the beginning of a new way of life, different from school, family, or peer relationships. The adjustment to these new relationships, responsibilities, and pressures may be difficult at first.

The Role of College in the Transition to Adulthood

In many ways, colleges and universities have become the headquarters for youth, providing the conditions under which young people come together to engage in educational and other stimulating endeavors while enjoying a relatively free and insulated environment. Often they do so with the blessing of parents who want to give their offspring a chance to develop the basis for a career and to find a desirable mate.

As we pointed out in Chapter 9, in this century, the number and characteristics of people attending college have expanded dramatically. At the beginning of this century, only a tiny percentage of Americans attended college of any kind, and these students were overwhelmingly white, well-to-do, urban, and male. The greatest increases in college attendance, coinciding with the opening of college to females and racial minorities, occurred in the post-World War II era. In 1947, 19% of all 18-year-olds were enrolled in some sort of college; the figure in 1977 had climbed to 45% (National Center for Educational Statistics, 1980).

The *number* of people in college also increased drastically in the 1960s and 1970s. From 1963 to 1973 the number of students in college rose 86% (Simon & Frankel, 1974). Thus, colleges grew dramatically to meet the demand of young people and the needs of society for higher education. After this trend peaked in the early 1970s, most growth in colleges involved older students, who are beyond the period of youth (most of whom had already been working and raising families).

Who goes to college depends upon a variety of factors. Three of the most important are academic ability, socioeconomic status, and gender (Bachman, O'Malley, & Johnston, 1978). Sewell and Shah (1967) showed that those who are the most likely to enroll in college are smart, upper-class males (90.7%); the least likely are intellectually marginal, poor females (3.7%). In later work Sewell (1971) refined his analysis of the effect of social status on college attendance. Citing the effects in terms of probability of attendance, he finds that, comparing students of equal academic ability, the high SES student will enjoy a 4-to-1 advantage in access to college, a 6-to-1 advantage in probability of graduating, and a 9-to-1 chance of entering graduate or professional school. Furthermore, people from lower SES backgrounds (of equal academic ability) are less likely to enroll in college immediately after high school, are less likely to attend a prestigious school, are more likely to drop out, and are less likely to return to school if they do drop out.

College, Youth, and Social Change

As we mentioned earlier in the discussion of youth, the forerunners of this new period in the life course were generally college students, and college remains the primary microsystem for large numbers of post-adolescents. This is true because of the large number of students in college and because the college atmosphere tends to reflect the predominant mood of the times. This is not to say that other areas of society do not also represent social concerns of the moment. But college is one domain where change in social attitudes is easily and clearly manifested since it is based on a new population every four years, its mission is preparing youth for the society of its future, and it offers so many opportunities for unregulated discussion, commentary, and information gathering.

Studies of college students at different times demonstrate this. For example, in the 1950s Jacob (1957) found that as students moved from freshman to senior year, they became more tolerant and able to apply critical thinking to judgments. However, they also become more conforming; students who had espoused more unorthodox views tended to become more conventional. This combination of responsible conformity epitomizes the image of the 1950s as the *silent generation.*

In the 1960s, surveys found college attendance was associated with a lessening of prejudice and authoritarianism, along with an increased appreciation of aesthetic phenomena and a more liberal attitude toward political and social issues (Feldman & Newcomb, 1969). Yankelovich (1974) saw 1960s college students as forerunners, espousing two strong values—personal desire for fulfillment through the full expression of life and a belief in social justice, peace, and freedom throughout society. Though never more than a minority of students, these forerunners dominated the public perception of youth at that time, embodied the era's most important concerns, and served as opinion leaders.

In the 1970s our public themes changed drastically, and college students reflected this vividly. Yankelovich (1974) surveyed 1,000 college students in 1973 and found that while some of the political and social liberalism of the 1960s was still present on campus, it was much less prominent. In its place was a passion for individual fulfillment, but without the impetus for social justice that had accompanied it in the 1960s. What Yankelovich calls "New Values" of this time include liberal and tolerant ideas about personal life-styles and morals combined with a return of support for such standard values as money, work, marriage, and family, and a concern for self-fulfillment. Yankelovich estimates that one-third of college students support these "New Values," one-third of college students espouse primarily materialistic goals, and the remaining third support some combination of traditional career and "New Values." The 1970s *Me Decade* preoccupation seems well exemplified by the students Yankelovich describes.

Data from the American Council of Education's annual survey of college freshmen provides a good summary of the shift in attitudes among the college population. Among other questions, the Council asked freshmen to rate a list of objectives on the basis of their importance in their lives. The results over the last ten years indicate that "being well off financially" was cited as important by 62% in 1979 versus 19% in 1969, and that the importance of personal growth and civic responsibility had declined over those ten years by 50% (Butler, 1980). The trends of the 1970s seem to have continued in the 1980s and demonstrate a greater preoccupation with career and economic gain, with a further diminution in emphasis of social justice in the pursuit of personal fulfillment and a strengthening of more conservative political and social values.

How does the experience of college affect the transition to adulthood? Of course this varies tremendously by the type of college, student, and, as we have seen, historical period, but there are certain generalities that will apply to most instances. Since the overwhelming majority of college students are young (although 35% were over 24 years old in 1978 [Garbarino & Asp, 1981]), college is a stepping-stone microsystem between the family and the adult world. Erikson's concept of the *psychosocial moratorium* (see Chapter 7) applies best to college; it is a refuge from adult roles, a time to try out the styles and to make the decisions that will set the course for adulthood. Hence it is a time of *both* freedom and pressure, with the future depending heavily on the successful navigation of courses, activities, and a commitment to adult roles.

For those students who live away from home, either in a college dormitory or off-campus with other students, another important learning experience is learning to live with others and to take care of oneself. There is more diversity of opinion and taste at college than in one's family. No one makes the student study, go to class, get enough sleep, or eat properly, and this lack of control requires that students learn some sort of self-reliance if they want to complete school successfully. Many personal value issues, such as the use of drugs and alcohol, religious involvement, participation in sexual activities, and academic honesty must be resolved by students without direct parental influence, and they are faced with the consequences of their choices. For these and other reasons, college can be a stressful time of life, and many students at one time or another become depressed or confused, try to escape through alcohol or other drugs, seek advice through campus counseling services, or contemplate leaving college.

The Variety of Colleges

Because the *type* of college makes such a difference in the experience of attending college, we should examine the variety of institutions more closely. The traditional liberal arts college in this country began its evolution during the beginning of English settlement and has always stressed the preparation of a small number of students through a broad exposure of the intellectual heritage of Western civilization and a strong moral-religious foundation. Today, these schools maintain a commitment to liberal arts education and the development of the whole person, while trying to keep abreast of social changes favoring technical mastery such as computer literacy. Liberal arts colleges tend to be moderately to highly expensive and tend to attract the upper-middle and upper-class student.

The growth of colleges that are large public institutions has made possible the tremendous increase in the numbers and proportion of people who attend college. Primarily attended by the middle and working classes, public universities offer an astonishingly wide range of courses and majors that includes the liberal arts as well as technical and professional training. This curricular diversity is reflected in great student diversity. The state school often is a microcosm of the ethnic, social, and cultural composition of the state it serves.

The growth of community and junior colleges has also contributed to the growing college population by making college attendance possible for people who are also involved with work and family responsibilities or who have a weak academic record in high school. Many two-year institutions serve mainly commuters who are able to work and raise families while they attend school, often part-time. Education is often oriented toward vocational advancement, with less emphasis on the liberal arts and an absence of the campus-based activities. Students are often older than the typical 18–22 year old college student. Indeed, almost all the growth in the number of college students in the 1970s derived from an expansion of the role played by older students, many of them on commuter campuses and in community colleges.

What are the consequences of a college education? Aside from the personal experiences of college, there are some measurable differences between groups of noncollege and college people that continue through life. Not surprisingly, college-educated people have higher incomes. Of course, as more people go to college, these differences diminish because college-educated people will include more people previously in the noncollege group. College-educated people often marry people they meet at college, so that attending college may affect who one marries. College is one of the most important of settings for youth development along a whole range of personal and role dimensions.

The Role of Marriage and Parenthood in the Transition to Adulthood

As we said earlier, the assumption of family roles is another primary task of early adulthood. Like the transition from student to worker, the transition from son or daughter (in the family of origin) to husband or wife and parent (in the family of procreation) is a movement from one microsystem to another (an *ecological transition*) that creates mesosystems. And, like the entrance into the work force, the entrance into marriage is one step in a process that begins years earlier with dating, continues with gradual learning about the opposite sex, a developing sense of how one wants to live as an adult, and how a relationship comes to be part of that life (the topics of Chapter 8). And, of course, marriage and parenthood continue as a process of mutual adjustment, as couples seek to balance their needs, responsibilities, and goals together and independently.

In recent years much has been said about the imminent death of the family, based on such alternatives as childless couples, cohabitation, homosexuality, and a divorce rate that has doubled in the past 20 years (Reiss, 1980) so that now the Census Bureau estimates that between 40% to 50% of present marriages will end in divorce (Spanier, 1980). Yet the experience of living in families is in no danger of extinction. As Mary Jo Bane has shown in her book *Here to Stay* (1976), the percentage of people who eventually do marry is quite high; by age 30 over 90% of men and women have been married at least once. Moreover, while many people delay childbearing, few give it up completely. And, although divorce is increasingly common, remarriage awaits 80% of currently divorced partners (Reiss, 1980), one-half within three years. Thus, marriage and parenthood are central life involvements for the majority of adult men and women.

As key transitions in the process of becoming adult, marriage and parenthood raise basic and important issues concerning autonomy and responsibility. Couples are expected to develop a unified emotional and financial identity and to turn their primary allegiance from parents and friends to the marital union. Marriage and parenthood take place in the context of other developmental processes—psychological, emotional, and social—that influence when and how the events occur. Most experts believe that marriage and parenthood should come *after* adolescence, as a way of solidifying the transition from youth into adulthood.

Following from our earlier discussion on maturity we can say that marriage and parenthood require a deep psychological commitment quite unlike relationships during childhood and adolescence. Adolescent relationships within the family of origin are not based on the adolescent's choice. Rather they are based on relationships begun at birth. At least as seen by North American ideals, the family of procreation, on the other hand, is based on commitments that are freely and consciously made. Clearly the commitment to start a family carries with it both emotional and economic responsibilities.

In both of these areas, individuals need the support of the entire human ecosystem, for although the creation of a family is a turning inward on the couple's part, parents, friends, and social institutions can play a major role in helping the young family. Marriage or parenthood that occurs when young people as individuals and as a couple have already passed through other adult transitions may be enhanced by the experience, and social competence gained in other areas. The issue of marital timing and its relation to adulthood is a key to the transition to adulthood, and we will examine it further.

Historical Trends in Adolescent Marriage and Parenting

Earlier we talked about historical trends in adolescent and youth development in patterns of work and education. The trend in the timing of marriage too has changed, gradually occurring at an earlier age over the past century, and possibly starting to reverse during the last 20 years. Currently, the average (median age) of first marriage is 24.4 years for men and 22.5 years for women, up almost two years for both sexes since the 1950s (U. S. Census, 1980).

The reasons for these historical shifts are complex and involve economic conditions as well as changing cultural practices, which may work in opposite directions. In years past, marriage occurred relatively late because it depended upon the couple's ability to establish economic independence, quite often with the help of parents at the start. Earlier marriages generally have been related to the strength of the economy; good and plentiful employment allows people to marry earlier (Hogan, 1981). Thus, the growing affluence of American society in this century (with the exception of the Depression of the 1930s) has made it possible for many couples to marry at an earlier age with the confidence that they could make their way financially. On the other hand, alternatives to marriage (such as cohabitation) have made marriage less automatic and provide other experiences that tend to take place before marriage, thus raising the age at which people do marry. The net effect on the age of marriage depends on the degree to which economic and cultural forces balance each other. Women born in the United States from 1910 to 1940 showed a trend towards earlier marriage. Women born after World War II have been marrying later.

Adolescent parenthood also reveals historical trends that have a bearing on the transition to adulthood. Although information is sketchy on the incidence of adolescent childbearing in the 19th century, available data indicate that it was less common then than it is today. A census in Massachusetts in 1885 reported that the total number of children born to teenage mothers was less than 20 per 1,000 women (Taeuber & Taeuber, 1971). Like teenage marriage, parenting was unusual and out of step with economic and cultural forces. Between 1915 and World War II, the birth rate among 15- to 19-year-old women ranged between 50 to 60 births per 1,000 women (Furstenberg, 1976).

Following World War II the teenage birthrate increased dramatically. The baby boom was definitely affected by teenage mothers (most of whom were married, *at least when the child was born, if not when it was conceived*). In 1945 the teenage birthrate was 51 births per 1,000 women; in 1957 (the peak baby boom year) it was 96.3 (Furstenberg, 1977).

The birthrate for teenagers has declined since then, once again reaching pre-World War II levels. Yet what has changed most since the 1940s is a sharp rise in the rate of births to *unmarried* teenagers, who are thus making one part of the transition to adulthood out of order (before the transition to the role of spouse). The number of births to teenagers who are unmarried in relation to the total number of births to adolescents has increased substantially. Between 1950 and 1977 the rate of births to unmarried teenagers more than doubled and the number of out-of-wedlock births in relation to all *married* births among 15–19-year-old mothers tripled. We cannot account for this increase solely by increased sexual activity or more pregnancies among teenagers. It reflects a decreased tendency to marry following conception and before the birth of the child. Even though fewer pregnant adolescents are choosing to marry, a higher percentage of first births to married white teenagers were *premaritally* conceived. This relative difference derives from the fact that the percentage of teenagers who are not pregnant but who do choose to marry dropped markedly (FLM, 1981). Generally, the younger the age of the couple at marriage, the more likely it is that pregnancy is a factor.

Significant racial differences have been found in rates of teenage pregnancy, with blacks pregnant at a higher level than whites. However, the trend since World War II has been toward a lessening of some racial differences. For example, since 1950 the white illegitimacy rate has increased by 66% while the black rate has increased a more modest 36%. Also, premarital sexual participation increased between 1971–1979 among white females at a far higher rate than among black females (85% versus 23%), so that by 1979, 40% of white and 63% of nonwhite unmarried 15- to 19-year-old females had had intercourse (Zelnik & Kanter, 1980). These racial differences have begun to decline.

The increase in incidence of nonmarital intercourse among youth began during the mid- and late 1960s and continued through the 1970s, a critical time for extensive changes in the sexual attitudes and behavior of youth (Chilman, 1978). In Chapter 8 we began to explore the many causes for this rise in nonmarital coitus, including low levels of religiousness, a relaxing of the sexual norms of society, peer group pressure, the increased use of drugs and alcohol, permissive attitudes of parents, little child-parent communication, strained parent-child relationships, and the earlier onset of puberty.

The trend since the early 1970s has been for fewer and fewer adolescents to marry when faced with a pregnancy. What used to be called a *shot gun wedding* is disappearing. Instead, adolescents resort to abortions or to having and keeping babies out of wedlock. Two studies by Zelnick and Kantner (1974, 1978) on premarital pregnancy based on nationally representative samples of 15- to 19-year-old females yields some interesting changes during the 1970s. The 1971 data showed that for whites, 52.2% were married before the pregnancy came to term, 12.3% married after the birth of the child, and 35.5% never married. This is in marked contrast to the 1976 sample, where 36.5% married before the birth of the child, 9.4% married after the pregnancy outcome, and 54.1% never married. Thus, we see that fewer pregnant teenagers opted to marry as the 1970s proceeded, a trend that appears to continue in the 1980s (see Zelnick and Kantner, 1981).

This may be because of a greater acceptance of single mothers. This might lead to less pressure being brought to bear on single mothers to get married. There is little evidence of change among blacks (among whom there has been greater acceptance of unmarried parenthood) along these dimensions. All of this represents the human ecology of youthful parenthood.

When we look at the distribution of premarital pregnancies of 15–19-year-old women who were unmarried at pregnancy, we find some interesting results.

The most striking change is in the number of induced abortions for whites, increasing from 32.9% for whites in 1971 to 44.9% for whites in 1976. Again, blacks show little change. The point is that marriage has become less linked to parenthood, and that pregnancy no longer leads to parenthood among many adolescents and youth.

Abortion was also chosen more frequently in the 1976 sample than in the 1971 sample. Of course, this probably reflects the 1973 decision by the U. S. Supreme Court that effectively legalized abortion throughout the United States. Baldwin (1976) reports that between 1972 and 1975 the abortion rate among adolescents climbed by over 60% and that this rate almost doubled for teenagers under 15. There were more abortions than live births for this age group in 1974 through 1976. Although the reverse seemed to be true in the past, national data for 1973–1977 revealed that more blacks received abortions during this period than whites (Forrest, Sullivan, & Tietze, 1979).

According to Zelnick and Kantner's data, it is clear that while the rate of abortion is increasing, the number of children being given up for adoption is decreasing. In 1971, about 18% of live births to white unmarried mothers had been placed for adoption, whereas in 1976, this percentage dropped to 7%. Notice that for this same group, in 1971 about 72% of the babies were living with the mother, while in 1976, about 87% of the babies were living with the mother. This pattern in the data is thought by the investigators to be caused by the availability of abortion. The option of abortion enables the pregnant teenager who does *not* want the child to not have it, while those who *do* want the child, whether they are married or not, tend to keep it rather than put it up for adoption.

Each year about one million 15–19-year-olds become pregnant (Stuart & Wells, 1982). Fewer than half the pregnancies result in live births, and over one-third of the pregnancies end in abortion. The great majority of the pregnancies occur among unmarried women. Because unmarried adolescents were much more likely to abort, 56% of births to adolescent mothers were to *married* adolescents. Yet, it is estimated that 60% of these were premaritally conceived.

Adolescent Marriage and Parenthood: Who and Why

In this section we will be focusing on couples who marry relatively early in life. As a group they tend to enter into marriage before they assume other major adult roles, and thus their experience is often quite different from that of couples who marry later. This special case, the early marriage, although not the predominant pattern in today's society, is nevertheless instructive because it demonstrates the connections between life choices and social options. It is difficult to draw any hard and fast rule, but we can tentatively define early marriage as a marriage in which the bride is 18 or under and the groom is 20 or younger (Bartz & Nye, 1970).

Who Marries Early?

The question of who tends to marry early includes three interrelated dimensions: social, personal, and circumstantial. On all dimensions there are characteristics that distinguish those who marry early from others of their age group who do not. Beginning with social factors, several researchers report that adolescent marriages take place more commonly among young people from lower socioeconomic levels (Bayer, 1968; Burchinal, 1965; Elder, 1972). The major roles of adolescence—family member and student—are more often problematic among those who marry early. Inselberg (1961) and Havighurst (1962) report married adolescents more often come from broken homes. Martinson (1955) associated early marriage with poor home adjustment, and Elder (1972) reported more estrangement from parents than those who marry later. At school, early marriage is associated with lower academic success, dropping out, and lower school satisfaction (Havighurst, 1962; Burchinal, 1965; deLissovoy, 1973). Family influence can operate through establishing norms for appropriate timing and sequencing of adult transitions. In addition, the quality of the parents' marriage may be related to children's age at marriage. Lowrie (1965) found that teenage brides reported lower parental marital happiness than did older brides.

Several studies have found specific personality and attitudes characteristic of those who marry early. Moss and Gingles (1959) and Havighurst (1962) found a positive relationship between emotional adjustment and age at marriage; those with poorer emotional adjustment tended to marry earlier. Two very different attitudes may be present among adolescent couples. One, consistent with low social and emotional adjustment, is *escapism*, in which unhappy youths seek marriage as a way out of unsatisfactory home or school settings. The other is a highly optimistic, even idealized, view of marriage that can neutralize opposition from parents, teachers, and friends, even when a marriage looks to others to be quite shaky. In general, though, many young people (especially females) marry because it is a long-held goal that surpasses academic and vocational interests. For those who have little interest in further work or school, marriage and parenthood become goals for which there may be no reason to delay beyond the teenage years. Not seeing either an intrinsic appeal to youth or a future-oriented rationale for it, they opt for an early exit from adolescence in the expectation of an early transition into adulthood.

In looking at circumstances or life events associated with early marriage, the most powerful is premarital involvement with the opposite sex. Bayer (1968) analyzed a sample of 33,000 high school students (from Project TALENT) and found that for adolescents of all social classes, beginning to date before age 15 was associated with a higher chance of marrying by age 23 for men and age 21 for women. Marini (1978) reported that those who date early and the most in high school tend to marry earlier, especially females. Elder (1972) also found an association between early sexual involvement and early age at marriage. In light of what we learned in Chapter 8 about the scripts of courtship and sexuality, this suggests that one way to postpone adulthood is to postpone dating.

Why Do People Marry Early?

The question of *why* people marry early is closely related to the question of *who* marries early. Early marriage can be said to be a function of causes that follow from the personal, social, and circumstantial characteristics of those people most likely to marry young. In fact, much research indicates that the principal reason adolescents marry is premarital pregnancy. As we mentioned in our discussion on teenage parenthood, fewer adolescents have been choosing to marry when pregnancy is not a factor, so those who do marry as teenagers are more likely to do so following discovery of a pregnancy. Among adolescent mothers, social and personal factors distinguishing those who marry and those who remain single include ambition. In Furstenberg's (1977) study of adolescent mothers in inner-city Baltimore, half were married by age 18. Ambition was a major determinant: only 10% of the most ambitious mothers married before delivery and 53% were married five years later, while among the least ambitious, 43% were married before the birth of their baby and 77% by five years later (Furstenberg, 1977).

The issue of strained parent-child relationships leading to pregnancy exemplifies a pattern of neurotic delinquency, which was identified in Chapter 11 (Wiener, 1982). Some teenagers appear to marry or become pregnant as a means of expressing rebelliousness against their parents and as a means to punish their mothers for not communicating with them satisfactorily (Barglow, Bornstein, Exum, Wright, & Visotsky, 1967; Meyerowitz & Maley, 1973; Roberts, Abrams, & Finch, 1973). Other teenagers marry or become pregnant in order to enhance their feelings of attractiveness and sexuality or to bolster peer-group attention and respect (Gottschalk, Titchener, Piker, & Stewart, 1964; Visotsky, 1966). Kaplan, Smith, and Pokorney (1979) report that low self-esteem and feelings of peer group rejection predicted a higher probability of teenagers becoming pregnant over one year in advance.

These all can involve egocentric, maladaptive, indirect ways of dealing with psychological needs. Marrying or becoming pregnant to "get back at Mom" is not an adaptive way of dealing with anger. The far-reaching consequences of such action are often not anticipated or thought out in advance. Because of the maladaptiveness of this behavior, we might consider getting married or pregnant for these reasons a serious manifestation of adolescent egocentrism.

Consequences of Adolescent Marriage and Parenthood

We can understand adolescent marriage and parenthood as a series of choices facing the adolescent, only some of which may be meaningful choices for any particular adolescent. First, there is the choice of whether or not to become sexually active, and, if so, whether and what kind of birth control to use. This was our topic in Chapter 8. (There may be no choices for the victim of sexual abuse.) If a pregnancy occurs, the adolescent will bear the baby, choose to undergo an abortion, or she may miscarry. During this same period, decisions about the nature of the adolescent's heterosexual relationship must be made, and that process continues before and after the birth of the baby. Following birth, the decision-making process repeats itself with regard to additional children, and this approach extends to life choices in other areas, such as education, employment, and marital stability (Elder, 1980). Those adolescents who preempt the experience of youth and choose marriage as the tactic for resolving these issues are embarking upon a risky course.

Confining our discussion at this point to those adolescents who have become pregnant and given birth, we can now examine some of the personal and social consequences of teenage childbearing. The most-studied consequences of teenage parenthood have been the health of mother and child, the educational and occupational attainment of teenage parents, and their marital stability. Teenage pregnancies have long been thought to be problematic medically, both to mother and child (Sacker & Newhoff, 1982). Life-style factors harmful to pregnancy like poor nutrition, smoking, and drug abuse are more common among teenagers who get pregnant than among older pregnant women, perhaps in part because of egocentric inability to plan for the well-being of the fetus. Prematurity and low birth weight are serious problems of teenage pregnancies, especially among young adolescents who do not get medical prenatal care, which many do not for a variety of reasons. However, when teenagers *do* get adequate prenatal care, they and their babies are quite healthy.

Several studies (Morrison, 1978; Furstenburg, 1977; Pressler, 1976, 1980; Maracek, 1979; Russ-Eft, Springer, & Beever, 1979) reviewed by Chilman (1980) have addressed the effect of early marriage and pregnancy on education. Because of the mother's greater involvement and responsibility for childcare, adolescent females are usually far more affected socially by the birth of a child than are adolescent males. Furstenberg (1977) examined several hypotheses concerning why teenage parenthood so adversely affects school attendance. In his study, one-half of the young mothers eventually graduated from high school. The young mothers were not markedly inferior students as compared to their classmates, so prior academic failure leading to pregnancy did not seem to be a strong explanation. Marriage, more than parenthood, was related to dropping out of school: one-half of the women who married before delivery dropped out, versus one-third of the unmarried mothers. It may be that establishing the role of husband and wife independent of parents or others encourages the young people to work rather than attend school. Of course, the mother and father often have no choice but to work and care for the child themselves, and thus are unable to attend school. High ambition and parental support to stay in school were also important. When the adolescent mother wanted to stay in school and her family was disposed to help her by helping with childcare, she was in a better position to be able to continue her education.

The link between teenage parenthood and education is further clarified when we consider racial differences. Furstenberg (1977) noted that the white adolescents in his sample were much more likely to marry before the child's birth than were blacks (70% versus 16%). A study of Southern adolescents (Howell & Frese, 1982) found that whites, more than blacks, dropped out of school following childbirth. Again, it is the decision to marry, and not parenthood *per se*, which often signals the end of the adolescent mother's education.

Another study (Card & Wise, 1981) based on a national sample of youth (Project TALENT) matched adolescents at age 15 in the early 1960s on social class, race, grades, and educational aspirations. Those who became adolescent parents had significantly lower educational and occupational status, as well as lower income and job satisfaction by age 29 (a joint product of where they started out and how being a teenage parent affected them). The authors concluded that early parenthood in itself (and the early marriage that often follows) limits educational and occupational accomplishment by cutting short education and putting pressure on adolescents for short-term economic payoffs before they are sufficiently prepared to begin work in a way that produces long-term payoffs. Thus, the life-course paths embarked upon in the teenage years can have long-term consequences for the kind of adult choices available years later (Card & Wise, 1981).

Other Consequences of Teenage Marriage

There is abundant evidence supporting the position that teenage marriages suffer from low satisfaction and stability, when compared to marriages begun after adolescence. Burchinal (1965) reported that marital satisfaction is markedly lower among teenage couples, and this difference is still present 15 years after marriage. He found their divorce rate was double that of couples who married in their 20s. Among all couples, marrying during pregnancy was associated with a divorce rate twice as high as marriages not begun during a pregnancy. Teenage couples are disproportionately made up of premaritally pregnant brides (Lowrie, 1965). Elder's study of marriage among people raised in the Great Depression found that 35% of the women married as teenagers were divorced by age 44, as compared to 15% of women married between 20 and 22, and 6% of the women married at 23 or later (Elder, 1972). Using marriage as part of the transition from youth into adulthood seem to work better than using it to exit adolescence.

Among Furstenberg's (1977) inner-city sample of adolescent mothers, 41% were married by age 18, and the instability rate was very high (60%) over the next five years. This was twice as high as nonpregnant classmates who married during the study (and after graduation). The factor that best separates those who managed to stay together from those who broke up was the husband's status. Among couples in which the husband had a high school degree and/or a skilled job, only one-fifth were separated within the first two years of marriage, whereas couples with a husband with neither a degree nor a skilled job had a two-year separation rate of 45%. All in all, the odds against the teenage marriages in Furstenberg's sample were so great that he concluded:

> Ironically, most young mothers who managed to avoid single parenthood by marrying either before or shortly after delivery ended up as single parents several years later. . . . Therefore it might be said that once an unplanned pregnancy occurs in adolescence, it hardly matters whether or not the young mother marries. In time, she may be almost as likely to bear the major, if not the sole, responsibility for supporting her child. (Furstenberg, 1977, p. 98)

The issue thus becomes the kind of support the mother receives, from all her micro-, meso-, exo-, and macrosystems.

Resources for Adolescent Marriages and Parenthood

The first news of an adolescent's pregnancy is usually deeply traumatic to her family. However, some families overcome their shock. Family relationships before and after the pregnancy are an important factor influencing the adolescent's choices, behaviors, and success in meeting the challenges before her. Thus, we must consider the adolescent's family as a mediator of the antecedents of teenage marriage and parenthood as well as of their consequences. The same goes for other microsystems, such as schools and churches.

According to Labarre (1972), parents are generally supportive and helpful toward pregnant daughters, but only after a brief period of shock "and intense feelings of grief, anger, hopelessness, and disbelief" (Authier & Authier, 1982). While it may be deeply disturbing to parents, their daughter's and future grandchild's well-being are strong motivations for adapting constructively in most cases. The adolescent, for her part, may need parental support more at this time than ever before, and her subsequent relationship with her parents may play a major role in her child's development. In Furstenberg's study, for example, family support was a major aid in the younger mothers' adjustment to motherhood. Of those who did not marry, remaining at home made it much easier for them to continue in school, to become employed, and be less likely to go on public assistance. Family support played a major role in the adolescent's career development. It bridged the life crisis represented by teenage parenthood, and could allow an adolescent to stay on track.

Yet there are problems inherent in the family microsystem when an adolescent pregnancy occurs. Adolescence is normally a time of redefining relationships, and a pregnancy can alter the fragile dynamics and send a family into chaos. In some ways the adolescent parent is now an adult, but may be still emotionally and financially dependent on her parents. This ambivalence between autonomy and dependence can be very difficult for adolescents and parents alike (Authier & Authier, 1982).

The aftermath of an adolescent pregnancy is also fraught with problems. If the daughter remains unmarried and in her parent's house, she and her parents must see to her baby's care. In some cases an immature teenage mother may abdicate parenting and the reluctant grandmother may find herself in charge of raising a new generation. Or, a dominant grandmother may seek to take control of the baby, claiming she knows best and that her daughter is too young to be a responsible parent. Either pattern can be the source of serious problems.

If the young couple is considering marriage, the families of both boy and girl are likely to be involved. Conflicts can arise if members of either family oppose the marriage. The result can be bitter fighting that destroys family support and makes the new family's future that much more difficult. An adolescent's legal status changes if she marries or leaves her parents' home. A baby born to a married teenage couple is solely the legal responsibility of the parents, and the young couple may be eligible for welfare payments as a separate unit. If the adolescent mother is not married and is living at home, her parents are responsible for her and the baby's support. Of course, she may be eligible for public aid whether she is living with her parents or not. When the parents of a child are not married, the paternity of the child must be established in order for the child's father to be legally responsible for the child's welfare.

Teenage parenthood clearly complicates the already challenging task of making the transition from adolescence to adulthood. It challenges family microsystems as well as schools, churches, and peer groups. It tests mesosystems. Will they hold together or will some microsystems try to cut the pregnant adolescent off? Whether or not this happens reflects the working of exosystems and macrosystems, through institutional policies and practices.

Social History and the Transition to Adulthood

Now that we have explored the various components of the transition to adulthood, let us consider some important issues in the relationship between the young adult and society. The legal system provides one major determinant of when people gain the social status of adults. In recent years, society's confusion about the proper age to grant adult status has been vividly evident in the controversy over the drinking age. At one time most states prohibited the purchase of alcoholic beverages until age 21. The obvious discrepancy between being liable for the draft at age 18 during the Vietnam War and not being permitted to buy a beer at that age impelled many states to lower the drinking age to 18 or 19 in the 1960s and 1970s.

Since then public debate has focused on the advisability of this change. The role of alcohol in adolescent motor vehicle deaths became the focal point. Concerned citizens cited accidents occurring when youths were returning to a state with a higher drinking age from another with a lower legal age. A national lobbying effort by Mothers Against Drunken Driving (MADD) pressed for tougher legislation. This has prompted states to return the drinking age to 19, 20, or 21, and in 1983 a Presidential Commission on Alcohol supported the 21-year-old limit. In 1984, President Reagen added his weight to this cause by supporting legislation that would withdraw federal funds for states that refused to raise their drinking age. The controversy continues, with forces on one side arguing for the adult rights of youth, and the other side arguing that the recklessness of a few make it necessary to restrict the rights of an entire age group in order to protect the community and the adolescents themselves. Of course, the fact that adults constitute the bulk of the drunken driving population is overlooked or discounted in much of this debate. People are much more ready to regulate youth.

The voting age, too, has changed. The 26th amendment to the United States Constitution passed in 1971 lowered the voting age to 18 in all national elections. At the time, many thought the youth vote would dramatically affect the face of American politics, but the effect thus far has been minimal, with 18- to 21-year-olds voting at the lowest rates of any age group and rarely voting very differently from the population as a whole.

Another issue concerning youth and society is the existence of a *youth culture*, or a set of values and behaviors shared by youth apart from or opposed to the rest of society. In our earlier discussion of youth and history, the concept of cohort was introduced to account for intergenerational differences in values, attitudes, and behavior between youth and older poeple. Yet a youth culture that emphasizes distinguishing young and old can arise in response to a variety of factors.

The Youth Culture

Our earlier discussion of the rise of youth described conditions likely to produce a youth culture. When large numbers of youth are detached and alienated from the larger society, they naturally look to their like-minded peers for confirming values, attitudes, and life-styles. An emerging youth culture expresses a collective set of issues and also becomes a rallying point that attracts new youth to it and strengthens even those older individuals who subscribe to its ideas. Thus, a youth culture can be seen as a spontaneous expression of many people's ideas and feelings that, while it lives, unites people and serves as a focus for identity, belief, and action. Certain symbols come to be recognized as associated with a particular youth culture and people can easily determine who belongs and who does not.

Style also characterizes a youth culture and this style is a constantly evolving phenomenon. New and unique expressions in clothes, music, recreation, and language are a staple of adolescence in this country. The lifespan of such styles varies from a few years to a few weeks, and the range of expression from the predictable (cars, hip music, and fraternity rituals) to the outlandish

Rock and roll concerts stand out as the most exciting events of my adolescent years. The music was electrifying, the crowds endlessly fascinating, and the whole atmosphere so alive that it seemed to me that this must surely be the center of the universe.

When I was 15, a friend and I went together to see a concert at the Fillmore East in New York's East Village for the first time. We took the train into the city from the suburbs, and as we rode downtown on the subway we planned the evening's adventure. We decided to celebrate with a bottle of wine, Boone's Farm Apple, of course, which we bought without problem from a Village liquor store whose main clientele appeared to be underage kids and winos. We drank some of the wine in an alley and tried to smuggle the bottle into the concert under a heavy coat. As a precaution we also filled two water pistols with wine.

As you can probably guess, we were not successful in bringing the wine past security. (At $1 a bottle; no great loss.) We still had our water pistols, though, and in the hour before the concert we walked around the lobby like two little kids at a circus. The mostly older audience seemed to me almost mythical: the colorful, free, high, music-loving hippies of paradise. At one point I began saying hello to everyone who walked by, until Jeff told me to quit acting "immature." Between the wine and the anticipation, I could barely control myself.

Although I don't remember much about the music itself, the spell it cast is still with me. Quicksilver Messenger Service, a psychedelic San Francisco band, was the headliner. They filled the stage with tie-dyed sheets and put candles everywhere. Sitting in the front (the best seats cost $5.50), we were enveloped in the rich, layered sound and the fantastic, hypnotizing colors of the light show.

During one of the lighter songs, the brilliant idea occurred to us to shoot wine at the band. Dino Valenti, the lead singer and guitarist, was doing his stuff when we commenced firing. At first he paid no attention, but then he looked straight at us, and without breaking from the song, gave us a look that spoke loud and clear. When the song ended, he said, away from the mike, "Look, I don't mind you shooting me, but not my guitar." We desisted, feeling both stupid and heroic. Without quite knowing why, we had become a small part of the life of the concert. We felt immortal, magical.

I went to a lot of other concerts over the next few years. The Fillmore closed, new bands came and went. Yet I don't think I ever equaled, in sheer excitement and wonder, the experience of that night, feeling like I was part of something very special.

Robert Abramowitz

(e.g., safety pins in ears or toga parties). Youth culture places a premium on novelty *and* conformity. What matters is that something is new and different (*and* that everyone is doing it).

The more serious aspects of youth culture may be no more permanent than those of style, but can constitute a profound and lasting influence on the lives and development of young people. According to Keniston's (1974) analysis, the expansion of affluence and advanced education became prime breeding grounds for a youth culture founded not only on new styles but on new ideas. Coleman's (1974) summation of the characteristics of the youth culture of the late 1960s emphasized the extent to which youth became independent of the adult world, seeking to form personal and cultural bonds with other youth. The college atmosphere made this possible because it offered intimate, protected interpersonal contact. The mushrooming of music, art, literature, films, and clothes created by and for young people became cultural legitimization and proof that youth were different and had something important to say. Coleman (1974) completed his analysis of the youth culture by noting its identification with the underdog, a commitment to change inspired by a sense of social injustice, and an alienation from the status-quo.

Since Keniston and Coleman wrote in the early 1970s, America has been grappling with prolonged and deep economic recession that has dampened the spread of the youth culture in its 1960s incarnation. Perhaps the phenomenon will remain limited to a few elite students or perhaps economic recovery will spur new waves of youth. For now, it seems that the majority of young people are quite concerned with the entrance into adult roles and do not have the luxury of ambivalent postponement and detached idealism.

Intergenerational Conflict

What are some of the reasons for intergenerational discontinuities or conflict? The historical perspective we have taken in this chapter has emphasized broad trends that have worked to create conditions likely to spark a generation gap. These conditions include the increasing separation between young and old, the expansion of affluence and education that keep young people out of the work force, and the whole array of modern technological advances from motor scooters to video games that facilitate adolescent peer-group involvement and create behavioral and stylistic divisions between generations.

Kingsley Davis (1940) examined the factors responsible for parent-youth conflict. He distinguished between constants, those factors that are intrinsically part of intergenerational conflict, and variables, the factors that differ from time to time and place to place. Although his analysis concerns parents and their children, much of what he says applies to the larger question of the generation gap between young and old. The constants mentioned by Davis center around the age difference between generations, and the fact that as adolescents are reaching their mental and physical peaks, adults are beginning to become aware of loss in their powers. As we noted in earlier chapters, McMorrow (1977) referred to this adult decline as *midolescence*. Youth (we hope) are naturally idealistic, having been brought up on a society's best hopes and wishes about itself, while adults see the world through the lens of experience and realism. These factors are natural and inevitable grounds for conflict and opposing points of view.

The variables noted by Davis have to do with the rate and intensity of social change. The more the world has changed between the parents' adolescence and their children's, the more a gulf divides them, a gulf based on separate attitudes, demands, and by a lack of understanding about the other. Thus, the historical developments of this century make it all but certain that many parents and children will see the world differently, and will have trouble understanding one another, even when they are motivated to seek consensus.

Youth and the Future

In a chapter that has examined the changing nature of youth in an historical perspective, we should conclude by looking forward into the future. Just as we have seen the effect of past economic and cultural changes on the experiences of adolescence, we can assume that a changing society will continue to provide new influences for tomorrow's youth, our children and grandchildren.

The broad historical trend has been toward liberating men and women from the drudgery and danger of menial work, replacing it instead with an increasingly technological, bureacratized, and urban society. Dramatic increases in education and affluence have created the phenomenon of adolescence and youth. The future promises further reductions in the need for unskilled labor; education, affluence, and freedom from drudgery will doubtless continue and expand as central themes for youth. Like the engines of industrialization, the computers and robots of tomorrow beckon a new future, one that we must strive to make as healthy and habitable for people as possible, particularly if fewer and fewer people are truly needed to run society's productive enterprises.

Despite widespread changes in society, however, the needs of youth will remain basically the same. The need to see the connection between one's experiences as an adolescent and one's future adult roles will continue to exist. The needs of youth to make their way in the world, learn the skills needed for adulthood, and resolve their complex feelings about independence and dependence, all will exist in the future as they always have (at least since society created adolescence). It is reassuring to know that the *fundamental* needs and developmental tasks of adolescents and youth remain the same from generation to generation. Yet as society changes we may have to find new ways to meet these needs. How will the world of youth change? The family, the neighborhood, and the school are the settings in which adolescents live on a day-to-day basis. Changes in these settings will have the most direct impact on the lives of young people.

We can pinpoint three social trends likely to continue into the future that pose challenges to youth and the social environment that surrounds and sustains them. Each can become either an opportunity to enhance the lives of youth or a risk for alienation, isolation, and frustration. The first is the trend toward greater demands placed on youth to compete and succeed. Some already believe childhood has become a "luxury" that few can afford and must be hurried out of (Elkind, 1981; Packard, 1983; Winn, 1983). The fact that future economic growth will be largely in high-technology areas pressures young people to succeed in school or be left behind. The pressure cannot help but intensify. While the opportunities will exist for those with the skills, training, and motivation to enjoy highly satisfying and rewarding work, the danger is that there will be fewer and fewer meaningful places for the large number of people who may not excel in high technology fields. It is up to future educational and occupation leaders to ensure that the demands on youth to succeed are not overwhelming, and that everyone has the chance to become a productive member of society. If a larger and larger proportion of youth are losers, society will pay a high price in terms of delinquency, alienation, drug abuse, and irresponsible sexuality.

The second challenge arises from the trend toward greater freedom and flexibility with regard to social roles. In the recent past, youth have exploded in a burst of personal and cultural freedoms. More and more young people questioned who they were and could be, and questioned customs that formerly guided behavior and belief. The benefits of this openness are clear: an end to narrowly defined sex-role stereotypes for women, greater opportunity for minorities, and cultural support for individual self-fulfillment and nonconformity. In short, the result has been increased pluralism. Yet, such freedom may prove perilous to youths seeking some anchor of stability as they reach toward personal identity in a complex world. Too much freedom may be more threatening and destructive than too little. It remains to be seen how well society will be able to strike a balance between tradition and change, stability and experimentation.

Finally, the world of tomorrow seems likely to be organized in a highly bureaucratic, impersonal fashion. The shift from particularistic to universalistic standards (see Chapter 2), like the previous two challenges, portends both good and bad possibilities. A bureaucratic social system discourages prejudice and will supply equal opportunity to all. Yet we stand to lose the small town and regional control over local institutions that has allowed them to be responsive to human needs. It is another case where the positive and negative possibilities coexist, and only time can tell whether this process improves or hampers the development of tomorrow's youth.

In conclusion, the future promises many profound changes, of unpredictable magnitude, scope, and direction. At the heart of adolescent development is a need for young people to be trusted to find themselves as they discover the world around them. If we work toward meeting this eternal need—if the family, school, work place and larger society aid adolescents in their search for a meaningful personal and social identity—the world of tomorrow will have a better chance of offering youth the possibility of becoming all that they are able to become. In so doing the social environment will be doing all it can to promote competence by providing developmental opportunity and preventing developmental risk. What more could we ask for?

Ecological Wrap-Up

Organism.   The lack of physical markers to indicate the end of adolescence focuses attention on social factors and sets the stage for the action of historical forces in shaping the experience of adolescence. In particular, the modern era contains a natural tension because puberty comes earlier than before, while the demands of social competence are greater. Thus there is much more time between childhood and adulthood.

Microsystems.   The socializing influence of higher education is one of the major influences on youth that is linked to historical change. Another is the constantly recurring challenge of forming new families—life's most rewarding and demanding *ecological transition*. The key issue is life-course timing. When does one leave one microsystem and seek to enter or establish another?

Mesosystems.   We see history at work in the way mesosystems arise involving family of origin and family of procreation, adolescent work and adult work, and school and home. Youth as a period in the life-course demands that mesosystems hold together under intense pressures generated by the individual wrestling with issues of identity and future life-course.

Exosystems.   Those who make laws regarding adult status (e.g., drinking ages) and individual discretion (e.g., abortion) play a vital role in the experience of youth. They do much to shape the choices and options adolescents face as they encounter the outskirts of adulthood. The same is true of those who make policy for educational institutions.

Macrosystems.   The broad trends in social history that influence youth operate particularly through demography (changing sizes of cohort groups) and economy (expanding and contracting employment prospects). Historical changes show up very quickly among adolescents, so quickly we can refer to them as social weathervanes. Macrosystems do much to create the odds for or against a particular cohort.

Epilogue: A Personal Statement on the Meaning of Adolescence

Let me speak directly and in the first person to conclude this text. When all is said and done, what is the meaning of adolescence? We began with this question in Chapter 1, and I return us to it again as a way of concluding our discussion because it *is*, after all, the central question. If you come away from this text with a good answer to this question I will feel that we have succeeded.

In this I harken back to a skit written by comedian Don Novello. Speaking in the guise of Father Guido Sarducci (a character he made famous on the television series "Saturday Night Live"), Novello described his plan for the "Five Minute University." Novello notes that everyone forgets most of what they learn in college and all they can remember is one phrase or idea from each course. Thus, he explains, at his Five Minute University he will only teach what people will remember. In economics you will learn the line "Supply and Demand;" in business "Buy low; sell high;" in Spanish "Como esta usted? Bien gracias;" in religion "Where is God? God is everywhere;" and so on. In the spirit of Novello's skit, the adolescence course might consist of "Storm and Stress," but I'd like to go beyond that. This is *my* Five Minute University course on adolescence: What is the meaning of adolescence? *It depends*. Let me elaborate in the hope that you'll remember what the question and the answer signify.

I think that the meaning of adolescence is immensely variable. It depends upon who you are and where and when you live through it. It can be a time of torment or a time of triumph. It can be a time of storm and stress or it can be clear sailing and full speed ahead. But however it is experienced, it usually sets your agenda for years to come. It sets the tone for your adulthood. It establishes themes that you embellish or work against for years, perhaps decades to follow. Do you ever get over being taller or shorter than all the other kids? Do you ever stop reliving in your daydreams being prom queen or scoring the winning touchdown? Have you stopped hating your parents? Do you ever really get over your first real love affair? Can you forget your first sexual experience?

But there's more to it than these personal experiences. Your adolescence marks you culturally. *Your* music, *your* films, *your* television programs, *your* slang, *your* clothes, your *style*; all these are a vital part of your adolescence, and they become a reference point for the rest of your life. Where and when you are an adolescent sticks with you; it organizes each new "present" as you experience it in terms of *your* past. I felt this keenly when I read the following piece in *The New Yorker* magazine in August 1983:

> A young friend writes:
>
> The other day, I was listening to FM radio, and the disc jockey was playing a lot of Byrds and Jefferson Airplane and some Jimi Hendrix, and he was talking about "the Sixties" as if they took place a long time ago, which in fact they did. I was born in 1960, and hence was a technical participant in the decade, but since I eluded awareness of the world around me for ten or eleven years, it might as well have been the Gay Nineties, or even the Big Band Era. By the time I got to the Sixties, everyone else was looking for his coat; the first L.P. in my collection, "Abbey Road," was the last the Beatles recorded, the first election I can recall featured a man named George McGovern, and the war in Vietnam, which began without my knowledge, ended, no thanks to me, not long after I learned which side we were on. So I missed all the fuss, and the only consolation (besides having avoided all the traumas heaped on those who lived in chaotic times) lies in belonging to the first generation that can begin to think about the Sixties as history of the sort one reads in books, instead of the sort one puts in resumes or recalls in dreams. Of course, the price of relative objectivity is relative ignorance, and the chance exists that all my reading and film-watching and record-listening have poisonously romanticized the period for me. Still, as the last few months wore on, I've found myself thinking more and more often of the silhouette of that decade. What looms as so novel and attractive about the Sixties, to one used only to the lower case seventies and early eighties, is that a number of people appear to have been thinking about and asking fundamental questions in that period—asking them insistently, and as if the answers mattered. And surely for a little while it must have looked as if the nation's politics and ways of life were fluid enough to flow in new directions. . . .
>
> My time has been a limp time. Even the music. Last week on TV, there was a rock-and-roll salute to the seventies, which listed the biggest song of the decade as Debby Boone's "You Light Up My Life," with the Bee Gees' smash "Stayin' Alive" just behind. If the world were as it should be, such limpness—and even Debby Boone—would make no difference. But last week's newspapers reported that the gap between black and white incomes remains exactly as wide as it was in 1960, the year that four black students refused to leave a Greensboro lunch counter and in so doing touched off a movement. And late last week President Reagan said he "would hope" that a naval blockade of Nicaragua would not prove necessary. Fundamental questions disappeared at the end of the Sixties not be-

cause they were settled but because they could not be settled without huge changes in the way America and Americans operate. The same mixture of affluence and fear that raised the questions in the first place prevented people from taking those huge steps—and, in fact, encouraged them to shy away, with the kind of sentiments that brought Ronald Reagan to power. The questions—about economic and racial justice, about war, about being rich in a poor world—were passed on to the future, which, for the moment, I belong to. Because upheavals like the Sixties', with the corresponding opportunities for real change, happen rarely in America, my generation may not get a chance at providing lasting answers. And if the chance came to us, there is no reason to imagine we'd do any better than our older brothers and sisters did. But the chance to make history is better than reflecting on it, and there are times when I wish that I'd been born ten years earlier.*

I was born in 1947, so the Sixties was precisely the decade of my adolescence and youth. I was part of that Baby Boom that we mentioned several times in this text. I watched the Beatles live on the Ed Sullivan show. A friend of mine went to the Beatles' first U.S. concert as her sweet sixteen present. I was in my high school English class when John F. Kennedy was assassinated in Dallas, Texas. As editor of my high school year book I joined thousands of my counterparts across the country in writing eulogies and dedicating the volume to J.F.K. In the midst of the Civil Rights Movement I was asked to take my turn doing the "inspirational reading" for the school assembly and chose a section from Thoreau's *On Civil Disobedience*. I had a "We Shall Overcome" bumper sticker on my suitcase. And, as I left high school and entered college the war in Vietnam became the dominant public issue shaping the consciousness and political behavior of me and my peers, some of whom died in the jungle, some of whom left the country, some of whom went to jail, some of whom found a way to avoid it all. It is through the lens of these experiences of my adolescence that I view my life and yours.

My adolescence reverberates through the years of my life as an adult, in what music "sounds right," in what kind of hair styles "look right," in what research results "seem right," in what kind of politics "feel right." Adolescence is the time in your life when you come to social consciousness, when you absorb images, symbols, highs and lows that can last, or at least shape, a lifetime. Don't forget that as you live out your life, particularly when and if you assume some responsibility for someone else's adolescence, be it as a parent, a teacher, or a human service professional.

The meaning of adolescence? It all depends upon who you are and where and when you live through it. Puberty and cognitive maturation are our constants as we grow up; the whole dazzling array of what *else* goes on belongs to us embedded as we are in the various systems this book has attempted to make clear. So we are and we aren't what we make of ourselves—but adolescence, in any case, is the launching pad.

Glossary

Accommodation (in Piaget) Modifying the existing psychological structures in order to adapt to an event.

Adaptation (in Piaget) The individual's general tendency to interact with or adapt to the environment.

Adolescence The period of life between childhood and adulthood.

Adolescent egocentrism The condition in which an individual recognizes that other people have their own unique thoughts, perspectives, and experiences, but believes that their focus is him- or herself.

Adrenalcortotropic hormone (ACTH) A pituitary hormone that controls secretions of the adrenal gland, including estrogen, progesterone, and testosterone.

Adulthood Someone who is physically, mentally, culturally, and emotionally mature, and who is involved in responsible work and family roles.

Age-differentiation hypothesis Theory proposing that a generalized intelligence in youth becomes composed of ever-more diverse specific abilities as one ages. Differentiation occurs at adolescence.

Alienation A sense of estrangement, of isolation, of being perilously alone.

Amai The idea of (desirable) dependency, fostered in Japan (in contrast to the Western-favored independence).

Ambisexuality (bisexuality) Sexual relations with both genders.

Amenorrhea Failure to menstruate.

Androgyny Having both masculine and feminine characteristics.

Anomic setting (for moral development) Rather disorganized setting with no integration of principles or goals.

Anomie Sense of powerlessness.

Anorexia nervosa Self-induced starvation.

Anthropological theory of development Emphasizes *continuity* of experience (Mead, Benedict).

Anti-hero image of adolescence Image of the adolescent as a *victimizer* of society.

Apathy-futility syndrome Exhibited by neglectful parents. The elements of this pattern are a kind of emotional deadness, an unwillingness to initiate or respond to actions, a pervasive sense of ineffectiveness, and a general unresponsiveness to the initiatives of other family members.

Aristotle's theory of human development Much like Plato's theory, this theory proposes the duality of mind and body but compares development to the natural biological order.

Assimilation (in Piaget)   The process in which the child interprets an environmental event through mental structures that already exist.

Authoritarian style   A style that violates the principle of reciprocity by loading excessive power in the hands of the parent and placing the youth in a passive role.

Authoritative orientation   Reciprocity in day-to-day (parent and child) interaction.

Autonomous reality   In Piaget's moral theory: the second stage, in which a child judges actions on the basis of the actor's intentions and the consequences for others, rather than by rigid adherence to laws.

Autopoietic   The ability of a living system to adjust, form new automatic responses, when faced with a new situation.

The Baby Boom generation   An overwhelming increase in the number of births in the wake of World War II, brought about, in part, by economic affluence.

Basal metabolism rate   (BMR)   The minimum amount of energy a person uses in a resting state.

Bandura's Social Learning Theory   Application of learning concepts (modeling, reinforcement, behavior, performance) to circumstances that range from social interaction to career choice.

Behavior settings   The different formal and informal activities that make up the school or other social unit.

Bicultural competence   The ability to function successfully in two or more contrasting cultures or ethnic groups.

Brain growth periodization   Spurts of brain weight increase, followed by periods of no change.

Bulimia   Binging on huge amounts of food; sometimes followed by self-induced vomiting or laxative use (purging).

Calvin's view of human development   One of preformation theories, Calvin's theory claims that the human mind and soul are completely preformed, prenatally.

Centration (in Piaget)   Tendency of child (approximately 4–7 years) to focus on only one dimension of an object.

Characterological delinquency   A group of personal characteristics exhibited in some delinquents, including showing no regard for the rights of others, trusting no one, and being unable or unwilling to control their behavior.

Class inclusion   The ability to see that objects can be part of a larger category of objects (e.g., strawberries, apples, and peaches are understood as also being *fruits*).

Clitoris   A small organ composed of erectile tissue, located toward the front of the vulva in females (homologous to the penis).

Co-construction   Process in which two individuals discover procedures for interaction by creating them through reciprocal exchange and cooperation.

Cognitive development   Changes in the way individuals acquire and use knowledge.

Cognitive-disequilibrium theories (e.g., Piaget, Kohlberg)   The systems orientations that focus on the way individuals negotiate their way through life by moving in and out of equilibrium.

Cognitive theories of human development   In this paradigm, both genetic and environmental forces shape the development of the capacity to understand reality, and they are engaged in significant interplay over the entire lifespan (Piaget, Kohlberg).

Cohort   Most commonly used to describe a birth cohort, e.g., all those born in 1966. It is the term used for all those people who experience a common event in a given time period. Another example: the "class of 1985" is a school cohort.

Community links   Any mechanisms that join or connect a child or youth service to its sources of community support (e.g., foster grandparents for status offenders).

Competence   The ability to succeed in the world; means sufficient for the necessities of a good life.

Confidentiality   The right to protection of personal information that is given to professionals by individuals in the process of seeking help.

Conservation (in Piaget)   Mental ability to recognize that, although the shape of a substance has changed, the quantity remains the same.

Contest mobility   Outcomes of one's school and career depend on a series of objective competitions.

Continuous growth   A gradual, smooth transition from adolescence to young adulthood.

Convergent thinking   Ability to solve a problem that has only one specific answer.

Credentialization   Acquiring the educational credentials necessary and/or desirable for occupational entry.

Critical weight hypothesis (Frisch and Revel's)   The theory that the onset of puberty occurs when a youngster reaches a certain critical weight.

Cultural lag   Gap between changes in broader social context and changes in social institutions (usually the latter lag behind the former).

Cultural relativism   Conception that all cultures are equivalent; no one is better or more moral than another.

Decentration (in Piaget)   Child can focus on more than one attribute or dimension of an object.

Deductive approach   Begins with the principles, ideas, and concepts and applies them to understand specific phenomena.

Delinquency (from Gold and Petronio)   Behavior by a juvenile that is in deliberate violation of the law and is believed by the juvenile to make him or her liable to adjudication if it comes to the attention of a law-enforcement agency.

Demography   The study of the population characteristics, including size, density, and distribution. In this text, we discuss the demography of youth.

Differentiation   The process of separating *self* from *other*.

Dimorphism   The full flowering of adult sex differences in appearance and physiology (at puberty).

Divergent thinking   In a test of creativity, seeking multiple, new, or unusual answers or solutions.

Domestic violence   Use and approval of violence in domestic relations.

Double binds   Irreconcilable conflict between two or more alternatives in a person's life.

DSM III. Diagnostic and Statistical Manual of Mental Disorders (American Psychiatric Association, 1980).

Dysfunctional state   Discrepancy between the way the person perceives him/herself and the way he/she would rather be.

Dysmenorrhea   Painful menstruation.

Early marriage   A tentative definition would be a marriage in which the bride is 18 or under and the groom is 20 or under.

Ecological perspective   The interplay of individual characteristics and the social systems in which the individual participates directly (family, school, church, peer group, etc.) or which have an indirect effect upon the individual's behavior and development (the parent's work place, the school board, the legislature).

Ecological transition   Movement from one microsystem to another (as when one marries, leaving the *family of origin* and establishing the *family of procreation*).

Ecology   The study of interrelationships of organisms and their environment.

Ego (Freud)   Operates according to the reality principle because it seeks to accomplish the individual's goals through socially acceptable and appropriate means.

Egocentric   Limited ability of a child to take another's perspective.

Ego-identity   Erik Erikson's idea that encouragement, self-mastery, and social recognition for development result in ego-identity (a social, externally-oriented perspective).

Ego strength   The individual's skills in handling the real world, and the individual's sense of confidence about those skills.

Eichmann Effect (after the World War II Nazi death camp commander)   The observed reaction of subjects told to give electrical shocks to a helpless victim: they (as he) did, saying they *were just following orders*.

Electra Complex   According to Freud, the desire of girls age 3–5½ years to marry their fathers and get rid of their mothers.

Empathy   The ability to accurately take the role of the other.

Endocrine glands   Groups of hormone-producing cells closely packed together to form glands or distributed throughout an organ whose primary function is not endocrinal. They have no ducts (unlike other bodily glands).

Epigenesis (John Locke)   A gradual unfolding, progressing toward complexity and organization in development.

Epiphyseal growing plates   The ends of long bones of the body where most growth occurs at puberty.

Epistemology The philosophical analysis of knowledge.

Erogenous zones (Freud) The libido becomes concentrated in these particular portions of the anatomy. There are five: oral, anal, phallic, latency (diffused libidinal energy), genital.

Estrogen General name for a group of hormones; the major female sex hormone.

Exosystems Situations having a bearing on the development of adolescents but in which they do not play a direct role, such as the workplace of parents, school board, planning commissions.

Fading In skills training intervention, the process in which the prompting stimulus for a desirable behavior is gradually removed.

Family of origin The family a person is born into, or brought up and shaped by.

Family of procreation The family an individual creates, by marrying (or cohabiting) and having (or adopting) children.

Follicle stimulating hormone (FSH) Gonadotropic hormone (whose target is the gonads stimulating the production of mature sex cells).

Fool stereotype The age of 'pre-responsibility.'

Formal operational period (in Piaget) (Age 11–adult) A transformation of thought that permits the handling of hypotheses and reasoning with regard to propositions removed from concrete and present observations.

Formal support systems Organized service agencies that serve the individual an the family-centered social services, foster homes, community, including specialized group homes.

Freudian slip A revealing misstatement—supposedly the voice of the subconscious breaking through the individual's social guards.

"G" factor A theory of Louis Terman that proposes that there is an inherited general factor that determines an individual's ability to verbalize and think abstractly.

Gender identity The internal, personal sense of being male or female.

Gender role Learning and performing the socially accepted characteristics and behavior of a given gender.

Generation gap The hypothesis that there is a large gap between the attitudes, ideas, and values of parents and their children.

Genotype Our underlying biological makeup.

Graafian follicle The site on an ovary where the mature egg erupts.

Growth hormone (GH) A nontropic hormone that stimulates growth.

Heterosexual dyads Boy-girl relationships.

Homeostasis The endocrine glands form a linked set of systems in dynamic equilibrium or homeostasis. They interact with each other in a way that strives for overall system balance.

Hormones Network of specialized chemicals produced by the endocrine glands; they act as messengers for these glands.

Humanistic psychology An approach that emphasizes the development of positive ideas and feelings about self through increased sensitivity.

"Hydraulic model" of personality (S. Freud) So-called because pressure on one part is transmitted to another, as happens in a car when pressure on the brake pedal is transmitted hydraulically to the brakes.

Hypothalamus Small portion of the underside of the brain that secretes hormones.

Id Unrestricted sexual drive.

Identity formation The way a person goes about deciding who he or she is.

Imaginary audience (Elkind) Young teenager's belief that all eyes are focused on him or her.

Impression formation An application of reasoning in social competence. It has five categories: differentiation, decentration, abstraction, inference, and organization.

Incest A form of sexual abuse; involvement between two family members.

Incongruity mechanism An inherent ability to recognize when forms have changed.

Inductive approach Specific aspects of an issue are discussed first, then general principles are introduced. Observing specifics of a phenomenon forms the basis for developing general principles.

Informal support system The natural support systems of an individual. These include relatives, churches, and neighbors. Informal support systems need to be drawn into collaborative relationships with public services such as social agencies or community programs.

Information-processing approaches (to IQ)   The view of the mind as a computer, focusing on the mind's encoding, storage, and retrieval of information abilities.

Informed consent   The process by which clients (or research participants) are informed of all aspects of the intervention procedures and provide consent for participation.

Intellectual abililty   The ability to acquire and use knowledge.

Intergenerational transmission   The idea that children from abusive families tend to model their parents' behavior and abuse their own children. Also applied to any family styles/values that are repeated by the next generation.

Internal locus of control   Belief in self-responsibility.

Interview or survey method   In research, the method by which the researcher collects data by asking the subject questions rather than by observing.

IQ   Intelligence quotient, as indicated by standardized tests, adjusted for chronological age, with a score of 100 indicating normal performance for age.

Kohlberg's six stages of moral reasoning   Two stages within each of three levels: preconventional, conventional, and postconventional.

Laboratory analogues   In research, the method by which researchers present subjects with a situation or controlled event in a laboratory and observes how the subject reacts; supposedly in a manner *analogous* to what behavior in real life would be.

Language codes   The characteristic way that an individual or group uses language in day-to-day life and in problem-solving situations.

Latency period   Period from age 5 to puberty, in which Oedipal feelings are subdued.

Lay helper   Member of a person's social network who helps him/her to resolve problems, though not a professional psychologist, social worker, etc.

Learning theory (in development)   Emphasizes content and contingencies of experience (Skinner).

Least restrictive treatment   The guideline that the therapist must use minimally intrusive procedures first before proceeding to more intrusive or controlling measures.

Libido   Psychic energy that drives the human personality (Freud).

Life-course perspective   Looks at three distinct levels of analysis: individual lifetime, social time, historical time.

Longitudinal studies   Empirical research that continues to study the same people for a period of time long enough to measure change in the variables of interest.

Looking-glass self   Using responses of others to us as we would use a mirror.

Luteinizing hormone (LH).   Gonadotropic hormone that stimulates the release of mature sex cells.

Macrosystems   The broad ideological and institutional patterns of a particular culture or subculture. (e.g., orientations such as Judeo-Christian, Communist, or Democratic).

Male prostitution   The exchange of money for sexual activities between males.

Marginal students   Adolescents whose background places them at high risk for academic failure.

Maturity   A full flowering of all that a person can be, biologically, psychologically, and socially.

Maturity gradient   Difference in rates of growth of different parts of the body (e.g., hands and feet growing larger first).

Menarche   The onset of menstruation.

Menstruation   Discharge of the uterine lining when an ovum has not been fertilized.

Mesosystem   Relationships *between* microsystems in which the adolescent experiences reality. (e.g., link of peer group and home, or of home and school: do they overlap?)

Microsystem   The immediate setting in which the adolescent develops and in doing so experiences and creates reality.

Midolescence (term coined by McMurrow)   Midlife (45–60) crisis, often occurring for parents while their children are experiencing adolescence.

Modal adolescent   Typical adolescent.

Monolithic setting (for moral development)   One overriding set of goals or principles.

Moral realism (or heteronomous mortality)   In Piaget's theory of morality: the first stage of moral reasoning, in which the child views actions as either right or wrong according to the standards set by law.

NCP   National Crime Panel.

Naturalistic observations   In research, the process of recording and counting well-defined, naturally occurring behaviors.

Neglecting or erratic (Baumrind)   Parental behavior involving few rules or guidelines, inconsistently enforced.

Neurotic delinquency   Sudden, situationally-provoked delinquency; not part of a consistent personal or social pattern.

Oedipus Complex/Electra Complex   Strong sexual attachment of child to the opposite-sex parent and desire to get rid of the same-sex parent.

Ontogeny   (the biological development of an organism) *Recapitulates* (mirrors or reflects) *phylogeny* (the historical evolution of a species).

Oocytes   Immature ovum (egg cells).

Optimal discrepancy   A balance of the familiar and the different that enhances perception.

Organization (in Piaget)   The tendency to integrate structures, which may be physical or psychological, into higher-order systems or structures.

Ova ducts   Transport the ova (mature egg) to the uterus.

Paradigm   A broad framework for viewing particular phenomena and for conducting research; more general and inclusive than a theory.

Parricide   When adolescents kill their parents.

Particularism   Looks at each person inividually (*who* you are).

Patriarchal family   A strong family unit dominated by the father.

Permissive style   Inappropriately gives *carte blanche* to the adolescent and his/her unformed drives and, thus, places the parent in a passive role.

Personal fable (Elkind)   A story that adolescents believe to be true of themselves by virtue of their immortality, uniqueness, or other special qualities.

Phenotype   The outward, visible person.

Phylogenetic change (Darwin)   A cycle of gradual biological change and adaptation of all species (that culminates in the formation of all modern species, including homo sapiens). This includes random biological variation and survival of the fittest.

Piaget's theory of intellectual functioning   That every individual's cognitive growth proceeds in four stages: sensorimotor (birth to two years); preoperational (2 to 7 years); the concrete operational (7 to 11 years); and the formal operational (11 to adult).

Pituitary gland   Bean-sized gland that most controls pubertal development.

Plato's theory of human development.   The belief that every individual is the product of two distinct entities, the body and the soul.

Pleasure principle   The libido constantly demands expression in the form of immediate gratification.

Pluralistic society   The middle ground between irreconcilably intense conflict on the one hand and the extreme absence of conflict on the other.

Political socialization   Youth *learn* their politics rather than creating or discovering them.

Precocious puberty   Onset of puberty occurring much earlier than usual (about age 8 for girls and 9 for boys).

Premenstrual syndrome   Series of problems (lower back pain, feeling of heaviness, headache, fluid retention, feeling of fatigue) that sometimes appear a few days before menstruation.

Prevention   One of three main goals of intervention; aims at creating conditions that will reduce the likelihood that a dysfunction will occur. The other two are remediation and rehabilitation.

Primary sex characteristics   Structures directly related to reproduction, e.g., the sex organs.

Privacy   In intervention, the assurance to the client that only personal information necessary to successful intervention will be requested.

Prompting   In skills training intervention, the technique of providing a condition that will increase the probability that a new behavior is performed.

Psychoanalytic view of adolescence   "Adolescence constitutes by definition an interruption of peaceful growth . . ." (A. Freud)

Psychodynamic approach to moral development (draws on Freud's theory of development)   By adolescence, an individual has developed a conscience (superego), incorporating and reformulating the moral lessons of parents and society.

Psychometric approach (to IQ)   An approach in which performance on intellectual and abilities tests is examined for shifts at various age levels.

Psychometric approach   Movement toward developing tests to measure an individual's intellect.

Puberty   Physical maturation. From the Latin *pubescere*, meaning to be covered with hair. The physique and physiological capabilities of an adult, including reproductive capacity.

Qualitative approach to knowledge   Emphasizes the types and styles of knowing that people exhibit.

Quantitative approach to intelligence   Concentrates on quantity of knowledge.

Racism   A set of values, beliefs, and expectations that defines one racial group as being inferior to another.

The Rationalist movement   A movement in which faith in science and reason replaced faith in religious dogma and governmental mandates.

Rebellion   Period of upheaval in which adolescent children reject their parents (in the psychoanalytic view).

Recapitulation Theory (G. Stanley Hall)   Ontogeny (individual organismic development) recapitulates (repeats the steps of) phylogeny (the evolution of species).

Regression   Exhibiting behaviors appropriate to an earlier developmental stage.

Rehabilitation   One of three main goals of intervention; aims to alleviate the surrounding conditions of the dysfunction. The other two goals are remediation and prevention.

Remediation   One of three main goals of intervention; aims to correct a problem already in existence. The other two are rehabilitation and prevention.

Reversibility   The permanent possibility of returning to the starting point of an operation in question.

Rites of passage   Ceremonies marking transition from childhood to adulthood.

Rousseau   A view of human development that promotes an interaction of nature and nurture with the idea that there are discrete stages of development.

Running away   Youth absent without parental permission over at least one night, intending to remove themselves from parental supervision and control.

"S" factor   Accounts for specific aptitudes of the individual, such as mathematical or spatial abilities; theory of Charles Spearman.

SES   Socioeconomic status: determined by income, education, occupational prestige.

Schaefer's circumplex of parental behaviors   A way to show schematically parenting style based on a control dimension and a love-hostility dimension.

Scheme (in Piaget)   Organized patterns of behavior, both physical and intellectual.

Scripts   Learned rules of sexual behavior.

Secondary sex characteristics   Features that contribute to the differences in appearance between the sexes such as facial hair in males.

Second Oedipal Complex   Anna Freud's idea of an upsurge in attraction to the opposite sex parent at adolescence that is rejected by the conscience.

Self-reinforcement   In which the subject rewards himself.

Seriation   The ability to rank objects on a scale of large to small, short to tall, etc.

Severe violence (domestic)   Kicking, biting, hitting with a fist or an object, beating up, threatening or using a gun or a knife.

Sexism   A set of values, beliefs, and expectations that place one sex (ordinarily females) as subordinate to the other.

Sexual infantilism   When a person never, or only partially, becomes sexually mature.

Shaping   In skills training intervention, the process of providing systematic positive reinforcements to parts of the entire complex behavior until the whole behavior is consistently established.

Single-track system   In American schools, the students following one pathway from first to last year of school (rather than dividing up a high school into vo-tech schools, teacher preparation schools, university prep schools, etc.).

Social puberty   The direct involvement in some way with members of the opposite sex before physical-sexual maturation.

Socialization (moral)   The child internalizes values in response to three kinds of discipline: power, love withdrawal, and induction.

Sociobiology   Efforts to explain social structure and values on the basis of biological evolution.

Sociocultural risk   An event or condition that impoverishes the adolescent's world of essential experiences and relationships.

Sociological delinquency   Illegal behavior that is encouraged by membership in a gang or group.

Sociometric status   How well accepted or rejected an individual is by his/her relevant peer group.

Sponsored mobility   Children being identified early as part of an elite group, and given extra opportunity thereafter.

Squeal rule   A proposal that publically-supported facilities be required to inform parents when adolescents requested contraception.

Status offense   A crime that is one only because the perpetrator is underage, e.g., running away from home, using tobacco or alcohol, engaging in sexual intercourse.

Stereotypes   Generalized conceptions not subject to easy correction modification through empirical observation.

Strategic interactions (Goffman)   Interpersonal encounters that have as their aim the acquisition, concealment, or revelation of information.

Structure-of-intellect model   A model that conceptualizes intelligence; at least 120 factors or abilities postulated by Guilford.

Sturm und drang (German)   Stormy and stressful characterization of adolescence.

Subcutaneous fat   Fat in layers beneath the skin (girls have more than boys).

Substance abuse   Misuse of drugs and alcohol.

Superego (Freud)   Creation of an ego-ideal (role model of same sex) and the conscience, incorporating societal morals and principles.

Surgent growth   Less gradual developmental pattern, where growth occurs in spurts.

Systems approach   Efforts to understand all beings or collections of operating parts in terms of a set of general principles.

Tabula rasa (John Locke)   The *blank page*; supposedly the child's mind at birth.

Temperament   Differences in behavioral style linked to overall differences in activity level and reactiveness.

Testosterone   The male sex hormone; produced by interstitial cells of the testes.

Theocracy   A political condition in which the church and state are under the same rulers (e.g., Iran under the Ayatollah Khomeini).

Thyroid stimulating hormone (TSH)   A tropic hormone (having a specific target) that stimulates the thyroid to produce its hormones.

Tracking   Ability grouping in schools.

Tumultuous growth   Inner turmoil and crisis pattern (storm and stress).

UCR   Uniform Crime Reports.

Universalism   Based on treating everyone by the same standards (*what* you are).

Value codes   The characteristic beliefs an individual or group holds about the right and wrong way to treat people and approach situations.

Vicarious reinforcement   Witnessing someone else being reinforced.

Wechsler scale   Series of subtests testing multiple aptitudes.

Youth culture   A spontaneous expression of many people's ideas and feelings that, while it lasts, unites people and serves as a focus for identity, belief, and action.

References

Achenbach, T. M. (1978). The child behavior profile: I. Boys aged 6–11. *Journal of Consulting and Clinical Psychology, 46*(3), 478–488.

Achenbach, T. M. (1982). *Developmental Psychopathology.* New York: John Wiley & Sons, Inc.

Ackerman, N. W. (1962). Adolescent problems: A symptom of family disorder. *Family Process, 1,* 202–213.

Acock, A. C., & Bengston, V. L. (1974). *On the relative influence of mothers or fathers: A covariance analysis of political and religious socialization.* Paper presented at the American Sociological Association annual meeting, New York.

Adams, G. R., & Gullotta, T. (1983). *Adolescent life experiences.* Monterey, CA: Brooks/Cole Publishing Co.

Adams, J. F. (1964). Adolescent personal problems as a function of age and sex. *Journal of Genetic Psychology, 104,* 207–214.

Adams, R. L., & Phillips, B. N. (1972). Motivational and achievement differences among children of various ordinal positions. *Child Development, 43,* 155–164.

Adams, V. (1981, June). The sibling bond. *Psychology Today,* 32–47.

Adelson, J. (1964). The mystique of adolescence. *Psychiatry, 27,* 1–5.

Adelson, J. (1975). The development of ideology in adolescence. In S. E. Dragastin & G. H. Elder, Jr. (Eds.), *Adolescence in the life cycle: Psychological change and the social context.* Washington, DC: Hemisphere.

Adelson, J. (Ed.). (1980). *Handbook of adolescent psychology.* New York: Wiley-Interscience.

Adorno, T. W., Frenkel-Brunswick, E., Levinson, D. J., & Sanford, R. N. (1950). *The authoritarian personality.* New York: Harper & Row.

Ahlgren, A., & Johnson, D. W. (1979). Sex differences in cooperative and competitive attitudes from the 2nd through the 12th grades. *Developmental Psychology, 15,* 45–49.

Ahlstrom, W. M., & Havighurst, R. J. (1971). *400 losers.* San Francisco: Jossey-Bass.

Ahrendt, K. M. (1970). Reading ability and the potential dropout. *Education Canada, 10,* 13–15.

Alan Guttmacher Institute. (1976). *11 million teenagers: What can be done about the epidemic of adolescent pregnancies in the United States.* New York: Alan Guttmacher Institute.

Alan Guttmacher Institute. (1981). *Teenage pregnancy: The problem that hasn't gone away.* New York: Alan Guttmacher Institute.

Albee, G. W. (1963). American Psychology in the 60's. *American Psychologist, 18,* 90–95.

Albee, G. W. (1980). Primary prevention and social problems. In G. Gerbner, C. J. Ross, & E. Zigler (Eds.), *Child abuse: An agenda for action.* New York: Oxford University Press.

Albert, N., & Beck, A. T. (1975). Incidence of depression in early adolescence: A preliminary study. *Journal of Youth and Adolescence, 4,* 301–308.

Alexander, J. F. (1982). Toughlove approach is not for everyone. *Developmental Psychology.* Washington DC: American Psychological Association.

Alexander, K. L., Cook, M., & McDill, E. L. (1978). Curriculum tracking and educational stratification: Some further evidence. *American Sociological Review, 43,* 47–66.

Alexander, W. M., & Hines, V. A. (1966). *Independent study in secondary schools.* University of Florida Research Project No. 2969.

Allen, D. M. (1980). Young male prostitutes: A psychosocial study. *Archives of Sexual Behavior, 9*(5), 399–426.

Allgeier, E. R., Przylyla, D. P., & Thompson, M. E. (1977, November). *Planned sin: The influence of sex guilt on premarital sexual and contraceptive behavior.* Paper presented at the convention of the Psychonomic Society, Washington, DC.

Allport, G. W. (1950). *The individual and his religion.* New York: Macmillan.

Allport, G. W. (1961). *Pattern and growth in personality.* New York: Holt.

Almond, G., & Verba, S. (1965). *The civic culture.* Boston: Little, Brown & Co.

Almquist, E., & Angrist, S. S. (1970). Career salience and atypicality of occupational choice among college women. *Journal of Marriage and the Family, 32,* 242–249.

Altman, S. L., & Grossman, F. K. (1971). Women's career plans and maternal employment. *Psychology of Women Quarterly, 1,* 365–375.

Altus, W. D. (1965). Birth order and academic primogenitive. *Journal of Personality and Social Psychology, 2,* 872–874.

Altus, W. D. (1967). Birth order and its sequelae. *International Journal of Psychiatry, 3,* 23–32.

Ambrosino, L. (1971). *Runaways.* Boston: Beacon Press.

American Psychiatric Association. (1980). *Diagnostic and statistical manual of mental disorders* (3rd ed.). Washington, DC: American Psychiatric Association.

Amini, F., Salasneck, S., & Burke, E. L. (1976). Adolescent drug abuse: Etiological and treatment considerations. *Adolescence, 11,* 281–299.

Anastasi, A. (1976). *Psychological testing* (4th ed.). New York: MacMillan.

Anderson, R. E., & Carter, F. (1974). *Human behavior in the social environment: A social systems approach* (3rd ed.). New York: Aldine.

Anderson, S., & Messick, S. (1974). Social competency in young children. *Developmental Psychology, 10,* 282–293.

Andrews, J. (1973). The relationship of values to identity achievement status. *Journal of Youth and Adolescence, 2*(2), 133–138.

Annesley, P. T. (1961). Psychiatric illness in adolescence: Presentation and prognosis. *Journal of Mental Science, 106,* 268–278.

Anthony, E. J., & Benedek, T. (Eds.). (1970). *Parenthood: Its psychology and psychopathology.* Boston: Little, Brown & Co.

Anthony, E. J., & Koupernik, C. (Eds.). (1974). *The child in his family: Children at risk* (Vol. 3). John Wiley & Sons.

Anthony, J. (1969). The reactions of adults to adolescents and their behavior. In G. Caplan & S. Lebovici (Eds.), *Adolescence.* New York: Basic Books.

Aries, P. (1962). *Centuries of childhood.* New York: Knopf.

Arieti, S. (1974). *Interpretation of schizophrenia* (2nd ed.). New York: Basic Books.

Arlin, P. K. (1975). Cognitive development in adulthood: A fifth stage? *Developmental Psychology, 11,* 602–606.

Armstrong, C. (1964). *Patterns in achievement in selected New York State schools.* Albany, NY: New York State University, Division of Research.

Aronowitz, S. (1973). *False promises: The shaping of American working class consciousness.* New York: McGraw–Hill.

Asher, S. R., Oden, S. L., & Gottman, J. M. (1977). Children's friendships in school settings. In L. G. Katz (Ed.), *Current topics in early childhood education* (Vol. 1). Norwood, NJ: Ablex.

Atwater, E. (1983). *Adolescence.* Englewood Cliffs, NJ: Prentice-Hall.

Ausburn, L., & Ausburn, F. (1978). Cognitive styles: Some information and implications for instructional design. *Education and Communication Technology, 26,* 337–354.

Ausubel, D. P., Montemeyer, R., & Svajian, P. (1977). *Theory and problems in adolescent development* (2nd ed.). New York: Grune & Stratton.

Authier, K., & Authier, J. (1982). Intervention with families of pregnant adolescents. In I. R. Stuart, & C. F. Wells (Eds.), *Pregnancy in adolescence: Needs, problems, and management.* New York: Van Nostrand Reinhold.

Averch, H. (1974). *How effective is schooling? A critical review of research.* Englewood Cliffs, NJ: Educational Technology Publications.

Ayllon, T., & Azrin, N. H. (1968). *The token economy: Motivational system for therapy and rehabilitation.* New York: Appleton-Century-Crofts.

Bachman, J. G., Green, S., & Johnston, J. (1978). *Youth in transition: Vol. IV.* Ann Arbor: Institute for Social Research, University of Michigan.

Bachman, J. G., Green, S., & Wirtanen, I. D. (1970). *Youth in transition: Vol. II.* Ann Arbor: Institute for Social Research, University of Michigan.

Bachman, J. G., Green, S., & Wirtanen, I. D. (1971). *Youth in transition: Vol. III.* Ann Arbor: Institute for Social Research, University of Michigan.

Bachman, J. G., O'Malley, P. M., & Johnston, J. (1979). Adolescence to adulthood: *Youth in transition: Volume VI.* Ann Arbor: Institute for Social Research, University of Michigan.

Badwin, H., & McLaughlin, S. (1964). Secular increments in height: Is the end in site? *Lancet, 2,* 1195–1196.

Bahr, H. (1978, August). *Change in family life in Middletown: 1924-1977.* Paper presented at the annual meeting of the American Sociological Association, Chicago.

Bailyn, B. (1960). *Education in the forming of American societies.* New York: Vintage.

Baizerman, M., Thompson, J., & Stafford-White, K. (1979). Adolescent prostitution. *Children Today, 8* (5), 20-24.

Bakan, D. (1966). *The duality of human existence.* Chicago: Rand McNally.

Bakan, D. (1971, Fall). Adolescence in America: From idea to social fact. *Daedalus,* 979-995.

Bakan, D. (1972). Adolescence in America: From idea to social fact. In J. Kagan & R. Coles (Eds.), *Twelve to sixteen: Early adolescence.* New York: W. W. Norton.

Baker, K., & Rubel, R. (Eds.). (1980). *Violence and crime in the schools.* Lexington, MA: Lexington Books.

Baldwin, C. P., & Baldwin, A. L. (1970). Children's judgments of kindness. *Child Development, 41,* 29-47.

Baldwin, W. H. (1976). Adolescent pregnancy and childbearing—Growing concerns for Americans. *Population Bulletin, 31,* 1-34.

Baldwin, W. H. (1982). Trends in adolescent contraceptives, pregnancy, and abortion. In E. R. McAnarney (Ed.), *Preventive adolescent pregnancy and parenthood.* New York: Gruve & Strottors.

Ball, J. C., & Logan, N. (1970). Early sexual behavior of lower-class delinquent girls. In A. Shiloh (Ed.), *Studies in human sexual behavior: The American scene* Springfield, IL: C. C.Thomas.

Balswick, J. O., & Macrides, C. (1975). Parental stimulus for adolescent rebellion. *Adolescence, 10,* 253-266.

Ban, J., & Ciminillo, L. (1977). *Violence and vandalism in public education.* Danville, IL: Interstate Printers and Publishers, Inc.

Banducci, R. (1967). The effects of mother's employment on achievement, aspiration, and expectations of the child. *Personnel and Guidance Journal, 46,* 263-267.

Bandura, A. (1964). The stormy decade: Fact or fiction? *Psychology in the School, 1,* 224-231.

Bandura, A., & Walters, R. H. (1959). *Adolescent aggression.* New York: Ronald.

Bandura, A., & Walters, R. H. (1963). *Social learning and personality development.* New York: Holt, Rinehart & Winston.

Bane, M. J. (1976). *Here to stay: American families in the twentieth century.* New York: Basic Books.

Bardwick, J. M., & Douvan, E. (1977). Ambivalence: The socialization of women. In V. Gornich & B. K. Moren (Eds.), *Women in sexist society.* New York: Basic Books.

Barglos, P., Bornstein, M. B., Exum, D. B., Wright, M. K., & Visotsky, H. M. (1967). Some psychiatric aspects of illegitimate pregnancy during early adolescence. *American Journal of Orthopsychiatry, 37,* 266-267.

Barker, R., & Gump, P. (1964). *Big school, small school.* Stanford, CA: Stanford University Press.

Barter, J. C., Swaback, D. C., & Todd, D. (1968). Adolescent suicide attempts. *Archives of General Psychiatry, 19,* 523-527.

Bartz, K., & Nye, I. (1970). Early marriage: A propositional formulation. *Journal of Marriage and the Family, 32,* 258-268.

Baruch, G. K. (1972). Maternal influences upon college women's attitudes towards women and work. *Developmental Psychology, 6,* 32-37.

Bateson, G. (1972). *Steps to an ecology of mind.* New York: Chandler.

Bauman, K. E., & Wilson, R. (1974). Contraceptive practices of white unmarried university students: The significance of four years at one university. *American Journal of Obstetrics and Gynecology, 118,* 190-194.

Baumrind, D. (1967). Child care practices anteceding three patterns of preschool behavior. *Genetic Psychology Monographs, 75,* 43-88.

Baumrind, D. (1968). Authoritarian vs. authoritative parental control. *Adolescence, 3,* 255-272.

Baumrind, D. (1971). Current patterns of parental authority. *Developmental Psychology, 4* (Monograph I, pt. 2), 1-103.

Baumrind, D. (1975). Early socialization and adolescent competence. In S. Dragastin & G. H. Elder, Jr. (Eds.), *Adolescence in the life cycle: Psychological change and social content.* New York: Wiley.

Baumrind, D. (1979). Parental disciplinary patterns and social competence in children. *Youth and Society, 9,* 239-270.

Bavolek, S., Kline, D., McLaughlin, J., & Publicover, P. (1979). Primary prevention of child abuse and neglect: Identification of high-risk adolescence. *Child Abuse and Neglect, 3,* 1071-1080.

Bayer, A. E. (1966). Birth order and college attendance. *Journal of Marriage and the Family, 28,* 480-484.

Bayer, A. E. (1968). Early dating and early marriage. *Journal of Marriage and the Family, 30,* 628-632.

Bayer, L. M., & Bayley, N. (1959). *Growth diagnosis.* Chicago: The University of Chicago Press.

Beck, A. T. (1970). *Depression: Causes and treatment.* Philadelphia: University of Pennsylvania Press.

Beck, A. T. (1971). Cognition, affect, and psychopathology. *Archives of General Psychiatry, 24,* 295-500.

Beck, A. T. (1974). The development of depression: A cognitive model. In R. J. Friedman & M. M. Katz (Eds.), *The psychology of depression.* Washington, DC: Winston.

Beck, A. T., Beck, R., & Kovacs, M. (1975). Classification of suicidal behaviors: I. Quantifying interest and medical lethality. *American Journal of Psychiatry, 132,* 285-287.

Beck, A. T., Kovacs, M., & Weissman, A. (1979). Assessment of suicidal intention: The scale for suicidal ideation. *Journal of Consulting and Clinical Psychology, 47*, 343–352.

Becker, W. C. (1964). Consequences of different kinds of parental discipline. In M. L. Hoffman & L. W. Hoffman (Eds.), *Review of Child Developmental Research*, Vol. I. New York: Russel Sage Foundation.

Bell, A. P. (1969). Role modeling of fathers in adolescence and young adulthood. *Journal of Counseling Psychology, 16*, 30–35.

Bell, A. P. (1974, Summer). *Childhood and adolescent sexuality*. An address delivered at the Institute for Sex Research, Indiana University, Bloomington, IN.

Bell, G. D. (1963). Processes in the formation of adolescents' aspirations. *Social Forces, 42*, 179–195.

Bell, N. W., & Vogel, E. F. (1968). Toward a framework for functional analysis of family behavior. In N. W. Bell & E. F. Vogel (Eds.), *A modern introduction to the family*. New York: Free Press.

Bell, R. Q. (1964). Structuring parent-child interaction situations for direct observations. *Child Development, 35*, 1009–1020.

Bell, R. Q. (1968). A reinterpretation of the direction of effects in studies of socialization. *Psychological Review, 75*, 81–95.

Belmont, L., & Marolla, F. (1973). Birth order, family size, and intelligence. *Science, 182*, 1096–1101.

Bem, D. J. (1974). Cognitive alteration of feeling states. In H. London & R. E. Nisbett (Eds.), *Thought and feeling*. Chicago: Aldine.

Bem, S. (1974). The measurement of psychological androgeny. *Journal of Consulting and Clinical Psychology, 42*, 155–162.

Bender, L., & Grugett, J. (1952). A follow up report on children who had atypical sexual experiences. *American Journal of Orthopsychiatry, 22*, 825–837.

Bengtston, V. L. (1970). The generation gap: A review and typology of social-psychological perspectives. *Youth and Society, 2*, 7–32.

Bengston, V. L., Furlong, M. J., & Laufer, R. S. (1974). Time, aging, and the continuity of social structure: Themes and issues in generational analysis. *Journal of Social Issues, 30*(2), 1–30.

Bennett, S. M., & Dickinson, W. B. (1980). Student-parent rapport and parent involvement in sex, birth control, and venereal disease education. *Journal of Sex Research, 16*, 114–130.

Benward, J., & Densen-Gerber, J. (1975). *Incest as a causative factor in anti-social behavior: An exploratory study*. New York: Odyssey Institute.

Berg, I. (1970). *Education and jobs: The great training robbery*. New York: Praeger.

Berger, I., and Schmidt, R. M. (1958). Results of child psychiatric and psychological investigations of spontaneous and reactive runaways. *Prox. Kinderpsychol : Kinderpsychiat, 1*, 206–210.

Berndt, T. J. (1982). The features and effects of friendship in early adolescence. *Child Development, 53*, 1447–1460.

Bernfeld, S. (1938). Types of adolescence. *Psychoanalytic Quarterly, 7*, 243–253.

Berzonsky, W. M., Weiner, A. S., & Rapball, D. (1975). Interdependence of formal reasoning. *Developmental Psychology, 11*, 258.

Bielby, D. D. (1978). Maternal employment and socioeconomic status as factors in daughters' career salience: Some substantive refinements. *Sex Roles, 4*, 249–265.

Bigelow, B. J., & LaGaipa, J. J. (1980). The development of friendship values and choice. In H. C. Foot, A. J. Chapman, & J. R. Smith (Eds.), *Friendship and social relations in children*. Chichester, England: Wiley.

Bigner, J. A. (1974). A Wernerian developmental analysis of children's descriptions of siblings. *Child Development, 45*, 317–323.

Biller, H. B. (1971). *Father, child, and sex-roles*. Lexington, MA: Heath.

Bixenstine, V. E., DeCorte, M. S., & Bixenstine, B. A. (1976). Conformity to peer sponsored misconduct at four grade levels. *Developmental Psychology, 12*, 226–236.

Blaine, G. B., & Carman, L. R. (1968). Causal factors in suicidal attempts by male and female college students. *American Journal of Psychiatry, 125*, 146–149.

Blake, J. (1979). Is zero preferred? American attitudes toward childlessness in the 1970's. *Journal of Marriage and the Family, 41*, 245–265.

Blasi, A. (1980). Bridging moral cognition and moral action: A critical review of the literature. *Psychological Bulletin, 88*, 1–45.

Blau, P. M., & Duncan, O. D. (1967). *The American occupational structure*. New York: Wiley.

Blauner, R. (1964). *Alienation and freedom*. Chicago: University of Chicago Press.

Blizzard, R., Thompson, R., Baghdassarian, A., Kowarski, A., Migeon, C., & Rodriguez, P. (1974). The interrelationship of steroids, growth hormones, and other hormones on pubertal growth. In M. Grumbach, G. Grane, & F. Mayer (Eds.), *The control of the onset of puberty*. New York: Wiley.

Block, J. H. (1973). Conceptions of sex role: Some cross-cultural and longitudinal perspectives. *American Psychologist, 28*, 512–526.

Bloom, B. L. (1979). Prevention of mental disorders: Recent advances in theory and practice. *Community Mental Health Journal, 15*, 179–191.

Blos, P. (1962). *On adolescence: A psychoanalytic interpretation*. New York: Free Press.

Blos, P. (1976). The split parental image in adolescent social relations. *Psychoanalytic Study of the Child, 31*, 7–33.

Blos, P. (1979). *The adolescent passage*. New York: International Universities Press.

Blumstein, P., & Schwartz, P. (1977). Bisexuality: Some social psychological issues. *Journal of Social Issues, 33*, 30–45.

Blyth, D., Simmons, R., & Bush, D. (1978). The transition into early adolescence: A longitudinal comparison of youth in two educational contexts. *Sociology of Education, 51,* 149–162.

Bob, S. (1968). *An investigation of the relationship between identity status, cognitive style, and stress.* Unpublished doctoral dissertation, State University of New York at Buffalo.

Bolton, F. G., (1980). *The pregnant adolescent.* Beverly Hills, CA: Sage.

Borkovec, T., & Bauer, R. (1980). Experimental designs in therapy outcome research. In Bellak, Hersen, & Kazdin (Eds.), *International handbook of behavior modification and therapy.* New York: Plenum Press.

Boskind-Lodahl, M. (1976). Cinderella's stepsisters: A feminist perspective on anorexia nervosa and bulimia. *Signs: Journal of Women in Cultural and Society, 2,* 342–356.

Boskind-Lodahl, M., & Sirlin, J. (1977) The gorging purging syndrome. *Psychology Today, 11,* 50.

Bossard, J. H., & Boll, T. S. (1954). *The larger family system.* Philadelphia: University of Pennsylvania Press.

Bossard, J. H., & Sorger, W. P. (1952). The large family system: A research report. *American Sociological Review, 17,* 3–9.

Bott, E. (1971). *Family and social network.* London: Tavistock.

Bouvier, L. F. (1980). America's baby boom generation: The fateful bulge. *Population Bulletin, 35*(1), 6–7.

Bowerman, C. E., & Dobash, R. M. (1974). Structural variation in intersibling affect. *Journal of Marriage and the Family, 36,* 48–54.

Bowerman, C. E., & Elder, G. H. (1964). Variations in adolescent perception of family power structure. *American Sociological Review, 29,* 551–667.

Bowerman, C. E., & Kinch, J. W. (1959). Changes in family and peer orientation of children between fourth and tenth grades. *Social Forces, 37,* 206–211.

Bowman, H., & Spanier, G. (1978). *Modern marriage.* New York: McGraw–Hill.

Boyd, W. (1978). The politics of curriculum policy making for American schools. *Review of Educational Research, 48,* 577–628.

Boyer, W. H. (1959). A survey of youth attitudes, opinion, and objectives of high school students in the Milwaukee area. *Journal of Educational Sociology, 32*(5), 344–348.

Brazee, E. N. & Brazee, P. E. (1979). Cognitive development in the middle school. *Colorado Journal of Educational Research, 19,* 6–8.

Breasted, M. (1970). *Oh, sex education.* New York: Praeger.

Breger, L. (1974). *From instinct to identity: The development of personality.* Englewood Cliffs, NJ: Prentice-Hall, Inc.

Breland, H. M. (1978). Birth order, family configuration, and verbal achievement. In M. S. Smart & R. C.

Smart (Eds.), *Adolescents* (2nd ed.). New York: Macmillan.

Bremmer, R. (Ed.). (1970). *Children and youth in America.* Cambridge, MA: Harvard University Press.

Brennan, J., Huizenga, D., & Elliott, D. S. (1978). *The social psychology of runaways.* Lexington, MA: D. C. Heath.

Brennan, T. (1980). Mapping the diversity among runaways: A descriptive multivariate analysis of selected social psychological background conditions. *Journal of Family Issues, 1*(2), 189–209.

Breuer, H. (1973). *Ego identity status in late adolescent college males, as measured by a group administered incomplete sentences blank and related to inferred stance toward authority.* Unpublished doctoral dissertation, New York University, New York.

Brim, O. G., Jr. (1956). Family structure and sex role learning by children: A further analysis of Alan Koch's data. *Sociometry, 21,* 1–16.

Brim, O. G., & Kagan, J. (1980). *Constancy and change in human development.* Cambridge, MA: Harvard University Press.

Brittain, C. V. (1963). Adolescent choices and parent-peer cross-pressures. *American Sociological Review, 28,* 385–39.

Bronfenbrenner, U. (1958). Socialization and social class through time and space. In E. Maccoby, T. Newcombe, & E. Hartley (Eds.), *Readings in social psychology.* New York: Rinehart & Winston.

Bronfenbrenner, U. (1970). *Two worlds of childhood.* New York: Free Press.

Bronfenbrenner, U. (1974). The origins of alienation. *Scientific American, 231,* 53–61.

Bronfenbrenner, U. (1975). Is 80% of intelligence genetically determined? In U. Bronfenbrenner & M. Mahoney (Eds.), *Influences on human development.* Hinsdale, IL: The Dryden Press.

Bronfenbrenner, U. (1975). The origins of alienation. In U. Bronfenbrenner & M. Mahoney (Eds.), *Influences on human development.* Hinsdale, IL: Dryden Press.

Bronfenbrenner, U. (1979). *The ecology of human development: Experiments by nature and design.* Cambridge: MA.: Harvard University Press.

Bronfenbrenner, U., & Crouter, A. C. (1982). Work and family through time and space. In S. B. Kamerman & C. D. Hayes (Eds.), *Families that work: Children in a changing environment of work, family, and community.* Washington, D.C.: National Academy of Science.

Bronte, C. *Jane Eyre.* (1847, reprinted 1911). Edinburgh: John Grant.

Brooks-Gunn, J., & Petersen, A. (Eds.). (1983). *Girls at puberty.* New York: Plenum Press.

Brooks-Gunn, J., & Ruble, D. (1983) The experience of menarche from a developmental perspective. In J. Brooks-Gunn & A. Petersen (Eds.), *Girls at puberty* New York: Plenum Press.

Brooks, K., & Edwards, F. (1978). The middle school in transition. *CPD Memorandum*, Center for Professional Development, College of Education, University of Kentucky.

Broughton, J. (1978). Development of concepts of self, mind, reality, and knowledge. *New Directions for Child Development, 1*, 75–100.

Brown, M. (1979). Teenage prostitution. *Adolescence, 14*(56), 665–680.

Brown, L. (1981). *Building a sustainable society.* New York: Norton & Co.

Browning, D. H., & Boatman, B. (1977). Incest: Children at risk. *American Journal of Psychiatry, 134*, 69–72.

Brownstone, J. E., & Willis, K. H. (1971). Conformity in early and late adolescence. *Developmental Psychology, 4*, 334–337.

Bruch, H. (1943). Psychiatric aspects of obesity in children. *American Journal of Psychiatry, 99*, 752–757.

Bruch, H. (1970). Changing approaches to anorexia nervosa. *International Psychiatry Clinics, 7*, 3–24.

Bruch, H. (1973). *Eating disorders: Obesity, anorexia nervosa and the person within.* New York: Basic Books.

Bruch, H. (1976). Anorexia nervosa in adolescence. In J. R. Gallagher, F. P. Heald, & D. C. Garell (Eds.), *Medical care of the adolescent* (3rd ed.). New York: Appleton–Century–Crofts.

Buhler, C. (1969). Loneliness in maturity. *Journal of Humanistic Psychology, 9*, 167–181.

Bunt, M. (1968). Ego identity: Its relationship to the discrepancy between how an adolescent views himself and how he perceives that others view him. *Psychology, 5*(3), 14–25.

Burchinal, L. G. (1965). Trends and prospects for young marriages in the United States. *Journal of Marriage and the Family, 27*, 243–254.

Burgdorff, K. (1980). *Recognition and reporting of child maltreatment: Findings from the National Incidence Study.* Washington, DC: National Center on Child Abuse and Neglect.

Burgdorff, K. (1982). *The national study of the incidence and severity of child abuse and neglect.* Washington, DC: National Center on Child Abuse and Neglect.

Burgess, A. W., & Holmstrom, L. L. (1974). *Rape: Victims of crisis.* Bowie, MD: Robert Brady.

Burgess, R., & Conger, R. (1978). Family interaction patterns in abusive, neglectful, and normal families. *Child Development, 49*, 163–173.

Burlin, F. (1976). The relationship of parental education and maternal work and occupational status to occupational aspirations in adolescent females. *Journal of Vocational Behavior, 9*, 99–104.

Burnham, D. (1984, July 29). F.B.I. arrest data found inaccurate. *The New York Times.*

Burnstein, E. (1963). Fear of failure, achievement, motivation, and aspiring to prestigeful occupations. *Journal of Abnormal and Social Psychology, 67*, 189–193.

Burt, C. (1954). The differentiation of intellectual abilities. *British Journal of Educational Psychology, 24*, 76–90.

Burt, C. (1955). The evidence for the concept of intelligence. *British Journal of Educational Psychology, 25*, 159–197.

Burt, C. (1966). The genetic determination of differences in intelligence: A study of monozygotic twins reared together and apart. *British Journal of Psychology, 57*, 137–153.

Burton, L. (1968). *Vulnerable children.* London: Routledge and Kegan Paul.

Burtz, K. W., & Nye, F. I. (1970). Early marriage: A propositional formulation. *Journal of Marriage and the Family, 32*, 258–268.

Butler, J. (1980). Portrait of an era. *Educational Record, 61*, 73–75.

Butts, W. H. (1947). Boy prostitutes of the metropolis. *Journal of Clinical Psychopathology, 8*, 674.

Califano, J. (1978). Keynote address, conference on adolescent behavior and health. National Academy of Sciences, Institute of Medicine, Washington, DC.

Campbell, A., Converse, P. E., & Rodgers, W. L. (1976). *The quality of American life: Perceptions, evaluations, and satisfactions.* New York: Russell Sage Foundation.

Campbell, B., & Barnlund, D. (1977). Communication patterns and problems of pregnancy. *American Journal of Orthopsychiatry, 47*, 134–139.

Campbell, D. T., & Stanley, J. C. (1963). *Experimental and quasi-experimental designs for research.* Chicago: Rand McNally.

Caplan, C. (1974). *Support systems and community mental health.* New York: Behavioral.

Caplan, G., & Killilea, M. (Eds.). (1976). *Support systems and mutual help: Multidisciplinary explorations.* New York: Grune & Stratton.

Card, J. J., & Wise, L. L. (1981). Teenage mothers and teenage fathers: The impact of early childbearing on the parents' personal and professional lives. In F. F. Furstenberg, R. Lincoln, & J. Menken (Eds.), *Teenage sexuality, pregnancy, and childbearing.* Philadelphia: University of Pennsylvania Press.

Carkhuff, R. R., & Berenson, B. G. (1967). *Beyond counseling and therapy.* New York: Holt, Rinehart, & Winston.

Carlson, R. (1971). Sex differences in ego functioning. *Journal of Consulting and Clinical Psychology, 37*, 267–277.

Carnegie Commission on Higher Education. (1973). *The purposes and the performance of higher education in the United States.* New York: McGraw-Hill Book Co.

Carns, D. E. (1973). Talking about sex: Notes on first coitus and the double standard. *Journal of Marriage and the Family, 35*, 677–688.

Caro, F. G. (1966). Social class and attitudes of youth relevant for the realization of adult goals. *Social Forces, 44*, 492–498.

Case, B. J. (1981). Lasting alternatives: A lesson in survival. *Phi Delta Kappan, 62*, 554–557.

Casper, R. C., Halmi, K. A., Goldberg, S. C., & Davis, W. (1979). Disturbances in body image estimation as related to other characteristics in outcome in anorexia nervosa. *British Journal of Psychiatry, 134,* 60–66.

Cass, L. K., & Thomas, C. B. (1979). *Childhood pathology and later adjustment.* New York: Wiley.

Cassel, J. (1974). Psychosocial processes and "stress": Theoretical foundations. *International Journal of Health Services, 4,* 471–482.

Casteel, J., & Doyle, P. (1974). *Valuing exercises for the middle school.* Resource Monograph No. 11, Florida University, Gainesville.

Cauble, M. A. (1976). Formal operations, ego identity, and principled morality: Are they related? *Developmental Psychology, 12,* 363–364.

Cauce, A. M., Felner, R. D., & Primavera, J. (1982). Social support in high-risk adolescents: Structural components and adaptive impact. *American Journal of Community Psychology, 10,* 417–428.

Caukins, S. E., & Coombs, N. R. (1976). The psychodynamics of male prostitution. *American Journal of Psychotherapy, 30*(3), 441–451.

Cawelti, G. (1968). Youth assess the American high school. *PTA Magazine, 62,* 16–19.

Center for Disease Control. (1979). Basic statistics on the sexually transmitted disease problem in the United States. *Sexually transmitted disease fact sheet, 34th edition.* (HEW Publication No. CDC 79-8195 pp. 1–37). Atlanta, GA: Center for Disease Control, U.S.

Chandler, M. J. (1973). Egocentrism and antisocial behavior: The assessment and training of social perspective-taking skills. *Developmental Psychology, 9,* 326–332.

Cherlin, A. J. (1981). *Marriage, divorce, remarriage.* Cambridge, MA: Harvard University Press.

Children's Defense Fund. (1981). *Children out of school in America.* Washington, D.C.: Children's Defense Fund.

Chilman, C. S. (1978). Adolescent sexuality in a changing American society: Social and psychological perspectives. (NIH Publication No. 79-1426. Department of Health, Education, and Welfare). Washington, DC: U.S. Government Printing Office.

Chilman, C. S. (1979). *Adolescent sexuality in a changing American society: Social and psychological perspectives.* Washington, DC: U.S. Department of Health, Education, and Welfare.

Chilman, C. S. (1980). *Adolescent sexuality in a changing American society: Social and psychological perspectives.* Washington, DC: U.S. Department of Health, Education, and Welfare.

Chilman, C. S. (1980). Social and psychological research concerning adolescent childbearing: 1970–1980. *Journal of Marriage and the Family, 42*(4), 793–805.

Chilman, C. S. (1980, December). Toward a reconceptualization of adolescent sexuality. In C. S. Chilman (Ed.), *Adolescent pregnancy and childbearing.* (NIH Publication No. 81-2077).

Washington, DC: U.S. Department of Health and Human Services.

Chilton, R. J., & Markle, G. E. (1972). Family disruption, delinquent conduct, and the effect of subclassification. *American Sociological Review, 37,* 93–99.

Chodorow, N. (1978). *The reproduction of mothering.* Berkeley: University of California Press.

Cicirelli, V. (1975). Effect of mother and older sibling on the problem solving behavior of the younger child. *Developmental Psychology, 11,* 749–756.

Clark, E. T. (1929). *The psychology of religion awakening.* New York: Macmillan.

Clark, M. (1969). Cultural values and dependency in later life. In R. Kalish (Ed.), *The dependencies of old people.* Ann Arbor, MI: Institute for Gerontology.

Clark, R. W. (1980). *Freud, the man and the cause.* New York: Random House.

Clark, S. D., Zabin, L., & Hardy, S. (1984). Sex, contraception and parenthood: Experience and attitudes among urban black young men. *Family Planning Perspectives, 16,* 77–82.

Clausen, J. A. (1975). The social meaning of differential physical and sexual maturation. In S. E. Dragistin & G. H. Elder, Jr. (Eds.), *Adolescence in the life cycle.* New York: Halsted.

Clawar, S. S. (1977). Resistance to sex education: A constituency perspective. *Journal of Sex Education and Therapy, 3,* 28–32.

Cloward, R., & Ohlen, L. (1960). *Delinquency and opportunity.* New York: Free Press of Glencoe.

Cobb, S. (1976). Social support as a moderator of life stress. *Psychosomatic Medicine, 38,* 1980, *9,* 258–284.

Cohn, A., & Andrews, L. (1978, August 14). Person in need of supervision. *The New Yorker,* 45ff.

Cole, M., & Scribner, S. (1974). *Culture and thought: A psychological introduction.* New York: John Wiley & Sons, Inc.

Coleman, J. S. (1961). *The adolescent society: The social life of the teenager and its impact on education.* New York: The Free Press of Glencoe.

Coleman, J. S. (1966). *Equality of educational opportunity.* (Report of the Office of Education to Congress and the President). Washington, D.C.: U.S. Government Printing Office.

Coleman, J. S. (1974). *Relationships in adolescence.* Boston and London: Routledge and Kegan Paul.

Coleman, J. S. (1974). Youth culture. In J. Coleman (Ed.), *Youth: Transition to adulthood.* Chicago: University of Chicago Press.

Coleman, J. S. (1980). Friendship and the peer group in adolescence. In J. Adelson (Ed.), *Handbook of adolescent psychology.* New York: Wiley.

Coles, R. (1980). *Children of crisis: Privileged ones.* Boston: Little, Brown, & Co.

Collins, A., & Pancoast, P. (1976). *National helping network.* Washington, DC: National Association of Social Workers.

Collins, J. K. (1972). Age and susceptibility to same sex peer pressure. *British Journal of Educational Psychology, 42,* 83–85.

Collins, W. A., Berndt, T. J., & Hess, V. L. (1974). Observational learning and consequences for television aggression: A developmental study. *Child Development, 45,* 799–802.

Combs, A. (1974). *The professional education of teachers.* Boston: Allyn and Bacon.

Conant, J. B. (1959). *The American high school today: A first report to interested citizens.* New York: McGraw–Hill Book Company, Inc.

Conger, J. J. (1977). *Adolescence and youth: Psychological development in a changing world.* New York: Harper & Row.

Conger, J. J., & Miller, W. S. (1966). *Personality, social class, and delinquency.* New York: Wiley.

Conger, J. J., Miller, W. C., & Walsmith, C. R. (1965). Antecedents of delinquency, personality, social class, and intelligence. In P. H. Mussen, J. J. Conger, & J. Kagan (Eds.), *Readings in child development and personality.* New York: Harper & Row.

Cooley, C. H. (1964). *Human nature and the social order.* New York: Schocken.

Coombs, N. R. (1974). Male prostitution: A psychosocial view of behavior. *American Journal of Ortho-psychiatry, 44,* 782.

Coombs, R. (1962). Reinforcement of values in the parental home as a factor in mate selection. *Marriage and Family Living, 24,* 155–157.

Cooper, D. (1970). *Death of the family.* New York: Pantheon.

Coopersmith, S. (1967). *The antecedents of self-esteem.* San Francisco: Freeman.

Copeland, A. D. (1974). *Textbook of adolescent psychopathology and treatment.* Springfield, IL: Charles C. Thomas.

Costanzo, P. R. (1970). Conformity development as a function of self-blame. *Journal of Personality and Social Psychology, 14,* 336–374.

Costanzo, P. R., & Shaw, M. E. (1967). Conformity as a function of age level. *Child Development, 37,* 967–975.

Courmier, B., Kennedy, M., & Saugovicz, J. (1962). Psychodynamics of father–daughter incest. *Canadian Psychiatric Association Journal, 7,* 203–217.

Cowen, E. L., & Gesten, E. L. (1978). Community approaches to intervention. In B. B. Wolmann, J. Egan, & A. O. Ross (Eds.), *Handbook of treatment of mental disorders in childhood and adolescence.* Englewood Cliffs, NJ: Prentice–Hall.

Cowen, E., Pederson, A., Babigian, H., Izzo, L., & Trost, M. (1973). Long-term follow-up of early detected vulnerable children. *Journal of Consulting and Clinical Psychology, 41,* 438–446.

Crisp, A. H., Palmer, R. L., & Kalney, R. S. (1976). How common is anorexia nervosa? A prevalence study. *British Journal of Psychiatry, 128,* 549–554.

Crisp, A. H., & Toms, D. A. (1972). Primary anorexia nervosa or weight phobia in the male. (Report on 13 cases). *British Medical Journal, i,* 334–338.

Cross, J. H., & Allen, J. G. (1970). Ego identity status, adjustment, and academic achievement. *Journal of Consulting and Clinical Psychology, 34,* 288.

Curren, J. P. (1977). Convergence toward a single sexual standard? In D. Byrne & L. Byrne (Eds.), *Exploring human sexuality.* New York: Thomas Y. Cravell.

Cusick, P. (1973). *Inside high school: The student's world.* New York: Holt, Rinehart, & Winston.

Cutler, G., Comite, F., Rivier, J., Vale, W., Loriaux, L., & Crowley, W. (1983). Pituitary desensitization with a long-acting Luteinizing-Hormone-Releasing Hormone Analog: A potential new treatment for ideopathic precocious puberty. In J. Brooks-Gunn & A. Petersen (Eds.), *Girls at puberty* (pp. 89–102). New York: Plenum Press.

Cvetkovich, G., & Grote, B. (1975). *Antecedents of responsible family formations.* Paper presented at the National Institute of Child Health and Human Development, Bethesda, MD.

Cvetkovich, G., Grote, B., Bjorseth, A., & Sarkissian, J. (1975). On the psychology of adolescents' use of contraceptives. *Journal of Sex Research, 11,* 256–270.

Dahlen, N. W. (1970). Young American's reported perceptions of their parents. *Journal of Psychology, 74,* 187–194.

Daly, H. (1980). *Economics, ecology, and ethics.* San Francisco: W. H. Freeman.

Daly, M. (1966). Physical and psychological development of the adolescent female. *Clinical Obstetrics and Gynecology, 9,* 711–721.

Daly, S. J. (1963). *Questions teenagers ask.* New York: Dodd, Mead, & Co.

Damon, A. (1977). *Human biology and ecology.* New York: Norton.

Damon, L. W., & Hart, D. (1982). The development of self-understanding from infancy through adolescence. *Child Development, 53,* 841–864.

D'Angelo, R. (1979). *Families of sand: A report concerning the flight of adolescents from their families.* Columbus: School of Social Work, Ohio State University.

Danish, S. J., & D'Augelli, A. R. (1980). Promoting competence and enhancing development through life development intervention. In L. A. Bond & J. C. Rosen (Eds.), *Competence and coping during adulthood.* Hanover, NH: University Press of New England.

Darling, C. A., & Hicks, M. W. (1982). Parental influence on adolescent sexuality: Implications for parents as educators. *Journal of Youth and Adolescence, 11,* 231–244.

D'Augelli, J. F., & D'Augelli, A. R. (1977). Moral reasoning and premarital sexual behavior: Toward reasoning about relationships. *Journal of Social Issues, 33,* 46–66.

D'Augelli, J. F., & Gross, H. J. (1975). Relationship of sex-guilt and moral reasoning to premarital sex in college women and in couples. *Journal of Consulting and Clinical Psychology, 43,* 40–47.

Davis, K. (1940). The sociology of parent-youth conflict. *American Sociological Review, 5,* 523–535.

Davis, S. M., & Harris, M. B. (1982). Sexual knowledge, sexual interests, and sources of information of rural and urban adolescents from three cultures. *Adolescence, 17,* 471–492.

Davison, M. L., Robbins, S., & Swanson, D. B. (1978). Stage structure in objective moral judgments. *Developmental psychology, 14,* 137–146.

Davitz, J. R. (1955). Social perception and sociometric choice in children. *Journal of Abnormal and Social Psychology, 50,* 173–176.

Deal, J. (1975). An organizational explanation of the failure of alternative secondary schools. *Educational Researcher, 4*(4), 1017.

Dearman, N. B., & Plisko, V. W. (Eds.). (1979). *The condition of education: 1979 edition.* Washington, D.C.: U.S. Department of Health, Education, and Welfare, National Center for Educational Statistics.

DeFrancis, V. (1969). *Protecting the child victim of sex crimes committed by adults.* Denver, CO: American Humane Association.

Deisher, R., Eisner, V., & Sulzbacker, S. I. (1969). The young male prostitute. *Pediatrics, 43,* 936.

deLissovoy, V. (1973). High-school marriages: A longitudinal study. *Journal of Marriage and the Family, 35,* 245–255.

Dellinger, R. W. (1980). *Cults and kids: A study of coercion.* Boys Town, Nebraska: The Boys Town Center.

DeLora, J. S., & Warren, C. A. B. (1977). *Understanding sexual interaction.* Boston: Houghton Mifflin.

DeLuca, J. R. (1981). *Fourth special report to the U.S. Congress on alcohol and health.* (U.S. Public Health Service, DHHS Publication No. ADM 81-1080). Washington, DC: U.S. Government Printing Office.

Demos, J., & Demos, V. (1969). Adolescence in historical perspective. *Journal of Marriage and the Family, 31,* 632–638.

Derbyshire, R. L., & Brody, E. B. (1964). Marginality, identity, and behavior in the American Negro: A functional analysis. *International Journal of Social Psychiatry, 10,* 7–13.

Devereux, E. C. (1970). The role of peer-group experience in moral development. In J. P. Hill (Ed.), *Minnesota Symposia on Child Psychology* (Vol. 4). Minneapolis: University of Minnesota Press.

Devereux, E. C. et al. (1969). Child-rearing in England and the United States: A cross-national comparison. *Journal of Marriage and the Family, 31,* 257–270.

DeVos, G. A. (1973). *Socialization for achievement.* Berkeley: University of California Press.

Dewhurst, C. J. (1969). Variations in physical signs in pubertal girls. *Journal of Obstetrics and Gynecology of the British Commonwealth, 76,* 831–833.

Dickinson, G. E. (1975). Dating behavior of black and white adolescents before and after desegregation. *Journal of Marriage and the Family, 37,* 605.

Diepold, J. Jr., & Young, R. D. (1979). Empirical studies of adolescent sexual behavior: A critical review. *Adolescence, 14,* 45–64.

Dillard, J. M., & Perrin, D. W. (1980). Puerto Rican, Black, and Anglo adolescents' career aspirations, expectations, and maturity. *The Vocational Guidance Quarterly, 28,* 313–321.

Dilley, J. S. (1965). Decision-making ability and vocational maturity. *Personnel and Guidance Journal, 44,* 423–427.

Doi, T. (1973). *The anatomy of dependence.* Tokyo: Kodansha International Ltd.

Donovan, B. T. (1974). Concluding comments. In M. M. Grumbach, G. D. Grave, & F. E. Mayer (Eds.), *Control of the onset of puberty.* New York: Wiley.

Donovan, B. T., & Van der Werff Ten, G., Bosch, J. J. (1965). *Physiology of puberty.* London: Williams and Wilkins.

Donovan, J. M. (1975). Identity status and interpersonal style. *Journal of Youth and Adolescence, 4*(1), 37–55.

Doroff, D. (1969). Attempted and gestural suicides in adolescent girls. *Dissertation Abstracts International, 29,* 2631.

Douglas, J., & Simpson, H. (1964). Height in relation to puberty, family size, and social class. *Milbank Memorial Fund Quarterly, 42,* 20–35.

Douvan, E. (1963). Employment and the adolescent. In F. I. Nye & L. W. Hoffman (Eds.), *The employed mother in America.* Chicago: Rand McNally.

Douvan, E., & Adelson, J. (1969). *The adolescent experience.* New York: John Wiley & Sons.

Dreeben, R. (1968). *On what is learned in school.* Reading, MA: Addison-Wesley Publishing Co.

Dreikurs, R. (1953). *Fundamentals of Adlerian Psychology.* Chicago: Alfred Adler Institute.

Dreyer, P. H. (1982). Sexuality during adolescence. In B. B. Wolman (Ed.), *Handbook of developmental psychology.* Englewood Cliffs, NJ: Prentice-Hall.

Dreyfus, E. A. (1976). *Adolescence: Theory and experience.* Columbus, OH: Charles E. Merrill.

Dryfous, J. (1982). The epidemiology of adolescent pregnancy: Incidence, outcomes, and interventions. In I. R. Stuart & C. F. Wells (Eds.), *Pregnancy in adolescence: Needs, problems, and management.* New York: Van Nostrand Reinhold.

Ducharme, H. R., Forest, M. O., de Pieretti, E., Sempe, M., Collin, R., & Betrand, J. (1976). Plasma adrenal and gonadal sex steroids in human pubertal development. *Journal of Clinical Endocrinology and Metabolism, 42,* 468–476.

Duke, D. C. (1978). Why don't girls misbehave more than boys in school? *Journal of Youth and Adolescence, 7,* 141–157.

Dulit, E. (1972). Adolescent thinking ala Piaget: The formal stage. *Journal of Youth and Adolescence, 1,* 281–301.

Dunphy, D. (1963). The social structure of urban adolescent peer groups. *Sociometry, 26,* 230–246.

Dupold, J., & Young, D. (1979). Empirical studies of adolescent sexual behavior: A critical review. *Adolescence, 14,* 45–63.

Durkheim, E. (1951). *Suicide: A study of sociology.* New York: Free Press of Glencoe.

Eagly, A. H., & Carli, L. L. (1981). Sex of researchers and sex-typed communications as determinants of sex differences in influenceability. *Psychological Bulletin, 90,* 1–20.

Easton, D., & Hess, R. D. (1961). Youth and the political system. In S. M. Lipset & L. Lowenthal (Eds.), *Cultural and social character.* Glencoe, IL: Free Press.

Edelbrock, C. (1980). Running away from home: Incidence and correlates among children and youth referred for mental health services. *Journal of Family Issues, 2,* 210–228.

Edelbrock, C., & Achenbach, T. M. (1980). A typology of child behavior profile patterns: Distribution and correlates for disturbed children ages 6-16. *Journal of Abnormal Child Psychology, 8,* 441–470.

Edwards, C. P. (1975). Society complexity and moral development: A Kenyan study. *Ethos, 3,* 505–527.

Edwards, J. N., & Brauburger, M. B. (1973). Exchange and parent-youth conflict. *Journal of Marriage and the Family, 35,* 101–107.

Eisenberg, L. (1962). Possibilities for a preventive psychiatry. *Pediatrics, 30,* 815–828.

Eisenstadt, S. N. (1972). Archetypal patterns of youth. In S. M. Clark & J. P. Clarke (Eds.), *Youth in modern society.* New York: Holt, Rinehart, & Winston.

Eissler, K. R. (1958). Notes on problems of technique in the psychoanalytic treatment of adolescents. *Psychoanalytic Study of the Child, 13,* 223–254.

Elder, G. H., Jr. (1963). Parental power legitimation and its effects on the adolescent. *Sociometry, 26,* 50–65.

Elder, G. H. (1968). Democratic parent-youth relations in cross-national perspectives. *Social Science Quarterly, 49,* 216–228.

Elder, G. H., Jr. (1968). Parent-youth relations in cross-national perspective. *Social Science Quarterly, 49,* 216–228.

Elder, G. H., Jr. (1972). Role orientation, marital age, and life patterns in adulthood. *Merrill-Palmer Quarterly, 18,* 3–23.

Elder, G. H., Jr. (1974). *Children of the Great Depression.* Chicago: University of Chicago Press.

Elder, G. H., Jr. (1975). Adolescence in the life-cycle. In S. Dragastin & G. Elder (Eds.), *Adolescence in the life cycle.* Washington, D.C.: Hemisphere.

Elder, G. H., Jr. (1980). Adolescence in historical perspective. In J. Adelson (Ed.), *Handbook of adolescent psychology.* New York: John Wiley & Sons.

Elias, J. E. (1978, March/April). Adolescents and sex. *The Humanist.*

Elkind, D. (1967). Egocentrism in adolescence. *Child Development, 38,* 1025–1034.

Elkind, D. (1967). Middle-class delinquency. *Mental Health, 5,* 80–84.

Elkind, D. (1968). Combinatorial thinking in adolescents from graded and ungraded classrooms. *Perceptual and Motor Skills, 27,* 1015–1018.

Elkind, D. (1975). Recent research on cognitive development in adolescence. In S. E. Dragastin & G. H. Elder, Jr. (Eds.), *Adolescence in the life cycle: Psychological change and social context.* Washington, DC: Hemisphere.

Elkind, D. (1980) Strategic interactions in early adolescence. In J. Adelson (Ed.), *Handbook of adolescent psychology.* New York: Wiley.

Elkind, D. (1981). *A sympathetic understanding of the child six to sixteen.* Boston: Allyn & Bacon.

Elkind, D. (1981). *The hurried child.* Boston: Addison Wesley.

Elkind, D. (1984) *All grown up and nowhere to go.* Boston: Addison Wesley.

Elliott, D. S., & Ageton, S. (1980). Reconciling differences in estimates of delinquency. *American Sociological Review, 45,* 95–110.

Elliott, D. S., & Voss, H. L. (1974). *Delinquency and dropout.* Lexington, MA: D.C. Heath.

Elliott, D. S., Voss, H. L., & Wendling, A. (1966). Capable dropouts and the social milieu of the high school. *Journal of Educational Research, 60,* 181–185.

Ellison, R. (1964). *Shadow and act.* New York: Random House.

Empey, L. T. (1969). Delinquent subcultures: Theory and recent research. In C. R. Cressey & D. A. Ward (Eds.), *Delinquency, crime, and social process.* New York: Harper & Row.

Enright, R. D., Lapsley, D. K., Drivas, A. E., & Fehr, L. A. (1980). Parental influences on the development of adolescent autonomy and identity. *Journal of Youth and Adolescence, 9(6),* 529–545.

Epstein, A. (1980). Adolescent pregnancy: A report on the ACYF-Funded Research and demonstration projects. *Children Today,* 10–35.

Epstein, H. (1977). A neuroscience framework for restructuring middle school curricula. *Transescence: The Journal on Emerging Adolescent Education, 5,* 6–11.

Epstein, J., & McPartlaud, J. (1976). The concept and measurement of the quality of school life. *American Educational Research Journal, 13,* 15–30.

Epstein, S. (1973). The self-concept revisited. *American Psychologist, 28,* 404–416.

Erikson, E. H. (1956). The problem of ego identity. *Journal of the American Psychoanalytic Association, 4,* 56–121.

Erikson, E. H. (1959). Identity and the life cycle. *Psychological Issues, 1,* 1–171.

Erikson, E. H. (1963). *Childhood and society* (2nd ed.). New York: Norton.

Erikson, E. H. (1968). *Identity: Youth and crisis.* New York: W. W. Norton & Co.

Erikson, E. H. (1970). Reflections on the dissent of contemporary youth. *International Journal of Psycho-Analysis, 51*, 11–22.

Ernsberger, D. J. (1974). *Adolescent conversion and the existential task.* Unpublished manuscript, University of Texas, Austin.

Evans, J., Selstad, G., & Welcher, W. (1976). Teenagers: Fertility control behavior and attitudes before and after abortion, childbearing, or negative pregnancy test. *Family Planning Perspectives, 8,* 192–200.

Ewens, W. P. (1970). Relationship of interest to aptitude by profiles and by interest areas. In R. F. Purnell (Ed.), *Adolescents and the American high school.* New York: Holt, Rinehart, & Winston.

Eysenck, H. J. (1961). The effects of psychotherapy. In H. J. Eysenck (Ed.), *Handbook of abnormal psychology.* New York: Basic Books.

Faiman, C., & Winter, J. S. D. (1974). Gonadotropins and sex hormone patterns in puberty: Clinical data. In M. M. Grumbach, G. D. Grave, & F. E. Mayer (Eds.), *Control of the onset of puberty.* New York: Wiley.

Fakouri, M. (1976). Cognitive development in adulthood: A fifth stage? A critique. *Developmental Psychology, 12,* 472.

Falkner, F. (1972). Physical growth. In H. L. Barneett & A. H. Einhorn (Eds.), *Pediatrics* (15th ed.). Appleton-Century Crofts.

Fantini, M. (1973). Alternatives within public schools. *Phi Delta Kappan, 54*(7), 444–449.

Farnsworth, D. L. (1968). Sexual morality and the dilemma of the colleges. In A. E. Winder & D. L. Angus (Eds.), *Adolescence: Contemporary studies.* New York: American Books.

Farnsworth, D. L. (1974). The young adult: An overview. *American Journal of Psychiatry, 131*(8), 845–852.

Faust, D., & Arbuthnot, J. (1978). Relationship between moral and Piagetian reasoning and the effectiveness of moral education. *Developmental Psychology, 14,* 435–436.

Faust, M. S. (1960). Developmental maturity as a determinant in prestige of adolescent girls. *Child Development, 31,* 173–184.

Faust, M. S. (1983). Alternative constructions of adolescent growth. In J. Brooks-Gunn & A. Petersen (Eds.), *Girls at Puberty.* New York: Plenum Press.

Faw, T. (1980). *Child psychology.* New York: McGraw-Hill.

Feinstein, S. C., & Ardon, M. S. (1973). Trends in dating patterns and adolescent development. *Journal of Youth and Adolescence, 2,* 157–166.

Feinstein, S. C., & Miller, D. (1979). Psychoses of adolescence. In J. D. Noshpitz (Ed.), *Basic handbook of child psychiatry,* Vol. 2. New York: Basic Books.

Feldman, H., & Feldman, M. (1979). The effect of father absence on adolescents. In B. M. Newman & P. R. Newman (Eds.), *An introduction to the psychology of adolescence.* Homewood, IL: Dorsey Press.

Feldman, K., & Newcomb, J. (1969). *The impact of college on students: An analysis of four decades of research.* San Francisco: Jossey-Bass.

Feldman, R. A. (1972). Normative integration, alienation, and conformity in adolescent groups. *Adolescence, 12,* 327–341.

Feldman, R. A., & Wodarski, J. S. (1975). *Contemporary approaches to group treatment.* San Francisco: Jossey-Bass.

Fernbach, D., & Starling, K. (1975). Acute leukemia in children. In M. Levine (Ed.), *Clinical Review Series: Pediatric Medicine.* New York: Publishing Sciences Group.

Feshbach, S. (1970). Aggression. In P. H. Mussen (Ed.), *Carmichael's manual of child psychology* (3rd ed.), Vol. 2, pp. 159–259. New York: Wiley.

Festinger, L. (1954). A theory of social comparison processes. *Human Relations, 7,* 117–140.

Feuer, L. S. (1969). *The conflict of generations.* New York: Basic Books.

Field, I. (1980). Adolescent pregnancy: A report on ACYF-Funded research and demonstration projects. *Children Today,* 10–35.

Fine, G. A. (1981). Friends, impression management, and preadolescent behavior. In S. R. Asher & J. M. Gottman (Eds.), *The development of children's friendships.* Cambridge: Cambridge University Press.

Finger, J., & Silverman, M. (1966). Changes in academic performance in the junior high school. *Personnel and Guidance Journal, 45,* 157–164.

Finkel, M., & Finkel, D. (1975). Sexual and contraceptive knowledge, attitudes and behaviors of male adolescents. *Family Planning Perspectives, 7,* 256–260.

Finkelhor, D. (1979). *Sexually victimized children.* New York: The Free Press.

Finkelstein, J. (1980). The endocrinology of adolescence. *Pediatric Clinics of North America, 27,* 53–69.

Fish, K. D. (1970). Paternal availability, family role structure, maternal employment, and personality development in adolescent females. *Dissertation Abstracts International,* (University Microfilms, No. 70-53, 24).

Fischer, J. L. (1981). Transition in relationship style from adolescence to young adulthood. *Journal of Youth and Adolescence, 10,* 11–24.

Fisher, B., & Berdie, J. (1978). Adolescent abuse and neglect: Issues of incidence; intervention and service delivery. *Child Abuse and Neglect, 2,* 325–338.

Fisher, B., Fazio, E., Weisberg, D. K., Johnson, E., Marotta, T., & Jones, S. (1982). *Juvenile prostitution: A resource manual.* San Francisco: Urban and Rural Systems.

Fisher, W. A., Fisher, J. D., & Byrne, D. (1971). Consumer reactions to contraceptive purchasing. *Personality and Social Psychology Bulletin, 3,* 243–296.

Fishman, J. R., Denham, W. H., Levine, M., & Shatz, E. D. (1969). *New careers for the disadvantaged in*

human services: Report of social experiment.
Washington, D.C.: Howard University Institute for
Youth Studies.

Fitzgerald, J. M., Nesselroade, J. R., & Baltes, P. B.
(1973). Emergence of adult intellectual structure.
Developmental Psychology, 9, 114–119

Flacks, R. (1970, June). Youth intelligence in revolt. *Trans-Action,* 47–55.

Flacks, R. (1971). *Youth and social change.* Chicago:
Markham Publishing.

Flanagan, J. (Ed.). (1978). *Perspectives on improving
education.* New York: Praeger.

Flavell, J. H. (1970). Concept development. In P. H.
Mussen (Ed.), *Carmichael's manual of child
psychology* (3rd ed.). New York: Wiley.

Foote, N., & Cottrell, L., Jr. (1955). *Identity and
interpersonal competence: A new direction in family
research.* Chicago: University of Chicago Press.

Ford, C. S., & Beach, J. A. (1951). *Patterns of sexual
behavior.* New York: Harper & Row.

Forrest, H., Hermolin, J., & Henshaw, R. (1981). The
impact of family planning clinic programs on
adolescent pregnancy. *Family Planning Perspectives,
13,* 109–116.

Forrest, J., Sullivan, E., & Tietze, C. (1979). Abortions in
the United States, 1977–1979. *Family Planning
Perspectives, 11,* 329–341.

Forrester, J. (1969). *Urban dynamics.* Cambridge, MA:
The M.I.T. Press.

Fountain, G. (1961). Adolescent into adult: An inquiry.
*Journal of the American Psychoanalytic Association,
9,* 417–433.

Fox, G. L. (1980) The mother-adolescent daughter
relationship as a sexual socialization structure: A
research review. *Family Relations, 29,* 21–28.

Fox, G. L., & Inazu, J. K. (1980). Mother-daughter
communications about sex. *Family Relations, 29,* 347–352.

Frank. J. D. (1979). The present status of outcome studies.
Journal of Consulting and Clinical psychology, 47,
310–316.

Frazier, D., & De Blassie, R. (1982). Comparison of self-concept in Mexican American and non-Mexican
American late adolescents. *Adolescence, 17,* 327–334.

Freedman, D. G. (1974). *Human infancy: An evolutionary
perspective.* Hillsdale, NJ: Earlbaum.

Freeman, D. (1983). *Margaret Mead and Samoa: The
making and unmaking of an anthropological myth.*
Cambridge, MA: Harvard University Press.

Freud, A. (1958). Adolescence. *Psychoanalytic Study of
the Child, 13,* 255–278.

Freud, A. (1966). *The writings of Anna Freud. Vol. II. The
ego and the mechanisms of defense* (rev. ed., 1936).
New York: International Universities.

Freud, A., & Dann, S. (1951). An experiment in group
upbringing. In *Psychoanalytic Study of the Child* (Vol.
6). New York: International Universities Press.

Freud, E. L. (Ed.). (1960). *Letters of Sigmund Freud.* (T.
Stern & J. Stern, Trans.). New York: Basic Books.

Friedenberg, E. Z. (1959). *The vanishing adolescent.*
Boston: Beacon Press.

Friedenberg, E. Z. (1965). *The dignity of youth and other
atavisms.* Boston: Beacon Press.

Friedman, C. J., Mann, F., & Friedmann, A. S. (1975). A
profile of juvenile street gang members. *Adolescence,
10,* 563–607.

Friedman, R. (1978). Child abuse: A review of the
psychosocial research. In Herne & Co. (Eds.), *Four
perspectives on the status of child abuse and neglect
research.* Washington, D.C.: National Center on Child
Abuse and Neglect.

Friesen, D. (1968). Academic-athletic-popularity
syndrome in the Canadian high school society.
Adolescence, 63, 39–52.

Frish, R. E. (1978). Population, food intake, and fertility.
Science, 199, 22–30.

Frish, R. E., & Revelle, R. (1969). Height and weight of
adolescent boys and girls at the time of peak velocity
of growth in height and weight: Longitudinal data.
Human Biology, 41, 536–559.

Frisch, R. E., & Revelle, R. (1970). Height and weight,
menarche and a hypothesis of critical body weight and
adolescent events. *Science, 169,* 397–399.

Froland, C., Pancoast, D. L., Chapman, N. J., &
Kimboko, P. (1981). Linking formal and informal
support systems. In B. H. Gottlieb (Ed.), *Social
networks and social support.* Beverly Hills, CA: Sage
Publications.

Furman, W. (1980). Promoting social development:
Developmental implications for treatment. In B. B.
Lahey & A. E. Kazdin (Eds.), *Advances in Clinical
Child Psychology,* Vol. 3. New York: Plenum.

Furstenberg, F. F. (1977). *Unplanned parenthood: The
social consequences of teenage childbearing.* New
York: The Free Press.

Furstenberg, F. F., Lincoln, R., & Menken, J. (Eds.).
(1981). *Teenage sexuality, pregnancy, and childbearing.*
Philadelphia: University of Pennsylvania Press.

Gagnon, J. (1965). Female child victims of sex offenses.
Social Problems, 13, 176–192.

Gagnon, J. H., & Simon, W. (1973). *Sexual conduct: The
social origins of human sexuality.* Chicago:
Aldine.

Gallatin, J. E. (1975). *Adolescence and individuality.* New
York: Harper & Row.

Gallatin, J. E. (1980). Political thinking in adolescence. In
J. Adelson (Ed.), *Handbook of adolescent psychology.*
New York: Wiley.

Gallup, G. (1975). The public looks at education. *Today's
Education, 64,* 16–20.

Gallup, G. (1978). The tenth annual Gallup poll of the
public's attitudes toward the public schools. *Phi Delta
Kappan, 60,* 33–45.

Gallup, G. (1980). 12th annual Gallup Poll of the public's
attitude toward the public schools. *Phi Delta Kappan,
62,* 33–46.

Galton, F. (1896). *Hereditary genius: An inquiry into its
laws and consequences.* London: Macmillan.

Gandy, G. L. (1974). Ordinal position research related to vocational interest. *Journal of Counseling Psychology, 21,* 281–287.

Gandy, P., & Deisher, R. (1970). Young male prostitutes: The physician's role in social rehabilitation. *Journal of the American Medical Association, 212,* 1661.

Garbarino, J. (1968). *Religion and democracy.* Unpublished master's thesis, St. Lawrence University, Canton, New York.

Garbarino, J. (1973). High school size and adolescent social development. *Human Ecology Forum, 4,* 26–29.

Garbarino, J. (1978, January). The role of schools in socialization and adulthood. *Educational Forum,* 169–181.

Garbarino, J. (1980). An ecological approach to child maltreatment. In L. Pelton (Ed.), *The social context of child abuse and neglect.* New York: Human Sciences Press.

Garbarino, J. (1980). Some thoughts on school size and its effects on adolescent development. *Journal of Youth and Adolescence, 9,* 19–31.

Garbarino, J. (1980). The issue is human quality: In praise of children. *Children and Youth Services Review, 1,* 353–377.

Garbarino, J. (1982). *Children and families in the social environment.* New York: Aldine.

Garbarino, J. (1985). *Spaceship earth and the lifeboat family.* In press.

Garbarino, J., & Asp, C. E. (1981). *Successful schools and competent students.* Lexington, MA: Lexington Books.

Garbarino, J., & Bronfenbrenner, U. (1976). The socialization of moral judgment and behavior in cross-cultural perspective. In T. Lickona (Ed.), *Moral development and behavior.* New York: Holt, Rinehart, & Winston.

Garbarino, J., & Crouter, A. (1978). Defining the community context of parent-child relations: The correlates of child maltreatment. *Child Development, 49,* 604–616.

Garbarino, J., & Garbarino, A. C. (1980). *Emotional maltreatment of children.* Chicago: National Committee for Prevention of Child Abuse.

Garbarino, J., & Garbarino, A. C. (1982). *Maltreatment of adolescents.* Chicago: National Committee for Prevention of Child Abuse.

Garbarino, J., & Gilliam, G. (1980). *Understanding abusive families.* Lexington, MA: Lexington Books.

Garbarino, J., & Jacobson, N. (1978). Youth helping youth in cases of maltreatment of adolescents. *Child Welfare, 57,* 505–509.

Garbarino, J., Sebes, J., & Schellenbach, C. (1984). Families at risk for destructive parent-child relations in adolescence. *Child Development, 55,* 174–183.

Garbarino, J., & Vondra, J. (1983, August). Psychological maltreatment. Paper presented to the First International Conference on Psychological Abuse and Neglect. Indianapolis, IN.

Garbarino, J., Wilson, J., & Garbarino, A. C. (1986). The adolescent runaway. In J. Garbarino, C. Schellenbach, J. Sebes, and Associates, *Troubled Youth, Troubled Families.* New York: Aldine.

Garfinkel, P. E., Moldofsky, H., & Garner, P. M. (1977a). Prognosis in anorexia nervosa as influenced by clinical features, treatment, and self-perception. *Canadian Medical Association Journal, 117,* 1041–1045.

Garfinkel, P. E., Moldofsky, H., & Garner, D. M. (1977b). The outcome of anorexia nervosa: Significance of clinical features, body image, and behavior modification. In R. A. Vigersky (Ed.), *Anorexia Nervosa.* New York: Raven Press.

Garmezy, N. (1977). Observations on research with children at risk for child and adult psychopathology. In M. F. McMillan & S. Henao (Eds.), *Child psychiatry: Treatment and research.* New York: Brunner/Mazel.

Garmezy, N., & Nuechterlein, K. (1972). Vulnerability and invulnerable children: The fact and fiction of competence and disadvantage. *American Journal of Orthopsychiatry, 77.*

Garms, W., Gutherie, J., & Pierce, L. (1978). *School finance: The economics and politics of public education.* Englewood Cliffs, NJ: Prentice-Hall.

Garrett, H. E. (1946). A developmental theory of intelligence. *American Psychologist, 1,* 372–378.

Gebhard, P. H. (1969). Misconceptions about female prostitutes. *Medical Aspects of Human Sexuality, 3,* 24–30.

Gecas, V. (1979). The influence of social class on socialization. In W. R. Burr, R. Hill, F. I. Nye, & I. L. Reiss (Eds.), *Contemporary theories about the family: Research based theories,* Vol. 1. New York: The Free Press.

Geleerd, E. R. (1957). Some aspects of psychoanalytic technique in adolescence. *Psychoanalytic Study of the Child, 12,* 263–283.

Gelfand, D. M. (1962). The influence of self-esteem on rate of verbal conditioning and social matching behavior. *Journal of Abnormal and Social Psychology, 65,* 259–265.

Gelles, R. (1978). Violence toward children in the United States. *American Journal of Orthopsychiatry, 48,* 580–592.

Genshaft, J. L. (1980). Personality correlates of delinquent subtypes. *Journal of Abnormal Child Psychology, 8,* 279–283.

Gershon, E. S., Bunney, W. E., Leckman, J. F., VanEerdewegh, M., & DeBauche, B. A. (1976). The inheritance of affective disorders: A review of data and of hypotheses. *Behavior Genetics, 6,* 227–261.

Gesten, E. L., Flores de Apodaca, R., Rains, M., Weissberg, R. P., & Cowen, E. L. (1979). Promoting peer related social competence in schools. In M. W. Kent & J. E. Rolf (Eds.), *The primary prevention of psychopathology, Vol. 3: Social competence in children.* Hanover, NH: University Press of New England.

Getzels, J. W. (1974). Socialization and education: A note on discontinuities. *Teachers College Record, 76,* 218–225.

Getzels, J. W., & Csikszentmihalyi, M. (1976). *The creative vision.* New York: John Wiley & Sons.

Giaretto, H. (1976). The treatment of father-daughter incest: A psychosocial approach. *Children Today, 25,* 34, 35.

Gil, D. G. (1973). *Violence against children: Physical child abuse in the United States* (2nd ed.). Cambridge, MA: Harvard University Press.

Gilford, R., & Black, D. (1982). *The grandchild-grandparent dyad: Ritual or relationship.* Paper presented to the Gerontological Society, San Juan, Puerto Rico.

Gilligan, C. (1982). *In a different voice: Psychological theory and women's development.* Cambridge, MA: Harvard University Press.

Gilligan, C. (1982). New maps of development: New visions of maturity. *American Journal of Orthopsychiatry, 52,* 199–212.

Ginsburg, H., & Opper, S. (1969). *Piaget's theory of intellectual development: An introduction.* Englewood Cliffs, NJ: Prentice-Hall.

Ginsburg, K. N. (1967). The meat rack: A study of the male homosexual prostitute. *American Journal of Psychotherapy, 21,* 170.

Ginzberg, E. (1972). Toward a theory of occupational choice: A restatement. *Vocational Guidance Quarterly, 20,* 169–176.

Ginzberg, E., Ginsburg, S. W., Axelrod, S., & Herman, J. L. (1951). *Occupational choice: An approach to a general theory.* New York: Columbia University Press.

Glaser, D. (1965). Social disorganization and delinquent subcultures. In H. C. Quay (Ed.), *Juvenile delinquency: Research and theory.* Princeton, NJ: Van Nostrand.

Glasser, W. (1969). *Schools without failure.* New York: Harper & Row.

Gleser, G., Seligman, R., Winget, C., & Raub, J. (1977). Adolescents review their mental health. *Journal of Youth and Adolescence, 6,* 249–263.

Gleuck, S., & Gleuck, T. (1959). *Predicting delinquency and crime.* Cambridge, MA: Harvard University Press.

Goertzel, V., & Goertzel, M. (1972). *Cradles of balance.* Boston: Little, Brown, & Co.

Goffman, E. (1969). *Strategic interaction.* Philadelphia: University of Pennsylvania Press.

Gold, D., & Andres, D. (1978). Developmental comparisons between adolescent children with employed and non-employed mothers. *Merrill-Palmer Quarterly, 24,* 243–254.

Gold, M. (1973). *Status forces in delinquent boys.* Ann Arbor: University of Michigan Press.

Gold, M., & Douvan, E. (1969). *Adolescent development.* Boston: Allyn & Bacon.

Gold, M., & Petronio, R. J. (1980). Delinquent behavior in adolescence. In J. Adelson (Ed.), *Handbook of adolescent psychology.* New York: Wiley.

Gold, M., & Reimer, D. J. (1975). Changing patterns of delinquent behavior among Americans 13 throgh 16

years old: 1967–1972. *Crime and Delinquency Literature, 7,* 483–517.

Goldberg, M. (1971). Socio-psychological issues in the education of the disadvantaged. In A. Parsons (Eds.), *Urban education in the 1970's.* New York: Columbia University Press.

Goldberg, S. (1977). Social competence in infancy: A model of parent-infant interaction. *Merrill-Palmer Quarterly, 23,* 163–177.

Goldenberg, I. I. (1971). *Build me a mountain: Youth, poverty, and the creation of new settings.* Cambridge, MA: M.I.T. Press.

Golding, W. (1954). *Lord of the flies.* New York: Coward-McCann.

Goldsmith, S., Gabrielson, M., & Gabrielson, I. (1972). Teenagers, sex, and contraception. *Family Planning Perspectives, 4,* 32–38.

Goodman, E. (1982). *Decisions, decisions.* The Boston Globe Newspaper Co., Washington Post Writers Group.

Goodman, P. (1956). *Growing up absurd.* New York: Vintage.

Gordon, R. A. (1976). Prevalence: The rare datum in delinquency measurement and its implications for the theory of delinquency. In M. Klein (Ed.), *The juvenile justice system.* Beverly Hills, CA.: Sage Publications.

Gordon, S. (1973). *The sexual adolescent.* North Scituate, MA: Duxbury Press.

Gordon, S. (1977, November). But where is sex education? *APA Monitor,* 13.

Gordon, S. (1978). *You would if you loved me.* New York: Bantam.

Gordon, S., & Dickman, I. R. (1977). *Sex education: The parent's role.* (Public Affairs Pamphlet No. 549). New York: Public Affairs Committee.

Gorsuch, R., & Barnes, M. (1973). Stages of ethical reasoning and moral norms of Carib youths. *Journal of Cross-cultural Psychology, 4,* 283–301.

Gottlieb, D., & Ramsey, C. E. (1964). *The American adolescent.* Homewood, IL: Dorsey Press.

Gottman, J., Markham, H., & Notarius, C. (1977). The topography of marital conflicts: A sequential analysis of verbal and nonverbal behavior. *Journal of Marriage and the Family, 9,* 461–477.

Gottschalk, L. A., Titchener, J. L., Piker, H. N., & Stewart, S. S. (1964). Psychosocial factors associated with pregnancy in adolescent girls: A preliminary report. *Journal of Nervous and Mental Disease, 138,* 524–534.

Gould, R. E. (1965). Suicide problems in children and adolescents. *American Journal of Psychotherapy, 19,* 228–246.

Grabe, M. (1981). School size and the importance of school activities. *Adolescence, 16*(61), 21–31.

Gray, D. (1973). "Turning out: A study of teenage prostitution." *Urban Life and Culture,* 401–425.

Greenberger, E. (1982, June). Personal communication.

Greenberger, E., & Sorensen, A. B. (1973). Toward a concept of psychosocial maturity. *Journal of Youth and Adolescence, 3*, 329–356.

Greenberger, E., & Sorensen, A. B. (1974). Toward a concept of psychosocial maturity. *Journal of Youth and Adolescence, 3*, 329–358.

Greenberger, E., & Steinberg, L. D. (1981). The workplace as a context for the socialization of youth. *Journal of Youth and Adolescence, 10*, 185–210.

Greenberger, E., Steinberg, L., & Vaux, A. (1981). Adolescents who work: Health and behavioral consequences of job stress. *Developmental Psychology, 17*, 691–703.

Greene, B. (1982, August). Fifteen. *Esquire*, 17–18.

Greenleaf, W. (1968). *American economic development since 1860.* Columbia, SC: University of South Carolina Press.

Greenspan, S. (1979). Social intelligence in the retarded. In N. Ellis (Ed.), *Handbook of mental deficiency* (2nd ed.). Hillsdale, NJ: Lawrence Erlbaum Associates.

Greenwald, H. (1970). *The elegant prostitute: A social and psychoanalytic study.* New York: Walker.

Gregiore, J. C. (1976). *The development of ego identity in juvenile delinquents.* Unpublished doctoral dissertation, University of Michigan, Ann Arbor.

Gribbons, W. D., & Lohnes, P. (1966). Occupational preferences and measured intelligence. *Vocational Guidance Quarterly, 14*, 211–214.

Grinder, R. E. (1977). *Adolescence.* New York: Wiley.

Grinker, R. R., Sr., Grinker, R. R., Jr., & Timberlake, J. (1962). A study of mentally healthy young males (homoclites). *Archives of General Psychiatry, 6*, 405–453.

Gronlund, N. E., & Anderson, L. (1957). Personality characteristics of socially accepted, socially neglected, and socially rejected junior high school pupils. *Educational Administration and Supervision, 43*, 329–338.

Gross, M. (1967). *Learning readiness in two Jewish groups.* New York: Center for Urban Education, 1967.

Grotevant, H. D., Thorbecke, W., & Meyer, M. L. (1982). An extension of Marcia's identity status interview into the interpersonal domain. *Journal of Youth and Adolescence, 11*, 33–47.

Grow, B. K., Schwartz, A. H., Grinder, D. H., & Loreson, S. L. (1970). Psychological autopsy in two cases of reported suicides in early adolescence. *American Journal of Orthopsychiatry, 40*, 339–340.

Gruber, H. E. (1973). Courage and cognitive growth in children and scientists. In M. Schwebel & J. Raph (Eds.), *Piaget in the classroom.* New York: Basic Books.

Grumbach, M. M., Grave, G. D., & Mayer, F. E. (Eds.). (1982). *Control of the onset of puberty.* New York: Wiley.

Guardo, C., & Bohan, J. (1971). Development of self-identity in children. *Child Development, 42*, 1909–1921.

Guerney, B. G., Jr. (Ed.). (1969). *Psychotherapeutic agents: New roles for non-professionals, parents, and teachers.* New York: Holt, Rinehart, & Winston.

Guerney, L. F. (1976). Filial therapy program. In D. H. Olson (Ed.), *Treating relationships.* Lake Mills, MN: Graphic.

Guest, J. (1976). *Ordinary People.* New York: Viking.

Guibaldi, J. (1982). *Impact of divorce on children.* Report to the William T. Grant Foundation, Kent State University.

Guilford, J. P. (1967). *The nature of human intelligence.* New York: McGraw-Hill.

Guillemein, R., & Burgus, R. (1972). The hormones of the hypothalamus. *Scientific American, 227*, 24–33.

Gump, P. V. (1977). Big schools, small schools. In E. M. Hetherington & R. D. Parke (Eds.), *Contemporary readings in child psychology.* New York: McGraw-Hill.

Gunn, B. (1964). Children's conceptions of occupational prestige. *Personnel and Guidance Journal, 42*, 303–308.

Gupta, D., Attanasio, A., & Roaf, S. (1975). Plasma estrogen and androgen concentrations in children during adolescence. *Journal of Clinical Endocrinology and Metabolism, 40*, 636–643.

Gurin, G., Veroff, J., & Feld, S. (1960). *Americans view their mental health.* New York: Basic Books.

Gurney, L., & Jordon, L. (1979). Children of divorce: A community support group. *Journal of Divorce, 2*, 283–294.

Hagestad, G. O. (1981). Problems and promises in the social psychology of intergenerational relations. In Fogel et al. (Eds.), *Aging: Stability and change in the family.* New York: Academic Press.

Hagestad, G. O., & Speicher, J. L. (1981). *Grandparents and family influences: Views of three generations.* Paper presented to the Society for Research on Child Development, Boston.

Haider, I. (1968). Suicidal attempts in children and adolescents. *British Journal of Child Psychiatry, 114*, 1133–1134.

Halbrecht, I., Sklorowski, E., & Tsafriv, J. (1971). Menarche and menstruation in various ethnic groups in Israel. *Acta Geneticae Medicae et Gemellological, 20*, 384–391.

Haley, J. (1980). *Leaving home.* New York: McGraw-Hill.

Hall, G. S. (1904). *Adolescence: Its psychology and its relations to physiology, anthropology, sociology, sex, crime, religion, and education.* New York: Appleton.

Hall, R. V., Lund, D., & Jackson, D. (1968). Effects of teacher attention on study behavior. *Journal of Applied Behavior Analysis, 1*, 1–12.

Hallinan, M. T. (1978-1979). The process of friendship formation. *Social Networks, 1*, 193–210.

Halmi, K. A. (1974). Anorexia nervosa, demographic and clinical features in 94 cases. *Psychosomatic Medicine, 36*(1), 18–26.

Halmi, K. A., Falk, J. R., & Schwartz, E. (1981). Binge-eating and vomiting: A survey of a college population. *Psychological Medicine, 11,* 697–706.

Hamburg, D. A., Coelho, G. V., & Adams, J. E. (1974). Coping and adaptation: Steps toward a synthesis of biological and social adaptation. In G. V. Coelho, D. A. Hamburg, & J. E. Adams (Eds.), *Coping and adaptation.* New York: Basic Books.

Hamilton E. (1978). *Sex with love: A guide for young people.* Boston: Beacon Press.

Handlin, O. (1959). *Boston's immigrants: A study of acculturation.* Cambridge, MA: Cambridge University Press.

Haney, B., & Gold, M. (1977). The juvenile delinquent nobody knows. In D. Rogers (Ed.), *Issues in adolescent psychology.* Englewood Cliffs, NJ: Prentice–Hall.

Hanke, M., & Eckland, B. K. (1978). Adult voluntary associations and adolescent socialization. *Sociological Quarterly, 19,* 481–490.

Hansen, S. L. (1977). Dating choices of high school students. *Family Life Coordinator, 26,* 133–138.

Hanson, E. D. (1981). *Understanding evolution.* New York: Oxford University Press, Inc.

Hare, R. D., & Cox, D. N. (1978). Clinical and empirical conceptions of psychopathology, and the selection of subjects for research. In R. D. Hare & D. Schalling (Eds.), *Psychopathic behavior.* New York: Wiley.

Harley, M. (1961) Some observations on the relationship between genitality and structural development at adolescence. *Journal of the American Psychoanalytic Association, 9,* 434–460.

Harman, L. W. (1970). Anatomy of career commitment in women. *Journal of Counseling Psychology, 17,* 77–80.

Harms, E. (1944). The development of religious experience in children. *American Journal of Sociology, 50,* 112–122.

Harris, L. (1971, January 8). Change, yes—upheaval, no. *Life, 70,* 22–27.

Hart, R. (1978). *Children's sense of place.* New York: Halsted Press.

Hart, S. (1983). Proceedings of the first international conference on psychological abuse and neglect. Indiana University, Indianapolis.

Harter, S. (1978). Effectance motivation reconsidered: Toward a developmental model. *Human Development, 21,* 34–64.

Hartup, W. W. (1979). Two social worlds: Family relations and peer relations. In M. Rutter (Ed.), *Scientific foundations of developmental psychiatry.* London: Heinemann.

Hartup, W. W. (1979). The social world of children. *American Psychologist, 34,* 944–950.

Hartup, W. W., & Lempers, J. (1973). A problem in life-span development: The interactional analysis of family attachments. In P. B. Baltes & K. W. Schaie (Eds.), *Life-span developmental psychology* Vol. 3. New York: Academic Press.

Harvard Medical School Health Letter. (1981, April). Cambridge, Mass.: Department of Continuing Education, Harvard Medical School.

Harvey, O. J., & Rutterford, J. (1960). Status in the informal group. *Child Development, 31,* 337–385.

Hass, A. (1979). *Teenage sexuality: A survey of teenage sexual behavior.* New York: Macmillan.

Haupt, D., & Offord, D. R. (1972). Runaways from a residential treatment center: A preliminary report. *Journal of Social Therapy, 18*(3), 14–21.

Hauser, R. M. (1971). *Socioeconomic background and educational performance.* Washington, D.C.: Rose Monograph Series, American Sociological Association.

Hauser, R. M., & Featherman, D. L. (1974). White- non-white differentials in occupational mobility among men in the United States, 1962–1972. *Demography, 11,* 247–266.

Hauserman, N., Miller, J. S., & Bond, F. T. (1976). A behavioral approach to changing self-concept in elementary school children. *The Psychological Record, 26,* 111–116.

Havighurst, R. J. (1962). *Growing up in River city.* New York: Wiley.

Havighurst, R. J. (1964). Youth in exploration and man emergent. In H. Borow (Ed.), *Man in a world at work.* Boston: Houghton Mifflin.

Havighurst, R. J. (1972). *Developmental tasks and education.* New York: McKay.

Havighurst, R. J. (1975). Objectives for youth development. In R. J. Havighurst & P. H. Dreyer (Eds.), *Youth.* Chicago: University of Chicago Press.

Havighurst, R. J., & Gottlieb, D. (1975). Youth and the meaning of work. In R. J. Havighurst & P. H. Dreyer (Eds.), *Youth.* Chicago: University of Chicago Press.

Havighurst, R. J., & Neugarten, B. L. (1977). *Society and education* (4th ed.). Boston: Allyn & Bacon.

Hawkins, J. D., & Weis, J. G. (1980). *The social developmental model: An integrated approach to delinquency prevention.* Seattle, WA: University of Washington, Center for Law and Justice.

Hawkins, R. C., & Clement, P. F. (1980). Development and construct validation of a self-report measure of binge eating tendencies. *Addictive Behaviors, 5*(3), 219–226.

Hayes, N. (1974, December). Lady in a case, reprinted from *Philly Talk Magazine.*

Hayman, C. R., & Lanza, C. (1971). Sexual assault on women and girls. *American Journal of Obstetrics and Gynecology, 109,* 480.

Heald, F. P., & Hung, W. (Eds.). (1970). *Adolescent endocrinology.* New York: Appleton–Century–Crofts.

Heath, D. (1970). Student alienation and school. *School Review, 78,* 515–528.

Heath, D. (1977). *Maturity and competence: A transcultural view.* New York: Gardner.

Helfer, R., & Kempe, C. H. (1982). *Child abuse and neglect: The family and the community.* Cambridge, MA: Ballinger.

Henderson, J. (1972). Incest: A synthesis of data. *Canadian Psychiatric Journal, 17,* 299–313.

Herman, J., & Hirschman, L. (1977). Father-daughter incest. *Signs, 2,* 1–22.

Herman, J. L., & Hirschman, L. (1981). *Father-daughter incest.* Cambridge, MA: Harvard University Press.

Herold, E., & Goodwin, M. (1981). Premarital sexual guilt and contraceptive attitudes and behavior. *Family Relations, 30,* 247–253.

Herzog, E., & Saudia, C. E. (1973). Children in fatherless families. In B. M. Caldwell & N. H. Ricciutti (Eds.), *Review of child development research,* Vol. 3. Chicago: University of Chicago Press.

Hess, R. D., & Torney, J. V. (1967). *The development of political attitudes in children.* New York: Anchor.

Hetherington, E. M. (1972). Effects of father absence on personality development in adolescent daughters. *Developmental Psychology, 7,* 313–324.

Hetherington, E. M., Cox, M., & Cox, R. (1977). Beyond father absence. In E. M. Hetherington & R. D. Parke (Eds.), *Contemporary readings in child psychology.* New York: McGraw–Hill.

Hetherington, E. M., Cox, M., & Cox, R. (1978a). The development of children in mother-headed families. In H. Hoffman & D. Reiss (Eds.), *The American family: Dying or developing?* New York: Plenum Press.

Hetherington, E. M., Cox, M., & Cox, R. (1978b). The aftermath of divorce. In J. H. Stevens, Jr., & M. Matthews (Eds.), *Mother-child, father-child relations.* Washington: National Association for the Education of Young Children. (pp. 146–176).

Hiernaux, J. (1968). Ethnic difference in growth and development. *Eugenics Quarterly, 15,* 12–21.

Hill, J. P. (1980). The family. In M. Johnson (Ed.), *Seventy-ninth yearbook of the national society for the study of education.* Chicago: University of Chicago Press.

Hill, J. P., & Palmquist, W. J. (1978). Social cognition and social relations in early adolescence. *International Journal of Behavioral Development, 1,* 1–36.

Hill, R., Foote, N., Aldous, J., Carlson, R., & MacDonald, R. (1970). *Family development in three generations.* Cambridge, MA: Schenkman.

Hindelang, M. J. (1981). Variations in sex-race-age-specific incidence rates of offending. *American Sociological Review, 46,* 461–474.

Hindelang, M. J., Hirschi, T., & Weis, J. G. (1979). Correlates of delinquency: The illusion of discrepancy between self-report and official measures. *American Sociological Review, 44,* 955–1014.

Hindelang, M. J., Hirschi, T., & Weis, J. G. (1981). *Measuring delinquency.* Beverly Hills, CA: Sage Publications.

Hirschi, T. (1969). *Causes of delinquency.* Berkeley: University of California Press.

Hodgson, G. (1973). Do schools make a difference? *Atlantic, 231,* 35ff.

Hodgson, J. W., & Fischer, J. L. (1979). Sex differences in identity and intimacy development in college youth. *Journal of Youth and Adolescence, 8,* 37–50.

Hoffman, E. (1979). Young adults' relations with their grandparents: An exploratory study. *International Journal of Aging and Human Development, 10,* 299–310.

Hoffman, L. W. (1974). Effects of maternal employment on the child. A review of the literature. *Developmental Psychology, 10,* 201–228.

Hoffman, M. L. (1970). Moral development. In P. H. Mussen (Ed.), *Carmichael's manual of child psychology* (3rd ed.), Vol. 2. New York: Wiley.

Hoffman, M. L. (1977). Moral internalization: Current theory and research. In L. Berkowitz (Ed.), *Advances in experimental social psychology* (Vol. 10). New York: Academic.

Hoffman, M. L. (1980). Moral development in adolescence. In J. Adelson (Ed.), *Handbook of adolescent psychology.* New York: Wiley.

Hogan, D. P. (1981). *Transitions and social change: The early lives of American men.* New York: Academic Press.

Holland, J. L. (1963). Explorations of a theory of vocational choice: Part II. Self-description and vocational preferences. *Vocational Guidance Quarterly, 12,* 17–24.

Holland, J. L. (1973). *Making vocational choices: A theory of careers.* Englewood Cliffs, NJ: Prentice-Hall.

Hollingshead, A. (1961). *Elmtown's youth: The impact of social classes on adolescents.* New York: John Wiley.

Holmes, T. H., & Rahe, R. H. (1967). The social readjustment rating scale. *Journal of Psychosomatic Research, 11,* 213–218.

Holtzman, W. H., & Moore, B. M. (1965). Family structures and youth attitudes. In M. Sheriff & C. W. Sherif (Eds.), *Problems of youth: Transition to adulthood in a changing world.* Chicago: Aldine.

Holzman, P. S., & Grinker, R. R. (1974). Schizophrenia in adolescence. *Journal of Youth and Adolescence, 3,* 267–279.

Homer, L. E. (1973). Community-based resource for runaway girls. *Social Casework, 54,* 473–479.

Honigstein, S. B., & Thornburg, H. D. (1980). *Junior high students' and their parents' attitudes toward school.* Paper presented at the annual meeting of the Rocky Mountain Psychological Association, Denver, CO.

Horner, M. S. (1970). Femininity and successful achievement: A basic inconsistency. In J. M. Bardwick, W. Douvan, M. S. Horner, & D. Guttman (Ed.), *Feminine personality conflict.* Belmont, CA: Brooks/Cole.

Hornick, J., Doran, L., & Crawford, S. (1979). Premarital contraceptive usage among male and female adolescents. *Family Coordinator, 28,* 181–190.

Horrocks, J. E. (1969). *The psychology of adolescence: Behavior and development* (3rd ed.). Boston: Houghton Mifflin.

Horst, H. J., Bartsch, W., & Dirksen-Thedens, I. (1977). Plasma testosterone, sex hormone binding, globulin binding capacity and percent binding of testosterone and Sa-dihydrostesterone in prepubertal, pubertal, and adult males. *Journal of Clinical Endocrinology and Metabolism, 45*, 522–527.

Houten, J., & Golembiewski, M. (1976). *A study of runaway youth and their families.* Washington, D.C.: Youth Alternatives Project.

Howard, A., & Scott, R. A. (1980). The study of minority groups in complex societies. *Handbook of cross-cultural human development.*

Howard, A., & Wilson, J. (1982). Leadership and a Declining Work Ethic. *California Management Review, 24*, (4)33–46.

Howard, M. P., & Anderson, R. J. (1978). Early identification of potential high school dropouts: A literature review. *Child Welfare, 57*, 221–231.

Howard, S. (1983, May 29). "Sally forth" cartoon strip.

Howell, F. M., & Frese, W. (1982). Adult role transitions, parental influence, and status aspirations early in the life course. *Journal of Marriage and the Family, 44*, 35–49.

Hrdy, S. (1984). *The woman that never evolved.* Cambridge, MA: Harvard University Press.

Hsu, L. K., Harding, B., & Crisp, A. H. (1970). Outcome of anorexia nervosa. *Lancet, 1*, 61–65.

Hudgens, R. W. (1974). *Psychiatric disorders in adolescents.* Baltimore, MD: Williams & Wilkins.

Hunt, M. (1970, July). Special sex education survey. *Seventeen*, 94.

Hunt, M. (1974). *Sexual behavior in the 1970s.* Chicago: Playboy Press.

Huston-Stein, A., & Higgins-Trenk, A. (1978). Development for females from childhood through adulthood: Career and feminine orientation. In P. B. Baltes (Ed.), *Life-span development and behavior* (Vol. 1). New York: Academic press.

Huston, T. L., & Burgess, R. L. (1979). Social exchange in developing relationships: An overview. In R. L. Burgess & T. L. Huston (Eds.), *Social exchange in developing relationships.* New York: Academic Press.

Hutt, C. (1972). Sex differences in human development. *Human Development, 15*, 153–170.

Hyde, J. S. (1982). *Understanding human sexuality.* New York: McGraw-Hill.

Iacovetta, R. G. (1975). Adolescent-adult interaction and peer-group involvement. *Adolescence, 10*, 325–336.

Illinois Institute for Juvenile Research. (1973). *Juvenile delinquency in Illinois.* Chicago: Illinois Department of Mental Health.

Inhelder, B., & Piaget, J. (1958). *The growth of logical thinking from childhood to adolescence.* New York: Basic Books.

Inselberg, M. R. (1961). Social and psychological factors associated with high school marriage. *Journal of Home Economics, 53*, 766–772.

Jackman, N. R., O'Tolle, R., & Geis, G. (1963). The self image of the prostitute. *Sociological Quarterly, 4*(2), 150–161.

Jackson, J. L. (1969, January). *School size and program quality in southern high schools.* Nashville, TN: Center for Southern Education Studies, George Peabody College for Teachers.

Jacobinzer, J. (1965). Attempted suicides in adolescence. *Journal of the American Medical Association, 191*, 7–11.

Jacobs, J. I. (1978, July). Use of sex to ward off intimacy. *Medical Aspects of Human Sexuality*, 32–43.

Jacobs, J., & Teicher, J. D. (1967). Broken homes and social isolation in attempted suicides of adolescents. *International Journal of Social Psychiatry, 13*, 139–149.

Jaffe, A. C., Dynneson, L., & ten Bensel, R. W. (1975). Sexual abuse of children: An epidemiologic study. *American Journal of Diseases of Children, 129*, 690.

Jaffee, A., Adams, W., & Meyers, S. (1968). *Negro higher education in the 1960's.* New York: Praeger.

James, J. (1976). Motivations for entrance into prostitution. In L. Crites (Ed.), *The female offender.* Lexington, MA: D.C. Heath and Co., Lexington Books.

James, L. (1983, March 7). An abused son kills a father. *People*, 34–36.

James. W. (1961). *Psychology: The briefer course.* New York: Harper Bros. (Originally published 1892).

Janes, C. L., Hesselbrock, V. M., Myers, D. G., & Penniman, J. H. (1979). Problem boys in young adulthood: Teacher ratings and twelve-year follow-up. *Journal of Youth and Adolescence, 8*, 453–472.

Jayratne, S., Stuart, R. B., & Tripodi, T. (1974). Methodological issues and problems in evaluating treatment outcomes in the Family and School Consultation Project. In P. O. Davidson, F. W. Clark, & L. A. Hamerlynck (Eds.), *Evaluation of behavioral programs.* Champaign, IL: Research Press.

Jemail, J. A., & Geer, J. (1977). Sexual scripts. In R. Gemme & C. C. Wheeler (Eds.), *Progress in sexology.* New York: Plenum.

Jencks, C. (1979). *Who gets ahead?* New York: Basic Books.

Jencks, C., Smith, M., Acland, H., Bane, M. J., Cohen, D., Gintis, H., Hyens, B. and Michelson, S. (1972). *Inequality: A reassessment of the effect of family and schooling in America.* New York: Basic Books.

Jenkins, R. (1955). Adaptive and maladaptive delinquency. *Nervous Child, 11*, 9–11.

Jenkins, R. (1957). Motivation and frustration in delinquency. *American Journal of Orthopsychiatry, 27*, 528–537.

Jenkins, R. (1978). Special health-related concerns of socially disadvantaged adolescents. *Conference on Adolescent Behavior and Health* (conference summary). National Academy of Sciences, Institute of

Medicine. Washington, DC: National Academy of Science.

Jennings, M., & Langton, K. (1969). Mothers versus fathers: The formation of political orientations among young Americans. *Journal of Politics, 31*, 329–358.

Jennings, M. K., & Niemi, R. G. (1968a). Patterns of political learning. *Harvard Educational Review, 38*, 443–467.

Jennings, M. K., & Niemi, R. G. (1968b). The transmission of political values from parent to child. *American Political Science Review, 62*, 169–184.

Jensen, A. (1969). How much can we boost IQ and scholastic achievement? *Harvard Educational Review, 39*, 1–123.

Jersild, A. I., Brook, J. S., & Brook, D. W. (1978). *The Psychology of Adolescence*, 3rd Edition. New York: MacMillan.

Jessor, S. L., & Jessor, R. (1975). Adolescent development and onset of drinking: A longitudinal study. *Journal of Studies on Alcohol, 36*(1), 27–51.

Johnson, C., Walters, L. H., & McKenny, P. (1979). Trends in services for pregnant adolescents. *Health and Social Work, 4*, 27–43.

Johnson, F. E., Malina, R. M., & Galbraith, M. A. (1971). Height, weight, and age at menarche and the critical weight hypothesis. *Science, 174*, 1148–1149.

Johnson, R., & Leslie, J. (1982). Couple involvement and network structure: A test of the dyadic withdrawal hypothesis. *Social Psychology Quarterly, 45*, 34–43.

Johnston, D. F. (1973). Education of workers: Projection to 1990. *Monthly Labor Review, 96*, 22–31.

Johnston, L. D., Bachman, J. G., & O'Malley, P. M. (1980). *Highlights from "Student drug use in America," 1975–1980*. National Institute on Drug Abuse, (DHHS Publication No. ADM 81-1066). Washington, DC: U.S. Government Printing Office.

Jones, M. C. (1965). Psychological correlates of somatic development. *Child Development, 56*, 899–911.

Jones, M. C., & Bayley, N. (1950). Physical maturing among boys as related to behavior. *Journal of Educational Psychology, 41*, 129–148.

Jones, M. C., & Mussen, P. H. (1958). Self-conceptions, motivations, and interpersonal attitudes of early- and late-maturing girls. *Child Development, 29*, 491–501.

Jones, R. (1977). Human effects. In R. Peterson (Ed.), *Marijuana research findings: 1976 NIDA Research Monograph 14*. Washington, DC: U.S. Government Printing Office.

Jordan, C., and Tharp, R. G. (1979). Culture and education. In A. J. Marsella (Ed.), *Perspectives on cross-cultural psychology*. New York: Academic Press.

Jordan, D. (1971). *Parental antecedents and personality characteristics of ego identity statuses*. Unpublished doctoral dissertation, State University of New York at Buffalo.

Jorgensen, J. (1983). Beyond adolescent pregnancy: Research frontiers for early adolescent sexuality. *Journal of Early Adolescence, 3*, 141–155.

Jorgensen, S. (1981). Sex education and the reduction of adolescent pregnancies: Prospects for the 1980's. *Journal of Early Adolescence, 1*, 38–52.

Jorgenson, S., King, S., & Torrey, B. (1980).. Dyadic and social network influences on adolescent exposure to pregnancy risk. *Journal of Marriage and the Family, 41*, 141–155.

Josselson, R. (1980). Ego development in adolescence. In J. Adelson (Ed.), *Handbook of Adolescent Psychology*. New York: Wiley.

Josselson, R., Greenberger, E., & McConochie, D. (1977a). Phenomenological aspects of psychosocial maturity in adolescence. Part I. Boys. *Journal of Youth and Adolescence, 6*, 25–55.

Josselson, R., Greenberger, E., & McConochie, D. (1977b). Phenomenological aspects of psychological maturity in adolescence. Part II. Girls. *Journal of Youth and Adolescence, 6*, 145–167.

Jurich, A. P., & Jurich, J. A. (1974). The effect of cognitive moral development upon the selection of premarital sexual standards. *Journal of Marriage and the Family, 36*, 736–741.

Kacerguis, M. A., & Adams, G. R. (1980). Erikson stage resolution: The relationship between identity and intimacy. *Journal of Youth and Adolescence, 9*, 117–126.

Kaestle, C. F., & Vinouskis, M. A. (1980). *Education and school change in Nineteenth Century Massachusetts*. Cambridge, MA: Cambridge University Press.

Kagan, H. (1969). Prostitution and sexual promiscuity among adolescent female offenders. Unpublished doctoral dissertation, University of Arizona, Tucson, Arizona.

Kagan, J. (1964). Acquisition and significance of sex typing and sex role identity. In M. L. Hoffman & L. W. Hoffman (Eds.), *Review of child development research* Vol. 1. New York: Russell Sage Foundation.

Kagan, J. (Speaker). (1975). *Adolescence: Winds of change* (Film). Chicago: Motorola Films.

Kagan, J., & Moss, H. A. (1962). *Birth to maturity: The Fels study of psychological development*. New York: Wiley.

Kahana, B., & Kahana, E. (1970). Grandparenthood from the perspective of the developing grandchild. *Developmental Psychology, 1*, 98–105.

Kalter, N. (1977). Children of divorce in an outpatient psychiatric population. *American Journal of Orthopsychiatry, 47*, 40–51.

Kandel, D. B. (1978). Similarity in real life adolescent friendship peers. *Journal of Personality and Social Psychology, 36*, 306–312.

Kandel, D. B. (1978). Homophily, selection, and socialization in adolescent friendships. *American Journal of Sociology, 84*, 427–436.

Kandel, D. B., & Faust, R. (1975). Sequence and stages in patterns of adolescent drug use. *Archives of General Psychiatry, 32*, 923–932.

Kandel, D. B., & Lesser, G. S. (1969). Parent-adolescent relationships and adolescent independence in the United States and Denmark. *Journal of Marriage and the Family, 31*(2), 348–358.

Kandel, D. B., & Lesser, G. S. (1969). Parental and peer influences on educational plans of adolescents. *American Sociological Review, 34*, 213–223.

Kantero, R., & Windholm, O. (1971). The age of menarche in Finnish girls in 1969. *Acta Obstetrics and Gynecology Scandinavia, 14*, 7–18.

Kantner, J., & Zelnick, M. (1972). Sexual experiences of young unmarried women in the U.S. *Family Planning Perspectives, 4*, 9–17.

Kantner, J., & Zelnick, M. (1973). Contraception and pregnancy: Experience of young unmarried women in the United States. *Family Planning Perspectives, 5*, 21–35.

Kaplan, H. B., Smith, P. G., & Pokorny, A. D. (1979). Psychosocial antecedents of unwed motherhood among indigent adolescents. *Journal of Youth and Adolescence, 8*, 181–207.

Karabel, J., & Astin, A. W. (1975). Social class, academic ability, and college "quality." *Social Forces, 53*, 381–398.

Katchadourian, M. (1977). *The biology of adolescence.* San Francisco: Freeman.

Katz, M. B., & Davey, I. F. (1978). Youth and early industrialization in a Canadian city. *American Journal of Sociology, 84*, (special supplement).

Kaufman, I., Peck, A. L., & Tagiuri, C. K. (1954). The family constellation and overt incestuous relations between fathers and daughters. *American Journal of Orthopsychiatry, 24*, 266–277.

Keating, D. P. (1980). Thinking processes in adolescence. In J. Adelson (Ed.), *Handbook of adolescent psychology.* New York: Wiley.

Keating, D. P., & Bobbitt, B. L. (1978). Individual and developmental differences in cognitive processing components of ability. *Child Development, 49*, 155–167.

Keil, C. (1966). *Urban blues.* Chicago: University of Chicago Press.

Kellam, S. (1979). *Consequences of teenage motherhood for mother, child, and family in a black urban community.* Progress reports to Center for Population Research. Bethesda, MD: National Institute of Child Health and Human Development.

Kelly, G. A. (1955). *The psychology of personal constructs* (2 vols.). New York: Norton.

Keniston, K. (1963). Social change and youth in America. In E. H. Erikson (Ed.), *The challenge of youth.* Garden City, NY: Anchor.

Keniston, K. (1968). *Young radicals: Notes on committed youth.* New York: Harcourt Brace Jovanovich.

Keniston, K. (1969). Moral development, youthful activism, and modern society. *Youth and Society, 1*, 110–127.

Keniston, K. (1970). Youth as a stage of life. *American Scholar, 39*, 631–634.

Keniston, K. (1971). Idealists: The perils of principle. In K. Keniston (Ed.), *Youth and dissent: The rise of a new opposition.* New York: Harcourt, Brace, Jovanovich.

Keniston, K. (1974). Psychological development and historical change. In R. J. Lifton (Ed.), *Explorations in psychohistory.* New York: Simon & Schuster.

Keniston, K. (1977). *All our children.* New York: Harcourt, Brace, Jovanovich.

Kenney, A., & Alexander, S. (1980). Sex/family life education in the schools: An analysis of state policies. *Family Planning/Population Reporter, 9*, 44–52.

Kestenberg, J. (1967a). Phases of adolescence with suggestions for correlation of psychic and hormonal organizations. Part I: Antecedents of adolescent organizations in childhood. *Journal of the American Academy of Child Psychiatry, 6*, 426–463.

Kestenberg, J. (1967b). Phases of adolescence with suggestions for correlation of psychic and hormonal organizations. Part II. Prepuberty, diffusion, and reintegration. *Journal of the American Academy of Child Psychiatry, 6*, 577–614.

Kestenberg, J. (1968). Phases of adolescence with suggestions for correlation of psychic and hormonal organizations. Part III. Puberty growth, differentiation, and consolidation. *Journal of the American Academy of Child Psychiatry, 7*, 108–511.

Kett, J. F. (1977). *Rites of passage.* New York: Basic Books.

Kilmann, P. R., Wanlass, R. J., Sabalis, R. F., & Sullivan, B. (1981). Sex education: A review of its effects. *Archives of Sexual Behavior, 10*, 177–205.

Kinsey, A. C., Pomeroy, W., & Martin, C. E. (1948). *Sexual behavior in the human male.* Philadelphia: Saunders.

Kinsey, A. C., Pomeroy, W. B., Martin, C. E., & Gebhard, P. H. (1953). *Sexual behavior in the human female.* Philadelphia: Saunders.

Kinsler, P. (1972). *Ego identity status and intimacy.* Unpublished doctoral dissertation, State University of New York at Buffalo.

Kirby, C. S. (1977). *Complexity-simplicity as a dimension of identity formation.* Unpublished doctoral dissertation, Michigan State University, East Lansing.

Kirby, D., Alter, J., & Scales, P. (1979). *An analysis of United States sex education programs and evaluation methods.* (Department of Health, Education, and Welfare Report No. CDC-2021-79-DK-FR). Washington DC: U.S. Government Printing Office.

Klein, J., & Litt, I. (1983). Menarche and dysmenorrhea. In J. Brooks-Gunn & A. Petersen (Eds.), *Girls at puberty.* New York: Plenum Press.

Klever, G. L., Woods, R. T., & Chapman, W. T. (1971). *The world of church youth.* Philadelphia: Board of Christian Education, United Presbyterian Church U.S.A.

Knorr, D., Bidlingmaier, F., Butenaudt, O., Feudel, H., & Ehrt-Wehle, R. (1974). Plasma testosterone in male puberty. 1. Physiology of plasma testosterone. *Acta Endocrinology, 75,* 181–194.

Knutson, J. (1972). *The human basis of polity: A psychological study of political men.* Chicago: Aldine-Atherton.

Kohlberg, L. (1958). *The development of modes of moral thinking and choice in the years 10 to 16.* Unpublished doctoral dissertation, University of Chicago.

Kohlberg, L. (1963). The development of children's orientations toward a moral order: I. Sequence in the development of moral thought. *Vita Humana, 6,* 11–33.

Kohlberg, L. (1966). A cognitive-developmental analysis of children's sex-role concepts and attitudes. In E. E. Maccoby (Ed.), *The development of sex differences.* Stanford, CA: Stanford University Press.

Kohlberg, L. (1973). The contribution of developmental psychology to education: Examples from moral education. *Educational Psychologist, 10,* 2–14.

Kohlberg, L. (1975, March). *The cognitive-developmental approach: New developments and a response to criticism.* Paper presented at the meeting of the Society for Research in Child Development, Denver, CO.

Kohlberg, L. (1976). Moral stages and moralization. The cognitive-developmental approach. In T. Lickona (Ed.), *Moral development and behavior.* New York: Holt, Rinehart, & Winston.

Kohlberg, L. (1978). Revisions in the theory and practice of moral development. *New Directions for Child Development, 2,* 83–88.

Kohlberg, L., & Gilligan, C. (1971). The adolescent as philosopher: The discovery of self in a post-conventional world. *Daedalus, 100,* 1051–1086.

Kohlberg, L., & Kramer, R. B. (1969). Continuities and discontinuities in childhood and adult moral development. *Human Development, 12,* 93–120.

Kohlberg, L., LaCrosse, J., & Ricks, D. (1972). The predictability of adult mental health from childhood behavior. In B. Wolman (Eds.), *Manual of Child Psychopathology.* New York: McGraw-Hill.

Kohlberg, L., & Mayer, R. (1972). Development as the aim of education. *Harvard Educational Review, 42,* 449–496.

Kohn, M. L. (1977). *Class and conformity: A study in values* (2nd ed.). Chicago: University of Chicago Press.

Kohn, M. L., & Clausen, J. (1955). Social isolation and schizophrenia. *American Sociological Review, 20,* 265–273.

Konopka, G. (1966). *The adolescent girl in conflict.* Englewood Cliffs, NJ: Prentice-Hall.

Korbin, J. (1977). Anthropological contributions to the study of child abuse. *Child Abuse and Neglect: The International Journal, 1,* 7–24.

Korbin, J. (1982). *Cross-cultural perspectives on child abuse.* Berkeley: University of California Press.

Kovar, M. (1979). Some indicators of health-related behavior among adolescents in the United States. *Public Health Reports, 94,* 109–118.

Kuhlen, R. G., & Lee, B. J. (1943). Personality characteristics and social acceptability in adolescence. *Journal of Educational Psychology, 34,* 321–340.

Kuhn, D. (1976). Short-term longitudinal evidence for the sequentiality of Kohlberg's early stages of moral development. *Developmental Psychology, 12,* 162–166.

Kuhn, T. (1962). *The structure of scientific revolutions.* Chicago: University of Chicago Press.

Kulin, H. E. (1972). Endocrine changes at puberty. In H. B. Barnett & A. H. Einhorn (Eds.), *Pediatrics,* (15th ed.). New York: Appleton-Century-Crofts.

Kurtines, W. (1978). A measure of autonomy. *Journal of Personality Assessment, 42,* 253–257.

LaBarre, M. (1972). Pregnancy experiences among married adolescents. *American Journal of Orthopsychiatry, 11,* 537–557.

L'Abata, L. (1971). The status of adolescent psychology. *Developmental Psychology, 4,* 201–205.

Ladner, J. (1971). *Tomorrow's tomorrow: The black women.* Garden City, NY: Doubleday & Company.

Lamb, M. E. (1976). The role of the father: An overview. In M. E. Lamb (Ed.), *The role of the father on child development.* New York: Wiley.

Lambert, T. A. (1972). Generations of change: Toward a theory of generations as a force in historical process. *Youth and Society, 4,* 21–34.

Landis, J. T. (1956). Experience of 500 children with adult sexual deviants. *Psychiatric Quarterly Supplement, 30,* 91–109.

Landis, J. T. (1970). A comparison of children for divorced and nondivorced unhappy marriages. *Family Life Coordinator, 11,* 61–65.

Landsbaum, J., & Willis, R. (1971). Conformity in early and late adolescence. *Developmental Psychology, 4,* 334–337.

Langford, P. E., & George, S. (1975). Intellectual and moral development in adolescence. *British Journal of Educational Psychology, 45,* 330–332.

Langton, K. P., & Jennings, M. K. (1968). Political socialization and the high-school civics curriculum in the United States. *American Political Science Review, 62,* 852–867.

Lanier, L. (1982). America's cults: Gaining ground again. *U.S. News and World Report, 93,* 37–41.

Laosa, L. M. (1979). Social competence in childhood: Toward a developmental, socioculturally relativistic paradigm. In M. W. Kent & J. E. Rolf (Eds.), *Primary prevention of psychopathology. Vol. III. Social competence in children.* Hanover, New Hampshire: University Press of New England.

Lasch, C. (1979). *The culture of narcissism.* New York: Norton.

Leadbetter, B. J., & Dionne, J. P. (1981). The adolescent's use of formal operational thinking in solving problems related to identity resolution. *Adolescence, 16(61),* 112–121.

LeBaron, R. (1972). *Hormones: A delicate balance.* New York: Pegasus.

Lecky, P. (1945). *Self-consistency: A theory of personality.* New York: Island Press.

Lefkowitz, M. M. (1977). Discussion of Dr. Gittelman-Klein's chapter. In S. G. Schulterbrandt & A. Raskin (Eds.), *Depression in childhood: Diagnosis, treatment, and conceptual models.* New York: Raven Press.

Leifer, A. D., & Lessor, G. S. (1976). *The development of career awareness in young children.* Washington, DC: National Institute of Education.

Lerner, R. M. (1969). The development of stereotyped expectancies of body build-behavior relations. *Child Development, 40,* 137–141.

Lerner, R. M. (1975). Showdown at generation gap: Attitudes of adolescents and their parents toward contemporary issues. In H. D. Thornburg (Ed.), *Contemporary adolescence: Readings* (2nd ed.). Belmont, CA: Brooks/Cole.

Lerner, R. M. (1982). Children and adolescents as producers of their own development. *Developmental Review, 2,* 342–370.

Lerner, R. M., & Busch-Rossnagel (Eds.). (1981). *Individuals as producers of their own development: A life-span perspective.* New York: Academic Press.

Lerner, R. M., & Hultsch, D. F. (1983). *Human development: A life-span perspective.* New York: McGraw-Hill.

Lerner, R. M., & Karabenick, S. (1974). Physical attractiveness, body attitudes, and self-concept in late adolescents. *Journal of Youth and Adolescence, 3,* 307–316.

Lerner, R. M., Karson, M., Meisels, M., & Knapp, J. R. (1975). Actual and perceived attitudes of late adolescents and their parents: The phenomenon of the generation gaps. *The Journal of Genetic Psychology, 126,* 195–207.

Lerner, R. M., & Knapp, J. R. (1975). Actual and perceived intrafamilial attitudes of late adolescents and their parents. *Journal of Adolescence, 4,* 17–36.

Lerner, R. M., Orlos, J. B., & Knapp, J. R. (1976). Physical attractiveness, physical effectivenss, and self-concept in late adolescents. *Adolescence, 11,* 313–326.

Lerner, R. M., Palermo, M., Spiro, A., & Nesselroade, J. R. (1982). Assessing the dimensions of temperamental individuality across the life span: The dimensions of temperament survey (DOTS). *Child Development, 53,* 149–159.

Lerner, R. M., & Spanier, G. B. (Eds.). (1978). *Child influences on marital and family interaction: a life-span perspective.* New York: Academic Press.

Lerner, R. M., & Spanier, G. B. (1980). *Adolescent development: A life-span perspective.* New York: McGraw-Hill.

Lester, D. (1979). Sex differences in suicidal behavior. In E. S. Gomberg & V. Franks (Eds.), *Gender and disordered behavior.* New York: Bruner/Mazel.

Levenkron, S. (1982). *Treating and overcoming anorexia nervosa.* New York: Warner Books.

Levine, D. V., Mitchell, E. S., & Havighurst, R. J. (1971). Opportunities for higher education in metropolitan area: A study of high school seniors in Kansas City, 1967. *Phi Delta Kappan.*

Levine, M. I. (1970). Sex education in the public elementary and high school curriculum. In D. L. Taylor (Ed.), *Human sexual developmment.* Philadelphia: Davis.

Levinson, D. J. (1978). *The seasons of a man's life.* New York: Ballantine.

Lewinsohn, P. M. (1974a). A behavioral approach to depression. In R. J. Friedman & M. M. Katz (Eds.), *The psychology of depression.* Washington, DC: Winston.

Lewinsohn, P. M. (1974b). Clinical and theoretical aspects of depression. In K. S. Calhoun, H. E. Adams, & K. M. Mitchell (Eds.), *Innovative treatment methods in psychopathology.* New York: Wiley & Sons.

Lewis, K. (1939). Field theory and experiment in social psychology: Concepts and methods. *American Journal of Sociology, 44,* 868–897.

Lewis, M., & Feiring, C. (1979). The child's social world. In R. Lerner & G. Spanier (Eds.), *Contributions of the child to marital quality and family interaction through the life-span.* New York: Academic Press.

Lewis, R. A. (1975). Social influences on marital choice. In S. E. Dragastin & G. H. Elder, Jr. (Eds.), *Adolescence in the life cycle.* New York: Wiley & Sons.

Libby, R. W.(1976). Social scripts for sexual relationships. In S. Gordan & R. W. Libby (Eds.), *Sexuality today and tomorrow.* North Scituate, MA: Duxbury Press.

Libertoff, K. (1980). The runaway child in America: A social history. *Journal of Family Issues, 1,* 151–164.

Liebert, R. N., Poulos, R. W., & Marmor, G. S. (1977). *Developmental Psychology.* Englewood Cliffs, NJ: Prentice-Hall.

Liebow, E. (1967). *Tally's corner.* Boston: Brown, Little, & Co.

Light, D., Jr., & Laufer, R. S. (1975). College youth: Psychohistory and prospects. In R. J. Havighurst & P. H. Drayer (Eds.), *Youth.* The seventy-fourth Yearbook of the National Society for the Study of Education. Chicago: University of Chicago Press.

Lindemann, C. (1974). *Birth control and unmarried young women.* New York: Springer Publishing Company.

Lips, H., & Colwill, N. (1978). *The psychology of sex differences.* Englewood Cliffs, NJ: Prentice-Hall.

Lipsitz, J. S. (1979). Adolescent development: Myths and realities. *Children Today, 8*(5), 2–7.

Livesley, W. J., & Bromley, D. B. (1973). *Person perception in childhood and adolescence.* New York: Wiley & Sons.

Lloyd, J. A. (1980, June). Education about sex in medical schools. *Medical Aspects of Human Sexuality, 131.*

Lockwood, A. (1976). Moral reasoning and public policy debate. In T. Lickona (Ed.), *Moral developmental behavior.* New York: Holt, Rinehart & Winston.

Loeber, R. (1982). The stability of antisocial and delinquent child behavior: A review. *Child Development, 53,* 1431–1446.

London, H., & Nisbett, R. E. (Eds.). (1974). *Thought and feeling.* Chicago: Aldine.

Longberg, B., Bickerstaff, M., & Fishbach, M. (1981). *Youth helping youth.* Boys Town, NE: Boys Town Center.

Lovell, K. A. (1961). A follow-up study of Inhelder and Piaget's "The growth of longitudinal thinking." *British Journal of Psychology, 52,* 143–153.

Lowrie, S. (1965). Early marriage: Premarital pregnancy and associated history. *Journal of Marriage and the Family, 27,* 49–56.

Luffman, D., & Parcel, G. S. (1979). Adaptation of an instrument to measure premarital sexual permissiveness attitudes in young adolescents. *Journal of Sex Education and Therapy, 6,* 21–24.

Luker, K. (1975). *Taking chances: Abortion and the decision not to contracept.* Berkeley: University of California Press.

Lynd, R. S., & Lynd, H. M. (1929). *Middletown: A study in modern American culture.* New York: Harcourt, Brace, & World.

Maccoby, E. E., & Jacklin, C. N. (1974). *The psychology of sex differences.* Stanford, CA: Stanford University Press.

MacFarlane, J. W., Allen, L., & Honzik, M. P. (1954). *A developmental study of the behavior problems of normal children.* Berkeley: University of California Press.

MacNamera, D. E. J. (1965). Male prostitution in American cities: A socioeconomic or pathological phenomenon? *American Journal of Orthopsychiatry, 35,* 204.

McAnarney, E. R. (1975). Suicidal behavior of children and youth. *Pediatric Clinics of North America, 22,* 595–604.

McCall, C., & Mark, M. E. (1983, July). Streets of the lost: Runaway kids eke out a mean life in Seattle. *Life,* 34–42.

McCandless, B. R. (1970). *Adolescents: Behavior and development.* Hinsdale, IL: Dryden Press.

McCary, J. L., & McCary, S. P. (1982). *McCary's human sexuality* (4th ed.). Belmont, CA: Wadsworth.

McClelland, D. C. (1973). Testing for competence rather than for "intelligence." *American Psychologist, 28,* 1–14.

McCord, J., & McCord, W. (1964). The effects of parental role model in criminality. In R. Carrin (Ed.), *Readings in Juvenile Delinquency.* Philadelphia: J. B. Lippincott.

McCord, J., McCord, W., & Thurber, E. (1963). Effects of maternal employment in lower-class boys. *Journal of Abnormal and Social Psychology, 76*(2), 177–182.

McGuire, R. J., Carlisle, J. M, & Young, B. G. (1965). Sexual deviations as conditioned behavior: A hypothesis. *Behavioral Research and Therapy, 2,* 185–190.

McLaughlin, G. W., Hunt, W. K., & Montgomery, J. R. (1976). Socioeconomic status and the career aspirations and perceptions of women seniors in high school. *Vocational Guidance Quarterly, 25,* 155–162.

McMorrow, F. (1977). *Midolescence: The dangerous years.* New York: Strawberry Hills Publishing Co.

Maddi, S. (1968). *Personality theories: A comparative analysis.* Homewood, IL: Dorsey Press.

Mahler, M., Pine, F., & Bergman, A. (1975). *The psychological birth of the human infant.* New York: Basic Books.

Malinowski, B. (1955). *The father in primitive psychology.* New York: Norton.

Maloney, D., Fixin, D., & Maloney, K. (1979). Behavior technology in child care: The Teaching-Parent and the Teaching-Family Model. In J. Beker (Ed.), *The child-care worker in the U.S.: A comparative analysis of involving role models.* New York: Human Sciences Press.

Manaster, G. (1977). *Adolescent development and the life tasks.* Boston: Allyn & Bacon.

Mannheim, K. (1952). The problem of generations. In K. Mannheim (Ed.), *Essays on the sociology of knowledge.* London: Routledge.

Maracek, J. (1979). *Economic, social and psychological consequences of adolescent childbearing.* Report to the Center for Population Research. Bethesda, MD: National Institute for Child Health and Human Development.

Marcia, J. E. (1966). Development and validation of ego-identity status. *Journal of Personality and Social Psychology, 3,* 551–558.

Marcia, J. (1967). Ego identity status: Relationship to change in self-esteem, "general maladjustment," and authoritarianism. *Journal of Personality, 35*(1), 119–133.

Marcia, J. (1976). *Studies in ego identity.* Unpublished research monograph. Simon Fraser University, Vancouver, British Columbia, Canada.

Marcia, J. (1980). Identity in adolescence. In J. Adelson (Ed.), *Handbook of Adolescent Psychology.* New York: John Wiley & Sons.

Marcia, J., & Friedman, M. L. (1970). Ego identity status in college women. *Journal of Personality, 38*(2), 249–263.

Maresh, M. (1972). A forty-five year investigation for secular changes in physical maturation. *American Journal of Physical Anthropology, 36,* 103–110.

Marini, M. M. (1978). Sex differences in the determination of adolescent aspirations: A review of the research. *Sex Roles, 4,* 723–753.

Marini, M. M. (1978). The transition to adulthood: Sex differences in educational attainment and age at marriage. *American Sociological Review, 43,* 484–507.

Marini, M. M., & Greenberger, E. (1978). Sex differences in occupational aspirations and expectations. *Sociology of Work and Occupations, 5,* 147–178.

Marks, A. (1977). Sex differences and their effects upon cultural evaluations of methods of self-destruction. *Omega, 8,* 65–70.

Marshall, D. S., & Suggs, R. C. (Eds.). (1971). *Harvard sexual behavior.* New York: Basic Books.

Marshall, W. A., & Tanner, J. M. (1970). Variations in the pattern of pubertal changes in boys. *Archives of Disabled Children, 45,* 13–23.

Marshall, W. A., & Tanner, J. M. (1974). Puberty. In J. D. Douvis & J. Drobeing (Eds.), *Scientific Foundation of Pediatrics.* London: William Heinemann Medical Books.

Martin, B. (1975). Parent-child relations. In F. D. Horowitz (Ed.), *Review of Child Development Research,* Vol. 4 (pp. 463–540). Chicago: University of Chicago Press.

Martin, J. E., & Kourany, R. F. C. (1980). Child abuse by adolescent babysitters. *Child Abuse and Neglect, 4,* 15–22.

Martinsen, F. M. (1955). Ego deficiency as a factor in marriage. *American Sociological Review, 20,* 161–164.

Martorano, S. (1974). *The developmental formal operational thought.* Unpublished doctoral dissertation, Rutgers University, New Brunswick, NJ.

Mass, G. D., Libby, R. W., & Fisher, M. P. (1981). *Sexual Choices.* Belmont, CA: Wadsworth Publishing Co.

Massachusetts Advocacy Center. (1980). *Delinquent justice: Juvenile detention practice in Massachusetts.* Boston, MA: Massachusetts Advocacy Center.

Master, W., & Johnson, V. (1970). *Human sexual inadequacy.* Boston: Little, Brown, & Co.

Masterson, J. F. (1967a). *The psychiatric dilemma of adolescence.* Boston: Little, Brown, & Co.

Masterson, J. F. (1967b). The symptomatic adolescent five years later: He didn't grow out of it. *American Journal of Psychiatry, 123,* 1338–1345.

Masterson, J. F. (1968). The psychiatric significance of adolescent turmoil. *American Journal of Psychiatry, 124,* 1549–1554.

Masterson, J. F. (1972). *Treatment of the borderline adolescent.* New York: Wiley.

Matteson, D. (1974). *Alienation vs. exploration and commitment: Personality and family correlates of adolescent identity statuses.* Report from the Project for Youth Research. Copenhagen: Royal Danish School of Educational Studies.

Maturana, H. (1975). The organization of the living: A theory of living organizations. *International Journal of Man-Machine Studies, 7,* 313–332.

Mead, G. H. (1934). *Mind, self, and society.* Chicago: University of Chicago Press.

Mead, M. (1929). *Coming of age in Samoa,* New York: Mentor.

Mead, M. (1952). Adolescence in primitive and modern society. In G. E. Swanson, T. M. Newcombe, & E. K. Hartley (Eds.), *Readings in social psychology,* (rev. ed.). New York: Henry Holt.

Mead, M. (1958). Adolescence in primitive and modern society. In G. E. Swanson, T. M. Newcombe, & E. K. Hartley (Eds.), *Readings in social psychology.* New York: Henry Holt.

Mead, M. (1970). *Culture and commitment: A study of the generation gap.* New York: Columbia University Press.

Mednick, S. A., & Schulsinger, F. (1970). Factors related to breakdown in children at high risk for schizophrenia. In M. Roff & D. F. Ricks (Eds.), *Life history research in psychopathology.* Minneapolis: University of Minnesota Press.

Meiselman, K. (1978). *Incest: A psychological study of causes and effects with treatment recommendation.* San Francisco: Jossey–Bass.

Melton, G. B. (1981). Children's participation in treatment planning: Psychological and legal issues. *Professional Psychology, 12,* 246–252.

Melton, G. (1983). Toward "personhood" for adolescents: Autonomy and privacy as values in public policy. *American Psychologist, 38,* 99–103.

Merton, R. (1961). *Social theory and social structure.* New York: Free Press of Glencoe.

Meyerding, J. (1977). Early sexual experience and prostitution. *American Journal of Psychiatry,* 1381–1385.

Meyerowitz, J. H., & Maler, J. S. (1973). Pubescent attitudinal correlates antecedent to adolescent illegitimate pregnancy. *Journal of Youth and Adolescence, 2,* 251–258.

Michael, C. M. (1957, January). Relative incidence of criminal behavior in long term follow-up studies of shy children. *Dallas Medical Journal.*

Michael, C. M., Morris, D. P., & Soroker, E. (1957). Follow-up studies of shy, withdrawn children II: Relative incidence of schizophrenia. *The American Journal of Orthopsychiatry, 27,* 331–337.

Milgram, S. (1974). *Obedience to authority: An experimental view.* New York: Harper & Row.

Miller, D., & Swanson, G. (1958). *The changing American parent.* New York: Wiley & Sons.

Miller, P. Y., & Simon, W. (1980). The development of sexuality in adolescence. In J. Adelson (Ed.), *Handbook of adolescent psychology.* New York: Wiley & Sons.

Miller, R. (1980). A decade of data on adult learners. *College Board Review, 114,* 16–17.

Miller, W. (1976). *Some psychological factors in undergraduate contraceptive use.* Paper presented at the 84th Convention of the American Psychological Association, Washington, DC.

Miller, W. (1980). Sexual and contraceptive behavior in young, unmarried women. In D. D. Young & A. Ehrhardt (Eds.), *Psychomatic obstetrics and gynecology.* New York: Appleton–Century–Crofts.

Millman, R. B. (1978). Drug and alcohol abuse. In B. Wolman, J. Egan, & A. O. Ross (Eds.), *Handbook of treatment of mental disorders in childhood and adolescence.* Englewood Cliffs, NJ: Prentice–Hall.

Miner, H. (1956). Body ritual among the Nacirema. *American Anthropologist, 58,* 352–369.

Minuchin, S., Baker, L., Rosman, B. L., Liebman, R., Milman, L., & Todd, T. C. (1975). A conceptual model of psychosomatic illness in children. *Archives of General Psychiatry, 32,* 1031–1038.

Molner, B., & Cameron, P. (1975). Incest syndromes: Observations in a general hospital psychiatric unit. *Canadian Psychiatric Association Journal, 20,* 1–24.

Money, J., & Erhardt, A. (1972). *Man and woman, boy and girl.* Baltimore: Johns Hopkins University Press.

Monge, R. H. (1973). Developmental trends in factors of adolescent self-concept. *Developmental Psychology, 8*(3), 382–393.

Montagu, A. (1972). Sociogenic brain damage. *American Anthropoligist, 74,* 1045–1061.

Montemayor, R., & Eisen, M. (1977). The development of self-conceptions from childhood to adolescence. *Developmental Psychology, 13,* 314–319.

Moore, K., & Hofferth, S. (1978). *Consequences of age at first childbirth: Final research summary.* Washington, DC: The Urban Institute.

Moos, R. (1969). A typology of menstrual cycle symptoms. *American Journal of Obstetrics and Gynecology, 103,* 390–402.

Morris, D. (1970). *The human zoo.* New York: Dell.

Morrison, P. (1978). *Consequences of late adolescent childbearing.* Preliminary report to Center for Population Research. Bethesda, MD: National Institute of Child Health and Human Development.

Morse, N. C., & Weiss, R. S. (1968). The function and measuring of work and the job. In D. G. Zytowski (Ed.), *Vocational behavior.* New York: Holt, Rinehart, & Winston.

Mortimer, J. T. (1974). Patterns of intergenerational occupational movements: A smallest spare analysis. *American Journal of Sociology, 5,* 1278–1295.

Mortimer, J. T. (1975). Occupational value socialization in business and professional families. *Sociology of Work and Occupation, 2,* 29–53.

Mortimer, J. T. (1976). Social class, work, and family: Some implications of the father's occupation for family relationships and son's career decisions. *Journal of Marriage and the Family, 38,* 241–254.

Mortimer, J. T., & Kumka, D. (1982). A further examination of the "occupational linkage hypothesis." *The Sociological Quarterly,* 3–16.

Moss, J. J., & Gingles, R. (1959). The relationship of personality and the incidence of early marriage. *Marriage and Family Living, 21,* 373–377.

Mullener, N., & Laird, J. D. (1971). Some developmental changes in the organization of self-evaluations. *Developmental Psychology, 5,* 233–236.

Murdock, G. P. (1949). *Social structure.* New York: Macmillan.

Musante, G. J. (1975). Behavior modification in prisons and correctional facilities. In W. Doyle Gentry (Ed.), *Applied behavior modification.* St. Louis, MO: C. V. Mosby.

Muuss, R. E. (1975). *Theories of adolescence.* New York: Random House.

NIAID Study Group. (1981). *Sexually transmitted diseases: 1980 status report.* (NIH Publications No. 81-2213). Washington, DC: U.S. Government Printing Office.

Nass, G. D., Libby, R. W., & Fisher, M. P. (1981). *Sexual choices.* Belmont, CA: Wadsworth.

National Abortion Rights Action League. (1979). *The Facts About Rape and Incest.* Washington, DC: National Abortion Rights Action League.

National Academy of Sciences. (1976). *Toward a national family policy.* Washington, DC: National Academy of Sciences.

National Center for Educational Statistics (NCES). (1980). *The condition of education: A statistical report on the condition of American education.* Washington, DC: U.S. Government Printing Office.

National Center for Health Statistics. (1976). *Physical characteristics of U.S. children.* Washington, DC: U.S. Government Printing Office.

National Center on Child Abuse and Neglect. (1978). *Child Sexual Abuse: Incest, Assault, and Sexual Exploitation.* (Publication No. 79-30166). Washington, DC: Department of Health, Education, and Welfare.

National Education Association. (1980). 1979 Teachers Poll. *Today's Education, 68,* 10.

Neimark, E. D. (1975). Intellectual development during adolescence. In F. D. Horowitz (Ed.), *Review of child development research* (Vol. 4). Chicago: University of Chicago Press.

Nelson, D. D. (1971). A study of personality adjustment among adolescent children with working and nonworking mothers. *Journal of Educational Research, 64,* 328–331.

Nesselroade, J., & Baltes, P. (1974). Adolescent personality development and historical change: 1970–1972. *SRCD Monographs, 39*(1), 1–80.

Neuber, K. A., & Guenther, R. W. (1977). The relationship between ego identity, personal responsibility, and facilitative communication. *Journal of Psychology, 95,* 45–49.

Neutens, J. J. (1980, June). Intimacy is not for amateurs. *Sexology Today,* sff.

Newman, M. J. (1979). The labor market experience of Black youth. *Monthly Labor Review, 102,* 19–27.

Newson, J., & Newson, E. (1974). Cultural aspects of child rearing in the English-speaking world. In M. P. M. Richards (Ed.), *The integration of a child into a social world.* Cambridge, England: Cambridge University Press.

Nydick, M., Bustos, J., Dale, J. H., Jr., & Rawson, R. (1961). Gynecomastia in adolescent boys. *Journal of the American Medical Association, 178,* 449–454.

Nye, F. I. (1958). *Family relationships and delinquent behavior.* New York: John Wiley & Sons.

Nye, F. I., & Edelbrock, C. (1980). Introduction: Some social characteristics of runaways. *Journal of Family Issues, 1,* 165–188.

Nylander, I. (1971). The feeling of being fat and dieting in a school population. *Acta Sociomed. Scandinavia, 3,* 17–26.

Offer, D. (1969). *The psychological world of the teenager: A study of normal adolescent boys.* New York: Basic Books.

Offer, D., & Offer, J. (1975). Normal adolescence in perspective. In J. C. Schoolar (Ed.), *Current issues in adolescent psychiatry.* New York: Brunner/Mazel.

Offer, D., & Offer, J. D. (1974). Normal adolescent males: The high school and college years. *Journal of the American College Health Association, 22,* 209–215.

Offer, D., & Offer, J. D. (1975). *From teenager to young manhood: A psychological study.* New York: Basic Books.

Offer, D., Ostrov, E., & Howard, K. I. (1981). The mental health professional's concept of the normal adolescent. *Archives of General Psychiatry, 38,* 149–152.

Ogbu, J. U. (1981). Origins of human competence: A cultural-ecological perspective. *Child Development, 52,* 413–429.

O'Hara, R. P. (1962). Acceptance of vocational interest areas by high school students. *Vocational Guidance Quarterly, 1962, 10,* 101–105.

Oldham, D. G. (1978). Adolescent turmoil: A myth revisited. In S. C. Feinstein & P. L. Gioracchini (Eds.), *Adolescent psychiatry.* (Vol. VI). Chicago: University of Chicago Press.

Olson, D., Russell, C., & Sprenkle, D. (1979). Circumplex model of marital interaction and family systems. *Family Process, 18,* 3–29.

Olson, L. (1982). *Costs of children.* Lexington, MA: Lexington Books.

Olson, L., Liebow, E., Mannino, E. V., & Shore, M. F. (1980). Runaway children twelve years later: A follow-up. *Journal of Family Issues, 1,* 165–188.

O'Malley, J. M. (1977). Research perspective on social competence. *Merrill-Palmer Quarterly, 23,* 29–44.

Orleans, C. T., & Barnett, L. R. (1980). *Bulimarexia: Guidelines for behavioral assessment and treatment.* Paper presented at the 19th annual meeting of the Association for Advancement of Behavior Therapy. New York.

Orlofsky, J. L., Marcia, J. E., & Lesser, I. M. (1973). Ego identity status and the intimacy vs. isolation crisis of young adulthood. *Journal of Personality and Social Psychology, 27*(2), 211–219.

Orr, M. (1982). Sex education and contraceptive education in U.S. public high schools. *Family Planning Perspective, 14,* 305–313.

Oshman, H. P., & Manosevitz, M. (1974). The impact of the identity crisis on the adjustment of late-adolescent males. *Journal of Youth and Adolescence, 3,* 207–216.

Osipow, S. H. (1973). *Theories of career development* (2nd ed.). Englewood Cliffs, NJ: Prentice-Hall.

Oskamp, S., & Mindick, B. (1981). Personality and attitudinal barriers to contraception. In D. Byrne & W.A. Fisher (Eds.), *Adolescents, sex, and contraception.* New York: McGraw-Hill.

Osuji, O. N. (1976). Patterns of occupational drive and aspirations in conditions of economic and technological underdevelopment. *Journal of Vocational Behavior, 8,* 133–144.

Outpatient Psychiatric Services. (1969). U.S. Dept. of Health, Education, and Welfare, Public Health Service Publication No. 1982. Washington DC: U.S. Government Printing Office.

Packard, V. (1983). *Our endangered children: Growing up in a changing world.* Boston: Little & Brown.

Padin, M. A., Lerner, R. M., & Spiro, III. (1981). A stability of body attitudes and self-esteem in late adolescents. *Adolescence, 16*(62), 371–384.

Page, E. B., & Grandan, G. M. (1979). Family configuration and mental ability: Two theories contrasted with U.S. data. *American Educational Research Journal, 16,* 257–272.

Parke, R., & Collmer, C. W. (1975). Child abuse: An interdisciplinary analysis. In E. M. Hetherington (Ed.), *Review of child development research* (Vol. 5). Chicago: University of Chicago Press.

Parsons, T. (1960). *Essays in sociological theory.* New York: The Free Press.

Pasley, K., & Grecias, V. (1984, March). Stresses and Satisfactions of the Parental Role. *Personnel and Guidance Journal,* 400–404.

Patterson, G. (1976). *Living with children: New methods for parents and teachers.* New York: Research Press.

Peel, E. (1971). *The nature of adolescent judgment.* New York: Wiley–Interscience.

Peevers, B. H., & Secord, P. F. (1973). Developmental changes in attribution of descriptive concepts to persons. *Journal of Personality and Social Psychology, 27,* 120–128.

Pellegrino, E. D. (1981). The challenge of shaping a personal identity. In A. C. Eurich (Ed.), *Major transitions in the human life cycle.* Lexington, MA: Lexington.

Perkinson, H. J. (1977). *The imperfect panacea: American faith in education, 1865-1976* (2nd ed.). New York: Random House.

Peshkin, A. (1978). *Growing up American.* Chicago: University of Chicago Press.

Peskin, H. (1973). Pubertal onset and ego functioning. *Journal of Abnormal Psychology, 72,* 1–15.

Peters, J. J. (1976). Children who were victims of sexual assault and the psychology of offenders. *American Journal of Psychotherapy, 30,* 398–412.

Petersen, A. (1979). Can puberty come any earlier? *Psychology Today, 12*(9), 45–47.

Petersen, A. (1982). Adolescent health: Developmental issues. In T. Coates, A. Petersen, & C. Perry (Ed.), *Adolescent health: Crossing the barriers.* New York: Academic Press.

Petersen, A. (1983). Pubertal changes and cognition. In J. Brooks-Gunn & A. Petersen (Eds.), *Girls at puberty.* New York: Plenum Press.

Petersen, A., & Kellam, S. (1977). Measurement of the psychological well-being of adolescents: The psychometric properties of the How I Feel. *Journal of Youth and Adolescence, 6,* 229–247.

Petersen, A., & Taylor, B. (1980). The biological approach to adolescence: Biological change and psychological adaptation. In J. Adelson (Ed.),

Handbook of adolescent psychology. New York: Wiley & Sons.

Peterson, D. R., & Beecher, W. C. (1965). Family interaction and delinquency. In H. C. Quay (Ed.), *Juvenile delinquency: Research and theory* (pp. 36–99). Princeton: NJ: D. Van Nostrand Co.

Peterson, R. A., & Kunz, P. R. (1975). Parental control over adolescents according to family size. *Adolescence, 10,* 419–427.

Peterson, R. A., & Sharpe, L. K. (1972). Effects of ordinal position: Tri partite analysis. *Psychological Reports, 30*(3), 890.

Phillips, E. L., Phillips, E. A., Fixen, D. L., & Wolf, M. M. (1974). *The teaching-family handbook*. Lawrence, KS: University of Kansas Printing Services.

Piaget, J. (1932). *The moral judgment of the child*. New York: Harcourt.

Piaget, J. (1950). *The psychology of intelligence* (M. Percy & D.E. Berlyne, Trans.). London: Routledge & Kegan Paul.

Piaget, J. (1952). *The origins of intelligence in children* (M. Cook, Trans.). New York: International Press.

Piaget, J. (1960). *The child's conception of physical causality* (M. Gabain, Trans.). Totowa, NJ: Littlefield, Adams.

Piaget, J., & Inhelder, B. (1969). *The psychology of the child* (H. Weaver, Trans.). New York: Basic Books. (Originally published, 1966).

Pines, M. (1979, January). Superkids. *Psychology Today,* 53–63.

Pitt, R. B. (1976). *Toward a comprehensive model of problem-solving: Application to solutions of chemistry problems in high school and college students*. Unpublished doctoral dissertation, University of California, San Diego.

Piven, H. (1979). The status offender controversy: Changes and study evidence. *Child Welfare, 8,* 484–499.

Poffenberger, T. (1964). Three papers on going steady. *Family Life Coordinator, 13,* 7–13.

Polansky, N. (1976). Analysis of research on child neglect: The social work viewpoint. In Herner & Company (Eds.), *Four perspectives on the status of child abuse and neglect research*. Washington, DC: National Center on Child Abuse and Neglect.

Polory, P. (1980). A study of moral development and personality relationships in adolescents and young adult Catholic students. *Journal of Clinical Psychology, 36*(3), 752–757.

Pomeroy, B. (1965). Some aspects of prostitution. *The Journal of Sex Research, 1*(3), 117–187.

Ponzo, Z., & Strowig, R. W. (1973). Relations among self-role identity and selected intellectual and non-intellectual factors for high school freshman and seniors. *Journal of Educational Research, 67*(3), 137–141.

Popper, K. (1972). *Objective knowledge: An evolutionary approach*. London: Oxford University Press.

Post, S. (1982). Adolescent parricide in abusive families. *Child Welfare, 61,* 445–455.

Pounds, R. L., & Bryner, J. R. (1973). *The school in American society* (3rd ed.). New York: Macmillan.

Powell, G. J., & Fuller, M. (1970). Self-concept and school desegregation. *American Journal of Orthopsychiatry, 40,* 303–304.

Prabhaker, A. K., Sundaram, K. R., Ramanujacharyulu, T. K. T. S., & Taskour, A. D. (1972). Influence of socioeconomic factors on the age of the appearance of different puberty signs. *Indian Journal of Medical Research, 60,* 789–192.

Prescott, J. W. (1975). Body pleasure and the origins of violence. *The Futurist, 9,* 64–74.

Presser, H. (1974). Early motherhood: Ignorance or bliss? *Family Planning Perspectives, 6,* 2.

Pressler, H. (1976, March). *Social factors affecting the timing of the first child*. Paper presented at the conference on the First Child and Family Formation, Pacific Grove, CA.

Pressler, H. (1977, May/June). Guessing and misinformation about pregnancy risk among urban mothers. *Family Planning Perspectives, 9,* 234–236.

Pressler, H. (1980). *The social and demographic consequences of teenage childbearing for urban women*. Final report to Center for Population Research. Bethesda, MD: National Institute of Child Health and Human Development.

Price, J. (1968). The genetics of depressive disorder. In A. Coppen & A. Walk (Eds.), Recent developments in affective disorders: A symposium. *British Journal of Psychiatry Special Publication No. 2*. Ashford: Headley.

Profiles in ignorance. (1981, December 20). *The New York Times,* p. 20 ff.

Propper, A. M. (1972). The relationship of maternal employment to adolescent roles, activities, and parental relationships. *Journal of Marriage and the Family, 34,* 417–421.

Prostitutes: The new breed. (1971, July 12). *Newsweek, 78.*

Quay, H. C. (1979). Classification. In H. C. Quay & J. S. Werry (Eds.), *Psychopathological disorders of childhood* (2nd ed.). New York: Wiley & Sons.

Quay, H. C., & Werry, J. S. (Eds.). (1972). *Psychopathological disorders of childhood*. New York: Wiley & Sons.

Rains, P. (1971). *Becoming an unwed mother*. Chicago: Aldine.

Ramey, J. (1979, May). Dealing with the last taboo. *SIECUS Report 7.*

Ramirez, M. III., & Castenada, A. (1974). *Cultural democracy, biocognitive development, and education*. New York: Academic Press.

Raphael, D., & Xelowski, H. G. (1980). Identity status in high school students: Critique and a revised paradigm. *Journal of Youth and Adolescence, 9,* 383–389.

Raywid, M. A. (1981). The first decade of public school alternatives. *Phi Delta Kappan, 62,* 551–554.

Rees, A. N., & Palmer, F. H. (1970). Factors related to change in mental performance. *Developmental Psychology Monograph, 3*(2, Pt. 2).

Rehberg, R. A. (1969). Behavioral and attitudinal consequences of high school interscholastic sports: A speculative consideration. *Adolescence, 4*, 69–88.

Reich, C. A. (1970). *The greening of America.* New York: Random House.

Reiss, I. (1967). *The social context of sexual permissiveness.* New York: Holt, Rinehart, & Winston.

Reiss, I. (1980). *Family systems in America* (3rd ed.). New York: Holt, Rinehart, & Winston.

Reiss, I. (1981). Some observations on ideology and sexuality in America. *Journal of Marriage and the Family, 43*, 271–283.

Renshon, S. A. (1974). *Psychological needs and political behavior.* New York: Free Press.

Rest, J. R. (1975). Longitudinal study of the defining issues test of moral judgment: A strategy for analyzing developmental change. *Developmental Psychology, 11*, 738–748.

Rest, J. R. (1976). New approaches in the assessment of moral judgment. In T. Lickona (Ed.), *Moral development and behavior.* New York: Holt, Rinehart, & Winston.

Rest, J. R., Cooper, D., Coder, R., Masanz, J., & Anderson, D. (1976). Judging the important issues in moral dilemmas—an objective measure of development. *Developmental Psychology, 10*, 491–501.

Rheingold, H. C. (1969). The social and socializing infant. In D. A. Goslin (Ed.), *Handbook of socialization theory and research.* Chicago: Rand McNally.

Rhodes, W. C. (1970). A community participation analysis of emotional disturbance in children. *Exceptional Children, 34*, 309–314.

Rice, S. P. (1981). *The adolescent: Development, relationships, and culture* (3rd ed.). Boston: Allyn & Bacon.

Richardson, R. (1981). *Family size and parent-child interaction.* Unpublished master's thesis. Pennsylvania State University.

Richardson, R. A., & Pfeiffenberger, C. A. (1983). Social support networks for families of divorce and remarriage. In J. Whittaker & J. Garbarino (Eds.), *Social support networks: Informal helping in the human services.* New York: Aldine.

Ridgeway, C. (1978). Parental identification and patterns of career orientation in college women. *Journal of Vocational Behavior, 12*, 1–11.

Riegel, K. (1976). The dialectics of human development. *American Psychologist, 31*, 689–699.

Rivlin, R. S. (1969). Thyroid hormone and the adolescent growth spurt: Clinical and fundamental considerations. In F. Heald (Ed.), *Adolescent growth and nutrition.* New York: Appleton-Century-Crofts.

Roberts, R. E., Abrams, L., & Finch, J. R. (1973). "Delinquent" sexual behavior among adolescents. *Medical Aspects of Human Sexuality, 7*, 162–183.

Robins, L. N. (1966). *Deviant children grown up.* Baltimore, MD: Williams & Wilkins.

Robins, L. N. (1972). Follow-up studies of behavior disorders in children. In H. C. Quay & J. S. Wenny (Eds.), *Psychopathological disorders of childhood.* New York: Wiley.

Robins, L. N. (1979). Sturdy childhood predictors of adult antisocial behavior: Replications from longitudinal studies. *Psychological Medicine, 8*, 611–622.

Robins, L. N., & Wish, E. (1977). Childhood deviance as a developmental process: A study of 223 urban black men from birth to 18. *Social Forces, 56*, 448–473.

Robinson, I. E., & Jedlicka, D. (1982). Change in sexual attitudes and behavior in college students for 1965 to 1980: A research note. *Journal of Marriage and the Family, 44*, 237–240.

Roche, A., French, N., & DaVila, D. (1971). Areolar size during adolescence. *Human Biology, 43*, 210–223.

Rocnick, E. H., & Goldstein, M. J. (1974). A research strategy for studying risk for schizophrenia during adolescence and early adulthood. In J. Anthony & C. Koupernick (Eds.), *The child in his family: Children at psychiatric risk,* (Vol. 3). New York: Wiley.

Roff, M. (1972). Some life history factors in relation to various types of adult maladjustment. In M. Ross & D. Ricks (Eds.), *Life history research in psychopathology.* Minneapolis: University of Minnesota Press.

Roff, M., & Sells, S. B. (1968). Juvenile delinquency in relation to peer acceptance-rejection and socioeconomic status. *Psychology in the schools, 5*, 3–18.

Roff, M., Sells, S., & Golden, M. (1972). *Social adjustment and personality development in children.* Minneapolis: University of Minnesota Press.

Rogers, C. (1951). *Client-centered therapy.* New York: Houghton Mifflin.

Rogers, D. (1969). *Psychology of adolescence.* Albany: State University of New York.

Rogers, D. (1981). *Adolescents and youth* (4th ed.). Englewood Cliffs, NJ: Prentice-Hall.

Rogers, T. (1980). *At the shores.* New York: Simon & Schuster.

Rohner, R. (1975). *They love me, they love me not.* New Haven, CT: HRAF Press.

Rollins, B. C., & Thomas, D. L. (1979). Parental support, power, and control techniques in the socialization of children. In W. R. Burr, R. Hill, F. I. Nye, & I. L. Reiss (Eds.), *Contemporary theories about the family: Research based theories.* (Vol. 1). New York: The Free Press.

Root, A. W. (1973). Endocrinology of puberty 1. Normal sexual maturation. *Journal of Pediatrics, 83*, 187–200.

Rose, R., Holaday, J., & Bernstein, I. (1971). Plasma testosterone, dominance rank, and aggressive behavior in male rhesus monkeys. *Nature, 231*, 366–368.

Rosen, B. C. (1955). The reference group approach to the parental factor in attitude and behavior formation. *Social Forces, 34*, 137–144.

Rosen, B. M., Bahn, A. K., and Shellow, R. (1965). Adolescent patients served in outpatient psychiatric clinics. *American Journal of Public Health, 55*, 1563–1577.

Rosen, R., & Davidson, J. (Eds.). (1977). *The Maimie Papers.* Old Westbury, NY: The Feminist Press.

Rosen, R., Hudson, A., & Martindale, L. (1976). *Contraception, abortion, and self-concept.* Paper presented to the American Sociological Association, Washington, DC.

Rosen, R. A., Martindale, L., & Grisdela, M. (1976). *Pregnancy study report.* Detroit, MI: Wayne State University.

Rosenbach, D., Crockett, W. H., & Wapner, S. (1973). Developmental level, emotional involvement and the resolution of inconsistency in impression formation. *Developmental Psychology, 8,* 120–130.

Rosenbaum, J. (1975). The stratification of socialization processes. *American Sociological Review, 40,* 48–54.

Rosenberg, B., & Sutton-Smith, B. (1972). *Sex and identity.* New York: Holt, Rinehart, & Winston.

Rosenberg, M. (1965). *Society and the adolescent self-image.* Princeton, NJ: Princeton University Press.

Rosenblatt, R. (1983). *Children of war.* New York: Doubleday.

Rosenfeld, C., & Grover, K. F. (1972). Employment of school-age youth. *Monthly Labor Review, 95,* 26–30.

Rosenfeld, R. U. (1972). *The relationship of ego identity to similarity among self, ideal self, and probable occupational-role concept among college males.* Unpublished doctoral dissertation, University of Maryland, College Park.

Rosenkrantz, A. L. (1968). Sex-role stereotypes and self-concepts in college students. *Journal of Consulting and Clinical Psychology, 32*(3), 287–295.

Rosenthal, D. M. (1979). Working and nonworking mothers in intact and non-intact families. *Dissertation Abstracts International, 39*(8-A), 5152.

Rosenthal, N. H. (1973). The United States economy in 1985: Projected changes in occupations. *Monthly Labor Review, 96,* 18–26.

Ross, S. (1979). *The youth values project.* Washington, DC: Population Institute.

Rotenberg, M. (1977). "Alienating-individualism" and "reciprocal-individualism": A cross-cultural conceptualization. *Journal of Humanistic Psychology, 17*(3), 3–17.

Rouman, J. (1956). School children's problems as related to parental factors. *Journal of Educational Research, 50,* 105–112.

Rowe, I., & Marcia, J. E. (1980). Ego Identity status, formal operations, and moral development. *Journal of Youth and Adolescence, 9*(2), 87–99.

Royce, J. E. (1973). Does person or self imply dualism? *American Psychologist,* 883–886.

Rubenstein, J. S. (1976). Young adolescents' sexual interests. *Adolescence, 11,* 487–496.

Ruebans, B., Harrison, J., & Rupp, A. (1981). *The youth labor force 1945–1995: A cross national analysis.* Totowa, NJ: Alanheld, Ossman.

Russ-Eft, D., Sprenger, M., & Beever, A. (1979). Antecedents of adolescent parenthood and consequences at age 30. *Family Coordinator, 28,* 173–178.

Russel, D. H. (1971). On the psychopathology of boy prostitutes. *International Journal of Offender Therapy, 15,* 49.

Russell, G. F. M. (1979). Bulimia nervosa: An ominous variant of anorexia nervosa. *Psychological Medicine, 9,* 429–448.

Rutter, M., Graham, P., Chadwick, O. F. D., & Yule, W. (1976). Adolescent turmoil: Fact or fiction? *Journal of Child Psychology and Psychiatry, 17,* 35–56.

Rutter, M., Tizard, J., & Whitmore, K. (1970). *Education, health, and behaviour.* New York: Wiley.

Ryan, W. (1976). *Blaming the victim.* New York: Vintage Press.

Ryder, N. (1965). The cohort as a concept in the study of social change. *American Sociological Review, 30,* 843–861.

Ryder, R., Kafka, J., & Olson, D. (1971). Separating and joining influences in courtship and early marriage. *American Journal of Orthopsychiatry, 41,* 450–464.

Sacker, I. M., & Neuhoff, S. D. (1982). Medical and psychosocial risk factors in the pregnant adolescent. In I. R. Stuart & C. F. Wells (Eds.), *Pregnancy in adolescence.* New York: Van Nostrand Reinhold.

Sale, K. (1980). *Human scale.* New York: Coward, McCann, & Geoghegan.

Sameroff, A. J., & Chandler, M. (1975). Reproductive risk and the continuum of caretaking causality. In F. D. Horowitz, M. Heatherington, & S. G. Siget (Eds.), *Review of child development research* Chicago: University of Chicago Press.

Sampson, E. E. (1962). Birth order, need achievement, and conformity. *Journal of Abnormal and Social Psychology, 64,* 155–159.

Sanders, R., & Spanier, G. (1979). *Divorce, child custody, and child support.* (U.S. Bureau of the Census, Current Population Reports Series P-23, No. 84). Washington, DC: U.S. Government Printing Office.

Santrock, J. W. (1975). Father absence, perceived maternal behavior and moral development in boys. *Child Development, 46,* 753–757.

Santrock, J. W. (1981). *Adolescence: An introduction.* Dubuque, IA: William C. Brown Company.

Sarafino, J. (1979). An estimate of nationwide incidence of sexual offense against children. *Child Welfare, 58,* 127–134.

Sarason, S. B. (1971). *The culture of the school and the problem of change.* Boston: Allyn-Bacon.

Sarason, S. B. (1978). The nature of problem solving in social action. *American Psychologist, 33,* 370–380.

Sargent, W. (1971). *Battle for the mind: The physiology of conversion and brain washing.* New York: Harper & Row.

Sargent, W. (1975). *The mind possessed.* New York: Penguin Books.

Sarrel, L. J., & Sarrel, P. M. (1979). *Sexual unfolding: Sexual development and sex therapies in late adolescence.* Boston: Little, Brown.

Sarri, R. E. (1976). Juvenile law: How it penalizes females. In L. Cites (Ed.), *The female offender*. Lexington, MA: D.C. Heath & Co., Lexington Books.

Savin-Williams, R. (1976). An ethological study of dominance formation and maintenance in a group of human adolescents. *Child Development, 47,* 972–979

Scales, P. (1977). Males and morals: Teenage contraceptive behavior amid the double standard. *The Family Coordinator, 26,* 211–222.

Scales, P. (1981). Sex education in the '70's and '80's: Accomplishments, obstacles, and emerging results. *Family Relations, 30,* 557–566.

Scales, P., and Kirby, D. (1981). A review of exemplary sex education programs for teenagers offered by nonschool organizations. *Family Relations, 30,* 238–245.

Schacter, S., & Singer, J. E. (1962). Cognitive, social, and physiological determinants of emotional state. *Psychological Review, 69,* 379–399.

Schaefer, E. S. (1959). A circumplex model for maternal behavior. *Journal of Abnormal and Social Psychology, 59,* 226–235.

Schaefer, E. S., & Bayley, N. (1960). Consistency of maternal behavior from infancy to preadolescence. *Journal of Abnormal and Social Psychology, 61,* 1–6.

Schaefer, E. S., & Bayley, N. (1963). *Maternal behavior, child behavior, and their intercorrelations from infancy through adolescence.* Monographs of the Society for Research in Child Development, 28, 1–127.

Schaeffer, G. (1967, July). Sex and family milieu. *General Practitioner.*

Schafer, S. (1976). Sexual and social problems of lesbians. *Journal of Sex Research, 12,* 50–69.

Scharff, D., Silber, T., Tripp, G., McGee, Bowie, S., & Emerson, B. (1980). Use of a sex rap group in an adolescent medical clinic. *Adolescence, 15,* 751–762.

Scheck, D., Emerick, R., & El-Assal, M. (1973). Adolescents' perceptions of parent-child relations and the development of internal-external control orientation. *Journal of Marriage and the Family, 35,* 643–654.

Scheck, D. C., & Emerick, R. (1976). The young male adolescent's perception of early child rearing effects of socioeconomic status and family size. *Sociometry, 39,* 39–52.

Schein, E. H. (1971). *Coercive persuasion.* New York: W. Norton & Company, Inc.

Schein, E. H. (1978). *Career dynamics: Matching individual and organization needs.* Reading, MA: Addison Wesley.

Schell, J. (1982). *The fate of the Earth.* New York: Knopf.

Schellenbach, C. J., Sebes, J. M., Ford, D. H., Garbarino, J., & Guerney, L. (1982). *The human ecology of adolescent maltreatment: Prediction and assessment.* Unpublished manuscript, Pennsylvania State University, University Park.

Schenke, S. P., Gilchrist, L. D., & Small, R. W. (1979). Preventing unwanted adolescent pregnancy: A cognitive-behavioral approach. *American Journal of Orthopsychiatry, 49,* 81–88.

Schenkel, S. (1975). Relationship among ego identity status, field-independence, and traditional femininity. *Journal of Youth and Adolescence, 4,* 73–82.

Schilling, K. L. (1975). *Ego identity status: A reevaluation and extension of construct validity.* Unpublished doctoral dissertation, University of Florida, Gainesville.

Schneiders, A. (1965). *Adolescents and the challenge of maturity.* Milwaukee, WI: Bruce Publishing Company.

Schonfeld, W. (1966). Body-image disturbances in adolescents: Influence of family attitudes and psychopathology. *Archives of General Psychiatry, 15,* 16–21.

Schonfeld, W. (1969). The body and body image. In G. Caplan & S. Leibovici (Eds.), *Adolescence: Psychosocial perspectives.* New York: Basic Books.

Schrut, A. (1968). Some typical patterns in the behavior and background of adolescent girls who commit suicide. *American Journal of Psychiatry, 125,* 69–74.

Schulenberg, J. E., Vondracek, F. W., & Crouter, A. C. (1984). The influence of the family on vocational development. *Journal of Marriage and the Family, 46,* 366–374.

Schumacher, E. F. (1973). *Small is beautiful: Economics as if people mattered.* New York: Harper & Row.

Schumacher, E. F. (1979). *Good Work.* New York: Harper Colophon.

Schwartz, B. (1978). *Psychology of learning and behavior.* New York: W. W. Norton & Co.

Schwartz, D. M., Thompson, M. G., & Johnson, C. L. (1982). Anorexia nervosa and bulimia: The socio-cultural context. *International Journal of Eating Disorders, 1*(3), 20–36.

Schwartz, G. (1977). *Summary and policy implications of the youth and society in Illinois reports.* Chicago: Institute for Juvenile Research.

Schwartz, S. K. (1975). Preschoolers and politics. In D. C. Schwartz & S. K. Schwartz (Eds.), *New directions in political socialization.* New York: Free Press.

Scientific Analysis Corporation. (1976). Runaways: Illegal aliens in their own land—implications for service. Final report. Unpublished paper, Scientific Analysis Corporation, San Francisco.

Sears, R. R. (1951). A theoretical framework for personality and social behavior. *American Psychologist, 6,* 476–483.

Sebald, H. (1981). Adolescents' concept of popularity and unpopularity, comparing 1960 with 1976. *Adolescence, 16*(61), 187–193.

Sebes, J. (1983). *Determining probable risk for maltreatment in families with adolescents: The development of a predictor measure.* Unpublished dissertation, Pennsylvania State University, State College, PA.

Seiden, R. H. (1969). *Suicide among youth.* (Public Health Service Publication No. 1971). Washington

DC: U.S. Department of Health, Education, and Welfare.

Seligman, M. E. P. (1974). Depression and learned helplessness. In R. J. Friedman & M. M. Katz (Eds.), *The psychology of depression.* Washington, DC: Winston.

Seligman, M. E. P. (1975). *Helplessness: On depression, development, and death.* San Francisco: W. H. Freeman.

Sellin, T., & Wolfgang, M. (1964). *The measurement of delinquency.* New York: Wiley.

Selman, R. L. (1971). Taking another's perspective: Role-taking development in early childhood. *Child Development, 42,* 1721–1734.

Selman, R. L. (1976a). The development of social-cognitive understanding: A guide to educational and clinical practice. In T. Lickona (Ed.), *Moral development and behavior.* New York: Holt, Rinehart, & Winston.

Selman, R. L. (1976b). Toward a structural analysis of developing interpersonal relations concepts: Research with normal and disturbed preadolescent boys. In A. D. Pick (Ed.), *Minnesota Symposia on Child Psychology* (Vol. 10). Minneapolis: University of Minnesota Press.

Selman, R. L. (1977). A structural-developmental model of social cognition: Implications for intervention research. *The Counseling Psychologist, 6,* 3–6.

Selman, R. L. (1980). *The growth of interpersonal understanding: Developmental and clinical analyses.* New York: Academic Press.

Selman, R. L., & Byrne, D. F. (1974). A structural-developmental analysis of levels of role-taking in middle childhood. *Child Development, 45,* 803–806.

Selman, R. L., & Selman, A. P. (1979, October). Children's ideas about friendship: A new theory. *Psychology Today, 13*(4), 71–72.

Sewell, W. (1971). Inequality of opportunity for higher education. *American Sociological Review, 36,* 793–807.

Sewell, W., & Shah, V. (1967). Socioeconomic status, intelligence, and the attainment of higher education. *Sociology of Education, 40,* 1–23.

Shaftel, F. R., & Shaftel, G. (1967). *Role playing for social values: Decision making in the social studies.* Englewood Cliffs, NJ: Prentice–Hall.

Shah, F., Zelnick, M., & Kantner, J. (1975). Unprotected intercourse among unwed teenagers. *Family Planning Perspectives, 1,* 39.

Shellow, R., Schamp, J., Liebow, E., & Unger, E. (1967). Suburban runaways in the 1960's. *Monographs of the Society for Research in Child Development, 32.*

Shirer, W. (1960). *The rise and fall of the Third Reich: A history of Nazi Germany.* New York: Simon & Schuster.

Short, J. F. (1974). Youth, gangs, and society: Micro- and macrosociological processes. *Sociological Quarterly, 15,* 3–19.

Short, J. F., & Nye, F. I. (1957). Reported behavior as a criterion of deviant behavior. *Social Problems, 5,* 207–213.

Shrauger, J. S., & Schoeneman, T. J. (1979). Symbolic interactionist view of self-concept: Through the looking glass darkly. *Psychological Bulletin, 86,* 549–573.

Shribman, D. (1982, June 20). "When part-time work beats full-time school." *New York Times,* p. E-7.

Shultz, T. R., & Butkowsky, I. (1977). Young children's use of the scheme for multiple sufficient causes in the attribution of real and hypothetical behavior. *Child Development, 48,* 464–469.

Siegler, R. S., & Liebert, R. M. (1975). Acquisition of formal scientific reasoning by 10- and 13-year-olds: Designing a factorial experiment. *Developmental Psychology, 11,* 401–402.

Sigel, R. S. (1975). Psychological antecedents and political involvement: The utility of the concept of locus-of-control. *Social Science Quarterly, 56,* 315–322.

Silberman, C. (1970). *Crisis in the classroom: The remaking of American education.* New York: Random House.

Silbert, M., & Pines, A. (1981). Occupational hazards of street prostitutes. *Criminal Justice and Behavior, 8*(4), 395–399.

Silbert, M., & Pines, A. (1981). *Runaway prostitutes.* Unpublished manuscript, Delancey Street Foundation, San Francisco.

Simmons, D. (1970). Development of an objective measure of identity achievement status. *Journal of Projective Technical Personality Assessment, 34,* 241–244.

Simmons, D. D. (1973). Further psychometric correlates of the Identity Achievement Scale. *Psychological Reports, 32,* 1042.

Simmons, R. G., Blyth, D. A., Van Cleave, E. F., & Bush, D. M. (1979). Entry into early adolescence: The impact of school structure, puberty, and early dating on self-esteem. *American Sociological Review, 45,* 917–931.

Simon, K., & Frankel, M. (1974). NCCS, U.S. Department of Education. *Projections of Educational Statistics to 1983–1984.* Washington: U.S. Government Printing Office.

Simon, S. B., Howe, L. W., & Kirschenbaum, H. (1972). *Values clarification: A handbook of practical strategies for teachers and students.* New York: Hart Publishing Co., Inc.

Simpson, E. L. (1974). Moral development research: A case study of scientific cultural bias. *Human Development, 17,* 81–106.

Simpson, R. L. (1962). Parental influence, anticipatory socialization, and social mobility. *American Sociological Review, 27,* 517–522.

Sinclair, D. (1973). *Human growth after birth.* London: Oxford University Press.

Sinoway, C. (1982, August). *The incidence and characteristics of bulimarexia in Penn State students.* Paper presented at the convention of the American Psychological Association, Washington, DC.

Sistrunk, F., & McDavid, J. W. (1971). Sex variable in conforming behavior. *Journal of Personality and Social Psychology, 17,* 200–207.

Sizonenko, P. C., & Paunier, L. (1975). Hormonal changes in puberty, III, etc. *Journal of Clinical Endocrinology and Metabolism, 41,* 894–904.

Skeels, H. M. (1966). Adult status of children with contrasting early life experiences. *Monographs of the Society for Research in Child Development, 31,* (Serial No. 105).

Sklav, J., & Berkov, B. (1981). Teenage family formation in America. In F. F. Furstenberg, R. Lincoln, & J. Menken (Eds.), *Teenage sexuality, pregnancy, and childbearing.* Philadelphia: University of Pennsylvania Press.

Slater, P. E. (1970). *The pursuit of loneliness.* Boston: Beacon Press.

Sloane, P., & Karpinsky, F. (1942). Effects of incest on participants. *American Journal of Orthopsychiatry, 12,* 668–673.

Smart, M. S., & Smart, K. C. (1978). *Adolescents: Developmental relationships* (2nd ed.). New York: MacMillan.

Smiley, W. C. (1977). Classification and delinquency: A review. *Behavioral Disorders, 2,* 184–200.

Smith, E. J. (1981). Adolescent drug abuse and alcoholism. Directions for the school and the family. *Urban Education, 16*(3), 311–332.

Snyder, E. E. (1972). High school athletes and their coaches: Educational plans and advice. *Sociology of Education, 45,* 313–325.

Soares, A. T., & Soares, L. M. (1971). Comparative differences in the self-perceptions of disadvantaged and advantaged students. *Journal of School Psychology, 9,* 424–429.

Solnit, A. J. (1972). Youth and the campus: The search for social conscience. *Psychoanalytic Study of a Child, 27,* 98–105.

Sommer, B. (1978). *Puberty and adolescence.* New York: Oxford University Press.

Sones, G., & Feshbach, M. (1971). Sex differences in adolescent reactions towards new comers. *Developmental Psychology, 4,* 381–386.

Sorensen, R. C. (1973). *Adolescent sexuality in contemporary America.* New York: World.

Spanier, G. B. (1976). Formal and informal sex education as determinants of premarital sexual behavior. *Archives of Sexual Behavior, 5,* 39–67.

Spanier, G. B. (1977). Sources of sex information and premarital sexual behavior. *Journal of Sex Research, 13,* 73–88.

Spanier, G. B. (1980). The family: Alive but not well. *Wilson Quarterly,* Washington: Smithsonian Institute.

Spearman, C. (1927). *The abilities of man.* New York: Macmillan.

Spitzer, R. L., Andreasen, N., & Endicott, J. (1978). Schizophrenia and other psychotic disorders in DSM-III. *Schizophrenia Bulletin, 4,* 489–509.

Spitzer, R. L., Endicott, J., & Robins, E. (1978). Research diagnostic criteria: Rationale and reliability. *Archives of General Psychiatry, 35,* 773–782.

Spivack, G., Platt, J. J., & Shure, M. B. (1976). *The problem-solving approach to adjustment.* San Francisco: Jossey-Bass.

Spivack, G., & Shure, M. B. (1976). *Social adjustment of young children.* San Francisco: Jossey-Bass.

Squires, G. D. (1979). *Education and jobs.* New Brunswick, NJ: Transaction Books.

Staffieri, J. R. (1967). A study of social stereotype of body-image in children. *Journal of Personality and Social Psychology, 7,* 101–104.

Stark, P. A., & Traxler, A. J. (1974). Empirical validation of Erikson's theory of identity crises in late adolescence. *The Journal of Psychology, 86,* 25–33.

Statistical Abstracts of the United States. (1980). *National Data Book and Source Guide, 1980.* Washington, DC: U.S. Government Documents.

Steinberg, L. D. (1982). Jumping off the work experience bandwagon. *Journal of Youth and Adolescence, 11,* 183–205.

Steinberg, L. D., Greenberger, E., Garduque, L., Ruggiero, M., & Vaux, A. (1982). Effects of working on adolescent development. *Developmental Psychology, 18,* 385–395.

Steinberg, L., Greenberger, E., Vaux, A., & Ruggiero, M. (1982). Effects of early work experience on adolescent occupational socialization. *Youth and Society, 12,* 403–422.

Steinberg, L., & Hill, J. (1980). Family interaction patterns during early adolescence. In R. Muuss (Ed.), *Adolescent behavior and society: A book of readings* (3rd ed.). New York: Random House.

Stengel, E. (1964). *Suicide and attempted suicide.* Baltimore, MD: Penguin.

Stern, M. (1980). *Sex in the USSR.* New York: Times Books.

Stevenson, W. (1978). Career and consequences of youth unemployment. *USA Today, 107,* 46.

Stolz, R., & Stolz, L. (1951). *Somatic development of adolescent boys: A study of the growth of boys during the second decade of life.* New York: Macmillan.

Stoner, C., & Parke, J. (1979). *All God's children: The cult experience—Salvation or slavery?* New York: Penguin Books, Inc.

Stork, P. A., & Traxler, A. J. (1974). Empirical validation of Erikson's theory of identity crises in late adolescence. *The Journal of Psychology, 86,* 25–33.

Straus, M., Gelles, R., & Steinmetz, S. (1980). *Behind closed doors.* New York: Anchor/Doubleday.

Strober, M., Green, J., & Carlson, G. (1981). Reliability of psychiatric diagnosis in hospitalized adolescents. Interrater agreement using DSM-III. *Archives of General Psychiatry, 38,* 141–145.

Strommen, M. P. (1972). *A study of generations.* Minneapolis, MN: Augsburg.

Stuart, I. R., & Wells, C. F. (Eds.). (1982). *Pregnancy in adolescence: Needs, problems, and management.* New York: Van Nostrand Reinhold.

Suedfeld, P. (1967). Paternal absence and overseas success of Peace Corps volunteers. *Journal of Consulting Psychology, 31,* 424-425.

Sullivan, H. S. (1953). *The interpersonal theory of psychiatry.* New York: Norton.

Sulzer-Azaroff, B., & Mayer, G. R. (1977). *Applying behavior-analysis procedures with children and youth.* New York: Holt, Rinehart & Winston.

Super, C. M. (1981). Behavioral development in infancy. In R. H. Munroe, R. C. Munroe, & B. B. Whiting (Eds.), *Handbook of cross-cultural human development.* New York: Garland.

Super, D. E. (1953). A theory of vocational development. *American Psychologist, 8,* 185-190.

Super, D. E. (1957). *The psychology of careers.* New York: Harper & Row.

Super, D. E. (1973). The Career Development Inventory. *British Journal of Guidance and Counseling, 1,* 37-50.

Super, D. E. (1980). A life-span, life space approach to career development. *Journal of Vocational Behavior, 16,* 282-298.

Super, D. E., Crites, J., Hummel, R., Moser, H., Overstreet, P., & Warnath, C. (1957). *Vocational development: A framework for research.* New York: Bureau of Research, Teachers College, Columbia University.

Super, D. E., Starishevsky, R., Mattin, N., & Jordaan, J. P. (1963). *Career development: Self-concept theory.* (CEEB Research Monograph No. 4). New York: CEEB.

Surber, C. F. (1977). Developmental processes in social inference: Averaging of intentions and consequences in moral judgment. *Developmental Psychology, 13,* 654-665.

Surgeon General's Report on Health Promotion and Disease Prevention. (1979). *Healthy people.* Washington, D.C.: U.S. Government Printing Office.

Sussex, J. N. (1978, May). Adolescent sexuality. *Journal of the Florida Medical Association.*

Suttles, G. D. (1970). Friendship as a social institution. In G. J. McCall, M. M. McCall, N. K. Denzin, G. D. Suttles, & S. B. Kurth (Eds.), *Social relationships.* Chicago: Aldine.

Swift, C. (1977). Sexual victimization of children: An urban mental health center survey. *Victimology, 2,* 322-327.

Taeuber, I. B., & Taeuber, C. (1971). *People of the United States in the 20th century.* Washington, DC: U.S. Government Printing Office.

Talk of the Town, Notes and Comments. (1983, August 1). *The New Yorker,* v. LIX #24, pp. 25-26.

Tangri, S. S. (1972). Determinants of outpatient role innovation among college women. *Journal of Social Issues, 28,* 177-199.

Tanner, J. M. (1962). *Growth at adolescence* (2nd ed.). Oxford: Blackwell Scientific Publications, Ltd.

Tanner, J. M. (1970). Physical growth. In P. H. Mussen (Ed.), *Carmichael's manual of child psychology,* (Vol. 3). New York: Wiley.

Tanner, J. M. (1973). Growing up. *Scientific American, 229,* 34-43.

Taylor, C., Smith, W. R., & Ghiselin, B. (1963). The creative and other contributions of one sample of research scientists. In C. W. Taylor & F. Barron (Eds.), *Scientific creativity: Its recognition and development* New York: Wiley.

Teicher, J. (1973). Why adolescents kill themselves. In J. Segal (Ed.), *The mental health of the child.* New York: Arno Press.

Tenzer, A. (1977). Parental influences on the occupational choice of career women in male-dominated occupations. *Dissertation Abstracts International, 38(4-A),* 2014.

Tepperman, J. (1973). *Metabolic and endocrine physiology,* (3rd ed.). Year Book. New York: Medical Publishers.

Terkel, S. (1963). *Hard times.* New York: Pantheon.

Terman, L. M. (1916). *The measurement of intelligence.* Boston: Houghton Mifflin.

Terman, L. M., & Merrill, M. A. (1960). *Stanford-Binet Intelligence Scale: Manual for the third revision,* Form L-M. Boston: Houghton Mifflin.

Thomas, A., & Chess, S. (1980). *The dynamics of psychological development.* New York: Brunner/Mazel.

Thomas, L. E. (1971). Political attitude congruence between politically active parents and college-age children. *Journal of Marriage and the Family, 32,* 375-386.

Thomas, L. E. (1974). Generational continuity in beliefs: An exploration of the generation gap. *Journal of Social Issues, 30(3),* 1-22.

Thomas, W. I., & Thomas, D. S. (1928). *The child in America.* New York: Alfred Knopf.

Thornburg, H. D. (1971). *An investigation of attitudes among potential drop outs from minority groups during their freshman year in high school.* (Final report, U.S. Office of Education, Bureau of Research). Washington, DC: U.S. Government Printing Office.

Thornburg, H. D. (1972). A comparative study of sex information sources. *Journal of School Health, 42,* 88.

Thornburg, H. D. (1974). An investigation of a dropout program among Arizona's minority youth. *Education, 94,* 249-265.

Thornburg, H. D. (1981). The amount of sex information learning obtained during early adolescence. *Journal of Early Adolescence, 1,* 171-183.

Thornburg, H. D. (1982). *Development in adolescence.* Monterey, CA: Brooks/Cole.

Thorndike, E. L. (1904). The newest psychology. *Educational Review, 28,* 217-227.

Thurstone, L. L., & Thurstone, T. G. (1962). *SRA primary mental abilities.* Chicago: Science Research Associates.

Timmons, F. R. (1977). Incidence of withdrawal from college: An examination of some misconceptions. *Perceptual and Motor Skills, 45,* 651–654.

Today's Education, Research Notes. (1981). *Today's Education, 70,* 10.

Toman, W. (1980, December). Birth order rules all. *Psychology Today,* 45–49, 68–69.

Tomlinson-Keasey, C., & Keasey, C. B. (1974). The mediating role of cognitive development in moral judgment. *Child Development, 45,* 291–298.

Tracy, J. J., & Cross, H. J. (1973). Antecedents of shift in moral judgment. *Journal of Personality and Social Psychology, 26,* 238–244.

Trivers, B. L. (1972). Parental investment and sexual selection. In B. Campbell (Ed.), *Sexual selection and the descent of man* (pp. 136–179). Chicago: Aldine.

Troll, L., & Bengston, V. L. (1978). Generations in the family. In W. Burr, R. Hill, I. Reiss, & I. Nye (Eds.), *Handbook of contemporary family theory.* New York: The Free Press.

Troll, L. E., Neugarten, B. L., & Kraines, R. J. (1969). Similarities in values and other personality characteristics in college students and their parents. *Merrill-Palmer Quarterly, 15,* 323–334.

Trotter, S. (1976). Zajonc defuses IQ debate: Birth order work wins prize. *APA Monitor, 7*(5), 1, 10.

Trowbridge, N. T. (1970, March). *Self-concept of disadvantaged and advantaged children.* Paper presented at the annual meeting of the American Educational Research Association, Minneapolis.

Tsunt, M. (1966, March). Dropouts on the run. *Atlas,* 10–15.

Tulkin, S. (1972). An analysis of the concept of cultural deprivation. *Developmental Psychology, 6,* 236–239.

Tuma, N., & Hallinan, M. T. (1979). The effects of sex, race, and achievement in school children's friendships. *Social Forces, 57,* 1265–1285.

Turiel, E. (1974). Developmental processes in the child's moral thinking. In P. H. Mussen, J. Langer, & M. Covington (Eds.), *Trends and issues in developmental psychology.* New York: Holt, Rinehart, & Winston.

Turner, R. (1961). Modes of social ascent through education: Sponsored and contest mobility. In A. Halsey, J. Floud, & C. Anderson (Eds.), *Education, economy, and society: A reader in the sociology of education.* New York: Free Press.

Tyack, D. (1978). Socialization to what? *Phi Delta Kappan, 59*(5), 316–317.

Tzuriel, D., & Klein, M. M. (1977). Ego identity: Effects of ethnocentrism, ethnic identification, and cognitive complexity in Israeli, Oriental, and Western ethnic groups. *Psychological Reports, 40,* 1099–1110.

Ulrey, G. (1981). Emotional development of the young handicapped child. In N. J. Anastaslow (Ed.), *New Directions for Exceptional Children: Socioemotional Development, 5,* 33–52.

Unemployment reaches highest level since Great Depression. (1983, January 19). *The New York Times,* p. 1ff.

Uniform Crime Reports "Crime in the United States." (1981. Release date, 1982, August 26). Washington DC: U.S. Department of Justice, Federal Bureau of Investigation.

U.S. Bureau of the Census. (1978). *Statistical Abstract of the United States: 1978.* Washington, DC: Department of Commerce.

U.S. Bureau of the Census. (1980). *Current Population Reports: Population Characteristics.* Washington DC: U.S. Government Printing Office.

U.S. Bureau of the Census. (1981). *Statistical Abstract of the United States: 1981* (102nd edition). Washington, DC: U.S. Government Printing Office.

U.S. Department of Commerce, Bureau of the Census. (1981, June). *Population profile of the United States: 1980 population characteristics* (Current Population Report, Series P-20, No. 363). Washington, DC: U.S. Government Printing Office.

U.S. Department of Health and Human Services, Office of Human Development Services. (1980). *Status of children, youth, and families* (DHHS Publication No. OHDS 80-30274). Washington, DC: U.S. Government Printing Office.

U.S. Department of Health and Human Services, Public Health Service. (1980). National Survey of drug abuse: Main findings, 1979. Rockwell, MD: National Institute on Drug Abuse.

U.S. Department of Health and Human Services. (1980). *The status of children, youth, and families: 1979.* Washington, D.C.: U.S. Department of Health and Human Services.

U.S. Department of Health, Education and Welfare. (1977). *The safe schools study report to Congress.* Washington, DC: U.S. Government Printing Office.

U.S. Department of Labor Bureau of Labor Statistics. (1980). Family budgets. *Monthly Labor Review, 103,* 29.

U.S. Senate Subcommittee on the Judiciary. (1975). *Our nation's schools—A report card: "A" in school violence and vandalism.* (Preliminary report of the Subcommittee to Investigate Juvenile Delinquency, Committee Print, 94th Congress, 1st session). Washington, DC: U.S. Government Printing Office.

Urbain, E., & Kendall, P. (1980). Review of social-cognitive problem-solving interventions with children. *Psychological Bulletin, 88,* 109–143.

Urban, H. (1978). The concept of development from a systems perspective. In P. Baltes (Ed.), *Life-span development and behavior* (Vol. 1). New York: Academic Press.

Urban, H., & Vondracek, F. (1977). Intervention within individual and family development: When? What kind? And how? In S. R. Goldberg & F. Deutsch (Eds.), *Life- span individual and family development.* Monterey, CA: Brooks/Cole.

Valentine, C., & Valentine, B. (1975). Brain damage and the intellectual defense of inequality. *Current Anthropology, 16,* 117–150.

Valett, R. E. (1977). *Humanistic education: Developing the total person.* St. Louis, MO: C. V. Mosby Company.

van den Berghe, P. (1979). *Human family systems: An evolutionary view.* New York: Elsevier.

Verger, D. M. (1968). Birth order and sibling differences in interests. *Journal of Individual Psychology, 24,* 56–59.

Visotsky, H. M. (1966). A project for unwed pregnant adolescents in Chicago. *Clinical Pediatrics, 5,* 322–324.

Vital Statistics of the United States, 1976. (1979). Vol. II. Mortality (Part 3). Hyattsville, MD: National Center for Health Statistics.

Vondracek, F. W., & Lerner, R. M. (1982). Vocational role development in adolescence. In B. B. Wolman (Ed.), *Handbook of Developmental Psychology,* Englewood Cliffs, NJ: Prentice–Hall.

Vondracek, F. W., Lerner, R. M., & Schulenberg, J. E. (1983). The concept of development in vocational theory and intervention. *Journal of Vocational Behavior, 23,* 179–202.

Wachter, M. L. (1982). Economic challenges posed by demographic changes. In E. Ginzburg, D. O. Mills, J. D. Owens, H. C. Sheppard, & M. L. Wachter (Eds.), *Work decisions in the 1980's.* Boston: Auburn House.

Wagner, H. (1978). The adolescent and his religion. *Adolescence, 13,* 349–364.

Wagner, J. (1976). *A study of the relationship between formal operations and ego identity in adolescence.* Unpublished doctoral dissertation, State University of New York, Buffalo.

Waldrop, M. F., & Halverson, C. F. (1985). Intensive and extensive peer behavior: Longitudinal and cross-sectional behavior. *Child Development, 46,* 19–26.

Wallerstein, J. S., & Kelly, J. B. (1980). *Surviving the breakup: How children and parents cope with divorce.* New York: Basic Books.

Warren, M. (1983). Physical and biological aspects of puberty. In J. Brooks-Gunn & A. Petersen (Eds.), *Girls at puberty* (pp. 3–28). New York: Plenum Press.

Warren, W. (1965). A study of adolescent psychiatric in-patients and the outcome six or more years later. II: The follow-up study. *Journal of Child Psychology and Psychiatry, 6,* 141–160.

Waterbo, R. (1972). Experiential bases of the sense of self. *Journal of Personality, 40,* 162–179.

Waterman, A. S., Geary, P. S., & Waterman, C. K. (1974). A longitudinal study of changes in ego identity status from the freshman to the senior year at college. *Developmental Psychology, 10,* 387–392.

Waterman, A. S., & Waterman, C. K. (1974). A longitudinal study of changes in ego identity status during the freshman year at college. *Developmental Psychology, 5,* 167–173.

Watson, E. W., Maloney, D. M., Books, L. E., Blase, K. B., & Collins, L. B. (1980). *Teaching family bibliography.* Boys Town, NE: Father Flanagan's Boys Home, Youth Care Department, Child Care Assistance Program.

Watt, N. (1978). Patterns of childhood social development in adult schizophrenics. *Archives of General Psychiatry, 35,* 160–165.

Weber, E. (1977, April). Sexual abuse begins at home. *Ms. Magazine,* 64–67.

Wechsler, D. (1955). *Manual for the Wechsler Adult Intelligence Scale.* New York: Psychological Corporation.

Wechsler, D. (1974). *Manual: Wechsler Intelligence Scale for Children--Revised.* New York: Psychological Corporation.

Wechsler, D. (1967). *Wechsler Preschool and Primary Scale of Intelligence.* New York: Psychological Corporation.

Weiner, I. B. (1970). *Psychological disturbance in adolescence.* New York: John Wiley & Sons.

Weiner, I. B. (1975). Depression in adolescence. In F. Fisch & S. Draghi (Eds.), *The nature and treatment of depression.* New York: John Wiley & Sons.

Weiner, I. (1980). Psychopathy in adolescence. In J. Adelson (Ed.), *Handbook of adolescent psychology.* New York: John Wiley & Sons.

Weiner, I. B. (1982). *Child and adolescent psychopathology.* New York: John Wiley & Sons.

Weiner, I. B., & Del Gaudio, A. C. (1973). Psychopathology in adolescence: An epidemiological study. *Archives of General Psychiatry, 33,* 187–193.

Weinstein, E. A. (1969). The development of interpersonal competence. In D. Goslin (Ed.), *Handbook of socialization theory and research.* Chicago: Rand McNally.

Weinstein, G., & Fantini, M. D. (1970). *Toward humanizing education: A curriculum of affect.* New York: Praeger.

Weir, J., Dunn, J., & Jones, E. (1971). Race and age at menarche. *American Journal of Obstetrics and Gynecology, 111,* 594–596.

Weiss, R. (1979). *Going it alone: The family life and social situation of the single parent.* New York: Basic Books.

Weissberg, R. P., Gesten, E. L., Rapkin, B. D., Cowen, E. L., Davidson, E., Flores de Apodaca, R. F., & McKim, B. J. (1981). The evaluation of a social problem-solving training program for suburban and inner-city third grade children. *Journal of Consulting and Clinical Psychology, 49,* 251–261.

Weissman, M. M., & Myers, J. K. (1977). Affective disorders in a U.S. urban community: The use of research diagnostic criteria in an epidemiological survey. *Archives of General Psychiatry, 34,* 854–862.

Weissman, M. & Paykel, E. (1973). Moving and depression in women. In R. S. Weiss (Ed.), *Loneliness* Cambridge, MA: The MIT Press.

Weitz, S. (1977). *Sex Roles.* New York: Oxford University Press.

Welcher, D. (1980). Adolescent pregnancy: A report on ACYF-Funded research and demonstration projects. *Children Today,* 10–35.

Werner, C., & Parmlee, P. (1979). Similarity of activity preference among friends: Those who play together stay together. *Social Psychology Quarterly, 42,* 62–66.

Werner, E. E., Simonian, K., & Smith, R. S. (1968). Ethnic and socioeconomic status differences in abilities and achievement among preschool and school-age children in Hawaii. *Journal of Social Psychology, 75,* 43–59.

Werner, E. E., & Smith, R. S. (1982). *Vulnerable, but invincible: A longitudinal study of resilient children and youth.* New York: McGraw–Hill.

Werts, C. E. (1968). Paternal influence on career choice. *Journal of Counseling Psychology, 15,* 48–52.

Westley, W. A., & Elkin, F. (1956). The protective environment and adolescent socialization. *Social Forces, 35,* 243–249.

Westman, J., Rice, D., & Berman, E. (1967). Nursery school behavior and later school adjustment. *American Journal of Orthopsychiatry, 37,* 725–731.

Wheeler, D. K. (1961). Popularity among adolescents in Western Australia and in the United States of America. *The School Review, 49,* 67–81.

White, C. B. (1975). Moral development in Bahamian school children: A cross-cultural examination of Kohlberg's stages of moral reasoning. *Developmental Psychology, 11,* 535–536.

White, R. (1959). Motivation reconsidered: The concept of competence. *Psychological Review, 66,* 297–323.

Whiteside, M., & Merriman, G. (1976). Dropouts look at their teachers. *Phi Delta Kappan, 57,* 700–702.

Whittaker, J. K. (1980). *Community support systems for troubled children and youth: A preliminary concept paper.* The National Institute of Juvenile Justice and Delinquency Prevention.

Whittaker, J., Garbarino, J., & Associates. (1984). *Social support networks.* New York: Aldine.

Wieder, H., & Kaplan, E. H. (1969). Drug use in adolescents. *Psychoanalytic study of the child, 24,* 399–431.

Willems, E. (1967). Sense of obligation to high school activities is related to school size and marginality of students. *Child Development, 38,* 1247–1260.

Williams, J. R., & Gold, M. (1972). From delinquent behavior to official delinquency. *Social Problems, 20,* 209–229.

Wilson, K. L., Zurcher, L. A., McAdams, D. C., & Curtis, R. L. (1975). An exploratory analysis from two national samples. *Journal of Marriage and the Family, 37,* 526–536.

Wilson, M. T. (1974). Better training for junior high and middle school teachers. *National Association of Secondary School Principals Bulletin, 58,* 110–121.

Winchester, A. M. (1976). *Heredity, evolution, and humankind.* St. Paul, MN: West Publishing Company.

Winer, A. S. (1977). Cognitive and social-emotional development in adolescence. *Journal of Pediatric Psychology, 2,* 87–92.

Winetsky, C. S. (1978). Comparisons of the expectations of parents and teachers for the behavior of preschool children. *Child Development, 49,* 1146–1154.

Winick, C., & Kinsie, P. M. (1972). Prostitutes. *Psychology Today, 5*(9), 57.

Winikoff, S. A., & Resnick, H. L. (1971). Student suicide. *Today's Education,* 30–31.

Winter, J., & Faiman, C. (1972). Pituitary-gonadal relations in male children and adolescents. *Pediatric Research, 6,* 126–135.

Wolf, L. (1972). *A dream of Dracula: In search of the living dead.* Boston: Little, Brown, & Co.

Wolfgang, M., Figlio, R., & Sellin, T. (1972). *Delinquency in a birth cohort.* Chicago: University of Chicago Press.

Wolk, S., & Brandon, J. (1977). Runaway adolescents' perceptions of parents and self. *Adolescence, 46,* 185–197.

Wolman, R. N. (1967). A developmental study of the perception of people. *Genetic Psychology Monographs, 76,* 95–140.

Wooden, K. (1976). *Weeping in the playtime of others: America's incarcerated children.* New York: McGraw–Hill.

Wright, J. D., & Wright, S. R. (1976). Social class and parental values for children: A partial replication and extension of the Kohn thesis. *American Sociological Review, 41,* 527–537.

Wyatt vs. Stickney, 344 F. Supp. 373 (MD, AL, 1972).

Wylie, R. C. (1979). *The self-concept: Theory and research on selected topics.* (Revised ed.). Vol. 2. Lincoln: University of Nebraska Press.

Wynne, E. A. (1977). *Growing up suburban.* Austin: University of Texas Press.

Yamamoto, J. K. (1982). *Echoes from Gold Mountain.* Long Beach, CA: Asian-American Studies.

Yancy, W., Nader, P., & Burnham, K. (1972). Drug use and attitudes of high school students. *Pediatrics, 50,* 739–745.

Yankelovich, D. (1974). *The new morality: A profile of American youth in the 1970's.* New York: McGraw–Hill.

Yankelovich, D. (1981). New rules in American life: Searching for self-fulfillment in a world turned upside down. *Psychology Today, 15,* 35–91.

Yarber, W. L. (1979). Instructional emphasis in family life and sex education: Viewpoints of students, parents, teachers, and principals at four grade levels. *Journal of School Health, 49,* 263–265.

Yarrow, L. J. (1963). Research in dimensions of early maternal care. *Merrill-Palmer Quarterly, 9,* 101–114.

Yarrow, M. R., & Campbell, J. D. (1963). Person perception in children. *Merrill-Palmer Quarterly, 9,* 57–72.

York, O., York, P., & Wachtel, T. (1982). *Toughlove.* Garden City, NY: Doubleday.

Yorukoclu, A., & Kemph, J. (1969). Children not severely damaged by incest. *Journal of the Academy of Child Psychiatry, 8,* 606.

Youniss, J. (1980). *Parents and peers in the social environment: A Sullivan Piaget perspective.* Chicago: University of Chicago Press.

Youniss, J., & Volpe, J. (1978). A relational analysis of friendship. In W. Damon (Ed.), *Social cognition*. San Francisco: Jossey-Bass.

Zacharias, L., Rand, W. M., & Wurtman, R. J. (1976). A prospective study of sexual development and growth in American girls: The statistics of menarche. *Obstetrics and Gynecology Survey* (Supplement), *31*, 325–337.

Zajonc, R. B. (1976). Family configuration and intelligence. *Science, 192,* 227–235.

Zajonc, R. B., & Markers, G. B. (1975). Birth order and intellectual development. *Psychological Review, 82,* 74–85.

Zebin, L. (1981). The impact of early use of prescription contraceptives on reducing premarital teenage pregnancies. *Family Planning Perspectives, 13,* 72–74.

Zebin, L., & Clark, S. D. (1982). Why they delay: A study of teenage family planning clinic patients. *Family Planning Perspectives, 13,* 205–217.

Zebin, L., Kantner, J. F., & Zebink, M. (1979). The risk of adolescent pregnancy in the first months of intercourse. *Family Planning Perspectives, 1,* 215–222.

Zegoib, L. E., Arnold, S., & Forehand, R. (1975). An examination of observer effects in parent-child interactions. *Child Development, 46,* 509–512.

Zelditch, M., Jr. (1964). Family, marriage, and kinship. In R. E. L. Faris (Ed.), *Handbook of modern sociology*. Chicago: Rand McNally.

Zelnick, M., & Kantner, J. F. (1974, Spring). The resolution of teenage pregnancies. *Family Planning Perspectives, 6,* 74–80.

Zelnick, M., & Kantner, J. F. (1977). Sexual and contraceptive experience of young unmarried women in the United States, 1976 and 1971. *Family Planning Perspectives, 9,* 55–71.

Zelnick, M., & Kantner, J. F. (1978). Contraceptive patterns and premarital pregnancy among women aged 15–19 in 1976. *Family Planning Perspectives, 10,* 135–142.

Zelnick, M., & Kantner, J. F. (1978, January/February). First pregnancies to women aged 15–19: 1971-1976. *Family Planning Perspectives, 10,* 10–20.

Zelnick, M., & Kantner, J. F. (1979, September/October). Reasons for non-use of contraceptives by sexually active women, ages 15–19. *Family Planning Perspectives, 1979, 11,* 289–294.

Zelnick, M., & Kantner, J. F. (1980). Sexual activity, contraceptive use and pregnancy among metropolitan teenagers: 1971-1979. *Family Planning Perspectives, 12,* 230–237.

Zelnick, M., Kantner, J. F., & Ford, K. (1981). *Sex and pregnancy in adolescence*. Beverly Hills, CA: Sage.

Zelnick, M., & Kim, Y. Sex education and its association with teenage sexual activity, pregnancy, and contraceptive use. *Family Planning Perspective, 14,* 117–126.

Zelnick, M., & Shah, R. (1983). First intercourse among young Americans. *Family Planning Perspectives, 15,* 64–70.

Zieglar, S. (1980). Adolescents' inter-ethnic friendships. *Children Today, 9,* 22–25.

Zimbardo, P., Pilkonis, P., & Norwood, R. (1974). *The silent prison of shyness*. Glenview, IL: Scott, Foresman.

Zinn, D. (1980). Therapeutic and preventive interventions in juvenile delinquency. In Scholevan & G. Perooz (Eds.), *Emotional disorders in children and adolescents*. New York: Spectrum Publications.

Zuck, R. B., & Getz, G. A. (1968). *Christian youth—An in-depth study*. Chicago: Moody.

Author Index

Abrams, R., 592
Achenbach, T., 197, 513
Ackerman, N., 34
Acock, A., 273, 274
Adams, G., 273, 278, 311, 366, 392, 504, 507, 552
Adams, W., 425, 426
Adelson, J., 28, 29, 35, 186, 187, 258, 267, 268, 269, 272, 297, 414, 448
Ageton, S., 476, 477, 478
Ahlgren, A., 313
Ahlstrom, W., 392
Ahrendt, K., 392
Albee, G., 60, 536
Albert, N., 514
Alexander, J., 533
Alexander, K., 400
Alexander, S., 366
Alexander, W., 395
Allen, D., 494, 495, 496
Allen, J., 296
Allen, L., 473
Allgeier, E., 352
Allport, G., 317
Almond, G., 63, 403
Almquist, E., 415

Alter, J., 366, 368
Altman, S., 415
Ambrosino, L., 486
Amini, F., 506
Anastasi, A., 143
Anderson, D., 172
Anderson, L., 50, 74, 438
Andres, D., 255, 257
Andrews, J., 296
Andrews, L., 531
Angrist, S., 415
Annesley, P., 472
Anthony, E., 267
Anthony-Caplan, 29, 198
Arbuthnot, J., 170
Ardon, M., 340
Aries, P., 223
Aristotle, 42, 204, 207, 208, 209
Arlin, P., 153, 154
Armstrong, C., 397
Asher, S., 439
Asp, E., 17, 19, 58, 382, 387, 389, 394, 423, 425, 460, 537, 571, 585
Astin, A., 411
Atwater, E., 340, 365, 392, 435, 436

Austen, J., 5
Authier, J., 595
Authier, K., 595
Ayllon, T., 547
Azrin, N., 547

Bachman, J., 392, 478, 505, 507, 551, 583
Bahr, H., 246
Baizerman, M., 490
Bakan, D., 314, 571
Baker, K., 385
Baker, L., 560, 561
Baldwin, A., 161
Baldwin, C., 161
Baldwin, H., 94
Baldwin, W., 350, 356, 590
Ball, J., 345
Balswick, J., 267, 272
Baltes, P., 43, 143
Ban, J., 385
Banducci, R., 415
Bandura, A., 37, 225, 229, 330
Bardwick, J., 268
Barglos, P., 592
Barker, R., 17, 18, 59
Barnes, M., 171

Barnett, L., 560
Barnlund, D., 560
Barter, J., 563
Bartz, K., 590
Baruch, G., 257
Bateson, G., 63
Bauman, K., 350
Baumrind, D., 54, 176, 260, 261, 262, 264, 271
Bavolek, S., 446
Bayer, A., 247, 591
Bayley, N., 260, 273, 303
Beach, J., 334
Beck, A., 509, 514, 516
Beck, R., 509
Becker, W., 258, 261, 262, 264
Beever, A., 593
Bell, A., 275, 413, 417
Bell, N., 244
Bell, R., 53, 238, 267
Belmont, L., 247
Bem, S., 287, 311, 436
Bender, L., 502
Benedict, R., 34, 218, 221, 226
Benedict, T., 267
Bengston, V., 186, 273, 274, 275
Bennet, S., 365
Benward, J., 503
Berenson, B., 520
Berg, I., 388
Berger, I., 488
Berman, E., 79
Berndt, T., 161, 441, 443, 445, 448, 449
Bernfeld, S., 34
Bernstein, I., 103
Berzonsky, W., 304
Bickerstaff, M., 545, 546, 551
Bielby, D., 415
Bigelow, B., 445, 448
Bigner, J., 160
Biller, H., 413
Bixenstine, V., 436
Blaine, G., 563
Blake, J., 249
Blasi, A., 174
Blau, P., 410, 412, 413, 416
Blauner, R., 314
Block, J., 312, 313, 314, 322

Bloom, B., 537
Blos, P., 34, 179, 288, 290
Blumstein, P., 362
Blyth, D., 127, 301
Boatman, B., 500
Bob, S., 296
Bobbitt, B., 157
Bohan, J., 300
Bolton, F., 182, 350
Bond, F., 323
Borkovec, T., 324
Bornstein, M., 592
Boskind-Lodahl, M., 520
Bott, E., 244
Bower, R., 324
Bowerman, C., 265, 270, 278
Bowman, H., 130
Boxer, B., 101
Boyer, W., 317
Brandon, J., 485, 549
Brauberger, M., 246, 265, 272
Brazee, E., 152
Breland, H., 247
Bremmer, R., 482
Brennan, T., 485, 488, 489, 549
Breuer, H., 298
Brim, O., 196, 247
Brittain, C., 270
Bromley, D., 160, 161, 162, 447
Bronfenbrenner, U., 44, 45, 50, 51, 52, 53, 57, 59, 62, 63, 84, 170, 175, 176, 194, 240, 247, 256, 285, 290, 315, 380, 384
Brook, D., 398, 574
Brook, J., 574
Brooks-Gunn, J., 90, 105, 122, 124
Broughton, J., 298, 299
Broughton, T., 5
Brown, L., 21, 66, 67, 322
Brown, M., 490, 492
Brown, R., 5
Browning, D., 500
Bruch, H., 288, 560
Bryner, J., 14
Buhler, C., 285
Bunt, M., 298
Burchinal, L., 591, 594
Burgdorff, K., 248, 265, 497, 558

Burgess, A., 502
Burgess, R., 55, 439, 441
Burke, E., 506
Burlin, F., 415
Burnham, D., 474
Burnham, K., 135
Burnstein, E., 409
Burt, C., 144
Burton, L., 502
Busch-Rossnagel, W., 85
Butler, J., 585
Byrne, D., 355

Califano, J., 133, 135, 136, 138
Calvin, J., 205, 208
Campbell, A., 455, 456
Campbell, B., 560
Campbell, D., 324
Campbell, J., 68, 160
Caplan, G., 527, 534, 537
Card, J., 594
Carkuff, R., 526
Carli, L., 311, 436
Carlisle, J., 330
Carlson, R., 313
Carmen, L., 563
Carns, D., 341
Caro, F., 412
Carter, F., 50
Case, B., 395
Cass, L., 472
Cassel, J., 527
Castaneda, A., 321, 322
Casteel, J., 323
Cather, W., 5
Cauble, M., 304
Cauce, A., 453
Caukins, S., 494, 495, 497
Cawelti, G., 389
Chadwick, O., 473, 514
Chandler, M., 81, 455
Chapman, N., 527
Chapman, W., 317
Cherlin, A., 249, 250, 252
Chess, S., 82
Chilman, C., 246, 248, 353, 355, 362, 589, 593
Chilton, R., 250
Choderow, N., 80

Cicerelli, V., 278
Ciminillo, L., 385
Clark, E., 317
Clark, M., 279
Clark, S., 350
Clausen, J., 127, 288, 453
Clawar, S. S., 366
Cloward, R., 461, 466
Cobb, S., 526
Coder, R., 172
Coelho, R., 37
Cohn, A., 531
Cole, M., 159
Coleman, J., 19, 381, 388, 389, 401, 403, 449, 599
Coles, R., 80
Collins, A., 161, 541
Collmer, M., 69
Colwill, N., 311
Conant, J., 17
Conger, J., 258, 264, 280, 317, 336, 419, 453
Conger, R., 55
Converse, P., 68, 456
Cook, M., 400
Cooley, C., 291
Coombs, N., 340, 400, 494, 495, 497
Cooper, D., 172, 267
Coopersmith, J., 55
Costaneda, A., 402
Costanzo, P., 436
Cottsell, L., 78
Courmier, B., 500
Cowen, E., 79, 163, 453, 536, 537
Cox, D., 481
Cox, M., 252
Cox, R., 252
Crane, S., 5
Crisp, A., 518, 519
Crockett, W., 160
Cross, H., 172
Cross, J., 296
Crouter, A., 84, 256, 410, 411, 460
Csikszentmihalyi, M., 158
Curren, J., 347
Curtis, R., 250

Cusick, P., 464
Cutler, G., 129

Dahlen, N., 265
Daly, H., 322
Daly, M., 66, 96
Damon, A., 108
Damon, L., 286, 298, 300, 301, 302, 324
D'Angelo, B., 485, 486, 549
Daniel, J., 101, 107, 118, 129
Danish, S., 541
Dann, S., 432
Darling, C., 365
Darwin, C., 207
D'Augelli, A., 375, 541
D'Augelli, J., 375
Davey, I., 570
Davidson, E., 163
Davidson, J., 492
DaVila, D., 119
Davis, K., 599, 600
Davis, S., 342, 365
Davison, M., 171
Davitz, J., 443
Deal, J., 395
DeBlassie, R., 320
DeFrancis, V., 498, 499
Deisher, R., 494
Del Gaudio, A., 511, 512, 516
deLissovoy, V., 591
Dellinger, R., 319
DeLora, J., 339
DeLuca, J., 507
Demos, J., 570
Demos, V., 570
Denham, W., 539
Denson-Gerber, J., 503
Denton, J., 30
Devereux, E., 183, 272
DeVos, G., 315
Dewhurst, C., 93
Dickens, C., 5
Dickinson, G., 341, 365
Dickinson, W., 365
Diepold, J., Jr., 124, 363
Dillard, J., 417
Dilley, J., 408
Dionne, J., 304

Dobash, R., 278
Doi, T., 315
Donovan, J., 307
Doroff, D., 564
Douglas, J., 98
Douvan, E., 35, 180, 246, 256, 258, 267, 268, 269, 272, 297, 414, 440
Doyle, P., 323
Dreeban, J., 69
Dreikurs, R., 306
Dreyer, P., 246, 247, 248, 249, 356
Dreyfus, E., 270
Drivas, A., 307
Duke, D., 273
Dulit, E., 153
Duncan, O., 410, 412, 413, 416
Dunphy, D., 434, 448
Durkheim, E., 461, 463

Eagly, A., 311, 436
Easton, D., 184
Eckland, B., 380
Edelbrock, C., 273, 482, 483, 484, 488, 513
Edwards, F., 398
Edwards, J., 171, 246, 265, 272, 398
Eisen, M., 161
Eisenberg, L., 536
Eisenstadt, S., 572
Eissler, K., 34
Elder, G., 46, 47, 85, 240, 243, 258, 264, 265, 276, 397, 407, 460, 580, 591, 593, 594
Elias, J., 344
Elkin, F., 35
Elkind, D., 147, 148, 149, 150, 153, 155, 156, 159, 163, 164, 187, 304, 354, 387, 459, 601
Elliott, D., 392, 476, 477, 478, 479, 549
Ellis, N., 70
Ellison, R., 321
Emerich, W., 412
Empey, L., 480
Enright, R., 307
Epstein, A., 560

Epstein, H., 111, 153
Epstein, J., 460
Epstein, S., 286
Erhart, A., 310
Erikson, E., 179, 215, 216, 217, 218, 230, 292, 293, 451, 572
Ernsberger, D., 317
Evans, J., 356
Ewens, W., 408
Ewing, R., 159
Exum, D., 592
Eysenck, H., 536

Fakouri, M., 154
Falkner, F., 94
Fantini, M., 323, 395
Farnsworth, D., 344, 504
Faust, D., 170
Faust, M., 119, 124, 126, 288
Faust, R., 507
Faw, T., 152
Fehr, L., 307
Feinstein, S., 340
Feiring, C., 278
Feld, S., 253
Feldman, A., 254
Feldman, H., 254
Feldman, K., 584
Feldman, R., 436, 545
Felner, R., 457
Fernbach, D., 134
Feshbach, M., 450
Festinger, L., 193
Feuer, L., 273
Field, T., 560
Fine, G., 455
Finger, J., 397
Finkel, D., 348, 351
Finkel, M., 348, 351
Finkelhor, D., 497, 498, 502
Finkelstein, J., 96, 105
Fischer, J., 297, 311, 451, 452
Fish, K., 257
Fishbach, M., 545, 546, 551
Fisher, B., 486
Fisher, J., 355
Fisher, W., 355
Fishman, J., 539
Fitzgerald, J., 144, 157

Fixen, D., 546, 547, 557
Flacks, R., 272, 580
Flanagan, J., 387
Flavell, J., 303
Flores de Apodaca, R., 163
Foote, N., 78
Ford, C., 334
Ford, D., 239
Forrest, H., 350
Forrest, J., 590
Forrester, J., 50, 66
Fountain, G., 34
Fox, G., 365
Frank, J., 324
Franzier, D., 320
Freedman, D., 82
Freeman, D., 34, 220
French, N., 119
Frese, W., 594
Freud, A., 32, 33, 214, 215, 217, 432
Freud, S., 33, 52, 179, 180, 200, 202, 203, 211, 216, 218, 222
Friedenberg, E., 28
Friedman, A., 480
Friedman, C., 480
Friedman, M., 296
Friedman, R., 489, 551
Friesen, D., 18, 390
Frisch, R., 96, 97, 129
Froland, J., 527
Fuller, M., 320
Furlong, M., 186
Furman, W., 324
Furstenberg, F., 559, 588, 592, 593, 594, 595

Gagnon, J., 331, 502
Gallatin, J., 31, 184, 185, 186, 207, 215
Gallop, G., 385, 387
Galton, F., 247
Gandy, P., 413, 494
Gangelhoff, R., 227
Garbarino, J., 17, 19, 25, 26, 43, 50, 51, 55, 58, 59, 63, 66, 68, 170, 175, 176, 238, 239, 240, 241, 250, 266, 271, 316, 322, 323, 382, 387, 389, 391, 394,

423, 430, 460, 485, 486, 497, 498, 499, 513, 527, 532, 534, 537, 538, 545, 558, 571, 585
Garduque, L., 419, 421, 422
Garmezy, N., 81
Garms, W., 460
Garrett, H., 144
Gebhard, P., 492
Gecas, V., 26, 83, 84
Geis, G., 491
Geleerd, E., 34
Gelford, J., 437
Gelles, R., 22, 69, 278, 311, 499
Gelman, S., 227
George, S., 170
Gesten, E., 163, 536, 537
Getz, G., 317
Getzels, J., 58, 158, 265, 317, 403
Gil, D., 69
Gilchrist, L., 560
Gilliam, G., 25, 26, 266, 485, 497, 498, 499, 532, 558
Gilligan, C., 68, 69, 80, 176, 177, 179, 186, 188, 269, 295, 297, 304, 316, 356, 450, 451
Gingles, R., 591
Ginsburg, H., 146, 151, 152
Glasser, W., 314, 323
Goffman, E., 163
Gold, D., 58, 255, 257, 269, 393, 475, 476, 478, 538
Goldberg, S., 81, 384
Golden, M., 79, 453
Goldenberg, I., 539
Golding, W., 210
Goldwater, B., 30
Goodman, P., 28
Goodwin, M., 352
Gordon, S., 357, 366, 368
Gorsuch, R., 171
Gottlieb, D., 43, 410
Gottman, J., 239, 439
Gottschalk, L., 592
Gould, R., 564
Grabe, M., 19
Graham, P., 473, 514
Grandon, G., 248
Gray, D., 491, 492, 493

Greenberger, E., 79, 297, 419, 420, 421, 422
Greene, B., 27
Greenleaf, R., 13
Greenspan, S., 76
Greenwald, H., 491
Greer, J., 347
Gregoire, J., 295
Gribbons, W., 408
Grinder, D., 563
Grinker, R., 37
Gronlund, N., 438
Gross, M., 403
Grossman, F., 415
Grotevant, H., 451
Grover, K., 419
Grow, B., 563
Gruber, H., 153
Grugett, J., 502
Grumbach, M., 105
Guardo, C., 300
Guenthner, R., 296
Guerney, L., 239, 546
Guest, J., 5
Guibaldi, J., 251
Guildford, J., 143
Gullotta, T., 311, 366, 392, 504, 507, 552
Gump, P., 17, 18, 59, 401
Gunn, B., 408
Gurin, G., 253
Gutherie, J., 460

Haeckel, E., 31, 209
Hagestad, G., 279, 577
Halbrecht, I., 97
Hall, G., 31, 204, 209, 211, 547
Hallinan, M., 440
Halmi, K., 519
Hamburg, D., 37
Hamilton, E., 363
Hanke, M., 380
Hansen, S., 339
Hanshaw, R., 350
Hardy, S., 350
Hare, R., 481
Harley, M., 34
Harms, E., 317
Harris, L., 387, 409

Harris, M., 342, 365
Hart, D., 286, 298, 300, 301, 302, 324
Hart, R., 273
Hart, S., 497
Harter, S., 79
Hartup, R., 79
Hartup, W., 267
Harvey, O., 437
Hass, A., 345, 346, 361, 362, 363, 364
Haupt, D., 488
Hauser, R., 415
Hauserman, N., 323
Havisghurst, R., 15, 289, 382, 392, 399, 406, 409, 464, 572, 573, 591
Hawkins, J., 541
Hayes, N., 492
Heald, F., 108
Heath, D., 17, 79
Helfer, R., 558
Herman, J., 498, 501, 502, 503
Hermolin, J., 350
Herold, E., 352
Hess, R., 184, 185
Hess, V., 161
Hessey, J., 5
Hetherington, E., 252, 254
Hicks, M., 365
Hiernaux, J., 97
Higgins-Trenk, A., 415
Higham, S., 96
Hill, J., 24, 160, 269, 273
Hindelang, M., 477, 478, 479
Hines, V., 395
Hirschi, T., 476, 478, 479
Hirschman, L., 501, 502, 503
Hodgson, J., 297, 381, 451
Hoffman, M., 166, 170, 171, 180, 182, 255, 256, 257
Hogan, D., 158, 588
Holaday, J., 101
Holland, J., 405, 409
Hollingshead, A., 464
Holmes, T., 537
Honzik, M., 473
Horner, M., 409
Horrocks, J., 440

Howell, F., 594
Hrdy, S., 177
Huizinga, D., 549
Hung, W., 108
Hunt, M., 361, 362, 365, 366
Huston, T., 439, 441
Huston-Stein, A., 415
Hutt, C., 71
Hyde, J., 330

Inazu, J., 365
Inhelder, B., 149, 150, 152, 157, 303
Inselberg, M., 591

Jacklin, C., 71, 109, 308, 311
Jackman, N., 491, 492
Jackson, D., 547
Jackson, J., 464
Jacobinzer, J., 508
Jacobs, J., 334, 564
Jacobsen, N., 545
Jaffee, A., 425, 426
James, J., 491, 492
James, W., 298
Janes, C., 453
Jayaratne, S., 547
Jedlicka, D., 345
Jemail, J., 347
Jencks, C., 381, 391, 403, 423
Jenkins, R., 138, 480, 485
Jennings, M., 184, 274
Jensen, A., 322
Jersild, A., 574
Jessor, R., 504
Jessor, S., 504
Johnson, C., 559
Johnson, D., 313
Johnson, R., 340
Johnson, V., 113
Johnston, 392, 418, 506, 507, 551, 583
Jones, M., 126, 127, 288, 303, 392
Jordan, D., 307
Jorgensen, S., 327, 340, 350, 354, 363, 368
Josselson, R., 290, 297, 451

Jurich, A., 374
Jurich, J., 374

Kacerguis, M., 451
Kagan, H., 491
Kagan, J., 41, 196, 238, 268, 309
Kahana, B., 279
Kahana, E., 279
Kalter, N., 250, 252, 485
Kalucy, R., 518
Kandel, D., 273, 276, 417, 418, 440, 441, 443, 507
Kantner, J., 350, 354, 355, 589
Kaplan, E., 506
Kaplan, H., 592
Karabel, J., 411
Karabenick, S., 304
Karpinsky, F., 502
Katchadourian, M., 92, 93, 103, 104, 110, 111, 113, 119, 128, 130, 131, 134
Katz, M., 570
Kaufman, I., 500
Keasey, C., 170
Keating, D., 157, 303
Keil, C., 321
Kellam, S., 286
Kelly, G., 296
Kempe, H., 558
Keniston, K., 183, 184, 185, 186, 572, 578, 599
Kenney, A., 366
Kennedy, M., 500
Kestenberg, J., 288
Kett, J., 12, 14, 570, 571
Killilea, M., 534
Kilmann, P., 367
Kinch, J., 270
Kinsey, A., 361, 496, 502
Kinsler, P., 297
Kirby, C., 296
Kirby, D., 366, 368
Klein, J., 129, 130
Klever, G., 317
Knapp, J., 304
Knowles, J., 5
Knutsen, J., 185

Kohlberg, L., 77, 79, 166, 167, 170, 171, 172, 173, 183, 184, 186, 229, 310
Kohn M., 59, 80, 83, 411, 453, 463
Konopka, G., 124
Korbin, J., 70, 244
Kosawa, H., 222, 224
Kourney, R., 23, 24
Kovacs, M., 509
Kovar, M., 131
Kraines, R., 273
Kramer, R., 171, 186
Kuhlen, R., 438
Kuhn, D., 172
Kuhn, T., 193
Kumka, D., 414
Kunz, P., 246

Labarre, M., 595
L'Abata, L., 4
La Gaipa, J., 445, 448
Laird, J., 286
Lamb, M., 253
Lambert, T., 579
Landis, J., 251
Landsbaum, J., 437
Langford, P., 170
Langton, K., 184, 274
Lanier, L., 318
Laosa, L., 80
Lao-tzu, 1, 39
Lapsley, D., 307
Lasch, C., 66
Laufer, R., 186, 578
Lawrence, D., 5
Leadbetter, B., 304
LeBaron, R., 90, 100, 101, 108, 116
Lebovici, L., 29
Lecky, P., 291
Lee, B., 438
Lefkowitz, M., 514
Leifer, A., 417
Lempers, J., 267
Lerner, R., 82, 85, 124, 128, 171, 175, 186, 187, 214, 232, 267,

287, 288, 304, 336, 346, 362, 365, 436
Leslie, J., 340
Lesser, G., 273, 276, 296, 297, 417, 418
Levenkron, S., 561
Levine, M., 367, 381, 539
Levinson, D., 576
Lewin, K., 200
Lewinsohn, P., 514
Lewis, K., 289
Lewis, M., 278, 340
Libby, R., 336
Liebert, R., 303
Liebertoff, K., 481, 482, 486
Liebman, R., 560, 561
Liebow, E., 321, 488
Light, D., 578
Lincoln, R., 559
Lindemann, C., 532
Lips, H., 311
Lipsitz, J., 398
Litt, I., 129, 130
Livesley, W., 160, 161, 162
Llewellyn, R., 5
Lloyd, J., 365, 392
Locke, J., 206, 208
Lockwood, A., 324
Loeber, R., 454
Logan, N., 345
Lohner, P., 408
London, H., 287
Longberg, B., 545, 546, 551
Lorenson, S., 563
Lovell, K., 303
Lowrie, S., 591, 594
Luffman, D., 367
Luker, K., 354
Lund, D., 547
Lynd, H., 571
Lynd, R., 571

McAdams, D., 250
McAnarney, E., 508
McCandless, B., 80, 287, 430, 431, 460
McCary, J., 342, 344, 365, 368

McClelland, D., 55, 77, 387
Maccoby, E., 109, 308, 311
McConochie, D., 297
McCord, J., 257, 262
McCord, W., 257, 262
McCullers, C., 5
McDavid, J., 436
McDill, E., 400
MacFarlane, J., 473
McGuire, R., 330
McKenney, P., 559
McKim, B., 163
McLaughlin, S., 94, 411
McMorrow, F., 271, 532, 600
MacNamera, D., 494
McPartland, J., 460
Macrides, C., 267, 272
Maley, J., 592
Malinowski, B., 222
Maloney, D., 546
Maloney, K., 546
Manaster, G., 308, 317
Mann, F., 480
Mannheim, K., 578, 580
Mannino, E., 488
Manoservitz, M., 296
Maracek, J., 593
Marcia, J., 217, 218, 291, 292,
    293, 294, 295, 296, 297, 306,
    307, 316
Maresh, M., 94
Marini, M., 415, 417, 591
Markham, H., 239
Markle, G., 250
Marshall, W., 90, 93, 115,
    331
Martin, B., 258
Martin, J., 23, 24
Martinson, F., 591
Mark, K., 193
Masanz, J., 172
Maslow, A., 230
Masters, M., 113
Masterson, J., 471, 472, 517
Matteson, D., 307
Mayer, R., 77
Mead, G., 55

Mead, M., 34, 43, 218, 219, 220,
    221, 222, 225, 226, 451, 579
Mednick, S., 453
Meiselman, K., 499
Melton, G., 429, 529
Mendel, G., 209
Menken, J., 559
Merrill, M., 145
Merton, R., 461, 463
Meyer, M., 451
Meyerding, J., 487
Meyerowitz, J., 592
Michael, C., 480
Milgrim, S., 173
Miller, J., 323
Miller, P., 334, 341, 342
Miller, W., 84, 352, 453
Milman, R., 560, 561
Mindick, B., 353, 354
Minuchin, S., 560, 561
Money, J., 310
Monge, R., 286
Montagu, A., 322
Montemayor, R., 161
Moos, R., 103
Morolla, F., 247
Morris, D., 70, 488
Morrison, P., 593
Morrison, T., 5
Morse, N., 405
Mortimer, J., 414
Moss, H., 238, 268, 309
Moss, J., 591
Mullener, N., 286
Murdock, G., 244
Musante, G., 547
Mussen, P., 288, 303
Muuss, R., 199, 203, 206, 221,
    222

Nabakov, V., 5
Nader, P., 135
Nass, G., 362
Neimark, E., 303
Nelson, D., 257
Nesselroade, J., 43, 144
Neuber, K., 296

Neuchterlein, K., 81
Neugarten, B., 15, 273
Neutens, J., 334, 335
Newcomb, J., 301, 584
Newhoff, S., 593
Newman, M., 421
Newson, E., 241
Niemi, R., 184
Nisbett, R., 287
Notarius, C., 239
Nydick, M., 119
Nye, F., 253, 255, 256, 272, 273,
    478, 482, 483, 488, 590

Oden, S., 439
Offer, D., 36, 186, 265, 271, 287,
    532
Offer, J., 532
Offord, D., 488
Ogbu, J., 80, 289, 411, 456
Ohlin, L., 460, 461
Olson, L., 412, 488
O'Malley, J., 78, 392, 429, 505,
    507, 551, 583
Opper, S., 146, 151, 152
Orleans, C., 560
Orlofsky, J., 296, 297
Orlos, J., 304
Orr, M., 366
Oshman, H., 296
Osipow, S., 406
Oskamp, S., 353, 354
Osuji, O., 407
O'Toole, R., 491

Packard, V., 160
Packard, W., 601
Padin, M., 287
Page, E., 248
Palmer, F., 255
Palmer, R., 518
Palmquist, W., 160
Pancoast, D., 527
Parcel, G., 367
Parke, J., 319
Parke, R., 69
Parmlee, P., 443

Parsons, T., 80
Pasley, C., 26
Patterson, A., 485
Paykel, S., 68
Peck, A., 500
Peel, E., 153
Peevers, B., 160, 447
Pellegrino, E., 574
Pepper, K., 193
Perkinson, H., 14, 15, 347, 380
Perrin, D., 417
Peshkin, A., 303, 463, 464, 465
Peters, J., 497
Petersen, A., 90, 93, 94, 97, 98,
    99, 101, 105, 111, 122, 124,
    126, 137, 286, 287
Peterson, R., 246, 247, 264
Pfeiffenberger, C., 250
Phillips, E., 547, 557
Phillips, L., 547, 557
Piaget, J., 145, 147, 149, 150,
    152, 153, 157, 166, 167, 207,
    228, 230, 303
Pierce, L., 460
Piker, H., 592
Pines, A., 485, 486, 487, 490,
    493, 541
Pitt, R., 303
Piven, H., 531
Plato, 203, 204, 208
Platt, J., 163
Poffenberger, T., 339
Pokorney, A., 592
Polansky, N., 55
Polory, P., 436
Pomeroy, B., 492
Ponzo, Z., 313
Post, S., 23, 24
Potok, C., 5, 82, 240
Pounds, R., 14, 382
Powell, G., 320
Prescott, J., 375
Presser, H., 350
Pressler, H., 593
Price, J., 514
Primavera, J., 457
Propper, A., 256
Przylyla, D., 352

Quay, H., 480

Rahe, R., 537
Rains, M., 163, 352
Ramirez, M., 321, 322, 402
Ramsey, C., 410, 413
Rand, W., 94, 98
Raphael, D., 295, 304
Rapkin, D., 163
Raywid, M., 395
Rees, A., 255
Rehberg, R., 401
Reich, C., 316
Reimer, D., 475, 476, 478
Reiss, 11, 244, 344, 345, 346, 587
Renshon, S., 185
Rest, J., 172, 175
Revelle, F., 99
Rheingold, H., 267
Rhodes, W., 541
Rice, D., 79, 399, 400
Rice, S., 128, 438, 459
Richardson, R., 246, 250, 360,
    364
Richter, C., 5
Ridgeway, C., 415
Riesman, D., 68
Robbins, S., 171
Roberts, R., 592
Robins, L., 454, 472, 473, 480
Robinson, I., 345
Roche, A., 119
Rodgers, W., 68
Roff, M., 79, 453
Rogers, C., 230
Rogers, D., 92, 133, 158, 241,
    336, 395, 435
Rogers, T., 4, 11
Rogers, W., 455, 456
Rohner, R., 56, 230
Rollins, B., 82, 83
Root, A., 104, 108, 109
Rose, R., 101
Rosen, R., 492
Rosenbach, D., 160
Rosenbaum, J., 399
Rosenberg, M., 71, 286, 321
Rosenblatt, R., 62

Rosenfeld, C., 419
Rosenfeld, R., 298
Rosenkrantz, A., 313
Rosenthal, D., 413, 426
Rosman, B., 560, 561
Rotenberg, M., 67, 314
Rouman, J., 256
Rousseau, J., 206, 207, 208, 209
Rowe, I., 306
Rubel, D., 124, 385
Rubenstein, J., 366
Ruebans, B., 421
Rupp, A., 421
Russ-Eft, D., 593
Russel, D., 494
Russel, G., 560
Rutherford, J., 437
Rutter, M., 36, 473, 514
Ryan, W., 552
Ryder, N., 20, 340, 578

Sabalis, R., 367
Sacker, I., 593
Salasnek, S., 506
Sale, K., 17
Salinger, J., 5
Sameroff, A., 81
Sampson, E., 247
Sanger, W., 246
Santrock, J., 128
Sarafino, J., 497, 499
Sarason, S., 536
Sargent, W., 319
Sarrel, L., 328
Sarrel, P., 328
Sarri, R., 486
Saugouicz, J., 500
Savin-Williams, R., 435
Scales, P., 354, 366, 368
Schacter, S., 287
Schafer, E., 259, 260, 272, 362,
    368
Shatz, E., 539
Scharff, D., 367
Schein, E., 319, 407
Schell, J., 50
Schellenbach, C., 238, 239, 250,
    266, 271, 513, 537

Schenk, D., 272, 412
Schenke, S., 560
Schenkel, S., 296
Schilling, L., 307
Schmidt, R., 488
Schneiders, A., 262
Schoeneman, T., 452
Schonfeld, W., 288
Schrut, A., 563
Schulman, A., 5
Schulsinger, F., 453
Schultz, R., 161
Schumacher, E., 17, 582
Schwartz, A., 563
Schwartz, B., 522
Schwartz, J., 185
Schwartz, P., 362
Schulenberg, J., 410, 411
Scribner, S., 159
Sears, R., 267
Sebald, H., 435
Sebes, J., 238, 239, 250, 266, 271, 513, 537
Secord, P., 160, 447
Seligman, M., 286, 514
Sellin, T., 475
Sells, S., 79, 453
Selman, R., 162, 173, 299, 300, 445, 453, 455
Selstad, G., 356
Sewall, W., 583
Shaftel, F., 323, 324
Shaftel, G., 323, 324
Shah, F., 583
Shakespeare, W., 53
Sharpe, L., 247
Shellow, R., 485
Shirer, R., 64, 174
Shore, M., 488
Short, J., 478, 480
Shrauger, J., 452
Shure, M., 163
Sigel, R., 185
Siegler, R., 303
Silberman, C., 381, 384, 386
Silbert, M., 485, 486, 487, 490, 493, 551
Silverman, M., 397

Simmons, D., 295
Simmons, R., 301
Simon, S., 323
Simon, W., 334, 341, 342
Simpson, E., 172, 417, 418
Simpson, H., 98
Sinclair, D., 98, 107
Singer, J., 287
Sinoway, C., 519, 520
Sistrunk, F., 436
Skeels, H., 194, 197
Skinner, B., 224
Sklorowski, E., 97
Slater, P., 67, 68
Sloane, P., 502
Small, R., 560
Smart, K., 449
Smart, M., 449
Smiley, W., 481
Smith, A., 65
Smith, P., 592
Smith, R., 81, 454
Snyder, E., 401, 402
Soares, A., 320
Soares, L., 320
Solnit, A., 179
Sommer, B., 92
Sones, G., 450
Sorensen, A., 429
Sorensen, R., 79, 344, 346, 348, 350, 355, 361, 363, 364, 365, 366
Soroker, E., 480
Spanier, G., 128, 130, 171, 175, 214, 250, 267, 367, 587
Spearman, C., 143
Speicher, J., 279
Spivack, G., 163
Springer, M., 593
Staffieri, J., 288
Stafford-White, K., 490
Stanley, J., 324
Stark, P., 296
Starling, K., 135
Steinberg, L., 66, 419, 421, 422
Steinmetz, S., 22, 69, 278, 311
Stern, M., 334
Stevenson, H., 424

Stewart, S., 592
Stoner, C., 319
Stolz, L., 126
Stolz, R., 126
Straus, M., 22, 69, 278, 311
Strommen, M., 317
Strowig, R., 313
Suedfeld, P., 254
Sullivan, B., 367
Sullivan, E., 590
Sullivan, H., 79, 439, 451, 452
Stuart, R., 547
Super, C., 82, 407
Surber, C., 171
Sussex, J., 369
Suttles, G., 455
Sutton-Smith, B., 71
Swaback, D., 563
Swanson, D., 84, 171

Taeuber, C., 588
Taeuber, I., 588
Tagiuri, C., 500
Takaishi, T., 107
Tangri, S., 415
Tanner, J., 90, 93, 94, 95, 96, 98, 107, 112, 115, 119, 122, 123
Taylor, B., 90, 93, 97, 99, 101, 105, 122, 124, 126, 287, 388
Teicher, J., 564
Tenzer, A., 416
Terkel, S., 48
Terman, L., 143, 144
Thomas, C., 472
Thomas, D., 82, 83
Thomas, L., 186, 273
Thomas, W., 53
Thompson, J., 490
Thompson, M., 352
Thorbecke, W., 451
Thornburg, H., 92, 365, 366, 368, 392, 395, 396, 419
Thorndike, R., 32
Thurber, T., 257
Thurstone, L., 144, 145
Thurstone, T., 144, 145
Tietze, C., 590
Timberlake, J., 37

Timmons, F., 392
Titchener, J., 592
Tizard, J., 473
Todd, D., 563
Todd, T., 560, 651
Tolstoy, L., 242
Toman, W., 247, 278
Tomlinson-Keasey, C., 170
Toms, D., 518
Torney, J., 184, 185
Tracey, J., 172
Traxler, A., 296
Trivers, D., 450
Troll, L., 273, 274, 275
Trotter, S., 246
Trowbridge, N., 320
Tsafriv, J., 97
Tsunt, M., 488
Tulkin, S., 62, 71, 322, 403
Tully, B., 313
Tuma, N., 440
Turiel, E., 172, 175, 296
Turner, R., 383
Twain, M., 5, 60
Tyack, D., 13, 14, 15
Tyrodi, T., 547

Ulrey, G., 82
Urban, H., 50, 524, 528

Valentine, B., 322
Valentine, C., 322
Valett, R., 323
Valusek, J., 70
Verba, S., 63, 403
Verger, D., 413
Veroff, J., 253
Visotsky, H., 592
Vogel, E., 244
Volpe, J., 452, 453
Vondra, J., 534
Vondracek, F., 405, 407, 409, 410, 411, 524, 528
Voss, H., 476, 478, 479

Walters, L., 559
Walters, R., 37, 330
Wanless, R., 367
Wapner, S., 160
Warren, C., 339
Warren, M., 97, 98, 129, 130
Watson, E., 489
Watt, N., 79
Webb, J., 68
Weber, E., 497, 499, 502, 503, 504
Wechsler, J., 144
Weiner, A., 304
Weiner, I., 37, 272, 473, 479, 481, 506, 509, 511, 512, 514, 516, 517
Weinstein, E., 79, 429, 454
Weinstein, G., 323
Weis, J., 478, 479, 541
Weiss, R., 253, 405
Weissburg, R., 163
Weissman, M., 68
Weitz, S., 415
Welcher, D., 560
Welcher, W., 350
Werner, C., 443
Werner, E., 81, 454
Werry, J., 480
Werts, C., 413
Westly, W., 35
Westman, J., 79
Wheeler, D., 438
White, C., 171
White, R., 64, 79
Whiteside, M., 401
Whitmore, K., 473
Whittaker, J., 68, 241, 527, 541, 551, 559
Wieder, H., 506
Wiener, I., 592
Willems, E., 19
Williams, J., 476, 478
Willis, R., 437
Wilson, K., 250
Wilson, R., 350

Winetsky, S., 84
Winn, M., 160, 601
Wise, L., 594
Wish, E., 473
Wodarski, J., 436, 541
Wolf, M., 547, 557
Wolff, L., 28
Wolfgang, M., 475, 478
Wolk, S., 485, 549
Wolman, R., 160
Wooden, K., 486, 493
Woods, R., 317
Wordsworth, W., 26
Wright, J., 84
Wright, M., 592
Wright, S., 84
Wurtman, R., 94, 98
Wynne, E., 61, 78, 247, 580

Xelowski, H., 295

Yamamoto, J., 29
Yancy, W., 135
Yankelovich, D., 374, 410, 575, 580, 581, 584
Yarber, W., 360
Yarrow, L., 238
Yarrow, M., 160
York, O., 533
Young, B., 124, 320
Young, D., 363
Youniss, J., 79, 445, 452, 453
Yule, W., 473, 514

Zabin, L., 350
Zacharias, L., 94, 98
Zajonc, R., 404
Zelnick, M., 341, 345, 346, 348, 349, 350, 351, 352, 354, 355, 356, 367
Ziegler, S., 441
Zimbardo, P., 548
Zinn, D., 531
Zuck, R., 317
Zurcher, L., 250

Subject Index

Abuse. *See* Maltreatment
Adolescence
  definition, 11
  stereotypes, 28–29, 30–35, 137
  substages, 27
Anorexia nervosa, 128, 517–518,
  560–562. *See also* Bulimia;
  Psychopathology
Anthropological perspective,
  218–224. *See also* Cultural
  differences; Macrosystems
Apathy-futility syndrome, 55.
  See also Depression;
  Maltreatment
At the Shores, 4–11
Athletics, 91, 111, 130

Babysitting, 23
Behavioral settings, 17–18. *See
  also* Ecological perspective;
  Education; School size
Behaviorism, 224–228
Biological influences, 41, 44, 95,
  96, 129, 145, 176–177, 219–
  220, 230–232, 374

Bulimia, 518–520, 561–562. *See
  also* Anorexia nervosa;
  Psychopathology

Cognitive development, 141–142,
  145–152, 228–230, 296, 298–
  299, 310, 311, 370, 445–448
  cognitive style, 159
  formal operations, 150–154,
  163, 303–306
  Piaget's model of, 145–152, 157
Cohort, 576–579, 580
Competence, 73, 75–85, 162–163,
  411–412, 429
Contraception, 350–355, 368,
  371–372, 374. *See also*
  Sexuality
Creativity, 158
Cultural influences, 12, 14, 21,
  27, 34, 35, 41, 43, 58–59, 61,
  62, 73, 80, 90, 92, 94, 97,
  98, 107, 112, 124, 153, 159,
  170–171, 175, 188, 218–224,
  225, 226, 245, 259, 275–277,
  320–322, 325, 330, 331–334,

340–341, 346–347, 375, 381,
  383, 402–404, 407, 411, 416–
  417, 456–477, 466, 504, 579–
  580. *See also*
  Anthropological perspective;
  Macrosystems

Deductive approach, 3–4
Demography, 16, 19–21, 248. *See
  also* Cohort; Macrosystems
Depression, 500, 509, 512, 513–
  516. *See also*
  Psychopathology; Suicide
Depression, economic. *See* Great
  Depression of 1930s
Dimorphism, 93
Divorce, 159–160, 249–254
Drug use, 135–136, 503–507,
  551–557

Ecological perspective, 12, 42,
  45, 74, 89, 99, 127, 142, 175,
  192, 194, 230–232, 291, 524,
  534, 541. *See also*
  Exosystems; Macrosystems;
  Mesosystems; Microsystems

Economic issues, 26, 46, 47, 51, 65–67, 97–98, 247–248, 254–258, 407, 409–410, 418–419, 424–426, 459, 482, 570–571, 578, 581–583
    social class, 84, 391, 396, 400, 410–413, 414, 432, 440, 462–463, 475–479, 483, 583, 594–595
Education, 8, 12–16, 57–59, 458–460, 462–463, 570–571, 583–586, 593–594
    school size, 17–19, 59, 380–404, 538
    sex education, 364–368, 525
Egocentrism, 149–150, 154–157, 164. See also Cognitive development
Empathy, 78
Evolution, 31, 209
Exosystems, 92, 139, 183, 189, 233, 240, 281, 301–302, 325, 328, 376, 427, 429, 457, 470, 520, 524, 534–535, 565, 602. See also Ecological perspective

Fictional accounts, 4–5

Generation gap, 186–188, 596–600
Great Depression of 1930s, 7, 19, 46–49, 240, 243, 258, 407, 580
Growth spurt, 106–107. See also Puberty

Health, 21–22, 97, 128–131, 131–138
Historical influences, 12–16, 19, 30, 66. See also Macrosystems
Homosexuality, 361–362
Hormones, 99–101, 102–105. See also Puberty

Identity, 216–218, 227, 269, 532, 541, 585

Inductive approach, 3–4
Interdependence, 67–68
IQ (intelligence quotient), 18, 76, 77, 142–145, 158, 193, 194, 197, 247, 248, 389, 399, 410. See also Cognitive development; Competence

Juvenile delinquency, 174, 393, 473–481, 557–558

Lao-tzu, 3, 39

Macrosystems, 60–72, 92, 122, 139, 175, 183, 189, 192, 233, 240, 271, 282, 301–302, 312–313, 322–323, 325, 328, 331, 342–347, 376, 380, 427, 460–466, 467, 470, 504, 521, 523, 533, 534, 535, 560, 570–571, 574–575, 577–578, 587–590, 596–602. See also Cultural influences; Ecological perspective
Maltreatment, 55–56, 239, 248, 262, 265–266, 485–486, 491, 497–503, 529, 546, 558–559
Masturbation, 124, 363. See also Sexuality
Maturity, 79, 90–91, 96, 108, 429, 569, 573–576, 587
Menarche, 94, 97, 98, 114, 124, 125. See also Puberty
Mesosystems, 56, 139, 176, 189, 233, 281, 301–302, 325, 328, 376, 427, 429, 467, 470, 520, 534, 565, 602. See also Ecological perspective
Methods of studying adolescence, 26, 35–36, 44, 237, 259, 269, 273, 286, 287, 297–298, 307–308, 343, 347, 437–438, 475–479, 509–510
Microsystems, 51, 92, 123–124, 139, 175, 188–189, 192–232, 239, 281, 291, 301–302, 306, 325, 328, 376, 379, 404, 427, 429, 430, 467, 469, 472, 520,

524, 534, 542, 565, 595–596, 602. See also Ecological perspective; Phenomonological approach

Nature. See Biological influences
Neglect. See Maltreatment
1950s, 48
Nurture. See Ecological perspective
Nutrition, 92, 95, 97, 111, 128. See also Health

Ontogeny recapitulates phylogeny, 31, 209
Opportunity, 53. See also Exosystems; Macrosystems; Mesosystems; Microsystems

Paradigm, 193, 194. See also Methods of studying adolescence
Parenthood, 586–596. See also Maturity; Sexuality
Parricide, 23–24. See also Maltreatment; Violence
Particularism, 58, 265
Peer orientation, 6, 7, 336–337, 339–340, 363, 365, 389–390, 417–418, 430–467. See also Peers
Peers, 182–183. See also Peer orientation
Phenomenological approach, 52–53. See also Microsystems
Physical maturation, 6–7. See also Biological influences; Puberty
Political influences, 29–30, 60, 63–64, 228–229. See also Macrosystems
Political socialization, 182–186. See also Political influences
Premenstrual syndrome, 103, 130
Prostitution, 490–497, 503, 562
Psychoanalytic perspective, 32–34, 179–180, 211–215, 309–312, 329–330

Psychopathology, 31, 36, 60, 468–481, 484–485, 509–520, 531

Puberty, 89, 90, 92, 93, 95, 97, 101, 104–105, 106, 108, 118–119, 122, 126–127, 287
  timing, 94, 95, 99, 122, 126–127, 129, 288, 303. *See also* Growth spurt; Menarche

Race, 70, 96–97, 475–479
Rejection, 236–239. *See also* Maltreatment
Religion, 317–319
Rites of passage, 92
Runaways, 481–490, 548–551

Schools. *See* Education
Scientific study of adolescence, 4. *See also* Methods of studying adolescence
Self-concept, 159. *See also* Self-esteem
Self-esteem, 55, 164, 286, 298, 320–321. *See also* Self-concept

Sex differences in development, 9–10, 47, 68–69, 106–112, 118–120, 176–181, 265, 268, 269, 274, 286, 288, 295, 297, 300, 307, 308–314, 316, 322, 325, 329, 331, 341, 345, 362, 364, 414–416, 436, 448–450, 508, 514
Sexism, 70, 324, 345, 354. *See also* Macrosystems
Sexuality, 5, 8, 9, 10, 30,89, 90, 91, 96, 101, 105, 107, 112–122, 156, 213, 223, 280, 327–376, 437, 490–497, 559–560, 575, 586–596. *See also* Homosexuality; Masturbation; Sex differences in development
Siblings, 8
Social class. *See* Economic influences
Social competence. *See* Competence
Social puberty, 92. *See also* Puberty
Social systems, 46, 49–50. *See also* Ecological perspective

Sociobiology, 96. *See also* Evolution
Storm and stress hypothesis, 31, 32–34, 36, 37, 137, 471–473. *See also* Sturm und drang
Strategic interactions, 163, 354–355. *See also* Cognitive development; Egocentrism
Sturm und drang, 195, 221. *See also* Storm and stress
Suicide, 11, 21–22, 227, 507–509, 562–565. *See also* Depression; Maltreatment

Temperament, 82. *See also* Biological influences

Universalism, 58, 265. *See also* Particularism

Venereal disease, 356–360, 367. *See also* Sexuality
Violence, 22–23, 69–70, 133–134, 278, 385, 475–479, 493, 535. *See also* Maltreatment

Youth, 569, 571–573, 597–599

James T. Garbarino has pursued his commitment to understand adolescence in social context through several books, articles, and numerous speeches, consultations, and workshop experiences with diverse professionals, parents, and concerned citizens. *Protecting Children from Abuse and Neglect* (Jossey-Bass, 1980) and *Understanding Abusive Families* (Lexington, 1980) explored dysfunctional families, the latter book focusing on adolescent maltreatment. *Successful Schools and Competent Students* (Lexington, 1981) examined the social and psychological processes of schooling, with particular attention to adolescence. *Children and Families in the Social Environment* (Aldine, 1982) developed the model of sociocultural risk and opportunity for families from the ecological perspective used in this present text. *Troubled Youth, Troubled Families* (Aldine, in press) analyzes the results and implications of research on high-risk adolescents in high-risk families.

As a consultant, program advisor, and speaker, Dr. Gabarino has been involved with a wide variety of groups and organizations serving youth. These include Boys Town, The National Committee for the Prevention of Child Abuse, the American Medical Association, the National Institute of Mental Health, ABC Television's "Good Morning America" and NBC's "Magazine," the Society for Research in Child Development, the American Psychological Association, and state and community youth service agencies across the country, in big cities, small towns, and rural villages.

All these experiences contributed to this text, as they have his teaching—at Pennsylvania State University, his academic home, as well as at Cornell University, at SUNY's Empire State College, and at the University of Nebraska at Omaha.